T0338642

Integer Algorithms in Cryptology and Information Assurance

Integer Algorithms in Cryptology and Information Assurance

Boris S. Verkhovsky
New Jersey Institute of Technology, USA

World Scientific

NEW JERSEY · LONDON · SINGAPORE · BEIJING · SHANGHAI · HONG KONG · TAIPEI · CHENNAI

Published by

World Scientific Publishing Co. Pte. Ltd.
5 Toh Tuck Link, Singapore 596224
USA office: 27 Warren Street, Suite 401-402, Hackensack, NJ 07601
UK office: 57 Shelton Street, Covent Garden, London WC2H 9HE

Library of Congress Cataloging-in-Publication Data
Verkhovsky, Boris S.
  Integer algorithms in cryptology and information assurance / prof. Boris S. Verkhovsky,
New Jersey Institute of Technology, USA.
    pages cm
  Includes bibliographical references
  ISBN 978-9814623742 (hardback : alk. paper)
  1. Information technology--Mathematics. 2. Cryptography--Mathematics. 3. Data integrity.
4. Algorithms. 5. Numbers, Natural. 6. Number theory. I. Title.
  T58.5.V47 2014
  652'.8015181--dc23

                                                                      2014024555

British Library Cataloguing-in-Publication Data
A catalogue record for this book is available from the British Library.

In-house Editor: Amanda Yun

Typeset by Stallion Press
Email: enquiries@stallionpress.com

Printed in Singapore

About the Author

 Dr. Boris S. Verkhovsky is a Professor of Computer Science at the New Jersey Institute of Technology (NJIT). He received his PhD in Computer Science jointly from the Academy of Sciences of the USSR and the Latvia State University, Riga.

Professor Verkhovsky's research experience and interests span across communication security, design and analysis of cryptosystems and information assurance protocols, the design and control large-scale systems, optimization and algorithms, and the design and control of telecommunication networks.

His prior affiliations are: the Scientific Research Institute of Computers (Moscow), the Academy of Sciences of the USSR, Princeton University School of Engineering, IBM Thomas J. Watson Research Center (Yorktown Heights), Bell Laboratories, University of Colorado and, since 1986, the NJIT.

Professor Verkhovsky is a recipient of awards including the USSR Ministry of Radio-Electronics Award; the Academy of Sciences of the USSR Award; the Alvin Johnson Award; and the Millennium Award and Medal of Excellence. Professor Verkhovsky is also a recipient of Blasé Pascal Award and Medal, and is listed in Marquis *Who's Who in America*.

Verkhovsky was the Wallace J. Eckert Scientist at the IBM Thomas J. Watson Research Center, a Member of Technical Staff at Bell Labs, and held the Charles Dana Endowed Chair Professorship. In 2002 he was elected as a member, and in 2003, as a Fellow of the European Academy of Science (EAS). He served as the EAS's Vice President from 2003 till 2006.

Dedicated to my children
Ekaterina-Anastasia and Samuel,
And in memoriam of my parents
Samuel and Alla Verkhovsky

Preface

"If you are out to describe the truth,
Leave elegance to the tailor",

A. Einstein

This book is based on the author's research and computer experiments for the last several years. It is mostly devoted to the discussion of algorithmic aspects that were developed and analyzed by the author for secure and reliable transmission of information and digital authentication of senders over open communication channels. The book consists of several parts describing and analyzing basic algorithms in modular arithmetic; cryptographic protocols based on complex moduli; algorithms for information assurance; cryptanalytic algorithms solving discrete logarithm problem (DLP); methods of cryptanalysis for solution of integer factorization (iFac) based on a generalization of Gauss's theorem; hybrid algorithms for information assurance and cryptography; cryptographic algorithms based on three-dimensional elliptic surfaces; sender identification/digital signature algorithms; and search and design algorithms that are provided in the last several chapters.

The algorithms considered in this book are designed for integer arithmetic of multi-digit long numbers. The reason to consider integer arithmetic stems from the necessity to deal with extremely large integers, which are used for secure encryption of sensitive information transmitted via communication channels that are open both to designated receivers as well as to unauthorized intruders. Various arithmetic transformations based on additions, subtractions, multiplications and exponentiations of integers are used for the encryption. Although each of these operations preserve the integer character of numerically-presented information, the size of the resulting integers is far beyond what computers can handle unless we use scientific notations and round off the extremely large numbers consisting of tens of thousands or more digits. However, rounding off is absolutely unacceptable in our case, otherwise after numerous operations the rounding off errors will propagate and, as a result, we will not be able to recover on the decryption level the initially transmitted information and instead of encrypted and transmitted *"Princeton"* the receiver will decrypt *"Pinkerton"* or instead of encrypted and transmitted *"Evian Bonus"* the receiver will decrypt *"Naïve Lotus"*. Another obstacle in dealing with integers is that on the level of decryption we need to use *inverse* arithmetic operations (division, extraction of roots etc.). However, in the overwhelming majority of cases these inverse operations do not preserve integrality of inputs since in traditional arithmetic *seven divided by three* is not an integer, and in the relatively small interval $[1, 10^6]$ only one thousands integers have exact integer square roots, only one hundred of them have exact integer cubic roots etc. The magic of modular arithmetic resolves most of these "problems" very efficiently. Indeed, seven-divided-by-three only in exceptional cases does not have an integer output (and we are aware of these limitations). For the interval mentioned above exactly half a million integers (versus 1,000 in traditional arithmetic) have integer square roots (and, of course, we know under what conditions that happens). Certainly, to make everything work efficiently we need to address many other issues to be sure that all processes are executed fast enough, with assured correctness and without undesirable surprises.

Here it is important to mention that there is a substantially distinct methodology in dealing with problems in mathematics of real numbers and modular arithmetic of integers. In the former case many classes of problems are solvable via efficient algorithms because the class of objects in many problems has global characteristics like continuity, convexity or concavity, unimodality or bi-modality, separability, existence of contracting operators, etc. However, in the modular arithmetic in most of cases the class of objects under study does not have global properties with one important exception. In the middle of the seventeenth century Pierre Fermat noticed that if modulus p is a prime, then for every integer c not divisible by p holds a cyclic property that $c^p \bmod p = c$. This is known as Fermat Little Theorem that was generalized by the Swiss mathematician Leonhard Euler: if $n = pq$, where p and q are primes, then for every c relatively prime with n the cyclic property holds: $c^{n-p-q+2} \bmod n = c$.

This property is in the core of RSA public-key cryptography. As it is shown in several chapters of this book, there are analogous cyclic properties in modular arithmetic based on complex integers and on complex moduli.

In dealing with efficiency and correctness of computation and other goals an inventive approach is a must. Such an approach is presented in this book for readers, who are interested in the proposed algorithms. The stress in the presentation of these algorithms is mostly on the descriptive and constructive levels rather than on the validation of algorithms (the mathematical proofs). Only in exceptional cases are the proofs presented. That is why many statements in the books are provided as conjectures or like propositions without proofs.

The proposed algorithms have numerous applications in business, banking, engineering, telemedicine (in laparoscopic surgery and implantable medical devices), in monitoring of containers in foreign trade exchange, in the national system of cybersecurity, in military systems, in interplanetary Internet developed by NASA for space research (monitoring and control of space vehicles, rovers/robots, and telemedicinal monitoring of astronauts), and many other areas of communication and control.

In the first several chapters of the book we describe various algorithms in modular arithmetic (modular multiplicative inverse algorithm, deterministic selection of generators, multiplication of multi-digit large integers, primality-testing procedures, etc.). These algorithms play significant roles in modern cryptographic protocols. Many combinatorial problems can be solved via a sequential analysis of permutations in conjunction with the branch-and-bound approach. The traveling salesman problem is an example of such a problem. Random permutations are used for inter-processor communication (randomized routing algorithm), in parallel computers and in various cryptographic schemes: substitution, transposition or permutation. Chapter 5 describes algorithms that both generate the permutations and count them.

In the second part of the book we provide various encryption/ decryption algorithms based on complex moduli rather than on real moduli. As we show in the book, the modular arithmetic based on the complex integer modulus (p, q) creates cycles of order $p^2 + q^2$ while the arithmetic with real modulus p has cycles of order p. Therefore, for potential intruders/cryptanalysts the computational complexity to solve inverse problems like the iFac of semi-primes or the DLP is significantly higher in the complex-moduli arithmetic than in the arithmetic based on real moduli. For instance, if both p and q are one hundred decimal-digits long integers, then the modulus (p, q) creates a cycle of 200-digit long, while in real-modulus arithmetic the cycle is the same as modulus p, i.e., 100 digits large. Hence, if the size of the cycle is a measure of cryptographic protection (crypto-immunity), then in the complex modular arithmetic we have 100-digit large cycle if either p or q or both are 50-digit long integers. As a result, we need to perform all computations with integers that are 10^{50} times smaller than their counterparts in the arithmetic based on the real moduli. Therefore, the time complexity of encryption and decryption can be substantially reduced, i.e., the cryptographic protocols can be executed faster, which is important if we wish to eventually implement them in a real-time mode.

A hybrid cryptographic system described in Chapter 13 provides also digital signature of the sender (sender identification) that transmits the information.

In modern communication networks two major requirements must be satisfied: the reliability of connection and the security of delivery. The implementation of these two requirements of information processing consumes extra time and additional bandwidth. These are major drawbacks if rapid delivery is essential. Information transmissions in a military environment and in financial exchanges are examples in which delay is a sensitive issue.

In the third part we describe several algorithms for reliable and secure transmission of information via open communication channels with random errors. These algorithms are based on various protocols of the information assurance and recovery of initially-transmitted data. Several reliability protocols are described in this part. Their characteristics (probabilities of protocol failure, specific bandwidth requirement per block of transmitted information and complexity of recovery) are analyzed and compared.

In addition to reliability and security, real-time communication in a voice network over the Internet is the time constraint that is even tighter since a delay larger than a quarter of a second is not acceptable. The efficiency of these protocols from various points of view, including the probability of failure and bandwidth requirement, we discuss in that part of the book. We also demonstrate that in some specially-tailored protocols, proposed by the author of this book, the information recovery is a straightforward process, while in other cases it is extremely tedious.

In the book we describe and analyze algorithms that assure a high probability of information transmission over unreliable channels and simultaneously provide protection of information from uninitiated and sometimes malicious intruders. It is shown that hybrid algorithms dealing simultaneously with information assurance and security are synergistically more efficient from a computational point of view in comparison with separate application of security and information assurance protocols. Tables, figures and numerous examples illustrate various concepts described in this part of the book.

In the fourth part, we dedicated to the system design and cryptanalytic algorithms dealing primarily with computational complexity of iFac and DLP. On the system design level of cryptographic protocols it is essential to select their basic parameters that satisfy certain conditions. For instance, in the classical Diffie–Hellman key exchange (DHKE) protocol, as well as in the RSA, Rabin, ElGamal and other cryptographic protocols it is required that the corresponding keys of the communicating parties must be prime integers. In the algorithms that we discuss in the second part it is essential to select, on the system design level, complex integers that are primes. Although it is not computationally difficult to verify whether given (p, q) is a complex prime, it is much more challenging to directly select a large (p, q) that *is* a complex prime. Chapter 22 provides an indirect and computationally efficient algorithm that solves this problem. That algorithm is based on the author's generalizations of Gauss's Theorem (GGT) and on the existing algorithms that count how many points has a specially-selected elliptic curve. These GGT are also applicable in the fourth part of the book where in Chapters 17 and 18 we describe several approaches for iFac of semi-primes. In Chapter 19 a relationship between a *constrained* DLP and iFac is shown. An approach that allows decomposition of large DLP into smaller DLPs is discussed in Chapter 20.

In the fifth part, we provide the description of various problems and related integer algorithms. For instance, we show that some algorithms can be characterized by a set of small integer parameters. As a result, the search for these algorithms can be reduced to the solution of rather simple although computationally-formidable combinatorial problems. However, after they are solved once, these problems lead to the discovery of new algorithms.

The book contains constructive ideas that can be effective in multitude of applications in various business, engineering, financial (EFT), military command/communication/control problems, in deep space exploration and control, in diplomatic exchange, in litigation and other legal actions, in robotic engineering, in remote health care technologies and services in telemedicine (diagnostics, telemonitoring and invasive actions/surgeries, etc.). These ideas can be helpful for studying in depth the computer science and mathematics of the modern cryptographic and information assurance algorithms.

The book should be of interest to cryptographic experts, communication and network cybersecurity professionals, mathematicians, and students studying theories of information transmission. Results of research, computer experiments and development in these areas that we provide in this book can be instrumental to graduate, postgraduate and PhD students, and their advisors in selecting theses and even PhD topics, semester projects or as guidance for an independent study. The topics and especially the approaches described and analyzed in the book can be instructive for those who are planning to teach advanced-level courses for graduate or PhD students in Computer Science, Electrical Engineering, Telecommunication or Applied Math Departments, as well as for those members of public who have general interest in science and technology. The ideas that we provided and discuss in this book can be helpful to specialists in R&D, who devote their efforts in finding solutions to Big Data challenges in cybersecurity.

Acknowledgments

I express my gratitude to internal and external reviewers for their constructive criticism and suggestions that improved the quality of this book.

Several colleagues, scientists, research collaborators and former undergraduate, graduate and PhD students provided their comments and/or constructive suggestions to various chapters of this book or helped to run computer experiments. Although all remaining errors or ambiguities are mine, I express my deep appreciation to all of them listed here in alphabetic order: W. Amber, D. Chacrabarti, P. Choudhury, H. Cohen, P. Fay, P. Garrett, A. Gerbessiotis, W. Gruver, L. Hars, J. Jones, A. Joux, D. Kanevsky, N. Koblitz, A. Koripella, A. Koval, M. Linderman, X. Ma, M. Marks, S. Medicherla, A. Menezes, W. Miranker, A. Mirajkar, R. Mollin, D. Moody, D. Mozley, D. Murphy, A. Mutovic, S. Naredla, D. Nassimi, D. Nowak, J. Pearson, Y. Polyakov, C. Pomerance, D. Rodik, R. Rubino, J. Runnells, S. Sadik, B. Saraswat, K. Sauraj, J. Scher, I. Semushin, M. Sikorski, K. Skov, R. Statica, B. Tokay, E. Verkhovsky, C. Washington, S. Winograd and the last but not least H. Wozniakowski. And, needless to state that, if I overlooked to mention somebody, I hope for her or his forgiveness.

Contents

About the Author   v

Preface   ix

Acknowledgments   xv

0. Introductory Notes on Security and Reliability   xxxv

    1. Background xxxv
    2. Basics of Modular Arithmetic xxxvii
    3. Basic Properties in Modular Arithmetic xxxviii
    4. Direct and Inverse Problems xl
    5. Complexity Enhancement xli

1. Enhanced Algorithm for Modular Multiplicative Inverse   1

    1. Introduction: Division of Two Integers 1
    2. Basic Arrays and their Properties 1
    3. NEA for MMI 3
    4. Complexity Analysis of MMI Algorithm 4
    5. Extended-Euclid Algorithm (XEA) 7
    6. Comparative Analysis of NEA vs. XEA 7
    7. Average Complexity of XEA and NEA 8

2. Multiplication of Large-Integers Based on Homogeneous Polynomials   9

    1. Introduction and Basic Definitions 9
    2. Multiplication $C = AB$ based on Homogeneous Polynomials 11

3.   Separation of "Even" and "Odd" Coefficients
     in AHP   12
     3.1. Separation of unknowns: $n = 5$ 13
     3.2. AHP for multiplication
           of triple-large integers   13
4.   Reduction of Algebraic Additions   14
5.   Comparison of Evaluated Polynomials
     in TCA vs. AHP   16
6.   Comparison of TCA vs. AHP for $n = 6$ 17
     6.1. AHP framework   17
     6.2. Toom–Cook Algorithm   17
7.   AHP for $n = 7$ 18
8.   AHP for $n = 4$ in Details   18
9.   Solution of System of Eqs. (8.6)–(8.10)   19
10. Multistage Implementation of TCA and AHP   21
     10.1. Two-stage implementation (TSI)   21
     10.2. Multi-stage implementation   22
11. Number of Algebraic Additions   22
12. Analysis of TCA vs. AHP   23
13. Generalized Horner Rule for Homogeneous
     Polynomials   24
14. Values of (p, q) Simplifying Computation of $A(p, q)$
     and $B(p, q)$ 24
15. Optimized AHP   25
16. Concluding Remark   27

**3.   Deterministic Algorithms for Primitive Roots
       and Cyclic Groups with Mutual Generators   29**

1.   Introduction and Basic Definitions   29
2.   Schematic Illustration of Cycles   30
3.   Verification Procedure: Is g a Generator?   32
4.   Safe Primes and their Properties   33
5.   Computational Complexities   34
6.   Algorithm and its Validation   34
7.   Formula for Generator   35
8.   Multiplicative Groups with Common Generators   35
9.   Complex Generators and Super-safe Primes   38
10. Concluding Remarks   38

Appendix 39
   A.1. Proof of Theorem 6.2 39
   A.2. Deterministic computation of generators:
       Proof of Theorem 7.1 41
   A.3. Search for smaller generators 41

**4. Primality Testing via Complex Integers
and Pythagorean Triplets**   **43**

  1. Introduction 43
  2. Basic Properties of Primes 44
  3. Generalizations 45
  4. Arithmetic Operations on Complex Integers 45
     4.1. Multiplications of complex numbers 45
     4.2. Modular multiplicative inverse
        of complex integer 46
     4.3. Complex primes 46
  5. Fundamental Identity 47
  6. Major Results 48
  7. Carmichael Numbers 49
  8. Primality Tests 50
  9. Primality Testing with Quaternions 51
  10. Computer Experiments 51

5. Algorithm Generating Random Permutation   **55**

  1. Applications of Permutations 55
  2. Permutation Generation 55
  3. Counting the Permutations 57
  4. Counting the Inversions 57
  5. Inversions-Permutation Mapping 57
  6. The Algorithm 58
  7. Modified Algorithm for Large n 59
  8. Example 6.1 Revisited 60

6. Extractability of Square Roots and Divisibility Tests   **61**

  1. Introduction 61
  2. Divisibility Algorithms for $m = 7$ and $m = 13$ 61
  3. "Binary" Divisibility Test by *Seven* and 17 62
  4. Divisibility Algorithm 63

5.   Faster Divisibility Tests   63
6.   Modified Tests   64
7.   Validity of Divisibility Tests   64
8.   More General Divisibility Test   65
9.   Extractability of Integer Square Roots   66
     9.1.   Problem definition and basic properties   66
     9.2.   Numeric illustration   67
10. The Extractability Algorithm   68
     10.1. Special case: $M = 256$ 68
     10.2. General case   69

7. **Extraction of Roots of Higher Order
    in Modular Arithmetic**   **71**

1.   The Introductory Section   71
2.   Algorithm for n^{th} Root Extraction   72
     2.1.   General framework   72
     2.2.   Alternative extractor E   74
3.   Extraction of Cubic Roots   75
     3.1.   Cubic root extractor where $p \bmod 9 = 2$ 75
     3.2.   Cubic root extractor where $p \bmod 9 = 5$ 76
     3.3.   Cubic root extractor where $p \bmod 3 = 1$ 77
     3.4.   Alternative algorithms for cubic root extraction
            if $p \bmod 3 = 2$ 78
4.   Quintic Roots Extraction: Special Cases   78
5.   General Formula for Quintic Roots Extraction   79
6.   Root Extractor of nth Order   79
7.   General Case: Extraction of Roots of nth Order   80
8.   Algorithm for Extraction of Roots of nth Order   80
9.   Concluding Remark   81
Appendix   81

8. **Public-Key Cryptography Based on Square
    Roots and Complex Modulus**   **83**

1.   Introduction and Problem Statement   83
     1.1.   Complex moduli   83
     1.2.   General properties   84
     1.3.   Extractability of square roots   85
2.   Quadratic Root Extraction if $N \equiv 5 (\bmod 8)$ 86
     2.1.   Quadratic and quartic roots of $(1, 0)$
            modulo (p, q)   86

2.2. Quadratic root extractor (QRE-1)   87
2.3. Validation of algorithm QRE-1   87
2.4. Criterion of square root existence
      if $N \equiv 5 \pmod 8$ 88
2.5. Numeric illustrations   89
3. Quadratic Root Extraction (QRE-2)
    if $N \equiv 9 \pmod{16}$ 89
3.1. Gaussian generators   89
3.2. Basic properties   90
3.3. Octadic roots of $(1,0)$ modulo (p,q)   91
3.4. Computation of $\sqrt{i} \equiv \sqrt{(0,1)}$ modulo (p,q) . . .   92
3.5. Multiplicative inverse of 2 modulo (p,q)   92
3.6. Alternate computation   93
3.7. Algorithm for quadratic root extraction   93
3.8. Second numeric illustration   94
4. Quadratic Root Extraction (QRE-3)
    if $N \equiv 17 \pmod{32}$ 94
4.1. Basic property and roots of $(1,0)$ 94
4.2. Resolventa of quadratic root extractor   95
4.3. Sedonic roots of $(1,0)$ modulo G   96
4.4. Third numeric illustration   96
5. Comparison of Extractors   97
6. Cryptographic Algorithm   98
7. Reduction of Computational Complexity   99
8. The Case Where $N \equiv 3 \pmod 4$ 100
9. Applicability of QRE Algorithms   100
10. Concluding Remarks   101
Appendix   101
A.1. Classification of roots of $(1,0)$ modulo (p,q) . . .   101
A.2. Criterion of quadratic residuosity and algorithm
      if $N \equiv (2^{k-1} + 1) \pmod{2^k}$ 102
A.3. Algorithm validation   103
A.4. Special case: quadratic extractor
      modulo $(p,-1)$ 103
A.5. Special cyclic identity   105
A.6. Alternate extraction of square roots
      (illustrated in Table A.2)   106

9. **Cubic Roots of Complex Integers and Encryption
    with Digital Isotopes**   **109**

    1. Introduction   109
    2. Algorithm-1   110
    3. Algorithm-2   111
    4. Multiplicity of Cubic Roots   112
    5. Relationship between Cubic Roots   112
    6. Existence of $\sqrt{3} \bmod p$ or $\sqrt{-3} \bmod p$ 113
    7. Properties of Gaussian Cubes   113
    8. Cryptographic Protocol   113
    9. Efficient Encryption of Complex Integers   114
    10. Digital Isotopes   115
    11. Numeric Illustration   116
    12. Algorithm in Nutshell   117
    13. Optimized Recovery of Information   119
    14. Minimization of Erroneous Recovery of Original
        Information   120
    15. Third Numeric Illustration   120
    16. Algorithm Analysis   121
    17. Speedup of Communication   121
    18. Possible Applications and Concluding Remarks   122
    Appendix   122
        A.1. Validation of Algorithm-1   122
        A.2. Validation of Algorithm-2   123
        A.3. More on identities for cubic roots   123
        A.4. Proof of Proposition 5   124

10. **Exponentiation-Free Accelerated Encryption/
    Decryption Protocol**   **127**

    1. Introduction   127
    2. Primary Residues   127
        2.1. Complex modulo reduction   128
        2.2. Primary residues   129
        2.3. Plaintext as primary residue   129
        2.4. Geometric interpretation   130
    3. Cryptographic System Based on Primary Residues . . .   130
    4. Information Hiding and its Recovery   132

4.1.	Threshold parameter	132
4.2.	Sender's secret key	132
5.	Validation of Encryption/Decryption Algorithm	133
6.	Cryptosystem Design	134
7.	Equalizing the Feasibility Intervals	134
8.	Plaintext Preconditioning and Recovery	135
9.	Numeric Illustrations	136
10.	Algorithm for Multiplicative Inverse of P modulo Complex R	137
11.	Computational Complexity	140
12.	Concluding Remarks	140

11. Cryptocol Based on Three-Dimensional Elliptic Surface — **141**

1.	Introduction and Basic Concepts	141
2.	Computation of y_3 and u_3	142
3.	Computation of x_3 and z_3	143
4.	Solution of System of Equations	144
5.	Addition of Points on TDES: Numeric Illustration	144
6.	Alternative for Decomposition	145
7.	Extraction of Cubic Roots	146
7.1.	Cubic root extractor if $p \bmod 9 = 5$	146
7.2.	Cubic root extractor if $p \bmod 9 = 2$	147
7.3.	Cubic root extractor if $p \bmod 9 = 4$	148
7.4.	Cubic root extractor if $p \bmod 9 = r$	148
7.5.	Cubic extractor if $p \bmod 9 = 8$	150
7.6.	Alternative algorithms for cubic root extraction if $p \bmod 9 = 8$	151
7.7.	MMI of 3 modulo $p - 1$ if $p \bmod 3 = 2$	151
8.	Number of Points on TDES	152
9.	Triplet of Considerations	152
10.	Cryptographic Protocol	153
11.	Number of Points on TDES	154
Appendix		155
A.1.	Solution of system of equations $d := x_3^3 + v_3^3 = u_3^3$	155
A.2.	Alternative TDES	155

12. Multi-Parametric Cryptography for Rapid Transmission of Information   **157**

   1.   Introduction   157
   2.   Proposed Cryptographic Algorithm   158
   3.   Key-Exchange Mechanism (KEM)   158
       3.1. Options of system design   159
       3.2. Key-exchange mechanism via open communication channels   159
       3.3. Key exchange with complex modulus   161
       3.4. Factorization of $N - 1$ 162
       3.5. Complex modulo reduction mechanisms (CMRM)   162
   4.   "Sequential" Algorithm for Complex Modulo Reduction   163
   5.   Entanglement and Information Recovering Set of Entangs   164
   6.   Multi-Parametric System of Equations   165
   7.   Numeric Illustration   167
   8.   Numeric Illustration-2   168
   9.   Protocol with Twenty Encryptors and Twelve Entangs   169
  10.   Illustrative Example   170
  11.   Feasibility Analysis   171
  12.   Feasibility Analysis: $\{u, w, y\}$-Eqs.   172
  13.   Feasibility Analysis: $\{v, x, z\}$-Eqs.   173
  14.   Cryptanalysis of the MPA   176
       Appendix   176
       A.1. Parallel algorithm for complex modulo reduction: $(x, y) := (a, b) \bmod (p, q)$ 176

13. Scheme for Digital Signature that Always Works   **179**

   1.   RSA Public and Private Keys   179
   2.   Failure of RSA Signature Scheme   180
   3.   ElGamal Digital Signature Algorithm   181
   4.   Signature Scheme with Upper-and-Lower Keys   182
       4.1. System Design Level   182
       4.2. System Implementation   183
   5.   Computational Complexity   183

14. Hybrid Cryptographic Protocols Providing Digital Signature **185**

   1.   Introduction and Basic Definitions 185

   2.   Digital Signature Scheme 187

       2.1. System design module 187

       2.2. Encryption/Decryption module 187

       2.3. Selection of block size and matrix
            of entanglements 188

       2.4. Essence of RSA digital signature algorithm 189

   3.   Examples of Entangs 190

       3.1. Linear transformations 190

       3.2. Non-Linear transformations 190

       3.3. Improper entanglement 191

   4.   Trade-off Analysis 192

   5.   Decryption: Reduction of Complexity 193

   6.   Illustrative Example 193

   7.   Concluding Remarks 195

15. Control Protocols Providing Information Assurance **197**

   1.   Introduction 197

   2.   Basic Definitions 198

   3.   Information Assurance Protocols 199

       3.1. $P(3,2)$-Protocol 199

   4. $P(4,2)$-Protocol 200

   5. $\Gamma(0,3)$-Protocol 201

   6. $P(r,n)$-Protocol Attributes 201

   7.   Comparative Analysis of $P(r,n)$ 202

       7.1. PoF and bandwidth requirements 202

   8.   Comparison of Protocols $P(8,4)$, $P(8,5)$
        and $P(9,5)$ 203

   9.   Efficiency of Aggregation 203

  10.   First Illustrative Example 204

  11.   Second Illustrative Example 204

  12.   Choice of Entangs 205

  13.   Concluding Remarks 205

       Appendix 206

       A.1. Repeated-transmission protocol 206

       A.2. $F_{3,2}$ formula derivation 206

A.3. PoF in $P(4,2)$ 207

A.4. PoF in $P(6,3)$ and $P(6,4)$ protocols   207

A.5. Monotone attributes of PoF   208

A.6. Ranking the protocols   209

A.7. Selection of optimal protocol   209

A.8. PoF as function of redundancy   210

A.9. Diminishing effect of redundancy   210

**16. Information Assurance Based on Cubic Roots
of Integers**   **211**

1.   Introduction   211

2.   Problem Statement   212

3. $P(3,2)$-Protocol: Quadratic Root Implementation . . .   213

4.   Cubic Root Encryption/Decryption Algorithm   214

5.   Algorithm Verification   214

6.   Protocol $P(3,2)$: Cubic-Root Implementation   215

7.   Reliability Analysis   216

8.   Protocol $P(4,2)$: Cubic-Root Implementation   216

9. $P(6,3)$-Protocol   217

10. Reliability Analysis of $P(6,3)$-Protocol   217

11. Comparison of Protocols   217

12. Highly-Improbable Cases   220

13. Concluding Remarks: Adaptive vs. Non-Adaptive
     Transmission   221

**17. Simultaneous Information Assurance
and Encryption Based on Quintic Roots**   **223**

1.   Introduction   223

2.   Problem Statement   224

3.   Numeric Representation of Plaintext as Array
     of Complex Integers   225

4.   Cryptosystem Based on Quintic Roots   225

     4.1. Encryption/Decryption algorithm   225

     4.2. Algorithm verification   226

5.   Properties of $P(r,h)$-Protocol   227

     5.1. Reliability analysis   227

     5.2. Protocol $P(4,2)$ 228

     5.3. Reduction of decryption complexity   228

5.4. $P(6,3)$-Protocol 229

5.5. Reduction of decryption complexity 229

5.6. Reliability analysis of $P(6,3)$-protocol 229

5.7. $P(6,4)$-Protocol 230

6. Average Complexity of Decryption 230

7. Comparison of Protocols 230

8. Comparison of Failure Probabilities 231

9. General Case of $P(r,h)$ 234

9.1. Average complexity of decryption 234

10. Highly-Improbable Cases 235

11. Concluding Remarks: Adaptive vs. non-Adaptive
Transmission 236

18. Modular Equations and Integer Factorization   **237**

1. Introduction and Problem Statement 237

1.1. Proof of Proposition 1.5 239

1.2. Generalized modular reduction-in-exponent . . . 242

2. *iFac*1 Algorithm Based on ECs 242

2.1. iFac1 algorithm 242

3. *iFac*1 Validation 243

4. Modular Quadratic and Biquadratic Equations 244

5. *iFac*2 Algorithm 246

5.1. iFac2 algorithm 246

6. Properties of Modular Equations for $m \geq 2$:
Computer Experiments 247

7. *iFac*2 Algorithm Validation 247

8. Concluding Remarks 248

Appendix 248

A.1. Proof of Proposition 4.1 248

A.2. Complexity analysis 249

A.3. Proof of Proposition 1.10 250

A.4. Number of points on EC $y^2 = x(x^2 + 2^d)(\mod pq)$
and its factorization 251

A.5. Analysis of options in Table A.1. 251

A.6. Alternate algorithm for cases $2,4,5,7,10,12,13$
and 15 253

A.7. *iFac* algorithm {Cases 6 or 16} 256

19. Counting Points on Hyper-Elliptic Curves and Integer Factorization   **259**

  1.   Introduction and Modular Elliptic Curves (ECs)   259
       1.1.   Simple algorithm for integer factorization   261
  2.   Super-Singular ECs as Splitters   261
  3.   RSA Challenge   263
  4.   Number of Points on EC   265
  5.   Number of Points on Quadratic Curves (QCs)   265
  6.   Number of Points on HECs   266
       6.1.   Two basic algorithms for integer
              factorization   267
       6.2.   Quadratic splitter   267
  7.   Computer Experiments with $V(m,n)$ 269
  8.   Quadratic Splitters   269
  9.   Points Counting Algorithm on EC $y^2 = x^3 - x (\mod p)$,
       if $p \mod 4 = 1$ 270
  10. Properties of Factors of Semi-Prime n   271
  11. Integer Factorization *via* Counting Points
       on Special HEC   271
       Appendix   273
       A.1.   Points Counting on $V(n)$ 273

20. Integer Factorization *via* Constrained Discrete Logarithm Problem   **275**

  1.   Introduction   275
  2.   Reduction of IFP to DLP   276
  3.   Algorithm Validation   277
  4.   Modular Multiplicative Inverse (MMI)   277
  5.   Numeric Illustration   278
  6.   Multiplicity of DLP Solutions   278
  7.   Upper and Lower Bounds   279
  8.   Integer Factorization Algorithm (IFA)   280
  9.   Solution of DLP *via* Baby-Step Giant-Step (BSGS)
       Algorithm   281
  10. Complexity of IFA   282
  11. Balanced IFA   282
  12. Optimal Search Parameters   283

12.1. Solution of constrained DLP 284

12.2. Optimizing the IFA 284

13. Corollaries and Hypothesis 285

14. Refinements 285

14.1. IFA on expanded lattices 285

14.2. Adjustment of search parameter S 288

15. Harmonic Average Complexity 288

16. Concluding Remarks 290

Appendix 290

A.1. Algorithm in nutshell 290

21. Decomposability of Discrete Logarithm Problems   **293**

1. Introduction and Problem Statement 293

2. Divide-and-Conquer Decomposition 295

3. Decomposition of DLP 296

4. Multi-Level Decomposition 296

5. More about Multi-Level Decomposition 299

6. Comparison of Complexities 300

7. Second-Level Decomposition: Solution of $DLP(3)$ . . . 300

8. Computational Considerations 301

9. Algorithmic Decomposition of $DLP(k)$ 302

10. Conclusion 303

22. Detecting Intervals and Order of Point

on Elliptic Curve   **305**

1. Introduction 305

2. Properties of Scalar Multiplication kH 305

3. More Efficient Approach 306

4. Detection Algorithm 307

5. Analysis of Algorithm 309

6. Optimal Detection Algorithm 310

23. Generalization of Gauss Theorem

and Computation of Complex Primes   **313**

1. Introduction and Gauss Theorem

for Counting Points 313

2. Generalized Gauss Theorem 314

3. Examples of Points on ECs (2.1) 316

4.   Points Counting on ECs with $a = 2^d$ 316
5.   Points Counting on Dual EC with $a = -2^d$ 318
6.   Further Generalization of Gauss Theorem 319
7.   Counting of Points $V(p, a)$ on EC 320
8.   Effect of Doubling in EC 321
9.   Generation of Complex Primes via Points Counting
     on ECs 323
10. CEs 324
11. Complexity Analysis 324
12. Concluding Remarks 325
     Appendix 325
     A.1. Analysis of Periodicity in EC $y^2 = x^3 + b^d x (\bmod p)$
           with Base $b = 3, 7, 11, 13$ 325

**24. Space Complexity of Algorithm for Modular
     Multiplicative Inverse**   **329**

1.   Introduction 329
2.   Algorithm for MMI 329
     2.1. Definition 329
     2.2. EEA 330
3.   Bit-Storage Requirement for Stack 330
     3.1. Direct problem 330
     3.2. Dual problem 331
4.   Properties of Optimal Quotients 332
5.   Diagonally-Decreasing Matrices 333
     5.1. Definition 333
     5.2. Properties of D-matrices 333
6.   Decomposition 334
7.   Transposition 334
8.   Optimal Control Variables 335
     8.1. Cases $s = 0, 1, 2$ 335
     8.2. Case $s = 3$ 336
     8.3. Case $s = 4$ 336
     8.4. Case $s = 5$ 336
9.   Iterative Relations for Tight Upper Bound $n(s)$ . . . 339
10. Closed-Form Expressions for $n(s)$ 340
11. Asymptotic Rate of Growth per Bit 340
12. Concluding Remarks 341

Appendix 342
    A.1. Analysis and examples 342
    A.2. Separability: Proof of Proposition 8.1 343
    A.3. Exact Presentation for Tight Upper Bound 343
        A.3.1. Auxiliary arrays $t_i(k)$ 343

25. New Algorithm Can Be Computed   345

    1. Introduction 345
    2. Multiplication of Complex Numbers 345
    3. Multiplication of Polynomials of mth Degree 347
    4. Reduction of Complexity 348
    5. Meta-Algorithm 351
    6. Example of Feasible Solution 352
    7. Enumeration of Combinations of Variables . . . . . . : . 352
    8. Reduction of CPU Time 354

26. Search for Period of Odd Function   355

    1. Introduction and Problem Statement 355
    2. Search for Period p 356
    3. Selection of Optimal Search Parameters 356
    4. The Problem 357
    5. Search for Optimal Search Strategy σ^o 357

27. Optimized Search for Maximum of Function on Large Intervals   359

    1. Introduction and Problem Statement 359
    2. Choice of Next Evaluation Point 362
        2.1. Sequential search: (single processor case) 362
        2.2. Comparisons of possible scenarios
            and the outputs 363
        2.3. Multiprocessor case 363
        2.4. Possible outputs in the worst case 363
    3. Search as Two-Player Game with Referee 364
        3.1. Sequential search: ($p = 1$) 364
        3.2. Multiple-processor search: ($p \geq 2$) 364
    4. Structure of Unbounded Sequential Search 365
    5. Optimal Balanced Sequential Search 367
        5.1. The algorithm 367
        5.2. Optimality of sequential search 368

6.   Complexity of Sequential Minimax Search   369
7.   Estimated Interval of Uncertainty   371
8.   Parallel Search: Basic Properties   371
9.   Search on Finite Interval: Principle of Optimality   . . .   372
   9.1.   Properties of $I_m^p(u, v)$ 373
   9.2.   Case: $p = 2$ 373
   9.3.   Odd number of processors   375
   9.4.   Even number of processors   376
   9.5.   Optimal detecting states   376
   9.6.   Optimal detecting states: defining rules   377
10.   Search Diagrams   378
11.   Optimal Intervals between Evaluation Points   378
   11.1.   Linear programming problems   378
   11.2.   Search diagrams   379
12.   Search Diagrams for Optimal Algorithms   381
   12.1.   Odd p   381
      12.1.1.   Defining rules   381
      12.1.2. $p = 3$ 382
   12.2.   Even number of processors: $\{p = 2r\}$ 382
      12.2.1.   Detecting mode   382
      12.2.2.   Scanning mode   383
      12.2.3.   Detecting rules   384
      12.2.4. $p = 4$ 384
13.   Optimal Parallel Search   385
   13.1.   Inter-processor communication network   385
   13.2.   The algorithm   385
      13.2.1.   Inter-processor communication   385
      13.2.2.   Pseudo-code   385
   13.3.   Optimality of parallel search   386
14.   Basic Parameters and Relations   387
   14.1.   Basic parameters   387
   14.2.   Basic relations: $\{odd\ p\}$ 387
   14.3.   Basic relations: $\{even\ p\}$ 387
15.   Complexity Analysis   387
   15.1.   Fundamental relations   387
   15.2.   Maximal interval analyzed after
       m parallel probes   389
16.   Speed-up and Efficiency of Parallelization   389

**28. Topological Design of Satellite
Communication Networks** **391**

   1.   Introduction and Problem Definition   391

   2.   Problem Statement   392

   3.   Special Cases   393

   4.   Linear Switching Cost Function   393

   5.   Binary Parametric Partitioning   394

   6.   Complexity of Algorithm   395

   7.   Binary Partitioning and Associated Binary Tree   395

   8.   Non-Monotone Cost of Hardware   396

   9.   Dynamic Programming Algorithm   397

       9.1.   Bottom-up mode   397

       9.2.   Top-down-depth-first mode   397

       9.3.   Numerical example   397

  10.   Statistical Properties of Cost-Function $h(x)$ 398

  11.   Optimal Algorithm for Large n   399

  12.   Average Complexity of Parametric Partitioning   399

References   401

Chapter 0

Introductory Notes on Security and Reliability

1. Background

As a brief preview to this book, it is necessary to mention the comprehensive communication and information exchange via the Internet. Billions of people and hundreds of thousands of businesses and other organizations take advantage of the Internet transmission of information. The world's capacity to store, retrieve and transmit information has doubled every 40 months since 1980s; just in 2012 2.5×10^{18} bytes of data were created daily.

The information exchange is performed via open channels, which means that everybody has access to this information; and in many cases the transmitted information is highly sensitive. Therefore, it is reasonable to assume that the communicating parties expect that the content of their exchange is reliably protected from uninitiated and in some cases malicious intruders. While the passive intruders retrieve the information, the active ones either interrupt the exchange or partially alter it, or disseminate the information to make it public, or impersonate it, or completely fabricate their own messages. Needless to state that intruders' tactic of disinformation can be devastating to the communicating parties.

Securing large multinational corporate communication networks has become another increasingly difficult task. It is no longer sufficient to simply prevent intruders from penetrating an organization's network. Sensitive information routinely leaves the corporate network boundaries and falls into the hands of unauthorized users. Therefore, it is imperative to be protected not only from outside attackers, but also from insiders, who are either intentionally or unknowingly leaking data such as valuable intellectual property. Employing the cyber-techniques, such as those discussed in this book, is the premier defense against adversaries attempting to obtain sensitive corporate data.

The art and science of secret communication as means of protection from intruders, called *cryptography*, has a long history that goes back to antiquity. It was based on prior clandestine exchange of secret ciphers/keys between the parties intended to communicate. This private key cryptography was used for centuries in secret diplomatic exchanges, in merchandize delivery, as well as in military planning, espionage and in private messages. There are many publications where cryptographic ciphers are described (Caesar cipher, one-time pad also known as Vernam cipher, transposition cipher, mono-alphabetic substitution cipher, permutation cipher, affine cipher, polyalphabetic or Vigenere cipher, etc.) (Menezes *et al.*, 1997). However, since the middle of 1970s, the security of communication has been addressed in cryptographic systems that do not require exchange of secret keys between the parties prior to communication. Such systems are called *public-key* cryptography (PKC).

It is necessary to reiterate that private exchange of secret keys is a time consuming and costly enterprise, and not every sender and receiver have means to do that. Because the PKC does not require clandestine exchange of keys, it allows communication between the parties, who even do not know each other. That explains its obvious practical appeal and importance, and, as a result, its wide application. The drawback of the PKC stems from its sluggishness, which precludes information exchange in real-time mode. It is too slow in comparison with the traditional cryptography based on the private keys.

In parallel with the cryptographers' efforts to protect the information, the intruders are developing various algorithms and other cyber-techniques, called *cryptanalysis*, for breaking the keys.

Definition 1.1. A set of well-defined, unambiguous and efficiently executable rules is called an *algorithm* if, after finite number of steps, it provably delivers solution to a class of problems.

The art and science that deals with cryptography and cryptanalysis is called *cryptology*. In this book, we introduce new methods of information protection and analyze their efficiency. We also provide and discuss several algorithms that solve two challenging problems in cryptanalysis called *integer factorization* (*iFac*) and *discrete logarithm problem* (DLP).

Another class of problems that we discuss in this book deals with the transmission of information over unreliable channels with either human-induced errors or errors that stem from natural causes: thermal noise in channels, negative influence of cosmic rays, or combination of several of them. Modern multi-layered communication protocols adopt meticulous systems of acknowledgements that is either precluding or at least minimizing the probabilities of those errors. However, when the communicating parties are separated by interplanetary distances, the system of acknowledgements is not feasible due to round trip transmission propagation delays that might take hours for a message to "travel" between the sender and receiver. We address this set of problems in *information assurance* algorithms that are described in Chaps. 14–16 of this book.

The situation becomes even more challenging when we deal with both factors (security and information assurance). In this book, we demonstrate how to simultaneously tackle these two problems. The combined cyber-approach dealing with both problems creates a synergetic affect: it is not only addressing each problem, but speeding up the communication time.

2. Basics of Modular Arithmetic

In this book, we consider several public-key encryption/decryption algorithms for secure transmission of information over open communication channels. These algorithms are mostly arithmetic transformations based on additions, subtractions, multiplications and exponentiations of integers that are used for the encryption, and inverse arithmetic operations (division, extraction of roots, etc.) that are used for the decryption. Although the encryptional operations preserve integer character of numerically presented information, the size of the resulting integers is far beyond what computers can handle unless we use scientific notations and round off the extremely large numbers consisting of tens of thousands or more digits. However, rounding off is absolutely unacceptable in our case, otherwise after the decryption we will not be able to recover the initially transmitted *"Evian Bonus"* and will mistakenly decrypt *"Naïve Lotus"*.

Another difficulty in dealing with integers stems on the level of decryption where we need to use the *inverse* arithmetic operations, which in most of cases do not preserve integrality of outputs because in traditional arithmetic "five-divided-by-three" or "cubic root of 19" is not an integer. However, in the *modular arithmetic*, the notion of division allows to preserve the integrality of outputs if we keep in mind that c/d is the product of c and a multiplicative inverse of d, i.e., $c/d = cd^{-1}$.

Indeed, let us denote $R := (5/3) \bmod 16$; and let x be the inverse of 3 modulo 16. It means that the definition of the multiplicative inverse implies that $3x \bmod 16 = 1$. It is easy to verify that $x = 11$ satisfies this equation, since $33 \bmod 16 = 1$.

Therefore, $R = 5x \bmod 16 = 55 \bmod 16 = 7$. On the other hand, verification confirms that indeed $3R \bmod 16 = 5$.

Obviously, for small inputs it is not difficult to guess the inverse x; however, if the inputs are large, this is not a simple task. Indeed, try to guess an integer x such that $17x \bmod 45 = 1$.

It is also easy to check that cubic root of 19 in the arithmetic based on modulo 71 is equal to 9. Indeed, $9^3 \bmod 71 = 19$.

Definition 2.1. Let a, b and p be positive integers; then $a \bmod p = b$ if there exists a non-negative integer m such that $a = mp+b$ and $0 \le b \le p-1$. Here p is called a *modulus*.

The following formula shows how b is computed:

$$b := a \bmod p = a - \lfloor a/p \rfloor p. \tag{2.1}$$

In Chap. 1, we provide an algorithm that finds for two integers p_0 and p_1 an integer number x, satisfying the equation

$$p_1 x \bmod p_0 = 1. \tag{2.2}$$

Such integer x is called a multiplicative inverse of p_1 modulo p_0 or, for short, a *modular multiplicative inverse* (MMI). We also provide analysis of time complexity of this algorithm and in Chap. 23 its space complexity. The latter one can be critical if we intend to utilize it in smart phones, tablets and/or wearable computers.

3. Basic Properties in Modular Arithmetic

In this section, we provide examples of basic operations in modular arithmetic and their properties:

(a) $(c + d) \bmod p = (d + c) \bmod p = (c \bmod p + d \bmod p) \bmod p$,
(b) $(cd) \bmod p = (dc) \bmod p = [(c \bmod p)(d \bmod p)] \bmod p$,
(c) $e(c \pm d) \bmod p = [(ec) \bmod p \pm (ed) \bmod p] \bmod p$,
(d) $(c^n) \bmod p = [(c \bmod p)^n] \bmod p$,
(e) if p is a prime, then $(c^n) \bmod p = [(c \bmod p)^{n \bmod (p-1)}] \bmod p$,
(f) $(-c) \bmod p = p - (c \bmod p)$,
(h) if $(c + x) \bmod p = d$, then $x = (d - c) \bmod p$,

(i) if $(cx)\bmod p = d$, and $\gcd(c,p) = 1$, then there exists an integer y such that $(cy)\bmod p = 1$; and $x = (dy)\bmod p$.

Short-cut notations: Instead of writing $A \bmod p = B \bmod p$, as we did in (a)–(e), it is shorter to write $A = B(\bmod p)$. C. F. Gauss introduced an equivalent notation $A \equiv B(\bmod p)$.

The properties (a)–(i) and other properties that we discuss in this book simplify computations in the modular arithmetic.

Example 3.1. Let us compute $x = 18^{23} \bmod 13$. Using the direct computation, we derive that

$$x = 74347713614021927913318776832 \bmod 13 = 8. \tag{3.1}$$

However, the same result can be derived more efficiently via application of properties (d) and (e), namely, with smaller number of computations [compare (3.1) and (3.2)].

Indeed,

$$x = 5^{11} \bmod 13 = 48828125 \bmod 13 = 8. \tag{3.2}$$

Exercise 3.2. Compute $x = (1539^{243} + 1837 \times 2013^{1777}) \bmod 29$.

Example 3.3. Let us now try to find an integer x that satisfies the equation $3x^2 \bmod 11 = 5$, then $x = \sqrt{5/3} \bmod 11$. Here we face two problems: both $5/3$ and square root of $5/3$ are not integers in the traditional arithmetic. However, in modulo 11 arithmetic the inverse of 3 is 4. Therefore, $x = \sqrt{20} \bmod 11 = 2\sqrt{5} \bmod 11$. On the other hand, $\sqrt{5} \bmod 11 = \pm 4$, since $16 \bmod 11 = 5$. Thus, $x = \pm 8$, which is the same as $x_1 = 3$ and $x_2 = 8$. Indeed, both values of x satisfy the initial quadratic equation.

We provided more details in the introductory sections of Chap. 1 and other chapters.

As curiosity of the modular arithmetic, it is worth to mention that famous Fermat's Last Theorem (FLT) is not correct in that setting. Namely, for every positive integers a and b there exist integers $c > 1$ and $m > 2$ such that $a^m + b^m = c^m(\bmod n)$.

Indeed, if n is a prime, then $m = n$ and $c = a + b$.

Exercise 3.4. Demonstrate that if modulus n is a product of two positive primes p and q, then for every positive integers a and b there exist integers

$c > 0$ and $m > 2$ such that

$$a^m + b^m = c^m \pmod{pq} \{\text{Hint: revisit the Preface}\}. \tag{3.3}$$

4. Direct and Inverse Problems

The existing algorithms of public key cryptography are based on computational complexity of *inverse problems*. The direct and inverse problems can be formally described as the following frameworks.

Consider two arrays of variables $\{a_1, \ldots, a_r\}$, $\{b_1, \ldots, b_t\}$ and an array of procedures $\{\text{proc}_1, \ldots, \text{proc}_t\}$, where every procedure is well-defined and efficiently executable. Let $\{a_1, \ldots, a_r\}$ be *inputs*; and $\{b_1, \ldots, b_t\}$ be *outputs*.

Definition 4.1. A set of assignments where for every $k = 1, \ldots, t$

$$b_k := \text{proc}_k(a_1, \ldots, a_r) \tag{4.1}$$

is called a *direct* problem.

It is paramount to understand that the direct problem (4.1) is executable by almost every programming language. In addition, if every procedure in (4.1) is unambiguous and executable in finite number of steps, then the direct problem is solvable on computer or by an analogous device.

Definition 4.2. A set of assignments where for every $i = 1, \ldots, r$

$$a_i := \text{proc}_i(b_1, \ldots, b_t) \tag{4.2}$$

is called an *inverse* problem.

The inverse problem (4.2) in general *cannot* be solved via any existing programming language.

While the direct problems are in domain of software engineers and programmers, the inverse problems are in domain of mathematicians, algorithm designers and/or computer scientists. A mathematician tries to address it as a system of equations, and to find a way how to solve it. An algorithmist tries to find an algorithm that solves the class of similar problems. And, if such an algorithm is either unknown or does not exist, or has unacceptable time or space complexity, then a computer scientist tries to tackle the inverse problem via computer simulation.

5. Complexity Enhancement

From the point of view of system science, the direct problems are typical in evaluation of a system performance; and the inverse problems are characteristic in engineering and system design. On every stage of cryptographic algorithms (system design, encryption and decryption), we must solve the direct problems. Yet, cryptanalysts and uninitiated intruders/hackers must deal with the inverse problems. That is why the inverse problems must be intentionally pre-designed to make them as difficult as possible. There are at least two ways in achieving it on the design level of each cryptographic system: either to consider very large input parameters (100 or more decimal digits) or to select the *intrinsically* complex problem.

It is a "cat-and-mouse" process: when the methods of cryptanalysis become more sophisticated, the cryptographers must either increase the size of cryptographic parameters (to several hundred decimal digits) or to enhance the intrinsic complexity of the inverse problem. In this endeavor we deal with a delicate dilemma: if the inverse problem is too complex, it provides stronger crypto-immunity, yet, it consumes too much time for its implementation. The approach with larger input parameters was initially implemented in the RSA (Rivest *et al.*, 1978) until new cryptographic concepts based on modular arithmetic of elliptic curves were independently introduced in Koblitz (1985) and Miller (1985).

In this book, we consider three classes of complex inverse problems: *iFac* (Chaps. 17 and 18), DLP (Chaps. 19 and 20) and cryptography based on three-dimensional elliptic surfaces (Chap. 10). There exists several cryptographic algorithms (Diffie–Hellman Key Exchange, RSA, ElGamal, Rabin, NTRU, etc.) based on the arithmetic of real integers and real modulus. In this book, we consider the intrinsically more difficult inverse problems in the arithmetic based on complex moduli and other settings (Chaps. 7–9, 11 and 13). As another novelty, we consider four rather than two layers of information protection (Chap. 13).

In system design when we try to solve a problem, we use three conceptual levels: "what to do" (descriptive/managerial level), "how to do it" (constructive level/design of algorithm) and "why it works" (algorithm validation/mathematical proof). Although we consider problems, for which the algorithms exist, in general this is not always the case. And, if there are several available algorithms, it is not clear how to find them and how to select the best one. In the last part of this book, we provide examples of algorithms that can be *computed* (Chap. 24). We also demonstrate how to use dynamic programming (DP) approach in design of an optimal search algorithm (Chap. 26). An efficient DP algorithm solving a combinatorial problem of network design is provided in Chap. 27.

For additional details *about* this book read the Preface and Acknowledgments.

Chapter 1

Enhanced Algorithm for Modular Multiplicative Inverse

1. Introduction: Division of Two Integers

As it was indicated above, output of division of two integers in most of the cases is not integer in traditional arithmetic. However, in modular arithmetic, $(c/d) \bmod p$ is either integer if d and p are relatively prime, or it does not exist if d and p are not co-prime, i.e., if $\gcd(d, p) > 1$. Analogous case exists in traditional arithmetic:

For instance, if $dy = 1$ and $d = 0$, then there is no unique y that satisfies $0y = 1$.

In this chapter, we provide an Enhanced-Euclid algorithm (NEA) that finds for two relatively prime integers p_0 and p_1 an integer number x, satisfying the equation

$$p_1 x \bmod p_0 = 1. \tag{1.1}$$

This integer x is called a multiplicative inverse of p_1 modulo p_0 or, for short, a *Modular Multiplicative Inverse* (MMI). However, if p_0 and p_1 are not relatively prime, then the NEA finds a $\gcd(p_0, p_1)$. The Extended-Euclid algorithm (XEA) (Knuth, 1997) also finds a MMI of p_0 and p_1 if $\gcd(p_0, p_1) = 1$. Otherwise, the XEA finds $\gcd(p_0, p_1)$.

In this chapter, we prove a validity of the NEA and provide its analysis. The analysis demonstrates that the NEA is faster than the XEA.

2. Basic Arrays and their Properties

Let us consider *five* finite integer arrays:

$$\{p_i\}, \{c_i\}, \{t_k\}, \{w_k\}, \{z_k\}. \tag{2.1}$$

Definition 2.1. Let $\{p_i\}$ and $\{c_i\}$ be integer arrays defined according to the following generating rules:

given two relatively prime integers p_0 and p_1 such that $p_0 > p_1$,

> **for** $i \geq 1$ **while** $p_i \geq 2$,
>
> **do** $p_{i+1} := p_{i-1} \bmod p_i$ and $c_i := \lfloor p_{i-1}/p_i \rfloor$. (2.2)

Definition 2.2. Let for every $k \geq 1$ $\{t_k\}$ be an arbitrary array; let $\{w_k\}$ and $\{z_k\}$ be defined by the following generating rules: if w_0, w_1, z_0 and z_1 are initially specified,

then for every $k \geq 2$,

$$w_k := w_{k-1}t_{k-1} + w_{k-2} \text{ and } z_k := z_{k-1}t_{k-1} + z_{k-2}. (2.3)$$

Proposition 2.3. Let us consider a sequence of determinants $D_k := \begin{vmatrix} w_k & w_{k-1} \\ z_k & z_{k-1} \end{vmatrix}$, then for every $k \geq 1$,

$$D_k = (-1)^{k-1}D_1. (2.4)$$

Consider D_k and substitute in the left column the values of w_k and z_k defined in (2.3).

After simplifications, it follows that $D_k = -D_{k-1}$, then this relation, if applied telescopically, implies (2.4).

Proposition 2.4. Let all three arrays $\{t_k\}, \{w_k\}$ and $\{z_k\}$ be integer, and

$$w_0 := 1, z_0 := 0, |z_1| := 1.$$

Proposition 2.3 implies that for every w_1 $(-1)^{k-1}z_1z_k$ is a multiplicative inverse of w_{k-1} modulo w_k. Indeed, since $D_1 = -z_1$, then (2.4) implies that

$$w_k z_{k-1} - z_k w_{k-1} = (-1)^k z_1,$$

or that

$$w_{k-1}[(-1)^{k-1}z_1 z_k] - z_1^2 = w_k[(-1)^{k-1}z_1 z_{k-1}]. (2.5)$$

Therefore, (2.5) implies that $\{w_{k-1}[(-1)^{k-1}z_1 z_k]-1\}/w_k = (-1)^{k-1}z_1 z_{k-1}$, i.e., $x = (-1)^{k-1}z_1 z_k$.

Proposition 2.5. If for every $0 \leq k \leq r$, $t_k := c_{r-k}$, then $w_k := p_{r-k}$, i.e.,

$$\{w_k\} = \{p_i\}^R \text{ and } \{t_k\} = \{c_i\}^R, (2.6)$$

where the superscript R in (2.6) means that the arrays $\{c_i\}$ and $\{p_i\}$ are written in reverse.

Thus p_0 and p_1 are seeds that generate the arrays

$$\{p_i\}, \quad \{c_i\}, \quad \{t_k\} := \{c_{r-k}\} \quad \text{and} \quad \{w_k\} := \{p_{r-k}\}.$$

Theorem 2.6. *For every* $k = 1, \ldots, r, (-1)^{k-1} z_1 z_k$ *is the multiplicative inverse of* p_{r-k+1} *modulo* p_{r-k}, *i.e., if* (k *is odd* **and** $z_1 = 1$) **or** (k *is even* **and** $z_1 = -1$),

   then $x := z_k$ **else** $x := p_{r-k} - z_k$;

   if $k := r$ *and* $z_1 = (-1)^{r-1}$, **then** $x := z_r, i.e., p_1 z_r = 1 \bmod p_0.$

$$(2.7)$$

Proof follows from Propositions 2.3–2.5.

3. NEA for MMI

The proposed algorithm uses stack as a data structure. It solves Eq. (1.1).

vars: r, L, M, S, t: all integer numbers, b: boolean,

proc *FORWARD*:

    assign $L := p_0$, $M := p_1$, $b := 0$,

    $\{r := 0$, height of the stack, r is used only for the analysis of the algorithm$\}$,

repeat $t := \lfloor L/M \rfloor$, $S := L - Mt$, $b := 1 - b$, $\{r := r + 1\}$,   (3.1)

    push t $\{$onto the top of the stack$\}$, $L := M$, $M := S$,

$$(3.2)$$

until $S = 1$, (**if** $S = 0$, **then** $\gcd(p_0, p_1) = t$; no MMI)

proc *BACKTRACKING*:

    assign $S := 0$; $M := (-1)^b$ (by (2.7) in Theorem 2.6),

repeat   **pop** t $\{$from the top of the stack$\}$;

        $L := Mt + S$, $S := M$, $M := L$,   (3.3)

until   the stack is *empty*; **output** $x := L$; $\{$if $x < 0$, then $x := x + p_0\}$.

Table 3.1   NEA in progress.

$p_1 = 1973$	$p_0 = 1777$	196	13	1
Stack	1	9	15	—
151	136	15	1	0

Table 3.2   NEA algorithm with even number of columns.

2013	**1976**	37	15	7	1
Stack	1	53	2	2	—
272	267	5	2	1	0

Example 3.1. Let p_0 and p_1 be relatively prime integers; let us find an integer number x that is a MMI, i.e., satisfying the equation $p_1 x \bmod p_0 = 1$ (1.1).

Suppose that $p_0 = 1777$ and $p_1 = 1973$. Table 3.1 shows the algorithm in progress.

Since the right-most element in the first row is equal one, hence the MMI exists.

The second row stores the stack and the left-most element in the third row is equal to either x, if the number of columns is even, or it is equal to $p_1 - x$ if the number of columns is odd. Thus, in this example $x = 1973 - 151 = 1822$. Indeed, $1777 \times 1822 \bmod 1973 = 1$.

Example 3.2. Let now $p_0 = 1976$ and $p_1 = 2013$, let us determine an integer x that satisfies Eq. (1.1). Table 3.2 shows the algorithm in progress.

Since the number of columns is even, hence $x = 272$. Indeed, $1976 \times 272 \bmod 2013 = 1$.

Notice that the lengths of the stacks are very short in both examples: we need to store only three and four elements, respectively.

The space complexity of the NEA is analyzed in Chap. 24.

4. Complexity Analysis of MMI Algorithm

Let us consider four integer non-negative arrays: $\{p_i\}$ and $\{c_i\}$ as they defined in (2.2), and $\{q_k\}$ and $\{d_k\}$ defined in accordance with the rules:

$$d_k := \lfloor q_{k-1}/q_k \rfloor, \tag{4.1}$$

$$p_{i+1} := p_{i-1} - p_i c_i, \quad q_{k+1} := q_{k-1} - q_k d_k. \tag{4.2}$$

Here $\{c_i\}$ and $\{d_k\}$ are quotients; $\{p_i\}$ and $\{q_k\}$ are remainders. It is clear from (2.2) and (4.2) that $p_{i+1} := p_{i-1} - p_i c_i = p_{i-1} \bmod p_i$. Hence, both arrays $\{p_i\}$ and $\{q_k\}$ are strictly decreasing and all terms of the corresponding arrays $\{c_i\}$ and $\{d_k\}$ are positive integers.

Definition 4.1. $\{x_j\}_s$ is a $(s + 1)$-dimensional vector, consisting of first $s + 1$ terms of an array $x_0, x_1, \ldots, x_{j-1}, x_j, \ldots$, i.e., $\{x_j\}_s :=$ $(x_0, x_1, \ldots, x_{s-1}, x_s)$.

Theorem 4.2. *Consider* $\{c_i\}_r \geq 1, \{p_i\}_s, \{d_k\}_s, \{q_k\}_s \geq 1$ *and* $\{p_i\}_r \geq 1$.
Let $p_0 = q_0$, $\{c_i\}_s \leq \{d_k\}_s$, *i.e., for every* $j = 1, \ldots, s$ *there is at least one* $j = l$ *such that* $c_l < d_l$; *then for every* $1 \leq j \leq s$ *the following inequalities hold:*

$$\text{if } 1 \leq j \leq l - 1, \text{ then } p_j \geq q_j \text{ else } p_j > q_j. \tag{4.3}$$

Proof. Assuming that the statement (4.3) holds for every $i \leq j - 1$, let us demonstrate by induction that it also holds for $i = j$. Consider

$$t_j = d_j - c_j = \lfloor q_{j-1}/q_j \rfloor - \lfloor p_{j-1}/p_j \rfloor \leq \lfloor p_{j-1}/q_j \rfloor - \lfloor p_{j-1}/p_j \rfloor. \tag{4.4}$$

If $j \leq l - 1$, then $t_j \geq 0$ else $t_j > 0$. Hence, (4.4) implies that if $j \leq l - 1$, then $p_j \geq q_j$ else $p_j > q_j$. Since $p_0 = q_0$, therefore, (4.3) holds for every $j \leq s$. $\qquad\square$

Consider a pair of relatively prime seeds p_0 and p_1 that generates an array $\{c_i\}_r = 1$.

Let us also consider another pair of relatively prime seeds p_0 and q_1 that generates an array $\{d_k\}_s \geq 1$, i.e., such that *not* every term is equal to *one*. Let r and s be the number of steps required respectively to find the MMIs for the first and the second pair using either the XEA or the NEA. This assumption implies that $q_s = 1$.

Therefore, by Theorem 2.6 $\{p_i\}_s \geq \{q_k\}_s$ and $p_s > q_s = 1$. Hence, $r > s$.

Corollary 4.3. A pair of seeds that is required for a given p_0, which is the maximal number of steps for computation of a MMI, generates an unary array of quotients, where every components in $\{c_i\}_r = 1$. Thus, as it follows from (2.2) and (4.3), this pair of seeds must generate the following array of integer numbers: $p_2 := p_0 - p_1, p_3 := p_1 - p_2, \ldots, p_r := p_{r-2} - p_{r-1} = 1$. For instance, the array of the Fibonacci numbers $\{F_{r+2}, F_{r+1}, \ldots, F_4, F_3, F_2\}$

generates the former array where for every $i = 0, \ldots, r$ $p_i := F_{r+2-i}$ (Boncompagni, 1857; Harkin, 1957).

Remark 4.4. The pair $p_0 = F_{r+2}, p_1 = F_{r+1}$ is *not* the only one that generates (a) an unary array of quotients; (b) a decreasing integer array with the rth remainder equal to *one*.

The following pairs of seeds have the same property {for all non-negative integer numbers t and u}:

1. $p_0 = F_{r+2} + tF_r, p_1 = F_{r+1} + tF_{r-1}$, for $t = 1, \{p_i\}^R = \{L_1, L_2, \ldots, L_{r+1}\}$
   is a sequence of the Lucas numbers $1, 3, 4, 7, 11, 18, \ldots$ (Bressoud, 1989).
2. $p_0 = tF_{r+2} + (1-t)F_{r-1},$ $\qquad t \geq 1, \quad p_1 = tF_{r+1} + (1-t)F_{r-2}.$
3. $p_0 = F_{r+1} + tF_r,$ $\qquad\qquad\quad t \geq 1, \quad p_1 = F_r + tF_{r-1}.$
4. $p_0 = (1+t)F_{r+2} + tF_{r-2} + uF_r,$ $\quad p_1 = (1+t)F_{r+1} + tF_{r-3} + uF_{r-1}.$

Here the Fibonacci numbers with *zero* and *negative* indices are computed with the formula: $F_{-m} = (-1)^{m-1}F_m$. For all pairs, listed above, exactly r steps are required to find the MMI. However, all these pairs are special cases of a pair of seeds where $p_0 = bF_r + F_{r-1}$ and $p_1 = bF_{r-1} + F_{r-2}$. Then for all $0 \leq i \leq r$, $p_i = bF_{r-i} + F_{r-i-1}$, $p_{r-1} = b$ and $p_r = 1$. Let $v = (1 - \sqrt{5})/2$ and $w = (1 + \sqrt{5})/2$. Using a z-transform approach we deduce that for all $0 \leq k \leq r$

$$p_{r-k} = [(b - v)w^k + (w - b)v^k]/\sqrt{5} \quad \text{(Bressoud, 1989).} \qquad (4.5)$$

Therefore, for a large r

$$p_{r-k}\sqrt{5} - (b - v)w^k = (w - b)(-1)^k |v|^k \xrightarrow[k \to r]{} 0, \quad \text{since } |v| < 1. \ (4.6)$$

The relation (4.6) implies that for a large r,

$$p_0 = [w^r(b - v)/\sqrt{5}][1 + o(w)]. \qquad (4.7)$$

Let $z := \max_{b \geq 2} r(p_0, b)$.

Then

$$z \approx \max_{b \geq 2} \log_w[\sqrt{5}p_0/(b - v)] = \log_w[\sqrt{5}p_0/(\sqrt{5} - 1)]$$

$$= \lfloor \log_w p_0 \rfloor [1 + o(p_0)]. \qquad (4.8)$$

From (4.8) it follows that the height of a stack satisfies the following inequality:

$$r \leq (\lfloor \log_w p_0 \rfloor)[1 + o(p_0)] \quad \text{(Silverman and Tate, 1995).} \qquad (4.9)$$

Remark 4.5. Although this upper bound is achievable if $p_0 = bF_r + F_{r-1}$ and $p_1 = bF_{r-1} + F_{r-2}$, for this pair of seeds the *MMI* can be computed explicitly and is equal to $(-1)^{r-1}F_r$.

Remark 4.6. If in the RSA public-key encryption (Rivest *et al.*, 1978), $p_0 = c \times 10^{100}$, then $r \leq 100/\log_{10} w + \log_{10} c$ or $r \leq 479 + \log c$. Over a 1,000 computer experiments demonstrated that an average height of the stack is about 40% smaller than the upper bound in (4.9).

5. Extended-Euclid Algorithm (XEA)

XEA finds a multiplicative inverse of p_1 modulo p_0 provided that $\gcd(p_0, p_1) = 1$.

1. $(X1, X2, X3) := (1, 0, p_0)$, $(Y1, Y2, Y3) := (0, 1, p_1)$,
2. **if** $Y3 = 0$ **return** $X3 = \gcd(p_0, p_1)$; no inverse,
3. **if** $Y3 = 1$ **return** $Y3 = \gcd(p_0, p_1)$, the multiplicative inverse $Y2$,
4. $Q := \lfloor X3/Y3 \rfloor$, $\qquad\qquad\qquad\qquad\qquad\qquad\qquad$ (5.1)
5. $(T1, T2, T3) := (X1 - QY1, X2 - QY2, X3 - QY3)$, $\qquad\quad$ (5.2)
6. $(X1, X2, X3) := (Y1, Y2, Y3)$, $\qquad\qquad\qquad\qquad\qquad$ (5.3)
7. $(Y1, Y2, Y3) := (T1, T2, T3)$, $\qquad\qquad\qquad\qquad\qquad\quad$ (5.4)
8. **goto** 2 (Knuth, 1997; Silverman and Tate, 1992).

6. Comparative Analysis of NEA vs. XEA

Both algorithms require the same number of steps, r, to compute all quotients: the values of t in the *FORWARD* procedure in (3.1), and Q in (5.1), respectively. In addition, the NEA requires r more steps in the *BACKTRACKING* procedure to compute the values of L in (3.3). Thus, the r steps of the XEA require r divisions, $3r$ multiplications, $3r$ long algebraic additions and $10r$ assignments, see (5.1)–(5.4). The XEA uses 10 variables. Yet in both procedures the NEA uses r divisions, $2r$ multiplications, $2r$ long additions, $2r$ stack operations, (push and pop), and $8r$ assignments, see (3.1)–(3.3). The NEA uses *four* integer variables, one binary variable and, in addition, $O(\log_w p_0)$ of memory to store the stack. Note that if a MMI does not exist, then there is no necessity to use the *BACKTRACKING* procedure in the NEA. In this case, the NEA requires even fewer operations than the XEA: *one* division, *one* multiplication, *one* addition, *one* push operation and *five* assignments per every step. Yet the XEA still requires the same number of operations per step as in the case if a MMI does exist.

Thus, in overall the XEA uses more multiplications, more additions, more assignments and twice more variables than the proposed algorithm.

7. Average Complexity of XEA and NEA

If both seeds p_0 and p_1 are chosen randomly, then the probability that $\gcd(p_0, p_1) = 1$ is equal $6/\pi^2 = 0.608$ (Chesaro, 1881).

Let us consider the following notations:

w_{xea}-Worst-case specific complexity (per step) of XEA;
w_{nea}-Worst-case specific complexity of NEA;
a_{xea}-Average-case specific complexity of XEA;
a_{nea}-Average-case specific complexity of NEA;
$t_d, t_m, t_a, t_s, t_{st}$-time complexities of the operations of division, multiplication, addition, assignment and stack operations **push** and **pop**, respectively.

Then,

$$w_{\text{xea}} = t_d + 3t_m + 3t_a + 10t_s, \tag{7.1}$$

$$w_{\text{nea}} = t_d + 2t_m + 2t_a + 8t_s + 2t_{st}, \tag{7.2}$$

$$a_{\text{nea}} = (t_d + 2t_m + 2t_a + 8t_s + 2t_{st}) \times 6/\pi^2$$
$$+(t_d + t_m + t_a + 5t_s + t_{st}) \times (1 - 6/\pi^2). \tag{7.3}$$

Notice that

$$a_{\text{xea}} = w_{\text{xea}}, \quad \text{and} \quad t_d \approx t_m \gg t_a \approx t_s \approx t_{st}. \tag{7.4}$$

Thus,

$$R := a_{\text{xea}}/a_{\text{nea}} = 2\pi^2/(3 + \pi^2) = 1.533785. \tag{7.5}$$

Therefore, the execution of the NEA requires significantly less time than the execution of the XEA.

Chapter 2

Multiplication of Large-Integers Based on Homogeneous Polynomials

As it was stated in the Preface, computers can handle arithmetic operations over integers with limited number of digits. Several algorithms based on homogeneous polynomials for multiplication of large integers are described in this chapter. The homogeneity of polynomials provides several simplifications: reduction of system of equations and elimination of necessity to evaluate polynomials in points with larger coordinates. It is demonstrated that a two-stage implementation of the proposed and Toom–Cook algorithms asymptotically require twice as many standard multiplications than their direct implementation. Analysis of these algorithms revealed that a multistage implementation is also less efficient than their direct implementation.

Although the proposed algorithms as well as the corresponding Toom–Cook algorithms require numerous algebraic additions, the proposed *Generalized Horner rule* for evaluation of homogeneous polynomials, provided in the chapter, decrease this number twice.

1. Introduction and Basic Definitions

Crypto-immunity of various protocols of secure communication over open channels is based on modular arithmetic of large integers with hundreds of decimal digits. Multiplications and exponentiations of large integers are essential operations in this arithmetic. Yet, standard programming libraries in general-purpose computers handle multiplication of integers A and B if the number of decimal digits in each does not exceed m. Such integers we will refer to as *standard* integers. For instance, if a computer cannot multiply integers larger than 10^{30} without a specially written program, then in this case $m = 30$.

The first papers on multiplication of large integers were published by Karatsuba and Ofman (1963) and Toom (1963). Several years later Toom's scheme was improved by Cook (see Cook, 1966; Knuth, 1981). Analysis of computational complexity of Toom–Cook algorithm (TCA) is provided in Crandall and Pomerance (2001) and theoretical foundation for efficient multiplication of large integers is discussed in Bernstein (2004). An efficient implementation of the TCA in cryptographic systems is described in several patents (Crandall, 1994). Analysis of computational complexity of the TCA and its lower bound is provided in Ablayev and Karpinski (2003). A special case of the TCA, where one multiplier is significantly larger than another, is considered in Zanoni (2010). Consider two nm-digit-large integers.

$A = \overline{a_{n-1} \ldots a_2 a_1 a_0}$ and $B = \overline{b_{n-1} \ldots b_2 b_1 b_0}$, where every part a_k and b_k is a m-decimal-digit large *standard integer* (SI, for short). Let us represent A and B as

$$A = \sum_{k=0}^{n-1} (10^m)^k a_k \qquad (1.1)$$

and

$$B = \sum_{k=0}^{n-1} (10^m)^k b_k. \qquad (1.2)$$

Therefore, the product $C = AB$ is expressed as

$$C = \sum_{s=0}^{2(n-1)} (10^m)^s c_s, \qquad (1.3)$$

where $c_{2n-2}, c_{2n-3}, \ldots, c_1, c_0$ are $2n - 1$ unknown coefficients.

In order to compute the product C, these coefficients must be determined.

Example 1.1. Suppose we need to multiply two integers

$$A = 385, 495, 374, 109 \quad \text{and} \quad B = 608, 348, 696, 284$$

using a computing device that cannot multiply integers of order higher than $O(10^3)$. Therefore, in this example $m = 3$ and we split A and B into $n = 4$ parts, where

$$a_3 = 385, \quad a_2 = 495, \quad a_1 = 374, \quad a_0 = 109,$$
$$b_3 = 608, \quad b_2 = 348, \quad b_1 = 696, \quad b_0 = 284.$$

The algorithm provided in Sec. 2 demonstrates how to solve this problem by using a minimal number of multiplications of m-digit "SIs".

2. Multiplication $C = AB$ based on Homogeneous Polynomials

Consider two n^{th} degree homogeneous polynomials of two integer variables x and y:

$$A_n(x, y) := \sum_{i=0}^{n} a_i x^i y^{n-i} \qquad (2.1)$$

$$B_n(x, y) := \sum_{i=0}^{n} b_i x^i y^{n-i} \qquad (2.2)$$

and their product

$$C_{2n}(x, y) := A_n(x, y) B_n(x, y) = \sum_{k=0}^{2n} c_k x^k y^{2n-k}. \qquad (2.3)$$

Remark 2.1. All coefficients in polynomials $A_n(x, y)$ and $B_n(x, y)$ are *inputs*, and the coefficients in $C_{2n}(x, y)$ are *outputs*.

For short, the multiplication algorithm, based on homogeneous polynomials (HP), provided below is called the AHP.

First of all, definition (2.3) implies that

$$c_{2n} = a_n b_n \quad \text{and} \quad c_0 = a_0 b_0. \qquad (2.4)$$

Computation of the remaining $2n - 1$ coefficients in (2.3) is described in the algorithm. Prior to that, let us modify Eq. (2.3) for integers $|x| \geq 1, |y| \geq 1$. Consider

$$M_{2(n-1)}(x, y) := [C_{2n}(x, y) - c_{2n} x^{2n} - c_0 y^{2n}]/xy = \sum_{k=1}^{2n-1} c_k x^{k-1} y^{2n-1-k}. \qquad (2.5)$$

As it is shown in Sec. 3, we can separate "*odd*" coefficients $c_1, c_3, \ldots, c_{2n-1}$ and "*even*" coefficients $c_2, c_4, \ldots, c_{2n-2}$.

The following properties of homogeneous polynomials imply certain limitations on choice of evaluation points:

Property 2.2. If n is a degree of homogeneity of $H(x, y)$ and g is a nonzero real number, then

$$H(gx, gy) = g^n H(x, y). \qquad (2.6)$$

Therefore, if $g = -1$, then

$$H(-x, -y) = (-1)^n H(x, y). \tag{2.7}$$

Property 2.3. If the degree of homogeneity is *even*, then $H(-x, y) = H(x, -y)$, otherwise

$$H(-x, y) = -H(x, -y). \tag{2.8}$$

Corollary 2.4. Definition (2.3) implies that

$$C(-x, y) = C(x, -y), \tag{2.9}$$

since for every integer $nC_{2n}(x, y)$ has an even degree of homogeneity.

Corollary 2.5. Identity (2.9) implies that it is not advantageous to consider, for instance, both $C(p, -q)$ and $C(-p, q)$; neither it is advantageous to consider $C(p, q)$ and $C(gp, gq)$ for any non-zero integer g (2.6). Therefore, in this chapter are considered only the relatively prime pairs of integers p and q.

3. Separation of "Even" and "Odd" Coefficients in AHP

Step 3.1: Compute *sums*

$$S_{2(n-1)}(p, q) := [M_{2(n-1)}(p, q) + M_{2(n-1)}(p, -q)]/2pq, \tag{3.1}$$

for the first $n - 1$ relatively prime pairs of integers

$$(p, q) = \{(2, 1), (1, 2), (3, 1), (1, 3), (3, 2), (2, 3), (4, 1), (1, 4), \ldots\}. \tag{3.2}$$

Remark 3.1. Using (3.1) and (3.2), we create and solve $n - 1$ equations with $n - 1$ "even" unknowns $c_2, c_4, \ldots, c_{2(n-1)}$.

Step 3.2: Compute *differences*

$$D_{2(n-1)}(p, q) := [M_{2(n-1)}(p, q) - M_{2(n-1)}(p, -q)]/2(pq)^2, \tag{3.3}$$

for the same pairs $(p, q) = \{(2, 1), (1, 2), (3, 1), (1, 3), (3, 2), (2, 3), (4, 1), (1, 4), \ldots\}$.

Remark 3.2. As a result, in (3.3), we create $n - 1$ equations with n unknowns $c_1, c_3, \ldots, c_{2n-1}$.

Since by this time the values of all "even" coefficients $c_2, c_4, \ldots, c_{2n-2}$ are already computed, we use $M_{2(n-1)}(1,1)$ (3.5) as the nth equation for computation of n "odd" coefficients.

The following example illustrates a slightly different approach to separate "even" and "odd" variables.

3.1. *Separation of unknowns: $n = 5$*

First, compute $S_8(p,q)$ [see (3.1)] for $(p,q) = \{(1,1), (2,1), (1,2)\}$ and from three equations find c_2, c_4 and c_6.

Second, compute $D_8(p,q)$ [see (3.3)] for $(p,q) = \{(1,1), (2,1), (1,2)\}$ and derive three equations with four "odd" unknowns c_1, c_3, c_5, c_7. As the fourth ("missing") equation, we consider

$$M_8(3,1) := 3^7 c_7 + 3^6 c_6 + \cdots + 3 c_2 + c_1 \tag{3.4}$$

[see (2.5)]. After all "even" coefficients are computed, let

$$Z := M_8(3,1) - 3^2(3^4 c_6 + 3^2 c_4 + c_2). \tag{3.5}$$

Finally, we derive the *fourth* equation

$$3^7 c_7 + 3^5 c_5 + 3^3 c_3 + 3 c_1 = Z. \tag{3.6}$$

3.2. *AHP for multiplication of triple-large integers*

Let us consider a multiplication of triple-large integers, where

$$A(x,y) = a_2 x^2 + a_1 x y + a_0 y^2 \quad \text{and} \quad B(x,y) = b_2 x^2 + b_1 x y + b_0 y^2,$$

$$C(x,y) = A(x,y)B(x,y) = c_4 x^4 + c_3 x^3 y + c_2 x^2 y^2 + \cdots + c_0 y^4. \tag{3.7}$$

therefore,

Step 3.1:

$$c_4 := a_2 b_2, \quad \{= C(1,0) = A(1,0)B(1,0)\}. \tag{3.8}$$

Step 3.2:

$$c_0 := a_0 b_0, \quad \{= C(0,1) = A(0,1)B(0,1)\}. \tag{3.9}$$

Step 3.3:

$$F := (4a_2 + 2a_1 + a_0)(4b_2 + 2b_1 + b_0) \quad \{= C(2,1) = A(2,1)B(2,1)$$
$$= 16c_4 + 8c_3 + 4c_2 + 2c_1 + c_0\}. \tag{3.10}$$

Step 3.4:

$$G := (a_2 + a_1 + a_0)(b_2 + b_1 + b_0), \quad \{=C(1,1) = A(1,1)B(1,1)$$
$$= c_4 + c_3 + \cdots + c_0\}. \quad (3.11)$$

Step 3.5:

$$H := (a_2 + 2a_1 + 4a_0)(b_2 + 2b_1 + 4b_0), \quad \{=C(1,2) = A(1,2)B(1,2)$$
$$= c_4 + 2c_3 + \cdots + 16c_0\}. \quad (3.12)$$

Step 3.6:

$$K := G - c_4 - c_0, \quad \{=M(1,1) = c_3 + c_2 + c_1\}. \quad (3.13)$$

Step 3.7:

$$L := [F - 16c_4 - c_0]/2, \quad \{=M(2,1) = 4c_3 + 2c_2 + c_1\}. \quad (3.14)$$

Step 3.8:

$$M := [H - c_4 - 16c_0]/2, \quad \{=M(1,2) = c_3 + 2c_2 + 4c_1\}. \quad (3.15)$$

Remark 3.3. From the system of linear equations (3.13)–(3.15) we determine c_3, c_2 and c_1.

Step 3.9:

$$N := (L - M)/3 = c_3 - c_1 \quad \text{and} \quad P := L - 2K = 2c_3 - c_1. \quad (3.16)$$

Step 3.10:

$$c_3 = P - N, \quad c_1 = c_3 - N, \quad c_2 = K - c_1 - c_3. \quad (3.17)$$

The algorithm described in (3.8)–(3.17) requires 24 algebraic additions.

4. Reduction of Algebraic Additions

Let us consider a multiplication of two quatro-large integers

$$A = \overline{a_3 a_2 a_1 a_0} \quad \text{and} \quad B = \overline{b_3 b_2 b_1 b_0},$$

where every part a_k and b_k is a m-decimal-digit large SI.

Let us represent A and B as

$$A = (10^m)^3 a_3 + (10^m)^2 a_2 + 10^m a_1 + a_0 \tag{4.1}$$

and

$$B = 10^{3m} b_3 + 10^{2m} b_2 + 10^m b_1 + b_0. \tag{4.2}$$

Therefore, the product $C = AB$ can be expressed as

$$C = 10^{6m} c_6 + 10^{5m} c_5 + \cdots + 10^m c_1 + c_0, \tag{4.3}$$

where *seven* coefficients $c_6, c_5, \ldots, c_1, c_0$ must be determined.

The drawback of the TCA and AHP algorithms is the large number of required algebraic additions. The following algorithm shows how to decrease *twice* the number of these additions.

Step 4.0:

$$c_0 := a_0 b_0, \quad c_6 := a_3 b_3. \tag{4.4}$$

Step 4.1:

$$A_1 := a_3 + a_1, \quad B_1 := b_3 + b_1, \quad A_0 := a_2 + a_0, \quad B_0 := b_2 + b_0. \tag{4.5}$$

Step 4.2:

$$C_1 := (A_1 + A_0)(B_1 + B_0), \quad C_{-1} := (-A_1 + A_0)(-B_1 + B_0). \tag{4.6}$$

Step 4.3:

$$A_3 := 4a_3 + a_1, \quad A_2 := 4a_2 + a_0, \quad B_3 := 4b_3 + b_1, \quad B_2 := 4b_2 + b_0. \tag{4.7}$$

Step 4.4:

$$C_2 := (2A_3 + A_2)(2B_3 + B_2), \quad C_{-2} := (-2A_3 + A_2)(-2B_3 + B_2). \tag{4.8}$$

Step 4.5:

$$A_5 := 8a_3 + A_1, \quad A_4 := 8a_2 + A_0, \quad B_5 := 8b_3 + B_1, \quad B_4 := 8b_2 + B_0. \tag{4.9}$$

Step 4.6:

$$C_3 := (3A_5 + A_4)(3B_5 + B_4), \quad C_{-3} := (-3A_5 + A_4)(-3B_5 + B_4). \tag{4.10}$$

Remark 4.1. For every k the variables A_k and B_k are used twice [see (4.6)–(4.10)].

In order to decrease the amount of computation, we pre-compute them only once. Therefore, we reduce twice the number of algebraic additions in (4.6)–(4.10).

Step 4.7:

$$E_1 := (C_1 + C_{-1})/2 - c_0, \quad E_2 := (C_2 + C_{-2} - 2c_0)/8,$$
$$E_3 := (C_3 + C_{-3} - 2c_0)/18. \tag{4.11}$$

Step 4.8:

$$F_2 := (E_2 - E_1)/3, \quad F_3 := (E_3 - E_1)/8. \tag{4.12}$$

Step 4.9:

$$c_4 := F_2 - 5c_6, \quad c_2 := E_1 - c_4 - c_6. \tag{4.13}$$

Step 4.10:

$$e_1 := (C_1 - C_{-1})/2, \quad e_2 := (C_2 - C_{-2})/4, \quad e_3 := (C_3 - C_{-3})/6. \tag{4.14}$$

Step 4.11:

$$f_2 := (e_2 - e_1)/3, \quad f_3 := (e_3 - e_1)/8. \tag{4.15}$$

Step 4.12:

$$c_5 := (f_3 - f_2)/5, \quad c_3 := f_2 - 5c_5, \quad c_1 := e_1 - c_3 - c_5. \tag{4.16}$$

This algorithm computes the product $C = AB$ using *seven* multiplications of SIs instead of 16 such multiplications as required by "grammar-school" rules.

Further details on the AHP of quatro-large integers are provided in Secs. 8 and 9.

5. Comparison of Evaluated Polynomials in TCA vs. AHP

First of all, in the TCA

$$\Psi := \{C(0), C(1), C(-1)\} \tag{5.1}$$

are computed, and in the AHP

$$\Phi := \{C(1,0), C(0,1), C(1,1), C(1,-1)\} \tag{5.2}$$

are computed. Additional values of evaluated polynomials for $n \geq 3$ are provided in Table 5.1.

Table 5.1   Points of polynomial evaluation in TCA and AHP.

Splitting in	Toom–Cook algorithms	Algorithms based on HP
3 parts	$\Psi, C(2), C(-2)$	$\Phi, C(2,1)$
4 parts	$\Psi, C(2), C(-2), C(3), C(-3)$	$\Phi, C(2,1), C(2,-1), C(1,2)$
8 parts	$\Psi, C(2), C(-2), C(3), C(-3);$ $C(4), C(-4), C(5), C(-5);$ $C(6), C(-6), C(7), C(-7)$	$\Phi, C(2,1), C(2,-1), C(1,2);$ $C(1,-2), C(3,1), C(3,-1), C(1,3);$ $C(1,-3), C(3,2), C(3,-2), C(2,3)$

Remark 5.1. Observe the fast growth of the values of evaluation points in the TCA in comparison with corresponding points in the AHP.

The sets Ψ and Φ of polynomial evaluations in Table 5.1 are defined in (5.1) and (5.2).

6.   Comparison of TCA vs. AHP for $n = 6$

6.1.   *AHP framework*

Compute $C(1,0), C(01), C(1,1), C(1,-1), C(2,1), C(2,-1), C(1,2),$

$$C(-1,2), C(3,1), C(3,-1), C(1,3), \tag{6.1}$$

$$C(1,0) = A(1,0)B(1,0) = a_5 b_5 = c_{10},$$
$$C(0,1) = A(0,1)B(0,1) = a_0 b_0 = c_0. \tag{6.2}$$

Computation of $C(1,1)$ and $C(1,-1)$ has the same complexity as $C(1)$ in the TCA; and computation of $C(2,1)$, $C(2,-1)$, $C(1,2)$ and $C(1,-2)$ has the same complexity as $C(-2)$ in the TCA (see Table 5.1). For instance,

$$C(2,1) = A(2,1)B(2,1) = (2^5 a_5 + 2^4 a_4 + \cdots + a_0)(2^5 b_5 + 2^4 b_4 + \cdots + b_0)$$

$$= 2^{10}c_{10} + 2^9 c_9 + \cdots + 2^2 c_2 + 2c_1 + c0, \tag{6.3}$$

where all coefficients are merely binary shifts. Furthermore, computation of $C(3,1)$, $C(3,-1)$ and $C(1,3)$ has the same complexity as $C(3)$ in TCA (Table 5.1).

6.2.   *Toom–Cook Algorithm*

Compute $C(0), C(1), C(-1), C(2), C(-2),$

$$C(3), C(-3), C(4), C(-4), C(5) \text{ and } C(-5), \tag{6.4}$$

$$C(0) = A(0)B(0) = a_0 b_0 = c_0, \tag{6.5}$$

$$C(1) = A(1)B(1) = (a_5 + a_4 + \cdots + a_0)(b_5 + b_4 + \cdots + b_0)$$
$$= c_{10} + c_9 + \cdots + c_2 + c_1 + c_0, \qquad (6.6)$$

$$C(-1) = A(-1)B(-1) = (-a_5 + a_4 - \cdots + a_0)(-b_5 + b_4 - \cdots + b_0)$$
$$= c_{10} - c_9 + c_8 - \cdots - c_1 + c_0, \qquad (6.7)$$

where both $A(p)$ and $B(p)$ can be computed by Horner Rule [Horner, 1819].

7. AHP for $n = 7$

It is easy to see that

$$C(1,0) = a_7 b_7 = c_{14} \quad \text{and} \quad C(0,1) = a_0 b_0 = c_0, \qquad (7.1)$$

i.e., we need to compute 13 remaining coefficients $c_{13}, c_{12}, \ldots, c_1$.

Let

$$M(p,q) := [C(p,q) - c_{14}p^{14} - c_0 q^{14}]/pq \qquad (7.2)$$

(modified values of $C(p,q)$, see (2.5)).

In order to separate "odd" and "even" unknowns, compute

$$S(1,1) := [M(1,1) + M(1,-1)]/2 = c_{12} + c_{10} + c_8 + c_6 + c_4 + c_2,$$
$$S(2,1) := [M(2,1) + M(2,-1)]/8 = 2^{10}c_{12} + 2^8 c_{10} + \cdots + c_2. \qquad (7.3)$$

In general, by computing

$$S(p,q) := [M(p,q) + M(p,-q)]/2(pq)^2, \qquad (7.4)$$

for $(p,q) = \{(1,1),(2,1),(1,2),(3,1),(1,3),(3,2)\}$, we create *six* equations with *six* "even" unknowns $c_2, c_4, \ldots, c_{12}$. Analogously, by computing

$$D(p,q) := [M(p,q) - M(p,-q)]/2, \qquad (7.5)$$

for $(p,q) = \{(1,1),(2,1),(1,2),(3,1),(1,3),(3,2)\}$, we create *six* equations with *seven* "odd" unknowns $c_1, c_3, \ldots, c_{13}$.

After the values of "even" coefficients $c_2, c_4, \ldots, c_{12}$ are computed, we use $M(2,3)$ [see (7.2)] as the *seventh* equation for computation of all "odd" coefficients.

8. AHP for $n = 4$ in Details

Consider

$$C(x,y) := A(x,y)B(x,y), \qquad (8.1)$$

where

$$A(x,y) := \sum_{k=0}^{3} a_k x^k y^{3-k}, \tag{8.2}$$

$$B(x,y) := \sum_{k=0}^{3} b_k x^k y^{3-k}, \tag{8.3}$$

and

$$C(x,y) := \sum_{k=0}^{6} c_i x^i y^{6-i}, \tag{8.4}$$

then

$$C(0,1) = c_0 = a_0 b_0 \quad \text{and} \quad C(1,0) = c_6 = a_3 b_3, \tag{8.5}$$

$$C(1,1) := c_6 + c_5 + \cdots + c_1 + c_0 = (a_3 + \cdots + a_0)(b_3 + \cdots + b_0), \tag{8.6}$$

$$C(1,-1) := c_6 - c_5 + \cdots + c_0 = (-a_3 + \cdots + a_0)(-b_3 + \cdots + b_0), \tag{8.7}$$

$$C(2,1) := 64c_6 + 32c_5 + 16c_4 + \cdots + 2c_1 + c_0$$
$$= (8a_3 + 4a_2 + 2a_1 + a_0)(8b_3 + 4b_2 + 2b_1 + b_0), \tag{8.8}$$

$$C(2,-1) := 64c_6 - 32c_5 + \cdots - 2c_1 + c_0$$
$$= (-8a_3 + 4a_2 - 2a_1 + a_0)(-8b_3 + 4b_2 - 2b_1 + b_0), \tag{8.9}$$

$$C(1,2) := c_6 + 2c_5 + 4c_4 + \cdots + 32c_1 + 64c_0$$
$$= (a_3 + 2a_2 + 4a_1 + 8a_0)(b_3 + 2b_2 + 4b_1 + 8b_0). \tag{8.10}$$

9. Solution of System of Eqs. (8.6)–(8.10)

Step 9.1:

$$V_1 := C(1,1) - c_6 - c_0.$$

Step 9.2:

$$V_2 := c_6 + c_0 - C(1,-1).$$

Step 9.3:

$$V_3 := [C(2,1) - c_0]/2 - 32c_6.$$

Step 9.4:

$$V_4 := 32c_6 + [c_0 - C(2,-1)]/2.$$

Step 9.5:
$$V_5 := [C(1,2) - c_6]/2 - 32c_0.$$

Remark 9.1. Using $V_1, \ldots, V_5$, we find five unknowns $c_1, \ldots, c_5$ from five linear equations:

$$c_5 + c_4 + c_3 + c_2 + c_1 = V_1, \tag{9.1}$$

$$c_5 - c_4 + c_3 - c_2 + c_1 = V_2, \tag{9.2}$$

$$16c_5 + 8c_4 + 4c_3 + 2c_2 + c_1 = V_3, \tag{9.3}$$

$$16c_5 - 8c_4 + 4c_3 - 2c_2 + c_1 = V_4, \tag{9.4}$$

$$c_5 + 2c_4 + 4c_3 + 8c_2 + 16c_1 = V_5. \tag{9.5}$$

Step 9.6:
$$V_6 := (V_1 - V_2)/2 \quad \{=c_4 + c_2\}, \tag{9.6}$$

Step 9.7:
$$V_7 := (V_3 - V_4)/4 \quad \{=4c_4 + c_2\}, \tag{9.7}$$

Step 9.8:
$$c_4 := (V_7 - V_6)/3, \tag{9.8}$$

Step 9.9:
$$c_2 := V_6 - c_4, \tag{9.9}$$

Step 9.10:
$$B_1 := V_1 - c_2 - c_4, \quad B_2 := V_3 - 8c_4 - 2c_2, \quad B_3 := V_5 - 2c_4 - 8c_2.$$

Remark 9.2. Now we solve the system of three equations with three unknowns:

$$c_5 + c_3 + c_1 = B_1, \tag{9.10}$$

$$16c_5 + 4c_3 + c_1 = B_2, \tag{9.11}$$

$$c_5 + 4c_3 + 16c_1 = B_3. \tag{9.12}$$

Step 9.11:
$$B_4 := (B_2 - 4B_1)/3 \quad \{=4c_5 - c_1\}, \tag{9.13}$$

Step 9.12:
$$B_5 := (B_3 - 4B_1)/3 \quad \{=-c_5 + 4c_1\}, \tag{9.14}$$

Step 9.13:
$$B_6 := (B_4 + B_5)/3 \quad \{=c_5 + c_1\}, \tag{9.15}$$

Step 9.14:
$$c_1 := (B_5 + B_6)/5, \quad c_5 := B_6 - c_1, \tag{9.16}$$

Step 9.15:
$$c_3 = B_1 - c_5 - c_1. \tag{9.17}$$

10. Multistage Implementation of TCA and AHP

10.1. *Two-stage implementation (TSI)*

Let us consider $n = 6 = 2 \times 3$, and analyze how to multiply sextuple-large integers in two stages. On the first stage, we represent A and B as double long:

$$A = 10^{3m} A_1 + A_0, \quad B = 10^{3m} B_1 + B_0, \tag{10.1}$$

and compute AB applying the Karatsuba algorithm, which requires *three* multiplications of $3m$-long integers.

Hence, as the second stage, we compute every product of triple-long integers using either the TCA or AHP, each requiring *five* standard multiplications (SMs, for short). Therefore, the TSI requires 15 SMs rather than 11 SMs required by the TCA or by AHP. Table 10.1 provides comparison for several other cases, where

$$R(n) := \text{TSI}(n)/\text{DI}(n). \tag{10.2}$$

General case: Let us now analyze the TSI of a multiplication algorithm if $n = rs$.

First, we represent A and B as

$$A = \sum_{k=0}^{r-1} 10^{ksm} A_k, \tag{10.3}$$

and

$$B = \sum_{k=0}^{r-1} 10^{ksm} B_k. \tag{10.4}$$

Such an implementation requires $2r - 1$ multiplications each of SM-long integers. Then, on the second stage, we multiply SM-long integers. Every such multiplication requires $2s - 1$ SMs. Therefore, we need

$$(2r - 1)(2s - 1) = O(4n) \tag{10.5}$$

SMs in total. However, the direct (one-stage) multiplication requires only

$$D(n) = 2n - 1 = O(2n) \quad SMs. \tag{10.6}$$

Table 10.1   Number of SMs in TSI and DI.

n	4	6	9	15	21	25	35	49	121
TSI	9	15	25	45	65	81	117	169	441
DI	7	11	17	29	41	49	69	97	241
$R(n)$	1.29	1.36	1.47	1.55	1.59	1.65	1.70	1.74	1.83

It is easy to verify that both parts in the inequality

$$(2r - 1)(2s - 1) \geq 2rs - 1 \tag{10.7}$$

are equal if and only if either $r = 1$, or $s = 1$, or $r = s = 1$.

In all other cases

$$(2r - 1)(2s - 1) > 2rs - 1. \tag{10.8}$$

Thus, the TSI of either TCA or AHP for large r and s asymptotically requires twice as many SMs than the DI.

Example 10.1. Now let $m = 4$, $A = 385425374179$ and $B = 608368695784$.

Therefore, in this example we need to split A and B into three parts, i.e., $n = 3$. By the algorithm, described in Secs. 8 and 9 we can compute $C = AB$ using five multiplications of four-digit large integers. However, if the standard integers are only two-digit long, we can pre-compute each product recursively using the Karatsuba algorithm. Each of these five products requires three SMs, i.e., overall we need 15 SMs to compute $C = AB$. On the other hand, we can compute the same product AB splitting both A and B into *six* parts.

In this case $m = 2$. To compute AB, we need only 11 SMs by using the direct implementation vs. 15 SMs required in the recursive TSI implementation.

10.2. *Multi-stage implementation*

Let now $n = 8 = 2^3$. Therefore, we multiply A and B in either three stages using the Karatsuba algorithm or using the AHP or TCA directly. In the MSI, we need $3^3 = 27$ SMs; while in the DI we need only 15 SMs.

Remark 10.2. Since the number of algebraic additions in the DI asymptotically grows as function of n, it is essential to properly select the evaluation points (p, q) to implement symmetricity illustrated above in Sec. 4 [see (4.4)–(4.16)] and to simplify computational complexity stemming from the multiplication by constant coefficients. These issues are addressed in Secs. 11–13.

11. Number of Algebraic Additions

Notice that computation of $M(p, q)$ requires $2n$ additions of SIs. Since we need to compute $M(p, q)$ for $2n-3$ different values of (p, q), the total number of algebraic additions is of order $O(4n^2)$. This number can be reduced twice as demonstrated in Sec. 2. Since every addition of m-digit long integers has order $O(m)$, therefore the total complexity of all additions is of order $O(2mn^2)$. Hence, the overall complexity is equal

$$T(m,n) = O(2nm^2 + 2mn^2) = O[2nm(m+n)].$$

If $m \gg n$, then

$$T(m,n) = O(2nm^2). \tag{11.1}$$

12. Analysis of TCA vs. AHP

In large-integer multiplication, we addressed two sources of complexity: the number of standard multiplications and the number of algebraic additions. The third source of complexity is multiplication by constant coefficients when the polynomials $A(x,y)$ and $B(x,y)$ are evaluated at points $(x,y) = (p,q)$.

Table 12.1 compares the polynomial evaluations in the TCA and AHP frameworks respectively for various values of n. It means that if $n = 15$, then in TCA polynomials $C(p)$ are evaluated for $p = \{0, \pm 1, \pm 2, \ldots, \pm 14\}$ and in the corresponding AHP polynomials $C(p,q)$ are evaluated for

$$(p,q) = \{(0,1), (1,\pm 1), (2,\pm 1), (1,\pm 2), \ldots, (1,\pm 5),$$
$$(5,\pm 2), (2,\pm 5), (5,\pm 4), (4,\pm 5)\}.$$

Example 12.1. Compare the computation of $C(2,5)$ and $C(13)$ for $n = 14$:

$$C(13) = \sum_{k=0}^{13} 13^k a_k \times \sum_{k=0}^{13} 13^k b_k, \tag{12.1}$$

Table 12.1   Evaluations required in TCA's vs. AHP frameworks.

n	1	2	3	4	5	6	7	8
TCA	$C(0)$	$C(\pm 1)$	$C(\pm 2)$	$C(\pm 3)$	$C(\pm 4)$	$C(\pm 5)$	$C(\pm 6)$	$C(\pm 7)$
AHP	$C(0,1)$	$C(1,\pm 1)$	$C(2,\pm 1)$	$C(1,\pm 2)$	$C(3,\pm 1)$	$C(1,\pm 3)$	$C(3,\pm 2)$	$C(2,\pm 3)$
n	9	10	11	12	13	14	15	16
TCA	$C(\pm 8)$	$C(\pm 9)$	$C(\pm 10)$	$C(\pm 11)$	$C(\pm 12)$	$C(\pm 13)$	$C(\pm 14)$	$C(\pm 15)$
AHP	$C(4,\pm 1)$	$C(1,\pm 4)$	$C(5,\pm 1)$	$C(1,\pm 5)$	$C(5,\pm 2)$	$C(2,\pm 5)$	$C(5,\pm 4)$	$C(4,\pm 5)$

$$C(5,2) = \sum_{k=0}^{13} 2^k \times 5^{13-k} a_k \times \sum_{k=0}^{13} 2^k \times 5^{13-k} b_k. \qquad (12.2)$$

In the next section, we propose an iterative procedure that computes $C(p,q)$.

13.　Generalized Horner Rule for Homogeneous Polynomials

Let $R_0 := a_0, L_0 := a_n$, and for $k = 1, \ldots, n$

$$R_k := R_{k-1}q + a_k p^k \qquad (13.1)$$

and

$$L_k := L_{k-1}p + a_{n-k}q^k, \qquad (13.2)$$

therefore,

$$A(p,q) = L_n = R_n. \qquad (13.3)$$

Analogously, we can compute $B(p,q)$.

14.　Values of (p,q) Simplifying Computation of $A(p,q)$ and $B(p,q)$

Case 1: If $p = 2^s$ and $q = 2^t \pm 1$ in (13.1), then $a_k p^k$ requires a binary shift on sk positions, and $R_{k-1}q$ requires merely a binary shift on t positions and one algebraic addition.

Case 2: If $q = 2^s$ and $p = 2^t \pm 1$ in (13.2), then, analogously as in the Case 1, $a_{n-k}q^k$ requires a binary shift on sk positions, and $L_{k-1}p$ requires a binary shift on t positions and one algebraic addition.

Case 3: If $q = 2^r(2^t \pm 1)$ and $p = 1$ in (13.1), then it is necessary to use two binary shifts and one algebraic addition.

Case 4: If $p = 2^r(2^t \pm 1)$ and $q = 1$ in (13.2), then, analogously as in the Case 3, it is necessary to use two binary shifts and one algebraic addition.

Case 5: If $q = 2^r$ and $p = 1$ in (13.1), then it is necessary to use only one binary shift on r positions.

Case 6: If $p = 2^r$ and $q = 1$ in (13.2), then, analogously as in the Case 5, it is necessary to use only one binary shift.

Example 14.1. In the following set of 37 points each (p, q) satisfies one of six special cases listed above:

$$(p, q) \in \{(1, 1), (2, 1), (3, 1), \ldots, (10, 1), (12, 1), (14, 1), \ldots, (18, 1),$$
$$(20, 1), (24, 1), (28, 1), (30, 1), (31, 1), (3, 2), (5, 2), (7, 2), (9, 2),$$
$$(15, 2), (17, 2), (31, 2), (5, 4), (7, 4), (9, 4), (15, 4), (17, 4), (9, 8),$$
$$(15, 8), (17, 8), \text{ and } (17, 16).$$

Add to this set the other 111 points $(p, -q)$, (q, p) and $(q, -p)$. For each of these 148 points the number of required algebraic additions in the AHPs is smaller than in the corresponding TCAs.

Example 14.2. If $n = 22$, then for the TCA we need to evaluate $C(p)$ at 43 points $C(0), C(\pm 1), \ldots, C(\pm 21)$; yet, for the AHP we evaluate polynomial $C(p, q)$ at points

$$C(0, 1), C(1, 0), C(1, \pm 1), C(2, \pm 1), \ldots, C(7, \pm 1),$$
$$C(1, \pm 2), C(1, \pm 3), \ldots, C(1, \pm 7), C(3, \pm 2), C(5, \pm 2),$$
$$C(7, \pm 2), C(2, \pm 3), C(2, \pm 5), C(2, \pm 7),$$

and $C(5,4)$, where, for instance, the evaluation of $C(5,4)$ requires fewer basic operations than for $C(21)$ in the TCA.

15. Optimized AHP

In order to decrease twice the number of additions/subtractions, we need to adjust the Generalized Horner Rule for iterative computation of $A(x, y)$ and $B(x, y)$.

Notice that if n is *odd* $\{n = 2s - 1\}$, then

$$A_{2s-1}(p, q) = (a_{2(s-1)}p^{2(s-1)} + \cdots + a_2 p^2 q^{2(s-2)} + a_0 q^{2(s-1)})$$
$$+ (a_{2s-3}p^{2s-3}q + \cdots + a_1 p q^{2s-3})$$
$$= A_{2s-1}^{(0)}(p, q) + A_{2s-1}^{(1)}(p, q). \tag{15.1}$$

Otherwise, if n is *even*, i.e., if $n = 2s$, then

$$A_{2s}(p, q) = (a_{2s-1}p^{2s-1} + a_{2s-3}p^{2s-3}q^2 + \cdots + a_3 p^3 q^{2(s-2)} + a_1 p q^{2(s-1)})$$
$$+ (a_{2(s-1)}p^{2(s-1)}q + \cdots + a_2 p^2 q^{2s-3} + a_0 q^{2s-1})$$
$$= A_{2s}^{(0)}(p, q) + A_{2s}^{(1)}(p, q). \tag{15.2}$$

Therefore, for every even and odd n

$$A_n(p,q) = A_n^{(0)}(p,q) + A_n^{(1)}(p,q), \tag{15.3}$$

$$A_n(p,-q) = A_n^{(0)}(p,q) - A_n^{(1)}(p,q). \tag{15.4}$$

Let us show how to modify (13.1) for iterative computation of (15.1).

Consider $n = 2s - 1, d_i := a_{n-1-i}$, and assign $R_0^{(0)} := a_0, L_0^{(0)} := d_0$, for every $k = 1, 2, \ldots$ compute

$$R_{2k}^{(0)} := R_{2(k-1)}^{(0)} q^2 + a_{2k} p^{2k}, \tag{15.5}$$

$$L_{2k}^{(0)} := L_{2(k-1)}^{(0)} p^2 + d_{2k} q^{2k}, \tag{15.6}$$

hence

$$A_{2s-1}^{(0)}(p,q) = R_{2(s-1)}^{(0)} = L_{2(s-1)}^{(0)}. \tag{15.7}$$

Assign $R_0^{(1)} := 0, L_0^{(1)} := 0$, for every $k = 1, 2, \ldots$ compute

$$R_{2k}^{(1)} = R_{2(k-1)}^{(1)} q^2 + a_{2k-1} p^{2k-1} q, \quad L_{2k}^{(1)} = L_{2(k-1)}^{(1)} p^2 + d_{2k-1} q^{2k-1} p. \tag{15.8}$$

hence

$$A_{2s-1}^{(1)}(p,q) = R_{2(s-1)}^{(1)} = L_{2(s-1)}^{(1)}.$$

Thus,

$$A_{2s-1}(p,q) = R_{2(s-1)}^{(0)} + R_{2(s-1)}^{(1)} = L_{2(s-1)}^{(0)} + L_{2(s-1)}^{(1)}, \tag{15.9}$$

$$A_{2s-1}(p,-q) = R_{2(s-1)}^{(0)} - R_{2(s-1)}^{(1)}. \tag{15.10}$$

Example 15.1. Let us consider $n = 7$, then

$$A_7(p,q) = (a_6 p^6 + a_4 p^4 q^2 + a_2 p^2 q^4 + a_0 q^6)$$
$$+ (a_5 p^5 q + a_3 p^3 q^3 + a_1 p q^5)$$
$$= R_6^{(0)} + R_6^{(1)}.$$

The iterative procedures (15.5)–(15.8) are simplified if

(A) p is a power of 2 and $q = 2^t \pm 1, t \geq 1$ or

(B) $p = 1$ and $q = 2^r(2^t \pm 1)$

(see the corresponding Cases 1–6 in Sec. 13).

Equations (13.2), (15.5) and (15.6) can be analogously modified for iterative computation of $A_{2s}^{(0)}(p,q), A_{2s}^{(1)}(p,q), B_{2s-1}^{(0)}(p,q), B_{2s-1}^{(1)}(p,q)$, and $B_{2s}^{(0)}(p,q), B_{2s}^{(1)}(p,q)$.

16. Concluding Remark

It has been demonstrated that the overhead in the TCA is higher than in the proposed approach based on homogeneous polynomials $A(x, y)$ and $B(x, y)$.

Integrality of all coefficients in the TCA and AHP is demonstrated by the first author in Verkhovsky and Rubino (2012).

Chapter 3

Deterministic Algorithms for Primitive Roots and Cyclic Groups with Mutual Generators*

1. Introduction and Basic Definitions

Generators (primitive roots) play important roles in secret-key exchange between users that transmit information via insecure telecommunication channels. To select a generator for a large prime p is a formidable computational problem. Like many problems in integer arithmetic, search for a generator modulo prime p currently applicable to various non-deterministic procedures based on trial-and-error.

Generators (see Definition 1.1 below) are essential in public-key encryption-decryption protocols. They play an important role in Diffie–Hellman key establishment protocol (Diffie and Hellman, 1976), in ElGamal cryptosystem (ElGamal, 1985) and in elliptic curve public-key cryptography (Koblitz, 1994; Miller, 1986). In order to provide a high crypto-immunity to the communication-protecting protocols, it is essential to select a parameter g called a generator that has the largest possible cycle (Maurer and Wolf, 1999).

In this chapter is described a *deterministic* approach for computation of primitive roots (generators) modulo p. It provides a formula and algorithm for computation of generators and proofs of their validity. Several numerical examples and Table 1.1 illustrate the proposed algorithms.

---

*I express appreciation to D. Chakrabarti and D. Nowak for comments and suggestions that improved the style of this chapter, and especially to R. Rubino for his assistance in graphics.

Table 1.1   Lengths of cycles for $g = 2$ and $g = 3$.

$g = 2, k$	1	2	3	4	5	6	7	8
h	2	4	8	16	15	13	9	1
$g = 3, k$	1	2	3	4	5	6	7	8
h	3	9	10	13	5	15	11	16
$g = 3, k$	9	10	11	12	13	14	15	16
h	14	8	7	4	12	2	6	1

Definition 1.1. If p is a prime, the numbers $(1, 2, \ldots, p - 1)$ form a multiplicative group modulo p that is denoted as Z_p^*. This group is cyclic for a prime $p \geq 3$. An element g of a cyclic group is called a *primitive root* (or a generator) modulo p, or a primitive element of Z_p^* if it generates the largest cycle. In other words, a primitive root or generator modulo p is an integer g such that every positive integer $0 < b < p$ can be expressed as a power of g modulo p, i.e., if there exists a unique positive integer $k < p$ such that every integer b on the interval $[1, p - 1]$ can be expressed as $b = g^k \bmod p$.

Definition 1.2. A positive integer $2 \leq g \leq p - 2$ is called a primitive root (generator) modulo prime p if the smallest positive integer m, for which holds $g^m \bmod p = 1$, is equal to $p - 1$.

Example 1.3. Let us consider prime $p = 17$ and compute $h(k, g) := g^k \bmod 17$ for $g = 2$ and $g = 3$. Table 1.1 shows that for $g = 2$ function $h(k, 2)$ has cycle 8 and function $h(k, 3)$ has cycle 16.

It is easy to verify that $h(k, g)$ has cycle 16 for $g = 3, 5, 6, 7, 10, 11, 12$ and 14, and for $g = 2, 4, 8, 9, 13, 15$ and 16, $h(k, g)$ has cycles smaller than 16.

Therefore, any integer in set $\{3, 5, 6, 7, 10, 11, 12, 14\}$ can be selected as a generator in a group with modulus $p = 17$. If $p = 71$, then the smallest generator $g = 7$ and on interval $[14, 20]$ there are no generators.

2. Schematic Illustration of Cycles

In the following discussion, for illustration, there are considered two cycles: for $p = 11$ and $p = 13$. In the first cycle for $p = 11$ and $g = 3$, there are connected pairs of integers $(n_k, k) = \{(3, 1); (9, 2); (5, 3); (4, 4); (1, 5); (3, 6)\}$, where $n_k = g^k \bmod p$. This illustration shows that only a subset of all integers on interval $[1, 10]$ can be expressed as $n_k = 3^k \bmod 11$, which means that $g = 3$ is not a generator for modulus $p = 11$.

In the second cycle for $p = 13$ and $g = 6$, there are connected pairs of integers $(n_k, k) = \{(6,1), (10,2), (8,3), (9,4), (2,5), (12,6), (7,7), \ldots, (1,12)\}$, where $n_k = 6^k \bmod 13$. This illustration indicates that *every* integer on interval $[1,12]$ can be expressed as $n_k = 6^k \bmod 13$; therefore $g = 6$ is a generator for modulus $p = 13$.

As illustrations for $p = 13$, see Figs. 2.1 and 2.2 below. In Fig. 1.1 for $g = 4$, there are six connected pairs of integers $\{n_k, k\}$, where $n_k = g^k \bmod 13$. This illustration shows that only a subset of all integers on interval $[1,12]$ can be expressed as $n_k = 4^k \bmod 13$, which means that $g = 4$ is not a generator for modulus $p = 13$.

In Fig. 2.2, for $g = 6$ there are 12 connected pairs of integers

$$(n_k, k) = \{(6,1), (10,2), (8,3), (9,4), (2,5), (12,6), (7,7), (3,8), (5,9),$$
$$(4,10), (11,11), (1,12)\}.$$

This illustration demonstrates that *every* integer on interval $[1,12]$ can be expressed as $n_k = 6^k \bmod 13$; therefore $g = 6$ is a generator for modulus $p = 13$.

A non-deterministic algorithm to find a generator is provided in Menezes *et al.* (1997). Shoup (1992) is considered a task how to compute deterministically in polynomial time a *subset* that contains a generator.

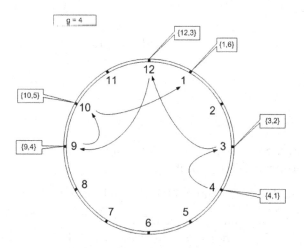

Fig. 2.1

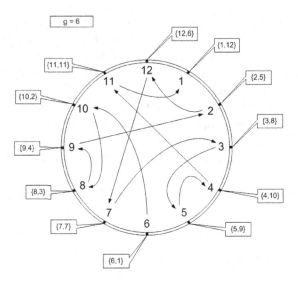

Fig. 2.2

3. Verification Procedure: Is g a Generator?

Suppose a positive integer g is randomly selected on the interval $3 \leq g \leq p - 2$ and

$$p - 1 = 2^{e_0} q_1^{e_1} \ldots q_r^{e_r}, \tag{3.1}$$

where all integer factors $q_1, \ldots, q_r$ are *odd* primes.

Proposition 3.1. If

$$g^{(p-1)/2} \bmod p = -1, \tag{3.2}$$

and for every $k = 1, \ldots, r$

$$g^{(p-1)/q_k} \bmod p \neq 1, \tag{3.3}$$

then g is a generator modulo p (Mollin, 1998).

Example 3.2. Suppose $p = 71$ let us find a generator. Since $p - 1 = 70 = 2 \times 5 \times 7$, then g is a generator if and only if

$$g^{35} \bmod 71 \neq 1, \quad g^{14} \bmod 71 \neq 1, \quad \text{and} \quad g^{10} \bmod 71 \neq 1. \tag{3.4}$$

Table 3.1 shows values of $g^n \bmod 71$.

Since $g = 7$ satisfies every condition in (3.4), therefore, after 15 *exponentiations* we find that it is the generator for $p = 71$.

Table 3.1   Choice of generator for $p = 71$

$g \backslash n$	$n = 10$	$n = 14$	$n = 35$
$g = 2$	30	54	1
$g = 3$	48	54	1
$g = 5$	1	57	1
$g = 6$	20	5	1
$g = 7$	45	54	70

Although the conditions (3.3) are straightforward to verify, if m is large, then (3.3) requires factorization of $p - 1$ and m exponentiations for each potential candidate. Also, if at least one of these conditions does not hold, it is necessary to consider the next candidate. In general, non-deterministic algorithms are typical for various problems in modular arithmetic.

Example 3.3 (Number of generators). Let $G(p)$ denote the number of generators as a function of modulus p. Then $G(11) = G(13) = 4$, $G(17) = G(31) = 8$, $G(61) = 16$, $G(211) = 48$, $G(331) = 80$, $G(2311) = 480$ and $G(2731) = 576$. Therefore, if an integer g is selected randomly, then the probability $F(p)$ that g is a generator equals $G(p)/(p - 3)$. For $p = 2311$, $F(2311) = 480/2308 = 0.2080$; for $p = 2711$, $F(2711) = 0.2111$, i.e., about every fifth integer on interval $[2, p - 2]$ is a generator. A deterministic algorithm computing generators (primitive roots) is provided in this chapter.

4. Safe Primes and their Properties

Definition 4.1. If both p and

$$q = (p - 1)/2 \tag{4.1}$$

are primes, then p is called a *safe* prime.

Example 4.2. $p = 5$, 7, 11, 23, 47, 59, 83, 107, 167, 179, 227, 263, 347, 359, 383, ..., 2903, 3023, 3119, 3167, 3203, 3467, 3623, 3779, 3803, 3863 are examples of safe primes.

Basic properties of safe primes: It is easy to verify that

1. Every safe prime is a Blum prime, i.e., it is congruent to 3 modulo 4.
2. Every safe prime greater than 7 is congruent to 11 modulo 12.   (4.2)
3. For every safe prime $p \geq 23$ holds that $p \bmod 20 = 3$ or 7 or 19.
4. Let $p_1 = 23 < \cdots < p_k < p_{k+1} < \cdots$ is the sequence of all safe primes.

If $p_k \bmod 20 = 7$, then $p_{k+1} - p_k \geq 12$ otherwise $p_{k+1} - p_k \geq 24$. $\qquad$ (4.3)

Indeed, 23, 47, 59, 83, 107 are safe primes. This property can be helpful to simplify search for a safe prime.

Although there is no known proof that there exist infinitely many safe primes, the largest known safe prime is

$$U = 48047305725 \times 2^{172404} - 1. \qquad (4.4)$$

It was discovered by D. Underbakke in 2007 (Singer and Whyte, 2003).

5. Computational Complexities

In this chapter, we reduce the complexity to find a generator to the complexity to find a safe prime. Although the method of verification in (3.2)–(3.3) is logically simple, it has the following disadvantages:

(a) It requires factorization of $p - 1$ (3.1).
(b) If an integer g does not satisfy at least one of the requirements in (3.2)–(3.3), then a new value of g must be tested, i.e., the procedure is not deterministic.
(c) If for a certain reason the generator is not suitable for implementation, we need to repeat the process again and again.
(d) For a large prime p the verification whether g is a generator requires $r + 1$ (1) modular exponentiations with overall complexity $O(r \log p)$.

Upper limit: If the Generalized Riemann Hypothesis is correct, then for every prime p there exists a generator g of the multiplicative group of integers modulo p, which is smaller than $70(\ln(p))^2$ (van der Linden, 1982).

On the other hand, in the proposed deterministic algorithm, the complexity is determined by the complexity of primality testing of $q = (p - 1)/2$. But primality testing of q is computationally simpler than its factorization (Ong and Kubiatowicz, 2005).

After a safe prime is determined, we can compute as many generators as necessary.

6. Algorithm and its Validation

Proposition 6.1. If p is a Blum prime, then

$$p \neq u^2 + w^2, \qquad (6.1)$$

where u and w are integers.

Proof. An assumption that there exists a Blum prime p_0 and two integers u and w such that $p_0 = u^2 + w^2$ leads to a contradiction.

Indeed, let us assume that there exist two such integers: one even $2j$ and another odd $2k + 1$ for which holds

$$p_0 = (2j)^2 + (2k+1)^2 = (4j^2) + (4k^2 + 4k + 1) = 4(j^2 + k^2 + k) + 1. \quad (6.2)$$

Therefore, (6.2) implies that $p_0 \bmod 4 = 1$. Hence p_0 is *not* a Blum prime, which contradicts with the above assumption in Proposition 6.1. $\square$

Fermat identity: For every prime p and an integer c co-prime with p holds that

$$c^{p-1} \bmod p = 1. \quad (6.3)$$

Theorem 6.2. If $p \geq 7$ is a safe prime (4.1), then for every integer on the interval

$$3 \leq v \leq p - 2, \quad (6.4)$$

$$g = p - v^2 \quad (6.5)$$

is a generator modulo p.

7. Formula for Generator

Theorem 7.1. Consider a safe prime $p \geq 7$, and let

$$b := [(3p - 1)/4] \bmod p \quad (7.1)$$

then b is a generator modulo p.

Proofs for both theorems are provided in the appendix.

Example 7.2. If $p = 2U + 1$ [see (4.4)], then

$$b = 144141917175 \times 2^{172402} - 1 \quad (7.2)$$

is a generator modulo p.

8. Multiplicative Groups with Common Generators

Under certain conditions on moduli p and s, there exists the same generator g that can be used in different groups. Indeed, since $p = 83$ and $s = 107$ are safe primes, then $g = 58$ is a generator in both groups (modulo $p = 83$ and modulo $s = 107$).

Theorem 8.1. Suppose that $7 < p < s$ are both safe primes and

$$m := (s - p)/12 \qquad (8.1)$$

then the following *four* identities hold:

T1: If $m \geq 7$, then

$$g := s - (m + 3)^2 = p - (m - 3)^2. \qquad (8.2)$$

Proof. m in (8.1) is always an integer because every safe prime is congruent to 11 modulo 12 (4.2). On the other hand, Eq. (8.2) holds if and only if (8.1) holds. □

Corollary 8.2. g in (8.2) is a mutual generator in groups with moduli p and s, if they satisfy (8.1).

T2: If m is an *even* integer and

$$|m/2 - 6| \geq 2,$$

then

$$g := s - (m/2 + 6)^2 = p - (m/2 - 6)^2. \qquad (8.3)$$

Proof. Equation (8.3) implies that $s - p = (m/2+6)^2 - (m/2-6)^2 = 12m$, which always holds (4.2).

It is essential that $0 \neq |m/2 - 6| \neq 1$, since neither $g = p$ nor $g = p - 1$ is a generator modulo p. □

Corollary 8.3. g in (8.3) is a mutual generator in groups with moduli p and s.

T3: If $m \geq 1$,

$$p > s - (3m + 1)^2 > 0 \quad \text{and} \quad p > (3m - 1)^2, \qquad (8.4)$$

then

$$g := s - (3m + 1)^2 = p - (3m - 1)^2 \qquad (8.5)$$

is a mutual generator modulo p and modulo s.

T4: If m is an *even* integer and $|3m/2 - 4| \geq 2$,
then

$$g := s - (3m/2 + 4)^2 = p - (3m/2 - 4)^2. \qquad (8.6)$$

Table 1.1 provides examples of different multiplicative groups sharing the same generators. From Table 1.1 it follows that

Table 8.1   Examples of mutual generators.

p	47	59	**83**	167	**263**	**263**	**3623**	**3623**	**3623**	**3623**	**3623**	**3623**
s	59	107	**107**	179	**479**	**479**	**3863**	**3863**	**3863**	**3863**	**3863**	**3863**
g	**43**	**43**	**58**	163	38	254	142	2839	3334	3502	3574	3607

A. There exist generators that are mutual for three and even more multiplicative groups. Indeed, $g = 43$ is a generator in *three* groups (modulo $p_1 = 47$, $p_2 = 59$, $p_3 = 107$):

$$g := p_1 - 2^2 = p_2 - 4^2 = p_3 - 8^2 = 43.$$

B. Two multiplicative groups (modulo 263 and modulo 479) have more than one mutual generator: indeed

$$g_1 = 263 - 15^2 = 479 - 21^2 = 38$$

and

$$g_2 = 263 - 3^2 = 479 - 15^2 = 254.$$

C. Two multiplicative groups (modulo $p = 3623$ and $s = 3863$) have *multiple* mutual generators:

$$g_1 = 3863 - 61^2 = 3623 - 59^2 = 142,$$
$$g_2 = 3863 - 32^2 = 3623 - 28^2 = 2839,$$
$$g_3 = 3863 - 23^2 = 3623 - 17^2 = 3334,$$
$$g_4 = 3863 - 19^2 = 3623 - 11^2 = 3502,$$
$$g_5 = 3863 - 17^2 = 3623 - 7^2 = 3574,$$
$$g_6 = 3863 - 16^2 = 3623 - 4^2 = 3607.$$

This property holds for every pair of safe primes if they satisfy the inequality

$$\sqrt{p} + 6 \geq \sqrt{s} > \sqrt{p}. \tag{8.7}$$

In this case the formula for a common generator is

$$g = \frac{p+s}{2} - \left(\frac{s-p}{12}\right)^2 - 9. \tag{8.8}$$

Example 8.4. Since (8.7) holds for $s = 383$ and $p = 227$, then from (8.8) $g = 127$ is a common generator for both groups based on moduli s and p.

9. Complex Generators and Super-safe Primes

Definition 9.1. Let $s := (a, b)$ and the norm

$$N = a^2 + b^2 > 0. \qquad (9.1)$$

A complex integer g is called a complex primitive root (*complex generator*) modulo prime p if the smallest positive integer m, for which holds

$$g^m \bmod p = 1 \text{ is equal to } p^2 - 1. \qquad (9.2)$$

Definition 9.2. A Blum prime p is a super-safe prime
    if

$$f := (p-1)/2; \quad \text{and} \quad h := (p+1)/4 \qquad (9.3)$$

are also primes.
     $p = 7$, 11 and 167 are examples of super-safe primes.

Proposition 9.3. Let p be a prime, c be an integer, and

$$\text{(A)} \quad s^f \bmod p = (c, 0), \qquad (9.4)$$
$$\text{(B)} \quad \text{or } s^h \bmod p = (0, c), \qquad (9.5)$$
$$\text{(C)} \quad \text{or } s^h \bmod p = (c, 0) \qquad (9.6)$$

then s is *not* a complex generator.

Otherwise, Eq. (9.4) implies that $(p-1)^2/2 < p^2 - 1$, i.e., (9.2) is not satisfied.
     Analogously, Eq. (9.5) implies that

$$s^{(p-1)(p+1)/2} \bmod p = (1, 0) = 1; \qquad (9.7)$$

and Eq. (9.6) implies that

$$s^{(p-1)(p+1)/4} \bmod p = (1, 0) = 1. \qquad (9.8)$$

Verkhovsky and Sadik (2010) provided a deterministic algorithm for selection of complex generators.

10. Concluding Remarks

Non-deterministic approaches to search for a generator can be fruitless or time consuming. Even for such small integer as $p = 71$ the first four square-free candidates $g = 2$, 3, 5, 6 are erroneous trials, and only $g = 7$ is a generator.

In this chapter are listed several ways to deterministically compute a generator g modulo prime p and how to find a mutual generator modulo primes p *and* s. Although the complexity to find a generator is reduced to the complexity to find a safe prime p, the latter problem is less complex since we know several properties of the safe primes. Besides, if a safe prime p is selected on a system-design level, we can dynamically change the generator g to ensure a higher crypto-immunity of communication. Or, if two or more groups, based on different moduli, have g as their mutual generator, then the communicating parties can periodically switch from one group to another.

The overall results of research in this chapter provide insights into the potential algorithms for the security and information assurance systems of the future IT communication.

Appendix

A.1. *Proof of Theorem 6.2*

If $p \geq 7$ is a safe prime (3.2), then for every integer v on the interval $3 \leq v \leq p - 2$, (6.4) $g = p - v^2$, (6.5) is a generator modulo p.

Remark A.1. The formulas (A.13) and (A.15) provided below illustrate the concept.

Proof. Let us demonstrate that g defined in (6.5) satisfies conditions (3.2) and (3.3).

Suppose the condition (3.2) does not hold, i.e., there exists a safe prime p_0 and an integer v_0, for which holds

$$g_0^{(p_0-1)/2} \bmod p_0 = 1. \tag{A.1}$$

Here

$$g_0 = p_0 - v_0^2 \ (6.4).$$

Since a safe prime $q_0 = (p_0 - 1)/2$ is an *odd* integer, then (A.1) implies that

$$g_0^{(p_0-1)/2} \equiv (p_0 - v^2)^{q_0} \equiv (-1)^{q_0} v^{p_0-1} \equiv -1 (\bmod p_0) = -1. \tag{A.2}$$

Suppose now the condition (3.3) does not hold, i.e., there exist integers p_1 and v_1 such that

$$g_1^{(p_1-1)/q_1} \equiv g_1^2 \bmod p_1 = 1, \tag{A.3}$$

then (A.3) implies that

$$(g_1^2 - 1) \equiv (g_1 + 1)(g_1 - 1) \bmod p_1 = 0. \qquad (A.4)$$

Since p_1 is a prime, hence (A.4) holds if and only if one of the following *four* conditions holds: either

$$(g_1 - 1) \bmod p_1 = 0, \qquad (A.5)$$

or

$$(g_1 + 1) \bmod p_1 = 0, \qquad (A.6)$$

or

$$p_1 \quad \text{divides} \quad (g_1 + 1), \qquad (A.7)$$

or

$$p_1 \quad \text{divides} \quad (g_1 - 1). \qquad (A.8)$$

Let us consider each case and show that an assumption that at least one of them holds leads to a contradiction. Indeed:

if $\quad g_1 = 1 (\bmod p_1)$ holds in (A.5), then $p_1 = 1 + v_1^2 = 1^2 + v_1^2$, $\quad$ (A.9)

which is impossible by Proposition 1.2, since p_1 is a Blum prime (6.1),

if $\quad g_1 = -1$ holds in (A.6), then (6.5) implies that

$$p_1 = v_1^2 - 1 = (v_1 - 1)(v_1 + 1), \qquad (A.10)$$

which is impossible because $v_1 - 1 > 1$ in (6.4) and p_1 is a prime.

If $\quad p_1 | (g_1 + 1)$ holds (A.7), then $p_1 | (p_1 - v_1^2 + 1)$, which implies that

$$p_1 | (v_1^2 - 1). \qquad (A.11)$$

Therefore, either $p_1 | (v_1 - 1)$ or $p_1 | (v_1 + 1)$ must hold. However, neither of these options is feasible, because

$$p_1 > v_1 + 1 > v_1 - 1,$$

i.e., a larger integer cannot divide a smaller integer.

Finally, if $\quad p_1 | (g_1 - 1)$ holds, then $p_1 | (p_1 - v_1^2 - 1)$, which implies that

$$p_1 | (v_1^2 + 1). \qquad (A.12)$$

Hence,

$$v_1^2 \bmod p_1 = -1.$$

However, since p_1 is a Blum prime, then by Euler criterion (Menezes *et al.*, 1997)

$$(-1)^{(p_1 - 1)/2} = -1,$$

i.e., -1 does not have a square root modulo Blum prime.

In other words, there is no integer v_1 that satisfies (A.12). $\qquad \square$

A.2. Deterministic computation of generators: Proof of Theorem 7.1

Let us prove that, if p is a safe prime and $p \geq 7$, then $b := [(3p-1)/4] \bmod p$ (7.1) is a generator modulo p.

Remark A.2. For further clarifications see also (A.15) and Examples A.1 and A.2.

Proof. First of all, for every Blum prime $(3p - 1)/4$ is an integer.
Since

$$(2^{-1})^2 \equiv \left(\frac{p+1}{4}\right) (\bmod p), \tag{A.13}$$

then

$$b = (3p - 1)/4 \equiv [p - (p + 1)/4] \equiv [p - (2^{-1})^2] \bmod p. \tag{A.14}$$

Therefore, by Theorem 6.2 b is a generator modulo safe prime p.   □

A.3. Search for smaller generators

For a large prime p, the formula (7.1) provides large generators. However, in some cases a substantially smaller generator provides certain computational advantages.

Example A.1 provided below demonstrates that the formula

$$g = p - \lfloor \sqrt{p} \rfloor^2 \tag{A.15}$$

can be applied in search for smaller generators

Example A.3.

If $p = 83$, then from (7.1) $g_1 = 62$, and from (A.15) $g_2 = 2$.

If $p = 467$, then from (7.1) $g_1 = 350$, and from (A.15) $g_2 = 26$.

Preliminary results of this chapter were published in Verkhovsky (2012).

Chapter 4

Primality Testing via Complex Integers and Pythagorean Triplets

"Mathematicians have tried in vain to this day to discover some order in the sequence of prime numbers, and we have reason to believe that it is a mystery, into which the human mind will never penetrate."

— Leonard Euler

1. Introduction

Prime integers and their generalizations play important roles in protocols for secure transmission of information via open channels of telecommunication networks. Large prime numbers are at the core of every modern cryptographic protocol. These protocols rely on multi-digit long primes to ensure that the cryptanalysis of an encrypted message is too complicated to break in any relevant time. Therefore, the efficiency of primality tests is important (Adleman *et al.*, 1983).

Generation of multi-digit long primes in the design stage of a cryptographic system is a formidable task. There are many ways to test an integer for primality. The Sieve of Eratosthenes, although able to detect all primes, has a time complexity in the order of n (Agrawal *et al.*, 2002). Fermat's Little Theorem (FLT) can be used to test for primality. Although the Fermat test is very simple, there exists an infinite set of composite integers, (called Carmichael numbers or CMNs, for short), that are not detectable by the Fermat test (Alford *et al.*, 1994).

In this chapter, we consider modular arithmetic based on complex integers and provide several tests that verify the primality of real integers. Although the new tests detect most CMNs, there is a small percentage of them, which we call *the Carmichael numbers of the second order* (CMN2),

43

they escape these tests. Numerous computer experiments demonstrate that there are fewer CMN2 than the ordinary CMN.

Primality testing has a long history. Paul Erdös, rephrasing Einstein's famous statement, expressed his view as *"God may not play dice with the Universe, but something strange is going on with the prime numbers"* (Pomerance, 1998). I believe that the following proposition explains the views of L. Euler and P. Erdös:

Conjecture 1.1. If there exists an algorithm that describes an order in the sequence of primes smaller than n, it has complexity $\Omega[f(n)]$, where $f(n)$ is a monotone non-decreasing function of n (Verkhovsky, 2004).

2. Basic Properties of Primes

Euclid Lemma. If p is a prime number and p divides a product ab of integers, then p divides a or p divides b. This is used in some proofs of the uniqueness of prime factorizations.

Fermat Little Theorem (FLT). If p is a prime that does not divide an integer a, then $a^{p-1} - 1$ is divisible by p, otherwise

$$(a^p - a) \bmod p = 0. \qquad (2.1)$$

Wilson Theorem (provides necessary and sufficient conditions for primality testing). An integer $p \geq 2$ is a prime if and only if

$$(p - 1)! + 1 \text{ is divisible by } p. \qquad (2.2)$$

However, since the Wilson Theorem has complexity $O(p)$, it is not computationally efficient.

Prime Number Theorem. The number of primes smaller than x is asymptotic to

$$O(x/\ln x) \quad \text{(Gauss, 1986).} \qquad (2.3)$$

Dirichlet Theorem. In every arithmetic progression $a, a + q, a + 2q, \ldots,$ $a+kq, \ldots,$ where the positive integers a and $q \geq 1$ are relatively prime, there are infinitely many primes. This property can be applied to generate large primes (greater than 10^{100}), which are important components in public-key cryptography.

Existence of Generator. For every prime p there exists an integer $1 < g < p$, called a *generator*, such that every integer $1 \leq b \leq p - 1$ can be expressed as

$$b = g^d \bmod p. \tag{2.4}$$

Here d is called a *discrete logarithm* of b modulo p. This property plays an important role in the ElGamal cryptographic algorithm (ElGamal, 1985) and in elliptic-curve cryptography (Koblitz *et al.*, 2000).

3. Generalizations

The concept of prime numbers is so important that it has been generalized in different ways in various branches of mathematics. For example, we can define complex primes. Notice that 5 is not a complex prime, because it is the product of two complex integers $(1 + 2i)$ and $(1 - 2i)$.

Another observation:

$$5 = (2 + i)(2 - i) = (1 + 2i)(1 - 2i);$$

which means that complex factorization is not unique. However, integer 3 is a complex prime. In general, every real prime n that satisfies $n \bmod 4 = 3$ (called *Blum prime*) is also a complex prime. Yet, every real prime n that satisfies $n \bmod 4 = 1$ is the complex composite (Gethner *et al.*, 1998). A public-key cryptographic algorithm based on complex moduli is described in Verkhovsky (2011a).

4. Arithmetic Operations on Complex Integers

Modular arithmetic with modulus n, unlike the "school-grade" arithmetic, operates on a finite set of integers in the interval $[0, n - 1]$.

4.1. *Multiplications of complex numbers*

Let $\quad L := a + bi \quad$ and $\quad R := c + di$

consider $\quad LR = (a + bi)(c + di) = m + wi$,

where $\quad m := ac - bd \quad$ and $\quad w := ad + bc$.

Hence, the computation of m and w requires *four* multiplications of real numbers, where integers in a cryptographic scheme might be of size 10^{100} or larger. However, Karatsuba and Ofman (1963) describe an algorithm that computes LR using only *three* multiplications. Indeed, let $P := (a + b)(c+d)$, $Q := ab$ and $S := bd$, then $m = Q - S$ and $w = P - Q - S$.

Consider now the squaring of a complex integer:

$$(a + bi)^2 = a^2 - b^2 + 2abi = m + wi,$$

$$p := a - b, \quad r := a + b \quad \text{and} \quad q := ab.$$

Then $m := pr$ and $w := 2q$, where the latter can be performed by left shift, if integers are in binary form. Therefore, squaring is done using *two* multiplications and *two* additions. If each integers A and B have s decimal digits, then algebraic addition $A \pm B$ requires $O(s)$ digital operations and multiplication AB has complexity $O(s^2)$.

4.2. *Modular multiplicative inverse of complex integer*

Definition 4.1. Let b and d be complex integers, where $bd \bmod n = 1$; then b and d are called mutually multiplicative inverse modulo n.

Let

$$b := c + fi \quad \text{and} \quad d := g + hi, \tag{4.1}$$

compute

$$s := c^2 + f^2 \quad \text{and} \quad t := s^{-1}. \tag{4.2}$$

If $\gcd(s, n) = 1$, then the inverse of s can be computed using either the extended Euclid algorithm (Knuth, 1973) or the algorithms in Pomerance (1998), and Verkhovsky (2011b).

Finally,

$$g := ct \quad \text{and} \quad h := (n - f)t. \tag{4.3}$$

4.3. *Complex primes*

It is known that for every prime p congruent to 1 modulo 4 (non-Blum prime) there exists two real integers u and w such that

$$p = u^2 + w^2. \tag{4.4}$$

Thus, every such prime can be presented as two products of two factors each:

$$p = (u + wi)(u - wi) = (w + ui)(w - ui). \tag{4.5}$$

Therefore, there are no complex primes among non-Blum integers.

However, every Blum prime is also a complex prime (Gauss, 1986): it cannot be presented as a product of two complex integers except as $p = (\pm pi)(\pm i)$.

In the following consideration, we are using the notation:

$$(a, b) := a + bi. \tag{4.6}$$

5. Fundamental Identity

Proposition 5.1. If p is a real prime, then for every complex integer (a, b), where

$$\gcd(a^2 + b^2, p) = 1. \tag{5.1}$$

The following identity holds

$$(a, b)^{p^2 - 1} \bmod p = (1, 0) = 1. \tag{5.2}$$

Proof. First of all, if $(a, b) \neq (0, 0)$, then

$$(a, b)(u, v) \equiv (a, b)(x, y)(\bmod p) \tag{5.3}$$

implies that

$$(u, v) \equiv (x, y)(\bmod p). \tag{5.4}$$

Indeed, there exists a complex integer

$$(a, b)^{-1} \equiv (a, p - b)(a^2 + b^2)^{-1}(\bmod p), \tag{5.5}$$

such that

$$(a, b)^{-1}(a, b) \bmod p = (1, 0).$$

By multiplying both parts of (5.3) with $(a, b)^{-1}$, we prove (5.4).

Let us consider a product A of all complex numbers (j, k) with components

$$0 \leq j, k \leq p - 1 \quad \text{and} \quad j + k > 0, \tag{5.6}$$

i.e., at least one of the components is strictly *positive*:

$$A := \prod_{\substack{0 \leq j, k \leq p-1 \\ (j,k) \neq 0}} (j, k) \bmod p. \tag{5.7}$$

Consider now

$$B := \prod_{\substack{0 \leq j, k \leq p-1 \\ (j,k) \neq 0}} (j, k)(a, b)^{p^2 - 1} \bmod p, \tag{5.8}$$

then

$$B := (a, b)^{p^2 - 1} \left[\prod_{\substack{0 \leq j, k \leq p-1 \\ (j,k) \neq 0}} (j, k) \bmod p \right] = \prod_{\substack{0 \leq j, k \leq p-1 \\ (j,k) \neq 0}} [(a, b)(j, k)] \bmod p.$$

$$\tag{5.9}$$

Since every (j, k) satisfying (5.6) is an element of a cyclic group, then all $(a, b)(j, k)$ are a permutation of the elements of the same group.

Hence,

$$A := \prod_{\substack{0 \leq j, k \leq p-1 \\ (j,k) \neq 0}} (j, k) \bmod p = B. \tag{5.10}$$

Therefore, (5.7), (5.8) and (5.10) imply that

$$(a, b)^{p^2 - 1} \bmod p = 1. \tag{5.11}$$

$\square$

Remark 5.2. If p is not a prime, then there exists (a, b), for which neither (5.1) holds nor (5.3) implies (5.4).

However, if $p = qr$, then

$$(a, b)^{(q^2 - 1)(r^2 - 1)} \bmod p = (1, 0). \tag{5.12}$$

Proposition 5.3. For every real prime p there exists a complex integer G, called a complex generator, such that every complex integer (a, b), where (5.1) holds, can be expressed as

$$G^d \equiv (a, b)(\bmod \ p), \tag{5.13}$$

here d is called a discrete logarithm of (a, b) modulo p.

6. Major Results

Proposition 6.1. Let (a, b) be a complex integer, satisfying (5.1), and p be a Blum prime $\{p \bmod 4 = 3\}$, then Proposition 5.1 implies the following identity for every a, b and p:

$$(a, b)^{(p+1)/2} \bmod p = (d, e), \tag{6.1}$$

where either $d = 0$ or $e = 0$, but $d + e \neq 0$.

Furthermore, if

$$\sqrt{(a^2 + b^2)} \bmod p \text{ exists,}$$

then

$$d + e = \pm\sqrt{(a^2 + b^2)} \bmod p, \tag{6.2}$$

otherwise

$$d + e = \pm\sqrt{-(a^2 + b^2)} \bmod p. \tag{6.3}$$

Remark 6.2. $\sqrt{a^2 + b^2}$ is the absolute value of (a, b). The alternative in (6.3) is based on the following observation: if p is a Blum prime, and $1 \leq q \leq p - 1$; then from the Euler criterion of quadratic residuosity either q or $p - q$, but not both, is a quadratic residue modulo p (Gauss, 1986).

The identity (6.1) in the following text is called the *BV-3 primality test*. Thousands of computer experiments have demonstrated that this test detects the overwhelming majority of CMNs (see Sec. 7 for details).

Definition 6.3. A triplet $\{a, b, c\}$ of positive integers where a and b are co-prime and satisfy

$$a^2 + b^2 = c^2 \qquad (6.4)$$

is called a *Pythagorean triplet*.

Proposition 6.4. For every Pythagorean triplet $\{a, b, c\}$, and every Blum prime p the following identity holds

$$(a, b)^{(p+1)/2} \equiv c(\mathrm{mod}\ p). \qquad (6.5)$$

Example 6.5. Let $p = 2011$, $a = 5$ and $b = 12$, then

$$(5, 12)^{1006} \equiv 13(\mathrm{mod}\ 2011),$$

where $5^2 + 12^2 = 13^2$. More examples are provided in Table 10.2.

7. Carmichael Numbers

CMNs are *composite* integers that nevertheless satisfy FLT (Carmichael, 1910). Carmichael found that 561 is the smallest integer, which escapes the primality test of FLT (Alford *et al.*, 1994). Indeed, for every $0 < a < 561$, co-prime with 561, holds:

$$(a^{561} - a)\ \mathrm{mod}\ 561 = 0.$$

According to Pinch (1993), there are 8,241 CMNs smaller than 10^{12}, 19,279 CMNs smaller than 10^{13}, 44,706 smaller than 10^{14}, 105,212 smaller than 10^{15}, 246,683 smaller than 10^{16} and 585,355 CMNs smaller than 10^{17}.

For the experiments provided below in this chapter, CMNs numbers used are smaller than 10^{16}. An algorithm that generates large CMNs is provided in Dubner (1989).

Proposition 7.1. Since every CMN is a product of at least three primes, i.e., CMN $= p_1 p_2 p_3$, therefore, at least one of these factors is smaller than the cubic root of this CMN:

$$p_k \leq \sqrt[3]{\text{CMN}}. \tag{7.1}$$

Therefore, (2.3) and (7.1) imply that the complexity to find the smallest factor f of a CMN is of order

$$f = O\left(\sqrt[3]{n}/\ln\sqrt[3]{n}\right). \tag{7.2}$$

The smallest factors of each CMN are shown in the left-most column of Table 10.5.

Example 7.2. If $n = 612816751$ (see Table 10.3) is a CMN, then in order to find its smallest factor f it is sufficient to check whether n is divisible by at most one of the first 140 primes. It is easy to verify that $f = 251$.

Computer experiments indicate that for numerous CMNs, the smallest factor of a CMN does not exceed $\sqrt[4]{\text{CMN}}$, i.e., the *fourth* root of the CMN (see Tables 10.5 and A.1).

8. Primality Tests

BV-3 test: If n is a Blum prime, a and b are distinct positive integers

$$0 < a < n, \quad 0 < b < n, \quad \text{and} \quad a + b \neq n,$$

then for every complex (a, b) holds that

$$(a, b)^{(n+1)/2} \bmod n = (c, d), \tag{8.1}$$

where either c or d, but not both, are equal to *zero*.

BV-1 test: If n is a non-Blum prime, a and b are distinct positive integers: $0 < a < n$, $0 < b < n$ and $a + b \neq n$, then for every complex (a, b) holds that

$$(a, b)^{(n-1)/2} \bmod n = (c, d), \tag{8.2}$$

where either c or d, but not both, are equal to *zero*.

Remark 8.1. Notice that the exponent in (8.2) equals $(n - 1)/2$.

Example 8.2. Let $n = 561$ and $(a, b) := (2, 3)$, then

$$(2, 3)^{280} \bmod 561 = (16, 459).$$

Therefore, 561 is not a prime, because (8.2) does not hold.

Additional numeric examples are provided in Table 10.5.

9. Primality Testing with Quaternions

For integers congruent to 1 modulo 4, we introduce a primality test based on quaternions

$$(a, b, c, d) := a + bi + cj + dk, \tag{9.1}$$

where

$$i^2 = j^2 = k^2 = -1,$$
$$ij = k, \quad jk = i, \quad ki = j, \tag{9.2}$$
$$ji = -k, \quad kj = -i, \quad ik = -j.$$

Conjecture 9.1. If n is a prime, then for every quaternion (a, b, c, d) holds

$$(a, b, c, d)^{n+1} \bmod n = (h, 0, 0, 0), \tag{9.3}$$

where

$$a^2 + b^2 + c^2 + d^2 = h. \tag{9.4}$$

10. Computer Experiments

The goal of these experiments is to verify the correctness of the primality tests.

The inputs for the experiments included all 246,683 CMNs smaller than 10^{16}. For other inputs, we only considered complex primes for verification of the tests (see Proposition 5.1). Table 10.1 provides the classification of integers.

In parallel, we tested various types of inputs using the Fermat test: In the two right-most columns of Tables 10.3–10.5 are computed $2^{p-1} \bmod p$ and $5^{p-1} \bmod p$.

Table 10.2 displays results of Pythagorean triplets (see Proposition 6.4). Each input represents (a, b) and the output is the corresponding c of the Pythagorean triplet

$$a^2 + b^2 = c^2. \tag{10.1}$$

Table 10.1 Classification of integers and Fermat Test (FT).

n	$n \bmod 4 = 1$	$n \bmod 4 = 3$
Primes	Pass the Fermat test	Pass the Fermat and BV-3 tests
Ordinary composites	Detectable by FT	Detectable by FT
CMNs: non-detectable by FT	Highly likely detectable by BV-1 test	Highly likely detectable by BV-3 test

Table 10.2   BV-3 test with primes and Pythagorean triplets $(3, 4)$, $(5, 12)$, $(8, 15)$ and $(21, 20)$ as testing inputs.

Primes	$(3, 4)$	$(5, 12)$	$(8, 15)$	$(21, 20)$	Primes	$(3, 4)$	$(5, 12)$	$(8, 15)$	$(21, 20)$
499	$(5, 0)$	$(13, 0)$	$(-17, 0)$	$(29, 0)$	827	$(5, 0)$	$(13, 0)$	$(-17, 0)$	$(29, 0)$
503	$(5, 0)$	$(13, 0)$	$(17, 0)$	$(29, 0)$	863	$(5, 0)$	$(13, 0)$	$(17, 0)$	$(29, 0)$
563	$(5, 0)$	$(13, 0)$	$(-17, 0)$	$(29, 0)$	1031	$(5, 0)$	$(13, 0)$	$(17, 0)$	$(29, 0)$
647	$(5, 0)$	$(13, 0)$	$(17, 0)$	$(29, 0)$	1051	$(5, 0)$	$(13, 0)$	$(-17, 0)$	$(29, 0)$
727	$(5, 0)$	$(13, 0)$	$(17, 0)$	$(29, 0)$	1063	$(5, 0)$	$(13, 0)$	$(17, 0)$	$(29, 0)$
739	$(5, 0)$	$(13, 0)$	$(-17, 0)$	$(29, 0)$	1999	$(5, 0)$	$(13, 0)$	$(17, 0)$	$(29, 0)$
823	$(5, 0)$	$(13, 0)$	$(17, 0)$	$(29, 0)$	2011	$(5, 0)$	$(13, 0)$	$(-17, 0)$	$(29, 0)$

Table 10.3   BV-3 test with CMNs and testing seeds $(3, 2), 2, 5$.

CMN m	$(3, 2)$	2	5
251|612816751	$(166608777, 8114326)$	1	1
7689096933451	$(711030612716, 887774073594)$	1	1
42057129199051	$(30876218159239, 23205152153739)$	1	1
160754105325451	$(157881729352807, 112064545099932)$	1	1
236807688261991	$(30786938340319, 53087149566046)$	1	1
3256635189018331	$(493659725299301, 3009342191292109)$	1	1
7655741140594051	$(5285004092343118, 512008698445306)$	1	1
9849406894481251	$(1060236062683878, 5602999134151296)$	1	1

Table 10.4   BV-1 test with CMNs and testing seeds $(4, 7), 2, 5$.

CMN m	$(4, 7)$	2	5
1742169256201	$(1722693465525, 772900186399)$	1	1
33812972024833	$(27880593218382, 28911607645602)$	1	1
74243421107857	$(56003783964933, 54351804989873)$	1	1
6876256816044001	$(5628728581599734, 1975253037870091)$	1	1
9996906808980001	$(6555953650183133, 1380686298748699)$	1	1
9997112118840001	$(298421257278807, 9251058975642986)$	1	1
9999568870200001	$(7972930190493543, 5790396227732740)$	1	1
9999731048186881	$(4457231781813884, 5226353781905389)$	1	1
9999924433632001	$(746295025284997, 8421553345672929)$	1	1

Remark 10.1. $3^2 + 4^2 = 5^2$, $5^2 + 12^2 = 13^2$, $8^2 + 15^2 = 17^2$ and $21^2 + 20^2 = 29^2$ are the Pythagorean triplets. More generally, for every pair $\{g, h\}$ of integer parameters, where $g > h > 0$ and

$$a := g^2 - h^2, \quad b := 2gh, \quad c := g^2 + h^2 \tag{10.2}$$

holds (10.1). For instance, if $\{g, h\} = \{5, 2\}$, then $a = 21$, $b = 20$ and $c = 29$.

Table 10.5   BV-1 test with CMNs and seeds $(2, 1)$, $(3, 2)$, $(3, 4)$, $(3, 5)$, $(8, 3), 2, 5$.

CMN n	$(2, 1)$	$(3, 2)$	$(3, 4)$	$(3, 5)$	$(8, 3)$	2	5
3|561	$(544, 327)$	$(16, 102)$	$(511, 102)$	$(280, 393)$	$(34, 429)$	1	1
5|1105	$(833, 429)$	$(696, 425)$	$(443, 884)$	$(586, 325)$	$(391, 650)$	1	1
7|1729	$(1275, 1638)$	$(995, 763)$	$(729, 1365)$	$(729, 364)$	$(1275, 1638)$	1	1
5|2465	$(1973, 1479)$	$\mathbf{(1, 0)}$	$(1973, 1479)$	$(2321, 1885)$	$\mathbf{(1, 0)}$	1	1
7|2821	$(2028, 317)$	$(2203, 1902)$	$(833, 2197)$	$(26, 2501)$	$(26, 1230)$	1	1
1|5441	$\mathbf{(1, 0)}$	$\mathbf{(0, 2989)}$	$\mathbf{(1, 0)}$	$\mathbf{(5440, 0)}$	$\mathbf{(0, 2989)}$	1	1
7|6601	$(2254, 4346)$	$(6027, 3312)$	$\mathbf{(2092, 0)}$	$\mathbf{(0, 2715)}$	$(2828, 2829)$	1	1

Thousands of computer experiments demonstrate that the BV-3 test detects every CMN. Several examples are provided in Table 10.3.

Indeed, in the Fermat tests $2^{n-1} \bmod n = 1$ and $5^{n-1} \bmod n = 1$.

However, $(3, 2)^{(n+1)/2} \bmod n$ does not satisfy (8.1), if n is a CMN (see Table 10.3).

The BV-1 test detects CMNs congruent to 1 modulo 4. Several examples are provided in Table 10.4. However, the BV-1 test is not reliable in all cases. Indeed, Table 10.5 shows the instance (CMN $= 2465$) where the BV-1 test fails. Numerous computer experiments with the BV-1 test detected CMNs in 95% of cases. More details on the experiments are provided in Verkhovsky and Mutovic (2005).

Remark 10.2. Table 10.3 shows the cases where every CMN is detected by the BV-3 test using one seed $(3, 2)$ only.

Remark 10.3. Table 10.4 shows the cases where every CMN is detected by BV-1 with one complex seed $(4, 7)$ only.

Remark 10.4. $n = 2465$ in Table 10.5 is a *strong* CMN since it escapes the BV-1 test with seeds $(3, 2)$ and $(8, 3)$. $n = 6601$ is another strong CMN since it escapes this test with seeds $(3, 4)$ and $(3, 5)$. Yet, $n = 5441$ is a prime, these cases are shown in bold in Table 10.5.

In the left-most column of Table 10.5 are shown minimal factors. For instance, in 1729 the factor 7 is the smallest one of this CMN.

Suppose $f(m)$ is the smallest factor of CMN m (see the first column in Table 10.5), and let

$$\exp(m) := \log_m f(m) = \ln f(m) / \ln m. \tag{10.3}$$

Example 10.5. If $m = 612816751$, then $f(m) = 251$, $\ln 251 = 5.525$ and $\ln 612816751 = 20.234$. Therefore, $\exp(m) = 0.2731$.

Table 10.6   Frequency distribution of $\exp(m)$ for CMNs m.

[0.03 0.06]	(0.06] 0.09]	(0.09] 0.12]	(0.12] 0.15]	(0.15] 0.18]	(0.18] 0.21]	(0.21] 0.24]	(0.24] 0.27]	(0.27] 0.3]	(0.3] 1/3]
12	230	252	139	64	38	45	63	34	2

Table 10.6 shows the distribution of these exponents in the interval $[10^9, 10^{10}]$.

Remark 10.6. Among CMNs m on the interval $[10^9, 10^{10}]$ there are no $f(m)$ with the corresponding $\exp(m) < 0.03$.

The average value of $\exp(m)$ is equal to 0.137, therefore,

$$f(m) = \Theta(m^{0.137}). \qquad (10.4)$$

Chapter 5

Algorithm Generating Random Permutation

1. Applications of Permutations

Many combinatorial problems can be solved via a systematic analysis of all permutations in conjunction with the branch-and-bound approach. The traveling salesman problem is one such problem. Random permutations are used as a tool to generate pseudo-random numbers for inter-processor communication (random routing algorithm) in parallel computers and in various cryptographic schemes: substitution, transposition and permutation. In the latter case, if two users want to communicate using one of these ciphers, they need to agree on a permutation. If the size of an alphabet is known (say, $n = 26$), then they can use the key-exchange scheme (Diffie and Hellman, 1976), where the secret key will be a permutation. To make this scheme more secure, they must frequently change the permutations. They can use two ways for representing the permutations of the 26 letters of the English alphabet: (1) as a sequence of 26 two-decimal-digit numbers, i.e., the key will be 52-digit long; (2) as an integer on interval $[1, n!]$, i.e., using a counting system for permutations (Khuth, 1998). In this case, the key will be 27-digit long, since $26! \cong 4.033 \times 10^{26}$, i.e., the counting system requires keys about half the length for $n = 26$.

2. Permutation Generation

In Sedgewick (1977, 1990), generation of permutations is considered "as an interesting computational puzzle". Namely, how one can write a program

(a) for a *random* permutation of n numbers,
(b) randomly generating *every* possible permutation of n distinct objects.

Both these problems are algorithmically addressed in this chapter.

Let us consider how to generate a random permutation of the first n natural numbers.

First, we generate randomly an integer R on interval $[1, n!]$ and then find a permutation corresponding to R. Hence, the problem is how to establish one-to-one correspondence between a set of all permutations S_n and integers on the interval $[1, n!]$. In a sense, we must find a way of *counting* the permutations. Consider an ordered set A of n distinct integer elements $a_1, a_2, \ldots, a_n$, where every element satisfies the inequality $1 \le a_k \le n$.

Definition 2.1. We say that A has an inversion if there exists at least one pair (a_i, a_j) such that $a_i > a_j$ and $i < j$.

It means that there is at least one pair $\{\ldots, c, \ldots, d, \ldots\}$ of elements in A such that $c > d$, i.e., a larger element c is located to the left of a smaller element d.

Example 2.2. The array of five elements $\{4, 1, 6, 3, 7\}$ has *three* inversions, since the element 1 is located to the right of the element 4, and the element 3 is located to the right of two elements 4 and 6.

Definition 2.3. We say that in the set $A = \{a_1, a_2, \ldots, a_n\}$ the element a_m has u inversions, if A has u elements each smaller than a_m and located to the right of a_m.

Example 2.4. Let $A = \{3, 1, 5, 4, 2\}$, then $u_1 = 0$, $u_2 = 0$, $u_3 = 2$, $u_4 = 1$, $\{u_5 = 2\}$.

The definition of inversion implies that for every m

$$0 \le u_m \le m - 1. \tag{2.1}$$

Remark 2.5. set of inversions $U = \{u_2, \ldots, u_n\}$ is a system of $n - 1$ coordinates that uniquely defines every permutation of n elements, $\{u_1 \equiv 0\}$. Using this system of coordinates we can establish one-to-one correspondence between the permutations and integers. An almost analogous system of coordinates is considered in Knuth (1998). On the other hand, by randomly generating a set of inversions $\{u_2, \ldots, u_n\}$, we can find a corresponding random permutation.

Hence, from the following mappings we can solve both problems:

All permutations $\leftrightarrow$ Random inversions $\leftrightarrow$ Random permutation.

Preliminary results are published in Verkhovsky (2000).

3. Counting the Permutations

For the counting system we use the identity $\sum_{k=1}^{n}(k-1)!(k-1)+1 = n!$.

Remark 3.1. For all $k \geq 2$, let M_k be the number assigned for a set of k distinct elements, u_k be the inversion of its kth element and let $M_1 = 1$, then

$$M_k = M_{k-1} + (k-1)!u_k. \tag{3.1}$$

Therefore, (3.1) implies that

$$M_n = 1 + \sum_{k=2}^{n}(k-1)!u_k. \tag{3.2}$$

4. Counting the Inversions

Step 4.1: Generate a random integer M_n: $1 \leq M_n \leq n!$.

Step 4.2: for $k = n$ **down to 2 do**

$$M_{k-1} := M_k \bmod (k-1)!, \quad u_k := (M_k - M_{k-1})/(k-1)!. \tag{4.1}$$

Step 4.3: **output** $U = \{u_1 = 0, u_2, \ldots, u_n\}$.

Although algorithmically it is a straightforward problem, division by $k!$ for a large k, if it is performed on computer, can become problematic and requires additional programming efforts. Besides, it remains to demonstrate how to convert U into a permutation.

5. Inversions-Permutation Mapping

Let $u_1 = 0, u_2 = 0, u_3 = 2, u_4 = 2, u_5 = 3, u_6 = 5, u_7 = 6, u_8 = 5$.

Definition 5.1. Let $V = \{v_1, v_2, \ldots, v_n\}$ be the set of inversions sorted in the increasing order of their values, i.e., $0 = v_1 \leq v_2 \leq \cdots \leq v_n$. For large n only, if there is a subset S of inversions with equal values, then sort them within S in a decreasing order of their indices. This type of sorting we call the *seesaw sorting*.

It is easy to check that the corresponding permutation is $\{7, 6, 8, 3, 5, 4, 1, 2\}$.

6. The Algorithm

Input: the set of inversions $U = \{u_2, \ldots, u_n\}$;

Output: the permutation $P = \{p_1, p_2, \ldots, p_n\}$.

for $r = 1$ **to** n **do**

Step 6.1 (Sort all inversions): Let after the sorting $\{u_{k(1)}, u_{k(2)}, \ldots, u_{k(n)}\}$,

i.e., $u_{k(i)} \leq u_{k(j)}$ **for every** $r \leq i < j \leq n$;

if $u_{k(i)} = u_{k(j)}$, **then** $k(i) > k(j)$ **for every** $i < j$;

(the extra sorting of equal inversions decreases the complexity of the algorithm);

$\quad$ *left* $:= k(1)$;

Step 6.2 (Modify the values of inversions and resort them):

$\quad$ **for** $i = r{+}1$ **to** n **do**

$\quad$ **if** $k(i) > $ *left*, **then** $u_{k(i)} := u_{k(i)} - 1$;

Step 6.3 (Move the left-most element to the permutation):

$\quad p_{n+1-r} := $ *left*;

(End of **for**).

Example 6.1. Input: $n = 8$ and $u_1 = 0$, $u_2 = 1$, $u_3 = 2$, $u_4 = 3$, $u_5 = 0$, $u_6 = 1$, $u_7 = 3$, $u_8 = 2$ (sort the inversions).

Remark 6.2. Notice that the contents of Tables 6.2–6.5 are shifted to the right ($\rightarrow$) to provide the outputs in the left parts ($\leftarrow$) of the tables.

Finally, the permutation is $\{4, 3, 2, 7, 1, 8, 6, 5\}$.

Table 6.1

$\leftarrow m$	$k \rightarrow$	5	1	6	2	8	3	7	4
$\leftarrow p_m$	$u_k \rightarrow$	0	0	1	1	2	2	3	3

Note: Move the left-most element (*left*) to the permutation, **output** $p_8 := 5$.

Table 6.2

8	← m	k →	6	1	8	2	7	3	4
5	← p_m	u_k →	**0**	**0**	**1**	**1**	**2**	**2**	**3**

Note: Modify the inversions and sort them, **output** $p_7 := 6$.

Table 6.3

7	8	← m	k →	8	1	7	2	3	4
6	**5**	← p_m	u_k →	**0**	**0**	**1**	**1**	**2**	**3**

Note: No sorting is necessary in the next two stages, **output** $p_6 := 8$ and $p_5 := 1$.

Table 6.4

5	6	7	8	← m	k →	7	2	3	4
1	**8**	**6**	**5**	← p_m	u_k →	**0**	**0**	**1**	**2**

Note: Modify the inversions, no sorting is necessary, **output** $p_4 := 7$ and $p_3 := 2$.

Table 6.5

3	4	5	6	7	8	← m	k →	3	4
2	**7**	**1**	**8**	**6**	**5**	← p_m	u_k →	**0**	**1**

Note: Modify the inversions, **output** $p_2 := 3$ and $p_1 := 4$.

7. Modified Algorithm for Large n

The seesaw sorting must be done explicitly only once. Sorting of inversions requires $O(n \log n)$ comparisons. Let for every k $0 \leq u_k \leq m$. Sorting of indices for equal inversions requires $O(n \log(n/m))$ comparisons. In order to decrease the number of required comparisons, consider

Step 7.1: if $u_k = j$, then $k \in S_j \{k \in S_j$ are sorted in decreasing order$\}$

Step 7.2:

for j **from** 1 **to** m **do**

    if $((k \in S_j)$ **and** $(k < left))$ **then** $k \in L_j$.

{End of **for**}.

Step 7.3:

$$S_0 := S_0 - \{\text{left}\} + L_1; \text{ MERGESORT } S_j \text{ and } R_{j+1};$$

for $l = 1$ to $m-1$, $S_j := S_j - L_j$; MERGESORT S_j and R_{j+1};

$$S_j := S_j - L_j$$

If $S_m = \emptyset$, $m = m-1$.

Go back to Step 7.2 for a new value of *left*.

After the next *left* is known, then every S_j can be represented as $S_j = \{L_j, R_j\}$ after at most $O(\log |S_j|)$ comparisons. The MERGESORT for all j requires in the worst case $n - r$ comparisons. The total number of comparisons for the MERGESORT is at most $n(n - 1)/2$.

8. Example 6.1 Revisited

1. After the seesaw sorting $S_0 = \{5,1\}$, $S_1 = \{6,2\}$, $S_2 = \{8,3\}$, $S_3 = \{7,4\}$, left $= \mathbf{5}$,
2. $S_0 := \{1\}$, $L_1 := \{6\}$, $R_1 := \{2\}$, $L_2 := \{8\}$, $R_2 := \{3\}$, $L_3 := \{7\}$, $R_3 := \{4\}$,
3. {MergeSort neighboring sets}: $S_0 = \{6,1\}$, $S_1 = \{8,2\}$, $S_2 = \{7,3\}$, $S_3 = \{4\}$; left $:= \mathbf{6}$,
4. $S_0 := \{1\}$, $L_1 := \{8\}$, $R_1 := \{2\}$, $L_2 := \{7\}$, $R_2 := \{3\}$, $L_3 := \emptyset$, $R_3 := \{4\}$,
5. {MergeSort neighboring sets}: $S_0 = \{8,1\}$, $S_1 = \{7,2\}$, $S_2 = \{3\}$, $S_3 = \{4\}$, left $:= \mathbf{8}$, etc.

Chapter 6

Extractability of Square Roots and Divisibility Tests

1. Introduction

In this chapter, two issues are addressed.

(a) We describe non-deterministic algorithms for quick testing whether a multi-digit long integer N is square free. These tests are called Las Vegas algorithms since they provide a correct answer if N is indeed squarefree, but do not determine whether N has an integer square root. Such algorithms accelerate solution of Diophantine equations. Applications of these algorithms are demonstrated in Chap. 16 where we discuss procedures for integer factoring of semi-primes.

(b) How to check whether a large integer N is divisible by a "small" integer m. Under certain conditions, it is necessary to check whether an integer D is divisible by a small integer $2 < m < 100$. There are known and simple criteria of divisibility by 2, 3, 4, 5, 6, 8, 9, 10, 11, 12, 15, 20 and 25 (Vorob'ev, 1980). In this chapter, we consider several algorithms for divisibility by many primes smaller than 100.

2. Divisibility Algorithms for $m = 7$ and $m = 13$

Definition 2.1. D is divisible by an integer m if and only if $D \bmod m = 0$.

Let $D = d_z d_{z-1} \ldots d_1$, where for every k $0 \le d_k \le 9$ are decimal digits.

Let us consider conditions of divisibility by 7, 13, 17 and other small primes.

If $m = 7$, then consider $d_k := d_k \bmod 7$ for every k.

Let us consider

$$F := d_1 - d_4 + d_7 - \ldots, \qquad (2.1)$$

$$S := d_2 - d_5 + d_8 - \ldots, \qquad (2.2)$$

$$T := d_3 - d_6 + d_9 - \ldots, \qquad (2.3)$$

$$Q := F + 3S + 2T. \qquad (2.4)$$

If $Q \bmod 7 = 0,$ **then** D is divisible by 7.   (2.5)

Let $R := Q + 2(T - F),$ (2.6)

If $R \bmod 13 = 0,$ **then** D is divisible by 13   (2.7)

(Rowland, 1997).

Remark 2.2. Both algorithms for $m = 7$ and $m = 13$ resemble a cryptographic transposition cipher in reverse (Menezes *et al.*, 1997):

(1) Consider a table with three rows and as many columns as necessary to fit the "plaintext" D.
(2) Write the "plaintext" D column after column starting from the right.
(3) For *seven*, use the "keyword" $\{1,3,2\}$ (2.4).
(4) For 13, use the "keyword" $\{-1, 3, 4\}$ (2.6).

3. "Binary" Divisibility Test by *Seven* and 17

If an integer B is represented in binary form $B = b_n\, b_{n-1}\, b_{n-2} \ldots b_6\, b_5\, b_4\, b_3\, b_2\, b_1$, then the algorithm is very simple:

(1) Consider sum T of triplets

$$T := (\ldots + b_9 b_8 b_7 + b_6 b_5 b_4 + b_3 b_2 b_1), \qquad (3.1)$$

(2) If $T \bmod 7 = 0$, then B is divisible by *seven*.

Example 3.1. Let $B = 10011111100110\{= 010, 011, 111, 100, 110\}$, then

$$T = 010 + 011 + 111 + 100 + 110 = 22 \text{ (in decimals)}.$$

Since $22 \bmod 7 = 1$, then B is not divisible by *seven*.

If an integer H is represented in binary form $H = h_n\, h_{n-1} \ldots h_8\, h_7\, h_6\, h_5\, h_4\, h_3\, h_2\, h_1$, then the algorithm is also very simple:

(1) Consider sum Q of quadruplets with *alternating* signs

$$Q := (\ldots + h_{12} h_{11} h_{10} h_9 - h_8 h_7 h_6 h_5 + h_4 h_3 h_2 h_1). \qquad (3.2)$$

(2) If $Q \bmod 17 = 0$, then H is divisible by 17.

Example 3.2. Let $H = 11111011110110101110 \{=1111, 1011, 1101, 1010, 1110\}$, then

$$Q = 1111 - 1011 + 1101 - 1010 + 1110 = 21 (\text{in decimal}).$$

Since $21 \bmod 17 = 4$, then H is not divisible by 17.

4. Divisibility Algorithm

If $\gcd(m, 10) = 1$, then the algorithm tests whether D is divisible by m; here D is multi-digit integer in the decimal base.

Step 4.1: For given m select a corresponding g from Table 4.1 below:

Step 4.2: Let $b := D \bmod 10, \quad a := (D - b)/10 (D = 10a + b)$ $\qquad$ (4.1)

Step 4.3: Compute $R := a + bg$ (R is called a *resolventa*)
Step 4.4: **if** $R \bmod m = 0$, **then** D is divisible by m
Step 4.5: **if** R is "large", **then** $D := R$; **goto** Step 4.2.

Example 4.1. Suppose $m = 19$ and $D = 3914$.
Compute the resolventa $R = 391 + 2 * 4 = 399 = 19 * 21$. Hence D is divisible by 19.

5. Faster Divisibility Tests

If D is h-digit decimal integer and h is large, then the algorithm requires $O(h)$ steps. The number of steps can be decreased by considering slightly modified computation in Step 4.2 in the algorithm provided above:

Step 5.1: $D = 100a + b$ $\qquad$ (5.1)

Step 5.2: Compute $R := a + bg$ $\qquad$ (5.2)

Step 5.3: **if** $R \bmod m = 0$; and $(100g - 1) \bmod m = 0$, $\qquad$ (5.3)

then D is divisible by m.

From the condition (5.3) it is easy to find the smallest values of g for which $100g - 1$ is divisible by m (see Table 5.1). In this case the number of steps is twice smaller than in the previous version of the algorithm.

Table 4.1 m and corresponding g.

m	3	7	11	13	17	19	23	29	31	41
g	1	-2	-1	4	-5	2	7	3	-3	-4

Table 5.1   Smallest g for which $100\,g^{-1}$ is divisible by m.

m	3	7	11	13	17	19	23	29	31	43
g	1	$-3, 4, -10$	$-10, 1$	$-10, 3$	$-9, 8$	4	$-20, 3$	$-20, 9$	9	-3

For $m = 7$, 11, 13, 17, 23 and 29 there are *several* values of g (negative and positive). Since the negative values of g also decrease the values of R, they are more preferable. Especially for $m = 7$, 11 and 13, $g = -10$, which does not require any explicit multiplication. Almost the same for $m = 23$ and 29: it is easier to multiply by -20, than by 3 and 9.

6. Modified Tests

If $m = 7$, 11 or 13, and $D = 100a + b$, then D is divisible by m if and only if

$$R = a - 10b \quad \text{is divisible by } m. \tag{6.1}$$

Example 6.1. Let $n = 5632116$, then $R = 56,321 - 160 = 56,161$.

Since R is large, repeat the test: $D := R = 56,161$, $R := 561 - 610 = -49$.

Therefore, D is divisible by 7 and *not* divisible by 11 and 13.

7. Validity of Divisibility Tests

Let for $5 < m < D$ find simple tests verifying whether integer D is divisible by m, i.e., whether $D \bmod m = 0$.

Let $D = 10a + b$, where D, a and b are decimal integers.

Remark 7.1. If $b = 0$ or $b = m$, then we test whether $D := a$ is divisible by m.

Consider integer R (an indicator of divisibility)

$$R := a + bg \quad \text{and} \quad \text{let } S := 10R.$$

If

$$\gcd(m, 10) = 1 \quad \text{and} \quad S = 10R \bmod m = 0, \text{ then } R \bmod m = 0. \tag{7.1}$$

And vice versa: if R is divisible by m, then S is also divisible by m. If $R \bmod m = 0$, then $R = km$, where k is an integer. Therefore,

$$a + bg = km. \tag{7.2}$$

Hence

$$S = 10km = 10a + b + 10bg - b = D + (10g - 1)b. \tag{7.3}$$

Since by assumption R and S are divisible by m, therefore,

$$D = S - (10g - 1)b \tag{7.4}$$

is divisible by m if $10g - 1$ is divisible by m.

8. More General Divisibility Test

Let

$$n = 10a + b \quad \text{and} \quad m = 10c + d, \text{ where } d > 0. \tag{8.1}$$

Proposition 8.1. If m divides $ad - bc$, then m divides n.

Proof. Consider a linear combination:

$$T := nx + my = (10a + b)x + (10c + d)y, \tag{8.2}$$

where

$$\gcd(x, m) = \gcd(y, m) = 1. \tag{8.3}$$

Therefore,

$$T = n(\text{mod } m). \tag{8.4}$$

Let

$$x := d \quad \text{and} \quad y := -b, \tag{8.5}$$

then

$$T = 10(ad - bc). \tag{8.6}$$

Since m is co-prime with 10 (7.1), then m divides T if
and only if m divides $ad - bc$. $\tag{8.7}$

Therefore, (8.6) implies that $m \mid T$ if and only if $m \mid (ad - bc)$.
On the other hand, if m divides T, then (8.4) implies that m divides n.
$\square$

Example 8.2. Let $n = 2003$ and $m = 47$, then

$$2003 \bmod 47 = (200 \times 7 - 3 \times 4) \bmod 47 = 1388 \bmod 47.$$

The universal test requires computation of ad, which is not so simple
if $d > 1$ and a is large. However, if $d = 1$ and c is a small integer, then the
testing is simplified.

For instance, if $m = 11, 31, 41, 61, 71, 101$, then the universal test is
very simple.

Example 8.3. Let $n = 4189$ and $m = 71$, then

$$4189 \bmod 71 = (418 \times 1 - 9 \times 7) \bmod 71 = 355 \bmod 71.$$

Since 71 divides 355, therefore, 71 divides 4189.

9. Extractability of Integer Square Roots

In Chap. 17, we consider Diophantine quadratic equation

$$z^2 - (QL + 2)z + SL^2/2 = 0, \qquad (9.1)$$

where Q and S are large even integers, L is an unknown integer parameter and z is a positive root of (9.1). In general, the interval of uncertainty for L can be very large.

Since

$$z_{1,2} = QL/2 + 1 \pm \sqrt{Q^2 L^2/4 + QL + 1 - SL^2/2}$$

$$= QL/2 + 1 \pm \sqrt{(Q^2 L/4 - SL/2 + Q)L + 1} \qquad (9.2)$$

the roots are integer if there exists an integer square root of the discriminant

$$K(L) := (Q^2 L/4 - SL/2 + Q)L + 1. \qquad (9.3)$$

The following tests eliminate numerous bad candidates and require minute memory.

9.1. *Problem definition and basic properties*

In general, let us find a computationally efficient test that checks whether a large integer N has an integer square root W, i.e., such that $W^2 = N$.

The following proposition is an example of simple rule to deduce that N does not have an integer square root.

Proposition 9.1. If N is represented in decimal base, r is the right-most digit of N, and $r = 2, 3, 7$ and 8, then W is not an integer.

Remark 9.2. It is easy to see that there is no analogue of Proposition 9.1 for a test of cubic root integer extractability, since $0^3 = 0$, $1^3 = 1$, $8^3 = 512$, $7^3 = 343$,

$$4^3 = 64, \quad 5^3 = 125, \quad 6^3 = 216, \quad 3^3 = 27, \quad 2^3 = 8, \quad 9^3 = 729.$$

The following procedures are based on modular reduction M. These procedures are non-deterministic algorithms with the following property: if procedure P determines for a fixed modulus $m = M$ that W is not an integer, then it provides the same output for every modulus m. However, the reverse is not always true, i.e., if for the fixed modulus M the procedure P does not determine that W is non-integer, then the output for other moduli is not definite. In this case there are two options: either to directly compute W or to apply P for several other moduli m. In the latter case, if for at least one modulus m1 the output of P is that W is not integer, then it implies that N does not have an integer square root (N is square free, for short). For instance, if $N = 2014$, then Proposition 9.1 does not provide an answer whether W is either an integer or N is square free. In this case further analysis is required. Let us define a *function of tails* for integers $z = 1, 2, \ldots, M - 1$:

$$f(z) := z^2 (\mathrm{mod}\ M). \tag{9.4}$$

Hence, the definition (9.4) implies that

$$f(M/2 \pm z) = z^2 = f(z). \tag{9.5}$$

Below are listed the tails for $z = 1, 2, \ldots, 4\sqrt{M} - 1$.

9.2. *Numeric illustration*

Let us consider modulus $M = 2^s = 256$. Notice that the tails in the rightmost column of Table 9.1 are the same as in the previous column, but listed in the reverse order. More generally,

$$\begin{aligned} f(48 + z) &= f(80 - z), \quad f(32 + z) = f(96 - z), \\ f(16 + z) &= f(112 - z), \quad f(z) = f(128 - z). \end{aligned} \tag{9.6}$$

All tails in this table can be sorted and represented as terms of five arithmetic progresssions A1, A2, A3, A5 and A7 with the difference $d = 2\sqrt{M} = 32$. For details, see Table 9.2.

Notice that the "progression" $A4 := \{16, 144\}$ has only two tails. The progression $A6 := \{36, 68, 100, 132, 164, 196, 228\}$ is already listed as the subset in $A2$, $A7 := \{49, 81, 113, 145, 177, 209, 241\}$ has 7 tails, and $A8 := \{64\}$ has one tail.

This observation eliminates necessity to store and retrieve later the tails if the modulus M is large. Thus, there are totally

$$\log_2(2\sqrt{M})\sqrt{M}/2 + 2 = (1 + s/2)2^{s/2-1} + 2 = 42 \tag{9.7}$$

feasible tails of 256 cases or $256/42 = 6.07$ times fewer. The tails indicated in bold font are the squares of integers.

Table 9.1　The function of tails.

	0	16	32	48	64
0	0	16	0	16	0
1	1	33	65	97	*129*
2	4	68	132	196	*4*
3	9	105	201	41	*137*
4	16	144	16	144	*16*
5	25	185	89	249	*153*
6	36	228	164	100	*36*
7	49	17	241	209	*177*
8	64	64	64	*64*	*64*
9	81	113	145	*177*	209
10	100	164	228	*36*	100
11	121	217	57	*153*	249
12	144	16	144	*16*	144
13	169	73	233	*137*	41
14	196	132	68	*4*	196
15	225	193	161	*129*	97

Table 9.2　Tails sorted as arithmetic progressions with $d = 32$.

$A1$	**1**	33	65	97	129	161	193	**225**
$A2$	**4**	**36**	68	**100**	132	164	**196**	228
$A3$	**9**	41	73	105	137	**169**	201	233
$A4$	**16**	—	—	—	144	—	—	—
$A5$	**25**	57	89	**121**	153	185	217	249
$A6$	**36**	68	**100**	132	164	196	228	—
$A7$	**49**	**81**	113	145	177	209	241	—
$A8$	**64**	—	—	—	—	—	—	—

Remark 9.3. Notice that the squares 64, 81, 100, 121, 144, 169, 196 and 225 are located on the diagonal in Table 4. The tails in the arithmetic progressions $A6$, $A9$, $A10$, $A11$, $A12$, $A13$, $A14$ and $A15$ are the subsets in $A2$, $A7$, $A6$, $A5$, $A4$, $A3$, $A2$ and $A1$.

Indeed, $A9 := \{81, 113, 145, \ldots\}$, $A10 := \{100, 132, 164, \ldots\}$, $A11 := \{121, 153, 185, 217, 249\}$, $A12 := \{144, 16, 144, 16\}$, $A13 := \{169, 201, 233\}$, $A14 := \{196, 228\}$, and $A15 := \{225\}$.

10. The Extractability Algorithm

10.1. *Special case: $M = 256$*

Suppose that we need to find an integer N on interval $[A, B]$ such that its square root W is integer. If $B - A$ is large, then N itself is large. For instance, if $A = 1$ and $B = 10^8$, then there are only 10,000 integers on $[1, 10^8]$ that have an integer square root.

In order to check whether integer W exists or to eliminate squarefree candidates, compute

$$R := N \bmod M = N \bmod 256, \tag{10.1}$$

if R has an *integer square root*, **then** compute W, $\tag{10.2}$

else compute $T := \sqrt{R \bmod 2\sqrt{M}} = \sqrt{R} \bmod 32, \tag{10.3}$

if T is an *integer*, **then** compute W **else** integer W does not exist.
$$\tag{10.4}$$

The procedure described above is a non-deterministic (Las Vegas) algorithm: it provides the correct answer if the integer N is squarefree, however, it responds that W "maybe exists" if R has an integer square root or T is an integer.

Remark 10.1. It is necessary to point out that the step (10.1) is essential. Otherwise, if $R = 81$, and the step (10.1) is not used, then the corresponding T is equal to $\sqrt{17}$, which falsely eliminates a good candidate.

Indeed, for every $N = (128k \pm 9)^2$ (9.5), $R = 81$ is the corresponding tail for every integer k. Therefore, it implies that the integer W does exist.

10.2. *General case*

Compute

$$R := N \bmod M, \tag{10.5}$$

if R has an *integer square root*, **then** compute W, $\tag{10.6}$

else compute $T := \sqrt{R \bmod 2\sqrt{M}}, \tag{10.7}$

if T is an *integer*, **then** compute W **else** integer W does not exist.
$$\tag{10.8}$$

The algorithm (10.5)–(10.8) is a set of necessary but not sufficient conditions that N has an integer square root.

Example 10.2. Let us check whether $N = 31415926$ has an integer square root W. Consider modulus $M = 400$. Compute $R = N \bmod 400 = 326$. Since 326 does not have an integer square root, then compute T. Since T is not an integer, then N does not have a square root.

Example 10.3. Let us now check whether $N = 31415924$ has an integer square root W; compute $R = N \bmod 400 = 324$. Since square root of 324 is equal to 18, then consider $M = 256$ and compute $R = N \bmod 256 = 116$. Since 116 does not have an integer square root, then compute T (10.3):

$$T := \sqrt{R \bmod 2\sqrt{M}} = \sqrt{R \bmod 32\sqrt{M}} = \sqrt{20}.$$

Since T is not an integer, then N does not have a square root.

Remark 10.4. The algorithm (10.5)–(10.8) can be applied if the number under the square root in (10.7) is itself a large integer.

Exercise 10.5. Check whether $N = 2718281828459045$ has an integer square root without direct computation of W (Hint: consider $M = 676$, 1024, 1600).

Exercise 10.6. Check whether $N = 73890632378665350600643 7476$ has an integer square root without direct computation of W (Hint: consider $M = 729$, 1600, 2500).

Chapter 7

Extraction of Roots of Higher Order in Modular Arithmetic

1. The Introductory Section

Computation of square roots in modular arithmetic was analyzed by Leonhard Euler.

He considered two cases: where modulus p is a non-Blum prime ($p \bmod 4 = 1$) and where p is a Blum prime ($p \bmod 4 = 3$). The latter case is solved via a simple formula:

$$u = \sqrt{w} = w^{(p+1)/4} \bmod p. \tag{1.1}$$

The computation of the square root for the former case ($p \bmod 4 = 1$) is based on two typical approaches: the Tonelli–Shanks method published in Tonelli (1891) and in Shanks (1973); and the Cipolla–Lehmer method published in Cipolla (1903) and Lehmer (1969). The Tonelli–Shanks method can be easily extended to the case of nth roots, which is called the Adleman–Manders–Miller method [Adleman et al., 1977], but it seems difficult to extend the Cipolla–Lehmer method to more general cases. In Nishihara et al. (2009), two explicit algorithms are proposed for implementation of the Cipolla–Lehmer approach in the case of cube roots for primes satisfying $p = 1 \pmod 3$.

Adleman–Manders–Miller method of the square root extraction can be generalized for the extraction of the nth root. In another paper (Nishihara et al., 2013), the Adleman–Manders–Miller method is implemented for the cubic root extraction.

For an application in cryptography or in information assurance, it is necessary to design a computationally efficient algorithm that finds a cubic root or roots of higher order of the integer w modulo prime p, for every w that is co-prime with p. Several non-deterministic algorithms for cubic roots where $p \bmod 3 = 1$ are presented in Adleman *et al.* (1977), Nishihara *et al.* (2009) and Cao *et al.* (2011).

The paper by Williams (1972) describes an algorithm, which determines a solution of the congruence $u^n \equiv w \pmod{p}$ provided that p is a prime such that $p \equiv 1 \pmod{n}$ and w is an integer such that $w^{(p-1)/n} = 1 \pmod{p}$, i.e., the nth root of w exists. The algorithm requires to find an integer b such that $(b^n - w)^{(p-1)/n} \neq 0, 1 \pmod{p}$. Williams's algorithm requires $O(n^3 \log p)$ steps. Williams and Hardy (1993) presented an improvement of this algorithm which determines a solution in $O(n^4) + O(n^2 \log p)$ steps, once b has been determined. Thus, the new algorithm is faster if $n^2 \ll \log p$. Adleman *et al.* (1977) described an algorithm for the general n^{th} root extraction in modular arithmetic, which requires solving a discrete logarithm problem. Barreto and Voloch (2006) provided algorithms that compute n^{th} roots modulo p^m, where m and p are co-prime and if either $\gcd[p(p-1), n] = 1$ or $n|(p-1)$ and $\gcd[(p-1)/n, n] = 1$, and $\gcd(m, n) = 1$.

In this paper, we present several new and deterministic algorithms for the cubic root extraction, where either $p \bmod 3 = 2$ or $p \bmod 3 = 1$, but $p \bmod 9 \neq 1$. We also provide deterministic algorithms for the quintic ($n = 5$) and general algorithms for the nth order roots modulo prime p. These algorithms have $\mathrm{O}(\log p)$ complexities. Most of the algorithms are illustrated in various numeric examples.

2. Algorithm for n^{th} Root Extraction

2.1. *General framework*

Definition 2.1. An integer u is an nth root of w modulo p:

$$u := \sqrt[n]{w} \bmod p,$$

if

$$u^n \bmod p = w. \tag{2.1}$$

Let us select an integer E and assign

$$v := w^E \bmod p, \tag{2.2}$$

such that

$$v^n = w^b \times w^F = w^b \pmod{p}, \tag{2.3}$$

i.e., where F is an integer and

$$w^F \bmod p = 1. \tag{2.4}$$

Hence, (2.2) and (2.3) imply that

$$nE = (F + b) \bmod (p - 1). \tag{2.5}$$

Therefore,

$$F = (nE - b) \bmod (p - 1). \tag{2.6}$$

If there exists an efficient algorithm that extracts a bth root modulo p, then

$$u = \sqrt[b]{v} \bmod p. \tag{2.7}$$

If $b = \pm 1$, then the case is trivial: $u := v^{\pm 1} \bmod p$. If $b = \pm 2$, then there are several square root algorithms (Tonelli–Shanks algorithm and Cipolla–Lehmer algorithm) that compute u in (2.7).

Let us consider $b = 1$ and select

$$E = [a(p - 1) + n^m]/n^{m+1}, \tag{2.8}$$

where a and m are integer parameters that must satisfy (2.4) and the integrality constraints on E and F. Hence,

$$nE = a(p - 1)/n^m + 1. \tag{2.9}$$

Finally, nE is an integer if and only if

$$F := a(p - 1)/n^m \text{ is integer.} \tag{2.10}$$

NB: (2.10) specifies the value of m.

Proposition 2.2. An integer u is the nth power of w if

$$w^{a(p-1)/n^m} \bmod p = 1. \tag{2.11}$$

In the following algorithms for extraction of the nth roots mod p, we consider two cases:

I. $p \bmod n \neq 1$, i.e., $p = fn + g$, $2 \leq g \leq n - 1$, $\gcd(p, g) = 1$. (2.12)

II. $p \bmod n = 1$, $p \bmod n^2 \neq 1$, i.e., $p = fn^2 + gn + 1$, $1 \leq g \leq n - 1$. (2.13)

In the latter case, w has a nth root u if and only if $w^{(p-1)/n} \bmod p = 1$.

Case I: Let $m = 0$, then the FLT implies that for every integer a (2.11) holds.

Case II: Let $m = 1$, then

$$E = [a(p-1) + n]/n^2 = [a(fn^2 + gn) + n]/n^2$$
$$= [a(fn + g) + 1]/n = af + (ag + 1)/n. \tag{2.14}$$

E is an integer if

$$(ag + 1) \bmod n = 0, \quad \text{i.e., if } a = (n-1)g^{-1}. \tag{2.15}$$

On the other hand, $nE = 1 + a(p-1)/n$.
Therefore,

$$w^{nE} = w \times [w^{(p-1)/n}]^a = w \times 1^a \bmod p = w. \tag{2.16}$$

2.2. *Alternative extractor E*

Let us consider

$$E = Q/n^2 = [a(p-1) + n]/n^2. \tag{2.17}$$

After substitution of $p - 1 = fn^2 + gn$ into (2.17), we derive that

$$E = [a(fn^2 + gn) + n]/n^2 = [a(fn + g) + 1]/n = af + (ag + 1)/n.$$

Therefore, E is an integer if $a = -g^{-1}n$.
On the other hand, $nE = Q/n = a(p-1)/n + 1$.

Proposition 2.3. If n^{th} root u of w exists, and (2.18) holds, then $u :=$ $w^E \bmod p$.
Indeed,

$$u^n = (w^E)^n = w \times [w^{(p-1)/n}]^a = w (\bmod p).$$

Example 2.4. Let $n = 3$ and $p = 6 \times 9 + 2 \times 3 + 1 = 61$, i.e., $g = 2$, and $(2a + 1) \bmod 3 = 0$ if $a = 1$.
Hence, $E = (1 \times 60 + 3)/9 = 7$. Let $w = 24$, since $24^{(p-1)/3} = 1$, then the cubic root u of w exists and $u = 24^7 \bmod 61 = 8$. Indeed, $8^3 = 512 \bmod 61 = 24$.
Table 2.1 provides several detailed examples for $n = 3, 5, 7$, and $p = 61, 31, 71$.

Table 2.1 Extractors E for cubic, quintic and heptadic ($n = 7$) roots of w modulo p.

p	n	g	a	E	w	u	$u^n = w \bmod p$?
61	3	2	1	7	24	8	$8^3 = 24$
31	5	1	4	5	25	5	$5^5 = 25$
71	7	3	2	3	54	57	$57^7 = 54$

3. Extraction of Cubic Roots

Definition 3.1. u is a cubic root of w modulo p,

$$u := \sqrt[3]{w} \bmod p, \quad \text{if } u^3 \bmod p = w. \tag{3.1}$$

Proposition 3.2. If

$$p \bmod 3 = 2, \tag{3.2}$$

then the cubic root (3.1) exists for every w co-prime with p and it is unique.

Proposition 3.3. If $p \bmod 3 = 1$, then the cubic root (3.1) of w exists if and only if w satisfies Euler's criterion:

$$w^{(p-1)/3} \bmod p = 1. \tag{3.3}$$

3.1. *Cubic root extractor where $p \bmod 9 = 2$*

Proposition 3.4. If p is a prime, $p \bmod 9 = 2$, then

$$u = w^E = w^{(2p^2+1)/9} \bmod p \tag{3.4}$$

is a cubic root of (3.1) for every w is co-prime with p,

Proof. First of all, $(2p^2+1)/9 = [2(p^2-1)+3]/9$ is an integer. Indeed, let $p = 9k + h$. Then $E = (2p^2 + 1)/9 = 18k^2 + 4kh + (2h^2 + 1)/9$; therefore, $9|2p^2 + 1$ if $9|2h^2 + 1$. Hence, if $h = 2$, then $2h^2 + 1 = 9$, i.e., $(2p^2 + 1)/9$ is the integer.

On the other hand, (3.4) implies that

$$u^3 = \{w^{2(p^2-1)/3} \times w\} \bmod p. \tag{3.5}$$

Since $3|(p + 1)$, then by Fermat's Little Theorem (FLT)

$$w^{2(p^2-1)/3} = [w^{2(p+1)/3}]^{p-1} \bmod p = 1. \tag{3.6}$$

Therefore,

$$u^3 = w^{2(p^2-1)/3} \times w = 1 \times w = w \bmod p. \tag{3.7}$$

$\square$

Table 3.1 $p = 11$, $n = 3$, $E = 27 \bmod (p - 1) = 7$.

w	2	3	4	5	6	7	8	9
$u \bmod p$	7	9	5	3	8	6	2	4

Example 3.5. Let $p = 29$, $w = 5$, then $E = 187$. Therefore,

$$u = 5^{187 \bmod 28} = 5^{19} \bmod 29 = 22. \tag{3.8}$$

More examples of the cubic root extractions are provided in Table 3.1.

Notice that for every odd n, every p and every w the following identity holds

$$(\sqrt[n]{w} + \sqrt[n]{p - w}) \bmod p = p. \tag{3.9}$$

3.2. *Cubic root extractor where $p \bmod 9 = 5$*

Proposition 3.6. If p is a prime, $p \bmod 9 = 5$, and w is co-prime with p, then

$$u = w^E = w^{(p^2+2)/9} = w^{[(p^2-1)+3]/9} \bmod p \tag{3.10}$$

is a cubic root of (3.1) for every w.

Notice that the extractor E is the same as in the case where $p \bmod 3 = 1$ (see Sec. 6).

Proof. First of all, $E = (p^2 + 2)/9$ is an integer. The proof proceeds analogously as in Proposition 3.2. On the other hand, (3.10) implies

$$u^3 = \{w^{(p^2-1)/3} \times w\} \bmod p. \tag{3.11}$$

Since $3 | (p + 1)$, then by FLT

$$w^{(p^2-1)/3} = [w^{(p+1)/3}]^{p-1} \bmod p = 1. \tag{3.12}$$

Therefore,

$$u^3 = w^{(p^2-1)/3} \times w = w \bmod p. \tag{3.13}$$

$\square$

Table 3.2 provides six examples for $p = 5, 23$ and 41.

Table 3.2 Cubic roots w of u modulo $p(u^3 \bmod p = w)$ where $p \bmod 9 = 5$.

p, w	$p = 5,$ $w = 2$	$p = 23,$ $w = 3$	$p = 23,$ $w = 5$	$p = 41,$ $w = 2$	$p = 41,$ $w = 3$	$p = 41,$ $w = 5$
$u = \sqrt[3]{w}$	$u = 3$	$u = 12$	$u = 19$	$u = 5$	$u = 27$	$u = 20$

3.3. *Cubic root extractor where p mod 3 = 1*

Here we consider only the cases where

$$p \bmod 9 \neq 1. \tag{3.14}$$

Proposition 3.7. If p is a prime, $p \bmod 9 = 4$, an integer w is co-prime with p and a cubic root u of w modulo p exists, then

$$u = w^E = w^{[(p^2-1)+3]/9} \bmod p. \tag{3.15}$$

Notice that the extractor E is the same as if $p \bmod 9 = 5$ (see Sec.n 3.2). However, the following proof is based on the FLT.

Proof. By Euler's criterion, w has a cubic root if and only if

$$w^{(p-1)/3} \bmod p = 1. \tag{3.16}$$

Then

$$u^3 = w^{(p^2+2)/3} = w \times w^{(p^2-1)/3} = w \times [w^{(p-1)/3}]^{p+1} \bmod p = w. \tag{3.17}$$

$\square$

Remark 3.8. Notice from Table 3.3 that $w = 5$ has three cubic roots: $u = \{7, 8, 11\}$.

Proposition 3.9. If p is a prime, $p \bmod 9 = 7$, an integer w is co-prime with p and a cubic root u of w modulo p exists, then

$$u = w^E = w^{(2p^2+1)/9} \bmod p. \tag{3.18}$$

Proof. By Euler's criterion w has a cubic root u modulo prime p if and only if (3.16) holds. Consider

$$u = w^E = w \times w^{2(p-1)(p+1)/9} \pmod{p} \tag{3.19}$$

and

$$u^3 = w^{(2p^2-2+3)/3} = w^{[(2p^2-2+3)/3] \bmod (p-1)} \pmod{p}, \tag{3.20}$$

where $E = [2(p^2 - 1) + 3]/9$ is integer, (3.18) and (3.19).

Let $p = 9k + 7$, then u is a cubic root of w if and only if

$$w^{a(p-1)(p+1)/3} \bmod p = 1. \tag{3.21}$$

Table 3.3 $p = 13$, $p \bmod 9 = 4$, $1 < u < p$.

u	2	3	4	5	6	7	8	9	10	11	12
u^3	8	1	12	8	8	5	5	1	12	5	12

The condition (3.21) holds if either $(p + 1)/3$ is an integer (i.e., if $p \bmod 3 = 2$), or if $(p - 1)/3$ is an integer (i.e., if $p \bmod 9 = 4, 7$) and (3.1) holds. □

Example 3.10. Let $p = 31$ and $w = 2$, since Euler's criterion holds for $w = 2$, then its cubic root exists, and its extractor equals $E = (p^2 + 2)/9 = 107$, i.e., $u = 2^{107 \bmod 30} \bmod 31 = 4$.

Example 3.11. Let $p = 61$ and $w = 8$ that has a cubic root. Since 61 mod $9 = 7$, $E = (2p^2 + 1)/9 \pmod{60} = 47$. Therefore, $u = 8^{827 \bmod 60} = 8^{47} \bmod 61 = 33$.

3.4. *Alternative algorithms for cubic root extraction if $p \bmod 3 = 2$*

Proposition 3.12. If p is a prime, $p \bmod 3 = 2$, then every integer w co-prime with p has a unique cubic root

$$u = w^{(2p-1)/3} \bmod p. \tag{3.22}$$

Proof. First of all, $(2p - 1)/3$ is an integer, since $(2p - 1) \bmod 3 = 0$. Indeed, let $p = 9k + h$, then E is an integer, if $(2p - 1) \bmod 3 = [2(9p + h) - 1] \bmod 3 = (2h - 1) \bmod 3 = 0$ for $h = 2, 5$ or 8.

On the other hand,

$$u^3 = w^{2(p-1) \bmod (p-1)} w \bmod p = w. \tag{3.23}$$

□

Table 3.4 contains all cases of the cubic extractors.

4. Quintic Roots Extraction: Special Cases

In the following consideration, we assume that $p \bmod 5 = 1$, $p \bmod 25 \neq 1$.

Proposition 4.1. If p is a prime, $p \bmod 25 = 5h + 1$, an integer w is co-prime with p and a quintic root u of w modulo p exists, then

$$u = w^E = w^{[a(p-1)+5]/25} \bmod p. \tag{4.1}$$

Let substitute $p - 1 = 25k + 5h$ into (4.1). Then $5(ah + 1) \bmod 25 = 0$.

Table 3.4   Cubic roots extractors for $p \bmod 9 = h$, $h \neq 3$, $h \neq 6$.

h	$2, 5, 8$	4	7
E	$[2(p - 1) + 1]/3$	$[(p^2 - 1) + 3]/9$	$[2(p^2 - 1) + 3]/9$
Existence	Always	If $(p - 1)/3 = 1$	If $(p - 1)/3 = 1$

The latter equation holds if $(ah + 1) \bmod 5 = 0$, where $h = 1, 2, 3, 4$. In general,

$$a = (-1)h^{-1} = 4h^{-1} = 4h^3 \bmod 5. \tag{4.2}$$

Proposition 4.2. If p is a prime, $p \bmod 5 = h \geq 2$, an integer w is co-prime with p, then a quintic root u of w modulo p exists, and

$$u = w^E = w^{(ap-a+1)/5} \bmod p. \tag{4.3}$$

Table 7.1 provides the formulas for the quintic extractors as a function of h.

5. General Formula for Quintic Roots Extraction

To derive a general formula for the quintic roots, consider

$$E = [a(p-1) + 1]/5, \tag{5.1}$$

where E is an integer, if $(ap - a + 1) \bmod 5 = 0$ or, if after the substitution of $p = 5k + h$, we derive that $(ah - a + 1) \bmod 5 = 0$ or $a(1 - h) \bmod 5 = 1$. Hence,

$$a = (6 - h)^{-1} = (6 - h)^3 \pmod{5}. \tag{5.2}$$

Therefore, if $p \bmod 5 = h$, then $E = \{[5 - (h-1)^{-1} \bmod 5](p-1)+1\}/5$. For instance, if $h = 2$, then $a = 4$; if $h = 3$, then $a = 2$; if $h = 4$, then $a = 3$ (see Table 3.1).

6. Root Extractor of nth Order

In this section, we consider the cases where n is a prime and

$$p \bmod n^2 = n + 1, 2n + 1, \ldots, (n - 1)n + 1, \tag{6.1}$$

i.e., where

$$p \bmod n = 1 \quad \text{but } p \bmod n^2 \neq 1. \tag{6.2}$$

Proposition 6.1. If p is a prime, $p \bmod n^2 = gn + 1$, an integer w is co-prime with p and a nth root u of w modulo p exists, then

$$u = w^E = w^{[a(p-1)+n]/n^2} \bmod p. \tag{6.3}$$

Let us substitute now $p - 1 = kn^2 + gn$ into (6.3). Then

$$u = w^E = w^{[an(kn+g)+n]/n^2} = w^{[a(kn+g)+1]/n} \bmod p$$

Table 7.1   Root extractors E and corresponding parameters a.

Prime n	3	5	n
$h := p \bmod n,$ $h = 2, \ldots, n-1$	$a = (1-h) \bmod 3,$ $E = [a(p-1)+1]/3$	$a = (1-h)^3 \bmod 5,$ $E = [a(p-1)+1]/5$	$a = (1-h)^{n-2} \bmod n,$ $E = [a(p-1)+1]/n$
$g := (p-1)/n,$ $g = 1, \ldots, n-1$ and if $w^{(p-1)/n}$ $\bmod p = 1$	$a = 2g \bmod 3,$ $E = [a(p-1)+3]/9$	$a = 4g^3 \bmod 5,$ $E = [a(p-1)+5]/25$	$a = (n-1)g^{n-2} \bmod n,$ $E = [a(p-1)+n]/n^2$

which holds if

$$(ag + 1) \bmod n = 0, \quad \text{and} \quad g = 1, 2, 3, \ldots, n-1. \tag{6.4}$$

In general,

$$a = (-1)g^{-1} = (n-1)g^{n-2} \pmod{n}. \tag{6.5}$$

7. General Case: Extraction of Roots of nth Order

The above table describes all cases of root extractions for $n = 3, 5$ and arbitrary prime n.

Remark 7.1. Of all n possible cases, where $p \bmod n^2 = gn + 1$, only a single one, where $g = 0$, is not solvable by the algorithm described in the second row of Table 7.1.

Example 7.2. Let us consider $p = 1933$, $n = 19$, and $w = 1913$; then $p \bmod n = g = 14$. Therefore, every w has a unique root of the 19th order. Hence, $a = (n+1-g)^{n-2} = 6^{17} \bmod 19 = 16$ and $E = [16(p-1)+1]/19 = 1627$. Finally, $u := 1913^{1627} \bmod 1933$.

8. Algorithm for Extraction of Roots of nth Order

Input: $p, n \geq 3$ and w; p and n are primes; $(\gcd(w, p) = 1)$;
Output: $u := \sqrt[n]{w} \bmod p$;
1. If $p \bmod n = 1$ then
       1.1. $z \leftarrow p \bmod n^2$;
       1.2. If $z = 1$ then end.   (algorithm is not applicable);
       1.3. If $w^{(p-1)/n} \bmod p = 1$ then $g \leftarrow (z-1)/n$;
       1.4. Else end   (w does not have n^{th} root);
       1.5. $a \leftarrow g^{-1}(n-1) = (n-1)g^{n-2} \pmod{n}$;
       1.6. $E \leftarrow \{[a(p-1)+n]/n^2\} \bmod (p-1)$;

2. Else

    2.1. $h \leftarrow p \bmod n;$ $(2 \leq h \leq n - 1)$

    2.2. $a \leftarrow (n + 1 - h)^{-1} = (n + 1 - h)^{n-2} \pmod{n};$

    2.3. $E \leftarrow \{[a(p - 1) + 1]/n\} \bmod (p - 1);$

3. $u \leftarrow w^E \bmod p$ $(u \leftarrow \sqrt[n]{w} \bmod p).$

Remark 8.1. If n is a composite and $n = rs$, then we separately extract the roots of the rth and s^{th} orders and then multiply the results modulo by p.

9. Concluding Remark

In this paper, we described the algorithms for extraction of roots of nth power modulo prime p. These algorithms find the roots via a polynomial exponentiation for all cases of prime p and arbitrary prime n with only one exception where $p \bmod n^2 = 1$. An analogous case exists for extraction of the square root $(n = 2)$, where Euler's algorithm is applicable for primes p, for which $p \bmod 4 = 3$ holds, and it is *not* applicable for $p \bmod 4 = 1$.

Appendix

Table A.1   Cycling properties $p = 3$, $R = b^e \pmod{p^2}$, $\gcd(b, p^2) = 1$.

$b \backslash e$	$e = 1$	$e = 2$	$e = 3$	$e = 4$	$e = 5$	$e = 6$
$b = 2$	2	4	8	7	5	1
$b = 5$	5	7	8	4	2	1
$b = 7$	7	4	1	7	4	1

Proposition A.1 (Equivalent of FLT). For every prime p, the following identity holds $b^{p(p-1)} \bmod p^2 = 1$ if and only if $\gcd(b - 1, p) = 1$ and $\gcd(b, p) = 1$. The last two conditions are equivalent to $\gcd[b(b - 1), p] = 1$ (illustrated in Table A.1).

Chapter 8

Public-Key Cryptography
Based on Square Roots
and Complex Modulus

1. Introduction and Problem Statement

In the next two chapters, we propose and analyze cryptographic algorithms based on two distinct concepts: square roots and cubic roots of complex integers in modular arithmetic with complex modulo reduction. Each of these algorithms has its advantages and drawbacks.

This chapter considers three algorithms for the extraction of square roots of complex integers (called Gaussians) using an arithmetic based on complex modulus $p + iq$. These algorithms are almost twice as fast as the analogous algorithms extracting square roots of either real or complex integers in arithmetic based on modulus p, where p is a real prime. A cryptographic system based on these algorithms is provided in this chapter.

A procedure reducing the computational complexity is described as well. Main results are explained in several numeric illustrations.

The concept of complex modulus was introduced by C. F. Gauss (Gauss, 1965). The set of complex integers is an infinite system of equidistant points located on parallel straight lines, such that the infinite plane is decomposable into infinitely many squares or rhombs. Analogously, every integer that is divisible by a complex integer $m = a + bi$ forms infinitely many squares or rhombs, with sides equal to $\sqrt{a^2 + b^2}$.

1.1. Complex moduli

Let us denote $(a, b) := a + bi$. Associates of $G := (p, q)$ are $-G, iG$ and $-iG$, they are the vertices of a square where $-G = (-p, -q), iG = (0, 1)(p, q) = (-q, p)$ and $-iG = (0, -1)(p, q) = (q, -p)$.

To understand the congruences, consider a system of integer Cartesian coordinates. The squares on this system of coordinates are inclined to the former squares if neither of integers a, b is equal to zero (Gauss, 1965; Kirsch, 2008). Then the associates of the modulus (p, q) are rotations of "vector" (p, q) at 90°. Let us consider the plane of complex numbers and as an example, the complex prime number $(1, 4)$. Let the left-most bottom point of the mesh be the origin of the coordinate system for Gaussians, and let $G := (1, 4)$ be the Gaussian modulus. Inside each square there is a number of Gaussian integers; plus every vertex of each square is also a Gaussian integer. In order to avoid multiple counting of the same vertex, we consider that only the left-most bottom vertex of each square belongs to that square (Gauss, 1965). For more insights and graphics, see Kirch (2008).

This chapter is a logical continuation of the paper by Verkhovsky (2011), which considered a cryptographic scheme based on complex integers modulo real semi-prime pq. The above mentioned paper describes an extractor of quadratic roots from complex integers. A slightly different approach is considered in Verkhovsky and Koval (2008). Several general ideas for computation of a square root in modular arithmetic are provided in Bach and Shallit (1996), Crandall and Pomerance (2001) and Schoof (1985).

This chapter considers arithmetic based on complex integers with *Gaussian modulus*. As demonstrated below, the extraction of square roots in such arithmetic requires a smaller number of basic operations. As a result, the described cryptographic system is almost twice faster than the analogous systems in Verkhovsky (2011) and Verkhovsky and Koval (2008).

Consider quadratic equation

$$(x, y)^2 = (c, d) \mod (p, q), \tag{1.1}$$

where modulus $G := (p, q)$ is a Gaussian prime, and let

$$N := \|(p, q)\| = p^2 + q^2. \tag{1.2}$$

1.2. General properties

Proposition 1.1. Gaussian (p, q) is a prime if and only if its norm N is a real prime (Gauss, 1965).

Remark 1.2. Since $\|(\pm p, \pm q)\| = \|(\pm q, \pm p)\|$, without loss of generality we assume that, if (p, q) is prime, then p is *odd* and q is *even* (unless it is stated otherwise).

Proposition 1.3. If norm $\|(p, q)\|$ is a prime (1.2), then for every (p, q) $N \bmod 4 = 1$.

Proof. Let $p := 2k + 1$ and $q := 2r$, then (1.2) implies that

$$N - 1 = 4[k(k + 1) + r^2]. \tag{1.3}$$

$\square$

Proposition 1.3 implies that there are no norms that are Blum primes, i.e., for every prime N, $N \bmod 4 \neq 3$.

Proposition 1.4 (cyclic identity). If $\gcd[(a, b), (p, q)] = (1, 0)$ and $\|G\|$ is a prime, then the following identity holds:

$$(a, b)^N \bmod (p, q) = (a, b). \tag{1.4}$$

Remark 1.5. More details about identity (1.4) are provided in Appendix.

Proposition 1.6 (Modular multiplicative inverse).
If

$$\gcd[(a, b), (p, q)] = (1, 0), \quad \text{then } (a, b)^{-1} \equiv (a, b)^{N-2} \bmod G. \tag{1.5}$$

Remark 1.7. Yet, more computationally efficient is to solve an appropriate Diophantine equation; this approach is discussed in another part of this book.

Definition 1.8. Gaussian (x, y) is called a quadratic root of (c, d) modulo G if (x, y) and (c, d) satisfy Eq. (1). We denote it as

$$(x, y) := \sqrt{(c, d)} \bmod G. \tag{1.6}$$

1.3. *Extractability of square roots*

In general, if $N \bmod 2^k = 1$, then the algorithms that extract square roots are not as simple as in the cases if $N \bmod 2^{k+1} = 2^k + 1$. For instance, if $N = 5, 13, 41, 113, 1777$, then $5 \bmod 4 = 13 \bmod 4 = 41 \bmod 4 = 41 \bmod 8 = 113 \bmod 4 = 113 \bmod 8 = 113 \bmod 16 = 1777 \bmod 16 = 1$.

However, $5 \bmod 8 = 13 \bmod 8 = 5$, $41 \bmod 16 = 9$ and $113 \bmod 32 = 1777 \bmod 32 = 17$.

In the following sections, we consider algorithms that extract quadratic roots where $N \bmod 8 = 5$, $N \bmod 16 = 9$, $N \bmod 32 = 17$, and in general, where $N \bmod 2^{k+1} = 2^k + 1$. For each of these cases, we provide a rather simple algorithm for square root extraction.

2. Quadratic Root Extraction if $N \equiv 5 (\mathrm{mod}\ 8)$

Lemma 2.1. Let $m := (N-1)/4$, if (p,q) is prime, $p \bmod 4 = \pm 1$, $q \bmod 4 = 2$ and $N \equiv 5 \ (\mathrm{mod}\ 8)$, then m is *odd*.

Proof. Let $p = 4k \pm 1, q = 4r + 2$, then $(N-1)/4 = 2(2k^2 \pm k + 2r^2 + 2r) + 1$. Therefore, the latter equation implies that m is odd.   □

Remark 2.2. The same holds for every odd p and $q = 4r + 2$, since $p = 4k \pm 1 = 4j \pm 3$.

Notice that, if $q \bmod 4 = 0$, then (1.3) implies that $N \equiv 1 \ (\mathrm{mod}\ 8)$.

2.1. *Quadratic and quartic roots of* $(1,0)$ *modulo* (p,q)

Consider a quadratic root (u,w) of $(1,0) \ \mathrm{mod}(p,q) : (u,w) := \sqrt{(1,0)} \ \mathrm{mod}(p,q)$, where u and w are real integers.

Therefore, $(u,w)^2 = (u^2 - w^2, 2uw) = (1,0) \ \mathrm{mod}(p,q)$.

This equation holds if either

$$w = 0 \quad \text{and} \quad u^2 = 1 \bmod G \quad \text{or} \quad u = 0 \quad \text{and} \quad w^2 = -1 \bmod G. \quad (2.1)$$

Since the last equation does not have a real integer solution for w, it implies that

$$(u,w) \equiv (\pm 1, 0) \equiv [(\pm 1, 0) + (p,q)] \equiv (p \pm 1, q) \bmod G. \quad (2.2)$$

Hence, if a root (x,y) is known, then another root of (c,d) is $(u,w)(x,y) \bmod G$.

Quartic roots: There are four quartic roots of $(1,0)$, each satisfying $q_k^4 \equiv (1,0)$:

$$q_1 = (1,0), \quad q_2 = (-1,0) \equiv (p-1,q), \quad q_3 = (0,1),$$
$$q_4 = (0,-1) \equiv (p,q-1), \quad (2.3)$$

where

$$q_{3,4}^2 \equiv q_2 \ (\mathrm{mod}\ G), \quad q_2^2 \equiv q_1 \equiv (1,0) \ (\mathrm{mod}\ G). \quad (2.4)$$

2.2. Quadratic root extractor (QRE-1)

The algorithm computes $(x, y) := \sqrt{(c, d)} \bmod G$ if such a square root exists.

Step 2.1: Compute

$$N := p^2 + q^2, \quad m := (N - 1)/4, \quad z := (N + 3)/8 \tag{2.5}$$

(if N is not a prime, then *QRE*-1 algorithm is not applicable).

Step 2.2: Compute

$$E := (c, d)^m \bmod G. \tag{2.6}$$

Step 2.3: if $E = (0, \pm 1)$**, then** (c, d) is a *Gaussian quadratic non-residue* (GQNR), i.e., its square root does not exist.

Step 2.4: if $E = (1, 0)$**, then**

$$(x, y) := (c, d)^z \bmod G. \tag{2.7}$$

Step 2.5: if $E = (-1, 0)$**, then**

$$R := \sqrt{E^{-1}} \bmod G \quad (R := (0, \pm 1)). \tag{2.8}$$

Step 2.6:

$$(x, y) := R \times (c, d)^z \bmod G \quad (R \text{ is called } resolventa). \tag{2.9}$$

Step 2.7: (2nd square root):

$$(t, v) := (p - 1, q)(x, y) \bmod G \ (2.3). \tag{2.10}$$

2.3. Validation of algorithm QRE-1

Proposition 2.3. Suppose that

(a)

$$(p, q) \text{ is a complex prime, where } p \text{ is odd and } q \equiv 2 \ (\bmod \ 4), \tag{2.11}$$

(b) let

$$m = (N - 1)/4, \quad z := (N + 3)/8, \quad E := (c, d)^{(N-1)/4} \bmod G, \tag{2.12}$$

(c)

$$R := \sqrt{E^{-1}} \bmod G, \tag{2.13}$$

if $E = (1,0)$ or $(-1,0)$, then

$$(x,y) := (c,d)^z R \equiv \sqrt{(c,d)} \ (\bmod \ G). \tag{2.14}$$

Proof. First of all, (2.13) implies that

$$ER^2 \bmod G = (1,0). \tag{2.15}$$

On the other hand, from Lemma 2.1 m is odd, and since

$$(m+1)/2 = [(N-1)/4 + 1]/2 = z, \quad (2.12),$$

hence z is an integer. At the same time,

$$(x,y)^2 = (c,d)^{(N+3)/4} R^2 \equiv (c,d)(c,d)^{(N-1)/4} R^2 \equiv (c,d)(ER^2)$$

$$\equiv (c,d) \ (\bmod \ G). \tag{2.16}$$

Therefore, (2.15) and (2.16) imply the identity

$$(c,d)^{2z} R^2 \equiv (c,d) \ (\bmod \ G) \tag{2.17}$$

which itself implies that (2.14) is correct. $\qquad\qquad\square$

2.4. *Criterion of square root existence if $N \equiv 5 \pmod 8$*

Proposition 2.4. Gaussian (c,d) has a quadratic root modulo Gaussian prime (p,q) if

$$E := (c,d)^m = (c,d)^{(N-1)/4} \bmod G = (\pm 1, 0). \tag{2.18}$$

If $E = (0, \pm 1)$, then (c,d) is a GQNR, i.e., its square root does not exist.

Proof. Suppose that the latter is not true and there exists a Gaussian (e,f) such that $(e,f)^2 \bmod G = (c,d)$. Then $E = (e,f)^{(N-1)/2} \bmod G = (0, \pm 1)$; i.e., $(e,f)^{N-1} \bmod G = (-1,0)$, which is in contradiction with (1.4).

     On the other hand, if $(c,d)^{(N-1)/4} \bmod G = (1,0)$, then $(x,y) := (c,d)^z \bmod G$, and if $(c,d)^{(N-1)/4} \bmod G = (-1,0)$, then $(x,y) := (c,d)^z (0, \pm 1) \bmod G$. $\qquad\qquad\square$

Table 2.1 Quadratic root extraction and verification, $N \bmod 8 = 5$.

(c, d)	$(3, 8)$	$(4, 8)$	$(6, 7)$	$(8, -2)$	$(9, 2)$	$(10, 5)$
$(c, d)^m$	$(1, 0)$	$(0, 1)$	$(-1, 0)$	$(-1, 0)$	$(0, -1)$	$(1, 0)$
$(c, d)^z$	$(9, -2)$	QNR	$(5, 3)$	$(11, 4)$	QNR	$(2, 2)$
$(c, d)^z R$	$(9, -2)$	n/a	$(7, 2)$	$(7, -1)$	n/a	$(2, 2)$
$(x, y)^2$	$(3, 8)$	—	$(6, 7)$	$(8, -2)$	—	$(10, 5)$

Example 2.5. Consider $p = 91, q = -6, N = \|(p, q)\| = 8317$, which is a prime, hence $(\pm 91, \pm 6)$ are Gaussian primes.

Compute

$$m := (N - 1)/4 = 2079, \quad z := (N + 3)/8 = 1040.$$

Let $(c, d) = (81, 71)$, since $(81, 71)^m \equiv (96, 85) \equiv (-1, 0)(\bmod (91, -6))$, therefore, $(81, 71)$ has a square root modulo $(91, -6)$, and

$$(x, y) = \sqrt{(81, 71)} = (81, 71)^{1040} \times (0, 1) = (57, 75) \ (\bmod(91, -6)). \quad (2.19)$$

Verification: Indeed,

$$(57, 75)^2 \bmod(91, -6) = (81, 71). \quad (2.20)$$

2.5. *Numeric illustrations*

Consider $p = 10, q = -3$, then $N = 109, m = 27, z = 14$. In this case, $p \bmod 4 = 2$ and $q \bmod 4 = \pm 1$. In Table 2.1, $(c, d)^m$ are the quartic roots q_k of unity (2.3), i.e.,

$$R := \{q_1 = (1, 0), q_2 = (12, 7) \equiv (-1, 0), q_3 = (3, 9) \equiv (0, -1),$$

$$q_4 = (10, -2) \equiv (0, 1) \ (\bmod(p, q))\}.$$

The step-by-step process of extraction of the square roots and criteria of quadratic residuosity is illustrated for several values of (c, d).

3. Quadratic Root Extraction (QRE-2) if $N \equiv 9 \pmod{16}$

3.1. *Gaussian generators*

Definition 3.1. Gaussian H is called a generator modulo G if every Gaussian (a, b) co-prime with G can be expressed as $H^x \equiv (a, b) \ (\bmod \ G)$, where x is a positive integer.

A Gaussian (c, d) has a square root if there exists an even integer w, for which holds

$$H^w \equiv (c, d) \pmod{G},$$

in that case

$$(x, y) \equiv \sqrt{(c, d)} \equiv H^{w/2} \pmod{G} \ (1.6).$$

3.2. Basic properties

Proposition 3.2. If $p \equiv \pm 3 \pmod 8$ and $q \equiv 4 \pmod 8$, then $m := (N - 1)/8$ is *odd* and $z := (N + 7)/16$ is an integer.

Proof. Since

$$p = 8w \pm 3 \quad \text{and} \quad q = 8r + 4, \quad N = 16(4w^2 \pm 3w + 4r^2 + 4r) + 25,$$
$$(3.1)$$

i.e., (3.1) implies that 16 divides $N + 7$. Hence, z is the integer. □

On the other hand, m is odd since $m = (N - 1)/8 = 2(4w^2 \pm 3w + 4r^2 + 4r) + 3$.

Proposition 3.3 (Criterion of square root existence). Let $\|\gcd((c, d), G)\| = 1$ and

$$(c, d)^{(N-1)/2} \bmod G = (1, 0), \tag{3.2}$$

then (c, d) has a quadratic root modulo Gaussian prime G.
   If

$$(c, d)^{(N-1)/2} \bmod G = (-1, 0), \tag{3.3}$$

then a quadratic root of (c, d) modulo Gaussian prime G does not exist.

Proof. Suppose that the latter is not true and there exists a Gaussian (e, f) such that $(e, f)^2 \bmod G = (c, d)$. Then (3.3) implies that $(e, f)^{N-1} \bmod G = (-1, 0)$ which is in contradiction with (1.4). □

Remark 3.4. Analogously, if $E := (c, d)^{(N-1)/8} \bmod G = \{(\pm 1, 0); (0, \pm 1)\}$, then (c, d) has a quadratic root modulo prime G (since $E^4 = (1, 0)$ (3.2)).
   Notice that $\{(\pm 1, 0); (0, \pm 1)\}$ are the quartic roots of $(1, 0)$.

Proposition 3.5 (Quadratic root extractor). Suppose that

(a) $$p \bmod 8 = \pm 3, \quad \text{and} \quad q \equiv 4 \ (\bmod \ 8), \tag{3.4}$$

(b) $$z = (N+7)/16, \tag{3.5}$$

(c) if resolventa R satisfies either (3.6), or (3.7) or (3.8):

$$R = \begin{cases} (\pm 1, 0) \bmod G & \text{if } E = (1,0), & (3.6) \\ (0, \pm 1) \bmod G & \text{if } E = (-1,0), & (3.7) \\ \sqrt{(0,\pm 1)} \bmod G & \text{if } E = (0,\pm 1), & (3.8) \end{cases}$$

then

$$\sqrt{(c,d)} \equiv (c,d)^z R \ (\bmod \ G). \tag{3.9}$$

Proof. Notice that $R \equiv \sqrt{E^{-1}} \bmod G$, then (3.9) implies that

$$(c,d)^{2z} R^2 \equiv (c,d) \ (\bmod \ G), \tag{3.10}$$

hence, (3.5) implies

$$(c,d)^{2z} R^2 \equiv (c,d)[(c,d)^{(N-1)/8} R^2] = (c,d)(ER^2) \ (\bmod \ G), \tag{3.11}$$

therefore, (3.2) and (3.6)–(3.8) imply that

$$ER^2 \bmod (p,q) = 1. \tag{3.12}$$

Finally, in (3.8) we need to pre-compute $\sqrt{(0,\pm 1)} = \sqrt[8]{(1,0)} \bmod G$.

Hence (3.10) is correct, in other words, it confirms the equality (3.9).

$\square$

3.3. *Octadic roots of $(1,0)$ modulo (p,q)*

Consider roots of 8th power (called the *octadic* roots) of unity, there are eight such roots: for $k = 1, \ldots, 8$

$$e_k := \sqrt[8]{(1,0)} = \{e_{1,2} := (\pm 1, 0), e_{3,4} := (0, \pm 1), e_{5,6} := \pm\sqrt{(0,1)},$$

$$e_{7,8} := \pm\sqrt{(0,-1)}\}. \tag{3.13}$$

Then

$$e_2^2 = (1,0) = e_1, \quad e_{3,4}^2 = (-1,0) = e_2,$$
$$e_{5,6}^2 = (0,1) = e_3, \quad e_{7,8}^2 = (0,-1) = e_4. \tag{40|3.14}$$

Notice that $\{e_1, e_2, e_3, e_4\}$ are also the quartic roots of $(1,0)$ modulo G, and $\{e_1, e_2\}$ are quadratic roots of unity $(1,0)$.

Therefore, the resolventa R in (3.6)–(3.8) must satisfy the following equations for $k = 1, 2, \ldots, 8$:

$$R^2 e_k \bmod G = (1,0) \quad \text{or} \quad R = \sqrt{e_k^{-1}} \ (\bmod\ G). \qquad (3.15)$$

Thus,

$$R^2 := e_k^{-1} = e_k \quad \text{if } k = 1, 2, \quad R^2 := e_k^{-1} = e_k^3 = e_k^2 e_k = -e_k \quad \text{if } k = 3, 4, \qquad (3.16)$$

and

$$R^2 := e_k^{-1} = e_k^7 = e_k^4 e_k^2 e_k = -e_k^2 e_k = \begin{cases} (0,-1)e_k & \text{if } k = 5, 6 \\ (0,1)e_k & \text{if } k = 7, 8 \end{cases}. \qquad (3.17)$$

3.4.   *Computation of $\sqrt{i} \equiv \sqrt{(0,1)}$ modulo (p,q)*

If (p,q) is fixed and $N \bmod 16 = 9$, then this root must be pre-computed in advance.

Direct computation: Since

$$\sqrt{i} = \sqrt{\cos \pi/2 + i \sin \pi/2} = \cos \pi/4 + i \sin \pi/4$$
$$= (\sqrt{2}/2, \sqrt{2}/2) = (\sqrt{2}/2)(1,1),$$

it is necessary to compute a square root of *two* modulo G and multiplicative inverse of *two* modulo G.

3.5.   *Multiplicative inverse of 2 modulo (p,q)*

The inverse of 2 always exists since p and q have opposite parities:
  If p is *odd* and q is *even*, then

$$2^{-1} \equiv ((p+1)/2, q/2) \ (\bmod(p,q));$$

if q is *odd* and p is *even*, then

$$2^{-1} \equiv ((1-q)/2, p/2) \ (\bmod(p,q)).$$

Example 3.6. Let $G = (8,-3)$; then $2^{-1} \equiv (2,4) \ (\bmod(8,-3))$ and $\sqrt{2} \equiv (5,1)(\bmod(8,-3))$.
  Hence, $\sqrt{i} \equiv (1,1)(5,1)(2,4) \equiv (2,3) \ (\bmod(8,-3))$ (Churchill *et al.*, 1976).
  Indeed,

$$(2,3)^8 \equiv (1,0) \ (\bmod(8,-3)).$$

3.6. *Alternate computation*

In general, observe that if a square root of 2 does not exist and for a Gaussian (a, b) holds the inequality

$$F := (a, b)^{(N-1)/8} \pmod{G} \neq \{(\pm 1, 0), (0, \pm 1)\}, \tag{3.18}$$

then

$$(a, b)^{(N-1)/8} \bmod G = \{\sqrt{i} \text{ or } \sqrt{-i}\}, \tag{3.19}$$

since

$$(a, b)^{N-1} = (\sqrt{\pm i})^8 = 1 \ (4). \tag{3.20}$$

Therefore,

$$F^2 \bmod G = (0, \pm 1) \ (44).$$

Hence,

$$R \equiv \sqrt{F^{-1}} \bmod G. \tag{3.21}$$

3.7. *Algorithm for quadratic root extraction*

Step 3.1:

$$N := p^2 + q^2, \quad m := (N-1)/8, \quad z := (N+7)/16. \tag{3.22}$$

Step 3.2: if N is not a prime, **then** the $QRE\text{-}2$ algorithm is not applicable.

Step 3.3: Find a Gaussian (a, b), for which

$$F := (a, b)^m \bmod G \neq \{(\pm 1, 0), (0, \pm 1)\}. \tag{3.23}$$

Step 3.4: if $F^2 = (0, 1)$, **then** $R := F \equiv \sqrt{i} \pmod{G}$,

if $F^2 = (0, -1)$, **then** $R := (0, -1)F \equiv \sqrt{i} \pmod{G}$.

Step 3.5: Compute

$$E := (c, d)^m \bmod G. \tag{3.24}$$

Step 3.6: if $E \neq \{(\pm 1, 0); (0, \pm 1)\}$ (2.16), **then** square root of (c, d) does not exist.

Step 3.7: if $E = (1, 0)$, **then** $(x, y) := (c, d)^z \bmod G$; **goto** Step 3.10.

Step 3.8: if $E = (-1, 0)$, **then** $(x, y) := (c, d)^z (0, 1) \bmod G$; **goto** Step 3.10.

Table 3.1   Quadratic root extractor where $N \equiv 9 \pmod{16}$.

(c,d)	$(1,1)$	$(3,-1)$	$(3,4)$	$(4,3)$	$(5,1)$	$(5,5)$	$(7,-1)$	$(8,5)$	$(10,3)$
$(c,d)^m$	$(2,3)$	$(0,1)$	$(0,-1)$	$(0,-1)$	$(1,0)$	$(0,1)$	$(9,2)$	$(8,-2)$	$(-1,0)$
$(c,d)^z$	n/a	$(8,5)$	$(3,6)$	$(5,7)$	$(1,2)$	$(8,1)$	n/a	$(3,-1)$	$(9,19)$
$(c,d)^z R$	n/a	$(4,5)$	$(9,4)$	$(4,1)$	$(1,2)$	$(5,4)$	n/a	$(2,2)$	$(7,6)$
$(x,y)^2$	n/a	$(3,-1)$	$(3,4)$	$(4,3)$	$(5,1)$	$(5,5)$	n/a	$(8,5)$	$(10,3)$

Step 3.9:

if $E = (0,1)$, **then** $(x,y) := (c,d)^z[(0,1)R] \bmod G$; **goto** Step 3.10;

$$(3.25)$$

else $(x,y) := (c,d)^z R \bmod G.$ $$(3.26)$$

Step 3.10: (2nd square root):

$$(t,v) := (p-1,q)(x,y) \bmod G. \tag{3.27}$$

3.8. *Second numeric illustration*

Consider $(p,q) = (8,-3)$, then $N = 73$, i.e.,

$$73 \equiv 9 \pmod{16}, \quad m = 9, \quad z = 5. \tag{3.28}$$

Octadic roots of **(1,0):**

$$e_1 = (10,5)^2 \equiv (1,0), \quad e_2 = (10,5) \equiv (-1,0) \ (\mathrm{mod}(8,-3)),$$

$$(8,-2)^2 \equiv (10,5), \quad e_3 = (8,-2) \equiv (0,1), \quad (3,7)^2 \equiv (10,5),$$

$$e_4 = (3,7) \equiv (0,-1), \quad (2,3)^2 \equiv (8,-2), \quad e_5 = (2,3) \equiv \sqrt{(0,1)},$$

$$(9,2)^2 \equiv (8,-2), \quad e_6 = (9,2) \equiv -\sqrt{(0,1)}, \quad (5,-1)^2 \equiv (3,7),$$

$$e_7 = (5,-1) \equiv \sqrt{(0,-1)}, \quad (6,6)^2 \equiv (3,7),$$

$$e_8 = (6,6) \equiv -\sqrt{(0,-1)}.$$

The following nine examples of (c,d) in Table 3.1 illustrate various cases of QRE-2 algorithm.

4. Quadratic Root Extraction (QRE-3) if $N \equiv 17 \pmod{32}$

4.1. *Basic property and roots of* **(1,0)**

Proposition 4.1. Analogously it can be proved that if $p \equiv \pm 7 \pmod{16}$ and $q \equiv 8 \ (\mathrm{mod}\,16)$, then $(N+15)/32$ is integer and $m := (N-1)/16$ is *odd*.

Proof. Let $p = 16k \pm 7$ and $q = 16r + 8$; then it is easy to verify that 32 divides $N + 15$.

Notice that $(N+15)/32 = (m+1)/2$. On the other hand, if m is an *even* integer, then $(m + 1)/2$ is not an integer, which implies that $(N + 15)/32$ is not an integer.   □

Definition 4.2. u_i is a *square* root of $(1,0)$ if

$$u_i^2 \equiv (1,0) \ (\mathrm{mod}\ G), \quad i = 1, 2. \tag{4.1}$$

Definition 4.3. q_j is a *quartic* root of $(1,0)$ if

$$q_j^4 \equiv (1,0) \ (\mathrm{mod}\ G), \quad j = 1, 2, 3, 4. \tag{4.2}$$

Definition 4.4. o_k is an *octadic* root of $(1,0)$ if

$$o_k^8 \equiv (1,0) \ (\mathrm{mod}\ G), \quad k = 1, 2, \ldots, 8. \tag{4.3}$$

Definition 4.5. s_l is a *sedonic* root of $(1,0)$ if

$$s_l^{16} \equiv (1,0) \ (\mathrm{mod}\ G), \quad l = 1, 2, \ldots, 16. \tag{4.4}$$

4.2. *Resolventa of quadratic root extractor*

Proposition 4.6. Suppose

(a)
$$p \equiv \pm 7 \ (\mathrm{mod}\ 16) \quad \text{and} \quad q \equiv 8 \ (\mathrm{mod}\ 16), \tag{4.5}$$

(b)
$$N := c^2 + d^2, \quad z := (N + 15)/32, \tag{4.6}$$

(c)
$$m := (N - 1)/16. \tag{4.7}$$

(d) Let $E := (c, d)^m \ \mathrm{mod}(p, q)$, and resolventa R satisfies the following conditions:

$$R := \pm \sqrt{u_i^{-1}} \equiv \pm \sqrt{u_i} \ (\mathrm{mod}\ G) \quad \text{if } E = u_i, \tag{4.8}$$

$$R := \pm \sqrt{q_j^{-1}} \equiv \pm \sqrt{q_j^3} \ (\mathrm{mod}\ G) \quad \text{if } E = q_j, \tag{4.9}$$

$$R := \pm \sqrt{o_k^{-1}} \equiv \pm \sqrt{o_k^7} \ (\mathrm{mod}\ G) \quad \text{if } E = o_k, \tag{4.10}$$

then

$$(c, d)^z R = \sqrt{(c, d)} \ (\mathrm{mod}\ G). \tag{4.11}$$

Proof. Let

$$(x, y) := (c, d)^z R = \sqrt{(c, d)} \pmod{G}, \tag{4.12}$$

therefore,

$$(c, d)^{(N+15)/16} R^2 = (c, d)ER^2 \pmod{G}. \tag{4.13}$$

If

$$E = u_i, \quad \text{then } ER^2 = E^2 = u_i^2 = (1, 0) \pmod{G}, \tag{4.14}$$

if

$$E = q_j, \quad \text{then } ER^2 = E^4 = q_j^4 = (1, 0) \pmod{G}, \tag{4.15}$$

if

$$E = o_k, \quad \text{then } ER^2 = E^8 = o_k^8 = (1, 0) \pmod{G}. \tag{4.16}$$

$\square$

4.3. *Sedonic roots of* $(1, 0)$ *modulo* G

Unity $(1, 0)$ has two square roots $\{(1, 0) \text{ and } (-1, 0)\}$, four quartic roots $\{(1, 0), (-1, 0), (0, 1), (0, -1)\}$, eight octadic roots $\{(1, 0), (-1, 0), (0, 1), (0, -1), e_5, e_6, e_7, e_8\}$ and 16 sedonic roots $\{(1, 0), (-1, 0), (0, 1), (0, -1), e_5, e_6, e_7, e_8, s_9, s_{10}, \ldots, s_{15}, s_{16}\}$, where

$$e_{5,6} = \pm\sqrt{(0, 1)}, \quad e_{7,8} = \pm\sqrt{(0, -1)},$$
$$s_{9,10,11,12} = \pm\sqrt{\pm\sqrt{(0, 1)}}, \quad s_{13,14,15,16} = \pm\sqrt{\pm\sqrt{(0, -1)}}. \tag{4.17}$$

4.4. *Third numeric illustration*

Consider $N = 113$, $(p, q) = (8, -7)$. Then $m := (N - 1)/16 = 7, z := (N + 15)/32 = 4$.

In Table 4.1,

$$(-1, 0) \equiv (14, 1), \quad (0, 1) \equiv (8, -6), \quad (0, -1) \equiv (7, 7) \pmod{(8, -7)}, \tag{4.18}$$

$$\sqrt{(0, -1)} \equiv (6, 5), \quad -\sqrt{(0, -1)} \equiv (9, -4), \quad \sqrt{(0, 1)} \equiv (3, -1),$$
$$-\sqrt{(0, 1)} \equiv (12, 2) \pmod{(8, -7)},$$

$$-\sqrt{\pm\sqrt{(0, \pm 1)}} \equiv \{(10, 5), (12, -2), (10, -2), (5, -2)\}$$
$$\pmod{(8, -7)}, \tag{4.19}$$

$$\sqrt{\pm\sqrt{(0, \pm 1)}} \equiv \{(5, -4), (3, 3), (5, 3), (10, 3)\} \pmod{(8, -7)}. \tag{4.20}$$

Table 4.1   Binary tree of sedonic roots of $(1,0)$ where modulus $G = (8,-7)$.

(g,h)	$(6,3)$	*	$(10,1)$	*	*	$(11,3)$	*	$(5,4)$	*
$E = \sqrt[16]{(1,0)}$	$(5,-4)$	$(10,5)$	$(3,3)$	$(12,-2)$	—	$(5,3)$	$(10,-2)$	$(10,3)$	$(5,-2)$
$E^2 = \sqrt[8]{(1,0)}$	—	$(6,5)$	$(9,-4)$	—	—	—	$(3,-1)$	$(12,2)$	—
$E^4 = \sqrt[4]{(1,0)}$	—	—	$(7,7)$	—	—	—	$(8,-6)$	—	—
$E^8 = \sqrt{(1,0)}$	—	—	—	—	$(-1,0)$	—	—	—	—
E^{16}	—	—	—	—	$(1,0)$	—	—	—	—

In (4.20), there are four sedonic roots of $(1,0)$ that must be pre-computed on the design stage of the QRE-3 algorithm. Although this is a non-deterministic process, each of these roots must be computed only once prior to using the extractor. These roots correspond to

$$E := (g,h)^m \equiv \sqrt[16]{(1,0)} \pmod{G},$$

where $m = 7, G = (p,q) = (8,-7)$ and Gaussians $(g,h) := \{(6,3),(10,1),$ $(11,3),(5,4)\}$.

The remaining four sedonic roots listed in (4.19) are equivalent to negative values of roots in (4.20):

$$(10,5) \equiv -(5,-4), \quad (12,-2) \equiv -(3,3),$$
$$(10,-2) \equiv -(5,3), \qquad (5,-2) \equiv -(10,3).$$

Remark 4.7. For the sake of brevity, only one-half of all roots are listed in every row of Table 4.1; all remaining roots are listed in the rows below. For instance,

$$\sqrt[0]{(1,0)} = \{(6,5),(9,-4),(3,-1),(12,2), and \ (7,7),(8,-6),$$
$$and \ (-1,0), and \ (1,0)\}.$$

5. Comparison of Extractors

The square root extractors work if for an *odd* component of modulus G holds

$$p \equiv \pm(2^k - 1) \pmod{2^{k+1}}; \quad \text{and for its } even \text{ component holds}$$
$$q \equiv 2^k \pmod{2^{k+1}}.$$

In Table 5.1, we provide major parameters of quadratic extractors that for every $k = 1,2,3,\ldots$ satisfy the following condition

$$N \equiv (2^{k+1} + 1) \pmod{2^{k+2}}.$$

Table 5.1   Main parameters of extractors.

k	m	z	$E = (c,d)^m$	(c,d) has square root if $E =$
QRE-1	$(N-1)/4$	$(N+3)/8$	$(c,d)^{(N-1)/4}$	$(1,0), (-1,0)$ (both quadratic roots of $(1,0)$)
QRE-2	$(N-1)/8$	$(N+7)/16$	$(c,d)^{(N-1)/8}$	$(1,0), (-1,0),$ $(0,1), (0,-1)$ (all four quartic roots of $(1,0)$)
QRE-3	$(N-1)/16$	$(N+15)/32$	$(c,d)^{(N-1)/16}$	$(1,0), (-1,0),$ $(0,1), (0,-1)$ $\pm\sqrt{(0,1)},$ $(0,\pm 1)\sqrt{(0,1)}$ (all eight octonic roots of $(1,0)$)
QRE-k	$(N-1)/2^{k+1}$	$(N+2^{k+1}-1)/2^{k+2}$	$(c,d)^{(N-1)/2^{k+1}}$	(all 16 sedonic roots of $(1,0)$ if $k=4$)

Remark 5.1. If $k = 1$, then the algorithm extracts all existing square roots in exactly half cases, where $N \bmod 8 = 5$ and does not work if $N \bmod 8 = 1$.

If $k = 1$ or $k = 2$, then in 75% we can extract the roots for $N \bmod 16 = 5$, $N \bmod 16 = 9$ and $N \bmod 16 = 13$; and only in 25% we cannot extract the square roots if $N \bmod 16 = 1$.

If $k = 1$ or $k = 2$ or $k = 3$, then in 7/8 cases we can extract the roots for $N \bmod 32 = 5$, $N \bmod 32 = 9$, $N \bmod 32 = 13$, $N \bmod 32 = 17$, $N \bmod 32 = 21$, $N \bmod 32 = 25$ and $N \bmod 32 = 29$, and only in 1/8 cases we cannot extract the square roots if $N \bmod 32 = 1$.

6. Cryptographic Algorithm

Step 6.1 (*System design*): Every user (Alice, Bob, ...) selects a pair of large Gaussian primes (p,q) and (r,s) as her/his private keys, and computes $n := (p,q)(r,s)$ as her/his public key; she/he pre-computes

$$N = p^2 + q^2, \quad m, z \text{ and } R$$

(for an algorithm that computes the large Gaussian primes see Chap. 11 of this book).

Step 6.2 (Generalized Chinese remainder Theorem modulo composite Gaussian n): Each user pre-computes his/her parameters of CRT:

$$M := (p, q)^{-1} \bmod (r, s), \quad W := (r, s)^{-1} \bmod (p, q). \tag{6.1}$$

Step 6.3 (*Encryption* by sender (Alice)): Alice represents the plaintext as an array of Gaussians and inserts digital isotopes into every Gaussian (a, b) (Verkhovsky, 2011).

Step 6.4: Using Bob's public key n, she computes ciphertext

$$C := (a, b)^2 \bmod n \tag{6.2}$$

and transmits C to receiver (Bob) via open channels of a communication network.

Step 6.5 (*Decryption* by receiver (Bob)): He computes square roots of $C \bmod (p, q)$ and $\bmod (r, s)$, where (p, q) and (r, s) are Bob's private keys.

Step 6.6: Using the CRT and *his* pre-computed M and W (6.1), Bob computes all quadratic roots of ciphertext C.

Step 6.7: Bob recovers the initial plaintext by selecting the quadratic root of C that has *digital isotopes* (for more details see Chap. 12).

This algorithm is a generalization of the cryptographic algorithm (Rabin, 1979), which employs the square root algorithm for encryption and decryption of real integers modulo semi-prime $n = pq$, where p and q are real primes.

7. Reduction of Computational Complexity

In Steps 2.2 (2.6) and 2.4 (2.7), two exponentiations are performed to compute (c, d) to the powers m and z, respectively; these operations are the most time consuming.

However, observe that there is a simple linear relationship between m and z:

$$2(z - 1) = m - 1, \quad (= (N - 5)/4). \tag{7.1}$$

This implies that it is sufficient to execute only one exponentiation. Indeed, we initially compute

$$A_1 := (c, d)^{z-1} \bmod G \quad \text{(one exponentiation)}, \tag{7.2}$$

then

$$A_2 := A_1^2 \bmod G = \{(c,d)^{2(z-1)}\} \quad \text{(one squaring)}, \tag{7.3}$$

after that

$$A_3 := A_2 \times (c,d) = \{(c,d)^m\} \quad \text{(one multiplication)}, \tag{7.4}$$

and finally

$$A_4 := A_1 \times (c,d) = \{(c,d)^z\} \quad \text{(one multiplication)}. \tag{7.5}$$

8. The Case Where $N \equiv 3$ (mod 4)

Let us consider the modulus $G = (p,q)$, where $p = 4k + g$ and $q = 4r + h$; g, h, k and r are integers; $1 \le g \le 3$ is *odd* and $0 \le h \le 2$ is *even*.
    Then

$$N = 8(2k^2 + gk + 2r^2 + hr) + g^2 + h^2, \tag{8.1}$$

where $g^2 + h^2 = \{1, 5, 9, 13\}$.
    Therefore, for every g, h, k and r,

$$N \bmod 4 \neq 3. \tag{8.2}$$

The same result we can deduce from an observation that every non-Blum prime n ($n \bmod 4 = 1$) can be expressed as a sum of two squares of integers; on the other hand, every Blum prime n ($n \bmod 4 = 3$) can be expressed as a *sum of at least three squares* of integers. The latter implies that $N \bmod 4 \neq 3$. For instances, $23 = 3^2 + 3^2 + 2^2 + 1^2$, $43 = 5^2 + 3^2 + 3^2$. See also Proposition 1.3 for further details.

9. Applicability of QRE Algorithms

Consider $A := N \bmod 32$, where N are primes, which can be represented as a sum of two integer squares. For such N, the residues are equal to $A := \{1, 5, 9, 13, 17, 21, 25$ and $29\}$.
    Therefore, the three algorithms provided in this chapter cover all cases of prime moduli with the exception of $N \equiv 1$ (mod 32). Table 9.1 indicates for which value of residue A the ORE algorithm is applicable.
    Yet, most of the moduli in the latter case can still be covered if we consider QRE algorithms, where the primes $N \equiv 33$ (mod 64), $N \equiv 65$ (mod 128), and in general, for integer $t \ge 5$ the algorithms described

Table 9.1 Residues, applicable square root extractors and examples of corresponding N.

$N \bmod 32$	5	9	13	17	21	25	29
QRE	QRE-1	QRE-2	QRE-1	QRE-3	QRE-1	QRE-2	QRE-1
N	260773	692969	432589	386641	612373	525913	906557
(p, q)	$(113, 498)$	$(212, 805)$	$(258, 605)$	$(375, 496)$	$(522, 583)$	$(157, 708)$	$(421, 854)$
N	812101	249257	360781	676337	159157	405529	750077
(p, q)	$(351, 830)$	$(16, 499)$	$(275, 534)$	$(464, 679)$	$(174, 359)$	$(48, 635)$	$(11, 866)$

above can be generalized for the cases where

$$N \equiv (2^t + 1) \ (\bmod \ 2^{t+1}). \tag{9.1}$$

The *even* component q in the corresponding modulus G is divisible by 2^{t-1}, and the odd component p in G satisfies $p \equiv \pm(2^t - 1)(\bmod \ 2^{t+1})$.

10. Concluding Remarks

Three algorithms, which extract square roots of Gaussians in arithmetic, based on complex modulo reduction, are considered and analyzed in this chapter. Their generalization is provided in Secs. A.2 and A.3 of Appendix.

Several numeric illustrations provide further explanation of these algorithms. A public key encryption/decryption protocol based on this arithmetic is described in this chapter. This cryptographic protocol is almost twice as fast as the analogous protocols described in Verkhovsky and Koval (2008) and Verkhovsky (2011).

Appendix

A.1. *Classification of roots of $(1,0)$ modulo (p, q)*

There are various types of unary roots:

Definitions and notations:

$$S_1 := \pm\sqrt{(1,0)} \bmod((p,q)) = \{s_{11}, s_{12}\}, \tag{A.1}$$

where

$$P_1 := -\sqrt{(1,0)} \bmod((p,q)) = \{p_{11}\} \tag{A.2}$$

is the set of *principal* square roots of $(1,0)$ of the first level.

Then

$$S_2 := \{\pm\sqrt{s_{1k}} \bmod((p,q))\}, \quad k = 1, 2, \tag{A.3}$$

where

$$P_2 := \pm\sqrt{p_{11}} \equiv \{p_{2k}\} \bmod((p,q)), \quad k = 1, 2 \tag{A.4}$$

is the set of *principal* square roots of $(1,0)$ of the second level.

In general,

$$S_i := \{\pm\sqrt{s_{i-1,k}}\} \bmod((p,q)), \tag{A.5}$$

where

$$P_i := \{\pm\sqrt{p_{i-1,k}} \bmod((p,q))\} \tag{A.6}$$

is the set of *principal* square roots of $(1,0)$ of the ith level.

A.2. Criterion of quadratic residuosity and algorithm if $N \equiv (2^{k-1} + 1) \pmod{2^k}$

Proposition A.1. If

$$p \equiv (2^{k-1} - 1) \pmod{2^k} \quad \text{and} \quad q \equiv 2^{k-1} \pmod{2^k}, \tag{A.7}$$

then

$$m = (N-1)/2^k \quad \text{is odd} \quad \text{and} \quad z := (N + 2^{k-1} - 1)/2^{k+1} \quad \text{is an integer.} \tag{A.8}$$

Proposition A.2 (Criterion of Gaussian quadratic residuosity). Let

$$\|\gcd((c,d),G)\| = 1$$

and

$$E := (c,d)^{(N-1)/2^k} \bmod G \tag{A.9}$$

if

$$(c,d)^{(N-1)/2} \equiv (1,0) \pmod{G}, \tag{A.10}$$

then (c,d) has a quadratic root modulo Gaussian prime G.

However, if

$$(c,d)^{(N-1)/2} \equiv (-1,0) \pmod{G},$$

then a quadratic root of (c,d) modulo Gaussian prime G does not exist.

Proposition A.3 (Quadratic root extractor). Suppose that (A.7) and (A.8) hold.

Then the square root of (c, d) (1) is equal to

$$(x, y) = R(c, d)^z \pmod{G}, \tag{A.11}$$

where

$$R := \pm\sqrt{E^{-1}} \bmod G \quad \text{and} \quad z := (N + 2^{k-1} - 1)/2^k. \tag{A.12}$$

A.3. *Algorithm validation*

Indeed,

$$R^2(c, d)^{2z} \equiv (c, d)[(c, d)^{(N-1)/2^k} R^2] \pmod{G}. \tag{A.13}$$

Therefore, (A.12) implies that

$$ER^2 \bmod (p, q) = 1. \tag{A.14}$$

In other words, it confirms the equality (A.11). □

A.4. *Special case: quadratic extractor modulo $(p, -1)$*

Here we consider a special case where p is even,

$$q = -1 \quad \text{and} \quad N \bmod 8 = 5. \tag{A.15}$$

$$p = 4w + 2, \quad N = p^2 + 1 = 16w^2 + 16w + 5,$$

$$(N - 5)/8 = 2w(w + 1) + 1,$$

and

$$(N - 1)/4 = 4w(w + 1) + 1.$$

Proposition A.4. Let $N = \|(p, -1)\|$ be a prime.

If the norm of (c, d) is co-prime with N, then square root (x, y) of (c, d) is equal to

$$(x, y) = R \times (c, d)^{(p^2+4)/8} \bmod (p, -1), \tag{A.16}$$

where

$$R = \left[\sqrt{[(c, d)^{p/2}]^{p/2}} \right]^{-1} \bmod (p, -1). \tag{A.17}$$

Proof. First of all, if $N = p^2 + 1$ is a prime integer, then p is *even*. Therefore, (A.15) implies that $p^2/4$ and $(p^2+4)/8$ are integers. Then (A.16) and (A.17) imply that

$$(x, y)^2 \equiv R^2 \times (c, d)^{p^2/4}(c, d) \equiv (c, d) \bmod(p, -1). \qquad (A.18)$$

Since the cyclic identity (1.4) implies that

$$(c, d)^{p^2} \equiv (1, 0) \ (\bmod(p, -1)),$$

then potentially

$$\sqrt{(c, d)^{p^2/4}} \bmod(p, -1) = \{(\pm 1, 0), (0, \pm 1), \ \pm\sqrt{(0, \pm 1)}\}. \qquad (A.19)$$

Therefore,

$$R = \begin{cases} (\pm 1, 0) & \text{if } (c, d)^{p^2/4} = (1, 0), \\ \pm(0, 1) & \text{if } (c, d)^{p^2/4} = (-1, 0), \\ \pm\sqrt{(0, 1)} & \text{if } (c, d)^{p^2/4} = (0, -1), \\ \pm(0, 1)\sqrt{(0, 1)} & \text{if } (c, d)^{p^2/4} = (0, 1) \end{cases} \qquad (A.20)$$

Since $\sqrt{(0, 1)} \equiv (1, 1)\sqrt{2}/2 \ (\bmod(p, -1))$ (see Sec. 5.3), then R does not exist if $\sqrt{2}$ does not exist. Therefore, (c, d) is the Gaussian QNR. For more details see (3.6)–(3.8), (A.16), (A.17), Sec. 5.4 and eight examples in Table A.1. □

Remark A.5. Here $\pm(1, 9)$ and $\pm(10, 0)$ are quartic roots of $(1, 0)$ modulo $(10, -1)$.

Indeed,

$$q_3 = (10, 0) \equiv (0, 1) \ (\bmod(10, -1)),$$
$$q_4 = (1, 9) \equiv (0, -1)(\bmod(10, -1)), (2.3)$$
$$q_3^2 = (10, 0)^2 \equiv (-1, 0) \ (\bmod(10, -1)) = q_2,$$
$$q_4^2 = (1, 9)^2 \equiv (-1, 0) \equiv (10, 9) = q_2.$$

Table A.1 (Quadratic root extraction where $N \bmod 8 = 5$): $(p, -1) = (10, -1)$, $m := (p/2)^2 = 25$, $z := (m + 1)/2 = 13$.

(c, d)	$(2, 0)$	$(3, 2)$	$(4, 8)$	$(6, 7)$	$(7, 4)$	$(9, 9)$	$(10, 1)$
$(c, d)^{(n/2)^2}$	$(0, -1)$	$(-1, 0)$	$(1, 0)$	$(-1, 0)$	$(-1, 0)$	$(0, 1)$	$(-1, 0)$
$(c, d)^z$	GQNR	$(9, 4)$	$(6, 3)$	$(6, 9)$	$(5, 8)$	GQNR	$(9, 0)$
R	n/a	$\pm(10, 0)$	$(1, 0)$	$\pm(1, 9)$	$\pm(10, 0)$	n/a	$\pm(1, 9)$
$(x, y) = (c, d)^z R$	n/a	$\pm(6, 8)$	$\pm(6, 3)$	$\pm(1, 5)$	$\pm(2, 4)$	n/a	$\pm(10, 8)$
$(x, y)^2$	—	$(3, 2)$	$(4, 8)$	$(6, 7)$	$(7, 4)$	—	$(10, 1)$

A.5. *Special cyclic identity*

Proposition A.6. If $N := \|(p, q)\|$ is prime, then

$$(q, p)^{N-1} \equiv (1, 0) \; (\text{mod}(p, q)). \tag{A.21}$$

Remark A.7. Although $\|(p, q)\| = \|(q, p)\|$, identity (A.21) holds because (p, q) and (q, p) are co-prime. Indeed, assumption that $(p, q)(u, w) \equiv (q, p) \; (\text{mod}(p, q))$, where both u and w are integers, implies that

$$u \equiv (p + q)/N \quad \text{and} \quad w \equiv (q - p)/N \; (\text{mod}(p, q)). \tag{A.22}$$

However, (A.22) is impossible since the inverse of N modulo (p, q) does not exist.

Example A.8. $(-4, 10)^{28} \; \text{mod}(5, -2) = (1, 0)$, although $\text{gcd}[\|(-4, 10)\|, \|(5, -2)\|] = 29 \neq 1$.

Corollary A.9. If $\text{gcd}[(s, t), (p, q)] = (1, 0)$, then

$$[(s, t)(q, p)]^{N-1} \equiv (1, 0) \; (\text{mod}(p, q)). \tag{A.23}$$

Proposition A.10. If n and r in modulus (n, r) have different parities, then multiplicative inverse of $(r, n) \, \text{mod}(n, r)$ exists and equals

$$(r, n)^{-1} \equiv (n + r)^{-1}[(n + r + 1, -n + r - 1)/2] \; (\text{mod}(n, r)). \tag{A.24}$$

Proof. First of all,

$$(r, n) \equiv (n + r)(1, 1) \; (\text{mod}(n, r)). \tag{A.25}$$

Now let us find integers x and y such that

$$(1, 1)(x, y) \equiv (1, 0) \equiv (n + 1, r) \; (\text{mod}(n, r)), \tag{A.26}$$

i.e., $x - y = n + 1, x + y = r$. Hence,

$$x = (n + r + 1)/2, \quad y = (-n + r - 1)/2. \tag{A.27}$$

Therefore, (A.25) and (A.27) imply $(r, n)(r, n)^{-1} \equiv [(n + r)(1, 1)] (n + r)^{-1}(1, 1)^{-1} \equiv$

$$\equiv (r, n)(n + r)^{-1}(n + r + 1, -n + r - 1)/2 \equiv$$

$$\equiv (1, 0) \; (\text{mod}(n, r)). \tag{A.28}$$

$$\square$$

Example A.11. Let $n = 10, r = -3$. Then $(-3, 10)^{-1} \equiv 7^{-1}(4, -7) \equiv (2, 1)(4, -7) \equiv (8, 3)$.

Indeed,

$$(-3, 10)(8, 3) \equiv (1, 0) \ (\mathrm{mod}(10, -3)).$$

Corollary A.12. If n and r in modulus (n, r) have different parities and there exists multiplicative inverse of (a, b), then multiplicative inverse of $(r, n)(a, b) \ \mathrm{mod}(n, r)$ also exists.

A.6. *Alternate extraction of square roots (illustrated in Table A.2)*

Consider $G := (p, q) = (9, -4)$. $\|G\| = 97$, i.e., G is Gaussian prime.

$$(-1, 0) = (12, 5), \quad (0, 1) = (9, -3), \quad (0, -1) = (4, 8),$$

$$(7, -2)^{16} = (12, 5) = (-1, 0), \quad (7, -2)^4 = (2, 3) = \pm\sqrt{i},$$

$$(7, -2)^2 = (4, 1) = \pm\sqrt{\pm\sqrt{i}} = \pm\{\sqrt[4]{i}, \sqrt[4]{i^5}\},$$

$$(7, -2) = \pm\sqrt{\{\pm\sqrt[4]{i}, \pm i\sqrt[4]{i}\}} = \pm\{\sqrt[8]{i}, \sqrt[8]{i^5}, \sqrt[8]{i^9}, \sqrt[8]{i^{13}}\},$$

$$(8, 0)^4 = (0, 1), \quad (8, 0)^2 = \pm\sqrt{i}, \quad (8, 0) = \pm\sqrt{\pm\sqrt{i}},$$

$$(3, 3)^8 = (4, 8) = (0, -1), \quad (3, 3)^4 = \pm\sqrt{-i},$$

$$(3, 3)^2 = \pm\sqrt{\pm\sqrt{i}}, \quad (3, 3) = \pm\sqrt{\pm\sqrt{\pm\sqrt{i}}},$$

$$(8, 6)^8 = (12, 5) = (-1, 0), \quad (8, 6)^4 = (9, -3) = (0, 1),$$

$$(8, 6)^2 = (6, -2) = \pm\sqrt{i},$$

$$(8, 6) = \pm\sqrt{\pm\sqrt{i}},$$

$$(11, 3)^8 = (4, 8) = (0, 1), \quad (7, 6)^{1}6 = (12, 5) = (-1, 0),$$

$$(7, 6)^8 = (4, 8, 5) = (0, 1).$$

Step A.1:

$$N := p^2 + q^2 = 97, \quad m := (N - 1)/32 = 3, \quad z := (N + 31)/64 = 2. \tag{A.29}$$

Step A.2: Find a Gaussian (a, b), for which

$$F := (a, b)^m \ \mathrm{mod} \ G \neq \{(\pm 1, 0), (0, \pm 1)\}. \tag{A.30}$$

Step A.3: **if** $F^2 = (0,1)$, **then** $R := F \equiv \sqrt{i} \pmod{G}$;

       if $F^2 = (0,-1)$, **then** $R := (0,-1)F \equiv \sqrt{i} \pmod{G}$.

Step A.4: Compute

$$E := (c,d)^m \bmod G. \tag{A.31}$$

Step A.5: **if** $E \neq \{(\pm1,0),(0,\pm1)\}$ (3.1), **then** square root of (c,d) does not exist.

Step A.6: **if** $E = (1,0)$, **then** $(x,y) := (c,d)^z \bmod G$.

Step A.7: **if** $E = (-1,0)$, **then** $(x,y) := (c,d)^z(0,1) \bmod G$.

Step A.8: **if** $E = (0,1)$, **then** $(x,y) := (c,d)^z[(0,1)R] \bmod G$, (3.25)

       else $(x,y) := (c,d)^z R \bmod G$. (A.32)

Table A.2   Quadratic root extractor where $G = (9,-4), N := p^2 + q^2 = 97, m := (N-1)/32 = 3, z := (N+31)/64 = 2$.

(c,d)	$(1,1)$	$(3,-1)$	$(3,4)$	$(4,3)$	$(5,1)$	$(5,5)$	$(7,-1)$	$(8,5)$	$(10,3)$
$(c,d)^3$	$(7,-2)$	$(8,0)$	$(4,1)$	$(1,0)$	$(3,3)$	$(8,6)$	$(11,3)$	$(7,6)$	$(7,-2)$
$(c,d)^2$	n/a	$(8,5)$	$(3,6)$	$(5,7)$	$(1,2)$	$(8,1)$	n/a	$(3,-1)$	$(9,19)$
$(c,d)^z R$	n/a	$(4,5)$	$(9,4)$	$(4,1)$	$(1,2)$	$(5,4)$	n/a	$(2,2)$	$(7,6)$
$(x,y)^2$	n/a	$(3,-1)$	$(3,4)$	$(4,3)$	$(5,1)$	$(5,5)$	n/a	$(8,5)$	$(10,3)$

Chapter 9

Cubic Roots of Complex Integers and Encryption with Digital Isotopes

There are settings where encryption must be performed by a sender under time constraint. This chapter describes an encryption/decryption algorithm based on modular arithmetic of complex integers. It is shown how cubic extractors operate and how to find all cubic roots of every complex integer. The validations (proofs) are provided in Appendix. Detailed numeric illustrations explain how to use the method of digital isotopes to avoid ambiguity in recovery of the original plaintext by the receiver.

1. Introduction

This chapter describes a cryptographic algorithm based on the extraction of cubic roots from complex numbers $a + bi$ with integer components a and b. Such complex integers are called Gaussian integers (Gauss, 1986). Let us denote $(a, b) := a + bi$ and $N := a^2 + b^2$, where N is called the norm of (a, b). In modular arithmetic based on Gaussians, if p is a prime and $N \bmod p \neq 0$, then for every integer a and b holds an equivalent of the Fermat identity (Cross, 1983):

$$(a, b)^{p^2 - 1} \bmod p = (1, 0) = 1. \tag{1.1}$$

It means that the cycles in Gaussian modular arithmetic have order $O(p^2)$, while the cycles in modular arithmetic based on real integers have order $O(p)$.

Application of Gaussians for ElGamal cryptosystem is considered in El-Kassar *et al.* (2001), and the RSA digital signature is described in

Elkamchouchi *et al.* (2002). Two distinct public key cryptographies based on cubic roots of real integers are provided in Kak (2006) and Verkhovsky (2009).

Definition 1.1. A Gaussian integer (x, y) is called the cubic root of (a, b) modulo integer n, and defined as

$$\sqrt[3]{(a, b)} \bmod n, \quad \text{if } (x, y)^3 = (a, b) \pmod{n}. \tag{1.2}$$

Proposition 1.2. If p is a prime, $p \bmod 12 = 1$, and

$$V := (a, b)^{(p-1)/3} \bmod p = (1, 0) = 1, \tag{1.3}$$

then there exists a cubic root of (a, b) modulo p.

Proposition 1.3. If $p \bmod 12 = 5$, then for *every* integer a and b there exists an unique cubic root of (a, b) modulo p.

Proposition 1.4. Let $p^2 \bmod 9 \neq 1$, then for *every* integer a and b, for which holds

$$W := V^{p+1} \bmod p = (1, 0) = 1, \ (1.3), \tag{1.4}$$

there exists a cubic root of (a, b) modulo prime p.

Remark 1.5. Here are examples where $p^2 \bmod 9 = 1 : p = 17, 19, 53, 71, 89, 107, 109, 179, 197, 199, 269, 271$.

In addition, for $p = 17, 53, 89, 197, 269$ hold both $p \bmod 12 = 5$ and $p^2 \bmod 9 = 1$.

The following two algorithms are constructive proofs of the propositions listed above.

2. Algorithm-1

Step 2.1: Compute

$$W := (a, b)^{(p^2-1)/3} \bmod p. \tag{2.1}$$

Step 2.2: if $W \neq (1, 0)$, **then** cubic root of (a, b) modulo p does not exist.

Step 2.3: Compute

$$s := p \bmod 9, \tag{2.2}$$

(there are six possibilities $s = \pm 1, \pm 2, \pm 4$).

Table 2.1   Cubic extractors Ep and m.

p	7	11	13	23
Ep, m	$(5,2)$	$(27,2)$	$(19,1)$	$(59,1)$
p	29	31	41	43
Ep, m	$(187,2)$	$(107,1)$	$(187,1)$	$(411,2)$

Step 2.4: if $s \neq \pm 1$, then assign

$$m := 4/|s|, \tag{2.3}$$

otherwise apply Algorithm-2.

Step 2.5: Compute

$$E_p := [m(p^2 - 1) + 3]/9 \tag{2.4}$$

(if $m = 1$ or 2, then see Table 2.1).

Step 2.6: Compute

$$(x, y) := (a, b)^{E_p} \bmod p. \tag{2.5}$$

Example 2.1. Let $p = 23$, $(a, b) = (19, 4)$, $W := (19, 4)^{(23^2 - 1)/3} = (19, 4)^{176} \bmod 23 = (1, 0)$, hence $(19, 4)$ is a cubic residue and the cubic extractor $Ep := 59$, therefore

$$(x, y) := \sqrt[3]{(19, 4)} = (19, 4)^{59} \bmod 23 = (16, 16).$$

Indeed, $(16, 16)^3 \bmod 23 = (19, 4)$. It is easy to verify that $(5, 2)$ and $(2, 5)$ are also cubic roots of $(19, 4)$. Hence, the Algorithm-1 computes only one of three cubic roots of (a, b). Computation of other two cubic roots is discussed in Secs. 5 and A.3.

3. Algorithm-2

If $q \bmod 12 = 5$, then a cubic root exists for every (a, b), and each Gaussian has a unique cubic root. The following algorithm computes such cubic root (1.1).

Step 3.1: Compute the cubic extractor

$$E_q := (2q - 1)/3.$$

Step 3.2: Compute

$$R := (a, b)^{E_q} \bmod q. \tag{3.1}$$

Step 3.3: Output $(x, y) := R$.

Several examples are illustrated in Table 3.1.

Table 3.1   Illustration of cubic root extractions, $q \bmod 12 = 5$.

q	53	89	269
(a, b)	$(19, 13)$	$(17, 77)$	$(19, 73)$
E_q	35	59	179
(x, y)	$(45, 28)$	$(6, 85)$	$(112, 124)$

4. Multiplicity of Cubic Roots

Proposition 4.1. Suppose C_1, C_2 and C_3 are three cubic roots of $L :=$ (a, b) modulo p, each satisfying the equation

$$(C^3 - L) \bmod p = 0, \tag{4.1}$$

then for every $i = 1, 2, 3$ the following identities hold:

1.
$$C_i^3 \equiv L \bmod p, \tag{4.2}$$

2.
$$(C_1 + C_2 + C_3) \bmod p = 0,$$

$$C_1 C_2 C_3 \bmod p = L \quad \text{(Hadden, 1994)} \quad \text{and} \tag{4.3}$$

$$(C_1 C_2 + C_1 C_3 + C_2 C_3) \bmod p = 0,$$

3.
$$(C_i C_j - C_k^2) \bmod p = 0, \tag{4.4}$$

4.
$$[(C_i + C_j)^2 - C_i C_j] \bmod p = 0, \tag{4.5}$$

where $\{i, j, k\}$ is every permutation of $\{1, 2, 3\}$ in (4.4) and (4.5).

5. Relationship between Cubic Roots

In order to find two other roots of (a, b), consider the cubic roots of unity:

$$(u, w) := \sqrt[3]{(1, 0)} \bmod n. \tag{5.1}$$

If (x, y) is a cubic root of (a, b), then $(u, w)(x, y)$ and $(u, w)^2(x, y) \bmod p$ are also its cubic roots modulo n.

Proposition 5.1. If p is a Blum prime, then either $\sqrt{3}$ or $\sqrt{-3}$ modulo p exists, but not both; if $\sqrt{3} \bmod p$ exists, then

$$u = [(p - 1)/2] \bmod p \quad \text{and} \quad w = [(p \pm 1)\sqrt{3}/2] \bmod p. \tag{5.2}$$

If $\sqrt{-3} \bmod p$ exists, then

$$u = (1 \pm \sqrt{-3}) \bmod p. \tag{5.3}$$

Proof is provided in Appendix.

6. Existence of $\sqrt{3}$ mod p or $\sqrt{-3}$ mod p

Jacoby symbols (Crandall and Pomerance, 2001; Menezes *et al.*, 1997) analyze whether a specified integer is quadratic residue (QR).

If p is a Blum prime, then

$$\left(\frac{3}{p}\right) = -\left(\frac{p \bmod 3}{3}\right) = \left\{-\left(\frac{1}{3}\right) = -1\right\} \quad \text{or}$$

$$= \left\{-\left(\frac{2}{3}\right) = -(-1)^{(3^2-1)/8} = 1\right\}. \tag{6.1}$$

Therefore, if p mod $12 = 11$, then 3 is QR (illustrated in Table 6.1). However,

$$\text{if } p \bmod 12 = 7, \text{ then } -3 \text{ is } QR. \tag{6.2}$$

Table 6.1 $\sqrt{3}$ mod p if p mod $12 = 11$.

p	11	23	47	59	71	83	107
$\sqrt{3}$	5	16	12	48	43	70	89

7. Properties of Gaussian Cubes

Consider $\quad (t, v) := (u, w)^3 = (u(u^2 - 3w^2), w(3u^2 - w^2)) \pmod p;$
$$\tag{7.1}$$

Property 1 : $(\pm u, \pm w)^3 = (\pm u(u^2 - 3w^2), \pm w(3u^2 - w^2))$
$$= (\pm t, \pm v) \pmod p; \tag{7.2}$$

Property 2 : $(w, u)^3 = (w(w^2 - 3u^2), u(3w^2 - u^2)) = -(v, t) \pmod p; \tag{7.3}$

Property 3 : If $u + w = p$, then $(u, w)^3 = (w, u)^3 = u^3(1, 1) \pmod p. \tag{7.4}$

8. Cryptographic Protocol

System design (for every user): The user

Step 8.1: Selects large distinct primes p and q,

where p mod $12 = 11$, p^2 mod $9 \neq 1$ and q mod $12 = 5$.

Step 8.2: Computes $n = pq$ (n is public key, p and q are private keys).

Step 8.3: Finds cubic root (u, w) of $(1, 0)$ modulo p:

$$u = (p-1)/2 (\text{mod } p), \quad w = (u\sqrt{3}) \text{ mod } p.$$

Step 8.4: Pre-computes $P := q(q^{-1} \text{ mod } p)$, $Q := p(p^{-1} \text{ mod } q)$.

Protocol implementation: Suppose a sender (Sam) wants to securely transmit a plaintext message F to receiver (Regina). Sam divides F into an array of blocks

$$\{(g_1, h_1), (g_2, h_2), \ldots, (g_k, h_k), \ldots\}$$

in such a way that every $g_k < n$ and $h_k < n$

Encryption (Sam's actions):

Step 8.5: He gets Regina's public key n,

computes the ciphertext $(a, b) := (g, h)^3 \text{ mod } n$

and sends (a, b) to her;

Decryption (Regina's actions):

Step 8.6: Using her private keys p and q, she extracts cubic roots

$$M_1 := \sqrt[3]{(a, b)} \text{ mod } p \quad \text{and} \quad R := \sqrt[3]{(a, b)} \text{ mod } q.$$

Step 8.7: She computes

$$M_2 := M_1 \times (u, w) \text{ mod } p \quad \text{and} \quad M_3 := M_2 \times (u, w) \text{ mod } p.$$

Step 8.8: Using Chinese Remainder Theorem (Knuth, 1998), Regina computes three cubic roots of (a, b) modulo semi-prime n:

$$\text{for } k = 1, 2, 3, \quad D_k := (M_k P + RQ) \text{ mod } n.$$

Step 8.9 (the original plaintext is recovered via digital isotopes — see Secs. 10 and 11).

9. Efficient Encryption of Complex Integers

Squaring of a Gaussian requires two multiplications of real integers (*MoRI*) and multiplication of two Gaussians requires three MoRI (Karatsuba and Ofman, 1962).

Therefore, the cubic power of Gaussian requires five MoRI.

Yet, encryption $(a, b) := (g, h)^3 = (g^3 - 3gh^2, 3g^2h - h^3) \bmod p$ in (6.2) requires only *four* MoRI:

$$P_1 := g^2 \bmod p, \quad P_2 := h^2 \bmod p,$$

$$S := P_1 - P_2, \quad A_3 := S - 2P_2, \quad A_4 := S + 2P_1,$$

$$P_3 := gA_3 \bmod p, \quad P_4 := hA_4 \bmod p$$

(notice that there are no A_1 and A_2), where the doublings $2P_1$ and $2P_2$ are achieved by binary shifting.

Therefore, $(a, b) := (P_3, P_4)$.

10. Digital Isotopes

In cryptographic algorithms based on extraction of square roots of real integers (Rabin, 1979) or Gaussians (Verkhovsky, 2009), there are four pairs of solutions, and only one of them is the original plaintext. To distinguish the original solution from the other three, the authors use methods of tails, which is an analogue of using isotopes to mark different chemical components. As shown below, a more elaborate strategy must be used to avoid ambiguity in the recovery of the original plaintext.

Proposition 10.1. If the square root of 3 modulo prime p exists, then there exist Gaussians with distinct components x and y such that

$$(x, y)^3 = (y, x)^3 \pmod{p}. \tag{10.1}$$

Proof. Since $(x - y) \bmod p \neq 0$, then (10.1) implies

$$(x - y)(1, -1)[(x, y)^2 + (x, y)(y, x) + (y, x)^2] = 0,$$

$$(x^2 - y^2, 2xy) + (0, x^2 + y^2) + (y^2 - x^2, 2xy)$$

$$= (0, 2xy + (x + y)^2) \bmod p = 0,$$

i.e.,

$$[(x + y)^2 + 2xy] \pmod{p} = 0. \tag{10.2}$$

Let

$$y := Tx \bmod p, \quad \text{then } x^2[(1 + T)^2 + 2T] \bmod p = 0,$$

i.e., $(T^2 + 4T + 1) \bmod p = 0$, which implies that $T = -2 \pm \sqrt{3} \bmod p$.

$\square$

Table 10.1   Cubic roots $\sqrt[3]{(a,b)}$ mod $83 = \{(x,y)$ and $(y,x)\}$, $x \neq y$.

(a,b)	$(27,56)$	$(31,52)$	$(26,57)$	$(2,81)$	$(78,5)$	$(53,30)$
$\sqrt[3]{(a,b)}$	$(22,76)$	$(15,24)$	$(46,8)$	$(77,7)$	$(8,5)$	$(1,11)$

Example 10.2. Let $p = 83$, then $\sqrt{3} = 70$, i.e., $T = -2 \pm 70 \bmod 83 = \{11$ or $68\}$. If $x = 1$, then $y = \{11$ or $68\}$, hence $(1,68)^3 = (68,1)^3 \pmod{83} = (73,10)$, and $(1,11)^3 = (11,1)^3 \pmod{83} = (53,30)$.

It means that $\sqrt[3]{(53,30)} \bmod 83$ equals either $(1,11)$ or $(11,1)$. Yet, if in both component the rightmost digit is "1", it is not clear whether the original plaintext is $(0,1)$ or $(1,0)$.

For every $p \bmod 12 = 11$ there exist $4(p-1)$ complex integers that satisfy (10.1) (examples are provided in Table 10.1).

11. Numeric Illustration

Let $F = (24,18)$, and with digital isotopes $Z := 10F + F \bmod 10 = (24\underline{4}, 18\underline{8})$.

Let $p = 23$ and $q = 17$, where $p^2 \bmod 9 = 7 \neq 1$, $q \bmod 12 = 5$ and $n = 391$, then Sam computes the ciphertext $(a,b) := Z^3 = (232,379)$ $\pmod{391}$ and transmits it to Regina.

Decryption: Regina computes $W := (a,b)^{(p^2-1)/3} \bmod p = (232,379)^{176}$ $\bmod 23 = 1$.

Hence, the cubic root of (a,b) exists

$$s := p \bmod 9 = -4 \quad \text{and} \quad m := 4/|-4| = 1, \quad \text{then } Ep := 59.$$

Regina pre-computes the cubic root of $(1,0)$ modulo p:

$$u = (p-1)/2 \pmod{p} = 11 \quad \text{and} \quad w = u\sqrt{3} = 11 \times 3^6 \bmod 23 = 15.$$

Therefore, $M_1 := (232,379)^{59} = (7,18) \pmod{23}$ and other two cubic roots are equal

$$M_2 := M_1 \times (u,w) = (7,18) \times (11,15) = (14,4),$$

$$M_3 := M_2 \times (u,w) = (14,4) \times (11,15) = (2,1).$$

Then Regina computes the cubic root extractor $E_q := (2q-1)/3$ and

$$R := (a,b)^{E_q} \bmod q = (232,379)^{11} \bmod 17 = (6,1)$$

$$\text{(cubic root } R \text{ is unique)}.$$

There are three potential plaintexts that must be recovered by Regina.

To do this, she solves three systems of modular equations

$$\begin{cases} (x,y) \bmod p = M_k, \quad k = 1,2,3 \\ (x,y) \bmod q = R. \end{cases} \tag{11.1}$$

Using the Chinese Remainder Theorem (Knuth, 1998)

$$(x,y)_k = (M_k P + RQ) \bmod n, \tag{11.2}$$

where P and Q are pre-computed earlier in Step 8.4:

$$P := q(q^{-1} \bmod p) \quad \text{and} \quad Q := p(p^{-1} \bmod q).$$

Then Regina computes (11.2) for $k = 1, 2, 3$:

$$(x,y)_1 = 323 M_1 + 69 \times (6,1)$$
$$= [323 \times (7,18) + (23,69)] \bmod 391 = (329, 18),$$
$$(x,y)_2 = 323 M_2 + 69 \times (6,1)$$
$$= [323 \times (14,4) + (23,69)] \ (\bmod \ 391) = (2\underline{4}4, 1\underline{8}8),$$
$$(x,y)_3 = 323 M_3 + 69 \times (6,1)$$
$$= [323 \times (2,1) + (23,69)] \bmod 391 = (278, 1).$$

$(x,y)_k = [M_k \times 17 \times (17^{-1} \bmod 23) + R \times 23 \times (23^{-1} \bmod 17)] \bmod n = (323 M_k + 69R) \bmod 391$. Hence, Regina recovers $F := [(x,y)_2 - (x,y)_2 \bmod 10]/10 = (24, 18)$.

Let assume that in this case the probability of error that the recovered "plaintext" is incorrect is equal to 1%. If the digital isotopes repeat r rightmost digits in each component of plaintext (g, h), then the probability of erroneous recovery of the "plaintext" is of order $O(1/10^{2r})$. For instance, if the length of isotope $r = 3$, then the probability of error is *one in one million*.

12. Algorithm in Nutshell

Design: $p, q, n, P, Q, u, w, s, m, E_p, E_q$;

Encryption: Plaintext Z with isotopes; Ciphertext (a, b);

Decryption: R, RQ, M_1, M_2, M_3.

System design: Let Regina's $p = 227$ and $q = 1109$,

where $p^2 \bmod 9 = 4 \neq 1$, $p \bmod 12 = 11$, $q \bmod 12 = 5$, then $n = pq = 251743$.

Regina pre-computes P and Q:

$$P := q(q^{-1} \bmod p) = 1109 \times (1109^{-1} \bmod 227) = 1109 \times 96 = 106464,$$

$$Q := p(p^{-1} \bmod q) = 227 \times (227^{-1} \bmod 1109) = 227 \times 640 = 145280,$$

and the cubic root (u, w) of $(1,0)$ modulo p:

$$u = (227 - 1)/2 \ (\bmod \ p) = 113,$$

$$w = u\sqrt{3} = 113 \times 3^{57} \bmod 227 = 25.$$

Remark 12.1. $(u, w)^2 = (u, p - w) \ (\bmod \ p)$.

Indeed, $(113, 25)^3 \bmod 227 \ = \ (1, 0)$ and $(113, 25)^2 \bmod 227 \ = \ (113, 202)$.

$$s := 227 \bmod 9 = 2, \quad m := 4/|2| = 2$$

and cubic root extractor (see Step 5.1)

$$E_p := [2 \times (227^2 - 1) + 3]/9 = 11451.$$

Finally, Regina (receiver) pre-computes another cubic extractor $E_q := (2q - 1)/3 = 739$.

Encryption: Suppose Sam (sender) wants to securely transmit message $F = (1941, 2487)$ to Regina using two-digit isotopes:

$$Z := 100F + F \bmod 100 = (1941\underline{\mathbf{41}}, 2487\underline{\mathbf{87}}).$$

In this case, the probability of erroneous recovery of the original message will not exceed $1/10,000$, i.e., it equals 0.01%.

Sam computes the ciphertext $(a, b) \ := \ Z^3 \bmod 251743 \ = (227258, 195067)$.

Decryption: Regina computes

$$M_1 := (227258, 195067)^{11451} \bmod 227 = (31, 74)^{11451} \bmod 227 = (74, 78)$$

and two other cubic roots:

$$M_2 := M_1 \times (u, w) = (74, 78) \times (113, 25) = (56, 222),$$

$$M_3 := M_2 \times (u, w) = (56, 222) \times (113, 25) = (97, 154),$$

and then unique cubic root R modulo q

$$R := (a, b)^{E_q} \bmod q = (227258, 195067)^{739} = (66, 371) \ (\bmod \ 1109).$$

Using the Chinese Remainder Theorem, Regina computes in accordance with (11.2):

$$(x, y)_k = [M_k \times 1109 \times (1109^{-1} \bmod 227) + R \times 227$$
$$\times (227^{-1} \bmod 1109)] \bmod 251743$$

$$= (106464 M_k + 145280 R) \bmod 251743,$$

$$(x, y)_1 = 106464 M_1 + 145280 \times (66, 371)$$

$$= [106464 \times (74, 78) + (22246, 25878)] \bmod n$$

$$= (96549, 274294), \quad \text{where } n = 251743,$$

$$(x, y)_2 = [106464 M_2 + (22246, 25878)] \bmod n$$

$$= [106464 \times (56, 222) + (22246, 25878)] \bmod n = (1941\underline{41}, 2487\underline{87}).$$

Therefore, Regina recovers the original Gaussian block of information, i.e., it is not necessary to compute $(x, y)_3$.

13. Optimized Recovery of Information

Let

$$M_k = (M_{k1}, M_{k2}), \quad R = (R_1, R_2),$$

then

$$x_k = M_{k1} P + R_1 Q, \quad y_k = M_{k2} P + R_2 Q.$$

$M_1 = (M_{11}, M_{12})$ is computed by cubic root extraction; if the isotopes in Z are detected, then the original information is recovered, otherwise we need to compute four components of two other cubic roots of (a, b):

$$M_2 = (M_{11}, M_{12})(u, w) = (M_{11} u - M_{12} w, M_{11} w + M_{12} u),$$
$$M_3 = (M_{11}, M_{12})(u, -w) = (M_{11} u + M_{12} w, -M_{11} w + M_{12} u).$$

Yet, to minimize computational burden, instead of computing M_2 and M_3, find $N_1 := M_{12} w P$ and then compute $x_2 = (M_{11} u P + R_{11} Q) - N_1$. If the isotopes are detected, then compute y_2, otherwise compute

$$x_3 = (M_{11} u P + R_{11} Q) + M_{12} w P = x_2 + 2N_1 \quad \text{and} \quad y_3.$$

14. Minimization of Erroneous Recovery of Original Information

The probability of erroneous recovery can be decreased if, instead of repeating r rightmost digits of g and h, the following procedure is applied:

- consider r *leftmost* digits (prefix P_r) of the first component g in plaintext (g, h) and post it as its digital isotope;
- consider r *rightmost* digits (suffix S_r) of the second component h of plaintext $F = (g, h)$ and repeat it as its digital isotope.

Example 14.1. If $(g, h) = (31415926, 27182845)$ and $r = 2$, then $(31\underline{31}415926, 2718284\underline{5}4\underline{5})$.

Remark 14.2. If n is f digits long and the number of digits in g is smaller than f, then the prefix $P_r = 00\ldots0$.

To avoid confusion, the sender must attach both digital isotopes P_r and S_r as suffixes.

Example 14.3. If $f = 8$, $(g, h) = (00415926, 07182845)$ and $r = 2$, then

$$Z := (g - g \bmod 10^6) \times 10^8 + g, (h - h \bmod 10^2) \times 10^2 + h \bmod 10^2)$$

$$= (\underline{00}41592600, 0718284\underline{5}4\underline{5}).$$

15. Third Numeric Illustration

Algorithm in nutshell

System design: $p, q, n, P, Q, u, w, s, m, E_p, E_q$;

Encryption: Plaintext Z with isotopes;

Ciphertext (a, b);

Decryption: R, QR, M_1, M_2, M_3,

System design: Let $p = 227$, $q = 1109$, $n = pq = 251743$, $P = 106464$, $Q = 145280$,

$$(u, w) = (113, 25), \quad s = 2, \quad m = 2,$$
$$E_p = 11451, \quad E_q = 739.$$

Encryption:

Plaintext	$F = (1756, 2011)$,
Plaintext with isotopes	$Z := (\underline{17}5617, 20\underline{11}11)$,
Ciphertext	$(a, b) = (57971, 209989)$

Decryption: $R = (395, 382)$, $M := (202, 137)$,

$$QR_1 \bmod n = 239939,$$

$$N_1 := M_{12}wP = 115336,$$

$$x_2 = M_{11}uP + QR_1 - N_1 = 196688,$$

since there is no isotope in x_2, then (x_3, y_3) is the original Gaussian.
Indeed, $x_3 = x_2 + 2N_1 = 1\,75617$.

16. Algorithm Analysis

The cryptographic algorithm described above is *neither* a generalization
nor a special case of the RSA protocol (Rivest *et al.*, 1978).

First of all, the following identity holds:

$$(a, b)^{(p^2-1)(q-1)} \bmod n = (1, 0) = 1. \tag{16.1}$$

In the RSA algorithm, each user selects a public key e that is co-prime with

$$z := (p - 1)(q - 1)$$

and then computes a multiplicative inverse d of e modulo z. In the algorithm
described above, the encryption key $e = 3$. However, the decryption key cannot be computed as a modular multiplicative inverse, because $\gcd(3, z) = 3$,
which means that such an inverse does not exist (Verkhovsky, 1999).

17. Speedup of Communication

Suppose it is necessary to transmit an H digit-long plaintext, where the
size of each block must not exceed 16 digits; in addition, suppose that we
want to ensure that the probability of erroneous recovery does not exceed
one in one million. There are two options.

Option 1: To select the size of each block equal to 10 digits and the size
of each tail equal to six digits;

Option 2: To select the size of each block equal to 13 digits and the size
of each tail equal to three digits.

In the first option, we will treat each block individually as a real integer;
which implies that we need to transmit $H/10$ real integers. In the second
option, we will treat a pair of blocks as a Gaussian; which implies that we
need to transmit $H/26$ Gaussians, i.e., $H/13$ real integers. Therefore, the
first option requires $13/10 = 1.3$ times more bandwidth, than the second

option. In other words, the bandwidth can be reduced by 30% if Gaussian integers are used.

18. Possible Applications and Concluding Remarks

The proposed cryptosystem has significant specifics: the encryption is substantially faster than the decryption. There are certain settings where the sender has limited time to transmit the message: visual images or video, and receiver does not have such restriction. For instance, the sender is a system that urgently needs to transmit information prior to either collision with a target or before it is destroyed by a hostile action (Verkhovsky, 2008a). In another example, the sender (say, an interplanetary or interstellar space station) detects an imminent collision with the asteroid and is programmed to report about such collision and transmit visual and other details about the asteroid (Verkhovsky, 2008d). In such case it is paramount to ensure the reliability of message delivery (Verkhovsky, 2008a, 2009b, 2009c). Yet, in the third example, a security camera that has detected an imminent explosion, is programmed to report the situation (audio, pictures and/or video) (Xu and Sun, 2010) prior to its own destruction from the explosion.

Appendix

A.1. *Validation of Algorithm-1*

If condition (2.1) holds, then

$$(x, y)^3 = (a, b)^{3E_p} = (a, b)^{m(p^2-1)/3+1} = [(a, b)^{(p^2-1)/3}]^m (a, b) \bmod p.$$

$$(A.1)$$

If $(a, b)^{(p^2-1)/3} \bmod p = (1, 0)$, then by definition (1.2) (x, y) is a cubic root of (a, b) modulo prime p. Hence, if $(p^2 - 1)/9$ is not an integer, then there exists an integer m such that Ep is an integer, i.e., there exists an integer solution of equation

$$[m(p^2 - 1) + 3] \bmod 9 = 0. \tag{A.2}$$

Indeed, observe that

1. every prime greater than 3 can be expressed either as $p = 6k + 1$ or as $p = 6k - 1$,
2. $(p^2 - 1)/3$ is an integer for every prime greater than 3,
3. if $(p^2 - 1)/9$ is not an integer, then $k \bmod 3 = 0$, and $(p^2 - 1)/3$ is not co-prime with 3.

Therefore, (A.2) can be rewritten as

$$m(p^2 - 1)/3 \bmod 3 = 2. \tag{A.3}$$

If there is no integer solution of Eq. (A.3), then the algorithm is not applicable for these cases. In other terms, if either $(p-1)/9$ or $(p+1)/9$ is an integer, then Ep is not an integer.

A.2. Validation of Algorithm-2

Let

$$R^3 = [(a,b)^{(q-1)}]^2 \times (a,b) \bmod q. \tag{A.4}$$

Since $q \bmod 12 = 5$, then $(q-1)/2$ is *even*.

Hence by Euler criterion of quadratic residuosity $(-1)^{(q-1)/2} \bmod q = 1$, i.e.,

$$i := \sqrt{p-1} \ (\bmod \ q) \tag{A.5}$$

is a real integer, and hence $(a,b) \bmod q$ is also a real integer.

Therefore, by the Fermat identity $R^3 \bmod q = (a,b)$.

A.3. More on identities for cubic roots

By the Vieta theorem (Knuth, 1981), the equation

$$(C^3 - L) \bmod p = 0 \tag{A.6}$$

implies that

$$(C - C_1)(C - C_2)(C - C_3) \bmod p = 0. \tag{A.7}$$

Hence, (A.6) and (A.7) imply

$$(C_1 + C_2 + C_3) \bmod p = 0, \quad C_1 C_2 C_3 \bmod p = L, \tag{A.8}$$

and for every permutation $\{i, j, k\}$ of $\{1, 2, 3\}$

$$(C_i C_j - C_k^2) \bmod p = 0. \tag{A.9}$$

On the other hand, (A.9) implies

$$[(C_i + C_j)^2 - C_i C_j] \bmod p = 0. \tag{A.10}$$

Yet, neither (A.9) nor (A.10) are instrumental in recovery of all cubic roots.

A.4. *Proof of Proposition 5*

Algebraic approach:

$$(u, w)^3 = (u^3 - 3uw^2, 3u^2w - w^3) \bmod p = (1, 0). \tag{A.11}$$

Therefore, from (A.6) we deduce two equations with unknown u and w:

$$u(u^2 - 3w^2) \bmod p = 1 \tag{A.12}$$

and

$$w(3u^2 - w^2) \bmod p = 0. \tag{A.13}$$

Since in (A.13) $w \bmod p \neq 0$, then

$$3u^2 = w^2 \ (\bmod \ p). \tag{A.14}$$

Hence, (A.12) and (A.14) imply that

$$8u^3 + 1 = 0 (\bmod \ p)$$

or

$$(2u + 1)(4u^2 - 2u + 1) \bmod p = 0. \tag{A.15}$$

Equation (A.15) holds if either

$$u = (p - 1)/2 \ (\bmod \ p) \tag{A.16}$$

or

$$(4u^2 - 2u + 1) \bmod p = 0. \tag{A.17}$$

Thus, in (A.16) case, if there exists square root of 3 modulo p, then from (A.14)

$$w = \pm u\sqrt{3} = \pm(p - 1)\sqrt{3}/2. \tag{A.18}$$

Otherwise, Eq. (A.17) implies that

$$u = 1 \pm \sqrt{-3} \bmod p \tag{A.19}$$

and finally from (A.12) we deduce w.

Trigonometric approach: Consider

$$(u^o, w^o) = \sqrt[3]{(1,0)} = \sqrt[3]{(\cos \pi + i \sin \pi)} = (\cos \pi/3 + i \sin \pi/3) = (1, \sqrt{3})/2. \tag{A.20}$$

Since $(u^o, w^o) \bmod p$ is a Gaussian integer, then

$$(u, w) = (u^o, w^o) \bmod p. \tag{A.21}$$

Proposition A.1. If (x, y) is a cubic root of (a, b) modulo p, then $(u, w)(x, y) \bmod p$ and $(u, w)^2(x, y) \bmod p$ are also cubic roots of (a, b).

Proof. From Definition 1.1 for $k = 1, 2, [(u, w)^k(x, y)]^3 = (1, 0)^k(a, b) = (a, b) \bmod p$ (1.2). $\qquad \square$

Chapter 10

Exponentiation-Free Accelerated Encryption/Decryption Protocol

1. Introduction

Most of the existing cryptographic algorithms require exponentiations on encryption and decryption stage, or, if they are based on elliptic curves (EC) require scalar multiplication of a point on the EC. In both cases, these operations are computationally intense, and as a result, the algorithms in questions are very sluggish.

An exponentiation-free encryption-decryption algorithm is described in this chapter. This algorithm is based on two moduli: one in the real field of integers and another in the field of complex integers that are also called *Gaussian* integers (or Gaussians, for short). The proper selection of cryptographic system parameters is provided and explained. In this chapter, we explain step-by-step how to

- precondition a plaintext,
- select secret control parameters,
- ensure feasibility of all private keys,
- avoid ambiguity in the process of information recovery.

The proposed cryptographic system is faster than most of the known *public key* cryptosystems, since it requires a small number of multiplications and additions, and does not require exponentiations for its implementation.

2. Primary Residues

This chapter describes and briefly analyzes a public key cryptography (PKC) based on *primary residues* and complex integer modulus. The framework of the proposed PKC partially resembles the NTRU PKC (Hoffstein *et al.*, 1998, 2001) (more details are provided in www.ntru.com), which was introduced in 1996 and later patented by three mathematicians from Brown University. Their PKC is analyzed in Coppersmith and Shamir (1997) and Jaulmes and Joux (2000). These papers provide several scenarios of cryptanalysis of the NTRU. It is pointed out in Howgrave-Graham *et al.* (2003) that the decryption does not always recover the initial plaintext.

In this chapter, we consider a public key cryptographic system with two modulo reductions:

- Real integer modulus n and
- Complex modulus R (Verkhovsky, 2011a).

As a result, all public and private keys of each user and secret controls S are also Gaussian integers. Since plaintext blocks are complex as well, in order to avoid ambiguity in information recovery we introduce a concept of primary residues in this chapter. We demonstrate how to ensure that all keys of the proposed cryptosystem provide unambiguous recovery of initially pre-conditioned and subsequently encrypted information.

Remark 2.1. In the proposed cryptosystem, there is no necessity to consider polynomials with binary coefficients as it is done in Hoffstein *et al.* (1998, 2001).

2.1. *Complex modulo reduction*

Real modulus: In a group based on real modulo reduction n there are two results, whether n is either prime or composite: if $a \bmod n = b > 0$, then $a \bmod n = b - n \leq 0$ is also correct.

In order to avoid ambiguity, we can stipulate that only non-negative results are feasible.

Complex modulus: Consider complex integers $B := (b_1, b_2)$ and $R := (r_1, r_2)$. In an arithmetic based on modulo reduction with complex integer R there are four possible results: if $A \bmod R = B$, where both A and B are complex integers, then

$$A \bmod R = \{(b_1, b_2), (b_1 - r_1, b_2 - r_2), (b_1 + r_2, b_2 - r_1),$$
$$(b_1 - r_1 + r_2, b_2 - r_1 - r_2)\}$$

are also correct. In order to avoid ambiguity in this case, it is stipulated in this chapter that only *primary residues* are feasible (a definition and details are provided below).

Let us define the norm N of R as

$$N := \|R\| := r_1^2 + r_2^2, \tag{2.1}$$

then

$$(x, y) := (a, b) \bmod (r_1, r_2) = (a, b) - \lfloor (a, b)(r_1, -r_2)/N \rfloor (r_1, r_2). \tag{2.2}$$

2.2. *Primary residues*

Let us consider two functions of integer variables x_1 and x_2 with integer parameters r_1 and r_2:

$$H(x_1, x_2) := r_1 x_2 - r_2 x_1 \tag{2.3}$$

and

$$V(x_1, x_2) := r_1 x_1 + r_2 x_2. \tag{2.4}$$

Definition 2.2 (primary residue). A complex integer $A = (a_1, a_2)$ is called primary residue modulo R if it satisfies four inequalities:

$$0 \le H(a_1, a_2) \le N - 1 \tag{2.5}$$

and

$$0 \le V(a_1, a_2) \le N - 1 \quad (2.1). \tag{2.6}$$

Property 2.3. If a Gaussian integer G is primary residue modulo Gaussian R, then

$$G \bmod R = G. \tag{2.7}$$

In the cryptographic scheme described below, a plaintext M is divided onto pairs of blocks $M = (m_1, m_2)$, where each pair is treated as a Gaussian integer. In the algorithm provided in Sec. 3, it is important to assure that the numeric representation $M = (m_1, m_2)$ is a *primary residue* modulo R.

2.3. *Plaintext as primary residue*

In general, $M = (m_1, m_2)$ is the *primary residue* modulo R, if m_1 and m_2 satisfy the following inequalities:

$$0 \le H(m_1, m_2) \le N - 1, \tag{2.8}$$

$$0 \le V(m_1, m_2) \le N - 1. \tag{2.9}$$

Remark 2.4. If both components in R are positive, then $(a_1, a_2) = (1, 0)$ is not a primary residue modulo R since (2.5) does not hold. Indeed, $(1, 0) \equiv (1 - r_2, r_1) \bmod (r_1, r_2)$ and, as a result, property (2.7) does not always hold.

However, **if** $r_2 < 0 < r_1$, then $(1,0)$ is the primary residue.

If $r_2 < 0$, then (2.8) implies

$$0 \le r_1 m_2 + |r_2| m_1 < r_1^2 + r_2^2, \tag{2.10}$$

and (2.9) implies that

$$0 \le r_1 m_1 - |r_2| m_2 < r_1^2 + r_2^2. \tag{2.11}$$

Therefore, the right inequalities in (2.10) and (2.11) are respectively equivalent to

$$0 \le r_1(r_1 - m_2) + |r_2|(|r_2| - m_1) \quad \text{and} \quad 0 \le r_1(r_1 - m_1) + |r_2|(|r_2| + m_2),$$

which hold **if**

$$m_2 \le r_1, \quad m_1 \le |r_2|, \quad m_1 \le r_1. \tag{2.12}$$

In addition, the left inequality in (2.11) holds **if**

$$(m_2 / m_1) \le (r_1 / |r_2|). \tag{2.13}$$

2.4. *Geometric interpretation*

All primary residues are located inside a tilted square (rhomb) with vertices $(0, 0), R, iR, (1 + i)R$ and with sides equal to $\sqrt{r_1^2 + r_2^2}$ (2.1).

If $\gcd(r_1, r_2) = 1$, then there are exactly $N - 1$ primary residues inside this rhomb.

3. **Cryptographic System Based on Primary Residues**

(1) All users ($i = 1, 2, \ldots$) agree to select a large real integer n (same for all of them).

(2) The ith user has private and public keys, and secret control P_i, R_i, U_i, Q_i, S_i with index i (in the forthcoming discussion index i is omitted for the sake of simplicity of notations).

(3) **Variables:** P, R, U, Q, S, F, W, where each of them is a complex (Gaussian) integer.

(4) User's **private** keys: $P = (p_1, p_2), R = (r_1, r_2)$, where R is a Gaussian prime and

$$\gcd(p_1, p_2) = 1, \quad \gcd(r_1, r_2) = 1. \tag{3.1}$$

The second condition in (3.1) holds if R is a Gaussian prime. An algorithm that computes large Gaussian primes is described in Chap. 22.

Remark 3.1. The stipulation that R is a Gaussian prime is sufficient to assure that certain conditions hold, but not necessary. Hence, it can be omitted under other considerations.

(5) Every user pre-computes a multiplicative inverse F of P modulo real integer n:

$$F := (f_1, f_2) := (p_1, p_2)^{-1} \bmod n. \qquad (3.2)$$

Remark 3.2. A Gaussian multiplicative inverse F of P modulo real integer n exists

$$\textbf{if} \quad \gcd(\|P\|, n) = 1, \quad \{\|P\| := p_1^2 + p_2^2\}. \qquad (3.3)$$

(6) Every user pre-computes her/his *public* key:

$$U := (u_1, u_2) := (f_1, f_2)(r_1, r_2) \bmod n. \qquad (3.4)$$

(7) Every user pre-computes a multiplicative inverse Q of P modulo Gaussian R:

$$Q := (q_1, q_2) := (p_1, p_2)^{-1} \bmod (r_1, r_2). \qquad (3.5)$$

Multiplicative inverse Q of P modulo R exists if

$$\gcd(P, R) = (1, 0). \qquad (3.6)$$

Remark 3.3. Notice that P has a multiplicative inverse modulo R even if $\gcd(\|P\|, \|R\|) > 1$. Indeed, although $\|(r_1, r_2)\| = \|(r_2, r_1)\|$ yet

$$\gcd[(r_1, r_2), (r_2, r_1)] = (1, 0). \qquad (3.7)$$

Therefore, **if** R is a Gaussian prime, then every Gaussian is co-prime with R, i.e., it has a multiplicative inverse modulo R. Primality of R is sufficient, but not necessary condition.

The algorithm for computation of Q in (3.5) is provided below in Sec. 10.

Remark 3.4. Condition (2.13) is not directly verifiable by a sender since R is the private key of the receiver. Yet, the sender has an option to *indirectly* satisfy (2.13). Indeed, **if** $|r_2| \leq r_1$ and $m_2/m_1 \leq 1$, then (2.13) holds, otherwise swap m_1 and m_2 in M:

$$w_2 := m_1, \quad w_1 := m_2. \qquad (3.8)$$

Then, as a result,

$$(w_2/w_1) \leq 1 \leq (r_1/|r_2|). \tag{3.9}$$

Remark 3.5. Since r_1 and r_2 are design *parameters* of the cryptographic algorithm, they can be properly selected. On the other hand, m_1 and m_2 are the *inputs* of the algorithm. As a result, a designer of this algorithm must ensure that both inequalities in (2.11) hold for every pair (m_1, m_2) by partitioning the plaintext onto blocks of appropriate sizes.

Remark 3.6. In the forthcoming discussion it is assumed that $W :=$ (w_1, w_2) is already *pre-conditioned* plaintext, i.e., in every Gaussian block $w_1 \geq w_2$.

4. Information Hiding and its Recovery

4.1. *Threshold parameter*

Suppose that a sender (Sam) transmits a plaintext message $M = (m_1, m_2)$ to a receiver (Rene). The size of plaintext blocks m_1 and m_2 must be selected in such a way that

$$0 \leq m_1, m_2 \leq u \leq r_1 \tag{4.1}$$

and plaintext M must be a primary residue modulo R [see (2.8)–(2.13)]. Here variable u (threshold) is the same for all users, its value is established below.

4.2. *Sender's secret key*

For security reason, the sender periodically selects a randomized secret key $S := (s_1, s_2)$. S plays two roles: it is a *screen/veil* that hides information; and at the same time it is a *control* that enables the system user to satisfy certain constraints. Proper selection of S is discussed below.

Encryption: Using Rene's public key U, Sam selects secret control S and computes ciphertext:

$$C := (M + SU) \bmod n. \tag{4.2}$$

Decryption (requires real and Gaussian modulo reductions):

Stage1 (Real modulo n reduction): $D := PC \bmod n,$ (4.3)

Stage2 (Gaussian modulo R reduction): $Z := QD \bmod R.$ (4.4)

5. Validation of Encryption/Decryption Algorithm

Proposition 5.1. If W is a primary residue and private keys P, R and secret control S are selected in such a way that holds

$$(PW + RS) \bmod n = PW + RS, \tag{5.1}$$

then in (4.4)

$$Z = W. \tag{5.2}$$

Proof. (3.2), (3.4), (3.5), (4.3) and (5.1) imply that

$$
\begin{aligned}
PW + RS \quad &\xrightleftharpoons{\;(5.1)\;}\quad (PW + (1,0)RS) \bmod n \\[2mm]
&\xrightleftharpoons{\;(3.2)\;}\quad [PW + (PF \bmod n) \times RS] \bmod n \\[2mm]
&\quad=\quad P[W + (FR \bmod n) \times S] \bmod n \\[2mm]
&\xrightleftharpoons{\;(3.4)\;}\quad P(W + US) \bmod n \\[2mm]
&\xrightleftharpoons{\;(4.2)\;}\quad PC \bmod n \\[2mm]
&\xrightleftharpoons{\;(4.3)\;}\quad D. \tag{5.3}
\end{aligned}
$$

Equation (5.3) holds since W, P, R, S are properly selected to ensure Eq. (5.1). Then

$$
\begin{aligned}
Z \quad &=\quad QD \bmod R \\[2mm]
&\xrightleftharpoons{\;(5.3)\;}\quad [Q(PW + RS)] \bmod R \\[2mm]
&=\quad (QP \bmod R)(W \bmod R) + (QS \bmod R)(R \bmod R) \\[2mm]
&\xrightleftharpoons{\;(3.5);(2.7)\;}\quad (1,0) \times W + (QS \bmod R) \times 0 = W. \tag{5.4}
\end{aligned}
$$

Finally, the latter equality in (5.4) holds since W is a primary residue modulo R (2.5)–(2.7), i.e., because $W \bmod R = W$. $\square$

Proposition 5.2. If

- absolute value of every component of private keys P and R is larger than threshold parameter $u = \sqrt{n/6}$ and does not exceed $2u$,
- each component of plaintext W is positive and does not exceed u, and
- absolute value of each component in secret control S does not exceed u,

then the encryption/decryption cryptosystem (4.2)–(4.4) provides unambiguous results.

6. Cryptosystem Design

Inputs m_1 and m_2 are independent variables known only to the sender (Sam). There are two types of variables: long-term static system parameters (strategic variables) and short-term dynamic controls (tactical variables):

System parameter n,

Strategic variables P and R,

Dynamic controls S, and

Observable inputs: $W(w_1 > w_2)$.

Here it is assumed that plaintext (w_1, w_2) is already preconditioned (more details are provided below).

In addition, every W must be a primary residue for the receiver, i.e., W and modulus R for every user must satisfy the following system of inequalities with eight integer variables:

$$0 \le w_1 \le u \le r_1, \quad 0 \le w_2 \le u \le |r_2|, \tag{6.1}$$

$$0 \le r_1 w_2 + |r_2| w_1, \quad r_1 w_2 + |r_2| w_1 < r_1^2 + r_2^2, \tag{6.2}$$

$$|r_2| w_2 \le r_1 w_1, \quad r_1 w_1 < r_1^2 + r_2^2 + |r_2| w_2. \tag{6.3}$$

(6.1)–(6.3) are conditions that ensure that W is a primary residue modulo R.

If $s_1 < 0$ and $p_2 < 0$, then controls S and private key P must satisfy constraints:

$$0 \le p_1 w_1 - r_1 |s_1| + |p_2| w_2 + |r_2| s_2, \tag{6.4}$$

$$p_1 w_1 - r_1 |s_1| + |p_2| w_2 + |r_2| s_2 \le n, \tag{6.5}$$

$$0 \le p_1 w_2 - |p_2| w_1 + r_1 s_2 + |r_2| |s_1|, \tag{6.6}$$

$$p_1 w_2 - |p_2| w_1 + r_1 s_2 + |r_2| |s_1| \le n. \tag{6.7}$$

If (6.4)–(6.7) hold, then (5.1) also holds.

7. Equalizing the Feasibility Intervals

Notice that at most three terms in (6.5) and (6.7) are positive. Hence, if every product does not exceed $n/3$, then the sum of three terms does not exceed n.

Let

$$0 < w_k \leq u, \quad |s_k| \leq u, \quad u \leq |p_k| \leq v, \quad u \leq |r_k| \leq v, \qquad (7.1)$$

where u and v are unknown real numbers. Hence

$$PC \leq 3uv \leq n, \quad \text{i.e., } uv \leq n/3. \qquad (7.2)$$

Select such u and v that the lengths of feasibility intervals for private keys P and R, secret key S and plaintext W are equal. Hence, $u = v - u$, which implies $2u = v$.

Thus,

$$2u^2 \leq n/3, \qquad (7.3)$$

hence

$$u \leq \sqrt{n/6} \quad \text{and} \quad v \leq \sqrt{2n/3}. \qquad (7.4)$$

Therefore, the following inequalities must hold:

$$0 < w_k \leq \sqrt{n/6}, \quad |s_k| \leq \sqrt{n/6}, \quad \sqrt{n/6} \leq |p_k| \leq \sqrt{2n/3},$$
$$\sqrt{n/6} \leq |r_k| \leq \sqrt{2n/3}. \qquad (7.5)$$

Notice that Sam (the sender)

- Knows input w_1 and w_2,
- Does not know P and R of Rene (the receiver's private keys),
- Dynamically selects controls s_1 and s_2.

Corollary 7.1. If $|p_i|w_j \leq n/3$ and $|r_k|s_l \leq n/3$, the value of each component in W and S is smaller than $\sqrt{n/6}$, p_1, $|p_2|$, r_1 and $|r_2|$ are on interval $[\sqrt{n/6}, \sqrt{2n/3}]$, then it ensures that W is a primary residue and that $(PW + RS) \bmod n = PW + RS$ (5.1).

Remark 7.2. By analogy with (6.1)–(6.3), (5.1) means that $PW + RS$ is a "primary residue" modulo n.

8. Plaintext Preconditioning and Recovery

Plaintext preconditioning: Compute

$$w_1 := m_1 + m_2, \qquad (8.1)$$

if $m_1 \geq m_2$, then

$$w_2 := m_1 - m_2 \quad \text{else } w_2 := m_2 - m_1 - 1. \tag{8.2}$$

Plaintext recovery: After decryption, the receiver compares parities of w_1 and w_2:

if $w_1 \equiv w_2 \pmod{2}$,

   then $m_1 := (w_1 + w_2)/2 \quad \text{and} \quad m_2 := w_1 - m_1,$ (8.3)

   else $m_1 := (w_1 - w_2 - 1)/2 \quad \text{and} \quad m_2 := w_1 - m_1 = (w_1 + w_2 + 1)/2.$

$$\tag{8.4}$$

9. Numeric Illustrations

Let $n = 10006001$, the user's private keys P, Q, R and public key U are listed in Table 9.1. Here $\|P\| = \|(2291, -2180)\| = 10001081$, P is a primary residue modulo R, $\|R\| = 10006109$; and feasibility threshold parameters are equal to $u = \sqrt{n/6} = 1291$ and $v := 2u = \sqrt{2n/3} = 2582$. In Table 9.2, every block of plaintext W is primary residue of R, and the following constraints are satisfied: $0 < |s_1| < s_2 \leq \sqrt{n/6}$, $0 < w_2 \leq w_1 \leq \sqrt{n/6}$.

Notice that for each of five blocks W we considered different secret controls S.

Table 9.1   Public keys (n-real, U-Gaussian) and private keys (P, Q, R-all Gaussian).

R Private key	P Private key	$Q = P^{-1} \pmod{R}$ Private key	$U = FR \bmod n$ Private key
$R = (2270, -2203)$	$P = (2291, -2180)$	$Q = (2858, 421)$	$U = (7624492, 258305)$

Table 9.2   Encryption/Decryption: $n = 10006001$, $0 \leq W \leq 1291$, $0 \leq |S| \leq 1291$.

$W = (w_1, w_2)$	$S = (s_1, s_2)$	$C = (W + SU) \bmod n$	$D = PC \bmod n$	$Z = QD \bmod R$	Plaintext M Recovered
$(1223, 973)$	$(-859, 949)$	$(9511830, 9559186)$	$(5063750, 3609610)$	$(1223, 973)$	$(1098, 125)$
$(959, 941)$	$(-999, 1234)$	$(9149875, 5092460)$	$(4699221, 5067188)$	$(959, 941)$	$(950, 9)$
$(1234, 95)$	$(-954, 1285)$	$(8880702, 5324391)$	$(3699469, 2546137)$	$(1234, 95)$	$(569, 665)$
$(1267, 1201)$	$(-999, 1234)$	$(9150183, 5092720)$	$(5971649, 4991408)$	$(1267, 1201)$	$(1234, 33)$
$(18, 17)$	$(-16, 1291)$	$(4812437, 3187326)$	$(2886051, 2965525)$	$(18, 17)$	$(0, 18)$

10. Algorithm for Multiplicative Inverse of P modulo Complex R

This algorithm computes

$$Q = P^{-1} \pmod{R}, \quad \text{where } R = (p, q). \tag{10.1}$$

If R is a Gaussian prime, then

$$Q = P^{N-2} \pmod{R}, \quad \text{where } N = \|R\| \ (2.1). \tag{10.2}$$

If $R = R_1 R_2$, where each factor in R is a Gaussian prime, then

$$Q = P^{\varphi(N)-1} \bmod R, \tag{10.3}$$

where $\varphi(N)$ is Euler totient function and

$$N = \|R\| = \|R_1\| \times \|R_2\|. \tag{10.4}$$

Computation (10.2) and (10.3) of multiplicative inverse (10.1) is based on the following cyclic identity.

Proposition 10.1. If $\gcd[(a, b), (p, q)] = (1, 0)$, then the following identity holds:

$$(a, b)^{\varphi(\|(p,q)\|)-1} \equiv (a, b)^{-1} \pmod{(p, q)}. \tag{10.5}$$

Proof follows from identity

$$(a, b)^{\varphi(\|(p,q)\|)} \bmod (p, q) = (1, 0) \quad \text{(Verkhovsky, 2011a)}. \tag{10.6}$$

Example 10.2. Suppose $R = (9, -2)$ and $P = (3, 2)$, then $N = \|(9, -2)\| = 85$ and $\varphi(85) = 64$.
Hence,

$$Q = P^{-1} \pmod{R} = (3, 2)^{63} \bmod (9, -2) = (4, 7).$$

Indeed,

$$(3, 2)(4, 7) = (1, 0) \pmod{R}.$$

Remark 10.3. Although in (10.2) and then in Example 10.2 we use exponentiation in order to compute multiplicative inverse of P modulo R, it is *performed only once* on the system design level, not on the operational level in the process of encryption and decryption.

Proposition 10.4. The inverse (x, y) of (a, b) modulo (p, q) can be also computed as

$$(x, y) := (a, -b)N^{-1}(a, b), \tag{10.7}$$

where

$$N^{-1}(a, b) := (a^2 + b^2)^{-1} \pmod{(p, q)}. \tag{10.8}$$

Particularly, if $(a, b) = (p_1, p_2) = P$, then

$$P^{-1} = (p_1, -p_2)\|P\|^{-1} \pmod{(p, q)}. \tag{10.9}$$

Computation of the multiplicative inverse (w, z) of real integer c modulo complex (p, q), [see (10.9)], can be performed taking into account that

$$c \times (w, z) \bmod (p, q) = (1, 0). \tag{10.10}$$

Remark 10.5. Let $R = (p, q)$ and $G = (a, b)$, then Sec. 2.1 implies that

$$G \bmod R = \{(a, b), (a - p, b - q), (a + q, b - p), (a - p + q, b - p - q)\}. \tag{10.11}$$

Remark 10.6. Recall that $(1, 0)$ is primary residue modulo (p, q) only if $pq < 0$.

Proposition 10.7. If the inverse (w, z) of a real integer c exists, then there exists an integer m such that holds

(a) either

$$(cw, cz) = [(1, 0) + m(p, q)] = (1 + mp, mq) \pmod{(p, q)}, \tag{10.12}$$

(b) or

$$(cw, cz) = [(1, 0) + m(q, -p)] = (1 + mq, -mp) \pmod{(p, q)}, \tag{10.13}$$

(c) or

$$(cw, cz) = [(1, 0) + m(-p + q, -p - q)]$$
$$= (1 - mp + mq, -mp - mq) \pmod{(p, q)}, \tag{10.14}$$

which imply that either

$$cw = 1 + pm \quad \text{and} \quad cz = qm, \tag{10.15}$$

or

$$cw = 1 + mq, \quad \text{and} \quad cz = -mp, \tag{10.16}$$

or

$$cw = 1 - mp + mq, \quad \text{and} \quad cz = -mp - mq. \tag{10.17}$$

Here we need to solve three systems (10.15)–(10.17) of two Diophantine equations each with inputs c, p and q, and three integer unknowns w, z and m.

Since (10.15) implies that $pqm = cqw - q = cpz$, therefore, we need to solve a Diophantine equation

$$cqw - cpz = q. \tag{10.18}$$

Analogously, (10.16) and (10.17) imply that we need to solve either

$$cpw + cqz = p, \tag{10.19}$$

or

$$cw + cz = 1 - 2mp \quad \text{and} \quad cw - cz = 1 + 2mq. \tag{10.20}$$

The latter yields to

$$cp(w - z) + cq(w + z) = p + q. \tag{10.21}$$

Therefore, the double moduli algorithm proposed in this chapter does not require any exponentiations even on the design level.

Example 10.8. Consider a complex prime modulo $(p, q) = (3, -2)$ and $c = 2$.

Then the multiplicative inverse (w, z) of c modulo $(3, -2)$ is equal to $(w, z) = (2, -1)$.

Indeed, $(2, 0)(2, -1) \bmod (3, -2) = (1, 0)$. Hence, from (10.15) $2 \times 2 + 3m = 1$ and $-2 \times 1 - 2m = 0$, which means that $m = -1$.

Consider now a table of MMI modulo $(11, -4)$ for $c = 2, 3, \ldots, 10$ (see Table 10.1).

Exercise 10.9. Consider $c = 7$ and $(p, q) = (11, -4)$. Verify that, if $(13, 6)$ is the MMI of 7, then there exists an integer m that satisfies either (10.15) or (10.16) or (10.17). Find this m. The solution is illustrated in Table 10.1.

Table 10.1 $(p, q) = (11, -4)$.

c	2	3	4	5	6	7	8	9	10
$c^{-1} \bmod (p, q)$	$(6, -2)$	$(9, 1)$	$(3, -1)$	$(7, 5)$	$(12, 4)$	$(13, 6)$	$(9, 3)$	$(13, 5)$	$(11, 6)$

11. Computational Complexity

Encryption of each W requires three multiplications and five additions of real integers. Decryption requires twice as many of these operations. Since additions/subtractions are much faster than multiplications, they can be neglected. Therefore, we need nine multiplication of $\log(\sqrt{n}/2)$-digit long integers, which means that bit-wise complexity is of order $O(\log^2 n)$. This complexity can be reduced if we apply more elaborate algorithms for multiplication of multi-digit long real integers (Toom, 1963; Bernstein, 2008).

12. Concluding Remarks

In this chapter, we considered and analyzed an encryption-decryption algorithm based on real and complex modulo reductions. A concept of primary residues was introduced to avoid ambiguity in information recovery. Several numeric illustrations explained step-by-step how to pre-condition a plaintext, how to select public and private keys for every user, and how to select secret controls for every block of the plaintext in order to ensure unambiguous recovery of the initial information. The proposed cryptosystem requires a small number of multiplications and additions, and does *not* require exponentiations on *operational levels* of encryption and decryption. As a result, it is extremely fast.

Although certain steps in the proposed cryptosystem resemble the NTRU cryptosystem, yet it differs from the NTRU in several features. One of them is the absence of polynomials.

Koblitz and Menezes (2004) provided a brief history on the NTRU, which is reiterated below. The NTRU that was initially presented at *Crypto'96*, was cryptanalyzed and broken in Coppersmith and Shamir (1997), by the method of lattice-basis reduction (Lenstra *et al.*, 1982) that determines short vectors in a lattice, which arise on the decryption stage. Soon after that Jaulmes and Joux (2000) and Howgrave-Graham *et al.* (2003) described two other successful attempts to break the NTRU. An NTRU signature scheme was proposed in Hoffstein *et al.* (2001), but that scheme and its revision were broken in Gentry *et al.* (2001) and Gentry and Szydlo (2002).

Chapter 11

Cryptocol Based on Three-Dimensional Elliptic Surface

1. Introduction and Basic Concepts

In this chapter, we consider three-dimensional elliptic modular equations {with three variables}, discuss their basic properties and describe a cryptographic algorithm based on these properties.

Definition 1.1. A modular Diophantine equation

$$y^2 + ay = x^3 + bz^3 + c(\text{mod } p), \qquad (1.1)$$

is called a *three-dimensional elliptic surface* (TDES), if $a^2 + 4c$ is a quadratic non-residue modulo p, i.e., if

$$(a^2 + 4c)^{(p-1)/2} \text{ mod } p = -1. \qquad (1.2)$$

Remark 1.2. Condition (1.2) implies that the eq.

$$y^2 + ay - c = 0(\text{mod } p) \qquad (1.3)$$

does not have real roots. If $a = 0$, then (1.1) is the TDES, if c is a quadratic non-residue modulo p (1.2).

The table below provides combinations of p, a and c, for which the modular Eq. (1.1) is or is not the TDES.

Table 1.1   Examples of TDES.

p, a, c	5, 2, 1	5, 1, 2	7, 1, 1	11, 1, 1	11, 2, 1	13, 1, 1	17, 1, 1	19, 1, 1	19, 2, 1	23, 1, 1
QNR?	Yes	*No*	Yes	*No*	Yes	Yes	Yes	*No*	Yes	Yes

Consider the elliptic curve (EC)

$$y^2 + ay = u^3 + c(\text{mod } p), \qquad (1.4)$$

where

$$u^3 = x^3 + bz^3(\text{mod } p). \qquad (1.5)$$

Remark 1.3. For the sake of simplicity, we consider

$$u^3 = x^3 + z^3(\text{mod } p), \qquad (1.6)$$

otherwise for every integer b that has a cubic root modulo p, we can substitute $z := \pm \sqrt[3]{b}z$.

Conditions of the cubic root existence and the algorithm for its extraction are considered below in the sec. 7 of this chapter.

Addition of points on the cubic surface (1.4)–(1.5) is defined by the following rule.

Suppose that $P = (x_1, y_1, z_1)$ and $Q = (x_2, y_2, z_2)$ are two points on the TDES (1.1).

Let us define $R := P + Q$ on the EC (1.4) as follows

$$(x_3, u_3) = (x_1, u_1) + (x_2, u_2). \qquad (1.7)$$

Since by (1.6)

$$u_1^3 = x_1^3 + z_1^3(\text{mod} p), \quad \text{and} \quad u_2^3 = x_2^3 + z_2^3(\text{mod} p), \qquad (1.8)$$

we can compute y_3 and u_3 by (1.4).

2. Computation of y_3 and u_3

Input: (x_1, y_1, z_1) and (x_2, y_2, z_2).

Step 2.1. {Computation of u_1 and u_2, (1.6)}:

for $k = 1, 2$

$$w_k := x_k^3 + z_k^3 \bmod p, \qquad (2.1)$$

$$u_k := \sqrt[3]{w_k} \bmod p. \qquad (2.2)$$

Remark 2.2. More details about extractors of cubic roots of w modulo prime p are provided in sec. 7 of this chapter.

Step 2.3. {Computation of a slope λ of the straight line containing P and Q}:

$$\text{If } P \neq \pm Q, \text{ then } \lambda := (y_1 - y_2)/(u_1 - u_2) \bmod p, \qquad (2.3)$$

$$\text{else } \lambda := (3u_1^2 + c)/(2y_1 + a) \bmod p, \qquad (2.4)$$

$$(\text{Menezes } et \ al. \ 1997).$$

Remark 2.4. In order to compute the slope in (2.3) or (2.4), we need to perform a cubic extraction in (2.2).

Step 2.5. Compute

$$u_3 = \lambda^2 - u_1 - u_2, \tag{2.5}$$

Step 2.6. Compute

$$y_3 = y_1 - \lambda(u_1 - u_3) \bmod p. \tag{2.6}$$

3. Computation of x_3 and z_3

Since for $k = 1, 2, 3$: hold the eqs.

$$u_k^3 = x_k^3 + z_k^3 = (x_k + z_k)(x_k^2 - x_k z_k + x_k^2) \bmod p. \tag{3.1}$$

consider the following three eqs. (3.1) for $k = 1, 2, 3$:

$$u_1^3 = x_1^3 + z_1^3 = (x_1 + z_1)(x_1^2 - x_1 z_1 + x_1^2) \bmod p,$$
$$u_2^3 = x_2^3 + z_2^3 = (x_2 + z_2)(x_2^2 - x_2 z_2 + x_2^2) \bmod p,$$
$$x_3^3 + z_3^3 = u_3^3 = (x_3 + z_3)(x_3^2 - x_3 z_3 + x_3^2) \bmod p,$$

and their product:

$$u_1^3 u_2^3 (x_3^3 + z_3^3) = u_1^3 u_2^3 (x_3 + z_3)(x_3^2 - x_3 z_3 + z_3^2)$$
$$= u_3^3 (x_1 + z_1)(x_2 + z_2)(x_1^2 - x_1 z_1 + z_1^2)(x_2^2 - x_2 z_2 + z_2^2)$$
$$= u_3^3 (x_1^3 + z_1^3)(x_2^3 + z_2^3)(\bmod p). \tag{3.2}$$

Thereforo,

$$x_3^3 + z_3^3 = [(x_1 + z_1)(x_2 + z_2)(u_1 u_2)^{-1} u_3]$$
$$\times [(x_1^2 - x_1 z_1 + z_1^2)(x_2^2 - x_2 z_2 + z_2^2)(u_1 u_2)^{-2} u_3^2](\bmod p).$$

Step 3.1. Assign

$$q := (u_1 u_2)^{-1} u_3 \bmod p, \tag{3.3}$$

Step 3.2.

$$r := (x_1 + z_1)(x_2 + z_2)q = (x_1 + z_1)(x_2 + z_2)(u_1 u_2)^{-1} u_3 \bmod p, \tag{3.4}$$

Step 3.3.

$$s := (x_1^2 - x_1 z_1 + z_1^2)(x_2^2 - x_2 z_2 + z_2^2)q^2$$
$$= (x_1^2 - x_1 z_1 + z_1^2)(x_2^2 - x_2 z_2 + z_2^2)(u_1 u_2)^{-2} u_3^2 \bmod p, \tag{3.5}$$

Thus,

$$x_3^3 + z_3^3 = (x_3 + z_3)(x_3^2 - x_3 z_3 + z_3^2) = rs \pmod{p}. \tag{3.6}$$

4. Solution of System of Equations

Let us consider

$$x_3 + z_3 = r \bmod p, \quad x_3^2 - x_3 z_3 + z_3^2 = s \bmod p. \tag{4.1}$$

Then

$$x_3^2 + 2x_3 z_3 + z_3^2 = r^2 \bmod p \quad \text{and} \quad x_3 z_3 = t := (r^2 - s)/3 \bmod p. \tag{4.2}$$

Hence, from Vieta theorem

$$x_{31} = -r/2 + \sqrt{r^2/4 - t} \pmod{p} \quad \text{and} \quad z_{31} = -r/2 - \sqrt{r^2/4 - t} \pmod{p}, \tag{4.3}$$

or

$$x_{32} = -r/2 - \sqrt{r^2/4 - t} \pmod{p} \quad \text{and} \quad z_{32} = -r/2 + \sqrt{r^2/4 - t} \pmod{p}. \tag{4.4}$$

5. Addition of Points on TDES: Numeric Illustration

Let us consider

$$y^2 + y = x^3 - z^3 + 1 \pmod{23}. \tag{5.1}$$

Remark 5.1. Notice that, if $p \bmod 18 = 5$, then for every *fixed* z, $\#E = p$. Here are seventeen examples of points on the elliptic surface (5.1):

$$\{(8,5,0), (1,1,0), (6,7,0), (5,7,1), (\boldsymbol{8,2,1}), (\boldsymbol{6,1,2}),$$
$$(5,8,2), (5,5,3), (8,8,3), (0,4,3), (0,2,4), (3,7,4),$$
$$(8,4,5), (9,5,5), (5,1,6), (3,6,6), (8,9,6)\}.$$

Let $P = (x_1, y_1, z_1) = (8,2,1)$ and $Q = (x_2, y_2, z_2) = (6,1,2)$.

Computation of w_1 and w_2:

$$w_1 := x_1^3 - z_1^3 = (512 - 1) \bmod 23 = 5,$$
$$w_2 := x_2^3 - z_2^3 = (216 - 8) \bmod 23 = 1.$$

Extraction of cubic roots:

$$u_1 := \sqrt[3]{w_1} = \sqrt[3]{5} \bmod p = 5^{(23^2+2)/9 \bmod 22} = 5^{15} \bmod 23 = 19,$$
$$u_2 := \sqrt[3]{w_2} = \sqrt[3]{1} \bmod p = 1.$$

Computation of slope λ:
　If $P \neq \pm Q$, then

$$\lambda := (y_1 - y_2)/(u_1 - u_2) = (2 - 1)/(19 - 1) \bmod 23 = 9.$$

Computation of u_3 and y_3:

$$u_3 = \lambda^2 - u_1 - u_2 = (81 - 19 - 1) \bmod 23 = 15,$$

$$y_3 = y_1 - \lambda(u_1 - u_3) = 2 - 9 \times (19 - 15) = 2 - 36 \bmod 23 = 12.$$

Computation of q:

$$q := (u_1 u_2)^{-1} u_3 \bmod p = 19^{-1} \times 15 = 17 \times 15 \bmod 23 = 2. \qquad (5.2)$$

Computation of r and s:

$$r := (x_1 - z_1)(x_2 - z_2)q \bmod p$$
$$= (8 - 1)(6 - 2) \times 2 = 7 \times 4 \times 2 (\bmod 23) = 10, \qquad (5.3)$$
$$s := (x_1^2 + x_1 z_1 + z_1^2)(x_2^2 + x_2 z_2 + z_2^2)q^2$$
$$= (64 + 8 + 1)(36 + 12 + 4) \times 4 (\bmod 23) = 4 \qquad (5.4)$$

Computation of x_3 and z_3:
　The first solution:

$$x_3 := (r + qt)/2 = (10 + 2 \times 1)/2 = 6,$$
$$z_3 := (r - qt)/2 = (10 - 2 \times 1)/2 = 4.$$

　The second solution:

$$x_3 := (r - qt)/2 = (10 - 2 \times 1)/2 = 4,$$
$$z_3 := (r + qt)/2 = (10 + 2 \times 1)/2 = 6.$$

By substitution into the eq. (5.1), we determine the correct solution.

Output:

$$R = (x_3, y_3, z_3) = (6, 12, 4).$$

6. Alternative for Decomposition

Consider

$$x_3^3 + z_3^3 = [(x_1 + z_1)(x_2^2 - x_2 z_2 + z_2^2)(u_1 u_2)^{-1} u_3^2]$$
$$\times [(x_1^2 - x_1 z_1 + z_1^2)(x_2 + z_2)(u_1 u_2)^{-2} u_3] (\bmod p).$$

$$r := (x_1 + z_1)(x_2^2 - x_2 z_2 + z_2^2)(u_1 u_2)^{-1} u_3^2 \bmod p, \qquad (6.1)$$

$$s := (x_1^2 - x_1 z_1 + z_1^2)(x_2 + z_2)(u_1 u_2)^{-2} u_3 \bmod p. \qquad (6.2)$$

Therefore,

$$x_3^3 + z_3^3 = (x_3 + z_3)(x_3^2 - x_3 z_3 + z_3^2) = rs (\bmod p). \qquad (6.3)$$

7. Extraction of Cubic Roots

Let

$$w_k := x_k^3 + z_k^3 \bmod p, \qquad (7.1)$$

then (1.6) implies that for $k = 1, 2$

$$u_k := \sqrt[3]{w_k} \bmod p. \qquad (7.2)$$

For our purpose we need an efficient algorithm that computes a cubic root of the integer w modulo prime p, for every w that is co-prime with p. Although such algorithms are presented in Adleman *et al.* (1977), Nishihara *et al.* (2009) and Cao *et al.* (2011), in this section we provide several algorithms that are substantially simpler.

If

$$p \bmod 3 = 2, \qquad (7.3)$$

then the cubic root (7.2) exists for every w_k and it is unique.

If $p \bmod 9 = 7$ or $p \bmod 9 = 4$, then the cubic root (7.2) does *not* exist for every w_k. However, if it does exist, then there are two other roots that satisfy (1.6).

7.1. *Cubic root extractor if $p \bmod 9 = 5$*

Proposition 7.1. If p is a prime, $p \bmod 9 = 5$, and w is co-prime with p, then

$$u = w^{(p^2+2)/9} \bmod p, \qquad (7.4)$$

is a cubic root of (7.1) for every w.

Proof. First of all, $(p^2 + 2)/9$ is an integer. Indeed, let $p = 9k + h$, then $(p^2 + 2)/9 = 9k^2 + 2kh + (h^2 + 2)/9$, therefore, $9 | p^2 + 2$ if $9 | h^2 + 2$.

Hence, if $h = 5$, then $h^2 + 2 = 27$, i.e., $(p^2 + 2)/9$ is an integer.

On the other hand, (7.4) implies that

$$u^3 = \{w^{(p^2-1)/3} \times w\} \bmod p. \qquad (7.5)$$

Table 7.1 Cubic roots w of u modulo p $\{u^3 \bmod p = w\}$ where $p \bmod 9 = 5$.

p, w	$P = 5,$ $w = 2$	$P = 23,$ $w = 3$	$P = 23,$ $w = 5$	$P = 41,$ $w = 2$	$P = 41,$ $w = 3$	$P = 41,$ $w = 5$
Cubic root	$u = 3$	$u = 12$	$u = 19$	$u = 5$	$u = 27$	$u = 20$
Verification	$u^3 = 2$	$u^3 = 3$	$u^3 = 5$	$u^3 = 2$	$u^3 = 3$	$u^3 = 5$

Since $3|(p+1)$, then by Fermat Little theorem

$$w^{(p^2-1)/3} = [w^{(p+1)/3}]^{p-1} \bmod p = 1. \qquad (7.6)$$

Therefore,

$$u^3 = w^{(p^2-1)/3} \times w = w \bmod p. \quad \text{quod erat demonstrandum (QED)} \qquad (7.7)$$

□

Several examples of taking the cubic root for the case when $p \bmod 9 = 5$ are illustrated in Table 7.1.

Remark 7.2. To simplify the exponentiation in (7.4), consider modular reduction in the exponent

$$u = w^{[(p^2+2)/9] \bmod (p-1)} \bmod p. \qquad (7.8)$$

Example 7.3. Let $p = 23$, $w = 7$, then

$$u := 7^{(23^2+2)/9 \bmod 22} = 7^{15}(\bmod 23) = 14.$$

Indeed, $14^3 \bmod 23 = 7$.

7.2. *Cubic root extractor if $p \bmod 9 = 2$*

Proposition 7.4. If p is a prime, $p \bmod 9 = 2$, then

$$u = w^{(2p^2+1)/9} \bmod p, \qquad (7.9)$$

is a cubic root of (7.1) for every w is co-prime with p.

Proof. First of all, $(2p^2 + 1)/9$ is an integer. Indeed, let $p = 9k + h$.

Then $(2p^2 + 1)/9 = 18k^2 + 4kh + (2h^2 + 1)/9$, therefore, $9|2p^2 + 1$ if $9|2h^2 + 1$.

Hence, if $h = 2$, then $2h^2 + 1 = 9$, i.e., $(2p^2 + 1)/9$ is an integer.

On the other hand, (7.4) implies that

$$u^3 = \{w^{2(p^2-1)/3} \times w\} \bmod p. \qquad (7.10)$$

Since $3|(p+1)$, then by Fermat Little theorem

$$w^{(p^2-1)/3} = [w^{2(p+1)/3}]^{p-1} \bmod p = 1. \qquad (7.11)$$

Therefore,

$$u^3 = w^{2(p^2-1)/3} \times w = 1 \times w = w \bmod p. \quad \text{QED} \tag{7.12}$$

$\square$

Remark 7.5. To simplify the exponentiation in (7.4), consider

$$u = w^{[2(p^2-1)/9] \bmod (p-1)} \bmod p. \tag{7.13}$$

Remark 7.6. Notice that if n is *odd*, then for every p

1) $$\sqrt[n]{p-1} \bmod p = p - 1.$$

2) and for every w

$$(\sqrt[n]{w} + \sqrt[n]{p-w}) \bmod p = p. \tag{7.14}$$

7.3. *Cubic root extractor if $p \bmod 9 = 4$*

Proposition 7.7. If p is a prime, $p \bmod 9 = 4$, an integer w is co-prime with p and a cubic root u of w modulo p exists, then

$$u = w^E = w^{(4p^2-1)/9}. \tag{7.15}$$

Proof. By Euler's criterion, w has a cubic root, if and only if

$$w^{(p-1)/3} \bmod p = 1. \tag{7.16}$$

Therefore,

$$u^3 = w^{(4p^2-1)/3} = w \times w^{4(p^2-1)/3} = w \times [w^{(p-1)/3}]^{4(p+1)}$$

$$= w \times 1 \bmod p = w. \tag{7.17}$$

$\square$

7.4. *Cubic root extractor if $p \bmod 9 = r$*

Here we consider three cases: $r = \{2, 5\}$, $r = \{4, 7\}$, and $r = 8$.

Proposition 7.8. If p is a prime, $p \bmod 9 = r = \{2, 5\}$, and an integer w is co-prime with p,

then

$$u = w^E = w^{(mp^2+3-m)/9} \bmod p, \tag{7.18}$$

where

$$m = 2 \text{ or } m = 5 \quad \text{if } r = 2, \tag{7.19}$$

and

$$m = 1 \text{ or } m = 4 \quad \text{if } r = 5. \tag{7.20}$$

Proposition 7.9. If p is a prime, $p \bmod 9 = r = \{4, 7\}$, an integer w is co-prime with p and a cubic root u of w modulo p exists, then

$$u = w^E = w^{(mp^2 + 3 - m)/9} \bmod p, \tag{7.21}$$

where

$$m = 1 \text{ or } m = 4, \quad \text{if } r = 4, \text{ and } m = 2 \text{ or } m = 5, \quad \text{if } r = 7. \tag{7.22}$$

Proof. By Euler's criterion, w has a cubic root u modulo prime p, if and only if

$$w^{(p-1)/3} \bmod p = 1, \tag{7.23}$$

otherwise

$$|w^{(p-1)/3} \bmod p| \neq 1.$$

Consider

$$u = w^E = w \times w^{m(p-1)(p+1)/9} (\bmod \ p), \quad (7.21), \tag{7.24}$$

and

$$u^3 = w \times w^{m(p^2-1)/3} = w^{(mp^2-m+3)/3}$$
$$= w^{[(mp^2-m+3)/3] \bmod (p-1)} (\bmod \ p), \tag{7.25}$$

where E in (7.21) is an integer.

Let $p = 9k + r$, then u is a cubic root of w, if and only if

$$w^{m(p-1)(p+1)/3} \bmod p = 1. \tag{7.26}$$

$\square$

Remark 7.10. Notice that r is an input and m is a control variable.

The condition (7.26) holds if either $(p + 1)/3$ is an integer, {i.e., if $p \bmod 9 = 2$ or 5}, or if $(p - 1)/3$ is an integer, {i.e., if $p \bmod 9 = 4, 7$} and (7.23) holds.

Since $E = m(9k^2 + 2kr) + D$, where $D := [m(r^2 - 1) + 3]/9$, then D is an integer, if (7.22) holds.

Remark 7.11. If $r = 2$ or $r = 5$, then every w co-prime with p has a cubic root u. In these cases $(p + 1)/3$ is an integer, if either $m = 1$ and $r = 5$, or if $m = 2$ and $r = 2$, or if $m = 4$ and $r = 5$, or if $m = 5$ and $r = 2$.

Example 7.12. Let $p = 61$, since Euler's criterion holds for $w = 8$, then the cubic root of w exists. Because $61 \bmod 9 = 7$, then the cubic extractor

$$E = (2p^2 + 1)/9 \bmod 60 = 47, \quad (7.22).$$

Therefore, $u = 8^{827 \bmod 60} \bmod 61 = 33$. Indeed, $33^3 \bmod 61 = 8$.

7.5. *Cubic extractor if p* mod 9 = 8

In this case, the search for the cubic extractor requires a more elaborate approach.

Proposition 7.13. Let p mod $9 = 8$, then for every w such that $\gcd(w, p) = 1$, the cubic root exists and it is unique.

Proof. Let us consider the cubic extractor

$$E := M/9 = (ap^3 + bp^2 + cp + d)/9. \tag{7.27}$$

Hence,

$$u^3 = w^{(ap^3 + bp^2 + cp + d)/3} = w \times w^{(fp^2 + gp + h)(p-1)/3} (\bmod p). \tag{7.28}$$

Here the coefficients a, b, c, d, f, g and h are subjects of the forthcoming analysis.

First of all, these coefficients must be selected in such a way that both E and

$$L := (fp^2 + gp + h)/3 \tag{7.29}$$

are integers. From substitution of $p = 9k + 8$ into L and E, we respectively derive that

$$[f(p \bmod 3)^2 + g(p \bmod 3) + h)] = (f + 2g + h)(\bmod 3) = 0. \tag{7.30}$$

and

$$[a(p \bmod 9)^3 + b(p \bmod 9)^2 + c(p \bmod 9) + d]$$
$$= (8a + b + 8c + d)(\bmod 9). \tag{7.31}$$

On the other hand, (7.28) implies that

$$u^3 = w^{[(fp^2 + gp + h)(p-1)+1]/3} = w \times w^{[(fp^2 + gp + h)(p-1)]/3}. \tag{7.32}$$

Therefore,

$$ap^3 + bp^2 + cp + d = (fp^2 + gp + h)(p - 1) + 3. \tag{7.33}$$

Hence,

$$a = f, \quad b = g - f, \quad c = h - g, \quad d = 3 - h.$$

Thus,

$$E = [fp^3 + (g - f)p^2 + (h - g)p + 3 - h]/9. \tag{7.34}$$

From (7.31)

$$M = [8f + (g - f) + 8(h - g) + 3 - h]/9 = [7(f - g + h) + 3)]/9.$$

For instance, if $f - g + h = 6, 15, 24, 33, 42, 51, 60, \ldots$, then every M is an integer, and from (7.30), if $f + 2g + h = 3, 6, 9, 12, 15, 18, 21, \ldots$, then $(fp^2 + gp + h)/3$ is also an integer.

Select $g = 1$ and $f + h = 7$, for instance, let $f = 3$ and $h = 4$. Then $f + h - g = 6$ and $f + h + 2g = 9$.

Finally, to simplify the computation, apply the FLT for modulo reduction in the exponent

$$u = w^E = [w^{E \bmod (p-1)}] \bmod p. \tag{7.35}$$

$\square$

7.6. *Alternative algorithms for cubic root extraction if $p \bmod 9 = 8$*

Let us select the cubic root extractors in such a way that either

$$V_1 := u^2 = w^{3E} = w^2 w^{(3E-6)/3} = w^2 \bmod p,$$

or

$$V_2 := u^{-1} = w^{3E} = w^{-1} w^{(3E+3)/3} = w^{-1} \bmod p.$$

If $p \bmod 9 = 8$ and $p \bmod 4 = 3$ {for instance, $p = 71, 107, 179$}, then V_1 is the square of u and the square root of V_1 is easy computable since p is a Blum prime.

V_2 is a modular multiplicative inverse (MMI) of u modulo p, which is also easy computable, {see the chapter 1 on the MMI algorithm}.

7.7. *MMI of 3 modulo $p - 1$ if $p \bmod 3 = 2$*

Let us consider

$$u = w^{1/3} \bmod (p - 1) = w^{3^{-1} \bmod (p-1)} \bmod p. \tag{7.36}$$

Then

$$u^3 = [w^{3^{-1} \bmod (p-1)}]^3 \bmod p = w. \tag{7.37}$$

The MMI of 3 modulo $p-1$ exists since $\gcd(3, p-1) = 1$, if $p \bmod 3 = 2$. It is easy to check that the MMI is equal $(2p - 1)/3$. Therefore,

$$u = w^{3^{-1} \bmod(p-1)} = w^{(2p-1)/3} (\bmod\ p).$$

Finally, $E = (2p - 1)/3$ is an integer, if $p \bmod 9 = 2$ or 5 or 8.

Indeed, let $p = 9k + r$, then E is an integer, if $(2p - 1) \bmod 3 = [2(9p + r) - 1] \bmod 3 = (2r - 1) \bmod 3 = 0$.

Example 7.14. Let $p = 179$, then the MMI of 3 modulo 178 is equal 119. Let $w = 5$, then $u = 5^{119} \bmod 179 = 156$. Indeed, $156^3 \bmod 179 = 5$.

8. Number of Points on TDES

The eq. (1.1) has $O(p^2)$ solutions, which is much larger than the number of solution $O(p)$ in EC. As a result, for the same level of cryptoimmunity we need smaller primes p, than for the Elliptic curve cryptography (ECC). It implies that we can substantially accelerate the speed of encryption and decryption, which is the ultimate goal of most innovations in the public key cryptography.

Example 8.1. In Koblitz–Buhler curve

$$y^2 + y \equiv x^3 + 1 (\bmod\ 11), \tag{8.1}$$

there are 11 points, but in the TDES (1.1)

$$y^2 + y = x^3 + (z^3 + 1)(\bmod\ 11),$$

there are 121 points.

If $p = 13$, then the EC (8.1) has 15 points and the corresponding TDES has 120 points.

This is the major advantage of the TDES cryptography vs. the ECC.

9. Triplet of Considerations

From mathematical point of view, we need to know how many solutions the eq. (1.1) has and provide a method to find at least one of them.

From cryptographic point of view, we need to show how these points on (1.1) can be used to assure security of communication.

From cryptanalytic point of view, for the sake of security/high crypto-immunity, we need to be sure that *all* points on the TDES are used, otherwise (in order to break the cryptographic protocol) an intruder needs to search not through the entire set of point $O(p^2)$, but through a smaller subset of it.

10. Cryptographic Protocol

1) Alice and Bob agree to select large prime p mod $36 = 23$ and a TDES, for which the right side never equals 0,
2) they select a point G on the TDES with a large order,
3) Alice and Bob select their private keys a and b {all notations of variables are local},
4) Alice and Bob compute their public keys

$$A := aG = (a_1, a_2, a_3) \bmod p \quad \text{and} \quad B := bG = (b_1, b_2, b_3) \bmod p, \tag{10.1}$$

5) let Alice intend to transmit to Bob a plain text $m = \{m_1, m_2, m_3\}$, where $0 < m_k < p$,

Encryption:

6) Alice selects a private key t and computes a secret key

$$S := tB = (s_1, s_2, s_3) \bmod p, \tag{10.2}$$

7) and a hint

$$H := tG \bmod p, \tag{10.3}$$

8) Alice computes a ciphertext

$$C := \{s_1 \times m_1, s_2 \times m_2, s_3 \times m_3\} = \{c_1, c_2, c_3\} \bmod p, \tag{10.4}$$

9) Alice sends $[C, H]$ to Bob,

Decryption {Bob decrypts the ciphertext}:

10) using his private key b and the hint H, Bob computes

$$L := bH = b(tG) \bmod p, \quad \{= S\}, \tag{10.5}$$

11) using the algorithm for MMI {see chapter 1}, Bob computes $\{s_1^{-1}, s_2^{-1}, s_3^{-1}\}$ and

$$D := \{c_1 s_1^{-1}, c_2 s_2^{-1}, c_3 s_3^{-1}\} \bmod p; \quad = \{m_1, m_2, m_3\}. \tag{10.6}$$

11. Number of Points on TDES

Conjecture 11.1. If

$$y^2 + ay = x^3 + b \bmod p; \; p \bmod 18 = 5 \text{ or } 11 \text{ or } 17, \text{ then } N = p^2$$

(illustrated in Tables 11.1–11.3).

Remark 11.2. If $a = 0$ and (x, y, z) is a point on a surface, then the $(x, \pm y, z)$ is also on this surface.

Table 11.1 $y^2 = x^3 + (1 + z^3) \bmod 5$; $b := 1 + z^3$; total # of points $N = 5^2 = 25$.

	$z=0,$ $b=1$	$z=1,$ $b=2$	$z=2,$ $b=4$	$z=3,$ $b=3$	$z=4,$ $b=0$
$x = 0$	0, 2	0, 1			0, 0
$x = 1$	1, 1		1, 0		1, 2
$x = 2$		2, 0	2, 1	2, 2	
$x = 3$			3, 2	3, 0	3, 1
$x = 4$	4, 0	4, 2		4, 1	

Table 11.2 $u^3 \equiv x^3 + z^3 \pmod 5$.

	$z=0$	$z=1$	$z=2$	$z=3$	$z=4$
$x = 0$	0	1	3	2	4
$x = 1$	1	2	4	3	0
$x = 2$	3	4	1	0	2
$x = 3$	2	3	0	4	1
$x = 4$	4	0	2	1	3

Table 11.3 $y^2 = x^3 + (1 + z^3) \bmod 11$, $b := 1 + z^3$, total # of points $N = 11^2 = 121$.

	$z=0,$ $b=1$	$z=1,$ $b=2$	$z=2,$ $b=9$	$z=3,$ $b=6$	$z=4,$ $b=10$	$z=5,$ $b=5$	$z=6,$ $b=8$	$z=7,$ $b=3$	$z=8,$ $b=7$	$z=9,$ $b=4$	$z=10,$ $b=0$
$x = 0$	0, 3	0, 1	0, 4	0, 2		0, 5					0, 0
$x = 1$	1, 1				1, 0	1, 2	1, 4		1, 5		1, 3
$x = 2$	2, 4		2, 2			2, 1		2, 0		2, 3	2, 5
$x = 3$				3, 0			3, 1	3, 5	3, 3	3, 4	
$x = 4$		4, 0			4, 5		4, 2	4, 3		4, 1	4, 4
$x = 5$		5, 2	5, 1			5, 4	5, 3		5, 0	5, 5	
$x = 6$	6, 5	6, 4		6, 1	6, 2	6, 3				6, 0	
$x = 7$			7, 0	7, 5	7, 3				7, 4	7, 2	7, 1
$x = 8$		8, 5		8, 3		8, 0		8, 4	8, 1		8, 2
$x = 9$			9, 3	9, 4	9, 1	9, 5	9, 0	9, 2			
$x = 10$	10, 0	10, 3	10, 5		10, 4			10, 1	10, 2		

Conjecture 11.3. If $y^2 + ay = x^3 + b \bmod p$, $p \bmod 18 = 1$ or 7 or 13, then $N = p(p+1)$.

Appendix

A.1. Solution of system of equations $d := x_3^3 + v_3^3 = u_3^3$

Let

$$r := x_3 + v_3, \quad s := x_3^2 - x_3 v_3 + v_3^2, \tag{A.1}$$

where $rs = d$, or $s = d/r$, (1.5).

Then $x_3^2 + 2x_3 v_3 + v_3^2 = r^2$ and, as a result,

$$x_3 v_3 = (r^2 - s)/3, \tag{A.2}$$

and

$$x_3^2 - 2x_3 v_3 + v_3^2 = s - (r^2 - s)/3 = (4s - r^2)/3. \tag{A.3}$$

Therefore,

$$x_3 - v_3 = \pm\sqrt{(4s - r^2)/3} = \pm\sqrt{(4d - r^3)/3r} = q \bmod p, \tag{A.4}$$

where

$$q := \pm\sqrt{(4d - r^3)/3r} \bmod p. \tag{A.5}$$

Select such an integer r that there exists a square root modulo p in (A.5).

In other words, q is a real integer, if and only if

$$[(4d - r^3)/3r]^{(p-1)/2} \bmod p = 1. \tag{A.6}$$

Let $x_3 - v_3 = q \bmod p$, then from (A.1),

$$x_3 = (q + r)/2 \bmod p, \quad v_3 = (q - r)/2 \bmod p. \tag{A.7}$$

Example A.1. Let $p = 23$ and $d = 15$, then $q(r) = \sqrt{(4d - r^3)/3r} \bmod p = \sqrt{(60 - r^3)/3r} \bmod 23$.

If $r = 1$, then $q(1) := \pm\sqrt{59 \times 8} = \pm\sqrt{12} = \pm 9 \pmod{23}$, i.e., because 12 is a quadratic residue modulo 23, then $q(1) = 9$ or $q(1) = 14$.

Therefore, in the latter case $x = (14 + 1)/2 \bmod 23 = 19$ and $v = (14 - 1)/2 \bmod 23 = 18$.

Verification: $(-4)^3 + (-5)^3 = -64 - 125 = -5 = 18 \pmod{23}$.

A.2. Alternative TDES

Let us consider another TDES, which we denote as TDES-2:

$$y^2 - z^2 = u^3 + au + c \pmod{p}. \tag{A.8}$$

Table A.1   Comparison of TDES-1 and TDES-2.

EC	TDES-2	TDES-1
Number of points	$P(p-1)/2$	p^2
Critical operations	square root extraction: can be a problem — does not always exist	cubic root extraction: always exists, if $p \bmod 3 = 2$
Choice of generator	Not easy to select a generator	Easy to select a generator

As we can see from the Table A.1., for large p, TDES-1 has twice more points than TDES-2. This and other considerations make the TDES-1 more suitable for cryptographic systems design than the TDES-2.

Consideration of TDES-1 was proposed by D. Kanevsky, [Kanevsky, private communication, 2009], who later provided several constructive comments.

Chapter 12

Multi-Parametric Cryptography for Rapid Transmission of Information

1. Introduction

As we demonstrate in this section, the entanglements used in the information assurance can be applied in *rapid* cryptographic exchange of sensitive information. In the description of multi-parametric algorithm and its application for secure transmission of information (MASTI) *via* open communication channels, the following features are provided:

- definition of MASTI terms,
- its major components,
- how the MASTI works {several numeric examples illustrate the algorithm},
- description of analogous mechanisms and their drawbacks,
- major advantages of MASTI,
- its possible variations.

Several apparata {called public key cryptographic schemes/protocols/ algorithms} providing secure transmission of information *via* open communication channels were published and/or patented for the last thirty five years. Their major common characteristic is that prior to secure communication, they do not require a *private* exchange of secret keys/codes/ciphers between communicating parties {traditionally called Alice and Bob}. Instead, the secret keys are established *publicly*, i.e., *via* open channels of internet, telephone, radio communication etc.

The MASTI consists of several stages that are periodically repeated until the entire file F is securely transmitted *via* open communication channels.

2. Proposed Cryptographic Algorithm

Suppose a sender (Alice) wants to securely transmit a file F {audio/voice, graphic images, text, video, etc.} to a receiver (Bob). In preparation to that Alice divides the file F onto a set of portions (blocks) $a_1, a_2, a_3, \ldots, a_i, \ldots$ and then represents each block in a numeric form $b_1, b_2, b_3, \ldots, b_i, \ldots$. Such blocks are called plaintext blocks {or plaintexts, for short}. In this chapter, we consider an encryption/decryption protocol based on solutions of sequence of systems of t linear equations (SOLE), where each SOLE has n variables:

$$h_k = N_k w_k \pmod{p}, \tag{2.1}$$

and for every $k = 1, \ldots, t$

- N_k is a $n \times n$ square matrix,
- w_k is a vector/array of n plaintext blocks,
- h_k is a vector of n encrypted blocks {called an array of ciphertext blocks or ciphertexts, for short} of transmitted information.

Prior to introduction of this protocol, it is necessary to explain several issues:

1. How Alice and Bob can secretly and efficiently exchange t matrices $N_1, N_2, \ldots, N_k, \ldots, N_t$ *via* open communication channels,
2. How they can periodically change these matrices to assure cryptoimmunity of communication,
3. How to ensure that the system of equations $N_k w_k = h_k$ has a unique solution for every $k = 1, 2, \ldots, t$,
4. How to find a computationally efficient method to solve such systems of linear equations provided that the integer solution exists.

All these issues we address in this chapter, and in some cases they are numerically illustrated.

3. Key-Exchange Mechanism (KEM)

First of all, on every stage of the protocol, the communicating parties Alice and Bob {the parties, for short} establish a secret key W between themselves, and t matrices for encryption/decryption.

Below is demonstrated how Alice and Bob are using the secret key W to establish secret matrices N_k *via* an open channel and a highly-efficient computational mechanism (decryptor) of solution

$$w_k = N_k^{-1} h_k \ (\text{mod } p), \tag{3.1}$$

that decrypts the ciphertext h_k and therefore recovers the plaintext w_k.

3.1. *Options of system design*

A system designer has two options:

(a) to select either $n \times t$ entanglements {entangs, for short} of n unknowns each and then to divide them onto t sets of *information recovering systems of equations* (IRSE),
(b) to consider a smaller set of entangs of n unknowns each and then to solve $2t$ subsets of linear equations each of size $\lfloor n/2 \rfloor \times \lfloor n/2 \rfloor$. The following examples illustrate the approach.

Example 3.1. If $t = 10$ and $n = 5$, we have at least two options:

(a) to select either fifty entangs each having five unknowns and then to divide them onto ten IRSEs,
(b) to consider a smaller set of entangs.

It is demonstrated in this chapter that it is sufficient to select much smaller number of SOLE. and then decompose them into ten systems each of only *two* unknowns, if $n = 4$ or $n = 5$, or SOLE each of three unknowns, if $n = 6$ or $n = 7$.

3.2. *Key-exchange mechanism via open communication channels*

Here we demonstrate how both Alice and Bob establish a common secret key.

Step 3.1. All communicating parties agree to use the same complex integer (p, q), where p and q are large integers, and complex integer generator $G := (g, h)$,

Remark 3.2. Further reduction of computation is possible, if in G either $h = 0$ or $h = 1$.

Step 3.2. Alice and Bob independently and randomly select large integers α and β, where α and β are respectively private keys of Alice and Bob.

Step 3.3. Alice computes

$$X_A = G^\alpha \bmod (p,q), \tag{3.2}$$

and Bob computes

$$X_B = G^\beta \bmod (p,q). \tag{3.3}$$

Notice that in (3.2) and (3.3), we use *complex* modulus (p,q).

Remark 3.3. In order to minimize the number of computations, all users have access to a database, where $G^2 \bmod (p,q)$, $(G^2)^2 \bmod (p,q)$, $(G^4)^2 \bmod (p,q), \ldots, (G^{2^k})^2 \bmod (p,q), \ldots$, are pre-computed and stored,

Step 3.4. Alice sends to Bob X_A *via* an open channel and Bob sends to Alice X_B also *via* an open channel,

Remark 3.4. A potential intruder knows complex modulus (p,q), G, X_A and X_B,

Step 3.5. Alice computes

$$K_A = X_B^\alpha \bmod (p,q), \tag{3.4}$$

and Bob computes

$$K_B = X_A^\beta \bmod (p,q); \tag{3.5}$$

Step 3.6. *The complex integer*

$$W = (W_1, W_2) = K_A = K_B, \tag{3.6}$$

is the secret key established by Alice and Bob.

Remark 3.5. Although there is no known procedure to assure proper selections of α and β guarantying that both components of W will be large integers, yet the possibility that they are small is minute if p and q, α and β are large, otherwise Alice and Bob will repeat Steps 3.2–3.6.

Remark 3.6. There are several KEM that are analogous to the procedure (3.2–3.6). The novelty here is that we are using computations based on complex modulo reduction (p,q). In 1976, Diffie and Hellman introduced a KEM, based on real integer generator g and real modulo reduction p. The drawback of Diffie–Hellman KEM is that currently there exists several computationally efficient algorithms for solution of discrete logarithm problem (DLP) that find α and β, if g, p, X_A and X_B are known to a potential intruder/cryptanalyst. The author of this book considered in the past, a KEM using a *complex* generator $G = (g, h)$ and a *real* modulo reduction p.

3.3. *Key exchange with complex modulus*

Each user selects randomly large integers {their own secret keys} and perform a sequence of computations described in the following Tables 3.1. and 3.2.

Therefore, the common secret key W equals $W := K_A = K_B = (W_1, W_2) = (4462, -1378)$.

In this example, as well as in the most of examples provided in this book, small integers are used for simplicity of illustration.

Remark 3.7. Below is illustrated how a concatenation $4462, -1378$ is used for two purposes:

- To select four secret parameters $\{Q = 44, R = 62, S = 13, T = 78\}$ and
- To select a secret sequence of SOLE, where the decimal digits $4, 4, 6, 2, 1, 3, 7, 8$ of W are used as the indices of encryption {or encryptors, for short}.

Therefore, the common secret key W equals $W := K_A = K_B = (W_1, W_2) = (\mathbf{632875}, \mathbf{083183})$.

Table 3.1   Let $G = (1913, 1999)$ and $(p, q) = (4111, 2777)$.

Both users actions	*Alice*'s action	*Bob*'s action
Selection of private keys	$\alpha = 79$	$\beta = 37$
1st exponentiation modulo (p, q)	$X_A = G^\alpha \bmod (p, q)$ $= (4465, -1867)$	$X_B = G^\beta \bmod (p, q)$ $= (2997, 1527)$
Swap of X_A and X_B	*Alice* sends X_A to *Bob*	*Bob* sends X_B to *Alice*
2nd exponentiation modulo (p, q) and secret key W	$K_A = X_B^\alpha \bmod (p, q)$ $= (\mathbf{4462}, \mathbf{-1378})$	$K_B = X_A^\beta = \bmod (p, q)$ $= (\mathbf{4462}, \mathbf{-1378})$

Table 3.2   Let $G = (293, 728)$ and $(p, q) = (236432, 779999)$.

Both users actions	*Alice*'s action	*Bob*'s action
Selection of private keys	$\alpha = 1913$	$\beta = 1756$
1st exponentiation modulo (p, q)	$X_A = G^\alpha \bmod (p, q)$ $= (595517, 318611)$	$X_B = G^\beta \bmod (p, q)$ $= (121926, 312155)$
Swap of X_A and X_B	*Alice* sends X_A to *Bob*	*Bob* sends X_B to *Alice*
2nd exponentiation modulo (p, q) and secret key W	$K_A = X_B^\alpha \bmod (p, q)$ $= (\mathbf{632875}, \mathbf{083183})$	$K_B = X_A^\beta = \bmod (p, q)$ $= (\mathbf{632875}, \mathbf{083183})$

The concatenation $632875, 083183$ is used for selection of four secret parameters

$$\{Q = 632, R = 875, S = 083, T = 183\},$$

and the decimal digits of W are used to create a secret sequence of encryptors

$$\{6, 3, 2, 8, 7, 5, 0, 8, 3, 1, 8, 3\}.$$

If $N := \|(p, q)\|$ is a prime, then (p, q) is a Gaussian prime and the group order equals $N - 1 = p^2 + q^2 - 1$. If both p and q are greater than 1, then in general the group order cannot be represented as a product of two polynomials {although $4|(N - 1)$ if N is a prime}. Therefore, solution of a DLP in a group, based on a complex modulus (p, q), is more complicated than solution of a DLP in a group based on complex integers modulo real prime p.

3.4.   *Factorization of* $N - 1$

Let us consider

$$q = kp + x, \tag{3.7}$$

where k is an integer and $|x| = 1$.

Then

$$N - 1 = p^2 + (kp)^2 + 2kpx + x^2 - 1 = p[p(k^2 + 1) + 2kx]. \tag{3.8}$$

Thus, $N - 1$ is divisible by p. In addition, if (p, q) is complex prime, then p and q must have distinct parity.

Hence (3.7) implies that, if p is even, then q is odd for every integer k, however, if p is odd, then q is even. if k is odd.

On the other hand, if N is a prime, then $N - 1$ is even. (3.8) implies that this condition holds if either p and k are odd or if p is even.

Therefore, if p is an even, then in order to avoid factorization of $N - 1$ consider $|kp - q| > 1$.

Example 3.8. Let $p = 4$ and $q = 11$, then $(4, 11)$ is complex prime since $N = 137$ is prime. At the same time, $N - 1 = 34p$.

3.5.   *Complex modulo reduction mechanisms* (*CMRM*)

Two such mechanisms/calculators are provided in this chapter: the first CMRM mechanism is sequentially executable, the second CMRM, {provided in the Appendix} is executable in parallel.

Two such calculators were independently developed by my collaborator Dr. S. Sadik and my former graduate student B. Saraswat. The following operations are performed by these calculators:

- Multiplication of two Gaussians (a, b) and (c, d) modulo (p, q),
- Exponentiation $(a, b)^m$ mod (p, q), {here m is a real positive integer},
- Multiplication of two Gaussians (a, b) and (c, d) modulo real integer n,
- Exponentiation $(a, b)^m$ mod n, {here m is a real positive integer},
- Exponentiation $(a, b)^m$ times (c, d) modulo (p, q),
- Verification whether (a, b) is a primary residue modulo (p, q),
- Modulo (p, q) reduction of (a, b) if it is not a primary residue.

Remark 3.9. The concept of primary residue is described in chapter 9, and in the following section, it is shown how to verify whether the output is a primary residue {see Step 4.7.}.

4. "Sequential" Algorithm for Complex Modulo Reduction

Remark 4.1. The algorithm computes a primary residue (x, y),

Input: $G := (a, b)$, $M := (p, q)$,

Step 4.2. If $q = 0$, then $(x, y) := (a, b)$ mod $p = (a$ mod $p, y = b$ mod $p)$,

Step 4.3. Compute $N := p^2 + q^2$, {N is norm of (p, q)},

Step 4.4. Compute $H_{ab} := ap + bq$,

Step 4.5. If $H_{ab} < 0$, then $J := \lfloor H_{ab}/N \rfloor$, go to Step 4.8,

Step 4.6. If $0 \le H_{ab} < N$, then $(c, d) := G$, go to Step 4.9;

Step 4.7. If $H_{ab} \ge N$, then $J := \lceil H_{ab}/N \rceil - 1$, {Notice that $\lceil z \rceil - 1 \le \lfloor z \rfloor$},

Step 4.8. Compute $(c, d) := G - JM$,

Step 4.9. Compute $V_{cd} := cq - dp$,

Step 4.10. If $V_{cd} < 0$, then $L := \lfloor V_{cd}/N \rfloor$, go to Step 4.13,

Step 4.11. If $0 \le V_{cd} < N$, then $(x, y) := G$; *output* (x, y), **stop**,

Step 4.12. If $V_{cd} \ge N$, then $L := \lceil V_{cd}/N \rceil - 1$,

Step 4.13. Compute $(x, y) := G - L(q, -p)$, *output* (x, y), **stop**.

5. Entanglement and Information Recovering Set of Entangs

Definition 5.1. A procedure that represents an array of n blocks as a system of r linear or non-linear combinations, {see Example 5.2 below}, is called the *entanglement* of the blocks, and every such combination is called an *entang*.

Without loss of generality, in this chapter all concepts are illustrated in the cases where $n = 5$ and $n = 6$ and for several values of r.

Example 5.2. Let us consider a system of *nine* entangs $A, B, C, D, E,$ F, G, H and K with *five* integer variables a, b, c, d, e and *three* secret integer parameters Q, R and S:

$$A = Qa + b, \quad B = a + b, \quad C = a - b + c, \quad D = a + Rb + c + d,$$
$$E = a - 2b + Sc - 2d + e, \quad F = b + c + Rd + e, \quad G = c - d + e,$$
$$H = d + e, \quad K = d + Qe. \tag{5.1}$$

Definition 5.3. A set of entangs that provide recovery of the plaintexts for every combination of parameters is called an IRSE.

In Example 5.2., every combination of five entangs $\{ABCDE,$ $ABCDF, \ldots, EFGHK$-there are 126 such combinations, many of them are listed below$\}$ is the IRSE, provided that it allows to recover the plaintexts a, b, c, d and e for every feasible combination of parameters Q, R and S. {*Warning*: not all of 126 combinations are IRSE!}.

Among all combinations we consider only ten: each of them is listed in the following table, where $1, 2, 3, \ldots, 8, 9, 0$ are called *indices of the encryptors* (IoEs).

Example 5.4. Suppose that

$$W = (W_1, W_2) = (2718281828459045, 0314159265367094).$$

Alice and Bob select $\{Q, R, S, T\} := \{27182818, 28459045, 03141592,$ $65367094\}$ and the concatenated W is used to create a secret sequence of 32 encryptors/CEDs:

$$\{2, 7, 1, 8, 2, 8, 1, 8, 2, 8, 4, 5, 9, 0, 4, 5, 0, 3, 1, 4, 1, 5, 9, 2, 6, 5, 3, 6, 7, 0, 9, 4\}.$$

These encryptors will be used to encrypt 32 arrays $\{a_i, b_i, c_i, d_i, e_i\}$ for $i = 1, 2, \ldots, 32$.

By using Table 5.1., each array is encrypted with the following sequence of the systems of equations: $\{2 = ACEGH, \quad 7 = BDEFK,$

Table 5.1   Ten subsets each having five entangs.

IoE	0	1	2	3	4
Combination	ABEHK	ACEFK	ACEGH	ADEFH	ADEGK
IoE	5	6	7	8	9
Combination	BCEFH	BCEGK	BDEFK	BDEGH	BDEGK

NB 5.1.: Notice that not every combination is symmetric.

$1 = $ ACEFK, $8 = $ BDEGH, $2 = $ ACEGH, $8 = $ BDEGH, $1 = $ ACEFK, $8 =$, $2 =$, $8 =$, $4 =$, $5 =$, $9 =$, $0 =$, $4 =$, $5 =$, $0 =$, $3 =$, $1 =$, $4 =$, $1 =$, $5 =$, $9 =$, $2 =$, $6 =$, $5 = $ BCEFH, $3 = $ ADEFH, $6 = $ BCEGK, $7 = $ BDEFK, $0 = $ ABEHK, $9 = $ BDEGK, $4 = $ ADEGK$\}$.

At the end of the cycle of 32 arrays, a cryptographer has an option: either to establish a new complex integer $W' = (W_1', W_2')$, or to reuse once more the same secret key W and the same sequence of encryptors.

6. Multi-Parametric System of Equations

Inputs: parameters Q, R, S, T and U, {real integers}, variables a, b, c, d and e, {real integers},

Remark 6.1. Although f_3 and f_5 are known to a cryptanalyst/intruder, yet this is insufficient information to recover the plaintext array $\{a, b, c, d, e\}$ or any part of it, if the entanglements E_5 and/or E_6 are encrypted.

Encryption {actions of sender}: Alice wants to send to Bob an array of plaintext blocks a, b, c, d and e,

Table 6.1   Computation of entangs.

$E_1 = Qa + b$	$E_{10} = Qe + d$
$E_2 = a + Rb - c$	$E_9 = e + Rd - c$
$E_3 = a + b + Sc$	$E_8 = e + d + Sc$
$E_4 = a - b + c + Td$	$E_7 = e + Tb + c - d$
$E_5 = 2a - b - c + d$	$E_6 = 2e + b - c - d$
$E_{11} = U(a + e) +$	$2(b + d) + c$

Table 6.2   Computation of f_i and s_i.

i, k	vars w and y	vars x and z
1	$f_1 := E_1 - E_{10}$	$s_1 := E_1 + E_{10}$
2	$f_2 := E_2 - E_9$	$s_2 := E_2 + E_9 + 2E_{11}$
3	$f_3 := E_3 - E_8$	$s_3 := E_3 + E_8 - 2SE_{11}$
4	$f_4 := E_4 - E_7$	$s_4 := E_4 + E_7 - 2E_{11}$
5	$f_5 := (E_5 - E_6)/2$	$s_5 := (E_5 + E_6)/2 + E_{11}$

Table 6.3 $\{w, y\}$-group and $\{x, z\}$-group of equations.

	$\{w, y\}$-group of equations		$\{x, z\}$-group of equations
$F(1)$	$Qw + y = f_1$	$S(1)$	$Qx + z = s_1$
$F(2)$	$w + Ry = f_2$	$S(2)$	$(2U + 1)x + (R + 4)z = s_2$
$F(3)$	$w + y = f_3$	$S(3)$	$(1 - 2SU)x + (1 - 4S)z = s_3$
$F(4)$	$w - (T + 1)y = f_4$	$S(4)$	$(1 - 2U)x + (T - 5)z = s_4$
$F(5)$	$w - y = f_5$	$S(5)$	$(U + 1)x + 2z = s_5$

Table 6.4   Combined Tables 6.2. and Table 6.3.

Eq.	Compute	Eqs.	Eq.	Compute	Eqs.
$F(1)$	$f_1 = E_1 - E_{10}$	$Qw + y = f_1$	$S(1)$	$s_1 = E_1 + E_{10}$	$Qx + z = s_1$
$F(2)$	$f_2 = E_2 - E_9$	$w + Ry = f_2$	$S(2)$	$s_2 = E_2 + E_9$ $+ 2E_{11}$	$(2U + 1)x$ $+ (R+4)z = s_2$
$F(3)$	$f_3 = E_3 - E_8$	$w + y = f_3$	$S(3)$	$s_3 = E_3 + E_8$ $- 2SE_{11}$	$(1 - 2SU)x$ $+(1-4S)z = s_3$
$F(4)$	$f_4 = E_4 - E_7$	$w - (T + 1)y = f_4$	$S(4)$	$s_4 = E_4 + E_7$ $- 2E_{11}$	$(1 - 2U)x$ $+ (T - 5)z = s_4$
$F(5)$	$f_5 = (E_5 - E_6)/2$	$w - y = f_5$	$S(5)$	$s_5 = (E_5 + E_6)/2$ $+ E_{11}$	$(U+1)x+2z = s_5$

Step 6.1. Sender (Alice) computes E_{11} and for a specified encryptor computes

$$E_i, E_k, E_{11-k}, E_{11-i} \text{ \{see Table 6.1\}},$$

Step 6.2. Alice transmits entanglements $\{E_i, E_k, E_{11-k}, E_{11-i}, E_{11}\}$ *via* open channels to the receiver (Bob),

Decryption {actions of receiver}:

Step 6.3. Receiver performs computations listed in Tables 6.2–6.4,

Step 6.4. Bob solves two systems of linear equations $F(i)$ and $F(k)$ with two unknowns w and y,

Step 6.5. Bob solves two systems of linear equations $S(i)$ and $S(k)$ with two unknowns x and z,

Step 6.6. Receiver recovers the plaintext array

$$a = (w + x)/2, \quad b = (y + z)/2, \quad c = E_{11} - (x + 2z),$$
$$d = (z - y)/2, \quad e = (x - w)/2.$$

Table 6.5   List of encryptors {indices of encryptors}.

$1, U = 1$	$2, U = 1$	$3, U = 1$	$4, U = 1$	$5, U = 1$
$\left\{ \begin{array}{l} E_1, E_2, E_9 \\ E_{10}, E_{11} \end{array} \right\}$	$\left\{ \begin{array}{l} E_1, E_3, E_8 \\ E_{10}, E_{11} \end{array} \right\}$	$\left\{ \begin{array}{l} E_1, E_4, E_7 \\ E_{10}, E_{11} \end{array} \right\}$	$\left\{ \begin{array}{l} E_1, E_5, E_6 \\ E_{10}, E_{11} \end{array} \right\}$	$\left\{ \begin{array}{l} E_2, E_3, E_8 \\ E_9, E_{11} \end{array} \right\}$
$6, U = 1$	$7, U = 1$	$8, U = 1$	$9, U = S$	$0, U = 1$
$\left\{ \begin{array}{l} E_2, E_4, E_7 \\ E_9, E_{11} \end{array} \right\}$	$\left\{ \begin{array}{l} E_2, E_5, E_6 \\ E_9, E_{11} \end{array} \right\}$	$\left\{ \begin{array}{l} E_3, E_4, E_7 \\ E_8, E_{11} \end{array} \right\}$	$\left\{ \begin{array}{l} E_3, E_5, E_6 \\ E_8, E_{11} \end{array} \right\}$	$\left\{ \begin{array}{l} E_4, E_5, E_6 \\ E_7, E_{11} \end{array} \right\}$

Table 6.5. provides a sequence of combination of linear equations, where $1, 2, 3, \ldots, 8, 9, 0$ are the *indices of the encryptors*. The sequence of encryptors is established using the KEM, {see **Remarks 3.5. and 3.6.**}.

Corollary 6.2. If $Q \geq 2$, $R \geq 3$, $S \geq 3$, $T \geq 6$ and $U = 1$, then all systems of eqs. listed in Table 6.5. are IRSE. Therefore, the decryption always recovers the plaintext for all cases.

7. Numeric Illustration

Let Alice transmit an array $a = 5$, $b = 3$, $c = 4$, $d = 2$, $e = 1$ to Bob, and let they establish secret parameters $Q = 2$, $R = 3$, $S = 3$, $T = 6$, $U = 1$, and let the *encryptor* = 1. From Tables 6.5. and 7.1, the sender must use entanglements $\{E_1, E_2, E_9, E_{10}, E_{11}\}$ for the encryption, and the table shows how to do it.

Alice (sender) transmits $\{E_1, E_2, E_9, E_{10}, E_{11}\} = \{13, 10, 3, 4, 20\}$ to Bob (receiver).

Remark 7.1. Notice that Bob also knows that encryptor $= 1$.

Bob performs decryption computations listed in Tables 7.2 and 7.3. Therefore, the receiver finds $w = 4$, $y = 1$, and $x = 6$, $z = 5$.

Finally, the receiver recovers $a = (w + x)/2 = 5$, $b = (y + z)/2 = 3$, $c = E_{11} - (x + 2z) = 20 - (6 + 10) = 4$, $d = (z - y)/2 = 2$, $e = (x - w)/2 = 1$.

Table 7.1   Encryption: computation of entanglements.

$E_1 = 2a + b = \mathbf{13}$	$E_{10} = 2e + d = \mathbf{4}$
$E_2 = a + 3b - c = \mathbf{10}$	$E_9 = e + 3d - c = \mathbf{3}$
$E_{11} = (a + e) + 2(b + d) + c = \mathbf{20}$	*****

Table 7.2   Decryption: computation of f_i and s_i.

i, k	**Variables w and y**	**Variables x and z**
1	$f_1 := E_1 - E_{10} = 9$	$s_1 := E_1 + E_{10} = 17$
2	$f_2 := E_2 - E_9 = 7$	$s_2 := E_2 + E_9 + 2E_{11} = 53$

Table 7.3 $\{w, y\}$-group and $\{x, z\}$-group of equations: $Q = 2$, $R = 3$, $U = 1$.

	$\{w, y\}$-group of equations		$\{x, z\}$-group of equations
$F(1)$	$2w + y = 9$	$S(1)$	$2x + z = 17$
$F(2)$	$w + 3y = 7$	$S(2)$	$3x + 7z = 53$

8. Numeric Illustration-2

Let Alice transmit an array $a = 27$, $b = 23$, $c = 14$, $d = 21$, $e = 19$.

Let $Q = 44$, $R = 62$, $S = 13$, $T = 78$, $U = 1$, and let *encryptor* $= 4$, then Tables 6.5. and 8.1. imply that the sender needs to use the entanglements $E_1, E_5, E_6, E_{10}, E_{11}$ for encryption.

Encryption:

Step 8.1. Sender computes the ciphertext array $\{E_1, E_5, E_6, E_{10}, E_{11}\}$ and sends it to the receiver,

Decryption {receiver's actions; summarized in Tables 8.2 and 8.3.}:

Step 8.2. Computes f_1 and f_5,

Step 8.3. Solves the system of two linear equations F_1 and F_5 with unknowns w and y,

Step 8.4. Computes s_1 and s_5,

Step 8.5. Solves the system of two linear equations S_1 and S_5 with unknowns x and z,

Step 8.6. Recovers $a = (w + x)/2$, $b = (y + z)/2$, $c = E_{11} - (x + 2z)$, $d = (z - y)/2$, $e = (x - w)/2$.

Table 8.1   {Encryption: computation of ciphertext array}.

$E_1 = 44a + b = \mathbf{1211}$	$E_{10} = 44e + d = \mathbf{857}$
$E_5 = 2a - b - c + d = \mathbf{38}$	$E_6 = 2e + b - c - d = \mathbf{26}$
$E_{11} = (a + e) + 2(b + d) + c = \mathbf{148}$	*****

Table 8.2   {Decryption: computation of f_i and s_i}.

i, k	Variables w and y	Variables x and z
1	$f_1 := E_1 - E_{10} = \mathbf{354}$	$s_1 := E_1 + E_{10} = \mathbf{2068}$
5	$f_5 := (E_5 - E_6)/2 = \mathbf{6}$	$s_5 := E_{11} + (E_5 + E_6)/2 = \mathbf{180}$

Table 8.3 {Decryption: solution of $\{w, y\}$-SOLE and $\{x, z\}$-SOLE}.

	$\{w, y\}$-group of eqs.		$\{x, z\}$-group of eqs.
$F(1)$	$44w + y = 354$	$S(1)$	$44x + z = 2068$
$F(5)$	$w - y = 6$	$S(5)$	$x + z = 90$

Remark 8.1. Although the cryptanalyst/intruder can find w and y, however, without knowing x and z, the intruder cannot deduce a, b, c, d and e.

Therefore, $w = 8$ and $y = 2$, $x = 46$, and $z = 44$,
Finally, $a = (w+x)/2 = \mathbf{27}$, $b = (y+z)/2 = \mathbf{23}$, $c = E_{11} - (x+2z) = \mathbf{14}$, $d = (z - y)/2 = \mathbf{21}$, $e = (x - w)/2 = \mathbf{19}$.

9. Protocol with Twenty Encryptors and Twelve Entangs

The following sections show how tedious is the information recovery procedure, in comparison with the straightforward recovery, demonstrated in the previous sections of this chapter. In the following table, we demonstrate twenty different encryptors.

Remark 9.1. In the concatenated secret key W the decimal digits are used in two cycles: in the 1st cycle are used the encryptors with suffix 1, in the 2nd cycle are used the encryptors with suffix 2 (see Table 9.1.).

$$u := a - f, \quad w := b - e, \quad y := c - d, \quad v := a + f,$$
$$x := b + e, \quad z := c + d, \tag{9.1}$$

There are $(6 \times 5 \times 4)/3! = 20$ combinations of 3×3 systems of linear equations, i.e., there are twenty encryptors.

Table 9.1 With entangs E_i, E_j, E_k are also sent entangs $E_{13-k}, E_{13-j}, E_{13-i}$.

1.1	2.1	3.1	4.1	5.1
$\{E_1, E_2, E_3\}$	$\{E_1, E_2, E_4\}$	$\{E_1, E_2, E_5\}$	$\{E_1, E_2, E_6\}$	$\{E_1, E_3, E_4\}$
$D_{123}, D_{10,11,12}$	$D_{124}, D_{9,11,12}$	$D_{125}, D_{8,11,12}$	$D_{126}, D_{7,11,12}$	$D_{134}, D_{9,10,12}$
6.1	7.1	8.1	9.1	0.1
$\{E_1, E_3, E_5\}$	$\{E_1, E_3, E_6\}$	$\{E_1, E_4, E_5\}$	$\{E_1, E_4, E_6\}$	$\{E_1, E_5, E_6\}$
$D_{135}, D_{8,10,12}$	$D_{136}, D_{7,10,12}$	$D_{145}, D_{8,9,12}$	$D_{146}, D_{7,9,12}$	$D_{156}, D_{7,8,12}$
1.2	2.2	3.2	4.2	5.2
$\{E_2, E_3, E_4\}$	$\{E_2, E_3, E_5\}$	$\{E_2, E_3, E_6\}$	$\{E_2, E_4, E_5\}$	$\{E_2, E_4, E_6\}$
$D_{234}, D_{9,10,11}$	$D_{235}, D_{8,10,11}$	$D_{236}, D_{7,10,11}$	$D_{245}, D_{8,9,11}$	$D_{246}, D_{7,9,11}$
6.2	7.2	8.2	9.2	0.2
$\{E_2, E_5, E_6\}$	$\{E_3, E_4, E_5\}$	$\{E_3, E_4, E_6\}$	$\{E_3, E_5, E_6\}$	$\{E_4, E_5, E_6\}$
$D_{256}, D_{7,8,11}$	$D_{345}, D_{8,9,10}$	$D_{346}, D_{7,9,10}$	$D_{356}, D_{7,8,10}$	D_{456}, D_{789}

Table 9.2　Encryption: computation of entangs.

$E_1 = Pa + e$	$E_{12} = b + Pf$
$E_2 = Qb - c + f$	$E_{11} = a - d + Qe$
$E_3 = b + Rd$	$E_{10} = Rc + e$
$E_4 = a + Sd$	$E_9 = Sc + f$
$E_5 = c - b + f$	$E_8 = a + d - e$
$E_6 = Ta + d + e$	$E_7 = b + c + Tf$

Table 9.3　Decryption: systems of parametric 3×3 linear equations.

$\{i, j, k\}$	$\{u, w, y\}$-eqs.	$\{i, j, k\}$	$\{v, x, z\}$-eqs.
1	$Pu - w = E_1 - E_{12}$	12	$Pv + x = E_1 + E_{12}$
2	$-u + Qw - y = E_2 - E_{11}$	11	$v + Qx - z = E_2 + E_{11}$
3	$w - Ry = E_3 - E_{10}$	10	$x + Rz = E_3 + E_{10}$
4	$u - Sy = E_4 - E_9$	9	$v + Sz = E_4 + E_9$
5	$-u - w + y = E_5 - E_8$	8	$v - x + z = E_5 + E_8$
6	$Tu - w - y = E_6 - E_7$	7	$Tv + x + z = E_6 + E_7$

For encryption, a sender computes six entangs $\{E_i, E_j, E_k, E_{13-k}, E_{13-j}, E_{13-i}\}$ for triads of integers $1 \le i < j < k \le 6$ listed in the Table 9.1. of encryptors. These computations are listed in Table 9.2.

For decryption, the receiver needs to solve two systems of linear equations each with three unknowns (Table 9.3):

- the first SOLE with unknowns u, w and y, and
- the second SOLE with unknowns v, x and z.

Finally, the receiver recovers the plaintext array $\{a, b, c, d, e, f\}$ using the recovery rules (9.1).

10. Illustrative Example

Suppose Alice and Bob established a secret key $W = \{8547097, 53207146\}$, selected secret parameters $P = 854$, $Q = 709$, $R = 753$, $S = 207$ and $T = 147$, and used W to create a sequence of thirty encryptors $\{8.1, 5.1, 4.1, 7.1, 0.1, 9.1, 7.1, 5.1, 3.1, 2.1, 0.1, 7.1, 1.1, 4.1, 6.1, \boldsymbol{8.2, 5.2, 4.2, 7.2, 0.2, 9.2, 7.2, 5.2, 3.2, 2.2, 0.2, 7.2, 1.2, 4.2, 6.2}$-see Table 9.1. listed above$\}$.

Suppose Alice needs to securely transmit a file F consisting of 900 blocks. She divides the file F onto 150 arrays each consisting of six plaintext blocks $\{a, b, c, d, e, f\}$.

Suppose the first plaintext block is

$$\{a, b, c, d, e, f\} := \{4310, 2111, 1913, 8341, 1973, 2010\}.$$

Table 10.1

$E_3 = b + Rd = 2111 + 753 \times 8341$	$E_{10} = Rc + e = 753 \times 1913 + 1973$
$E_5 = c - b + f = 1913 - 2111 + 2010$	$E_8 = a + d - e = 4310 + 8341 - 1973$
$E_6 = Ta + d + e$	$E_7 = b + c + Tf$
$\quad = 147 \times 4310 + 8341 + 1973$	$\quad = 2111 + 1913 + 147 \times 2010$

Table 10.2   Decryption: two systems of parametric 3×3 linear eqs.

$\{i, j, k\}$	$\{u, w, y\}$-eqs.	$\{v, x, z\}$-eqs.
3	$w - 753y = E_3 - E_{10}$	$x + 753z = E_3 + E_{10}$
5	$-u - w + y = E_5 - E_8$	$v - x + z = E_5 + E_8$
6	$147u - w - y = E_6 - E_7$	$147v + x + z = E_6 + E_7$

Let us demonstrate how it is encrypted by sender (Alice) and decrypted by receiver (Bob).

Let us assume that encryptor $= 9.2$.

From Table 10.1, Alice uses entanglements $\{E_3, E_5, E_6, E_7, E_8, E_{10}\}$ for encryption.

After Bob solves the SOLE listed in Table 10.2 and finds the unknown u, w, y and v, x, z, he recovers the plaintext blocks: $a = (u + v)/2$, $f = (v - u)/2$, $b = (w + x)/2$, $e = (x - w)/2$, $c = (y + z)/2$, $d = (z - y)/2$.

11. Feasibility Analysis

A system of two equations $\alpha_1 x + \beta_1 y = \lambda_1$ and $\alpha_2 x + \beta_2 y = \lambda_2$ has a unique solution if its determinant

$$\begin{vmatrix} \alpha_1 & \beta_1 \\ \alpha_2 & \beta_2 \end{vmatrix} \neq 0, \quad \text{or it } \alpha_1 \beta_2 - \alpha_2 \beta_1 \neq 0. \tag{11.1}$$

Equivalently, it means that a unique solution exists if

$$\alpha_1/\beta_1 \neq \alpha_2/\beta_2. \tag{11.2}$$

This inequality implies that the parameters Q, R, S, T and U must satisfy the following two chains of pair-wise inequalities:

$$Q \neq 1/R \neq 1 \neq -1/(T+1) \neq -1, \tag{11.3}$$

and

$$Q \neq (2U+1)/(R+4) \neq (2SU-1)/(4S-1)$$
$$\neq (2U-1)/(5-T) \neq (U+1)/2. \tag{11.4}$$

Analysis of (11.4) for $U = 1$ is provided in the next section.

12. Feasibility Analysis: $\{u, w, y\}$-Eqs.

Here are listed twenty determinants related with solution of eqs. in left column of Table 9.2., a unique solution exists, if the secret parameters P, Q, R, S, and T satisfy the following conditions:

1. $D_{123} := \begin{vmatrix} P & -1 & 0 \\ -1 & Q & -1 \\ 0 & 1 & -R \end{vmatrix} \neq 0,$ i.e., if $P, Q, R > 1,$

2. $D_{124} := \begin{vmatrix} P & -1 & 0 \\ -1 & Q & -1 \\ 1 & 0 & -S \end{vmatrix} \neq 0,$ i.e., if $P, Q > 1,$

3. $D_{125} := \begin{vmatrix} P & -1 & 0 \\ -1 & Q & -1 \\ -1 & -1 & 1 \end{vmatrix} \neq 0,$ i.e., $PQ + 2 \neq P,$ {always if $P, Q > 0$},

4. $D_{126} := \begin{vmatrix} P & -1 & 0 \\ -1 & Q & -1 \\ T & -1 & -1 \end{vmatrix} \neq 0,$ i.e., $T + 1 \neq P(Q + 1),$

5. $D_{134} := \begin{vmatrix} P & -1 & 0 \\ 0 & 1 & -R \\ 1 & 0 & -S \end{vmatrix} \neq 0,$ i.e., if $R \neq PS,$

6. $D_{135} := \begin{vmatrix} P & -1 & 0 \\ 0 & 1 & -R \\ -1 & -1 & 1 \end{vmatrix} \neq 0,$ i.e., $R(P + 1) \neq P,$

$$\{\text{always if } P > 0 \text{ and } R > 0\},$$

7. $D_{136} := \begin{vmatrix} P & -1 & 0 \\ 0 & 1 & -R \\ T & -1 & -1 \end{vmatrix} \neq 0,$ i.e., if $TR \neq P(R + 1),$

8. $D_{145} := \begin{vmatrix} P & -1 & 0 \\ 1 & 0 & -S \\ -1 & -1 & 1 \end{vmatrix} \neq 0,$ i.e., if $S > 1,$

9. $D_{146} := \begin{vmatrix} P & -1 & 0 \\ 1 & 0 & -S \\ T & -1 & -1 \end{vmatrix} \neq 0,$ if $S > 1,$

10. $D_{156} := \begin{vmatrix} P & -1 & 0 \\ -1 & -1 & 1 \\ T & -1 & -1 \end{vmatrix} \neq 0,$ i.e., $2P + 1 \neq T,$

11. $D_{234} := \begin{vmatrix} -1 & Q & -1 \\ 0 & 1 & -R \\ 1 & 0 & -S \end{vmatrix} \neq 0, \quad$ i.e., $S + 1 \neq QR$,

12. $D_{235} := \begin{vmatrix} -1 & Q & -1 \\ 0 & 1 & -R \\ -1 & -1 & 1 \end{vmatrix} \neq 0, \quad$ if $R, Q > 1$,

13. $D_{236} := \begin{vmatrix} -1 & Q & -1 \\ 0 & 1 & -R \\ T & -1 & -1 \end{vmatrix} \neq 0, \quad$ if $Q, R, T > 1$,

14. $D_{245} := \begin{vmatrix} -1 & Q & -1 \\ 1 & 0 & -S \\ -1 & -1 & 1 \end{vmatrix} \neq 0, \quad$ i.e., if $Q, S > 1$,

15. $D_{246} := \begin{vmatrix} -1 & Q & -1 \\ 1 & 0 & -S \\ T & -1 & -1 \end{vmatrix} \neq 0, \quad$ i.e., $Q + S + 1 \neq ST$,

16. $D_{256} := \begin{vmatrix} -1 & Q & -1 \\ -1 & -1 & 1 \\ T & -1 & -1 \end{vmatrix} \neq 0, \quad$ i.e., if $Q, T > 1$,

17. $D_{345} := \begin{vmatrix} 0 & 1 & -R \\ 1 & 0 & -S \\ -1 & -1 & 1 \end{vmatrix} \neq 0, \quad$ i.e., $R + S \neq 1$,

18. $D_{346} := \begin{vmatrix} 0 & 1 & -R \\ 1 & 0 & -S \\ T & -1 & -1 \end{vmatrix} \neq 0, \quad$ i.e., $TS \neq R + 1$,

19. $D_{356} := \begin{vmatrix} 0 & 1 & -R \\ -1 & -1 & 1 \\ T & -1 & -1 \end{vmatrix} \neq 0, \quad$ i.e., if $R, T > 1$,

20. $D_{456} := \begin{vmatrix} 1 & 0 & -S \\ -1 & -1 & 1 \\ T & -1 & -1 \end{vmatrix} \neq 0, \quad$ i.e., if $S, T > 1$.

13. Feasibility Analysis: $\{v, x, z\}$-Eqs.

Here are listed twenty determinants related with solution of the eqs. in the right column of Table 9.2., a unique solution exists if the secret parameters $P, Q, R, S,$ and T satisfy the following conditions:

21. $D_{10,11,12} := \begin{vmatrix} P & 1 & 0 \\ 1 & Q & -1 \\ 0 & 1 & R \end{vmatrix} \neq 0,$

22. $D_{9,11,12} := \begin{vmatrix} P & 1 & 0 \\ 1 & Q & -1 \\ 1 & 0 & S \end{vmatrix} \neq 0,$

23. $D_{8,11,12} := \begin{vmatrix} P & 1 & 0 \\ 1 & Q & -1 \\ 1 & -1 & 1 \end{vmatrix} \neq 0,$ i.e., $PQ \neq P + 2,$ or $P(Q - 1) <> 2,$

$$\text{or if } P > 0, Q > 1, \text{ and } P + Q > 4,$$

24. $D_{7,11,12} := \begin{vmatrix} P & 1 & 0 \\ 1 & Q & -1 \\ T & 1 & 1 \end{vmatrix} \neq 0,$ i.e., if $P + T + 1 \neq PQ,$

25. $D_{9,10,12} := \begin{vmatrix} P & 1 & 0 \\ 0 & 1 & R \\ 1 & 0 & S \end{vmatrix} \neq 0,$ if $P, R, S > 0,$

26. $D_{8,10,12} := \begin{vmatrix} P & 1 & 0 \\ 0 & 1 & R \\ 1 & -1 & 1 \end{vmatrix} \neq 0,$ i.e., if $P > 0,$

27. $D_{7,10,12} := \begin{vmatrix} P & 1 & 0 \\ 0 & 1 & R \\ T & 1 & 1 \end{vmatrix} \neq 0,$ i.e., if $P + RT \neq PR,$

28. $D_{8,9,12} := \begin{vmatrix} P & 1 & 0 \\ 1 & 0 & S \\ 1 & -1 & 1 \end{vmatrix} \neq 0,$ if $P, S > 0,$

29. $D_{7,9,12} := \begin{vmatrix} P & 1 & 0 \\ 1 & 0 & S \\ T & 1 & 1 \end{vmatrix} \neq 0,$ i.e., if $S > 1,$

30. $D_{7,8,12} := \begin{vmatrix} P & 1 & 0 \\ 1 & -1 & 1 \\ T & 1 & 1 \end{vmatrix} \neq 0,$ i.e., $T - 2P \neq 1,$

31. $D_{9,10,11} := \begin{vmatrix} 1 & Q & -1 \\ 0 & 1 & R \\ 1 & 0 & S \end{vmatrix} \neq 0,$ if $Q, R, S > 0,$

32. $D_{8,10,11} := \begin{vmatrix} 1 & Q & -1 \\ 0 & 1 & R \\ 1 & -1 & 1 \end{vmatrix} \neq 0,$ if $Q, R > 0,$

33. $D_{7,10,11} := \begin{vmatrix} 1 & Q & -1 \\ 0 & 1 & R \\ T & 1 & 1 \end{vmatrix} \neq 0,$ i.e., if $Q, R, T > 0,$

34. $D_{8,9,11} := \begin{vmatrix} 1 & Q & -1 \\ 1 & 0 & S \\ 1 & -1 & 1 \end{vmatrix} \neq 0,$ i.e., if $Q, S > 0,$

35. $D_{7,9,11} := \begin{vmatrix} 1 & Q & -1 \\ 1 & 0 & S \\ T & 1 & 1 \end{vmatrix} \neq 0,$ $Q + S = 1 \neq QST,$

36. $D_{7,8,11} := \begin{vmatrix} 1 & Q & -1 \\ 1 & -1 & 1 \\ T & 1 & 1 \end{vmatrix} \neq 0,$ i.e., if $QT \neq Q + T + 3,$

or if $Q > 3,$ and $T > 3,$

37. $D_{8,9,10} := \begin{vmatrix} 0 & 1 & R \\ 1 & 0 & S \\ 1 & -1 & 1 \end{vmatrix} \neq 0,$ i.e., $S \neq R + 1,$

38. $D_{7,9,10} := \begin{vmatrix} 0 & 1 & R \\ 1 & 0 & S \\ T & 1 & 1 \end{vmatrix} \neq 0,$ i.e., if $R > 1,$

39. $D_{7,8,10} := \begin{vmatrix} 0 & 1 & R \\ 1 & -1 & 1 \\ T & 1 & 1 \end{vmatrix} \neq 0,$ i.e., if $R > 1, T > 1,$

40. $D_{789} := \begin{vmatrix} 1 & 0 & S \\ 1 & -1 & 1 \\ T & 1 & 1 \end{vmatrix} \neq 0,$ i.e., $S(T + 1) \neq 2.$

Remark 13.1. Many determinants in 1–20 are the same or almost the same as in 21–40. If at least one of determinants equals zero, then parties must randomly select new α and β, and apply KEM. However, for large prime p the probability of such event is negligible.

14. Cryptanalysis of the MPA

If the *encryptor* = 9, then f_5 and f_6 are known to a cryptanalyst/intruder, since the entangs E_5 and E_6 are used in encryption. Yet this information is not sufficient for recovery of the plaintext array $\{a, b, c, d, e\}$ or any part of it. At the same time, in order to enhance cryptoimmunity of the MPA, the following modification is simple and easy to implement: If *encryptor* = 9, then $U := S$, else $U := 1$.

Appendix

A.1. *Parallel algorithm for complex modulo reduction:* $(x, y) := (a, b) \bmod (p, q)$

Input: a, b, p, q real integers,

Variables: H, J, L, V real integers,

Output: x, y real integers,

Step A.0. If $q = 0$, then $(x, y) := (a \bmod p, b \bmod p)$, **output** (x, y), **end** of algorithm,

Remark A.1. If $q = 0$, there is no necessity to compute H_{xy} and V_{xy}, {see Step A.7},

Step A.1. Compute

$$N := p^2 + q^2, \tag{A.1}$$

Step A.2. Compute

$$H_{ab} := ap + bq, \quad V_{ab} := aq - bp, \tag{A.2}$$

Step A.3. If $H_{ab} < 0$, then

$$J := \lfloor H_{ab}/N \rfloor, \tag{A.3}$$

If $H_{ab} \geq N$, then

$$J := \lceil H_{ab}/N \rceil - 1, \quad \textbf{else } J := 0, \tag{A.4}$$

Step A.4. If $V_{ab} < 0$, then

$$L := \lfloor V_{ab}/N \rfloor, \tag{A.5}$$

If $V_{ab} \geq N$, then

$$L := \lceil V_{ab}/N \rceil - 1, \quad \textbf{else } L := 0, \tag{A.6}$$

$$\{\text{Notice that } \lceil z \rceil - 1 \leq \lfloor z \rfloor, \quad \text{since } \lceil z \rceil - \lfloor z \rfloor \leq 1\},$$

Step A.5.

$$(x, y) := (a, b) - J \times (p, q) - L \times (q, -p), \quad output\ (x, y), \quad (A.7)$$

$$\{J \times (p, q) = (Jp, Jq); \quad L \times (q, -p) = (Lq, -Lp)\},$$

Step A.6.

$$H_{xy} := px + qy, \quad V_{xy} := qx - py, \quad output\ H_{xy}\ and\ V_{xy}, \quad (A.8)$$

{end of algorithm}.

Remark A.2. The Step A.7 is used for verification only: (x, y) is a primary residue, if the following inequalities are satisfied:

$$0 \le H_{xy} < N, \quad 0 \le V_{xy} < N. \quad (A.9)$$

Chapter 13

Scheme for Digital Signature that Always Works

1. RSA Public and Private Keys

As we demonstrate in this chapter, for certain values of transmitted plaintext, the RSA digital signature scheme (DSS) does not work. A new DSS is proposed below. The recommended scheme eliminates a source of protocol failure in the RSA-DSS. This signature scheme has the same computational complexity as the RSA-DSS. However, it requires that the public key for every user consists of *three* rather than *two* large integers, and the private key consists of *two* large integers.

Let us consider two users *Alice* and *Bob* and recall how they select their public and private keys in accordance with the RSA-DSS, (Rivest *et al.* 1978).

Let $p, q, r,$ and s be such primes that

1. $n = pq$, and $gcd[(p-1)(q-1), d] = 1$, $(de) \bmod n = 1$,
2. $t = rs$, and $gcd[(r-1)(s-1), g] = 1$, $(gh) \bmod t = 1$,
3. Then both public and private keys for *Alice* and *Bob* are provided in the Table 1.1.
4. In addition, let $n > t$ and a plaintext is divided onto such blocks that the length of every block $a < t$.

Table 1.1 Public and private keys of users.

Keys\Users	*Alice* is user	*Bob* is user
Public keys	$N = pq, e$	$t = rs, h$
Private keys	d	g

2. Failure of RSA Signature Scheme

Let *Alice* send an *intelligible* message a to *Bob,* then Table 2.1. describes all steps required by RSA-DSS for *signature, encryption, decryption* and *signature verification*:

Table 2.1   DSS stages for RSA.

Stages	Alice's actions
Signature	$u := a^d \bmod n$
Encryption	$v := u^h \bmod t$
	Bob's actions
Decryption	$w := v^g \bmod t, w < t$
signature verification	$x := w^e \bmod n$

Finally, if x is an intelligible message, then B accepts *Alice*'s signature and the initially-transmitted message $x = a$.

However, there exist values of message a for which this scheme does not work.

Indeed, let $u \geq t$, then by the Euler's theorem, (Menezes *et al.* 1997),

$$w = u^{hg} \bmod t = u \bmod t < t.$$

Thus, $w \neq u$, and as a result, $x \neq a$.

Let R be a set of all messages a for which $n > u(a) \geq t$. Hence for every message a of R the scheme does not work since $w < t \leq u$ and, as a result, x is not equal a. Besides, it is highly unlikely that x *is* intelligible.

Therefore, for large primes p, q, r, and s all messages of R

1. either will not be intelligible with a high probability and, as a consequence, will be rejected by the receiver {*Bob*},
2. or will be intelligible with a minute probability and as a result, will be accepted by *Bob*, however, these messages will not be the same as messages transmitted by the sender {Alice}.

Thus, in both cases the RSA signature protocol fails for every message a of R.

Example 2.1.

- Let $p = 5, q = 17, m = 85, z = 64$, select $e = 13$, then $d = 5$: $\{5d \bmod 64 = 1\}$.
- Let $r = 11, s = 3, t = 33, y = 20$, select $h = 7$, then $g = 3 : \{7g \bmod 20 = 1\}$.
- The signature scheme does not work because for the *twenty* listed messages $\{3 \leq a \leq 31$, see Table 2.2.$\}$ the values of $u(a)$ exceed $t = 33$:

Table 2.2

a	3	5	6	7	8	9	10	11	**12**	15
$u(a)$	73	65	41	62	43	59	40	61	**37**	70
a	19	22	23	24	25	26	27	28	29	31
$u(a)$	49	82	58	79	60	76	57	78	54	46

- Indeed, let us consider a message $a = \mathbf{12}$,
- then

$$u := 12^5 \bmod 85 = \mathbf{37} > t = 33, \quad v := 37^7 \bmod 33 = 16,$$
$$w := 16^3 \bmod 33 = 4 \neq 37.$$

- Since w is not equal u, hence x is not equal a. It means that the RSA signature protocol fails under certain conditions.

Verification:

$$4^{13} \bmod 85 = 4 \neq 12.$$

There are many digital signature algorithms (DSAs) that operate without failures. In 1991, The National Institute of Standards and Technology (NIST) proposed DSA, (Federal Register, 1991). Since the RSA signature scheme was considered as a de facto standard, many researchers and corporations (IBM, Motorola) pointed out that RSA is faster than the DSA, (Kaliski, 1991; Follett, 1991; Shroyer, 1992). The latest version of the NIST standard is published in NIST (1994). This version of the DSA is a modification of the ElGamal algorithm, (ElGamal, 1985).

3. ElGamal Digital Signature Algorithm

On the signature generation stage {Alice sends a message m to Bob} *Alice* performs the following steps:

1. Randomly chooses $r \in N$ such that $r < p - 1$ and $\gcd(r, p - 1) = 1$,
2. Computes $\beta \equiv \alpha^r \pmod{p}$,
3. Computes $r^{-1} \bmod (p - 1)$,
4. Computes $s = r^{-1}s = [h(m) - a\beta] \pmod{p}$, here $h(m)$ is a hash function,
5. The signature for m is (β, s) which is sent to B.
   On the verification stage, Bob performs the following steps:
6. Obtains A's public key (p, α, α^a),
7. Tests that $\beta \in N$ with $\beta < p$, and rejects, if it is not,

8. Computes $x \equiv \alpha^{a\beta}\beta^s \pmod{p}$,
9. Computes $h(a)$ and $z \equiv a^{h(m)} \pmod{p}$,
10. *Bob* accepts the signature if $x = z$, in which case m is a valid message.

This scheme requires a hash function h. Although the ElGamal signature schemes work without failure, computationally they are more time demanding than the RSA signature scheme.

4. Signature Scheme with Upper-and-Lower Keys

Let us consider *two* large numbers L and R, where $L < R$. Select a number M in the middle of interval $[L, R]$: $M := (L + R)/2$, i.e., M divides the interval $[L, R]$ onto two subintervals.

Remark 4.1. L determines a required minimal level of crypto-immunity, R establishes a maximal level of complexity beyond which the computational complexity of the cryptosystem becomes too large for its implementation.

4.1. *System Design Level*

Step 4.1. A user selects *two* primes p and q such that $L < pq < M$, let $m := pq$,

Table 4.1   Upper and lower keys.

keys\users	Alice : $\{i = 1\}$	Bob : $\{i = 2\}$
upper public key	$n_1 > M, e_1$	$n_2 > M, e_2$
upper private key	f_1	f_2
lower public key	$m_1 < M, e_1$	$m_2 < M, e_2$
lower private key	d_1	d_2

Step 4.2. The same user selects *two* primes r and s such that $M < rs < R$, let $n := rs$,

Step 4.3. Let $y := (p - 1)(q - 1)/2$, and $z := (r - 1)(s - 1)/2$,

Step 4.4. Select an integer e relatively prime with y and z, i.e., $gcd(e, y) = 1$, and $gcd(e, z) = 1$,

Step 4.5. Find $de \bmod y = 1$, and $ef \bmod z = 1$.

4.2. System Implementation

Step 4.6. $\{n, e\}$ is an *upper* public key and f is *upper* private key,

Table 4.2   Upper and lower keys in action.

Sender's actions	Alice is sender, a is message	Bob is sender, b is message
signature (*lower* key)	$u := a^{d_1} \bmod m_1 < M$	$u := b^{d_2} \bmod m_2 < M$
encryption (*upper* key)	$v := u^{e_2} \bmod n_2 > M$	$v := u^{e_1} \bmod n_1 > M$
Receiver's actions	Bob is receiver	Alice is receiver
decryption (*upper* key)	$w := v^{f_2} \bmod n_2 > M$	$w := v^{f_1} \bmod n_1 > M$
signature verification (*lower* key)	$x := w^{e_1} \bmod m_1 < M$, if x is intelligible, then Bob accepts that $x = a$.	$x := w^{e_2} \bmod m_2 < M$, if x is intelligible, then Alice accepts that $x = b$.

Step 4.7. and $\{m, e\}$ is a *lower* public key and d is *lower* private key, {see Table 4.1.}.

Step 4.8. The sender is using her/his *lower* keys and the receiver is using his/her *upper* keys {see Table 4.2.},

Remark 4.2. A sequence of keys applied in the proposed DSS resembles an *overpass crossing*: firstly, apply the lower key, then twice the upper keys, and finally the lower key again.

5. Computational Complexity

Notice that each user must have *two* private keys and *three* numbers as public keys, i.e., the overpass-crossing signature scheme requires 50% more storage for the public keys and twice more memory for the private keys. The time–complexity of the scheme is the same as for the RSA-DSS.

Chapter 14

Hybrid Cryptographic Protocols Providing Digital Signature

A hybrid cryptographic system, providing digital authentication, is described and analyzed in the chapter. The proposed cryptosystem incorporates three features: complexity of discrete logarithm problem, complexity of integer factorization of a product of two large primes, and a combination of symmetric and asymmetric keys. In order to make the cryptosystem less vulnerable to cryptanalytic attacks, a concept of digital *entanglements* is introduced. As a result, the proposed cryptographic system has *four layers* (entanglement–encryption–decryption–disentanglement). It is shown that in certain instances the proposed communication cryptocol is many times faster than the RSA cryptosystem. Examples provided in the chapter illustrate details of the proposed cryptographic protocol.

1. Introduction and Basic Definitions

In this chapter a hybrid digital signature, cyber-secure communication system is described and analyzed. In order to make this cryptosystem faster and less vulnerable to cryptanalytic attacks a concept of *entanglement* is introduced (Verkhovsky, 2008b; 2008d). Furthermore, in this cryptographic protocol there are *four* layers: entanglement–encryption–decryption–disentanglement. Since there is no one-to-one mapping between a plaintext block and the corresponding ciphertext block, this system of communication is less vulnerable to plaintext attacks. The overall cryptographic algorithm is a hybrid protocol that incorporates three features: discrete logarithm problem modulo large prime (Diffie–Hellman, 1976), factorization of a product of two large primes (Rivest *et al.* 1978), and a combination of symmetric and asymmetric keys.

To describe the proposed cryptosystem, let us consider

A.1. An array

$$m = (a_1, a_2, \ldots, a_r), \tag{1.1}$$

consisting of r blocks of a digitized plaintext that is to be transmitted from a sender (Alice) to a receiver (Bob),

B.1. A square $r \times r$ non-singular matrix E with

$$|E| \neq 0, \quad \text{and} \quad h = Em. \tag{1.2}$$

In this chapter

$$h = (h_1, \ldots, h_r), \tag{1.3}$$

and E are respectively called a vector and matrix of *entangs* (Verkhovsky, 2008b).

C.1. A sufficiently strong cryptographic protocol L, which is used for encryption of one of the entanglements, for example, h_1 with the corresponding ciphertext c_1.

In order to speed up the encryption/decryption procedure and, as a result, to minimize the entire communication time, it is necessary to minimize the amount of computations. For that reason there is no necessity to encrypt all other entanglements $h_{j \neq i}$, where $j = 1, 2, \ldots, i-1, i+1, \ldots, r$ and h_i is the only encrypted entang. Indeed, if h_i is not known to a potential intruder, then he or she cannot solve a system of r eqs., where only $r-1$ components of vector h are publicly known. In the cryptosystem described below, the size r of the array m is a trade-off between crypto-immunity and acceleration of the decryption: the larger the value of r, the faster is the overall communication protocol. On the other hand, the larger is r, the less time is required to cryptanalyze the entire message.

To **avoid confusions**, it is important to indicate the following distinctions:

- The matrix of entanglement E (and non-linear mappings) discussed below are not secret keys as in an affine cryptographic algorithm, all elements of matrix E are *publicly known*,
- In contrast to the RSA and Rabin algorithms, n_k is a *private* key of the k-th user, not a public key.

2. Digital Signature Scheme

2.1. *System design module*

{users establish their private and public keys}:

A.2. All users agree on a large prime p and a generator g, where

$$2 \leq g \leq p - 2, \tag{2.1}$$

Remark 2.1. Selection of a generator for a large prime p is a non-deterministic procedure. However, if both p and $(p-1)/2$ are primes, then

$$g := (3p - 1)/4, \tag{2.2}$$

is a generator. Other algorithms for selection of generators are described in (Verkhovsky, 2013), {see chapter 2},

B.2. Each user selects large primes p_k and q_k, such that

$$p_k \equiv q_k \equiv 2(\mathrm{mod}\ 3), \tag{2.3}$$

and that their product n_k satisfies two constraints:

$$\alpha p < n_k < p, \tag{2.4}$$

C.2. Each user selects her/his public key e_k {encryption key} co-prime with private key n_k, i.e.,

$$\gcd\ (n_k, e_k) = 1, \tag{2.5}$$

D.2. Every user computes a private key d_k, which is a multiplicative inverse of e_k modulo

$$z_k := (p_k - 1)(q_k - 1),$$

i.e., d_k satisfies the equation

$$d_k e_k \equiv 1(\mathrm{mod}\ z_k), \tag{2.6}$$

E.2. If Alice and Bob intend to secretly exchange authenticated information, they establish a secret key $w_{AB} := g^{ab}$ mod p by using the Diffie–Hellman key exchange, (Diffie–Hellman, 1976).

2.2. *Encryption/Decryption module*

{Alice sends to Bob a plaintext array m}:

F.2. Alice requests Bob to secretly send to her *via* an open channel Bob's private key n_B,

G.2. Bob computes $x := n_B w_{AB} \bmod p$ and sends x to Alice, she recovers $n_B := x w_{AB}^{-1} \bmod p$,

H.2. Using the RSA protocol, Alice encrypts h_i {see (1.2)}:

$$c_i := h_i^{e_B} \bmod n_B, \quad \text{(Rivest et al. 1978)}, \tag{2.7}$$

I.2. Alice transmits the array $\{h_1, \ldots, h_{i-1}, c_i, h_{i+1}, \ldots, h_r\}$ to Bob,

J.2. Bob decrypts c_i:

$$v := c_i^{d_B} \bmod n_B, \quad \{= h_i\}, \tag{2.8}$$

K.2. Using $h = (h_1, \ldots, h_r)$, Bob recovers all plaintext blocks $m = (a_1, a_2, \ldots, a_r)$,

L2. If the original array m is intelligible, but the recovered text is not, then Bob realizes that it was forged by an intruder, otherwise Bob accepts authenticity of the text.

2.3. *Selection of block size and matrix of entanglements*

To assure that the entanglements are smaller than every n_i, {otherwise the entire array $m = (a_1, a_2, \ldots, a_r)$ is not recoverable}, select the matrix of entanglement E and such division of a plaintext onto blocks that the maximal value of the i-th entang h_i does not exceed αp, (2.4)}.

Example 2.1. Let

$$m := (a, b, c, d, e), \quad \text{and} \quad h = (h_1, h_2, h_3, h_4, h_5), \tag{2.9}$$

where

$$h_1 := d + 2e, \quad h_2 := a - 2b, \quad h_3 := 2a - b + c,$$
$$h_4 := c - d + 2e, \quad h_5 := a + 2b + c + d. \tag{2.10}$$

Thus,

$$b = h_1 + 3h_3 - (4h_2 + h_4 + 2h_5), \quad a = h_2 + 2b,$$
$$c = h_3 - 2a + b, \quad d = h_5 - a - 2b - c, \quad e = (h_1 - d)/2. \tag{2.11}$$

Let us specify that every block in m must satisfy the threshold $a_k < t$, then (2.10) implies that

$$\max h_i = 3t \le \alpha p < n_i < p. \tag{2.12}$$

Therefore, for every $k = 1, \ldots, r$ must hold $a_k \le t \le \alpha p/3$, and if $\alpha = 3/4$, then $a_k \le t \le p/4$.

From the recovery procedure (2.11), it is clear that we can recover the initial blocks a, b, c, d and e **only if** we know every numeric value h_1, h_2, h_3, h_4, h_5 from (2.10). Henceforth, this fact implies that it is sufficient to encrypt at least one of these entanglements to securely protect all five plaintext blocks.

Furthermore, it is worth to notice that entanglements themselves do not provide secure protection. In the proposed cryptographic scheme instead of employing just one layer {plaintext–encryption–ciphertext} we propose **two layers** {plaintext–entanglement–encryption–ciphertext} between the plaintext array $(a, b, c, d, e, \ldots,)$ and ciphertext $(c_1, h_2, h_3, h_4, h_5, \ldots,)$.

Remark 2.2. The RSA discussed below is just an example of how h_i can be encrypted. Any strong cryptocol based on the complexity of factorization of $n = pq$ can be also used. The Rabin algorithm (Rabin, 1979) or (hyper)-elliptic–curve cryptography (Miller, 1985; Koblitz, 1987; 1989; Koblitz *et al.* 2000) based on modulo of composite n are other possible applications.

2.4. *Essence of RSA digital signature algorithm*

In order to demonstrate advantages of the proposed digital signature algorithm, let us recall the RSA digital signature algorithm (Rivest *et al.* 1978; Verkhovsky, 2001).

Suppose that Alice wants to send to Bob a message $m = (a_1, a_2, \ldots, a_r)$ with digital signature. Then for *every* $k = 1, 2, \ldots, r$, Alice signs $a_k f_k := a_k^{d_A} \bmod n_A$, with her private key, then encrypts it with Bob's public key

$$c_k := f_k^{e_B} \bmod n_B, \tag{2.13}$$

and transmits the ciphertext c_k to Bob over an open communication channel. Bob decrypts

$$x := c^{d_B} \bmod n_B,$$

and then verifies the signature:

$$y := x^{e_A} \bmod n_A, \quad \{y = m\}. \tag{2.14}$$

If y is intelligible, then Bob accepts it as an authenticated message from Alice {see chapter 23, describing the cases where it does not work and provide constructive approach how it should be executed to assure that it does work}.

3. Examples of Entangs

3.1. *Linear transformations*

Example 3.1. Let

$$h_0 := a_1 + \cdots + a_{r-1} + a_r, \quad h_1 := -a_1 + a_2 + \cdots + a_r,$$
$$h_2 := a_1 - a_2 + \cdots + a_r, \ldots, \quad h_{r-1} := a_1 + \cdots - a_{r-1} + a_r. \tag{3.1}$$

Proposition 3.2. If all entanglements $h_0, h_1, h_2, \ldots, h_{r-1}$ are known and integer, then for every $k = 1, \ldots, r-1$

$$a_k = (h_0 - h_k)/2, \tag{3.2}$$

$$a_r = h_0 - (a_1 + a_2 + \cdots + a_{r-1}) \tag{3.3}$$

and all a_k are integer as well.

Proof follows from two observations:

- for every $k = 1, \ldots, r-1$

$$h_k = h_0 - 2a_k, \tag{3.4}$$

- all $h_0, h_1, h_2, \ldots, h_{r-1}$ have the same parity, which implies that their pairwise differences are *even*. Therefore, every $a_1, a_2, \ldots$ and a_r is integer. quod erat demonstrandum (QED).

Complexity of recovery: It requires $r-1$ subtractions and divisions by two (binary shifts) to recover the first $r-1$ blocks in (3.2) and $r-1$ subtractions to recover the last block in (3.3).

If a sender (Alice) encrypts only s of all entanglements, where $0 < s < r$, then the intruder will not be able to deduce any blocks (provided that the matrix E is properly selected and a portion of entanglements is encrypted with a sufficiently strong public-key cryptography (PKC) protocol). In an extreme case, if $s = 1$, then the intruder must solve a system of eqs. $Ea = g$, where the matrix E is *known* but only $r-s$ elements of vector g are known. However, this is impossible, because to find the blocks $a_1, a_2, \ldots, a_r$, the intruder must know all r elements of vector g.

3.2. *Non-Linear transformations*

In the more general case, the entanglements can be non-linear, i.e., $h := E(a)$, and/or some components of the transformation $E(a)$ can also be encrypted. For example, if $h := Ea$, then we can encrypt several elements of matrix E. This approach is beyond the scope of this short discussion. It is important to bear in mind that the selection of the transformation $E(a)$ affects the computational complexity of the recovery process.

The choice of the mapping E is important. If E is a matrix, then it must be non-singular and selected in such a way that the recovery will not become computationally formidable.

Example 3.3. Let's consider an array of r plaintext blocks $h_1, h_2, \ldots,$ h_{r-1}, h_r and the following r entanglements:

$$
\begin{aligned}
h_1 &:= a_1^2 - a_2^2, & h_2 &:= a_2^2 - a_3^2, \ldots \\
h_{r-1} &:= a_{r-1}^2 - a_r^2, & h_r &:= a_1 + a_r.
\end{aligned}
\tag{3.5}
$$

It is obviously sufficient to encrypt only one of the entanglements. Then, after the decryption, we proceed as follows:

$$
w := h_1 + h_2 + \cdots + h_{r-1} = a_1^2 - a_r^2.
\tag{3.6}
$$

Therefore,

$$
a_1 = (h_r + w/h_r), \quad a_r = (h_r - w/h_r),
\tag{3.7}
$$

and for k from 2 to $r - 1$

$$
a_k = \sqrt{a_{k-1}^2 - h_{k-1}}.
\tag{3.8}
$$

In combination with encryption these non-linear entanglements provide secure protection and recovery for every transmitted array. Yet, they require divisions of integers and extraction of square roots, which are computationally more complicated procedures.

3.3. *Improper entanglement*

Example 3.4. Let

$$
\begin{aligned}
h_1 &:= 2a_1 + a_2, & h_2 &:= a_1 + a_2, \\
h_3 &:= a_1 + a_2 + a_3, \ldots, & h_r &:= a_1 + a_2 + \cdots + a_r.
\end{aligned}
\tag{3.9}
$$

If $r > 2$, then it is insufficient to encrypt only one of these entangs.

Indeed, if h_1 is encrypted, then for all $3 \leq k \leq r$,

$$
a_k = h_k - h_{k-1}.
\tag{3.10}
$$

In general, if i is fixed, $i \geq 2$, and only h_i is encrypted, then

$$
a_1 = h_1 - h_2;
\tag{3.11}
$$

and for all $3 \leq k \leq i - 1$ and $i + 2 \leq k \leq r$

$$a_k = h_k - h_{k-1}. \tag{3.12}$$

Therefore, $r - 2$ blocks are cryptographically unprotected in every array.

4. Trade-off Analysis

Every block in (2.13)–(2.14) requires *four* exponentiations for encryption and decryption. In contrast, in the protocol A.2–L.2 described above, (2.1)–(2.8), the *array* of r blocks requires only one exponentiation for its encryption and decryption. Therefore, the larger is the transmitted array r, the more efficient is speed-up of A.2–L.2. If $r = 100$, then A.2–L.2. is *four hundred* times faster than the RSA algorithm.

Furthermore, if $n_B \leq m \leq n_A$, then the RSA digital signature algorithm (2.13)–(2.14) fails to recover the original plaintext m unless special measures are taken, (Rivest *et al.* 1978; Verkhovsky, 2001). The application of entanglements (linear or non-linear transformations) is a tool that is proposed to accelerate the encryption/decryption process. Although the entanglements themselves do not provide protection, yet, when used in combination with other measures, they decrease the amount of computations necessary for the entire encryption/decryption process.

It is necessary to mention that every detailed and credible *quantification* of the trade-off between the size r of the array and crypto-immunity requires analysis of all strategies potentially available to the intruder. Yet, to *qualitatively* illustrate this point of view, let us consider an asymptotic case, where the size r of the transmitted array of plaintext blocks is very large. From one point of view, the larger is r, the more advantageous is the proposed cryptosystem. Indeed, only one entanglement is encrypted/decrypted instead of all r entanglements as it is done in the RSA, ElGamal, Rabin (Rabin, 1979), elliptic-curve cryptography (ECC) or (hyper)-ECC (Miller, 1985; Koblitz, 1987; Koblitz *et al.* 2000) and other public key cryptosystems (Koblitz, 1989). On the other hand, if the size r of the array is very large, then the intruder can invest required time and computing resources to cryptanalyze the encrypted entanglement.

Let us consider the extreme case, where the entire message M consists of N blocks. Let us select a square $N \times N$ non-singular matrix E, compute N entanglements $h_1, h_2, \ldots, h_N$ using (3.1) and encrypt only one of them, say, h_1. For instance, if the sender transmits information regarding highly-sensitive issues of long-term national policy or the details of a major corporate policy, the intruder will invest all available resources to break the encrypted entanglement h_1 (Odlyzko, 2000; Pollard, 2000; Stinson, 2002; Chateauneuf *et al.* 2003; Coron *et al.* 2005).

Therefore, for security purpose, it is safer to divide the entire file M onto several parts/arrays and securely protect each array.

5. Decryption: Reduction of Complexity

The most serious computational bottleneck of the present public-key cryptographic protocols is that they are notoriously slow and therefore cannot be used in the real-time exchange of sensitive information.

Although we are currently far away from completely eliminating this bottleneck, the proposed cryptosystem is a systemic tool that accelerates secure communication *via* open channels of the internet or within corporate networks.

Eliminating the bottleneck mentioned above is one of major research areas today and will likely occupy hundreds of communication specialists and system designers for years ahead. Various PKC algorithms were introduced in the last thirty years. ECC and its hyper-elliptic extension are vivid examples of research that accelerates the encryption/decryption process. The proposed cryptosystem is another illustration of how the PKC protocols can be accelerated if the entangled arrays rather than the individual blocks are encrypted.

6. Illustrative Example

The Steps A.6–H.6 describe a system *design* stage and the steps I.6–L.6 describe its implementation for signed encryption and authenticated decryption of arrays

$$m = (a_1, \ldots, a_r),$$

A.6. Let Alice and Bob select $p = 1907$, a generator $g = 1430, (2.2)$, and $\alpha = 2/3, (2.10\text{--}12)$,

B.6. Let each Alice and Bob select two pairs of primes:

$$\{p_A, q_A\} = \{29, 47\} \quad \text{and} \quad \{p_B, q_B\} = \{17, 89\},$$

where

$$p_A \equiv q_A \equiv p_B \equiv q_B \equiv 2 \pmod{3}, \tag{6.1}$$

and compute their products (Verkhovsky, 2008b):

$$n_A := p_A q_A = 1363 \quad \text{and} \quad n_B := p_B q_B = 1513, \tag{6.2}$$

then $\{p_A, q_A, n_A\}$ is the triad of Alice's *private* keys and $\{p_B, q_B, n_B\}$ is the triad of Bob's *private* keys,

C.6. {Establishment of a secret key w}: w must satisfy the inequality $w < \alpha p$, Alice and Bob randomly select secret integers $a = 7$ and $b = 10$ respectively and compute

$$u := g^a \bmod p = 1601,$$

and

$$y := g^b \bmod p = 1733,$$

D.6. Alice transmits u to Bob, who transmits y to Alice,

E.6. Alice and Bob compute respectively

$$w_A := y^a \bmod p \quad \text{and} \quad w_B := u^b \bmod p. \qquad (6.3)$$

As a result,

$$w_{AB} = w_A = w_B = g^{ab} \bmod p = 1118, \qquad (6.4)$$

is their secret key,

F.6. Alice and Bob compute the multiplicative inverse w_{AB}^{-1} of their secret key w_{AB}:

$$w_{AB}^{-1} = 1281, \quad \text{(Verkhovsky, 2001)},$$

G.6. {Alice requests that Bob transmits to her his *private* key n_B}:
   Bob computes v and sends it to Alice:

$$v := n_B w_{AB} \bmod p = 25,$$

H.6. Alice recovers Bob's private key

$$n_B = v w_{AB}^{-1} \bmod 1907 = 1513,$$

I.6. Suppose Alice and Bob select their public keys $e_A = e_B = 3$.
   Consequently,

$$d_A e_A \bmod z_A = 1,$$

and

$$d_B e_B \bmod z_B = 1,$$

implies that

$$d_A = 909 \quad \text{and} \quad d_B = 1009.$$

J.6. Suppose Alice intends to transmit to Bob over the internet an encrypted array

$$m := \{324, 241, 332, 108, 412\}$$

with her digital signature.

If she selects the entanglements (2.10), then

$$h = \{1234, 500, 568, 1350, 1588\}.$$

If $\alpha = 2/3$, then h_1 satisfies the requirement (2.12),

K.6. Alice encrypts h_1:

$$c_1 := h_1^{e_B} \bmod n_B = 1476,$$

and transmits $(c_1, h_2, h_3, h_4, h_5)$ to Bob,

L.6. Bob decrypts the ciphertext c_1:

$$x := c_1^{d_B} \bmod n_B = 1234 \quad \{= h_1\},$$

M.6. Using (2.11), Bob recovers $h = (h_1, \ldots, h_5)$. Because nobody except Bob knows his private key n_B, only he can recover the correct values of all plaintext blocks. If the recovered message is intelligible, Bob accepts it as the authentic message from Alice.

7. Concluding Remarks

This chapter describes the PKC that employs a combination of discrete logarithm problem (DLP), factorization and entanglements, which facilitates otherwise computationally difficult problem (Odlyzko, 2000). Let us summarize most important issues that were described and briefly discussed in this chapter:

A.7. In contrast to RSA, n_k is a private key of the k-th user, not the public key,

B.7. In another contrast, the encryption/decryption is applied not to every block of the plaintext, but to every *array* of the blocks; in other words, the *unit of cryptographic protection* is not a block, but every array consisting of several blocks (Verkhovsky, 2008a),

C.7. Within each array prior to encryption all blocks are entangled (Verkhovsky, 2008b),

D.7. The advantage of entanglements is that they are interdependent, the disadvantage is that if one entang is corrupted, it affects the entire array, namely, *that* array cannot be recovered by the receiver (Verkhovsky, 2008d),

E.7. If the information is transmitted in an aggressive media and subject to networking failures or errors, the proposed cryptosystem cannot be used unless additional measures of information assurance are applied, (Verkhovsky, 2009c; 2009e).

F.7. As a by-product of interdependence, there is no necessity to encrypt and decrypt each block or each entang. Instead it is sufficient to encrypt at least one of r entangs (Verkhovsky, 2009b). This is a substantial advantage of the proposed protocol.

G.7. The application of cryptography based on cubic roots provides another substantial advantage: the encryption requires only two multiplications (Verkhovsky, 2008b),

H.7. The overhead of the entanglements is on the stage of information recovery: it is necessary to solve a system of r eqs. with r unknowns. Yet, there are many ways how to select matrix E that will make these computations easier. Several linear and non-linear examples of entanglements are provided above for illustration. Additional examples of entanglements are described in (Verkhovsky, 2008a). The proposed cryptosystem also provides a digital signature protocol.

Chapter 15

Control Protocols Providing Information Assurance

1. Introduction

In modern communication networks two major requirements must be met: reliability of connection and security of delivery. Both requirements have been analyzed in communication theory (Curts, 2003; Gorodetsky *et al.*, 2001; Verkhovsky, 2008) and thoroughly developed in cryptography (Menezes *et al.*, 1997). The reliability is assured by communication protocols that provide a system of acknowledgments (ACKs). In these protocols, a sender repeatedly transmits a block of information until the intended receiver sends an ACK. In addition, prior to transmission, each block is cryptographically protected by the sender (Verkhovsky, 2008; Voas–Wilbanks, 2008).

The implementation of these two requirements of information processing consumes extra time and additional bandwidth (Hamill *et al.*, 2005). These are major drawbacks if rapid delivery is essential. Information transmissions in a military environment and in financial exchanges are examples in which delay is a sensitive issue. Security of voice communication over the internet is another example (Aldini *et al.*, 2003), where reliability, security and real-time communication in Voice-over-Internet protocol (VoIP) are paramount requirements. In voice networks the time constraints are even tighter, since a delay larger than a quarter of a second is not acceptable. In addition, in voice networks there are three other impairments: noise, losses and echo. In Brown *et al.* (2008), are considered capabilities of information assurance strategies in decision-making, which are critical to national infrastructures. These capabilities are subject 'to attack and compromise of data by globally dispersed threats'. A methodology generating the information assurance strategies and their assessment are discussed in Brown *et al.* (2008). Another example of one-way communication is the control of a deep-space robotic craft. This is an emerging field of communication technology, in which The National Aeronautics and Space Administration (NASA) created a communication protocol, that uses tandems of space probes and orbiters as deep space routers (Falby *et al.*, 2004). Currently more than forty interplanetary missions are supported by NASA. The Earth control center transmits information *via* the orbiter to the rover. Obviously, such information must be securely protected and highly reliable.

Several reliability protocols are described in this chapter. Their probabilities of failure (*PoFs*), bandwidth requirement per block of transmitted information and complexity of recovery are analyzed and compared. The chapter provides a further discussion and analysis of the information assurance (IA) protocols and corresponding algorithms for the information assurance previously considered in Verkhovsky (2008a; 2008d).

2. Basic Definitions

In this chapter, we discuss how to ensure that information is delivered to an intended receiver with the required probability of success (reliability consideration) (Hamill *et al.*, 2005). For the sake of simplicity, the security requirements and speech communication networks are not addressed in this chapter. Yet, even in this simplified setting the problem is far from trivial. In order to tackle this problem, redundancy protocols are introduced in this chapter and their performances are analyzed (Verkhovsky, 2008b).

Definition 2.1. A protocol, handling r channels/links over which an *array* of n blocks of information $\{a_1, \ldots, a_n\}$ is transmitted, is called $P(r, n)$-protocol. Here $1 \leq n \leq r$ and $R := r - n$ is defined as the *redundancy* of the protocol $P(r, n)$.

If every channel is absolutely reliable, i.e., its *PoF* $f = 0$, then the most efficient is a transmission protocol, where redundancy equals zero. However, in most system communications, a certain degree of redundancy is necessary, since there is always a chance of communication channel failure ($f > 0$), {i.e., probability of successful transmission is less than 100%}. Although redundancy does not provide absolute assurance of information delivery, yet, if properly handled, it can substantially increase the probability of successful transmission, if a suitable $P(r, n)$-protocol is used for communication.

Definition 2.2. In a $P(r,n)$-protocol, if all n blocks of information are received and recovered by the receiver (Bob), then such transmission is called successful.

Modern communication is an expensive and complex process, requiring financial resources, bandwidth and time. Therefore, it should be designed to satisfy all technical and other requirements and to optimize utilization of all systemic resources.

In this chapter, several IA protocols are described and their performance is analyzed.

3. Information Assurance Protocols

3.1. $P(3,2)$-Protocol

Consider a *pair* of plaintext blocks represented in a digital form as integers a and b on the interval $2 \leq a, b \leq n - 2$.

Suppose that

$$\{A, B, C\} := \{a + b, a - b, a^2 - b^2\} \tag{3.1}$$

are three corresponding *entanglements* {combinations} of blocks a and b. It is clear that, if any *two* out of three entanglements in Eq. (3.1) are successfully transmitted, then Bob is able to recover the original blocks. However, the $P(3,2)$-protocol fails if fewer than two entanglements are successfully transmitted. Thus, the *PoF* in the $P(3,2)$-protocol equals

$$F_{3,2} = f^3 + 3f^2(1 - f) = (3 - 2f)f^2. \tag{3.2}$$

If the probability of link failure is significantly smaller than *one*, $\{f \ll 1\}$, then Eq. (3.2) implies that, with high degree of accuracy:

$$F_{3,2} = 3f^2, \tag{3.3}$$

since $2f \ll 3$. In other words, the second term in Eq. (3.2) is substantially smaller than $3f^2$. In stricter terms it means that, if f is approaching *zero*, then the ratio $(3f^2 - 2f^3)/3f^2$ is approaching *one*, i.e.,:

$$F_{3,2}/3f^2 \to 1. \tag{3.4}$$

For example, if $f = 0.01$, $\{1\%\}$, then $3f^2 = 0.0003$ and $2f^3 = 0.000002$, i.e., the latter term is 150 times smaller than the former one.

If either (A and C) or (B and C) are successfully transmitted, then recovery of a and b requires *one* operation of division. The protocol provided

Table 3.1 $P(3, 2)$ recovery procedures.

FSE	Recovery procedure
$\{A, B\}$	$a := B - A,\ b := A - a$
$\{A, C\}$	$a := (A + C)/2,\ b := a - C$
$\{B, C\}$	$a := (B + C)/3,\ b := a - C$

in Eq. (3.1) is an example of a non-linear implementation. Here is a more efficient (faster) *linear* variation of the $P(3, 2)$-protocol:

$$\{A, B, C\} := \{a + b, 2a + b, a - b\}. \tag{3.5}$$

For instance, if the entanglements

$$A := a + b \quad \text{and} \quad B := 2a + b, \tag{3.6}$$

are successfully transmitted, then *Bob* computes $a := B - A$, and $b := A - a$.

Therefore, the implementation of Eq. (3.5) is more efficient since it requires addition, subtraction, and division by 2 and 3. All these operations have linear bit-wise complexity. In contrast, the recovery in the Eq. (3.1) version of the $P(3, 2)$-protocol requires one operation of division, which has quadratic bit-wise complexity.

Table 3.1. provides recovery procedures for every feasible set of entanglements (*FSEs*): $\{A, B\}$, $\{A, C\}$ and $\{B, C\}$.

Definition 3.1. Suppose that t is an *acceptable* probability of transmission failure $\{t$ is an acceptable *threshold*$\}$. If $F_{r,n} \leq t$, then the $P(r, n)$-protocol is feasible.

For instance, if $F_{3,2} \leq t$, then a $P(3, 2)$-protocol is feasible, otherwise a more elaborate protocol is required. Furthermore, if $f \ll 1$, then the inequalities

$$F_{3,2} = 3f^2 - 2f^3 < 3f^2 \leq t, \tag{3.7}$$

imply that $F_{3,2} < t$.

It is important to mention that

- $P(3, 2)$ is the simplest of all IA protocols,
- Although the *PoF* in $F_{3,2}$ is *three* times larger than in $F_{2,1}$, the $P(3, 2)$-protocol has its advantage over $P(2, 1)$, since $P(2, 1)$ requires 33.3% more bandwidth than the $P(3, 2)$-protocol.

4. $P(4, 2)$-Protocol

In this protocol, either *four* channels are used to transmit *two*-block array $\{a, b\}$ or, if time-division multiplexing mode is employed, *four* timeframes are used to transmit one array. Exact and approximate values for the *PoF*

Table 4.1 $P(4, 2)$ and recovery procedures.

FSE	Recovery procedures
$\{A, B\}$	$a := B - A,\ b := A - a$
$\{A, C\}$	$a := (A + C)/2,\ b := A - a$
$\{A, D\}$	$a := (A - D)/3,\ b := A - a$
$\{B, C\}$	$a := (B + C)/3,\ b := a - C$
$\{B, D\}$	$b := (B - 2D)/5,\ a := D + 2b$
$\{C, D\}$	$b := C - D,\ a := C + b$

are provided in Eqs. (A.3) and (A.4) in the appendix. Consider a set of *four* integers:

$$\{A, B, C, D\} := \{a + b, 2a + b, a - b, a - 2b\}. \tag{4.1}$$

In this protocol, a communication is successful if at least *two* out of *four* entanglements from Eq. (4.1) are successfully transmitted. It fails if fewer than *two* out of *four* entanglements in Eq. (4.1) are delivered to Bob.

Table 4.1. shows how to recover the initial blocks for every *FSE*, the recovery requires *two* additions/subtractions and at most one division by one-decimal-digit integer.

5. $P(6, 3)$-Protocol

Assuming that $\{a, b, c\}$ are *three* consecutive blocks of a plaintext, we now consider *six* entanglements of these blocks:

$$\{A := a, B := a - b, C := b - c, D := c, E := a + b + c, F := a + 2b + c\} \tag{5.1}$$

It is easy to verify that none of the above entanglements can be expressed as a linear combination of any other *two* entanglements, otherwise the original message (a, b, c) is not recoverable. In this protocol, the transmission is successful if at least *three* out of *six* values $\{A, B, C, D, E, F\}$ in Eq. (5.1) are successfully delivered to the receiver, otherwise, the $P(6, 3)$-protocol fails. For the exact and approximate *PoF* of $P(6, 3)$ see Eqs. (A.6)–(A.10) in the appendix and Fig. 6.1.

6. $P(r, n)$-Protocol Attributes

The probability of $P(r, n)$-protocol failure has monotone properties that can be instrumental in choice of an appropriate protocol. Indeed,

(1) If f is much smaller that 1, then with an increasing r, the *PoF* is decreasing,

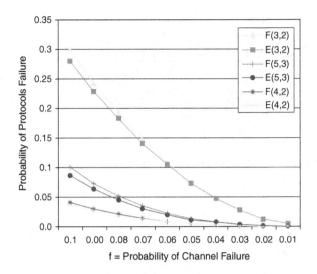

Fig. 6.1   Proximity of exact and approximate *PoF*.

Table 6.1   *PoF*.

f	0.09	0.07	0.05	0.03	0.01
$10E(3,2)$	0.228	0.140	0.073	0.026	0.003
$10F(3,2)$	0.243	0.147	0.075	0.027	0.003
$10E(4,2)$	0.027	0.013	0.005	0.0011	*insdif*
$10F(4,2)$	0.029	0.014	0.005	0.0011	*insdif*
$10E(5,3)$	0.063	0.031	0.012	0.0026	*insdif*
$10F(5,3)$	0.073	0.034	0.013	0.0027	*insdif*

(2) If the size of the array n is increasing, then the *PoF* is increasing,

(3) With simultaneous growth of both r and n, the *PoF* is increasing.

For illustration of these properties see Table 6.1. and Fig. 6.1., for proofs see the Appendix (A.11)–(A.26).

NB: The values of exact and approximate *PoF*s are multiplied by 10 to fit the outputs into Table 6.1., '*insdif*' means that the difference between the exact and approximate values of *PoF* is insignificant, i.e., substantially smaller than 10^{-5}. For further details see Fig. 6.1.

7. Comparative Analysis of $P(r, n)$

7.1. *PoF and bandwidth requirements*

Under assumption that $f \ll 1$, Table 7.1. provides data for comparison of *twenty four* information assurance protocols.

Table 7.1 *PoF* in $P(r,n)$-protocol.

$r\backslash n$	2	3	4	5	6
4	$4f^3$	$6f^2$	f	$* * *$	$* * *$
5	$5f^4$	$10f^3$	$10f^2$	f	$* * *$
6	$6f^5$	$15f^4$	$20f^3$	$15f^2$	f
7	$7f^6$	$21f^5$	$35f^4$	$35f^3$	$21f^2$
8	$8f^7$	$28f^6$	$56f^5$	$70f^4$	$56f^3$
9	$9f^8$	$36f^7$	$84f^6$	$126f^5$	$126f^4$
10	$10f^9$	$45f^8$	$120f^7$	$210f^6$	$252f^5$

8. Comparison of Protocols $P(8,4)$, $P(8,5)$ and $P(9,5)$

By decreasing the bandwidth on 20% and using $P(9,5)$ instead of $P(8,4)$, we increase the probability of link failure 2.25 times, i.e., on 125%.

On the other hand, the ratio of *PoF*s for $P(9,5)$ and $P(8,5)$ equals $(126/70)f = 1.8f$, then for $f = 0.01$, the ratio equals 0.0018.

Therefore, by increasing the bandwidth on 20% and using $P(9,5)$ instead of $P(8,5)$, we decrease the probability of link failure 55.6 times.

If $f = 0.001$, we decrease the *PoF* 555.6 times. The only drawback is that instead of 35 IRRs, it is necessary to consider 66 IRRs.

9. Efficiency of Aggregation

The protocols $P(3,2)$, $P(6,4)$ and $P(9,6)$ have the same bandwidth requirements $B_{3,2} = B_{6,4} = B_{9,6} = 1.5$, yet, if $f \ll 1/10$, then

$$F_{3,2} > F_{6,4} > F_{9,6}. \tag{9.1}$$

Analogously, the protocols $P(4,2)$, $P(6,3)$, $P(8,4)$ and $P(10,5)$ have the same bandwidth requirements

$$B_{4,2} = B_{6,3} = B_{8,4} = B_{10,5} = 2.0. \tag{9.2}$$

However, if $f \ll 1$, then

$$F_{4,2} > F_{6,3} > F_{8,4} > F_{10,5}, \tag{9.3}$$

i.e., the latter protocol has a substantially smaller *PoF* than the former ones. Therefore, certain protocols provide greater assurance than others. For details see Eqs. (A.14)–(A.16) in the appendix. In general, let us consider a $P(mr, mn)$-protocol, where m is a positive integer. If $m \geq 2$ and $f \ll 1$, then it is easy to verify that

$$B_{mr,mn} < B_{r,n}. \tag{9.4}$$

10. First Illustrative Example

Suppose that $f = 10^{-2}$, i.e., a link/channel of communication fails in 1% of the transmissions. Therefore, the *PoFs* in the protocols $P(4, 2)$, and $P(6, 3)$ are respectively about 25 (*twenty five*) times and 667 (*six hundred sixty seven*) times smaller than the *PoF* in the $P(2, 1)$-protocol. In general, the following ratios illustrate the efficiency of these protocols and corresponding aggregations:

$$F_{2,1} : F_{4,2} : F_{6,3} : F_{8,4} : F_{10,5} = 1 : 4f : 15f^2 : 56f^3 : 210f^4 \qquad (10.1)$$

For further details, see Table 7.1. If an acceptable threshold of protocol failure equals $t = 10^{-8}$, then $F_{8,4} = 0.56 \times 10^{-8} < t$, and $F_{10,5} = 0.21 \times 10^{-9} < t$.

If the probability of link failure f and acceptable threshold t are specified as system-performance parameters, then it is necessary to select an appropriate protocol $P(r, n)$ with parameters r and n. If more than one protocol satisfies the threshold requirement, then we select a protocol with smaller bandwidth requirement per block of transmitted information.

11. Second Illustrative Example

Now suppose that $f = 10^{-3}$ and $t = 10^{-10}$, then several information assurance protocols can be employed for solution of this problem. Indeed, the repeated-transmission protocol $P(4, 1)$ provides assurance $f = 10^{-12}$, which is one hundred times smaller than the acceptable threshold t. Yet the $P(4, 1)$-protocol is highly inefficient since it requires quadrupled repetition of each block of information, i.e., $B_{4,1} = 4$. Alternatively, we can select more efficient protocols with smaller bandwidth requirements.

Indeed, let us consider several options and their *PoFs*, {see the Table 7.1.}:

$$\begin{aligned}
\textit{Option I:} &\quad F_{5,2} = 0.05 \times 10^{-10} < t, \\
\textit{Option II:} &\quad F_{6,3} = 0.15 \times 10^{-10} < t, \\
\textit{Option III:} &\quad F_{7,4} = 0.35 \times 10^{-10} < t, \\
\textit{Option IV:} &\quad F_{8,5} = 0.70 \times 10^{-10} < t.
\end{aligned}$$

Yet, $F_{9,6} = 1.26 \times 10^{-10} > t$, i.e., $P(9, 6)$ does not satisfy the threshold t requirement.

Table 11.1 Number of recovery rules in $P(r, n)$-protocols.

$n \backslash r$	5	6	8	9	10	12	16
2	10	15	28	*	45	66	120
3	10	20	56	*	120	220	560
4	5	15	70	*	210	495	1820
5	1	6	56	**126**	252	792	4368

Notice that the bandwidth requirement $B_{r,n}$ per each block is respectively equal:

$$B_{5,2} = 2.5, \quad B_{6,3} = 2, \quad B_{7,4} = 1.75, \quad B_{8,5} = 1.60.$$

Therefore, by considering protocol $P(6, 3)$ instead of $P(4, 1)$, we can reduce *twice* the required bandwidth. Yet, the protocol $P(8, 5)$ is better than $P(6, 3)$ and $P(7, 4)$ because it requires a *minimal bandwidth* per block. There is one substantial drawback with larger arrays: the number of recovery rules for each of these protocols {see Table 11.1.} respectively equals $10, 20, 35$ (not shown in that table) and 56, i.e., progressively increasing.

Add to this a complexity concern. The recovery rules for each combination of the protocol parameters r and n must be computationally simple. There is a way for tackling this drawback. However, this is beyond the scope of this discussion and is addressed in another chapter.

12. Choice of Entangs

If in $P(8, 5)$, the entanglements are

$$\begin{aligned}
A &= a + b, \quad B = a - 2b, \quad C = 2a - b + c, \\
D &= a + 2b + c + d, \quad E = b + c + 2d + e, \\
F &= c - d + 2e, \quad G = e - 2d, \quad H := d - 2e,
\end{aligned} \tag{12.1}$$

then the original blocks $\{a, b, c, d, e\}$ are not recoverable from each of the fifty six *FSEs*. For example, if *BCDFH* or *ADEGH* is transmitted, then the receiver cannot recover the original array. However, if in Eq. (12.1), $A = 3a - b$ and $H := d + 2e$ are selected instead, then the protocol always recovers $\{a, b, c, d, e\}$.

13. Concluding Remarks

If adaptability is appropriate, more reliable transmission protocols can be introduced; however, there are systems that allow only one-way communication:

(a) steganographic protocol, where a receiver needs to keep 'radio' silence,
(b) weapon-guidance protocol, where requirements for real-time control combined with the possibility of high-level noise do not allow time for response and correction.

An example of one-way communication is control of a spacecraft. In the NASA communication protocol, a tandem of the space rover and orbiter is used as deep space switches. It is an extension of the internet into interplanetary space and, in the future, beyond the solar system (Falby *et al.*, 2004). Obviously, such information must be transmitted with high reliability and protected from any interference.

Several protocols concerning information assurance are considered in this chapter. Their efficiencies are analyzed in several examples. Monotonic properties of the IA protocols are formulated, efficiency of aggregation of information arrays is demonstrated and the diminishing effect of redundancy is discussed. As presented in this chapter, algorithm selects an optimal protocol taking into consideration the reliability of the transmission channels {the probability of link failure f}, the level of the IA requirements {the threshold t}, the simplicity of the recovery operations necessary to restore the messages from the entanglements, and finally minimizes the bandwidth requirement per block of transmitted data.

Appendix

A.1. *Repeated-transmission protocol*

Suppose that

$$f^m \le t < f^{m-1}. \tag{A.1}$$

Then for redundancy the same block a is transmitted m times in the $P(m, 1)$-protocol. If a time-division multiplexing protocol (Voas–Wilbanks, 2008) is used, then m time frames are used to transmit every block. Thus, the transmission fails only if all m attempts fail, hence the *PoF* equals

$$F_{m,1} := f^m. \tag{A.2}$$

A.2. *$F_{3,2}$ formula derivation*

In order to derive a formula for *PoF* in $P(3, 2)$-protocol, we need to consider every case where transmission of (a, b) fails. It occurs if either *none* of three entangs $\{A, B, C\}$ is transmitted or if only one out of three entangs $\{A, B, C\}$ is transmitted {see the table}.

Table A.1   Successes and failures.

	1	2	3	4	5	6	7	8
A	*F*	*S*	*F*	*F*	*S*	*S*	*F*	*S*
B	*F*	*F*	*S*	*F*	*S*	*F*	*S*	*S*
C	*F*	*F*	*F*	*S*	*F*	*S*	*S*	*S*

In the Table A.1., F means that transmission of an entang 'failed' and S means that the transmission of that entang was 'successful'. In the first four cases, (3.1)–(1.4), the overall transmission of blocks (a, b) fails, in the last four cases, (1.5)–(1.8), {shown in 'ice-blue' font} that transmission is successful. The first case when all three attempts failed occurs with probability f^3. The cases 2–4 occur with probability $3f^2(1 - f)$. The sum of these two probabilities is equal to $F_{3,2}$ (3.2).

Analogously, one can derive formula (A.3) for the *PoF* in $P(4, 2)$-protocol and formula (A.6) in $P(6, 3)$-protocol.

A.3. *PoF in $P(4, 2)$*

An exact *PoF* for $P(4, 2)$ is equal:

$$F_{4,2} = f^4 + 4f^3(1 - f) = 4f^3 - 3f^4, \tag{A.3}$$

and an approximate *PoF*:

$$F_{4,2} = 4f^3, \quad \text{if } f \ll 1. \tag{A.4}$$

Therefore, (A.3) implies that, if $4f^3 \leq t$ holds, then definitely

$$F_{4,2} < t. \text{ holds.} \tag{A.5}$$

A.4. *PoF in $P(6, 3)$ and $P(6, 4)$ protocols*

The *PoF* in $P(6, 3)$-protocol is equal to

$$F_{6,3} = 15f^4 - 2f^5(12 - 5f) < 15f^4. \tag{A.6}$$

If $f \ll 1$, then

$$F_{6,3} = 15f^4 - o(f). \tag{A.7}$$

Finally, since $F_{6,3} < 15f^4$, then $15f^4 \leq t$ implies that

$$F_{6,3} < t. \tag{A.8}$$

Suppose that $f \ll 1$, then the *PoF* in the $P(6, 3)$-protocol equals

$$F_{6,3} = 15f^4, \tag{A.9}$$

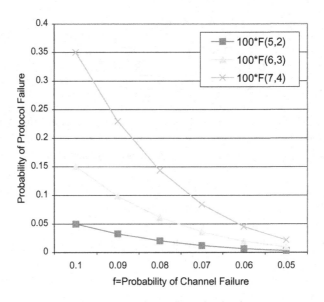

Fig. A.1 Diminishing effect of redundancy.

and in P(6,4)

$$F_{6,4} = 20f^3. \tag{A.10}$$

A.5. *Monotone attributes of PoF*

If $f \ll 1$, then the following inequalities hold:

$$F_{r+1,n} < F_{r,n} < F_{r+1,n+1} < F_{r,n+1}, \tag{A.11}$$

{for illustration see Table 6.1.}.

Indeed, let us show that, if $r > m + 1$, then

$$F_{r+1,m} < F_{r,m}. \tag{A.12}$$

(A.12) follows from two facts: the general formula for

$$F_{r,m} = \binom{r}{m-1} f^{r-(m-1)}, \tag{A.13}$$

and from the ratio

$$F_{r+1,m}/F_{r,m} = (r+1)f/(r-m+2). \tag{A.14}$$

Hence, if $f < 1 - (m-1)/(r+1)$, then

$$F_{r+1,m}/F_{r,m} < 1. \tag{A.15}$$

Therefore, the left-most inequality in (A.11) holds if $m = n$, and the right-most inequality in (A.11) holds if $m = n + 1$. The inequality $F_{r+1,n+1} < F_{r,n}$ follows from two facts:

(1) from the Pascal triangle identity: for every pair of integers r and m such that $r > m$ holds

$$\binom{r+1}{m+1} = \binom{r}{m+1} + \binom{r}{m},$$

(2) from an observation that

$$F_{r+1,n+1} - F_{r,n} = \binom{r}{n} f^{r-(n-1)} > 0. \tag{A.16}$$

A.6. *Ranking the protocols*

Definition A.1. A protocol $P(c,d)$ is more preferable than a protocol $P(g,h)$, {and it is indicated as $P(c,d) \succ P(g,h)$}, if

$$F_{c,d} < F_{g,h}, \tag{A.17}$$

and

$$c/d = g/h. \tag{A.18}$$

Proposition A.2. If $f \ll 1$, then the following properties hold:

$$P(6,3) \succ P(4,2) \succ P(2,1), \tag{A.19}$$

and

$$P(6,4) \succ P(3,2). \tag{A.20}$$

Indeed, let us consider ratios of *PoF*s for these protocols. If $f < 15 \ll 1$, then

$$F_{4,2}/F_{2,1} = 4f < 1, \quad F_{6,3}/F_{4,2} = 15f/4 < 1, \quad \text{and} \tag{A.21}$$
$$F_{6,4}/F_{3,2} = 20f/3 < 1.$$

A.7. *Selection of optimal protocol*

If both the probability of link failure f and the acceptable threshold t are specified as the system performance parameters, then it is necessary to select such r and the size n of the array that satisfy the inequalities:

$$F_{r,n} \leq t < F_{r-1,n} \quad \text{and} \quad F_{r,n} \leq t < F_{r,n+1}. \tag{A.22}$$

A.8. *PoF as function of redundancy*

Let consider

$$R := r - n, \tag{A.23}$$

as a measure of redundancy, and let

$$V(R) := F_{R+n,n} = \binom{R+n}{n-1} f^{R+1} \tag{A.24}$$

I. If $f \ll 1$, then $V(R)$ is a monotone decreasing function of redundancy R.

Indeed, R is increasing if either r is increasing or if the size n of the array of blocks is decreasing. Consider three redundancies $R_1 < R_2 < R_3$:

$$R_1 := r - n - 1, \quad R_2 := r - n = R_1 + 1, \quad R_3 := r + 1 - n = R_1 + 2,$$

and the corresponding *PoF*, $F_{r,n+1}$, $F_{r,n}$ and $F_{r,n+1}$.

Then inequalities (A.11) imply the following relations:

$$F_{r,n+1} > F_{r,n} > F_{r+1,n}. \tag{A.25}$$

II. Alternatively, if the redundancy R remains constant, but the size n of the array is increasing, then the *PoF* is increasing.

Indeed, the inequalities (A.11) implies that

$$F_{r,n} < F_{r+1,n+1}. \tag{A.26}$$

Additionally, if for instance $R = 3$, then the Table 4 shows growth of *PoFs*:

$$F_{5,2} = 5f^4, \quad F_{6,3} = 15f^4, \quad F_{7,4} = 35f^4, \quad F_{8,5} = 70f^4, \ldots \tag{A.27}$$

For illustration see also Fig. A.1.

A.9. *Diminishing effect of redundancy*

Inequality (A.26) indicates a *diminishing* effect of the redundancy R if the size n of the array of transmitted blocks is increasing.

Chapter 16

Information Assurance Based on Cubic Roots of Integers

1. Introduction

In this and other following chapters, we continue to discuss two issues: (1) security of communication; and (2) reliability of communication. A new public-key cryptography algorithm described in this chapter is based on cubic roots of modulo composite $n = pq$. This algorithm is compared with the Rabin algorithm based on square roots. The new algorithm is computationally more efficient than its Rabin counterpart.

The chapter demonstrates how to intertwine both the security requirement and communication assurance into one algorithmic protocol. Four reliability protocols are introduced and their efficiencies {probabilities of failure (*PoFs*), bandwidth requirement per block of transmitted ciphertext and number of exponentiations per block of ciphertext} are analyzed and compared.

In modern communication networks, for transmitting highly-sensitive commercial, financial, legal, military, etc. information, two major requirements must be met: reliability of connection and security of delivery (NIST, 2004; Garrett, 2004; Hardy–Walker, 2003; Menezes *et al.*, 1997; Rabin, 1979; Rivest *et al.*, 1978).

The reliability of connection and information transmission are assured by communication protocols that provide an elaborate system of acknowledgments (ACKs). The basic concept in these protocols is simple: a sender repeatedly transmits a block of information {packet or cell} to a receiver until the intended receiver sends an ACK. In addition, for security reasons each block of information is cryptographically protected by the sender prior to transmission.

In this chapter, we demonstrate how to intertwine the security requirement and communication assurance into one algorithmic protocol. In addition, an analysis of computational aspects of such 'symbiosis' and efficiency of its implementation is provided.

2. Problem Statement

In this chapter, we continue consideration of two major issues that are addressed in the previous chapter:

(1) How to protect information transmitted over open channels/links from a potential intruder {security consideration},
(2) How to ensure that the transmitted information is successfully delivered to an intended receiver with required probability.

Security issue: public-key cryptography algorithms are described, including the algorithms based on *cubic* roots of integers in modular arithmetic.

Reliability issue: redundancy protocols are provided.

Definition 2.1. A protocol, in which r channels/links are used to transmit h packets/blocks $\{u_1, u_2, \ldots, u_h\}$ of information, is called $P(r, h)$-protocol. Here, $1 \leq h \leq r$.

If in $P(r, h)$-protocol all h packages are recovered by the intended receiver, then such transmission is called successful.

If each channel is absolutely reliable, {its *PoF* $f = 0$}, then the most efficient protocol of transmission is $P(1, 1)$-protocol, i.e., where redundancy is absent.

However, in most of technological and/or human communication there is always a chance of communication failure, {i.e., *PoF* $f > 0$}, hence a certain degree of redundancy is necessary. Although there is no redundancy that provides absolute assurance of information delivery, under certain conditions, we can substantially decrease *PoF* $F_{r,h}$, if a proper $P(r, h)$-protocol is used for communication.

Since modern communication is an expensive and complex process, {it requires financial resources, bandwidth and time}, it should be organized to optimize usage of these resources and satisfy all technical and other requirements. In the following text, several protocols are described, their analysis is provided and their performances are compared.

3. $P(3, 2)$-Protocol: Quadratic Root Implementation

Consider a sequence of blocks of a plaintext $m_1, m_2, m_3, m_4, \ldots, m_{2t-1}, m_{2t}$ that must be transmitted from a sender to a receiver {respectively called *Alice* and *Bob* in cryptography}.

Let

$$a_1 := m_1, b_1 := m_2, \ldots, a_i := m_{2i-1}, b_i := m_{2i}, \ldots, a_t := m_{2t-1}, b_t := m_{2t}. \tag{3.1}$$

Consider *triads* of integers

$$\{u, v, w\} := \{a_i^2 \bmod n, (a_i + b_i)^2 \bmod n, b_i^2 \bmod n\}. \tag{3.2}$$

This approach is based on the application of the Rabin encryption (Rabin, 1979) of $a_i, a_i + b_i$ and b_i, where each decryption requires computation of *four* square roots.

It is clear that if any *two* of *three* components are successfully transmitted to *Bob*, then after appropriate decryption, *Bob* will be able to find a_i and b_i, i.e., to recover the plaintext blocks m_{2i-1} and m_{2i}.

For example, if the values of

$$u = a_i^2 \quad \text{and} \quad w = b_i^2 \tag{3.3}$$

are received, then, knowing u and w, Bob decrypts both of them independently {in parallel or sequentially}. Indeed, in knowing the values of p and q, Bob finds from u and respectively from w, the values of a_i and b_i modulo p and modulo q. Then, using the Chinese remainder theorem, Bob computes the values of a_i and b_i, both modulo composite n, (Rabin, 1979).

If

$$u = a_i^2 \bmod n \quad \text{and} \quad v = (a_i + b_i)^2 \bmod n \tag{3.4}$$

are reliably delivered, then after a decryption, Bob computes

$$b_i := \sqrt{v} \bmod n - a_i. \tag{3.5}$$

Bob analogously acts if w and v are transmitted, i.e.,

$$a_i := \sqrt{v} \bmod n - b_i. \tag{3.6}$$

Remark 3.1. Since in the process of decryption the square root modulo composite n provides *two* outputs, according to the Rabin algorithm it is necessary to add extra bits to each plaintext block m_i, otherwise it is not clear which of these two outputs is the original message.

Computational complexity of decryption can be substantially improved if instead of using squaring for encryption and square-root algorithm for decryption we use *cubic* power modulo composite n for encryption of the plaintext and then *directly* {without time consuming Chinese remainder theorem} extract the *cubic*-root for decryption modulo n, (Verkhovsky, 2007).

4. Cubic Root Encryption/Decryption Algorithm

Definition 4.1. An integer z is a cubic root of c modulo n if
$$z^3 \bmod n = c. \tag{4.1}$$

Encryption:

1. Each user selects two large distinct primes such that
$$p \equiv q \pmod 3 = 2, \tag{4.2}$$
   then $n := pq$ and $s := p + q$ are the user's public and private keys,
2. Let m be a plaintext message, $0 < m < n$, where
$$\gcd(m, n) = 1, \quad \text{and} \quad m^2 \bmod n \neq 1, \tag{4.3}$$
3. Compute
$$c := m^3 \bmod n, \quad \{c \text{ is a corresponding ciphertext}\}, \tag{4.4}$$

Decryption:

3. Compute
$$d := c^{(n-s)/3} \bmod n, \tag{4.5}$$

4. Then
$$m = cd^2 \bmod n. \tag{4.6}$$

5. Algorithm Verification

Proposition 5.1. Let $s := p + q$ and $g := 2(n - s)/3 + 1$, and (4.2) holds, then
$$z = c^g \bmod n, \tag{5.1}$$
is a cubic root of c modulo composite n (4.1).

Proof: First of all,
$$2(n - s)/3 + 1 = [2(p - 1)(q - 1) + 1]/3. \tag{5.2}$$
In addition, $(n - s)/3$ is an integer.

Indeed, if (4.2) holds, then

$$pq \equiv (p + q) \pmod 3. \tag{5.3}$$

Hence

$$[pq - (p + q)] \bmod 3 = 0, \tag{5.4}$$

which means that 3 divides $n - s$. Since by Euler's theorem, (Euler, 1911–1944), for every integer z co-prime with n holds that

$$z^{(p-1)(q-1)} \bmod pq = 1, \tag{5.5}$$

then

$$c^3 \equiv z^{1+2(p-1)(q-1)} \equiv z[z^{(p-1)(q-1)}]^2 \equiv z \times 1^2 \equiv z \bmod n. \tag{5.6}$$

Remark 5.2. The exponent g in (5.1) is computable if the *sum* s is known. However, if p and q are large private keys, then g is not known to the intruder.

Remark 5.3. It is essential that the integer $(n - s)/3$ in (4.5) is *odd* since for any a and any *odd* integer R holds

$$\sqrt[R]{-a} = - \sqrt[R]{a}.$$

The encryption/decryption algorithm based on cubic roots is *four times more efficient* than the Rabin algorithm, (Hamill *et al.*, 2005), since the decryption in (4.5) and (4.6) requires computation of *one* cubic root with time complexity equal O (log n) rather than *four* square roots of the same complexity in the Rabin algorithm. Besides, there is no necessity to consider additional bits {tails} as is done in the Rabin algorithm to decide which of the square roots corresponds to the original plaintext, {see the **Remark 3.1.**}.

6. Protocol $P(3, 2)$: Cubic-Root Implementation

Consider a triad of integers

$$\{u, v, w\} := \{a_i^3 \bmod n, (a_i + b_i)^3 \bmod n, b_i^3 \bmod n\}. \tag{6.1}$$

A pair $\{a_i, b_i\}$ is securely and successfully transmitted by the sender (*Alice*), if at least any two components of the triad $\{u, v, w\}$ are delivered to the receiver (*Bob*).

Indeed, if u and w are received by Bob, then he decrypts both u and w independently {sequentially or in parallel} and computes a_i and b_k:

$$a_i := u^g \bmod n, \tag{6.2}$$

and

$$b_i := w^g \bmod n, \quad (4.5)\text{-}(4.7). \tag{6.3}$$

However, if Bob receives u and v, then using (4.7) he first decrypts both u and v, and then recovers

$$b_i := (v^g - u^g) \bmod n, \quad \text{where } g = 2(n - s)/3 + 1. \tag{6.4}$$

The case of w and v is analogous to the previous one.

7. Reliability Analysis

Let f be a probability of link failure and let t be an acceptable probability of transmission failure {t is an acceptable *threshold*}. Then the probability S of successful transmission for $P(3, 2)$-protocol is equal

$$S_{3,2} := (1 - f)^3 + 3(1 - f)^2 f = 1 - F_{3,2}, \tag{7.1}$$

where

$$F_{3,2} = f^3 + 3f^2(1 - f) = f^2(3 - 2f) = 3f^2 + o_1(f). \tag{7.2}$$

Here $o(f)$ is a term that is substantially smaller in comparison with $3f^2$.

As we can see $P(3, 2)$-protocol has three times higher *PoF* than $P(2, 1)$-protocol, which has the *PoF* of failure equal to f^2. However, $P(3, 2)$-protocol is more efficient in terms of bandwidth requirement per block than $P(2, 1)$-protocol. Indeed, the former requires 50% extra bandwidth for reliability, while the latter requires additional 100% of bandwidth.

In general, if $F_{r,h} \le t < 1$, then a $P(r, h)$-protocol is acceptable. However, if the acceptable threshold of failure t is lower than the *PoF* $F_{r,h}$ in the $P(r, h)$-protocol, then a more elaborate approach is required.

8. Protocol $P(4, 2)$: Cubic-Root Implementation

Consider a combination of *four* integers:

$$\{u_1, u_2, u_3, u_4\}$$

$$:= \{a_i^3 \bmod n, (a_i + b_i)^3 \bmod n, (a_i - b_i)^3 \bmod n, b_i^3 \bmod n\}. \tag{8.1}$$

In this protocol, a communication is successful if at least *two* $\{u_i, u_j\}$ of *four* values $\{u_1, u_2, u_3, u_4\}$ in (8.1) are successfully transmitted, then $F_{4,2} = 4f^3 + o_2(f)$.

9. $P(6, 3)$-Protocol

Suppose that $\{a, b, c\}$ are *three* consecutive blocks of a plaintext. Consider again *six* combinations of these blocks that are considered in Chapter 14, (5.1):

$$\{a, a - b, b - c, c, a + b + c, a + 2b + c\}. \tag{9.1}$$

Remark 9.1. It is easy to verify that any subset consisting of three elements in (9.1) is *linearly independent*, which means that none of its elements can be expressed as a linear combination of other two. Otherwise the original message $\{a, b, c\}$ is not recoverable.

Let's consider six corresponding cipher-blocks:

$$u_1 := a^3 \bmod n, \qquad u_2 := (a - b)^3 \bmod n \tag{9.2}$$

$$u_3 := (b - c)^3 \bmod n, \qquad u_4 := c^3 \bmod n, \tag{9.3}$$

$$u_5 := (a + b + c)^3 \bmod n, \quad u_6 := (a + 2b + c)^3 \bmod n. \tag{9.4}$$

In this protocol, a communication is successful if at least *three* $\{u_i, u_j, u_k\}$ of *six* values $\{u_1, u_2, u_3, u_4, u_5, u_6\}$ in (9.2)–(9.4) are successfully transmitted.

10. Reliability Analysis of $P(6, 3)$-Protocol

The transmission fails if either all *six* links fail {with *PoF* f^6}, or any *five* links fail {with *PoF* $6f^5(1 - f)$, or any *four* links fail {with *PoF* $20f^4 (1 - f)^2$}. Hence, the overall *PoF* is equal to

$$F_{6,3} := f^6 + 6f^5(1 - f) + 20f^4(1 - f)^2 = 20f^4 + o_3(f), \tag{10.1}$$

where the term $o_3(f)$ is small in comparison with $20f^4$, if f itself is small.

11. Comparison of Protocols

$P(2, 1)$ is a repeated-message protocol. In this simple protocol, the same ciphertext $a^3 \bmod n$ is transmitted *twice* for redundancy over *two* links/channels. If a time-division multiplexing protocol is used, then two

Table 11.1   Comparison of protocols.

Protocols	$F_{r,h}$	$B_{r,h}$	$E_{r,h}$
$P(2, 1)$-cubic root	f^2	2	$O(2 \times \log n)$
$P(3, 2)$-quadratic root	$3f^2$	1.5	$O(6 \times \log n)$
$P(3, 2)$-cubic root	$3f^2$	1.5	$O(1.5 \times \log n)$
$P(4, 2)$	$4f^3$	2	$O(2 \times \log n)$
$P(6, 3)$	$15f^4$	2	$O(2 \times \log n)$

time frames are used to transmit each block of the ciphertext. Thus the transmission fails only if both channels/links fail. Hence, the *PoF* is equal to

$$F_{2,1} := f^2 \qquad (11.1)$$

Table 11.1. provides comparison of various information assurance protocols.

Here in $P(r, h)$ protocol, $F_{r,h} = PoF, B_{r,h} =$ bandwidth requirement per block of transmitted ciphertext, $E_{r,h} =$ required number of exponentiations per block of ciphertext.

The protocols $P(2, 1)$, {see (11.1)}, $P(4, 2)$, {see (8.1)}, and $P(6, 3)$, {see (9.1)–(9.4), (10.1)}, have the same bandwidth requirements and the same complexity of decryption. However, the latter protocol has a substantially smaller *PoF* than the other two. The protocol $P(3, 2)$, {see (3.1)–(3.6) and (7.2)}, combined with the cubic root algorithm, {see (6.1)–(6.4)}, and the $P(2, 1)$ protocol are different: the former is more efficient in bandwidth requirements and in the complexity of decryption. Yet, the latter protocol has three times smaller a *PoF* than the former one. Finally, the protocol $P(3, 2)$ combined with the square root algorithm is more time consuming for decryption than the protocol $P(3, 2)$ combined with the cubic root algorithm.

Example 11.1. Suppose a channel fails with the probability 1%, i.e., $f = 1/100$, then

$$F_{2,1} = f^2 = 1/10{,}000, \qquad\qquad F_{3,2} = 3f^2 \approx 3/10{,}000,$$

$$F_{4,2} = 4f^3 + o_2(f) \approx 1/250{,}000, \quad F_{6,3} = 20f^4 + o_3(f) \approx 1/5{,}000{,}000.$$

Thus, the *PoF* in the $P(6, 3)$ protocol is about *five hundred times* smaller than the *PoF* of the *repeated-transmission protocol*.

In general,

$$F_{6,3} : F_{4,2} : F_{3,2} : F_{2,1} = 20f^2 : 4f : 3 : 1.$$

Example 11.2. Suppose $p = 29$ and $q = 41$, {see the requirement (7.2)}, then $n = 1189$ and $s = p + q = 70$. Let $f = 1/10$ and the acceptable threshold of failure $t = 1/400$, then

$$F_{6,3} = 20f^4 + o_2(f) \approx 20/10{,}000 = 1/500.$$

Hence, the *PoF* in the $P(6,3)$-protocol is *fifty* times smaller than in the $P(2,1)$ protocol. Besides, $1/500 = F_{6,3} < t = 1/400$.

Thus, the $P(6,3)$ protocol is an appropriate procedure for information assurance.

Suppose $\{a, b, c\}$ are three consecutive blocks of plaintext and $\{a, b, c\} = \{52, 37, 20\}$.

Compute the combination $\{u_1, \ldots, u_6\}$:

$$u_1 := a^3 \equiv 52^3 \bmod 1189 = 306,$$

$$u_2 := (a - b)^3 \equiv (52 - 37)^3 \equiv 15^3 (\bmod 1189) = 997,$$

$$u_3 := (b - c)^3 \equiv 17^3 \bmod 1189 = 1346,$$

$$u_4 := c^3 \equiv 20^3 (\bmod 1189) = 866,$$

$$u_5 := (a + b + c)^3 \equiv 109^3 (\bmod 1189) = 208,$$

and

$$u_6 := (a + 2b + c)^3 \equiv (52 + 2 \times 37 + 20)^3 \equiv 146^3 (\bmod 1189) = 523, \quad (27)\text{--}(29).$$

Next, consider two cases illustrating how to decrypt and recover the original blocks of the plaintext. In each case the receiver, prior to recovery of all three blocks $\{a, b, c\}$ of the original plaintext, must apply the decryption protocol, i.e., *Bob* computes $2(n - s)/3 + 1 = 2(1189 - 70)/3 = 373$.

First case: Suppose that *three* messages $\{u_3, u_4, u_6\}$, out of *six* are successfully transmitted.

Then *Bob* decrypts $c \equiv 866^{373} (\bmod 1189) = 20,$

$$A := b - c \equiv 1346^{373} (\bmod 1189) = 17 \quad \text{and}$$

$$B := a + 2b + c \equiv 523^{373} (\bmod 1189) = 146.$$

Finally, Bob recovers

$$b \equiv (A + c)(\bmod 1189) = 37,$$

and

$$a \equiv (B - 2b - c)(\bmod 1189) = 52.$$

Second case: Now suppose that *three* messages $\{u_2, u_5, u_6\}$, out of *six* are successfully transmitted.

Then Bob decrypts

$$A := a - b \equiv 997^{373} (\text{mod } 1189),$$

$$B := a + b + c \equiv 208^{373} (\text{mod } 1189),$$

$$C := a + 2b + c \equiv 523^{373} (\text{mod } 1189),$$

and then recovers

$$b \equiv (C - B)(\text{mod } 1189), \quad a \equiv (A + b)(\text{mod } 1189),$$

and

$$c \equiv (C - a - 2b)(\text{mod } 1189).$$

In both cases the recovered plaintext blocks $\{a, b, c\}$ are the same.

12. Highly-Improbable Cases

There exist integers $m < pq$, for which

$$m^2 \text{ mod } n = 1. \tag{12.1}$$

In this case, a ciphertext and corresponding plaintext in the cubic-root algorithm, {see (4.1)–(4.6)}, are the same. An analogous phenomenon is also observed in the Rabin algorithm and in RSA cryptography, (Rivest *et al.*, 1978).

In the cubic-root algorithm, if (12.1) holds, then

$$m^3 \equiv m(\text{mod } n), \tag{12.2}$$

which implies that

$$pq \mid m(m - 1)(m + 1) \tag{12.3}$$

and, since p and q are primes,
  then

$$\{p \mid (m - 1) \text{ xor } p \mid m \text{ xor } p \mid (m + 1)\}$$

$$\textbf{and } \{q \mid (m - 1) \text{ xor } q \mid m \text{ xor } q \mid (m + 1)\}. \tag{12.4}$$

There are $2(p+q-2)$ integers m, that satisfy (12.1). In addition, among all positive integers smaller than $n = pq$, there are $(p + q - 2)$ integers m, that are *not* co-prime with n. Hence, if m is randomly selected among all $n - 1$ positive integers, then with probability

$$e = 3(1/p + 1/q - 1/n) + o(1/n) < 6/\min(p, q), \qquad (12.5)$$

it will not satisfy the condition (4.3) of the cubic-root algorithm. However, for large p and q, the probability e is extremely small, if, say, $p = q = O(10^{100})$, then

$$e \approx 6 \times 10^{-100}. \qquad (12.6)$$

Although there is a way to tackle this problem, handling these highly-improbable cases is beyond the scope of this chapter.

Example 12.1. Suppose $p = 9923$ and $q = 9929$, then $0 < e < 6/9923 = 0.000605$.

13. Concluding Remarks: Adaptive vs. Non-Adaptive Transmission

More reliable protocols of transmission can be introduced if adaptability is appropriate, which is not always the case. Indeed, there are circumstances, in which only one-way communication is feasible: communication with a deep-space craft whether it is man controlled or machine controlled, steganographic communication, where a receiver needs to keep 'radio' silence, weapon-control protocol, where real-time control requirement does not allow time for response and adjustment, one-way communication with submarines, etc.

Chapter 17

Simultaneous Information Assurance and Encryption Based on Quintic Roots

1. Introduction

In transmission of highly-sensitive commercial, financial, legal, military, etc. information, both criteria of reliability and security of delivery must be *simultaneously* satisfied (NIST, 2004). Both requirements have been well analyzed in communication theory (Garrett, 2004; Hardy–Walker, 2003) and thoroughly developed in traditional cryptosystems and public-key cryptography (PKC) (Rabin, 1979; Rivest *et al.* 1978).

Information transmission in a military environment and in financial exchanges between brokers and customers are examples in which delay is a sensitive issue (Schwartz, 1996). Another example is secure lines of a Voice-over-Internet protocol (VoIP), in which reliability, security and real-time communication are a must (Leon–Garcia *et al.* 2000).

In this chapter, we provide constructive measures illustrating how to interlink the communication assurance and security requirement into algorithmic protocols. An analysis of computational complexity of such a tandem and trade-off between level of crypto-immunity and bandwidth requirements of its implementation is provided.

It is demonstrated in Verkhovsky (2008), how to use complexity of square root extraction modulo composite $n = pq$ for encryption and decryption of Gaussian integers. Computational complexity of the decryption can be substantially improved if, instead of using squaring for encryption and square-root algorithm for decryption, the *cubic* power modulo *composite* n is used for encryption of the plaintext, represented as real integers, and then for decryption, the root of third power modulo n is extracted directly (without application of the Chinese remainder theorem, which is time consuming procedure).

However, if the plaintext is numerically represented as complex (Gaussian) integers, the *extraction of cubic roots* is computationally *challenging problem*. Instead, it is *more efficient* to deal with *extraction of quintic roots*, (i.e., roots of the *fifth* power).

The chapter demonstrates how to interlink both the security requirement and communication assurance into one algorithmic protocol. Several reliability protocols are introduced and their efficiencies (probabilities of failure (*PoFs*), bandwidth requirement per block of transmitted ciphertext and number of exponentiations per block of ciphertext) are analyzed and compared.

A novel PKC algorithm described in this chapter is based on *quintic* roots of Gaussian integers modulo semi-prime $n = pq$. The advantage of the quintic-root based encryption/decryption algorithm is that, it is *four* times more efficient than the algorithm based on square-root extraction because the decryption requires computation of *one* quintic root rather than *four* square roots. Besides, there is *no necessity to consider additional bits* to decide which of the multiple roots corresponds to the original plaintext.

2. Problem Statement

Two major concerns are addressed in this chapter: protection of information transmitted over open channels/links from a potential intruder (security consideration); and assurance of the transmitted information, i.e., how to guarantee that this information is successfully delivered to an intended receiver with required probability (reliability consideration) (Hamill *et al.* 2005).

Security protection: PKC algorithms are described; including the algorithms based on *cubic* roots in modular arithmetic.

Reliability mechanism: redundancy protocols are considered and analyzed.

A protocol, handling r channels/links over which h units of information $\{u_1, u_2, \ldots, u_h\}$ are transmitted $\{1 \leq h \leq r\}$, is called $P(r, h)$-protocol.

If each channel is absolutely reliable, (its *PoF* $f = 0$), then the most efficient protocol is $P(1, 1)$-transmission protocol, i.e., where redundancy is absent.

However, in most of system and/or human communication, a certain degree of redundancy is necessary, since there is always a chance of communication failure, i.e., probability of successful transmission is less than 100%. Although redundancy does not provide absolute assurance of information delivery, yet, if properly handled, it substantially increases probability $S_{r,h}$ of successful transmission if $P(r,h)$-protocol is used for communication. The transmission is called successful if in the $P(r,h)$-protocol all h blocks of information are received and recovered by the intended receiver.

Since modern communication is an expensive and complex process (it requires financial resources, bandwidth and time), it should be designed to satisfy all technical and other requirements and to optimize usage of these resources. Several algorithms are described in this chapter, and their performance is analyzed and compared.

3. Numeric Representation of Plaintext as Array of Complex Integers

In the chapter, we consider that the plaintext blocks are converted into numerical representation and then divided onto sequential pairs. For instance, if the plaintext is represented as a sequence of blocks $\{27, 65, 29, 63, 19, 14, 72, 69, \ldots, \}$, then we subdivide them onto pairs of blocks $\{(27, 65), (29, 63), (19, 14), (72, 69), \ldots, \}$, where every pair is treated as a complex number with integer components. Such complex integers are called Gaussian integers (Gauss, 1986). This presentation and processing of information has its own advantages, which become apparent below.

The ideas presented above are applicable to both cases: whether the plaintext blocks are presented as Gaussian integers or as real integers, the latter are just special cases of the complex integers.

4. Cryptosystem Based on Quintic Roots

Consider a sequence of blocks of a plaintext $m_1, m_2, \ldots, m_{t-1}, m_t$ that must be transmitted from a sender to a receiver (respectively called *Alice* and *Bob*).

4.1. *Encryption/Decryption algorithm*

Definition 4.1. A complex integer z is a quintic root of complex integer c modulo n if

$$z^5 \bmod n = c. \tag{4.1}$$

Encryption:

1. Each user selects two large distinct primes satisfying

$$p \equiv q \pmod{10} = 7, \tag{4.2}$$

and computes

$$n := pq, \quad N = n^2, \quad \text{and} \quad S = p^2 + q^2, \tag{4.3}$$

here n and S are respectively the user's public and private keys,

2. Let

$$m := (a, b), \tag{4.4}$$

be a plaintext message, $0 < a < n$, $0 < b < n$, where

$$(a^2 + b^2) \bmod n \neq 0, \quad \text{and}$$
$$(a^2 - b^2) \bmod n \neq \pm 1, \quad \text{and}$$
$$\gcd(ab, n) = 1, \tag{4.5}$$

3. Compute

$$c := m^5 \bmod n, \quad \{c \text{ is a corresponding ciphertext}\}, \tag{4.6}$$

Decryption:

4. Compute

$$w := (N - S + 2)/5, \tag{4.7}$$
$$d := c^w \bmod n. \tag{4.8}$$

4.2. *Algorithm verification*

Proposition 4.2. If the conditions (4.1)–(4.8) hold, then

$$d = m. \tag{4.9}$$

Proof. First of all,

$$(N - S + 2)/5 \quad \text{is an integer.} \tag{4.10}$$

Secondly,

$$(N - S + 2)/5 = [(p^2 - 1)(q^2 - 1) + 1]/5. \tag{4.11}$$

Indeed, if (4.2) holds, then

$$(pq)^2 - (p^2 + q^2) \equiv 3 \pmod{5}, \tag{4.12}$$

which means that $5 | (N - S + 2)$. □

Conjecture 4.3. For every integer z co-prime with pq holds that

$$z^{(p^2 - 1)(q^2 - 1)} \bmod pq = (1, 0) = 1. \tag{4.13}$$

Remark 4.4. $c^{-1} \equiv c^{N-S} \pmod{n}$.

Then

$$c^5 \equiv z^{N-S+2} \equiv [z^{(p^2-1)(q^2-1)}]z \equiv 1 \times z \equiv z \bmod n. \qquad (4.14)$$

Conjecture 4.3 is a generalization of the Euler's theorem (Euler, 1911–1944).

Remark 4.5. The exponent w in (4.8) is computable, if the sum of squares S is known. However, if p *and* q are large primes and are private keys, then w is not known to the intruder.

Since for every m and every *odd* integer R holds that $\sqrt[R]{-m} = -\sqrt[R]{m}$, it is essential to observe that the integer $(N - S + 2)/5$ in (4.11) is also *odd*.

The quintic-root based encryption/decryption algorithm is *four* times more efficient than the algorithm based on square-root extraction (Hamill *et al.* 2005), because the decryption in (4.16) requires computation of *one* quintic root with time complexity equal to $O(\log n)$ rather than *four* square roots of the same complexity as the Hamill algorithm. Besides, there is no necessity to consider additional bits to decide which of the several roots corresponds to the original plaintext.

5. Properties of $P(r, h)$-Protocol

Consider *pairs* of plaintext blocks represented as integers on interval $2 \leq a_i, b_i \leq n - 2$ and three corresponding ciphertext blocks

$$\{u, v, w\} := \{E(a_i) \bmod n, E(a_i + b_i) \bmod n, E(b_i) \bmod n\}.$$

It is clear that if any *two* of *three* components are successfully transmitted to *Bob*, then after appropriate decryption *Bob* will be able to find a_i and b_i, i.e., to recover the plaintext blocks m_{2i-1} and m_{2i}. For example, if the values of $u = a_i^3$ and $v = a_i + b_i$ are received, then Bob decrypts u, finds a_i and from v determines $b_i = v - a_i$. Bob analogously acts, if he receives v and w.

5.1. *Reliability analysis*

Let f be a probability of link failure. Then probability $S_{r,h}$ of successful transmission for $P(r, h)$-protocol equals

$$S_{r,h} := \sum_{k=0}^{r-h} \binom{r}{r-k} (1 - f)^{r-k} f^k = 1 - F_{r,h}, \qquad (5.1)$$

where $F_{r,h}$ is probability of link failure.

$$F_{r,h} := 1 - \sum_{k=r-h+1}^{r} \binom{r}{r-k} (1-f)^{r-k} f^k \tag{5.2}$$

If $f \ll 1$, then

$$F_{r,h} := \binom{r}{h-1} f^{r-(h-1)} + o(f), \tag{5.3}$$

where $o(f)$ term is substantially smaller in comparison with the first summand in (5.3).

Proposition 5.1. If $f < 1 - \frac{h-1}{r+1}$, then $F_{r,h}$ is a decreasing function of r.

Proposition 5.2. If $f + 1 < \frac{r+1}{h}$, then $F_{r,h}$ is an increasing function of h.

Definition 5.3. Suppose t is an *acceptable* probability of transmission failure (t is acceptable *threshold*). If $F_{r,h} \leq t$, then a $P(r,h)$-protocol is acceptable.

For example, if $F_{3,2} \leq t$, then a $P(3,2)$-protocol is acceptable. Otherwise a more elaborate approach is required.

5.2. *Protocol $P(4,2)$*

Consider a combination of *four* integers:

$$\{u_1, u_2, u_3, u_4\} := \{a_i^5 \bmod n, (a_i + b_i)^5 \bmod n, (a_i - b_i)^5 \bmod n, b_i^5 \bmod n\}. \tag{5.4}$$

In this protocol, a communication is successful if at least *two* $\{u_i, u_j\}$ of *four* values $\{u_1, u_2, u_3, u_4\}$ in (5.4) are successfully transmitted, then $F_{4,2} = 4f^3 + o_2(f)$.

5.3. *Reduction of decryption complexity*

In the Protocol $P(4,2)$, the extraction of two roots is required in decryption for every combination $\{u_i, u_j\}$. However, this requirement can be reduced by sending instead

$$\{u_1, u_2, u_3, u_4\} := \{a_i^5 \bmod n, (a_i + b_i)^5 \bmod n, a_i - b_i \bmod n, b_i^5 \bmod n\}.$$

Indeed, since there are six possible combinations, one half of them are combinations $\{u_3, u_{j \neq 3}\}$. In these combinations only one quintic root extraction is required, while each of three remaining combinations requires extraction of two quintic roots. It means that in average $3/2$ extractions are required for recovery in any case of successful transmission.

5.4. $P(6,3)$-*Protocol*

Suppose that $\{a, b, c\}$ are *three* consecutive blocks of a plaintext. Consider *six* combinations of these blocks:

$$\{a, c, a - b, a + 2b + c, a + b + c, b - c\}. \tag{5.5}$$

Remark 5.4. It is easy to verify that any subset consisting of three elements in (5.5) is *linearly independent*, which means that none of its elements can be expressed as a linear combination of other two. Otherwise the original message $\{a, b, c\}$ is not recoverable.

Let us consider six corresponding cipher-blocks:

$$u_1 := a^5 \bmod n, \qquad\qquad u_2 := c^5 \bmod n, \tag{5.6}$$

$$u_3 := (a - b)^5 \bmod n, \qquad u_4 := (a + 2b + c)^5 \bmod n, \tag{5.7}$$

$$u_5 := (a + b + c) \bmod n, \quad u_6 := (b - c) \bmod n. \tag{5.8}$$

In this protocol, a communication is successful if at least *three* $\{u_i, u_j, u_k\}$ of *six* values $\{u_1, u_2, u_3, u_4, u_5, u_6\}$ in (5.6)–(5.8) are successfully transmitted.

5.5. *Reduction of decryption complexity*

Notice that the last two entangs in (5.8) are not encrypted.

Then each of four feasible set of entanglements (*FSEs*) $= \{123, 124, 134, 234\}$ requires three decryptions, each of four *FSEs* $= \{156, 256, 356, 456\}$ requires one decryption and each of remaining twelve *FSEs* $= \{125, 135, 145, 235, 245, 345, 126, 136, 146, 236, 246, 346\}$ requires two decryption. Therefore, $(3 \times 4 + 2 \times 12 + 1 \times 4)/20 = 40/20 = 2$.

Hence, on average it takes *two* decryptions for recovery of three entangs on the basis of which the three blocks a, b and c will be recovered.

5.6. *Reliability analysis of* $P(6,3)$-*protocol*

The transmission fails if either all *six* links fail $\{$with *PoF* $f^6\}$, or any *five* links fail $\{$with *PoF* $6f^5(1 - f)\}$, or any *four* links fail $\{$with *PoF* $15f^4(1 - f)^2\}$. Hence, the overall *PoF* is equal to

$$F_{6,3} := f^6 + 6f^5(1 - f) + 15f^4(1 - f)^2 = 15f^4 + o_3(f), \tag{5.9}$$

where the term $o_3(f)$ is small in comparison with $20f^4$, if f itself is small.

5.7. $P(6,4)$-Protocol

The transmission fails if either all *six* links fail {with *PoF* f^6} or if any *five* links fail or any *four* links fail or any three links fail.

Hence,

$$F_{6,4} := f^6 + 6f^5(1-f) + 15f^4(1-f)^2 + 20f^3(1-f)^3 = 1 - (1-f)^5(1-7f).$$

6. Average Complexity of Decryption

Notice that in (5.8), we consider linear combinations of the original message $\{a,b,c\}$ without raising each to the third power. This reduces an average complexity of decryption. Indeed, there are $\binom{6}{3} = 20$ possible combinations of successful transmission. Of them there are *four* combinations

$$\{u_i, u_j, u_k\}, \quad \text{where } 1 \le i < j < k \le 4, \tag{6.1}$$

six combinations

$$\{u_i, u_j, u_5\}, \quad \text{where } 1 \le i < j \le 4, \tag{6.2}$$

another *six* combinations

$$\{u_i, u_j, u_6\}, \quad \text{where } 1 \le i < j \le 4, \tag{6.3}$$

and remaining *four* combinations

$$\{u_i, u_5, u_6\}, \quad \text{where } 1 \le i \le 4. \tag{6.4}$$

Each combination in (6.1) requires three extractions of the cubic root, each combination in (6.2) and (6.3) requires two extractions of the cubic root, and each combination in (6.4) requires one extraction of the cubic root. Hence, in average instead of *three* extractions per combination, we need only two extractions:

Indeed,

$$(4 \times 3 + 12 \times 2 + 4 \times 1)/20 = 2. \tag{6.5}$$

7. Comparison of Protocols

Table 7.1. provides comparison of various information assurance protocols.

Basic notations in $P(r,h)$-protocol:

$F_{r,h} = PoF,$
$B_{r,h} = $ bandwidth requirement per block of transmitted ciphertext,
$E_{r,h} = $ required number of exponentiations per block of ciphertext.

Table 7.1   Comparison of protocols.

Protocols	$F_{r,h}$	$B_{r,h}$	$E_{r,h}$
$P(2,1)$-cubic root	f^2	2	$O(2 \times \log n)$
$P(3,2)$-quadratic root	$3f^2$	1.5	$O(6 \times \log n)$
$P(3,2)$-cubic or quintic root	$3f^2$	1.5	$O(1.5 \times \log n)$
$P(4,2)$	$4f^3$	2	$O(2 \times \log n)$
$P(6,3)$	$15f^4$	2	$O(2 \times \log n)$
$P(6,4)$	$6f^5$	1.5	

The protocols $P(2,1)$, {see (6.2)}, $P(4,2)$, {see (5.4)}, and $P(6,3)$, {see (5.5)–(6.2)}, have the same bandwidth requirements and the same complexity of decryption. Yet, the latter protocol has a substantially smaller *PoF* than the other two.

The protocol $P(3,2)$, combined with the cubic root algorithm, and the $P(2,1)$-protocol are different: the former is more efficient in bandwidth requirements and in the complexity of decryption. Yet, the latter protocol has three times smaller a *PoF* than the former one. Finally, the protocol $P(3,2)$ combined with the square root algorithm is more time consuming for decryption than the protocol $P(3,2)$ combined with the quintic root algorithm.

Example 7.1. Let a channel fail with the probability f, then

$$F_{2,1} = f^2, \quad F_{3,2} = f^2(3 - 2f), \quad F_{4,2} = f^3(4 - 3f),$$

$$F_{6,3} = 15f^4(1 - f)^2 + 6f^5(1 - f) + f^6, \quad F_{6,4} = f^5(6 - 5f).$$

Suppose $f = 1/20$, then the *PoFs* in the $P(4,2)$-protocol and $P(6,3)$-protocol are respectively about 5 (*five*) *times and* 20 (*twenty*) *times* smaller than the *PoF* of the repeated-transmission protocol $P(2,1)$.

8.   Comparison of Failure Probabilities

Let's consider ratios of *PoFs* as functions of channel failure f:

$$F_{3,2}/F_{2,1} = 3(1 - f) + f = 3 - 2f \geq 1,$$

$$F_{4,2}/F_{2,1} = (4 - 3f)f \approx 4f < 1 \quad \text{if } f < 0.25,$$

$$F_{6,3}/F_{2,1} = f^2[15(1 - f)^2 + 6f(1 - f) + f^2]$$

$$= f^2(15 - 24f + 10f^2) \approx 15f^2 < 1 \quad \text{if } f < 0.25,$$

$$F_{6,4}/F_{3,2} = f^3(6 - 5f)/(3 - 2f) = 2f^2 - o_5(f),$$

where $F_{6,4}/F_{3,2} < 2f^2 < 1$. The right-most inequality holds, if $f < 1/\sqrt{2} \approx$ .7071.

The examples below shows how the probability in each protocol is changing as function of f and $\{0.01 \le f \le 0.25\}$:

Example 8.1. Let $f = 1/20$, then $F_{6,3} = 20f^4 + o_2(f) \approx 1/8,000$, and $F_{6,4} = 20f^3 + o_3(f) \approx 1/400$.

Hence the *PoF* in the $P(6,3)$-protocol is *twenty* times smaller than in the $P(2,1)$-protocol. And the *PoF* in the $P(6,4)$-protocol is *the same* as in the $P(2,1)$-protocol.

If an acceptable threshold of failure $t = 1/5000$, then $1/8000 = F_{6,3} < t = 1/5000$, and the $P(6,3)$-protocol is an appropriate procedure for information assurance.

However, if an acceptable threshold of failure $t = 1/500$, then $1/500 = t < F_{4,6} = 1/400$, and the $P(6,4)$ protocol is not an appropriate procedure for information assurance.

Example 8.2. Suppose $p = 17$ and $q = 7$, {see the requirement (3.2)}, then $N = 14,161$, $S = 338$ and $w = 2765$.

Suppose $\{a, b, c\}$ are three consecutive blocks of plaintext, where

$$a = 10, \quad b = 4 \quad \text{and} \quad c = 3.$$

Compute the combination $\{u_1, \ldots, u_6\}$, {see (5.6)–(5.8)}.

Here the first four entangs must be encrypted by raising each entang into fifth power:

$$u_1 := a^5 \equiv 10^5 \pmod{119} = 40,$$

$$u_2 := (a-b)^5 \equiv 6^5 \pmod{119} = 41,$$

$$u_3 := c^5 \equiv 3^5 \pmod{119} = 5,$$

$$u_4 := (a+b+c)^5 \equiv 17^5 \pmod{119} = 68,$$

$$u_5 := (b-c) \bmod 119 = 1, \quad \text{and}$$

$$u_6 := (a+2b+c) \pmod{119} = 21.$$

Next, consider two cases illustrating how to decrypt and recover the original blocks of the plaintext. In each case the receiver, prior to recovery of all three blocks $\{a, b, c\}$ of the original plaintext, must apply the decryption protocol, (3.16), i.e., *Bob* computes

$$N = n^2 = 119^2 = 14,161,$$

$$S = p^2 + q^2 = 7^2 + 17^2 = 338,$$

$$w := (N - S + 2)/5 = (14161 - 338 + 2)/5 = 2765.$$

If the blocks are real integers, then $w \bmod (p-1)(q-1) = 2765 \bmod 96 = 77$.

Hence, the decrypting key $w = 77 = 64 + 8 + 4 + 1$.

First case: Suppose that *three* messages $\{u_3, u_4, u_6\}$ out of *six* are successfully transmitted. Then *Bob* decrypts

$$c := u_3^w \ (\bmod \ 119) = 5^{77} \bmod 119 = (5^{11} \bmod 119)^7 \bmod 119 = 3,$$

and

$$B := u_4^w \ (\bmod \ 119) = 68^{77} = 17^7 \bmod 119 = 17$$

$$\{\text{both correctly decrypted!}\}.$$

Let

$$C := a + 2b + c,$$

then Bob recovers

$$b \equiv (C - B) \ (\bmod \ 119), \quad \text{and}$$

$$a \equiv (2B - C - c) \ (\bmod \ 119).$$

Second case: Now suppose that *three* messages $\{u_2, u_5, u_6\}$ out of *six* are successfully transmitted. Then Bob decrypts

$$A := u_2^w \ (\bmod \ 119).$$

Let

$$M := (b - c) \ (\bmod \ 119), \quad \text{and}$$

$$N := (a + 2b + c) \ (\bmod \ 119).$$

Then he recovers

$$a \equiv [(3A + u_5 + u_6)/4] \ (\bmod \ 119),$$

$$b \equiv (a - A) \ (\bmod \ 119), \quad \text{and}$$

$$c \equiv (b - u_5) \ (\bmod \ 119).$$

Verification: If all computations are correctly performed, then in both cases the recovered plaintext blocks $\{a, b, c\}$ must be the same.

Table 9.1

Number of entangs	Encrypted entangs $\{u_1, \ldots, u_{r-h+1}\}$	Non-encrypted entangs $\{u_{r-h+2}, u_{r-h+3}, \ldots, u_r\}$	Number i of required decryptions
$m = h - 1$	$\binom{r-h+1}{1}$	$\binom{h-1}{h-1}$	$i = 1$
...	...	...	...
$m = h - k$	$\binom{r-h+1}{h-k}$	$\binom{h-1}{k}$	$i = k$
...	...	...	...
$m = 0$	$\binom{r-h+1}{h}$	$\binom{h-1}{0}$	$i = h$

9. General Case of $P(r, h)$

Total number of possible combinations is equal to $\binom{r}{h}$.

In order to minimize complexity of decryption/recovery, not all r entanglements must be encrypted. It is sufficient to encrypt $r - (h - 1)$ entanglements.

Suppose that the first $r - (h - 1)$ entanglements $\{u_1, \ldots, u_{r-h+1}\}$ are encrypted and the remaining $\{u_{r-h+2}, u_{r-h+3}, \ldots, u_r\}$ are not.

9.1. *Average complexity of decryption*

Let us consider Table 9.1., which provides all details about required number of decryptions.

Then the average number of required decryptions

$$A_{hr} = \sum_{i=0}^{h-1} \binom{h-1}{i} \binom{r-(h-1)}{h-i} (h-i),$$

and average number of decryptions per transmitted block

$$\tilde{A}_{hr} = \left[\sum_{i=0}^{h-1} \binom{h-1}{i} \binom{r-(h-1)}{h-i} (h-i) \right] \bigg/ \left[h \binom{r}{h} \right].$$

Example 9.1. Let $h = 4$ and $r = 8$, then

$$A_{4,8} = \sum_{i=0}^{3} \binom{3}{i} \binom{5}{4-i} (4-i)$$

$$= \binom{3}{0}\binom{5}{4} \times 4 + \binom{3}{1}\binom{5}{3} \times 3 + \binom{3}{2}\binom{5}{2} \times 2 + \binom{3}{3}\binom{5}{1} \times 1$$

$$= 1 \times 5 \times 4 + 3 \times 10 \times 3 + 3 \times 10 \times 2 + 1 \times 5 \times 1$$

$$= 20 + 90 + 60 + 5 = 175.$$

Therefore, the average number of required decryptions per block is equal to

$$\tilde{A}_{4,8} = 175 \Big/ \left[4 \times \binom{8}{4} \right] = 175/(4 \times 70) = 5/8.$$

Example 9.2. Let $h = 3$ and $r = 6$, then

$$A_{3,6} = \sum_{i=0}^{2} \binom{2}{i} \binom{4}{3-i} (3-i)$$

$$= \binom{2}{0} \binom{4}{3} \times 3 + \binom{2}{1} \binom{4}{2} \times 2 + \binom{2}{2} \binom{4}{1} \times 1$$

$$= 1 \times 4 \times 3 + 2 \times 6 \times 2 + 1 \times 4 \times 1 = 12 + 24 + 4 = 40,$$

$$\tilde{A}_{3,6} = 40 \Big/ \left[3 \times \binom{6}{3} \right] = 40/(3 \times 20) = 2/3.$$

If $r = 2h$, then forever h holds that

$$\left[\sum_{i=0}^{h-1} \binom{h-1}{i} \binom{r-(h-1)}{h-i} (h-i) \right] \Big/ \left[h \binom{r}{h} \right] = 1/2.$$

10. Highly-Improbable Cases

There exist complex integers such that

$$m^5 \bmod n = (m, 0) = m. \tag{10.1}$$

which implies that

$$(m-1)m(m+1)(m^2+1) \bmod n = 0 \tag{10.2}$$

or that $pq|m(m-1)(m+1)(m^2+1)$.

Since p and q are primes, then (10.2) implies that

$$\{p|(m-1) \textbf{ xor } p|m \textbf{ xor } p|(m+1) \textbf{ xor } p|(m^2+1)\} \quad \textbf{and}$$
$$\{q|(m-1) \textbf{ xor } q|m \textbf{ xor } q|(m+1) \textbf{ xor } q|(m^2+1)\}. \tag{10.3}$$

In this case, a ciphertext and corresponding plaintext in the quintic-root algorithm, are the same. An analogous phenomenon is also observed in the Rabin algorithm (Rabin, 1979), and in RSA cryptography (Rivest *et al.* 1978).

There are $4(p+q) - 5$ complex integers m that satisfy (10.1).

Hence, if m is randomly selected among all $n-1$ positive integers, then with probability

$$e = 3(1/p + 1/q - 1/n) + o(1/n) < 6/\min(p, q), \qquad (10.4)$$

it will not satisfy the condition (3.3) of the cubic-root algorithm. However, for large p and q the probability e is extremely small. Indeed, if $p = q = O(10^{100})$, then

$$e \approx 6 \times 10^{-100}. \qquad (10.5)$$

Example 10.1. Suppose $p = 9923$ and $q = 9929$, then $0 < e < 6/9923 = 0.000605$.

11. Concluding Remarks: Adaptive vs. non-Adaptive Transmission

More reliable protocols of transmission can be introduced, if adaptability is appropriate, which is not always the case. Indeed, there are circumstances, in which only one-way communication is feasible: communication with a deep-space craft whether it is man controlled or machine controlled; steganographic communication, where a receiver needs to keep 'radio' silence, weapon-control protocol, where real-time control requirement does not allow time for response and adjustment, one-way communication with submarines, etc.

Chapter 18

Modular Equations and Integer Factorization

1. Introduction and Problem Statement

Security of modern communication based on RSA cryptographic protocols and their analogues is as cryptoimmune as integer factorization (*iFac*) is computationally difficult (Rivest *et al.* 1978; Elkamchouchi *et al.* 2002; Rabin, 1979). In this chapter, we consider enhanced algorithms for the *iFac* that are faster than the algorithms proposed in the previous chapter. Among these enhanced algorithms is the one that is based on the ability to count the number of integer solutions on quadratic and biquadratic modular equations. Therefore, the *iFac* complexity is at most as difficult as the problem of counting. Properties of various modular equations are provided and demonstrated in numerous computer experiments. These properties are instrumental in the proposed factorization algorithms, which are numerically illustrated in several examples. The paper (Verkhovsky, 2011c) considers a factorization algorithm of semi-prime $n = pq$ for two cases: where either both factors p and q are non-Blum primes, i.e.,

$$p = q = 1 (\mathrm{mod}\ 4), \tag{1.1}$$

or at least one factor is a non-Blum prime. In this chapter is provided the *iFac* algorithm, which also works if both factors p and q are Blum primes, i.e.,

$$p = q = 3 (\mathrm{mod}\ 4). \tag{1.2}$$

The algorithm, discussed in this chapter and preliminary in Verkhovsky (2011c), is based on several properties {formulated as propositions and conjectures} of dual modular elliptic curves (ECs), where b is an integer:

$$y^2 = x(x^2 + b^2)(\text{mod } n), \tag{1.3}$$

and

$$y^2 = x(x^2 - b^2)(\text{mod } n). \tag{1.4}$$

Let us reiterate some of these properties and then consider their generalizations.

Let $p = q = 1(\text{mod } 4), n = pq$, let $P(n, b)$ and $M(n, b)$ denote the number of points on ECs, (1.3) {EC with *plus* sign} and (1.4) {EC with *minus* sign}, respectively. For the sake of brevity, we call $P(n, b)$ and $M(n, b)$ the *counts*. There are several methods for counting the number of points on ECs (Schoof, 1995; Dewaghe, 1998; Rubin–Silverberg, 2009).

Conjecture 1.1. Consider $n = pq$, and let primes p and q satisfy (1.1),

(a) if

$$P(n, 1) \neq M(n, 1), \tag{1.5}$$

then for every integer b,

$$P(n, b) \neq M(n, b), \tag{1.6}$$

(b) if (1.5) does not hold, then for every integer b,

$$P(n, b) = M(n, b), \tag{1.7}$$

(c) if n is a prime and (1.5) holds, then for every b, it also holds

$$P(n, b) + M(n, b) = 2n. \tag{1.8}$$

Remark 1.2. Conjecture 1.1 plays an important role in the design of the *iFac*, {further details are provided in the appendix}.

If the factors p and q are congruent to 1 modulo $n = pq$, then the following two propositions hold.

Proposition 1.3. If m and s are non-negative integers and

$$|m - s| \bmod 4 = 2, \tag{1.9}$$

then

$$P(n, 2^m) = M(n, 2^s). \tag{1.10}$$

Proposition 1.4. If b_1 and b_2 are distinct integers and

$$P(n, b_1) = M(n, b_2),$$

then

$$M(n, b_1) = P(n, b_2). \tag{1.11}$$

Proposition 1.5. {modular *reduction-in-exponent*}: Consider the ECs

$$y^2 = x(x^2 + b^e)(\text{mod } n), \tag{1.12}$$

and

$$y^2 = x(x^2 - b^e)(\text{mod } n), \tag{1.13}$$

where $e \geq 4$, then for every integer $b \geq 2$, the following identities hold:

$$P(n, b^e) = P(n, b^{e \bmod 4}), \tag{1.14}$$

$$M(n, b^e) = M(n, b^{e \bmod 4}). \tag{1.15}$$

1.1. *Proof of Proposition 1.5*

Proof {by reduction}: Consider substitutions

$$y := Yb^3 \bmod n \quad \text{and} \quad x := Xb^2 \bmod n, \tag{1.16}$$

into (1.12). Then after cancellation of term b^6 in both parts of (1.12), we derive the EC

$$Y^2 = X(X^2 + b^{e-4})(\text{mod } n). \tag{1.17}$$

Repeating the substitutions (1.16) and cancellations of terms b^6, we derive the proof of (1.14). Analogously, we proceed with the proof of (1.15).

Consider $b = 2$ in (1.12)–(1.17) and two ECs for a positive integer m:

ECP:

$$y^2 = x(x^2 + 2^{m+1})(\text{mod } p), \tag{1.18}$$

ECM:

$$Y^2 = X(X^2 - 2^{m-1})(\text{mod } p). \tag{1.19}$$

Let us show that there exist such integers u and w that for every integer m the substitutions

$$x := uX \bmod p \quad \text{and} \quad y := wY \bmod p \tag{1.20}$$

establish a one-to-one correspondence between points of *ECP* and *ECM*.

First of all, (1.18)–(1.20) imply

$$w^2 Y^2 = uX(u^2 X^2 + 2^{m+1})(\text{mod } p). \qquad (1.21)$$

Let us select integers u and w, each co-prime with p, for which hold

$$w^2 = u^3 (\text{mod } p), \qquad (1.22)$$

and

$$u^2 = -4(\text{mod } p). \qquad (1.23)$$

If integer solutions of (1.22) and (1.23) exist, then after cancellation of equal terms in both sides of (1.21), we derive (1.19). Therefore, (1.23) implies that

$$u = 2\sqrt{p-1}(\text{mod } p), \qquad (1.24)$$

and (1.22) implies

$$w = \sqrt{u^3}(\text{mod } p). \qquad (1.25)$$

If $p \bmod 4 = 1$, then integer u exists, since $(p-1)/2$ is *even*. Indeed, by Euler's criterion of quadratic residuosity, $p-1$ is a quadratic residue (QR), if and only if

$$(p-1)^{(p-1)/2} = (-1)^{(p-1)/2}(\text{mod } p) = 1.$$

On the other hand, integer w also exists, because u itself is QR modulo p.

Indeed,

$$[2\sqrt{p-1}]^{(p-1)/2} \equiv 2^{(p-1)/2} \times \sqrt{p-1}^{(p-1)/2} \bmod p = 1, \qquad (1.26)$$

since, as is shown in Table 1.1., both 2 and $\sqrt{p-1}$ are simultaneously either QR or quadratic non-residue (QNR) modulo p. quod erat demonstrandum (QED).

Example 1.6. Let $p = 13$, find u and w, such that

$$w^2 = u^3 (\text{mod } 13),$$

and

$$u^2 = 9(\text{mod } 13), \quad \text{i.e., } u = 3, \text{ then } w^2 = u^3 = 27(\text{mod } 13) = 1.$$

Table 1.1   Parity of quadratic residuosity of 2 and $\sqrt{p-1}$.

* * *	$p \bmod 8 = 1$	$p \bmod 8 = 5$
2	QR	QNR
$\sqrt{p-1}$	QR	QNR

Table 1.2   Correspondence between (x, y) and (X, Y).

ECP	$(0,0)$	$(3,0)$	$(10,0)$	$(2,4)$	$(2,9)$	$(11,6)$	$(11,7)$
ECM	$(0,0)$	$(1,0)$	$(12,0)$	$(5,4)$	$(5,9)$	$(8,6)$	$(8,7)$

Hence, $w = \pm 1$ and $u = 3$. Indeed,

$$1^2 \equiv 3^3 (\text{mod } 13), \quad 3^3 \equiv -4 \times 3 (\text{mod } 13).$$

Therefore,

$$ECP \xleftarrow{\quad x=3X, y=Y (\text{mod } 13) \quad} ECM.$$

Table 1.2. shows examples of the one-to-one correspondence between the *ECP* and *ECM*.

Remark 1.7. We leave to the reader of this book to analyze the case where $u = -3$.

Example 1.8. Let $p = 41$, find u and w, such that

$$w^2 = u^3 (\text{mod } 41),$$

and

$$u^2 = -4 \equiv 37 (\text{mod } 41), \quad \text{i.e., } u = \pm 18.$$

Then

$$w^2 = u^3 = \pm 5832 = \pm 10 (\text{mod } 41),$$

where both 10 and 31 are QR modulo 41.

Therefore, $w = 16$, and $u = 18$.
Indeed,

$$16^2 \equiv 18^3 (\text{mod } 41), \quad 18^3 \equiv -4 \times 18 (\text{mod } 41).$$

Thus,

$$ECP \xleftarrow{\quad x=18X, y=16Y (\text{mod } 41) \quad} ECM.$$

Exercise 1.9. Analyze the case where $u = -18$ in the Example 1.8.

Table 1.3. shows one-to-one correspondence between points on *ECP* and *ECM* for several non-Blum primes.

Table 1.3 (u, w) as function of p.

p	13	29	37	41
(u, w)	$(3, \pm 1)$	$(5, \pm 3)$	$(12, \pm 10)$	$(18, \pm 16)$

1.2. Generalized modular reduction-in-exponent

Proposition 1.10. Consider hyper-elliptic curves (HECs)

$$y^r = (x^d \pm x^t b^e)(\bmod\ n), \tag{1.27}$$

and

$$Y^r = (X^d \pm X^t b^{e\ \bmod\ [(d-t)r/m]})(\bmod\ n). \tag{1.28}$$

If $0 \le t < d$ and gcd $(d, r) = m$, then both HECs have an equal number of points for every integer $b \ge 2$.

Proof. After appropriate substitutions, the proof is analogous to the proof of Proposition 1.5. {details of the proof and an example are provided in the appendix}.

Special case: if d and r are relatively prime and $t = 0$, then

$$Y^r = (X^d \pm b^{e\ \bmod\ dr})(\bmod\ n). \tag{1.29}$$

□

2. *iFac1* Algorithm Based on ECs

In this algorithm is considered a sequence of ECs with control parameter b. Namely, for every $b = 1, 2, 3, 5, \ldots$, we count the number of points on each EC until *four* distinct counts are found; {see Example 2.1. below}.

In the following algorithm we need *at most three* distinct counts.

Let

$$P_i := P(n, b_i).$$

2.1. *iFac1 algorithm*

1) Compute $P_1, P_2, \ldots, P_i \ne P_1$ until two distinct counts are found,
2) **if**

$$sign(P_1 - n) = sign(P_i - n), \tag{2.1}$$

then

$$p := \gcd(P_1 + P_i, n), \quad q = n/p, \tag{2.2}$$

else compute

$$w := \gcd(P_1 + P_i, n), \tag{2.3}$$

3) **if** $w > 1$,

$$\text{then } p := w, \tag{2.4}$$

$$\textbf{else find a 3rd distinct count } P_k,$$

4) Compute

$$p := \gcd(P_1 + P_k, n), \quad q = n/p. \tag{2.5}$$

Example 2.1. Consider semi-prime $n = 6525401$.
Since

$$P_1 \neq P_2, \quad \text{and} \quad P_1 \neq P_3 \neq P_2, \tag{2.6}$$

then

$$p = \gcd(P_1 + P_3, n).$$

3. *iFac*1 Validation

Definition 3.1. A pair of counts $\{P_i, P_j\}$ is called a *resolvent* A, if $\gcd(P_i + P_j, n) > 1$.

If $w = 1$ (2.3), then we need to compute the third distinct value {see Example 2.1.}.

However, if $w > 1$, then we compute the first factor, say, p, and then $q := n/p$.

Example 3.2. Consider $n = 9037729$, and EC

$$y^2 = x(x^2 + b^2)(\bmod n). \tag{3.1}$$

It $P_1 = A = 8894593, P_i = B = 9176905$, then compute $w := \gcd(A + B, n)$.

If $w = 1$, it means that we cannot find the factors of n. Yet, after we find the third distinct value $P_k = L = 9342205$, the factorization is accomplished: $p = 3361$ and $q = 2689$.

Example 3.3. Consider $n = 8405801$ and EC (3.1).
Compute

$$P_1 = 8387409, \quad P_2 = P_1, \quad P_3 = 8995597,$$

and

$$w := \gcd(P_1 + P_3, n) = 2801.$$

Because $w > 1$, therefore

$$p := w, \quad \text{and} \quad q := n/p = 3001.$$

Although the *iFac1* is computationally simple, we can further simplify the *iFac* algorithm *via* application of other modular equations.

4. Modular Quadratic and Biquadratic Equations

In this section, we consider properties of quadratic, biquadratic modular equations and equations with $m \geq 3$, where the moduli are prime or semi-prime.

Proposition 4.1. Consider a modular quadratic equation (MQE)

$$y^2 = x^2 - b(\bmod n). \tag{4.1}$$

Suppose that $G(n, b)$ denotes the number of integer pairs (x, y) {called points on the quadratic curve} that satisfy (4.1),
if n is a prime, then for every non-zero b co-prime with n,

$$G(n, b) = n - 1,$$

if n is a semi-prime and $n = pq$, then for every non-zero b co-prime with n,

$$G(pq, b) = (p - 1)(q - 1). \tag{4.2}$$

Proof is provided in the appendix.

Conjecture 4.2. Consider a modular equation $V(p, m, b)$:

$$y^2 = x^{2m} - b(\bmod p), \tag{4.3}$$

where p is a prime, and let $G(p, m, b)$ denote the number of points on (4.3),
if in (4.3) $m = 1$ and $p \bmod 4 = 1$, then

$$G(p, m, b) = p - 1, \tag{4.4}$$

if in (4.3) $m = 1$ or $m = 2$ and $p \bmod 4 = 3$, then (4.4) also holds.
If $m \geq 3$ and $\gcd(m, p - 1) = 1$, then $G(p, m, b) = p - 1$.
All cases are listed in the Table 4.1.
Consider a modular equation $V(n, m, b)$: let $b \geq 1$ and integer, $n = pq$,

$$y^2 = x^{2m} - b(\bmod n), \tag{4.5}$$

Table 4.1   Values of $G(p, m, b)$.

$p \bmod 4$	$m = 1$	$m = 2$	$m \geq 3$ and $\gcd(m, p - 1) = 1$
$p \bmod 4 = 1$	$p - 1$	$\neq p - 1$	$p - 1$
$p \bmod 4 = 3$	$p - 1$	$p - 1$	$p - 1$

and let $G(n, m, b)$ denote the number of points on (4.5), and factors p and q are primes.

Conjecture 4.3. If (4.5) is either a quadratic or biquadratic equation, {i.e., if $m = 1$ or $m = 2$}, then for every $b \geq 1$

$$G(pq, m, b) = (p - 1)(q - 1), \qquad (4.6)$$

if an odd prime m is co-prime with $(p - 1)(q - 1)$, then for every integer $b \geq 1$,

$$G(n, m, b) = (p - 1)(q - 1) = \varphi(n). \qquad (4.7)$$

Here, $\varphi(n)$ denotes the Euler's totient function (Gauss, 1965).

Numerous computer experiments for $m = 2, 3, 5, 7$ confirmed plausibility of this conjecture. The examples in Tables 4.2a. and 4.2b. demonstrate the correctness of the Conjecture 4.3. for $m = 1, 2, 3$ and 5. In bold italics are shown the cases, where $\gcd[m, \varphi(n)] > 1$, i.e., where (4.7) does *not* hold. {see also Tables 6.1. and 6.2. below}.

The *iFac2* algorithm described below is based on the Proposition 4.1. This algorithm is computationally efficient, if there exists an efficient procedure {an oracle} that counts the points on either the MQE ($m = 1$) or biquadratic equation ($m = 2$) (4.5).

Definition 4.4. {equivalence}: Problem A_1 is equivalent to problem A_2, if their time complexities satisfy the inequality $T(A_1) \leq T(A_2)$.

Definition 4.5. {strong equivalence}: Problems A_1 and A_2 are strongly equivalent, if their time complexities T_1 and T_2 satisfy $\Theta(T_1) = \Theta(T_2)$.

Table 4.2a   Values of $G(pq, m, b)$.

	$m = 1$	$m = 2$	$m \geq 3$ and $\gcd[m, \varphi(n)] = 1$
$p = q \pmod 4 = 1$	$\varphi(n)$	$\neq \varphi(n)$	$\varphi(n)$
$p = q \pmod 4 = 3$	$\varphi(n)$	$\varphi(n)$	$\varphi(n)$
$pq \bmod 4 = 3$	$\varphi(n)$	$\neq \varphi(n)$	$\varphi(n)$

Table 4.2b   Values of $G(pq, m, b)$, $m = 1, 2, 3, 5$ if $\gcd[m, \varphi(n)] = 1$.

$n = pq$		$m = 1$	$m = 2$	$m = 3$	$m = 5$
$65, 85, 377$	$p = q \pmod 4 = 1$	$48, 64, 336$	***36, 28, 324***	***32, 64, 224***	$48, 64, 336$
$77, 161, 209$	$p = q \pmod 4 = 3$	$60, 132, 180$	$60, 132, 180$	***140, 308, 20***	***12, 132, 36***
$55, 95, 187$	$pq \bmod 4 = 3$	$40, 72, 160$	***20, 36, 140***	$40, \mathbf{8}, 160$	***8, 72, 32***

In the sections below, Tables 6.1. and 6.2. illustrate Conjecture 4.2. and Conjecture 4.3.

5. *iFac2* Algorithm

Conjecture 4.3. can be applied to design an *iFac2* algorithm. As implied from the following discussion, this algorithm is more efficient than the algorithm proposed in Verkhovsky (2011c). Yet, for the seemingly simple *iFac2* algorithm, we need to know how to efficiently count the number of points $G(n, m, b)$ on modular Eq. (4.5) for $m = 1$ or $m = 2$.

5.1. *iFac2 algorithm*

1) Select $b = m = 1$, compute $G(n) := G(n, 1, 1)$ for $V(n, 1, 1)$ (4.5),
2) Compute

$$R := n - G(n) + 1, \qquad (5.1)$$

3) Solve quadratic equation

$$z^2 - Rz + n = 0, \qquad (5.2)$$

suppose z_1 and z_2 are its roots,
4) {Integer factors p and q}:

$$p := z_1, \quad \text{and} \quad q := z_2. \qquad (5.3)$$

Therefore, the *iFac2* problem is equivalent to the problem of counting points on the MQE (4.1). It is well-known that, if n is a semi-prime and if we know the value of the Euler's totient function $\varphi(n)$ (4.7), then we can find the factors of n.

The Conjecture 4.3. is the framework that allows us to compute $\varphi(n)$.

Example 5.1. Let $n = 98,743,069$, then

$$G(n) = 98,723,196,$$

and

$$R := n - G(n) + 1 = 19874.$$

The quadratic equation

$$z^2 - 19874z + 98743069 = 0, \qquad (5.4)$$

has two roots: $z_{1,2} = 9937 \pm 30$. Therefore, $p := z_1 = 9967$ and $q := z_2 = 9907$.

Table 6.1 $V(p, m, 1) : y^2 = x^{2m} + 1 (\bmod p)$.

p	$m = 2$	$m = 3$	$m = 5$	$m = 7$	**	p	$m = 2$	$m = 3$	$m = 5$	$m = 7$
59	58	58	58	58	**	**2011**	2010	*2186*	*2162*	2010
101	*98*	100	*92*	100	**	**2017**	*1998*	*2084*	2016	*2284*
1777	*1854*	*1748*	1776	1776	**	99923	*99992*	*99992*	*99992*	*99992*
1913	*1998*	1912	1912	1912	**	99991	99990	*101102*	*101102*	99990

Table 6.2 $V(p, m, 1)$ for $10^6 < p < 10^7$.

p	$m = 1$	$m = 2$	$m = 3$	$m = 5$	$m = 7$
2696527	2696526	2696526	*2689958*	2696526	*2701694*
5264647	5264646	5264646	*5273726*	5264646	5264646
6878407	6878406	6878406	*6875918*	6878406	6878406

6. Properties of Modular Equations for $m \geq 2$: Computer Experiments

Table 6.1. describes results of computer experiments for various primes p and modular equation

$$y^2 = x^{2m} + 1 (\bmod p). \tag{6.1}$$

Remark 6.1. In Tables 6.1. and 6.2., the cases in ***bold italic*** indicated where $G(p, m, b) \neq p - 1$, because $\gcd(m, p - 1) \neq 1$.

For instance, since

$$101 \equiv 1777 \equiv 1913 \equiv 2017 \equiv 1 (\bmod 4),$$

therefore, the number of points in the corresponding biquadratic modular equations is not equal to $p - 1$.

7. *iFac2* Algorithm Validation

From Conjecture 4.3., the number of points $G(n, m, b)$ on modular Eq. (4.5) is equal to

$$G(pq, m, b) = (p - 1)(q - 1). \tag{7.1}$$

If there is an efficient algorithm that computes $G(n, 1, b)$ or $G(n, 2, b)$, then it implies that for $m \leq 2$,

$$p + q = n + 1 - G(n, m, b). \tag{7.2}$$

Therefore, by the Vieta's theorem, p and q are the roots of quadratic equation

$$z^2 - [n + 1 - G(n, m, b)]z + n = 0. \quad \text{QED.} \tag{7.3}$$

Table 8.1 Algorithms and residues modulo 4.

Algorithm	$p = q = 1 \pmod 4$ or $(p + q) \bmod 4 = 0$	$p = q = 3 \pmod 4$
iFac1	Three ECs: (2.1)–(2.6)	*Not Applicable*
iFac2	One MQE: (5.1)–(5.4)	One MQE: (5.1)–(5.4)

8. Concluding Remarks

Several factorization algorithms were described and analyzed in this chapter and also described below in Table 8.1. It is obvious that modular Eq. (4.5) can be used for the *iFac2*, only if either $m = 1$ or $m = 2$. The above implies that the complexity of *iFac* is at most as difficult as the problem of counting how many solutions have modular Diophantine equations. Therefore, the problem of counting points on the MQE is equivalent to the *iFac2* problem.

Appendix

A.1. *Proof of Proposition 4.1*

Consider MQE:

$$y^2 = x^2 - b \,(\text{mod } n). \qquad (A.1)$$

If n is a prime, then the number of points with non-negative x and y on quadratic curve $Q(n)$ is equal to $n - 1$.

Proof. Consider an integer parameter t on interval $[1, n-1]$. The modular multiplicative inverse of t exists, if and only if $\gcd(t, n) = 1$.

Consider

$$v = (t + t^{-1}b)(n + 1)/2 \,(\text{mod } n),$$

and

$$w = (t^{-1}b - t)(n + 1)/2 \,(\text{mod } n). \qquad (A.2)$$

If n is a prime, then there are $n - 1$ integers that are co-prime with n, if n is a semi-prime and $n = pq$, then there are $\varphi(pq) = (p - 1)(q - 1)$ integers that are co-prime with n. If n is odd, then $(n + 1)/2$ is an integer, therefore both v and w are integers.

It is easy to verify that for every t, there exists a unique pair $\{v, w\}$ that satisfies (A.1). Therefore, we proved that (A.1) has at least $n - 1$ solutions for n prime and has at least $(p - 1)(q - 1)$ solutions, if $n = pq$. Let us show that there are no other solutions.

Suppose there *exists* a solution (g, h) that is distinct from every pair in (A.2).

First of all, $g^2 - h^2 = b(\text{mod } n)$, which implies that, if $1 \le b \le n - 1$, then neither

$$(g - h) \bmod n = 0, \quad \text{nor} \quad (g + h) \bmod n = 0. \tag{A.3}$$

Consider an integer

$$u := (g - h) \bmod n \ne 0, \tag{A.4}$$

where

$$1 \le u \le n - 1,$$

then

$$g + h = u^{-1}b \bmod n.$$

Therefore,

$$g = (u + u^{-1}b) \times 2^{-1} \bmod n,$$

and

$$h = (u^{-1}b - u) \times 2^{-1} \bmod n. \tag{A.5}$$

If n is *odd*, then the modular inverse of 2 exists and

$$2^{-1} \bmod n = (n + 1)/2 \bmod n. \tag{A.6}$$

Hence, the solution (g, h) has the same parametric representation as (v, w), if $u = t$.

The contradiction proves the Proposition 4.1. QED. ⊓

Example A.1. Consider Q (17):

$$y^2 = x^2 - 2(\text{mod } 17).$$

There are *sixteen* points on Q (17): $(\pm 6, 0), (0, \pm 7), (\pm 1, \pm 4), (\pm 2, \pm 6), (\pm 7, \pm 8)$.

A.2. *Complexity analysis*

There are several algorithms that count points on ECs and HECs. If some of these algorithms can be applied for counting points on quadratic or biquadratic modular equations with the same time complexities, then the Schoof–Elkies–Atkin (SEA) algorithm is currently the best known algorithm, that counts points on a modular cubic curve with expected running time $O(\log^4 p)$ (Schoof, 1995; Rubin–Silverberg, 2002). Therefore, if, for instance, p is of order $O(2^{1024}) = O(10^{307})$, then

$$O(\log^4 p) = O(2^{40}) = O(10^{12}).$$

Since the SEA algorithm does not work if $a = 1$ and $b = 0$ (Dewaghe, 1998), consider a modular equation $y^2 = x^2 + b^2 (\text{mod } p)$ with $b \neq 0$ and an algorithm with complexity $O(\log^s p)$ that counts points on this curve. Thus,

$$O(\log^s p) = O(2^{10s}) = O(10^{3s}).$$

A.3. *Proof of Proposition 1.10*

Consider HECs

$$y^r = (x^d + x^t b^e)(\text{mod } n), \tag{A.7}$$

and

$$Y^r = (X^d + X^t b^{e \bmod [(d-t)r/m]})(\text{mod } n) \quad (1.18)\text{--}(1.20). \tag{A.8}$$

If $0 \leq t < d$ and gcd $(d, r) = m$, then for every positive integer b, both HECs have equal number of points.

Proof {by reduction}: Consider substitutions

$$x := X b^w, \quad y := Y b^z, \tag{A.9}$$

into Eq. (A.7), then we derive

$$Y^r b^{rz} = (X^d b^{dw} \pm X^t b^{tw+e})(\text{mod } n). \tag{A.10}$$

Now let us find such integers w and z, for which the following equation holds.

$$rz = dw(\text{mod } \varphi(n)). \tag{A.11}$$

The case is simplified if

$$t \ll \varphi(n) \quad \text{and} \quad d \ll \varphi(n).$$

If

$$\gcd(r, d) = m, \quad \text{then } w = r/m \quad \text{and} \quad z = d/m.$$

Hence,

$$dr \leq rt + em, \quad \text{i.e., } (d - t)r/m \leq e.$$

Therefore, after cancellation of equal terms in both sides of the modular Eq. (A.10), we derive a HEC

$$Y^r = (X^d \pm X^t b^{e-(d-t)r/m})(\text{mod } n). \tag{A.12}$$

Example A.2. Let us consider HEC

$$y^6 = (x^{15} + b^{1777} x^{11})(\text{mod } 1913), \tag{A.13}$$

then HEC $Y^6 = (X^{15} + bX^{11})(\mathrm{mod}\ 1913)$ has the same number of points as (A.13).

A.4. *Number of points on EC* $y^2 = x(x^2 + 2^d)(\mathrm{mod}\ pq)$ *and its factorization*

In this section, we consider n with congruent factors p and q, where

$$p = q = 1(\mathrm{mod}\ 4), \quad p = C^2 + F^2, \quad q = D^2 + H^2,$$

and where C, D, F and H are odd integers.

For the sake of brevity, here we consider only the case where $C = D = 1$ (mod 4).

A.5. *Analysis of options in Table A.1.*

Notation: w is a factor of semi-prime $n = pq$, where p and q are primes. Hence, w is either p or q.

Cases 5, 7, 13, 15: Compute $E(n,0)$ and $E(n,2)$,

If $E(n,0) \neq E(n,2)$, compute $S := E(n,0) + E(n,2), \{= 2(q - 2D)p\}$, then $p := \gcd(S, n)$,

Cases 2, 4, 10, 12: Compute $E(n,0)$ and $E(n,2)$,

If $E(n,0) \neq E(n,2)$, compute $S := E(n,0) + E(n,2), \{- 2(p - 2C)q\}$, then $q := \gcd(S, n)$,

In general, if $E(n,0) \neq E(n,2)$, compute $S := E(n,0) + E(n,2)$, then $w := \gcd(S, n)$.

This algorithm covers all eight cases: 2, 4, 5, 7, 10, 12, 13, 15.

Case 1 $\{0, 0\}$: If $E(n,0) = E(n,2) = E(n,1)$, then the algorithm is not applicable,

Case 11 $\{4, 4\}$: If $E(n,0) = E(n,2) \neq E(n,1) = E(n,3)$, then the algorithm is not applicable,

Remark A.3. The cases $\{0,0\}$ and $\{4,4\}$ require another approach, it is discussed in chapter 4.

Table A.1   Number of points $E(n,d)$ on EC $y^2 = x(x^2 + 2^d) \pmod{n}$, $n = pq$.

	$\{F \bmod 8, H \bmod 8\}$	$d = 0$	$d = 1$	$d = 2$	$d = 3$
1	$\{0, 0\}$	$(p-2C)(q-2D)$	$(p-2C)(q-2D)$	$(p-2C)(q-2D)$	$(p-2C)(q-2D)$
2	$\{0, 2\}$	$(p-2C)(q-2D)$	$(p-2C)(q-2H)$	$(p-2C)(q+2D)$	$(p-2C)(q+2H)$
3	$\{0, 4\}$	$(p-2C)(q-2D)$	$(p-2C)(q-2H)$	$(p-2C)(q-2D)$	$(p-2C)(q-2H)$
4	$\{0, 6\}$	$(p-2C)(q+2D)$	$(p-2C)(q+2H)$	$(p-2C)(q-2D)$	$(p-2C)(q-2H)$
5	$\{2, 0\}$	$(p-2C)(q-2D)$	$(p-2F)(q-2D)$	$(p+2C)(q-2D)$	$(p+2F)(q-2D)$
6	$\{2, 2\}$	$(p-2C)(q-2D)$	$(p-2F)(q-2H)$	$(p+2C)(q+2D)$	$(p+2F)(q+2H)$
7	$\{2, 4\}$	$(p-2C)(q-2D)$	$(p-2F)(q-2H)$	$(p+2C)(q-2D)$	$(p+2F)(q-2H)$
8	$\{2, 6\}$	$(p-2C)(q+2D)$	$(p-2F)(q+2H)$	$(p+2C)(q-2D)$	$(p+2F)(q-2H)$
9	$\{4, 0\}$	$(p-2C)(q-2D)$	$(p-2F)(q-2D)$	$(p-2C)(q-2D)$	$(p-2F)(q-2D)$
10	$\{4, 2\}$	$(p-2C)(q-2D)$	$(p-2F)(q-2H)$	$(p-2C)(q+2D)$	$(p-2F)(q+2H)$
11	$\{4, 4\}$	$(p-2C)(q-2D)$	$(p-2F)(q-2H)$	$(p-2C)(q-2D)$	$(p-2F)(q-2H)$
12	$\{4, 6\}$	$(p-2C)(q+2D)$	$(p-2F)(q+2H)$	$(p-2C)(q-2D)$	$(p-2F)(q-2H)$
13	$\{6, 0\}$	$(p+2C)(q-2D)$	$(p+2F)(q-2D)$	$(p-2C)(q-2D)$	$(p-2F)(q-2D)$
14	$\{6, 2\}$	$(p+2C)(q-2D)$	$(p+2F)(q-2H)$	$(p-2C)(q+2D)$	$(p-2F)(q+2H)$
15	$\{6, 4\}$	$(p+2C)(q-2D)$	$(p+2F)(q-2H)$	$(p-2C)(q-2D)$	$(p-2F)(q-2H)$
16	$\{6, 6\}$	$(p+2C)(q+2D)$	$(p+2F)(q+2H)$	$(p-2C)(q-2D)$	$(p-2F)(q-2H)$

A.6. *Alternate algorithm for cases* 2, 4, 5, 7, 10, 12, 13 *and* 15

Here, we illustrate the algorithm using the case 15 as an example:

Compute $E(n, 0)$ and $E(n, 2)$,
  If

$$E(n, 0) \neq E(n, 2),$$

then compute

$$G := \gcd[E(n, 0), E(n, 2)], \quad \{= (q - 2D)L, \text{where } L := \gcd(p + 2C, p - 2C)\},$$

then

$$A := E(n, 0)/G, \quad \text{and} \quad B := E(n, 2)/G,$$
$$\{A = (p + 2C)/L, \quad B = (p - 2C)/L\}, \tag{A.14}$$

Lemma A.4. For every odd prime p and every integer C, holds that gcd $(p - 2C, p + 2C) = 1$.

Proof. Suppose that

$$\gcd(p - 2C, p + 2C) = L > 1. \tag{A.15}$$

Since $p + 2C = p - 2C = 1 \pmod 2$, then L is an odd integer.

Consider, $A := (p - 2C)/L$, $B := (p + 2C)/L$. The assumption (A.15) implies that A and B are integers, and from summation $A + B$, we derive that $L(A + B)/2 = p$.

Since L is odd and p is integer, then 2 divides $A + B$.

If $L > 1$, then $p = L(A + B)/2$ implies that p is not a prime. Contradiction proves that $L = 1$.

Cases 3 or 9:

| 3 | {0, 4} | $(p - 2C)(q - 2D)$ | $(p - 2C)(q - 2H)$ | $(p - 2C)(q - 2D)$ | $(p - 2C)(q - 2H)$ |

If

$$E(n, 0) = E(n, 2), \quad E(n, 1) = E(n, 3), \quad E(n, 0) \neq E(n, 1),$$
$$\gcd[E(n, 0), E(n, 1)] \geq p - 2C,$$

then compute $G := \gcd[E(n,0), E(n,1)], \{= (p-2C)L$, where $L := \gcd(q - 2D, q - 2H)$,

$$A := E(n,0)/G, \quad \{= (q - 2D)/L\},$$

$$B := E(n,1)/G, \quad \{= (q - 2H)/L\},$$

Since $q - 2D = q - 2H = 1 \pmod 2$, hence L is an odd integer.

Consider

$$R := A + B, \quad \{= 2[q - (D + H)]/L\}.$$

Since L does not divide 2 and does not divide prime q, hence L does not divide $D + H$.

Therefore,

$$2(D + H) = 2q - LR,$$

$$M := A^2, \quad \{= (q^2 - 4Dq + 4D^2)/L^2\},$$

$$N := B^2, \quad \{= (q^2 - 4Hq + 4H^2)/L^2\},$$

$$S := M + N, \quad \{= 2[q^2 - 2q(D + H) + 2q]/L^2\},$$

Thus,

$$(SL^2)/2 = q^2 - q(2q - LR) + 2q = -q^2 + LRq + 2q. \tag{A.16}$$

After simplifications, we derive the parametric quadratic equation

$$z^2 - (LR + 2)z + (SL^2)/2 = 0, \tag{A.17}$$

with odd integer parameter L.

Find an odd integer L that delivers integer solutions to the quadratic Diophantine equation, then one of its roots is the factor of n.

Case 9 {4, 0}: The algorithm for this case is analogous to the algorithm for the previous case.

As a result, we derive that

$$SL^2/2 = -p^2 + (LR + 2)p. \qquad \square$$

Remark A.5. {Computability}: $E(n,0), E(n,1), E(n,2)$ are directly computable, G, A, B, R, A^2, B^2 and S are also directly computable, however, L is *not* directly computable.

Therefore, we must solve the Diophantine quadratic Eq. (A.17), where z and L are unknown integers and L is odd.

Therefore,

$$z = (LR + 2)/2 \pm \sqrt{(LR + 2)^2/4 - SL^2/2},$$

where roots z_1 and z_2 are the factors of semi-prime n.

Remark A.6. If case 9 is correct and solvable, then case $\{0, 4\}$ is analogously solvable.

Example A.7. Consider $n = 1869001$, then $E(n, 0) = E(n, 2) = 815265$, $E(n, 1) = 931209, G := \gcd[E(n, 0), E(n, 1)] = 2673, A_1 := E(n, 0)/G = 305, B_1 := E(n, 1)/G = 323$ and $S_1 = A_1 + B_1 = 305 + 323 = 628$.

Therefore, p and odd L satisfy the quadratic Eq. (A.17):

if $L = 1$, then $z^2 - (R + 2)z + S/2 = 0$, does not have integer solutions.
However, if $L = 3$, then

$$z^2 - 1886z + 888093 = 0,$$

has integer solutions,

$$z = 943 \pm \sqrt{889249 - 888093} = 943 \pm \sqrt{1156} = 943 \pm 34,$$

where both roots are the factors of n.

Cases 6 $\{2, 2\}$, or 16 $\{6, 6\}$

6	$\{2, 2\}$	$(p - 2C)(q - 2D)$	$(p - 2F)(q - 2H)$	$(p + 2C)(q + 2D)$	$(p + 2F)(q + 2H)$
16	$\{6, 6\}$	$(p + 2C)(q + 2D)$	$(p + 2F)(q + 2H)$	$(p - 2C)(q - 2D)$	$(p - 2F)(q - 2H)$

Remark A.8. As demonstrated below, the case 16 is efficiently executable, the cases $\{2, 2\}, \{2, 6\}$ and $\{6, 2\}$ are solvable analogously.

Compute $E(n, 0), E(n, 1), E(n, 2)$ and $E(n, 3)$,
if

$$E(n, 0) \neq E(n, 2), \quad \text{and} \quad E(n, 1) \neq E(n, 3),$$

then compute

$$A := E(n, 0) + E(n, 2) + E(n, 1) + E(n, 3), \tag{A.18}$$

$$B := (A - 2n)/8, \tag{A.19}$$

$$n = pq, \tag{A.20}$$

$$R := E(n, 0) - E(n, 2), \tag{A.21}$$

$$S := E(n, 1) - E(n, 3). \tag{A.22}$$

$$R^2 = 16(C^2 q^2 + 2CDn + p^2 D^2), \tag{A.23}$$

$$S^2 = 16(F^2 q^2 + 2FHn + p^2 H^2). \tag{A.24}$$

Since

$$p = C^2 + F^2 \quad \text{and} \quad q = D^2 + H^2, \tag{A.25}$$

therefore,

$$R^2 + S^2 = 16n[q + 2(CD + FH) + p]. \qquad \text{(A.26)}$$

Consider

$$V := (R^2 + S^2)/16n - 2B, \quad \{= p + q\}. \qquad \text{(A.27)}$$

Hence, by the Vieta's theorem, we determine both factors $z_1 = p$ and $z_2 = q$ from the quadratic equation

$$z^2 - Vz + n = 0. \qquad \text{(A.28)}$$

A.7. *iFac algorithm* {*Cases* **6** *or* **16**}

Step A.1. Compute $E(n, 0)$ and $E(n, 2)$,

Step A.2. If $E(n, 0)$ and $E(n, 2)$ are distinct, compute $E(n, 1)$ and $E(n, 3)$,

Step A.3. If $E(n, 1)$ and $E(n, 3)$ are distinct, then compute

$$A := E(n, 0) + E(n, 1) + E(n, 2) + E(n, 3),$$

Step A.4. Compute

$$B := (A - 2n)/8,$$

$$R := E(n, 0) - E(n, 2), \quad \text{(A.21)},$$

and

$$S := E(n, 1) - E(n, 3), \quad \text{(A.22)},$$

Step A.5. Compute

$$V := (R^2 + S^2)/16n - 2B, \quad \text{(A.27)},$$

Step A.6. Solve the quadratic equation $z^2 - Vz + n = 0$,

Step A.7. Assign $p := z_1$, and $q := z_2$.

Example A.9. Consider $n = 49769$,

Compute $E(n, 0) = 60681, E(n, 2) = 39825, E(n, 1) = 58305, E(n, 3) = 41905$.

Since $E(n, 0)$ and $E(n, 2)$ are distinct, and $E(n, 1)$ and $E(n, 3)$ are distinct, then compute

$$A := E(n, 0) + E(n, 2) + E(n, 1) + E(n, 3) = 200716,$$

$$B := (A - 2n)/8 = 205,$$

$$R := E(n,0) - E(n,2) = 20856, \quad S := E(n,1) - E(n,3) = 16400,$$

$$R^2 = 434972736, \quad S^2 = 268960000,$$

$$V := 884 - 410 = 474, \quad \{= p + q\}.$$

Therefore, from the quadratic equation $z^2 - Vz + n = 0$, or

$$z^2 - 474z + 49769 = 0,$$

we derive that $z_{1,2} = 237 \pm \sqrt{56169 - 49769} = 237 \pm 80, z_1 = 317, z_2 = 157$.

Cases 8 $\{2, 6\}$ and 14 $\{6, 2\}$

6	$\{2,2\}$	$(p-2C)(q-2D)$	$(p-2F)(q-2H)$	$(p+2C)(q+2D)$	$(p+2F)(q+2H)$
8	$\{2,6\}$	$(p-2C)(q+2D)$	$(p-2F)(q+2H)$	$(p+2C)(q-2D)$	$(p+2F)(q-2H)$
14	$\{6,2\}$	$(p+2C)(q-2D)$	$(p+2F)(q-2H)$	$(p-2C)(q+2D)$	$(p-2F)(q+2H)$
16	$\{6,6\}$	$(p+2C)(q+2D)$	$(p+2F)(q+2H)$	$(p-2C)(q-2D)$	$(p-2F)(q-2H)$

Let us analyze the case $\{2,6\}$.
Compute $E(n,0), E(n,1), E(n,2)$ and $E(n,3)$,

$$T := E(n,0) + E(n,2) \quad \text{and} \quad N := E(n,1) + E(n,3).$$

Let

$$T := M + N, \quad G := (4n - T)/8,$$

if

$$\gcd(M,n) = 1 \quad \text{and} \quad \gcd(N,n) = 1,$$

then

$$R := |E(n,0) - E(n,2)|, \quad \text{and} \quad S := |E(n,1) - E(n,3)|.$$

Compute

$$A := R^2, \quad \text{and} \quad B := S^2.$$

Since

$$p = C^2 + F^2, \quad q = D^2 + H^2,$$

therefore,

$$U := A + B = 16n(p + q - 2G).$$

Consider

$$V := U/16n + 2G, \quad \{= p + q\}.$$

Hence, by Vieta's theorem, the quadratic equation $z^2 - Vz + n = 0$, determines the factors of n. Indeed, $z_1 = p$ and $z_2 = q$.

Example A.10. Let $n = 15857$, $\{F \mod 8 = 2, H \mod 8 = 6\}$.

$$T := M + N = E(n,0) + E(n,1) + E(n,2) + E(n,3) = 62860,$$

$$G := (4n - T)/8 = 71,$$

$$R := |E(n,0) - E(n,2)| = 3816, \quad S := |E(n,1) - E(n,3)| = 3856,$$

$$A := R^2 = 14561856, \qquad\qquad B := S^2 = 14868736,$$

$$U := A + B = 29430592, \qquad\qquad V := U/16n + 2G = 258,$$

$$z^2 - 258z + 15857 = 0, \quad \text{i.e., } z_{1,2} = 129 \pm \sqrt{16641 - 15857} = 129 \pm 28.$$

Therefore,

$$z_1 = 157 \quad \text{and} \quad z_2 = 101.$$

Analogous tables can be provided and analyzed for instances, where

$$C \mod 4 = 1, \quad D \mod 4 = 3,$$

$$C \mod 4 = 3, \quad D \mod 4 = 1,$$

and

$$C \mod 4 = 3, \quad D \mod 4 = 3.$$

Table A.2 　Semi-prime $n = pq$ and number of points on EC $y^2 = x(x^2 + 2^d)(\mod n)$.

	$H \mod 8 = 0$, $q = 1913$, $D = 43, H = 8$	$H \mod 8 = 2$, $q = 109$, $D = 3, H = 10$	$H \mod 8 = 4$, $q = 97$, $D = 9, H = 4$	$H \mod 8 = 6$, $q = 157$, $D = 11, H = 6$
$F \mod 8 = 0$, $p = 257, C = 1, F = 16$	$n = 491641$, $n \mod 8 = 1$	$n = 28013$, $n \mod 8 = 5$	$n = 24929$, $n \mod 8 = 5$	$n = 40349$, $n \mod 8 = 1$
$F \mod 8 = 2$, $p = 101, C = 1, F = 10$	$n = 193213$, $n \mod 8 = 5$	$n = 11009$, $n \mod 8 = 1$	$n = 9797, n$ $\mod 8 = 1$	$n = 15857$, $n \mod 8 = 1$
$F \mod 8 = 4$, $p = 977, C = 31, F = 4$	$n = 1869001$, $n \mod 8 = 1$	$n = 106493$, $n \mod 8 = 5$	$n = 94769, n$ $\mod 8 = 5$	$n = 153389, n$ $\mod 8 = 1$
$F \mod 8 = 6$, $p = 317, C = 11, F = 14$	$n = 721201$, $n \mod 8 = 1$	$n = 34553$, $n \mod 8 = 5$	$n = 30749$, $n \mod 8 = 1$	$n = 49769$, $n \mod 8 = 5$

Chapter 19

Counting Points on Hyper-Elliptic Curves and Integer Factorization

1. Introduction and Modular Elliptic Curves (ECs)

Security of information transmission *via* communication networks is provided by various cryptographic protocols. Crypto-immunity of these protocols is mostly based on hardness of either the integer factorization or the discrete logarithm problem.

There are several algorithms that factorize a semi-prime $n = pq$, where n is known, but its integer factors p and q are large and unknown. Fermat and Euler and other mathematicians and computer scientists and prior to them mathematicians of antiquity introduced various algorithms and proposed their methods for integer factorization. A survey of these methods is provided in Pomerance–Crandall (2001). Modern factoring algorithms are described in Cohen (1996). Various special methods are considered in Shanks (1969), Lehman (1974) and Pollard (1974). An application of cubic forms for factorization, as one of these special methods, is provided in Pollard (1993).

A comparison and analysis of factoring algorithms with exponential time complexity is provided in Pomerance (1982). Algorithms based on the quadratic sieve (QS) are discussed in Pomerance (1985) and Silverman (1987), while integer factoring *via* the number field sieve (NFS) is provided in Buhler *et al.* (1993). Both the QS and NFS are algorithms with sub-exponential time complexity.

The application of special devises for factoring is described in Lenstra–Shamir (2000) and analyzed in Shamir–Tromer (2003). A pioneering paper on the application of quantum computing for integer factorization is discussed in Schor (1997).

New factoring algorithms proposed in this chapter are based on the analysis of several modular elliptic and hyper-elliptic equations (respectively called ECs and hyper-elliptic curves, HECs) and counting how many integer points {integer pairs (x, y)} satisfy these curves. The application of ECs for factoring is described in Lenstra Jr. (1987), Schoof (1995), Montgomery (1992). Methods of counting points on ECs are considered in Lencier *et al.* (2006) and Lauder–Wan (2008), and more generally on modular equations with several variables in Weil (1949) and Lauder (2004). A relationship between integer factorization and constrained discrete logarithm problems is analyzed in Verkhovsky (2009d).

In this chapter and in other chapters of this book several algorithms that address the integer factorization problem are described. These algorithms are based on counting the number of points on specially-selected ECs and HECs. In the book, we do not discuss how to do the counting. This is a classical problem in itself and is addressed in Koblitz (1994), Cohen (1996), Gaudry (2003), Satoh (2000), Satoh *et al.* (2003), Furukawa *et al.* (2004).

In the first sections, we introduce several special ECs and HECs, describe their properties and demonstrate how these properties can be applied for integer factorization. In the third section, we demonstrate how these ideas can be used to factor several semi-primes proposed in the RSA challenge.

Conjecture 1.1. {multiplicaticity}: Consider a hyper-elliptic curve (HEC)

$$y^2 + dy = x^m + ax + b \bmod n_k, \quad k = 1, 2, 3, \tag{1.1}$$

where $a, b, d, m > 2$ and $n_k \geq 3$ are integers and known input parameters of the HEC, and let $\#E(n_k)$ be the number of integer points (x, y) that satisfy (1.1).

If $n_3 = n_1 n_2$, then

$$\#E(n_1 n_2) = \#E(n_1) \#E(n_2). \tag{1.2}$$

Consider elliptic curve

$$y^2 \equiv x^3 + 1 \pmod{n}, \tag{1.3}$$

then the following four points $(0, 1), (-1, 0)$ and $(2, \pm 3)$ satisfy (1.3) for *every* $n > 3$.

1.1. *Simple algorithm for integer factorization*

Consider $n = pq$, where both p and q are multi-digit long primes.

There are two special cases:

1) $$(p + q) \bmod 4 = 0, \tag{1.4}$$

2) $$p = q(\bmod 4). \tag{1.5}$$

Below is provided and discussed a factorization algorithm for (1.4) case only.

Consider an EC $E(n, b)$ modulo n:

$$y^2 = x(x^2 + b)(\bmod n), \quad b \neq 0. \tag{1.6}$$

Let $P(n, b)$ denote the number of points on the EC (1.6). It is easy to observe that (1.4) implies that,

$$\text{if } n = pq, \quad \text{then } n \bmod 4 = 3. \tag{1.7}$$

Definition 1.2. The product of two primes $n = pq$ is called a *semi-prime*.

Here is the simple algorithm that finds the integer factors p and q.

Input: n is a semi-prime,

Output: integer factors p and q of n,

1: **if** $n \bmod 4 = 3$, **then** for a randomly chosen b compute $P(n, b)$

                else output 'the algorithm is not applicable',

2: Assign

$$p := \gcd[P(n, b), n], \quad q := n/p, \tag{1.8}$$

{**end** of algorithm}.

2. Super-Singular ECs as Splitters

Definition 2.1. A procedure that finds a factor of semi-prime n is called a *splitter*.

The algorithm described in the previous section is an example of the splitter.

Let us consider two HEC:

$$E_b(m, n) : y^2 + dy = x^m + b(\bmod n), \tag{2.1}$$

$$E_a(m, n) : y^2 = x^m + ax(\bmod n), \tag{2.2}$$

Table 2.1   Number of points on ECs $y^2 = x^3 + ax \pmod{p}$ and $y^2 = x^3 + b \pmod{p}$.

p	5	7	11	13	17	19	23	29	31	37	41	43	47	61	71	139
$\#E_b(3,p)$	5	11	11	11	17	11	23	29	35	47	41	35	47	47	71	155
$\#E_a(3,p)$	3	7	11	11	15	19	23	23	31	35	31	43	47	51	71	139

Remark 2.2. if $m = 3$, then $Eb(3,n)$ and $Ea(3,n)$ are super-singular ECs (Koblitz, 1994).

Proposition 2.3. If p is a prime and $p \bmod 3 \neq 1$, then the number of points on $E_b(3,p)$ is equal p {excluding the point at infinity O}.

Proposition 2.4. If p is a Blum prime, i.e., $p \bmod 4 \neq 1$, then the number of points on $E_a(3,p)$ is equal p {excluding the point O}.
     Table 2.1. shows the number of points on $E_a(3,p)$ and $E_b(3,p)$, where $a = b = 1$.

Remark 2.5. if $p \bmod 3 \neq 1$ or $p \bmod 4 \neq 1$, then correspondingly for *every* a and b the number of points on each of these ECs is equal to p.

Proposition 2.6. If n is a semi-prime and $n \bmod 3 = 2$, then gcd [$\#$ $E_b(3,n), n] > 1$ is a proper factor of n. Here $n \bmod 3 = 2$ is called the *indicator*.

Proof. If $n \bmod 3 = 2$, hence $(p+q) \bmod 3 = 0$, which implies that either $p \bmod 3 = 1$ and $q \bmod 3 = 2$ or *vice versa*. Thus, either

$$\#E_b(3,q) = q \quad \text{or} \quad \#E_b(3,p) = p. \tag{2.3}$$

Therefore, by Conjecture1.1, either

$$\#E_b(3,n) = p\#E_b(3,q) \quad \text{xor} \ \# \ E_b(3,n) = \#E_b(3,p)q. \tag{2.4}$$

$\square$

Example 2.7. Let $n = pq = 5561$. Since $n \bmod 3 = 2$, then consider $Eb(3, 5561)$.
     If $b = 1$, then $\# \ Eb(3, 5561) = 6889$. Hence, gcd $(n, 6889) = 83$.
     Therefore, one factor of n, say $p = 83$, and another $q = n/p = 67$.
     If $b = 1001$, then $\# \ Eb(3, 5561) = 6474$. Therefore, again gcd$(n, 6474) = 83$.

Example 2.8. Let $n = pq = 3399401$. Since $n \bmod 3 = 2$, then for $b = 1$ $\# \; Eb(3, 3399401) = 3372619$, and gcd $(3399401, 3372619) = 1913$. Therefore, $p = 1913$ and $q = n/p = 1777$.

Remark 2.9. If $n \bmod 3 = 1$, then consider $n \bmod 4$.

Proposition 2.10. If n is a semi-prime and $n \bmod 4 = 3$, then gcd $[\# \; Ea(4, n), n] > 1$ is a proper factor of n. Here $n \bmod 4 = 3$ is called the *indicator*.

Proof. First of all, the indicator implies that one factor of n is a Blum prime and another is not, i.e., $(p + q) \bmod 4 = 0$. The analysis proceeds analogously as in Proposition 2.6., i.e., either $p \bmod 4 = 1$ and $q \bmod 4 = 3$ or *vice versa*.

Thus, either $\#E_a(3, q) = q$ or $\#E_a(3, p) = p$.

Therefore, by Conjecture 1.1., either

$$\#E_a(3, n) = \#E_a(3, q)p \quad \text{or} \quad \#E_a(3, n) = \#E_a(3, p)q. \tag{2.5}$$

$\square$

Example 2.11. Let $n = pq = 3967703$. Since $n \bmod 4 = 3$, consider $Ea(3, n)$.

If in (2.2) $a = 1$, then $\#E_a(3, 3967703) = 4141327$. Hence, gcd $(3967703, 4141327) = 1973$.

Thus, one factor of n, say $p = 1973$, and another $q = n/p = 2011$.

If in (2.2), $a = 1913$, then $\# \; E_a(3, 3967703) = 3910486$.

Thus, gcd $(3967703, 3910486) = 1973$.

Remark 2.12. In every case considered above, the choice of a or b in ECs (2.1) and (2.2) does not affect the final results.

3. RSA Challenge

Several years ago, RSA Corp. announced a challenge to factor multi-digit long integers. In the following examples we show how many of them could have been factored, using algorithms described above in Propositions 2.6. or 2.10.

Example 3.1. Consider RSA-100:

$$n := pq = 37975227936943673922808872755445627854565536638199$$

$$\times \; 40094690950920881030683735292761468389214899724061.$$

Since $n \bmod 3 = 2$, hence $p \neq q (\bmod 3)$.

Therefore, using Proposition 2.6., we can find p and q.

Example 3.2. Consider RSA-110:

$$n := pq = 6122421090493547576937037317561418841225758554253106999$$
$$\times 58464182144061546788365531829791623841986105056010623333,$$

where $n \bmod 4 = 3$, hence $p \neq q (\bmod 4)$.

Therefore, using Proposition 2.10., we can find p and q.

Example 3.3. Consider RSA-120:

$$n := pq$$
$$= 327414555693498015751146303749141488063642403240171463406883$$
$$\times 69334266711083018119732540189970064136196586312733668$$
$$0673013,$$

where $pq \bmod 4 = 3$. Therefore, as in the previous example, either $p \bmod 4 = 3$, and $q \bmod 4 = 1$, or *vice versa*. Thus, using Proposition 2.10., we can find p and q.

Example 3.4. Consider RSA-129:

$$n := pq$$
$$= 3490529510847650949147849619903898133417764638493387843990820577$$
$$\times 327691329932667095499619881908344614131776429679929425397$$
$$98288533,$$

where $n \bmod 3 = 1$ and $n \bmod 4 = 1$. Therefore, $p = q (\bmod 3)$ and $p = q (\bmod 4)$, hence neither Proposition 2.6. nor 2.10. is applicable. Below we consider another approach that addresses this case.

Example 3.5. Consider RSA-130. Since $n \bmod 3 = 2$. Hence, by Proposition 2.6., we can find p and q.

Proposition 3.6. $n \bmod 12 = 1$, if and only if $p = q (\bmod m)$, where $m = 3$ and $m = 4$.

Proof. Suppose that $p = 12K + y$ and $q = 12L + z$, where $1 \leq y, z \leq 11$, then $n = pq = 144KL + 12(Kz + Ly) + yz$. Therefore,

$n = yz(\mathrm{mod}\, 12)$

$$= \begin{cases} 1 & \text{if } (y, z) = \{(1, 1), (5, 5), (7, 7), (11, 11)\} \\ 5 & \text{if } (y, z) = \{(1, 5), (7, 11)\}, \text{ i.e., } y \neq z(\mathrm{mod}\, 3) \\ 7 & \text{if } (y, z) = \{(1, 7), (5, 11)\}, \text{ i.e., } y \neq z(\mathrm{mod}\, 4) \\ 11 & \text{if } (y, z) = \{(1, 11), (5, 7)\}, \text{ i.e., } y \neq z(\mathrm{mod}\, m), \ m = 3, 4 \end{cases} \tag{3.1}$$

$\square$

Corollary 3.7. Therefore, if $n \bmod 12 \neq 1$, then either Proposition 2.6. or Proposition 2.10. holds, and, as a result, the algorithms described above are applicable as the splitters.

4. Number of Points on EC

Proposition 4.1. Consider

$$y^2 + dy = x^3 - b(\mathrm{mod}\, p), \tag{4.1}$$

if p is an odd prime,

$$p \bmod 3 \neq 1, \tag{4.2}$$

then the curve (4.1) has p points.

Proof. (4.1) is equivalent to

$$x = \sqrt[3]{y^2 + dy + b}(\mathrm{mod}\, p), \tag{4.3}$$

and for every y on $[0, p-1]$, there exists a cubic root $x = \sqrt[3]{y^2 + dy + b}$ $(\mathrm{mod}\, p)$.

The algorithm that extracts the cubic root, if p satisfies (4.2), is provided in the appendix at the end of this chapter. $\square$

5. Number of Points on Quadratic Curves (QCs)

Let us consider a modular QC,

$$Q(n) : x^2 - y^2 = b(\mathrm{mod}\, n). \tag{5.1}$$

Proposition 5.1. If p is a prime, then the number of points on $Q(p)$ equals $p - 1$.

Table 5.1   Number of points on quadratic form $Q(n)$.

n	$91 = 7*13$	$111 = 3*37$	1777	1913	1973	2011	77711	99991
# Q (n)	$72 = 6*12$	$72 = 2*36$	1776	1912	1972	2010	77710	99990

Proof. Consider an integer parameter t on interval $[1, p-1]$.

Let $t := x + y$, then (5.1) implies that

$$x - y = bt^{-1}, \tag{5.2}$$

where the modular multiplicative inverse of t exists, if and only if $\gcd(t, p) = 1$ or if $t = 1$. Therefore,

$$\begin{aligned} x\,(t) &= (t^{-1}b + t)(p+1)/2(\bmod p), \quad \text{and} \\ y\,(t) &= (t^{-1}b - t)(p+1)/2(\bmod p). \end{aligned} \tag{5.3}$$

If p is odd, then $(p+1)/2$ is an integer, hence both $x(t)$ and $y(t)$ are integers.
$\square$

Example 5.2. Suppose $Q(11) : y^2 = x^2 + 2(\bmod 11)$.

There are *ten* points on $Q(11)$: $(\pm 3, 0), (\pm 1, \pm 5), (\pm 5, \pm 4)$.

Corollary 5.3. Proposition 5.1 can be used for the integer factorization: observe that, if p and q are primes, then

$$\#Q(pq) = \#Q(p)\#Q(q) = (p-1)(q-1). \tag{5.4}$$

For numeric illustration, see Table 5.1.

6. Number of Points on HECs

Proposition 6.1. Consider HEC

$$y^2 + dy = x^m + b(\bmod p), \quad \text{where } m \text{ is odd.} \tag{6.1}$$

If p is an odd prime such that

$$p \bmod m \neq 1, \tag{6.2}$$

then the HEC (6.1) has p points.

Proof. (6.1) is equivalent to

$$x = \sqrt[m]{y^2 + dy - b}(\bmod p), \tag{6.3}$$

and for every y on $[0, p-1]$ there exists an integer x that satisfies (6.3).
$\square$

Table 6.1 Number of points on curves $y^2 + dy = x^m + b(\mathrm{mod}\, p)$, $d = b = 1$.

$p;\ m$	37; 5	61; 5	61; 7	73; 5	97; 5	109; 5	157; 5	181; 7	241; 7
# HEC	37	66	61	73	97	109	157	181	241

Definition 6.2. HEC

$$y^2 = x^m + x(\mathrm{mod}\, n), \tag{6.4}$$

is called a Buhler–Koblitz HEC and is denoted as $BK\ (m, n)$.

Definition 6.3. HEC

$$y^2 + y = x^m + 1(\mathrm{mod}\, n), \tag{6.5}$$

is denoted as $V(m, n)$.

6.1. *Two basic algorithms for integer factorization*

Suppose that the splitter is an EC or HEC (6.1), where N is the number of points on this curve.

First Algorithm: If m is **odd** and (6.2) holds, then $p = \gcd\ (N, n)$, and $q := n/p$,

Second Algorithm: If m is **even,** then compute $V := n - N + 1$, and solve quadratic equation

$$z^2 - Vz + n = 0, \tag{6.6}$$

then $p := z_1$ and $q := z_2$.

Table 6.2. provides a list of various semi-primes n, their global indicators and the corresponding splitters.

Remark 6.4. {hidden relations between factors p and q}: in Case 1 p and q are not congruent modulo 3, in Case 2 p and q are not congruent modulo 4, in Cases 3 and 7 both factors are Blum primes, in Cases 6 and 8–13 both p and q are non-Blum primes.

6.2. *Quadratic splitter*

Example 6.5. $n = 25681$, use $E_b(2, n)$: $N = 25200$, $v = n - N + 1 = 482$, solve the quadratic equation: $z^2 - 482z + 25681 = 0$, $z = 241 \pm 180$;
Therefore, $p = 421, q = 61$.

Table 6.2   Factorable cases, splitters and indicators.

Factorable cases	Splitters to use	Indicators
1: $(p+q) \bmod 3 = 0$	$E_b(3, n)$	$n \bmod 3 = 2$
2: $(p+q) \bmod 4 = 0$	$E_a(3, n)$	$n \bmod 4 = 3$
3: $p = q (\bmod 3) = 2$	$V(6, n)$	$n \bmod 3 = 1$
4: $p = q \ (\bmod 4) = 3$	$BK \ (4, n)$ or $V(4, n)$	$n \bmod 4 = 1$
5: $p = q \ (\bmod 12) = 1$	see cases 6–8, 10, 12	$n \bmod 12 = 1$
6: $p = q \ (\bmod 12) = 5$	$V(6, n)$	$n \bmod 12 = 1$
7: $p = q \ (\bmod 12) = 7, 11$	$BK \ (4, n)$	$n \bmod 12 = 1$
8: $p = q \ (\bmod 60) = 1$	$BK \ (14, n)$ or $Q(n)$	$n \bmod 60 = 1$
9: $p = q \ (\bmod 60) = 13, 37$	$BK \ (10, n)$	$n \bmod 60 = 49$
10: $p = q \ (\bmod 60) = 49$	$BK \ (10, n)$	$n \bmod 60 = 1$
11: $p = 1, q = 13, 37, 49 \ (\bmod 60)$	$V(5, n)$	$n \bmod 60 = 13, 37, 49$
12: $p = 13, q = 37 \ (\bmod 60)$	$BK \ (10, n)$ or $V(10, n)$	$n \bmod 60 = 1$
13: $p = 13, 37, q = 49 \ (\bmod 60)$	$BK \ (10, n)$ or $V(10, n)$	$n \bmod 60 = 13, 37$
14: $p = q \ (\bmod 60) = 1$	$Q(n)$	$n \bmod 60 = 1$

Table 6.3   Splitters and recovery actions for odd and even m.

HEC modulo n	Recovery actions	Remarks
EC $Ea(n)$: $y^2 = (x^3 + ax)(\bmod n)$	Find $\# \ Ea(n)$, $z := \gcd[n, \# \ Ea(n)]$, if $z > 1$, then $p := z$, else compute $\# \ Eb(n)$	$q := n/p$
EC $Eb(n)$: $y^2 = (x^3 + b)(\bmod n)$	Find $\# \ Eb(n)$, $z := \gcd[n, \# \ Eb(n)]$, if $z > 1$, then $p := z$, else compute $\# \ Ea(n)$	$q := n/p$
HEC $BK \ (m, n)$: $y^2 + y = x^m (\bmod n)$	Find $N := \# \ BK \ (m, n)$, $V := n - N + 1$, Solve $z^2 - Vz + n = 0$, $p := z_1, q := z_2$	m even
HEC $V(m, n)$: $y^2 + y = (x^m + 1)(\bmod n)$	Find $N := \# \ V(m, n)$, $V := n - N + 1$, Solve $z^2 - Vz + n = 0$, $p := z_1, q := z_2$	m even
HEC $BK \ (m, n)$: $y^2 + y = x^m (\bmod n)$	Find $N := \# \ BK \ (m, n)$, $z := \gcd(n, N)$, if $z > 1$, then $p := z$, else compute $\# \ V(m, n)$	m odd,, $q := n/p$
HEC $V(m, n)$: $y^2 + y = (x^m + 1)(\bmod n)$	Find $N := \# \ V(m, n)$, $z := \gcd(n, N)$, if $z > 1$, then $p := z$, else compute $\# \ BK \ (m, n)$	m odd, $q := n/p$

Table 6.4 $\{p = q \bmod 12 = 1, p \bmod 60, q \bmod 60, n \bmod 60\}$.

$p \bmod 60$	$q \bmod 60 = 1$	$q \bmod 60 = 13$	$q \bmod 60 = 37$	$q \bmod 60 = 49$
1	1: $BK \ (14, n)$ or $V(14, n)$ or $Q(n)$	13: $BK \ (5, n)$	37: $BK \ (5, n)$	49: $BK \ (5, n)$
13	13: $BK \ (5, n)$ or $V(5, n)$	49: $BK \ (10, n)$ or $V(10, n)$	1: $V(5, n)$	37: $BK \ (5, n)$
37	37: $BK \ (5, n)$ or $V(5, n)$	1: $V(5, n)$	49: $BK \ (10, n)$ or $V(10, n)$	13: $BK \ (5, n)$
49	49: $BK \ (5, n)$ or $V(5, n)$	37: $BK \ (5, n)$	13: $BK \ (5, n)$	1: $BK \ (10, n)$ or $V(10, n)$

Table 6.5 Integer factorization using HEC with odd m.

$n = 11773$	$n = 9577$	$n = 11773$	$n = 19729$	$n = 12871$
$n \bmod 60 = 13$	$n \bmod 60 = 37$	$n \bmod 60 = 13$	$n \bmod 60 = 49$	$n \bmod 4 = 3$
$BK\ (5, n)$	$BK\ (5, n)$	$BK\ (5, n)$	$V(5, n)$	$E_b(3, n)$
$N = 11966$	$N = 9734$	$N = 14861$	$N = 23108$	$N = ?$
$gcd\ (n, N) = p = 193$	$p = 157$	$p = 193$	$p = 109$	$p = ?$

Table 6.6 Integer factorization using HEC with even m.

$n = 11041$	$n = 5293$	$n = 4897$	$n = 14089$	$n = 24961$	$n = 21037$
$n \bmod 60 = 1$	$n \bmod 60 = 13$	$n \bmod 60 = 37$	$n \bmod 60 = 49$	$n \bmod 60 = 1$	$n \bmod 60 = 37$
$BK\ (14, n)$	$BK\ (4, n)$	$BK\ (6, n)$	$BK\ (10, n)$	$V(10, n)$	$V(10, n)$
$N = 10800$	$N = 5148$	$N = 4756$	$N = 13824$	$N = 24624$	$N = 20736$
$v = 242$	$v = 146$	$v = 142$	$v = 266$	$v = 338$	$v = 302$
$p = 181$	$p = 79$	$p = 83$	$p = 193$	$p = 229$	$p = 193$

Example 6.6. {alternate approach-see Table 6.6.}: $n = 24961$, $n \bmod 60 = 1 : \{n \bmod 4 = 1, n \bmod 3 = 1\}$, compute $\#E_b(2, n) = N = 24624$, {CPU = 1 minute}, then compute v, solve the quadratic equation and proceed as in Example 6.5.

7. Computer Experiments with $V(m, n)$

The outputs with even m in Table 7.1. are especially interesting:
$\# V\ (4, p) = p - 1$, if $p \bmod 4 = 3$ {Blum prime},
$\# V\ (6, p) = p - 1$, if $p \bmod 6 \neq 1$ {plus additional cases where $p \bmod 6 = 1 : 37, 73, 103, 127, \ldots,$}

Conjecture 7.1. Suppose that m_1 divides m_2, and N_1, N_2 are the number of points on the corresponding curves $V(m, n)$, then

$$(m_2 - m_1) \mid (N_2 - N_1). \tag{7.1}$$

In more general form,

$$\gcd(m_1, m_2) \mid (N_2 - N_1). \tag{7.2}$$

For numerical illustrations of this conjecture, see Table 7.1.

8. Quadratic Splitters

Conjecture 8.1. If n is a prime and $n \bmod 60 > 1$, then the number of points on EC is equal to $n - 1$.

Table 7.1　*HEC* $y^2 + y = x^m + 1 (\mod n)$ and number of points $\# V(m, n)$ on it.

$n \backslash m$	$m = 4$	$m = 5$	$m = 6$	$m = 7$	$m = 10$	$m = 14$
13	16	13	24	13	12	12
17	24	17	16	17	16	16
29	18	29	28	44	28	58
31	30	42	26	31	42	30
37	48	37	36	37	36	36
41	50	57	40	41	72	40
43	42	43	60	42	42	28
61	50	77	74	61	92	60
67	66	67	60	67	66	66
71	70	72	70	86	62	114
73	88	73	72	73	72	72
97	88	97	120	97	96	96
101	102	92	100	101	62	100
109	102	109	110	109	108	108
113	96	113	112	112	112	84
131	130	132	130	131	102	130
N	$n \bmod 4 = 3$	$n \bmod 10 > 1$	$n \bmod 6 > 1$	$n \bmod 7 > 1$	$n \bmod 10 > 1$	$n \bmod 14 > 1$

Table 8.1

n	$E_a(2, n)$	$E_b(2, n)$	$BK(2, n)$	$V(2, n)$
47	46	46	46	46
49	42	42	42	42
59	58	58	58	58
61	61	61	61	61
67	66	66	66	66

Table 9.1　$E(p, 0)$ as function of c and d.

$C \backslash F$	$F \bmod 4 = 0$	$F \bmod 4 = 2$
$C \bmod 4 = 1$	$\#E = p - 2C$	$\#E = p + 2C$
$C \bmod 4 = 3$	$\#E = p + 2C$	$\#E = p - 2C$

9. Points Counting Algorithm on EC $y^2 = x^3 - x (\mod p)$, if $p \bmod 4 = 1$

Every non-Blum prime p can be uniquely represented as $p = C^2 + F^2$, where C is *odd* and F is *even* integer. Then the number of points $E(p, 0)$ is given in the Table 9.1. However, if p is a Blum prime, then it cannot be presented as a sum of two integer squares.

The Table 9.1. implies that if $(C + F) \bmod 4 = 2 \pm 1$, then $\#E = p \pm 2C$.

Example 9.1. Let $p = 109$, then $p = 3^2 + 10^2$. Hence $E = p - 2C = 109 - 6 = 103$.

Example 9.2. Let $p = 1913$, then $1913 = 43^2 + 8^2$. Therefore, $E = p + 2C = 1913 + 86 = 1999$.

Exercise 9.3. Find E for $p = 11777$. {Hint: solve Diophantine equation $C^2 + F^2 = 11777$}.

10. Properties of Factors of Semi-Prime n

Proposition 10.1. If n is a semi-prime and $n \bmod 4 = 1$, then $p = q (\bmod 4)$, therefore, either both p and q or none are Blum primes.

Proposition 10.2. If n is a semi-prime, $n \bmod 4 = 1$ and $\#E_a(3, n) = n$, then both factors p and q of n are Blum primes.

Proposition 10.3. If n is a semi-prime and $n \bmod 4 = 3$, then p **xor** q is a Blum prime.

Proposition 10.4. If n is a semi-prime, $n \bmod 3 = 1$ and $\#E_b(3, n) = n$, then its factors

$$p = q(\bmod 3) = 2.$$

Proposition 10.5. If $n \bmod 4 = 3$, and $\#E_a(3, n) = n$, then n is either a prime or a product of more than two integer factors.

Proposition 10.6. If $n \bmod 3 = 2$ and $\#E_b(3, n) = n$, then n is either a prime or a product of more than two integer factors.

11. Integer Factorization *via* Counting Points on Special HEC

Proposition 11.1. Suppose

$$C(n) : y^2 = x^5 + b \bmod n, \quad r := p \bmod 60, \quad s := q \bmod 60, \qquad (11.1)$$

consider the following short-hand notations:

$$cc := \#C(p)\#C(q), \quad cq := \#C(p)q, \quad pc := \#C(q)p, \qquad (11.2)$$

if $r \bmod 5 = 2, 3, 4$ and $s \bmod 5 = 1$, then $\#C(n) = pc$, $\qquad (11.3)$

if $r \bmod 5 = 1$ and $s \bmod 5 = 2, 3, 4$, then $\#C(n) = cq$. $\qquad (11.4)$

All other cases are shown in the Table 11.1.

Table 11.1

$n = pq$	$s = 1$	$s = 7$	$s = 11$	$s = 13$	$s = 17$	$s = 19$	$s = 23$	29	31	37	41	43	47	49	53	$s = 59$
$r = 1$	cc	cq	cc	cq	cq	cq	cq	cq	cc	cq	cc	cq	cq	cq	cq	cq
$r = 7$	pc	n	pc	n	n	n	n	n	pc	n	pc	n	n	n	n	n
$r = 11$	cc	cq	cc	cq	cq	cq	cq	cq	cc	cq	cc	cq	cq	cq	cq	cq
$r = 13$	pc	n	pc	n	n	n	n	n	pc	n	pc	n	n	n	n	n
$r = 17$	pc	n	pc	n	n	n	n	n	pc	n	pc	n	n	n	n	n
$r = 19$	pc	n	pc	n	n	n	n	n	pc	n	pc	n	n	n	n	n
$r = 23$	pc	n	pc	n	n	n	n	n	pc	n	pc	n	n	n	n	n
$r = 29$	pc	n	pc	n	n	n	n	n	pc	n	pc	n	n	n	n	n
$r = 31$	cc	cq	cc	cq	cq	cq	cq	cq	cc	cq	cc	cq	cq	cq	cq	cq
$r = 37$	pc	n	pc	n	n	n	n	n	pc	n	pc	n	n	n	n	n
$r = 41$	cc	cq	cc	cq	cq	cq	cq	cq	cc	cq	cc	cq	cq	cq	cq	cq
$r = 43$	pc	n	pc	n	n	n	n	n	pc	n	pc	n	n	n	n	n
$r = 47$	pc	n	pc	n	n	n	n	n	pc	n	pc	n	n	n	n	n
$r = 49$	pc	n	pc	n	n	n	n	n	pc	n	pc	n	n	n	n	n
$r = 53$	pc	n	pc	n	n	n	n	n	pc	n	pc	n	n	n	n	n
$r = 59$	pc	n	pc	n	n	n	n	n	pc	n	pc	n	n	n	n	n

Therefore, of all 256 combinations of $\{r, s\}$, only some of them can be used for integer factorization:

a. The combinations that output either n (144 cases) or cc (16 cases) are not constructive for the integer factorization.
b. Thus, in $96/256 = 3/8$ cases, we can use the points counting on the HEC (11.1), as a tool for the integer factorization of semi-primes.

Appendix

A.1. *Points Counting on* V (n)

$$y^2 = (x^3 + b^2) \bmod n, \quad \text{if } n \bmod 3 = 1. \tag{A.1}$$

Proposition A.1. If n is a semi-prime, $\{n = pq\}$ and $p \equiv q(\bmod 3) = 2$, then the elliptic curve (A.1) has n points.

Proof. Let us show that there exists a unique cubic root for every integer d co-prime with n. Indeed, let

$$s := p + q \quad \text{and} \quad g := 2(n - s)/3 + 1, \tag{A.2}$$

then

$$z = d^g \bmod n, \tag{A.3}$$

is a cubic root of d modulo composite n.

First of all, $(n - s)/3$ is an integer. Therefore, if $p \equiv q(\bmod 3) = 2$, then

$$pq \equiv (p + q)(\bmod 3). \tag{A.4}$$

Hence, $[pq - (p + q)] \bmod 3 = 0$, this means that 3 divides $(n - s)$.
At the same time,

$$g = 2(n - s)/3 + 1 = [2\varphi(n) + 1]/3. \tag{A.5}$$

Since the Euler's totient theorem (Euler, 1911–1944), implies that for every integer x co-prime with n, holds that

$$x^{(p-1)(q-1)} \bmod pq = 1, \tag{A.6}$$

then

$$z^3 \equiv d^{3g} \equiv d^{1+2(p-1)(q-1)} \equiv d[d^{\varphi(n)}]^2 \equiv d \times 1^2 \equiv d(\bmod n). \tag{A.7}$$

Thus, z is a cubic root of d (A.3), i.e., the Eq. (A.1) implies that

$$x = \sqrt[3]{y^2 - b^2} = \sqrt[3]{d} = d^g (\text{mod } n), \ (A.2)\text{-}(A.3).$$

Therefore, the elliptic curve $V(n)$ has n points, if n is a semi-prime $\{n = pq\}$ and $p \equiv q(\text{mod} 3) = 2$, i.e., this cubic root exists for every y on the interval $[0, n-1]$.   quod erat demonstrandum (QED).   □

Chapter 20

Integer Factorization *via* Constrained Discrete Logarithm Problem

Since the end of 1970s, various public-key cryptographic algorithms/ protocols have been developed. The cryptanalysis of several of these protocols require integer factorization of large semi-primes. The chapter provides a framework for design and analysis of algorithms for integer factorization: it demonstrates how to find integer factors of semi-prime n using an algorithm for constrained discrete logarithm problem (DLP). It is demonstrated that the time complexity of the proposed algorithm that solves this problem is of order $\Theta(\sqrt{n/\log n})$. Details of the algorithm are illustrated in several numerical examples.

1. Introduction

Attempts to find efficient algorithms for integer factorization of a semi-prime $n = pq$ have a long history. Pierre Fermat (McKee, 1999), Leonhard Euler (McKee, 1996) and other great mathematicians of the past suggested various algorithms. However, their algorithms cannot efficiently factor semi-primes with hundreds of decimal digits. During the last 25 years, various factorization algorithms were discovered or improved (Atkin and Bernstein, 2004; Bach, 1984; Lenstra, 2000; Lenstra Jr., 1987; Pollard, 1975; Pomerance *et al.* 1988; Seysen, 1987; Verkhovsky, 2008). Several of these algorithms have a sub-exponential complexity (Lenstra and Lenstra, 1993; McKee, 1996; Pollard, 1993). Yet, the RSA factoring challenge (Frenke, 2004) showed that it required the coordinated efforts of many researchers, using several thousand computers for many months, to factor a single semi-prime.

Factorization:

If the product n of two distinct primes p and q is known: $n = pq$, 　(1.1)

but the factors p and q are *unknown*, the goal of the integer factorization problem (IFP) is to determine these primes p and q. For the sake of simplicity and without loss of generality, throughout this paper it is assumed that $p < q$.

2. Reduction of IFP to DLP

Modular multiplicative inverse: If g and n are co-prime, then there exists an integer $0 < b < n$ such that

$$bg \bmod n = 1, \tag{2.1}$$

b is called a multiplicative inverse of g modulo n, (Gauss, 1986; Knuth, 1997).

DLP: Suppose that g, h and n are known integers that satisfy the equation

$$g^x = h(\bmod n), \tag{2.2}$$

where x is an unknown integer. If such x exists, then the DL algorithm is a method to find x.

Framework of IFP and algorithm: Solve the DLP

$$g^v = b(\bmod n), \tag{2.3}$$

where b satisfies (2.1),

solve the quadratic equation:

$$z^2 - (n - v)z + n = 0, \tag{2.4}$$

then

$$p := z_1, \quad q := z_2. \tag{2.5}$$

Although the algorithm (2.3)–(2.5) appears straightforward, it can be computationally complex. This chapter demonstrates how its computational complexity can be reduced.

3. Algorithm Validation

Lemma 3.1. If b is a multiplicative inverse of g modulo $n = pq$, and g is co-prime with n, then

$$b = g^{n-p-q} (\text{mod } pq). \tag{3.1}$$

Proof. follows from Euler's identity

$$g^{(p-1)(q-1)} \text{ mod } n = 1, \tag{3.2}$$

which implies that

$$bg = g^{n-p-q} g (\text{mod } pq) = 1, \tag{3.3}$$

therefore,

$$v = n - p - q \ (2.3). \tag{3.4}$$

Thus, Eq. (2.4) can be rewritten as

$$z^2 - (p+q)z + pq = 0. \tag{3.5}$$

Finally, Viète's theorem (Viète, 1579) implies the validity of (2.5). Moreover, (3.3) implies that the solution of Eq. (2.3) exists for every n and every g co-prime with n. quod erat demonstrandum (QED). □

4. Modular Multiplicative Inverse (MMI)

The MMI algorithm described below is proposed by the author of this book and analyzed in Verkhovsky (1999). It consists of two stages: *Down-stage* and *Up-stage*.

Step 4.1. $\qquad\qquad count := 0, \quad T := n, \quad B := b, \tag{4.1}$

Step 4.2. {*Down-stage*}: $count := count + 1$,

$$H := T \text{ mod } B, \quad F := (T - H)/B \tag{4.2}$$

store all values of F in a *stack*,

Step 4.3. If $H = 0$, then the MMI inverse does not exist,

{as a result, $F = \gcd(n, b)$},

while $H > 1$, reassign $\qquad T := B, \quad B := H, \tag{4.3}$

repeat **Step 4.2.**, $kount := count$, $\tag{4.4}$

Initialize $\qquad\qquad T := 0, \quad B := 1, \tag{4.5}$

Step 4.4. {*Up-stage*}: $count := count - 1$,

pop F off the *stack*, $\qquad\qquad H := BF + T$, $\qquad\qquad$ (4.6)

Step 4.5. while $count > 1$, re-assign $T := B$, $\quad B := H$, $\qquad$ (4.7)

repeat **Step 4.4.**, if $count = 0$ and *kount* is *odd*, then $MMI := H$,

if $count = 0$ and *kount* is *even*, then $\qquad MMI := n - H$. $\qquad$ (4.8)

For further details, see chapters 1 and 23.

5. Numeric Illustration

Let $n = 97965643$. Select an integer $g = 22$.

The multiplicative inverse of g modulo n equals $\quad b = 40076854$.

Applying an algorithm (Adleman and DeMarrais, 1993; Enge and Gaudry, 2000; LaMacchia and Odlyzko, 1991; Schirokauer, 2000) to solve the DLP

$$22^v \bmod 97965643 = 40076854,$$

we find that

$$v = 97945847 \quad \text{and} \quad R = n - v = 19796.$$

Solving the quadratic equation

$$z^2 - Rz + n = z^2 - 19796z + 97965643 = 0,$$

we determine $z_{1,2} = 9898 \pm 69$. Therefore,

$$p := z_1 = 9829, \quad q := z_2 = 9967.$$

6. Multiplicity of DLP Solutions

If n is a prime and g is a primitive root (Lenstra and Lenstra, 1993), then the DLP (2.2) has a unique solution and there is a unique multiplicative inverse (2.1).

However, if n is a semi-prime, $n = pq$, and

$$L := (p-1)(q-1)/\gcd(p-1, q-1), \qquad (6.1)$$

then for every g relatively prime with n, the following identity holds:

$$g^L \bmod pq = 1. \qquad (6.2)$$

Therefore, there exists more then one solution to Eq. (2.3).

Indeed, if

$$b = g^{L-1} \bmod pq, \tag{6.3}$$

then for every integer $t = 1, 2, \ldots, \gcd(p-1, q-1)$ also holds

$$b = g^{tL-1} \bmod pq. \tag{6.4}$$

Example 6.1. Let $n = 91 = 7 \times 13$ and $g = 5$, then $L = 12$ (20) and $5^{12} = 1 (\bmod 91)$. Since $b := 5^{11} = 73 (\bmod 91)$, then $b = 5^{11} = 5^{23} = 5^{35} = 5^{47} = 5^{59} = 5^{71} = 5^{83} (\bmod 91)$. $\tag{6.5}$

7. Upper and Lower Bounds

Theorem 7.1. Let $n = pq$,

$$T := (\sqrt{n} - 1)^2, \tag{7.1}$$

then

$$\varphi(n) < T, \tag{7.2}$$

where $\varphi(n)$ is called *Euler's totient function* and

$$\varphi(pq) := (p-1)(q-1). \tag{7.3}$$

Proof. Since

$$(p+q)/2 \geq \sqrt{pq} \text{ and because } p \neq q,$$

hence

$$T = n + 1 - 2\sqrt{n} = pq + 1 - 2\sqrt{pq} > pq + 1 - (p+q) = \varphi(pq), \quad \text{QED.} \tag{7.4}$$

$\square$

Theorem 7.2. Let

$$2 \leq m \leq \min(p, q), \tag{7.5}$$

and

$$D := (\sqrt{n/m} - \sqrt{m})^2 + 1, \tag{7.6}$$

then

$$T - D < \varphi(n) < T. \tag{7.7}$$

Proof. Consider

$$f(x, n) := (x - 1)(n/x - 1), \quad \text{then } f'(x, n) = n/x^2 - 1. \tag{7.8}$$

If $1 \leq x < \sqrt{n}$, then $f'(x, n) > 0$, i.e., $f(x, n)$ is a monotone increasing function of x. Let

$$E := n - n/m - m, \tag{7.9}$$

then from (7.5), (7.8) and (7.9)

$$E = (m - 1)(n/m - 1) - 1 \leq \varphi(n) - 1. \tag{7.10}$$

Therefore, (7.5) and (7.8) imply that

$$E + 1 = f(m, n) < f(p, n) \equiv \varphi(n). \tag{7.11}$$

Thus,

$$T - E = n - 2\sqrt{n} + 1 - (n - m - n/m)$$
$$= n/m - 2\sqrt{n} + m + 1 = (\sqrt{n/m} - \sqrt{m})^2 + 1 = D, \tag{7.12}$$

i.e., (7.11) and (7.12) imply the left inequality in (7.7):

$$T - D < E + 1 < \varphi(n). \qquad \square$$

Remark 7.3. It is essential to find the *largest* integer v that satisfies (2.3) on the interval $[E, T]$.

Example 7.4. Let $n = 868575847$, select $g = 2$, then its multiplicative inverse $b = 434287924$.

There are sixteen solutions that satisfy the equation $g^v \bmod n = 434287924$. These solutions are terms of an arithmetic progression with step 54280435. Here are three terms: $v = 54280434, 108560869, \dots, \mathbf{868486959}$ (the boldface integer is the largest term that is smaller than n).

The search for v must be strictly on the interval $[E, T]$, where $T = 868516903$.

On the other hand, if

$$m = \lfloor \sqrt[3]{n} \rfloor = 954, \quad \text{then from (7.9)}, E = 867664550.$$

8. Integer Factorization Algorithm (IFA)

Step 8.1. Verify that n is not divisible by primes smaller than or equal to m, otherwise n is factorized after at most $m/\log m$ trials,

Step 8.2. Compute the lower bound E (7.9) and upper bound T on $\varphi(n)$:
$T = \lceil (\sqrt{n} - 1)^2 \rceil$,

Step 8.3. Select an integer $2 \leq g < m$, {all integers smaller than m are co-prime with n},

Step 8.4. Using the algorithm (4.1)–(4.8), find the multiplicative inverse b of g,

$$\text{if } g = 2, \quad \text{then } b = (n + 1)/2,$$

Step 8.5. Solve the DLP: $g^v = b(\text{mod } n)$, (2.3), where $v \in [E, T]$.

Remark 8.1. The DLP problem (2.3) may be solved using any known algorithm for the DLP, (Adleman and DeMarrais, 1993; Enge and Gaudry, 2000; LaMacchia and Odlyzko, 1991; Schirokauer, 2000; Silverman, 2000; Verkhovsky, 2008). The overall complexity of the algorithm (2.3)–(2.5) depends on two factors: the complexity of the algorithm that is used to solve the DLP (2.3) and the complexity of the algorithm to estimate the value of m in (7.5).

Step 8.6. Compute v and $R := n - v$,

Step 8.7. Solve the equation $z^2 - Rz + n = 0$ (2.4).

9. Solution of DLP *via* Baby-Step Giant-Step (BSGS) Algorithm

Consider

$$v := T - Sy - w, \tag{9.1}$$

where

$$S := \lceil \sqrt{D} \rceil = \lceil \sqrt{T - E} \rceil, \quad 1 \leq w \leq S, \ 0 \leq y \leq S - 1. \tag{9.2}$$

Here, w and y are unknown integers.

Remark 9.1. If the BSGS algorithm is used (LaMacchia and Odlyzko, 1991; Verkhovsky, 2008), then for every w, the values $g^{w-1} \text{mod } n$ are pre-computed {these are the *baby* steps} and stored and $g^T (b^S)^y \text{mod } n$ are computed {these are the *giant* steps}.
Solve the problem

$$g^T (b^S)^y = g^{w-1}(\text{mod } n).$$

10. Complexity of IFA

If $m = \sqrt[3]{n}$ and both variables y and w (7.13) are changing on the interval $[1, S]$, then

$$S := \lceil \sqrt{D} \rceil = \sqrt{(\sqrt[3]{n} - \sqrt[6]{n})^2 + 1} = \Theta(\sqrt[3]{n}). \tag{10.1}$$

In addition, $O\ (m/\log m)$ trial divisions are used in Step 8.1. Therefore, the algorithm described in Steps 8.1.–8.8. has time-space complexity

$$\Theta(\sqrt[3]{n}/\log n) + \Theta(\sqrt[3]{n}) = \Theta(\sqrt[3]{n}). \tag{10.2}$$

11. Balanced IFA

Proposition 11.1.

$$\text{If } m := \sqrt[3]{n\log^2 n}, \quad \text{then } S(n) = \Theta(\sqrt[3]{n/\log n}). \tag{11.1}$$

Proof. Let us directly verify divisibility of n by every prime smaller than

$$m := \sqrt[3]{n}\log^u n, \tag{11.2}$$

where we have a choice in selection of exponent u since m itself in (11.2) is a control parameter.

There are

$$\pi(m) := (m/\log m)[1 + o(m)] \tag{11.3}$$

primes smaller than m, where for every large m, $m/\log m < \pi(m) < 1.04423 \times m/\log m$, (Lagaris *et al.* 1985). The complexity of such verification (11.2) is of order

$$V(n) = \Theta[(\sqrt[3]{n}\log^u n)/(\log\sqrt[3]{n} + \log\log^u n)] \quad (11.3).$$

Therefore,

$$\text{if } \sqrt[3]{n} \gg \log^u n, \quad \text{then } V(n) = \Theta(3 \times \sqrt[3]{n}\log^{u-1} n). \tag{11.4}$$

On the other hand, if it is verified that n has no factors smaller than m, then (7.6) implies that

$$D = (\sqrt{n/m} - \sqrt{m})^2 + 1.$$

Thus

$$S(n) \approx \sqrt{n/m} - \sqrt{m} = \sqrt{n/(\sqrt[3]{n}\log^u n)} - \sqrt{\sqrt[3]{n}\log^u n}$$

$$= (\sqrt[3]{n}\log^{-u/2} n)[1 - o(n)]. \tag{11.5}$$

Let us select a value of exponent u, for which the trials in (11.2) have the same complexity as the algorithm solving the DLP (Adleman and DeMarrais, 1993; LaMacchia and Odlyzko, 1991; Schirokauer, 2000; Silverman, 2000).

In other words, let

$$\Theta(\sqrt[3]{n}\log^{-u/2} n) = \Theta(3 \times \sqrt[3]{n}\log^{u-1} n).$$

Hence, $u = 2/3$ for large n, therefore, the time complexity of the search algorithm is

$$S(n) = \Theta(\sqrt[3]{n/\log n}). \tag{11.6}$$

$\square$

12. Optimal Search Parameters

Let us analyze all control parameters on every stage of the IFA.

There are two stages: probing stage verifying whether the first m primes divide n and the stage where we solving the DLP.

Probing stage:

1. Let us verify that none of the first m primes divides n,
2. There are about $d := \Theta(m/\log m)$ such primes {*divisors* to test},
3. Let us select

$$m = n^\lambda \log^\mu n, \tag{12.1}$$

where the exponents λ and μ are selected below, then

$$m/\log m = (n^\lambda \log^\mu n)/(\lambda \log n + \mu \log \log n).$$

If $\lambda \log n \gg \mu \log \log n$, then

$$d = \Theta(m/\log m) = \Theta(n^\lambda \log^{\mu-1} n). \tag{12.2}$$

4. Further improvement of the IFA might arise from observing that $m/\log m$ division trials of n is a much simpler task than multiplying an equal number of e-digit long integers, where $e := \lceil \log n \rceil$. Let the overall complexity of the above mentioned verification be equal to

$$V(d,n) := O(d^\alpha / \log^\beta d), \tag{12.3}$$

then

$$V(d,n) = O\{[n^\lambda \log^{\mu-1} n]^\alpha / [\log(n^\lambda \log^{\mu-1} n)]^\beta\}.$$

Let's denote

$$V(n) := O(n^{\alpha\lambda}\log^{\alpha\mu-\alpha-\beta} n). \tag{12.4}$$

12.1. *Solution of constrained DLP*

Let the complexity of the *DLP* (n) to solve DLP (2.3) on the set of D integers be equal

$$DLP(n) := O(D^\gamma \log^\delta D), \qquad (12.5)$$

then

$$D = O\left[\left(\sqrt{n/m} - \sqrt{m}\right)^2\right]$$

$$= O\left(\sqrt{n/(n^\lambda \log^\mu n)} - \sqrt{n^\lambda \log^\mu n}\right)^2 = O(n^{1-\lambda} \log^{-\mu} n), \quad (12.6)$$

and

$$DLP(n) = O[(n^{(1-\lambda)\gamma} \log^{-\mu\gamma} n) \log^\delta(n^{1-\lambda} \log^{-\mu} n)]$$

$$= O[(n^{(1-\lambda)\gamma} \log^{-\mu\gamma} n) \log^\delta n]. \qquad (12.7)$$

Therefore,

$$DLP(n) = O(n^{\gamma(1-\lambda)} \log^{\delta-\gamma\mu} n). \qquad (12.8)$$

12.2. *Optimizing the IFA*

In order to optimize the IFA algorithm let us select the parameters λ and μ in m, for which the probing stage and the corresponding DLP have the same complexities, i.e., for which holds

$$O[DLP(n)] = O[V(n)]. \qquad (12.9)$$

Therefore, λ and μ must satisfy the following equations for every large $n = pq$:

$$\gamma(1 - \lambda) = \alpha\lambda, \quad \delta - \gamma\mu = \alpha\mu - \alpha - \beta. \qquad (12.10)$$

As a result,

$$\lambda = \gamma/(\alpha + \gamma), \quad \mu = (\alpha + \beta + \delta)/(\alpha/\gamma).$$

Therefore, the overall complexity $T(n)$ of the IF algorithm equals

$$T(n) = O(n^\sigma \log^\omega n) = O(n^{\gamma(1-\lambda)} \log^{\alpha\mu-\alpha-\beta} n), \qquad (12.11)$$

provided that (12.10) hold, then

$$\sigma = \gamma(1 - \lambda) = \alpha\lambda, \quad \omega = \delta - \gamma\mu = \alpha\mu - \alpha - \beta. \qquad (12.12)$$

The goal in the algorithm design is to minimize σ (12.12) by appropriate selection of optimal values of control variables λ and μ, provided that all variables satisfy constraints (12.10), and α, β, γ and δ satisfy lower bounds constraints: $\alpha_* \le a \le 1$, $\beta_* \le \beta \le 1$, $\gamma_* \le \gamma \le 1/2$, $\delta_* \le \delta \le 1$. In addition, it is appropriate to impose an upper bound constraint on the variable $\omega \le \omega^*$. If some of the bounds are unknown, then the minimal value of σ is expressible in a parametric form.

13. Corollaries and Hypothesis

Corollary 13.1. If $\alpha = \delta = 1$, $\beta > 0$, $\gamma = 1/2$, then

$$\lambda = 1/3 \quad \text{and} \quad T(n) = O\left(\sqrt[3]{n \log^{1-\beta} n}\right). \tag{13.1}$$

Corollary 13.2. If $m := \sqrt[3]{n \log^2 n}$, then (11.6) implies

$$T(n) = S(n) = O\left(\sqrt[3]{n/\log n}\right). \tag{13.2}$$

Hypothesis 13.3. If $\alpha = 1$, $\beta > 0$, and the algorithm for the CDLP has complexity $O(\sqrt[3]{n \log^2 n})$, i.e., if $\gamma = 1/3$, $\delta = 2/3$, then the optimal $\lambda = 1/4$, $\mu = (5 + 3\beta)/4$. Hence,

$$m := \sqrt[4]{n \log^{5+3\beta} n}. \tag{13.3}$$

Therefore, $\sigma = 1/4$, $\omega = (1 - \beta)/4$. As a result,

$$T(n) = O\left(\sqrt[4]{n \log^{1-\beta} n}\right). \tag{13.4}$$

14. Refinements

14.1. *IFA on expanded lattices*

Prior to the following discussion, we need to introduce a special rounding off procedure.

Definition 14.1.

$$\lceil c \rceil_{(r,s)} := \{\min \text{ integer } t \ge c : t \bmod s = r\}. \tag{14.1}$$

For instance,

$$\lceil \sqrt{567} \rceil_{(3,5)} = 28, \quad \text{since } 28 \bmod 5 = 3,$$

and

$$\lceil \sqrt{567} \rceil_{(4,9)} = 31, \quad \text{since } 31 \bmod 9 = 4.$$

Lemma 14.2. If $b \, g \bmod n = 1$, then the largest solution v of the DLP (2.3) is congruent to 3 modulo 4.

Proof. Since both p and q are odd, then *four* divides *Euler's totient function* $\varphi(n)$. Thus

$$v \equiv \varphi(n) - 1 \equiv [(p-1)(q-1) - 1](\bmod 4) = 3. \tag{14.2}$$

As a result, only *one-fourth* of the integers on the interval $[E, T]$ must be probed. Therefore,

1. Compute

$$T := \lceil T \rceil_{(3,4)}, \tag{14.3}$$

2. Compute

$$S := \left\lceil \sqrt{Dc} \right\rceil_{(0,4)}, \tag{14.4}$$

3. y is changing on interval $[0, S-1]$ with step 1, and w is changing on interval $[4, S-4]$ with step 4.

For a further refinement of the IFA algorithm, consider the following lemmas. $\square$

Lemma 14.3. If

$$n \bmod 4 = 3, \tag{14.5}$$

then the largest solution v of the DLP (2.3) is congruent to 7 modulo 8.

Proof. follows from the observation that

$$8|\varphi(n). \tag{14.6}$$

Therefore,

$$v = \varphi(n) - 1 = [(p-1)(q-1) - 1](\bmod 8) = 7. \tag{14.7}$$

As a result, only *one-eighth* of all integers on the interval $[E, T]$ must be probed. $\square$

Lemma 14.4. If

$$n \bmod 3 = 2, \tag{14.8}$$

then the largest solution v of the DLP (2.3) is congruent to 11 modulo 12.

Proof. First of all, if p and q are odd, then $4|\varphi(n)$.

Furthermore, (14.8) implies that $(p+q)\bmod 3 = 0$, i.e.,

$$n - p - q = n(\bmod 3) = 2.$$

Hence, $3|\varphi(n)$ and Lemma 4 implies that

$$12|\varphi(n). \tag{14.9}$$

Table 14.1   Minimal divisors c.

	$n \bmod 3 = 1$	$N \bmod 3 = 2$
$n \bmod 4 = 1$	4	12
$n \bmod 4 = 3$	8	24

Therefore,

$$v \equiv \varphi(n) - 1 \equiv [(p-1)(q-1) - 1]11 (\bmod 12). \tag{14.10}$$

As a result, only *one-twelfth* of all integers on the interval $[E, T]$ must be probed. □

Lemma 14.5. If $n \bmod 3 = 2$ and $n \bmod 4 = 3$, then $24|\varphi(n)$. As a result, the IFA can be further accelerated, since only $1/24$th of all integers on the interval $[E, T]$ must be probed.

Let's consider the following

Remark 14.6. In Table 14.1., only the smallest divisors of $\varphi(n)$ are provided. Indeed, if $n \bmod = 1$ and $n \bmod 4 = 1$, then in one of several options $p \bmod 12 = 1$ and $q \bmod 12 = 1$ satisfy these conditions. As a result, $144|\varphi(n)$. However, this option occurs only with probability $1/4$, if p and q are selected randomly. Therefore,

1. Compute

$$T := \lceil T \rceil_{(c-1,c)}, \tag{14.11}$$

2. Compute

$$S := \lceil \sqrt{Dc} \rceil_{(0,c)}, \tag{14.12}$$

3. y is changing on interval $[0, S-1]$ with step 1 and w is changing on interval $[c, S-c]$ with step c.

Example 14.7.
Consider $n = 868575847$. Since $n \bmod 3 = 1$ and $n \bmod 4 = 3$, then $c = 8$. Therefore,

$$T = \lceil (\sqrt{n} - 1)^2 \rceil_{(7,8)} = \lceil (\sqrt{868575847} - 1)^2 \rceil_{(7,8)}$$

$$= \lceil 868516904.778 \rceil_{(7,8)} = 868516911.$$

Now consider

$$m = \sqrt[3]{n} = \lceil \sqrt[3]{868575847} \rceil = 954.$$

Then $D := (\sqrt{n/m} - \sqrt{m})^2 + 1 = (n/m)(1 - m/\sqrt{n})^2 + 1 \approx \lceil n/m \rceil + 1 = 910457$, (7.6). As a result, $S := \lceil \sqrt{Dc} \rceil_{(0.8)} = 2696$. Therefore, Sy is changing from 0 to 910457 with step 2696, {hence, y is changing from 0 to 337 with the step 1}, and w is changing from 8 to 2688 with step 8, {i.e., assuming 336 values}.

14.2. *Adjustment of search parameter S*

Let, for instance, $n = 996412403$. Since $n \bmod 3 = 2$ and $n \bmod 4 = 3$, then $c = 24$.

In general, because the search in the DLP stage is on the expanded lattice, then $D := D/c$. Therefore, from (12.8) the complexity of *DLP* (n) must be adjusted to

$$DLP(n) = O[(n^{\gamma(1-\lambda)} \log^{\delta-\gamma\mu} n)/\sqrt{c}]. \tag{14.13}$$

However, for large values of the semi-prime n this adjustment does not affect the asymptotic results that are provided above.

15. Harmonic Average Complexity

If p and q are selected randomly, then the properties, listed below in Table 15.1., hold. The table shows all cases where $n \bmod 12 = k$, where $k = 1, 5, 7, 11$, although for every k the corresponding values of $p \bmod 12$ and $q \bmod 12$ are unknown, yet for every k we know all possible combinations of $p \bmod 12$ and $q \bmod 12$.

Example 15.1. If $n \bmod 12 = 1$, then $\{p \bmod 12, q \bmod 12\}$ is equal either $\{1, 1\}$ or $\{5, 5\}$, or $\{7, 7\}$, or $\{11, 11\}$. Hence, in average the number of required steps is equal

$$S/w = (S/144 + S/36 + S/16 + S/4)/4.$$

Table 15.1 $n \bmod 12 = k$ and divisibility of *Euler's function.*

	$p \bmod 12 = 1$	$p \bmod 12 = 7$	$p \bmod 12 = 5$	$p \bmod 12 = 11$
$q \bmod 12 = 1$	$n \bmod 12 = 1$: $144|\varphi(n)$	$n \bmod 12 = 7$: $72|\varphi(n)$	$n \bmod 12 = 5$: $48|\varphi(n)$	$n \bmod 12 = 11$: $24|\varphi(n)$
$q \bmod 12 = 7$	$n \bmod 12 = 7$: $72|\varphi(n)$	$n \bmod 12 = 1$: $36|\varphi(n)$	$n \bmod 12 = 11$: $24|\varphi(n)$	$n \bmod 12 = 5$: $12|\varphi(n)$
$q \bmod 12 = 5$	$n \bmod 12 = 5$: $48|\varphi(n)$	$n \bmod 12 = 11$: $24|\varphi(n)$	$n \bmod 12 = 1$: $16|\varphi(n)$	$n \bmod 12 = 7$: $8|\varphi(n)$
$q \bmod 12 = 11$	$n \bmod 12 = 11$: $24|\varphi(n)$	$n \bmod 12 = 5$: $12|\varphi(n)$	$n \bmod 12 = 7$: $8|\varphi(n)$	$n \bmod 12 = 1$: $4|\varphi(n)$

Therefore,

$$w = 4/(1/144 + 1/36 + 1/16 + 1/4) = 576/49 = 11.76,$$

i.e., w is a *harmonic average* of 144, 36, 16 and 4.

Remark 15.2. As a result, in all cases listed above, the IFA can be accelerated on average. Let's describe the strategy that implements the acceleration in case considered in Example 4. First we search for a solution of the DLP with step 144, if a solution does not exist, we search with step 36, then with step 16 and finally with step 4.

Example 15.3. If $n \bmod 12 = 7$, then $\{p \bmod 12, q \bmod 12\}$ = either $\{1, 7\}$ or $\{7, 1\}$, or $\{5, 11\}$, or $\{11, 5\}$. Hence, in average the number of required steps is equal to $S/w = (S/72 + S/72 + S/8 + S/8)/4$. Therefore, $w = 4/(1/36 + 1/4) = 144/10 = 14.4$, i.e., w is the harmonic average of 72, 72, 8 and 8.

Example 15.4. If $n \bmod 12 = 5$, then $\{p \bmod 12, q \bmod 12\}$ = either $\{1, 5\}$ or $\{5, 1\}$, or $\{7, 11\}$, or $\{11, 7\}$. Hence, in average the number of required steps is equal to

$$S/w = (S/48 + S/48 + S/12 + S/12)/4.$$

Therefore, $w = 4/(1/24 + 1/6) = 96/5 = 19.2$, i.e., w is the harmonic average of 48, 48, 12 and 12.

Example 15.5. If $n \bmod 12 = 11$, then $\{p \bmod 12, q \bmod 12\}$ = either $\{1, 11\}$ or $\{11, 1\}$, or $\{7, 5\}$, or $\{5, 7\}$. Hence, the number of required steps is equal to $S/w = (S/24 + S/24 + S/24 + S/24)/4$. Therefore, $w = 4/(1/6) = 24$.

Example 15.6.

$$n = 19729, \quad \sqrt[3]{n} = 27, \quad T := 19449, \quad D = 475(7.6), \quad n \bmod 12 = 1.$$

Let $c = 4$, then

$$S := \lceil \sqrt{4D} \rceil = 44, \quad T \bmod 12 = 9, \quad T := T - T \bmod 12 + 11 = 19451,$$

$$v := T - Sy - w = 19451 - 44y - w, \quad y = 0, \quad w = 12, \quad v = 19439,$$

$$R = n - v = 19729 - v = 290, \quad z = 145 \pm 36, \quad z_1 = 109, \quad z_2 = 181.$$

16. Concluding Remarks

It is essential to stress that the algorithm for IFP is based on the assumption that we know a computationally efficient algorithm A for solution of the DLP. This assumption implies that the complexity of the IFP cannot be higher than the complexity of the DLP. It is also important to emphasize that we are comparing the information-based complexities of the problems, not the algorithms used to solve them. A specific algorithm is a method that after a finite number of well-defined and executable steps provably delivers a solution to a class of problems. Unless it is an optimal algorithm (Traub and Wozniakowski, 1980; Veroy, 1986; 1988; 1989), it is plausible that its computational complexity can be later improved.

In contrast, the information-based complexity of a specific problem is an intrinsic characteristic of the problem itself. Presently, there are no strict proofs demonstrating that DLP and IFP *problems are intrinsically* complex. We can only plausibly assume that they are not computationally 'simple' problems. The proposed general-purpose IFA (GPIFA) implies that the IFP has either the same complexity as the DLP or is less complex than the DLP. Furthermore, if the search is balanced, and the constrained DLP algorithm has complexity $\mathrm{O}(\sqrt[3]{n \log^2 n})$, then the IFA has time-space complexity

$$T(n) = \mathrm{O}\left(\sqrt[4]{n \log^{1-\beta} n}\right). \tag{16.1}$$

Preliminary results of this paper are published in Verkhovsky (2009a).

I express my appreciation to A. J. Menezes for advice, X. Ma and S. Sadik for assistance in computer experiments, and P. Fay for corrections that improved the style of this chapter.

Appendix

A.1. *Algorithm in nutshell*

Input: semi-prime n,

Output: its factors p and q,

1. Compute $m < \min(p, q)$,
2. Solve the *decision problem*: check whether primes smaller than m divide n,
3. Compute $n \bmod 12$, and find c,
4. Compute $T := (\sqrt{n} - 1)^2$, round off T appropriately {see (14.1) and (14.11)},

5. Compute D (7.6) and $S := \sqrt{D/c}$,
6. Round off S up to the nearest integer divisible by c,
7. Select an integer $g < m$, if $g = 2$, then the inverse $b := (n+1)/2$,
8. Use the most efficient DLP algorithm to find maximal solution x of constrained DLP:

$$g^x \bmod n = b, \quad \text{where } x \text{ is on the interval } [T - D, T],$$

9. Let $x = v$ be the solution, compute the resolvent A $R := n - v$,
11. Solve the equation:

$$z^2 - Rz + n = 0, \quad \text{then } p := z_1, \quad q := z_2.$$

Remark A.1. A solution of the Constrained DLP does not exist if $p < Q$, but we verified that at the very beginning of the algorithm.

Example A.2. Let

$$n = 3649, \quad T = 3529, \quad \text{compute } n \bmod 12 = 1, \quad c = 4,$$

then

$$T := T - T \bmod c + c - 1 = 3531, \quad m = 16, \quad D = 64, \quad S = 8,$$

$$g := 2, \quad b = (n+1)/2 = 1825,$$

$$P := 2^{T+1} = 2^{3532} \bmod 3649, \quad \text{and} \quad L := b^S = 1825^8 \bmod 3649,$$

assign

$$w := 0, \quad M(0) := 1,$$

while $w < S$, compute

$$M(w+2) := 4M(w) \bmod n, \quad \{\text{two binary shifts}\}, \quad \textbf{sort} \text{ and store}$$
$$\{M(w), w\}, \quad \text{and assign } y := 0, \quad H(0) := P,$$

while $\{w < S \textbf{ and } H(y) \neq M(w)\}$, compute

$$H(y+1) := LH(y) \bmod n,$$

since $H(1) = M(2)$, then $y = 1$, $w = 4$,

$$v = 3531 - 8 \times 1 - 4 = 3519, \quad R = 3649 - 3519 = 130, \quad \text{and}$$

$$z^2 - 130z + 3649 = 0.$$

Therefore $p = 41$, $q = 89$.

Table A.1   IFPs and their solutions, where $g = 2$.

n	**77**	**253**	**4033**	**1003939**	**868575847**
T	61	223	3907	1001837	868516904
E_{-odd}	47	207	3763	993811	867664551
D	14	16	144	8025	852353
S_{-even}	**4**	**4**	**12**	**90**	**924**
b	39	127	2017	501970	434287924
y	0	3	10	73	890
w_{-even}	2	0	4	74	48
v	59	219	3887	1000455	868486959
R	18	34	146	3484	88888
p	**7**	**11**	**37**	**317**	**11177**
q	**11**	**23**	**109**	**3167**	**77711**

Table A.2   IFPs and their solutions, where $g = 2, S := \sqrt{D/2}, v := T - Sy - w$.

n	**39**	**4033**	**1003939**	**3824087**	**868575847**
$T\text{-}odd$	3529	3907	1001837		868516905
E	3397	3763	993811		867664551
D	66	72	4013		852353
$S\text{-}even$	**8**	**8**	**64**		**652**
b	1825	2017	501970		434287924
y	1	2	21		45
$w\text{-}even$	2	4	38		606
v	3519	3887	1000455		868486959
R	130	146	3484		88888
p	**41**	**37**	**317**		**11177**
q	**89**	**109**	**3167**		**77711**

Exercise A.3. Find parameters of the search in Tables A.1. and A.2. for the following semi-primes $n = 3824087, 55631203, 95930287$ and 97965643.

Chapter 21

Decomposability of Discrete Logarithm Problems

1. Introduction and Problem Statement

A framework that reduces the computational complexity of the discrete logarithm problem (DLP) is provided in this chapter. Here, we consider how to decompose the initial DLP onto several DLPs of smaller dimensions. Decomposability of the DLP is an indicator of potential vulnerability of encrypted messages transmitted via open channels of the Internet or within corporate networks. Several numerical examples illustrate the framework and show its computational efficiency.

Crypto-immunity of numerous public key cryptographic protocols is based on the computational hardness of the DLP (Diffie-Hellman, 1976; ElGamal, 1985). A DLP finds an integer x satisfying the equation

$$g^x \bmod p = h, \qquad (1.1)$$

where

$$2 \leq g \leq p - 1, \quad 1 \leq h \leq p - 1, \qquad (1.2)$$

and p is a large prime. In (1.1) g, p and h are inputs, and the unknown integer x must be selected on interval $[1, p - 1]$. If g is a generator {see Chapter 2 in this book}, then (1.1) has a solution for every h, otherwise the existence of a solution is not guaranteed.

For instance, if $p = 7$ and $g = 2$, then the DLP $2^x \bmod 7 = 5$ does not have a solution.

Various algorithms for the solution of the DLP were proposed and their computational complexities were analyzed for the last 40 years (Adleman and DeMarrais, 1993; Bach, 1984; Crandall and Pomerance, 2001; Enge and

Gaudry, 2000; LaMacchia and Odlyzko, 1991; Lenstra and Lenstra, 1993; Müller *et al.*, 1999; Schirokauer, 2000; Shanks, 1971; Silverman, 2000; Terr, 2000; Verkhovsky, 2008c; Zuccherato, 1998).

This chapter provides a framework for the algorithm that reduces the computational complexity of the DLP. It describes step-by-step how to decompose the initial DLP into several DLPs of smaller dimensions. Numerous examples illustrate the decomposition algorithm and show its computational efficiency.

Let us denote

$$g_1 := g; \quad h_1 := h; \quad x_1 := x; \quad q_1 := p - 1 \quad \text{and} \quad p - 1 = 2r_1 r_2. \qquad (1.3)$$

Here, it is assumed that integer factors r_1 and r_2 in $(3|1.3)$ are known or can be determined using algorithms for integer factorization (Crandall-Pomerance, 2001; Pollard, 1975; Pomerance *et al.*, 1988).

Proposition 1.1. Let

$$R_1 := (p - 1)/q, \qquad (1.4)$$

if $q \mid (p - 1)$, then R_1 is an integer (1.4).

Let define

$$g_2 := g_1^{R_1} \bmod p, \qquad (1.5)$$

$$h_2 := h_1^{R_1} \bmod p. \qquad (1.6)$$

If an integer x_2 is a solution of equation

$$g_2^{x_2} \bmod p = h_2; \quad \text{where } x_2 \in [0, q], \qquad (1.7)$$

then q divides $x_1 - x_2$.

Proof. Let us multiply both sides of Eq. $(1|1.1)$ by $g_1^{-x_2} \bmod p$ (Verkhovsky, 1999), and find such x_2, for which

$$h_1 g_1^{-x_2} \bmod p \qquad (1.8)$$

has a root of power q. By Euler criterion (Crandall and Pomerance, 2001) such a root exists if and only if

$$(h_1 g_1^{-x_2})^{(p-1)/q} \bmod p = 1. \qquad (1.9)$$

Using notations (1.4)–(1.6), we rewrite (1.8) as

$$h_2 g_2^{-x_2} \bmod p = 1 \qquad (1.10)$$

or as Eq. (1.7). Q.E.D

Therefore, the unknown x_1 can be represented as

$$x_1 = x_2 + qx_3, \qquad (1.11)$$

where an integer x_3 must be on interval

$$x_3 \in [0, (p-1)/q] = [0, q_3]. \qquad (1.12)$$

After x_2 is determined, we need to find an integer x_3, for which holds

$$g_1^{x_2 + qx_3} \bmod p = h_1. \qquad (1.13)$$

This equation can be rewritten as

$$(g_1^q)^{x_3} = h_1 g_1^{-x_2} (\bmod p), \qquad (1.14)$$

where in contrast with the BSGS algorithm, the value of x_2 is already known.

Let

$$g_3 := g_1^{(p-1)/q_3} \bmod p, \qquad (1.15)$$

and

$$h_3 := h_1 g_1^{-x_2} \bmod p. \qquad (1.16)$$

2. Divide-and-Conquer Decomposition

Example 2.1. Let us consider how to solve

$$2^{x_1} \bmod 947 = 273, \qquad (2.1)$$

i.e., $g_1 = 2$, $p = 947$, $h_1 = 273$, and $x_1 \in [1, 946]$.

Let

$$q_1 := p - 1.$$

Since

$$q_1 = 2r_1 r_2 = 2 \times 11 \times 43,$$

select

$$q_2 = \min_{0 \leq z \leq \sqrt{p-1}} \max(z, (p-1)/z) = 43,$$

then

$$R_1 := q_1/q_2 = 22, \quad g_2 := g_1^{R_1} \bmod p = 2^{22} \bmod 947 = 41,$$

and

$$h_2 := h_1^{R_1} \bmod p = 273^{22} \bmod 947 = 283.$$

Therefore, we need to solve

$$DLP(2) : 41^{x_2} \bmod 947 = 283(7|1.7), \tag{2.2}$$

where $x_2 \in [1, 42]$.

Remark 2.2. Notice that the interval of uncertainty $[1, 42]$ for x_2 is much smaller than the corresponding interval of uncertainty $[1, 946]$ for x_1.

Equation (2.2) can be solved using any algorithm for the DLP (Adleman and DeMarrais, 1993; Enge and Gaudry, 2000; Lenstra and Lenstra, 1993; Müller *et al.*, 1999; Schirokauer, 2000; Silverman, 2000).

In this example $x_2 = 39$ and $q_2 = 43$.
Therefore,

$$x_1 = 39 + 43x_3, \quad \text{where } x_3 \in [0, (p - 1/q_2)] = [0, 22].$$

To find x_3 solve

$$DLP(3) : \ (2^{43})^{x_3} = 273 \times 2^{-39} \pmod{947},$$

which is equivalent to

$$367^{x_3} = 273 \times 111 = 946 \pmod{947}. \tag{2.3}$$

Therefore, $x_3 = 11$.

$$\text{Verification: } 367^{11} \bmod 947 = 946. \tag{2.4}$$

Finally, $x_1 = 39 + 43 \times 11 = 512$.

3. Decomposition of DLP

In order to describe the concept of decomposition, a more suitable system of notations is considered below in Table 4.1. These notations are used to describe the process of solving three DLPs A, B and C. A reader has an opportunity for exercise since in the problem B not all intermediate values are listed, yet the solutions of $DLP(2)$ and $DLP(3)$ are provided for the sake of verification.

4. Multi-Level Decomposition

Initial DLP(1): Find an integer x_1, for which holds

$$30^{x_1} \bmod 99991 = 45636, \tag{4.1}$$

where $x_1 \in [1, 99990]$.

Table 4.1   Solutions of $DLP(1)$ via decompositions $DLP(2)$ and $DLP(3)$.

	Problem A	Problem B	Problem C
$DLP(1)$: $g_1^{x_1} \bmod p = h_1$ Inputs $\{g_1; p; h_1\}$	$\{2; 947; 273\}$	$\{2; 500491; 1020305\}$	$\{30; 99991; 45636\}$
$q_1 := p - 1 = 2r_1 r_2 \ldots r_t$	$2 \times 11 \times 43$	$p - 1 = 990 \times 5051$	$2 \times 3^2 \times 11 \times 101$
$DLP(2)$: $q_2 = \min_z \max(z, q_1/z)$	$q_2 = 43$	$q_2 = 5051$	$q_2 = 330$
$R_2 := (p-1)/q_2$	$R_2 = 22$	$R_2 = 990$	$R_2 = 303$
$g_2 := g_1^{R_2} \bmod p$	$g_2 = 41$	$g_2 =$	$g_2 = 30^{303} \bmod 99991 = 151$
$h_2 := h_1^{R_2} \bmod p$	$h_2 = 283$	$h_2 =$	$h_2 = 45636^{303} \bmod 99991 = 64099$
$g_2^{x_2} \bmod p = h_2$ $x_2 \in [0, q_2]$	$x_2 \in [0, 43]$; $x_2 = 39$	$x_2 \in [0, 5051]$; $x_2 = 1947$	$x_2 \in [0, 330]$; $x_2 = 115$
$DLP(3)$: $q_1 = q_2 q_3$ $R_3 := (p-1)/q_3$	$R_3 = 43$	$R_3 =$	$R_3 = 330$
$g_3 := g_1^{R_3} \bmod p$	$g_3 = 36$	$g_3 =$	$g_3 = 30^{330} \bmod 99991 = 2593$
$h_3 := h_1 g_1^{-x_2} \bmod p$	$h_3 = 946$	$h_3 =$	$f = 30^{-1} \bmod p = 96658$ $h_3 = 96658^{x_2} \bmod p = 9381$
$g_3^{x_3} \bmod p = h_3$, $x_3 \in [0, q_3]$	$x_3 \in [0, 22]$, $x_3 = 11$	$x_3 \in [0, 990]$, $x_3 = 470$	$x_3 \in [0, 303]$, $x_3 = 47$
Solution of $DLP(1)$: $x_1 = x_2 + q_2 x_3$	$x_1 = 39 + 43 \times 11 = 512$	$x_1 = 1947 + 5051 \times 470 = 2375917$	$x_1 = 115 + 330 \times 47 = 15625$

Since $99990 = 303 \times 330$, then select $q_2 = 330$, and represent the unknown x_1 as $x_1 = x_2 + 330x_3$. Since $R_1 := (p-1)/q_2 = 303$; then $g_2 := g_1^{303} \bmod 99991 = 151$; and $h_2 := h_1^{303} \bmod 99991 = 64099$.

DLP(2): Solve

$$g_2^{x_2} \bmod 99991 = h_2, \quad \text{i.e.,} \quad 151^{x_2} \bmod 99991 = 64099; \tag{4.2}$$

where $x_2 \in [0, 330]$.

The solution is $x_2 = 115$, indeed $151^{115} \bmod 99991 = 64099$. Therefore,

$$30^{x_1} = 30^{115+330x_3} \bmod 99991 = 45636.$$

Consider equation

$$(30^{330})^{x_3} = 30^{-115} \times 45636 \pmod{99991}.$$

Let

$$g_3 := 30^{330} \bmod 99991 = 2593;$$

and

$$h_3 := 30^{-115} \times 45636 = 96658^{115} \times 45636 \pmod{99991} = 49845.$$

Therefore, we need to solve

DLP(3):

$$2593^{x_3} \bmod 99991 = 49845, \quad \text{where } x_3 \in [0, 303]. \tag{4.3}$$

It is easy to verify that $x_3 = 47$. Finally, $x_1 = x_2 + q_2 x_3 = 115 + 330 \times 47 = 15625$.

Decomposition of DLP(2): Let solve

$$g_2^{x_2} \bmod p = h_2, \tag{4.4}$$

where $x_2 \in [0, q_2] = [0, 330]$.

Remark 4.1. Notice that the interval for unknown in $DLP(2)$ is not $[1, p-1]$, but $x_2 \in [1, q_2]$, which is much smaller than $[1, p-1]$.

Instead of solving (4.4) directly by using an algorithm for DLP, we can apply the method of decomposition described previously. Consider a factor q_4 of q_2 that is close to the square root of $q_2 = 330$:

$$q_4 = \min_{0 \leq z \leq \sqrt{q_2}} \max(z, q_2/z) = \min_z \max(z, 330/z) = 30. \tag{4.5}$$

Let represent the unknown in (4.4) as

$$x_2 = x_4 + q_4 x_5, \tag{4.6}$$

where

$$x_4 \in [1, q_4] = [1, 30]; \quad \text{and} \quad x_5 \in [1, q_5 := q_2/q_4] = [1, 11]. \tag{4.7}$$

Let us now find whether h_2 has an integer root of power 30 modulo p. By Euler's criterion, such root exists if and only if

$$h_2^{(p-1)/q_4} \bmod p = 1. \tag{4.8}$$

However, if $h_2^{(p-1)/q_4} \bmod p \neq 1$, find an integer x_4, for which the following equation holds

$$(h_2 g_2^{-x_4})^{(p-1)/q_4} \bmod p = 1. \tag{4.9}$$

Let

$$g_4 := g_2^{(p-1)/q_4} \bmod p \tag{4.10}$$

and

$$h_4 := h_2^{(p-1)/q_4} \bmod p. \tag{4.11}$$

Then we need to solve equation

$$g_4^{x_4} \bmod p = h_4, \tag{4.12}$$

where $x_4 \in [0, 30]$. And again, the Eq. (4.12) itself is also a DLP with much smaller interval (4.7) for x_4, than the interval for x_2 in (4.4), and so on.

5. More about Multi-Level Decomposition

First level: Let us solve the equation $g_1^{x_1} \bmod p = h_1$, where $g = 2$, $p = 4{,}000{,}000{,}003{,}231$, and $h = 3{,}024{,}336{,}139{,}227$.

Then $p-1 = 863 \times 2310 \times 2006491$, where 863 and 2,006,491 are primes.

In this case the initial $DLP(1)$ $g_1^{x_1} \bmod p = h_1$, is decomposable onto two sub-problems: $DLP(2)$ and $DLP(3)$.

$DLP(2)$: Compute

$$g_2 := g_1^{(p-1)/q_2} = 2^{1993530} \bmod 4000000003231 = 3278213345371,$$

$$h_2 := h_1^{(p-1)/q_2} = 3024336139227^{1993530} \bmod 4000000003231$$

$$= 2084778340641.$$

Solve

$$g_2^{x_2} \bmod 4000000003231 = h_2, \quad \text{where } 0 \leq x_2 \leq q_2 = 2006491.$$

It is easy to verify that the solution $x_2 = 1853979 \leq 2006491$.

DLP(3): Compute

$$g_3 := g_1^{(p-1)/q_3} = 2^{2006491} \bmod 4000000003231 = 3767306619080;$$

$$h_3 := h_1 g_1^{-x_2} = 3024336139227 \times 2000000001616^{1853979}$$

$$\bmod 4000000003231 = 3024336139227 \times 629308445687$$

$$\bmod 4000000003231 = 2623468766941.$$

Now solve $g_3^{x_3} = h_3 (\bmod\, p)$, where

$$0 \leq x_3 = 14622 \leq q_3 = (p-1)/q_2 = 1993530; \quad \text{and} \quad q_1 = q_2 q_3.$$

Then

$$x_1 = x_2 + q_2 x_3 = 1{,}853{,}979 + 2{,}006{,}491 \times 14{,}622 = 29{,}340{,}765{,}381.$$

It is easy to verify that the solution $x_3 = 14622 \leq 1993530$.

6. Comparison of Complexities

While the size of required storage for $DLP(1)$ equals $T_1 = \lfloor \sqrt{p-1} \rfloor = 2000000$; the corresponding sizes of required memory/storage for $DLP(2)$ and $DLP(3)$ are respectively equal

$$T_2 = \lfloor \sqrt{q_2 - 1} \rfloor = \lfloor \sqrt{2006491} \rfloor = 1416,$$

and

$$T_3 = \lfloor \sqrt{q_3 - 1} \rfloor = \lfloor \sqrt{1993530} \rfloor = 1411.$$

Therefore, the speed-up ratio $S = T_1/(T_2 + T_3) = 2000000/(1416 + 1411) = 707$.

Thus, the decomposition algorithm for solving $DLP(1)$ via $DLP(2)$ and $DLP(3)$ is 707 times faster than a direct solution of the $DLP(1)$.

7. Second-Level Decomposition: Solution of $DLP(3)$

Remark 7.1. Although the $DLP(2)$ problem cannot be solved by decomposition since $q_2 = 2{,}006{,}491$ is a prime integer, yet, the problem $DLP(3)$ is decomposable, therefore the speed-up ratio S can be further increased.

Indeed, select

$$q_6 := \min_{0 \leq z \leq \sqrt{q_3}} \max(q_3/z, z) = 2310.$$

Let us represent x_3 as $x_3 = x_6 + q_6 x_7$, where

$$0 < x_6 < q_6 = 2310 \quad \text{and} \quad 0 < x_7 < q_7 = 863,$$

and solve DLP(3) by decomposition. Then $DLP(6)$ and $DLP(7)$ are as follows:

$DLP(6)$: Compute

$$g_6 := g_3^{(p-1)/q_6} \bmod p, \quad \text{and} \quad h_6 := h_3^{(p-1)/q_6} \bmod p,$$

where $q_6 q_7 = q_3 = 1993530$, and solve

$$g_6^{x_6} = h_6 (\bmod 1993531), \quad \{0 < x_6 < q_6 = 2310\}.$$

$DLP(7)$: Compute

$$g_7 := g_3^{(p-1)/q_7} \bmod p, \quad \text{and} \quad h_7 := h_3 g_3^{-x_6} \bmod p,$$

and solve

$$g_7^{x_7} = h_7 (\bmod 1993531), \quad \{0 < x_7 < q_7 = 863\}.$$

Then

$$T_6 = \lfloor \sqrt{q_6} \rfloor = 48 \quad \text{and} \quad T_7 = \lceil \sqrt{q_7} \rceil = 29.$$

Therefore,

$$S = T_1/(T_2 + T_6 + T_7) = 2000000/(1416 + 48 + 29)$$
$$= 2000000/1493 = \mathbf{1339.6},$$

which implies that by decomposing the problem $DLP(1)$ on three sub-problems $\{DLP(2), DLP(6) \text{ and } DLP(7)\}$, we can solve the initial $DLP(1)$ 1340 times faster than if we directly solve it without the decomposition.

In general, the speed-up is increasing if the size of p is increasing.

8. Computational Considerations

It is quite reasonable to raise the question: under what conditions should we stop the decomposition of a $DLP(k)$ and try to solve it directly. Here are the major issues that must be taken into consideration:

(1) Feasibility to factor $q_k = q_{2k} q_{2k+1}$ in such a way that

$$g_{2k} := g_k^{(p-1)/q_{2k}} \bmod p \neq \pm 1. \tag{8.1}$$

For instance, if $q_2 q_4 | 2(p-1)$, then

$$w_4 := w_2^{(p-1)/q_4} = [w_1^{(p-1)/q_2}]^{(p-1)/q_4}$$
$$= [w_1^{2(p-1)/q_2 q_4}]^{(p-1)/2} = \pm 1 (\bmod p), \qquad (8.2)$$

where $w = \{g, h\}$. In such case Eq. (4.12) has only trivial solutions $\{0 \text{ or } 1\}$ or no solution if $g_4 = 1$ and $h_4 = -1$.

(2) Overhead computations required to find g_{2k} and g_{2k+1} and then to solve two DLPs do not become too "costly".

Remark 8.1. Analogously, we can solve $DLP(3)$ by decomposing it onto two DLPs with smaller intervals of uncertainty for the corresponding unknowns.

9. Algorithmic Decomposition of $DLP(k)$

Suppose that we need to solve $DLP(k)$

$$g_k^{u_k} \bmod p = h_k, \qquad (9.1)$$

where $u_k \in [0, q_k]$. If q_k is a prime or if factors of q_k are unknown, then (9.1) can be solved by an algorithm for DLP: BSGS, Pollard's rho-algorithm, Lenstra's number field algorithm etc. However, if $q_k = cd$, where both c and d are integers, then $DLP(k)$ can be reduced to solutions of two DLPs: $DLP(2k)$ and $DLP(2k+1)$.

Let

$$q_k = q_{2k} q_{2k+1},$$

DLP(2k): Solve

$$g_{2k}^{u_{2k}} \bmod p = h_{2k}, \qquad (9.2)$$

where

$$q_{2k} := c \quad \text{and} \quad u_{2k} \in [0, c], \qquad (9.3)$$

$$R_k := (p-1)/q_k, \qquad (9.4)$$

$$g_{2k} := g_k^{R_k} \bmod p, \qquad (9.5)$$

and

$$h_{2k} := h_k^{R_k} \bmod p, \qquad (9.6)$$

DLP(2k + 1): Solve

$$g_{2k+1}^{u_{2k+1}} \bmod p = h_{2k+1}, \qquad (9.7)$$

where

$$u_{2k+1} \in [0, q_k/c], \tag{9.8}$$

$$R_{2k+1} := (p-1)/q_{2k+1}, \tag{9.9}$$

$$g_{2k+1} := g_k^{R_{2k+1}} \bmod p, \tag{9.10}$$

and

$$h_{2k+1} := h_k g_k^{-u_{2k}} \bmod p. \tag{9.11}$$

10. Conclusion

Provided that we know how to factor $p-1$, we can reduce the initial $DLP(1)$ to two DLPs: $DLP(2)$ and $DLP(3)$, which can be solved by applying the best known algorithms. The decomposition can be applied recursively to solve $DLP(k)$ by reducing it to a pair of $DLP(2k)$ and $DLP(2k+1)$.

Chapter 22

Detecting Intervals and Order of Point on Elliptic Curve

1. Introduction

In certain cases it is either important or computationally beneficial to know how many points there are on a specific elliptic curve.

Let us consider an elliptic curve E: $y^2 \equiv x^3 + ax + b(\bmod p)$ with parameters a, b, p.

Definition 1.1. Let $H = (u, v)$ be a point on E (Menezes *et al.*, 1993), and let q be the smallest integer such that $qH = O$, where O is the point at infinity. Then we say that q is the *order* of H on E, and write $ord(H) = q$.

Although an algorithm finding the order of E, $\#E$, is computationally difficult, for the purpose of this chapter $\#E$ can be evaluated using Hasse's inequality

$$(\sqrt{p} - 1)^2 \leq \#E \leq (\sqrt{p} + 1)^2, \quad \text{(Menezes et al., 1993).} \quad (1.1)$$

In order to use an elliptic curve public-key cryptography, it is important to find a point G on the elliptic curve E, which has a large $ord(G)$. This point G is called a *generator* for this curve. As it is demonstrated below, we do not need to compute kH for *every* $k = 2, 3, \ldots, q$ in order to find $ord(H)$. Indeed, let $H_k := kH$.

2. Properties of Scalar Multiplication kH

Let N be the number of points on EC. If we can find an EC for which there exists a generator G such that for all $k = 1, 2, \ldots, N - 1$ $kG \neq O$, then the point G is an *ideal* generator.

Theorem 2.1. Let $H = (u, v)$ be a point on EC and $q(u, v) = O$. Then, for every $k < p$ the following equation holds:

$$k(u, v) = (q - k)(u, p - v). \tag{2.1}$$

The Proof follows from the definition of the order of H and from periodicity of EC points.

This property can be employed to decrease the number of points that must be computed before we will find $ord(H)$.

Proposition 2.2. If q is *odd*, then there exists a pair of points (u, v) and $(u, p - v)$ such that $s(u, v) = (s + 1)(u, p - v)$. In this case $q = 2s + 1$.

Proposition 2.3. If q is *even*, then there exists a point such that $s(u, v) = (w, 0)$. In this case $q = 2s$.

In both cases, we *twice* decrease the number of points to be checked before we find the order of H.

3. More Efficient Approach

We are going to compute a subset of points kH (one at a time). Every time after a new point is computed, the set of all already-computed points is presorted with respect to their first coordinates as a sorting key.

Let Z be a point on the EC with the second coordinate equal *zero*, i.e., $Z = (z, 0)$.

If $H_1 = Z$, then $q = 2$. Otherwise let us compute H_2.

If $H_2 = -H_1$, then $q = 3$. If $H_2 = Z$, then $q = 4$. After one doubling we can check *two* additional values $k = 3$ and $k = 4$. Totally *three* candidates are checked.

If $2 \times 2 < p$, then compute H_4.

If $H_4 = -H_1$, then $q = 5$. If $H_4 = -H_2$, then $q = 6$. If $H_4 = Z$, then $q = 8$. After *one* additional doubling we can check *three* additional values $k = 5$, $k = 6$ and $k = 8$. Totally *six* candidates are checked.

If $2 \times 4 < p$, then compute H_8.

If $H_8 = H_1$, then $q = 7$ (and $H_3 = -H_4$). If $H_8 = -H_1$, then $q = 9$. If $H_8 = -H_2$, then $q = 10$. If $H_8 = -H_4$, then $q = 12$. If $H_8 = Z$, then $q = 16$. After *one* additional doubling we can check *five* additional values $k = 7$, $k = 9$, $k = 10$, $k = 12$ and $k = 16$. Totally 11 candidates are checked.

4. Detection Algorithm

Basic notations:

D is a detecting point (detector),
Z is an EC point with zero y-coordinate,
$H_k := kH$, where $H = (u, v)$.

In addition, we assume that $H \neq O$, otherwise $ord(H) = 1$; $H \neq Z$, otherwise if $H = Z$, then $ord(H) = 2$, since $2Z = O$.

Let $N(m, H)$ be the set of the first m points $H_1, H_2, \ldots, H_m$.

$T(p, H)$ is the total number of the EC points computed for detection of the order of point H as a function of p.

$C(p, H)$ is the total number of comparisons of the EC points for detection of the order of point H as a function of p.

Definition 4.1. Two EC points $A = (x_1, y_1)$ and $B = (x_2, y_2)$ are equal if and only if both their corresponding coordinates are equal, i.e., $A = B \leftrightarrow x_1 = x_2$ and $y_1 = y_2$.

Definition 4.2. Let $A = (x_1, y_1)$ and $B = (x_2, y_2)$. Then $A = -B \leftrightarrow x_1 = x_2$ and $y_1 = p - y_2$.

Definition 4.3. A pair of points $\{A, B\}$ on E are *twins* if either $A = B$ or $A = -B$.

Let t be the number of additional EC points computed after the set $N(m, H)$ is computed.

1. Compute for $k = 2$ to m $H_k = H_{k-1} + H$, $\{H_1 := H; m < p\}$.
2. Sort the set $N(m, H)$ and store it in a table where $x_1 < x_2 < \cdots < x_{m-1} < x_m$.
3. Compute $C := 2H_m$, if

$$
C = \begin{cases}
Z, & \text{then } ord(H) = 2m; \\
H_k\ 1 \leq k \leq m, & \text{then } ord(H) = m - k; \\
-H_k\ 1 \leq k \leq m, & \text{then } ord(H) = m + k.
\end{cases}
\qquad (4.1)
$$

4. Compute $D := 2C$, if

$$
D = \begin{cases}
Z, & \text{then } ord(H) = 4m; \\
H_k, & \text{then } ord(H) = 2m - k; \\
-H_k, & \text{then } ord(H) = 2m + k.
\end{cases}
\qquad (4.2)
$$

5. While $2t + 1 < p/2$ and $D \neq \{Z, H_k, -H_k\}$, compute $D := D + tC$.

$$\text{(4.3)}$$

6. If $(2t + 1)m \geq p/2$ and

$$D = \begin{cases} Z, & \text{then } ord(H) = 2(2t + 1); \\ H_k, & \text{then } ord(H) = 2t - k + 1; \\ -H_k, & \text{then } ord(H) = 2t + k + 1. \end{cases} \quad \text{(4.4)}$$

{A curve, where for every $k = 1, 2, \ldots, m$ $D \neq \{Z, H_k, -H_k\}$, is impossible, otherwise $ord(H) = \infty$}.

Remark 4.4. In some cases the time-"cost" of addition (a) and doubling (d) are not the same. There are EC for which $a \gg d$. In these cases the computation of the first m EC points $\{2H, 3H, \ldots, mH\}$ can be performed twice faster. Indeed, let $m = 2r$. Then compute H_2 by doubling. And for every integer $I = 2, \ldots, r$ compute

$$H_{2i-1} = H_{2(i-1)} + H \quad \{\text{by addition}\} \quad \text{(4.5)}$$

and

$$H_{2i} = 2H_i. \quad \{\text{by doubling}\} \quad \text{(4.6)}$$

This approach requires r doublings and $r - 1$ additions, i.e., it "costs" $r(a + d) - a$ which is about twice smaller than $(2r - 1)a$ if additions only are used to compute all EC points.

Example 4.5. $a = b = 1$; $p = 23$ and let $H = (18, 3)$. Generate kH for $k = 2, 3, 4, 5, 10, 20, 30, 40$ (see Table 4.1). Then compare them: if there is a *twin* for newly computed kH, then compute the $ord(H)$, else do *Insert Sorting*.

Since $New\_k = (12, 4)$, then $q = 30 - 2 = 28$. Thus, the order of H is computed after only *eight* points of the EC were checked.

Example 4.6. Let $H = (6, 4)$. *Compare-and-Insert*: search for a twin (see Table 4.2); if there is a twin, then *FindOrder* else *InsertSort*. The procedure *FindOrder* is described earlier in the chapter.

Table 4.1

x-coord	3	5	7	9	$x = \mathbf{12}$	17	18	$x = \mathbf{12}$
y-coord	10	4	12	7	$y = \mathbf{4}$	3	3	$y = \mathbf{4}$
k	5	4	10	3	2	20	1	$k = \mathbf{30}$
								New_k

Table 4.2

x-coordinate	5	6	7	12	13	5
y-coordinate	4	4	12	19	7	19
k	4	1	3	5	2	10

Since $(5, 19) = -(5, 4)$, {i.e., $10H = -4H$}, then $q(H) = 10 + 4 = 14$. Hence, the order of H is found after only *six* points on the EC were checked. In general, if $i > j$ and $iH = jH$ then $ord(H) = i - j$.

5. Analysis of Algorithm

In the worst case the total number of computed EC points $T(p) = m + t$, where the inequality $(2t + 1)(m + 1) \geq 2p$ holds.

The left side of the inequality is the total number of the EC points checked in the worst case. From this inequality we find that $m \geq 2p/(2t + 1) - 1$.

Therefore, $m + t \geq t + 2p/(2t + 1) - 1$.

Let us select such a value of t that minimizes the right side of this inequality.

Let $f(t) := t + 2p/(2t + 1)$, then $f'(t) = 0$ implies that the optimal $t^o = \sqrt{p} - 1/2$ and $m^o = \sqrt{p} - 1$. Finally, the total number of computed EC points equals

$$T(p) = f(t^o) = 2\sqrt{p} - 3/2. \qquad (5.1)$$

Therefore, for large p

$$T(p) = 2\sqrt{p}[1 + o(p)]. \qquad (5.2)$$

If m is large, then the algorithm can be recursively applied by assigning $p := m$.

Example 5.1. Let $p = 2^{64}$; then $m^o = 2^{32}$, which is still a large number.

By letting $p := m = 2^{32}$, we find that the next $m = 2^{16}$.

If this is still large, select $p := m = 2^8$, then next $m = 2^4 = 16$.

Consider an EC1 with parameters $a = 1$, $b = 1$, $p = 1021$. Then $(1, 32)$ is a point on the EC1.

If $a = 1$, $b = 3$, $p = 1019$, then the point $(1, 32)$ also belongs to the curve EC2.

6. Optimal Detection Algorithm

Let N be the number of points on EC; $\{N < 2p\}$.

Let $P_{z_i} := z_i H$, where for every $i \in I$, $2 \le z_i \le N$, and let $N(H, p)$ be the minimal number of EC points that must be computed in the worst case in order to find the order of point H.

Consider

$$n(p) = \min_{z} \max_{H,a,b} = N(H,p); \tag{6.1}$$

where $\{z_1, \ldots, z_n\}$ is the set of unknowns:

$$2 \le z_1 < \cdots < z_n \le N. \tag{6.2}$$

q can be detected either when z_i is computed, or if $q = z_i + z_j$, or if $q = |z_i - z_j|$.

Thus, there are totally n^2 possible conditions, from which q can be detected. It means that all unknowns $\{z_1, \ldots, z_n\}$ must be selected in such a way that the values $z_i + z_j$ and $|z_i - z_j|$ cover the entire set of integer numbers on the interval

$$\{2, 3, \ldots, 2p - 1, 2p\}. \tag{6.3}$$

Hence,

$$n^2 \ge 2p - 1 \text{ or } n \ge \sqrt{2p - 1}. \tag{6.4}$$

In addition, for every $i \in I$ z_i is computable.

Definition 6.1. z_1 is computable; if z_j is computable, then $z_{2j} = 2z_j$ is also computable; If z_i and z_j are computable, then $z_{i+j} = z_i + z_j$ is also computable.

Example 6.2. Let $p = 25$; then $n \ge 7$, let $z_0 := H$; $z_1 = 2H$; $z_2 = z_1 + z_0 = 3H$; $z_3 = 4H$; $z_4 = 5H$; $z_5 = 10H$; $z_6 = 20H$; $z_7 = 30H$; $z_8 = 40H$; $z_9 = 50H$, where for every $i \in I z_i$ is computable and integers on the interval (13) can be presented either as a sum $z_i + z_j$ or as a difference $|z_i - z_j|$.

Eight EC points $\{2, 3, 4, 5, 10, 20, 30, 40\}$ detect the order of any point on interval $[1, 45]$ (see Table 6.1).

Table 6.1   Selection of $z_i + z_j$ and $|z_i - z_j|$ for interval $[1, 45]$.

5	6	7	8	9	10	11	12	13	14	15
15	16	17	18	19	20	21	22	23	24	25
25	26	27	28	29	30	31	32	33	34	35
35	36	37	38	39	40	41	42	43	44	45
−5	−4	−3	−2	−1	0	1	2	3	4	5

Nine EC points $\{2, 3, 4, 5, 10, 20, 30, 40, 50\}$ detect the order of any point on interval $[1, 55]$;

Ten EC points $\{2, 3, 4, 5, 6, 12, 24, 36, 48, 60\}$ detect the order of every point on interval $[1, 66]$;

$2m - 1$ EC points $\{2, 3, \ldots, m, 2m, 4m, 6m, \ldots, 2m^2\}$ detect the order of every point on the interval $[1, 2m(m + 1)]$;

$2m$ EC points $\{2, 3, \ldots, m, m + 1; 2(m + 1), 4(m + 1), 6(m + 1), \ldots, 2m(m + 1)\}$ detect the order of every point on interval $[1, 2(m + 1)^2 + 1]$;

$m + z$ EC points: $\{2, 3, \ldots, m + 1; 2(m+1), 4(m+1), 6(m+1), \ldots, 2z(m+1)\}$ detect the order of every point on interval $[1, (m + 1)(2z + 1)]$.

If the interval that must be covered in the worst case is $[1, 2p]$, then $(m + 1)(2z + 1) \geq 2p$. Therefore, the optimal parameters are

$$z^o = \sqrt{p} - 1/2; \quad \text{and} \quad m^o = 2p/(2\sqrt{p} - 1 + 1) - 1 = \sqrt{p} - 1. \quad (6.5)$$

Thus, the total minimal number of points

$$\min_z (m + z) = 2\sqrt{p} - 3/2 = 2\sqrt{p}[1 - o(p)]. \quad (6.6)$$

Here, $o(p)$ is a negligibly small value in comparison with p.

Since both m and z must be integers, then select

$$m^o = \lceil \sqrt{p} \rceil - 1, \quad (6.7)$$

and because $(m + 1)(2z + 1) \geq 2p$, then

$$z^o = \lceil p/(m^o + 1) - 1/2 \rceil. \quad (6.8)$$

For instance, if $p = 31$, then $m^o = \cdot \lceil \sqrt{31} \rceil - 1 = 5$, and $z^o = \lceil 31/6 - 1/2 \rceil = 5$.

Or, if $p = 1021$, then $m^o = 31$ and $z^o = 32$. For every m we generate $2m$ points with $k = 2, \ldots, m + 1, 2(m + 1), 4(m + 1), 6(m + 1), \ldots, 2(m + 1)m$. These $2m$ points detect the order of every EC point on the interval $[1, (2m + 1)(m + 1)]$, which is illustrated in Table 6.2.

Table 6.2

$m+1$	$3(m+1)$	...	$(2m-3)(m+1)$	$(2m-1)(m+1)$	$-m-1$
$m+2$	$3m+4$	...	$2(m^2-1)-m$	$2m(m+1)-m$	$-m$
...	...	...	...	...	...
$2m$	$4m+2$	...	$2(m^2-1)-2$	$2m(m+1)-2$	-2
$2m+1$	$4m+3$	...	$2(m^2-1)-1$	$2m(m+1)-1$	-1
$\mathbf{2(m+1)}$	$\mathbf{4(m+1)}$	...	$\mathbf{2(m-1)(m+1)}$	$\mathbf{2m(m+1)}$	
$2m+3$	$4m+5$	...	$2(m^2-1)+1$	$2m(m+1)+1$	1
$2m+4$	$4m+6$	...	$2(m^2-1)+2$	$2m(m+1)+2$	2
...	...	...	...	...	...
$3m+2$	$5m+4$	...	$2(m^2-1)+m$	$(2m+1)(m+1)-1$	$\boldsymbol{m}$
$3(m+1)$	$5(m+1)$	...	$(2m-1)(m+1)$	$(2m+1)(m+1)$	$\boldsymbol{m+1}$

Let

$$p := (2m+1)(m+1) = 2m^2[1 + o(m)], \qquad (6.9)$$

therefore, from computational point of view, on the interval $[1, p]$ we detect the order of a point on the elliptic curve after at most

$$2m = \sqrt{2p} + o_1(p). \qquad (6.10)$$

This complexity resembles the baby-step-giant-step algorithm for solution of the discrete logarithm problem (Shanks, 1969).

In **bold italics** are the values of k for which points kH are *computed*.

For example, if $6(m+1)H = -2H$, then $q = 6m+8$. Or if $4(m+1)H = mH$, then $q = 3m+4$.

Chapter 23

Generalization of Gauss Theorem and Computation of Complex Primes

1. Introduction and Gauss Theorem for Counting Points

This chapter provides several generalizations of Gauss theorem that counts points on special elliptic and hyper-elliptic curves (ECs). It is demonstrated how to apply these generalizations in design of cryptographic algorithms, and in computation of complex primes, which are applicable in several protocols providing security in communication networks. These generalizations are based on intensive computer experiments (CEs). As a result, in this chapter we provide conjectures that are supported by results of these CEs. Numerical examples illustrate the ideas discussed in this chapter.

Knowledge of how many points are on an EC provides certain advantages in cryptography. In general, counting points on an EC is domain of algebraic number theory (Lercier *et al.*, 2006; Rubin-Silverberg, 2009) and algorithmic number theory (Lauder and Wan, 2008). Only in special cases it is possible to provide a closed-form solution (Gauss, 1863) or a rather simple algorithm (Rubin and Silverberg, 2002). Although validation of these algorithms requires application of algebraic number theory, their description is easy to understand for cryptographers and application-oriented computer scientists.

Gauss theorem: Consider

$$\text{EC } y^2 = (x^3 - x)(\bmod p), \tag{1.1}$$

where p is a real prime.

(1) If $p \bmod 4 = 3$, then EC (1.1) is super-singular and has $\#E = p + 1$ points {including the point at infinity O}.

(2) If $p \bmod 4 = 1$, $p = C^2 + F^2$; where C and F are integers, C is *odd*,

$$(1.2)$$

and

$$(C + F) \bmod 4 = 1; \tag{1.3}$$

then

$$\#E = p + 1 - 2C, \{\text{including the point at infinity O}\} \text{(Schoof, 1995)}. \quad (1.4)$$

If condition (1.3) holds, Gauss formula (1.4) can be applied to compute a complex prime (C, F). This application is based on the fact that an ordered pair of integers $(C, F) := C + iF$ is a complex prime if and only if its norm $C^2 + F^2$ is a prime.

However, not all complex primes have components C and F that satisfy (1.3).

For instance, $(C, F) = (5, 2)$ is the complex prime; yet $(5 + 2) \bmod 4 = 3$, i.e., (1.3) does not hold. The following conjectures generalize Gaussian theorem and, as a byproduct, allow to design a deterministic algorithm that computes complex primes for every real prime p if $p \bmod 4 = 1$.

2. Generalized Gauss Theorem

As it is shown below, in certain cases the number of points $\#E$ on EC

$$y^2 = x^3 + ax \bmod p, \tag{2.1}$$

can be represented as

$$\#E = p + 2C \times G(a, C, F), \tag{2.2}$$

where $G(a, C, F)$ is equal either 1 or -1. In the following discussion the point at infinity O is excluded in the counting.

Conjecture 2.1. Consider

$$\text{EC } y^2 = (x^3 - x)(\bmod p), \tag{2.3}$$

where p is a prime and $p \bmod 4 = 1$.

Let

$$p = C^2 + F^2, \quad \text{where } C \text{ is } odd, \text{ and } (C + F) \bmod 4 = 2 \pm 1, \tag{2.4}$$

then respectively

$$\#E = p \pm 2C. \tag{2.5}$$

Analogous results are provided in Rubin and Silverberg (2009).

Table 2.1 Generalized Gauss theorem if EC: $y^2 = (x^3 + ax) \bmod p$.

a	p	**1,777**	1,913	2,029	4,133	5,501	6,101	11,777	514,229	919,393
	$C; F$	39; 16	43; 8	45; 2	17; 62	5; 74	25; 74	31; 104	377; 610	823; 492
-1	$\#E(-1)$	**1,855**	1,999	2,119	4,167	5,511	6,151	11,839	514,983	921,039
1	$\#E(1)$	**1,855**	*1,999*	1,939	4,099	5,491	6,051	*11,839*	513,475	*921,039*

Remark 2.2. In an equivalent form (2.5) can be rewritten as

$$\#E = p + 2C \times [(C + F) \bmod 4 - 2]. \tag{2.6}$$

Table 2.1 provides examples of randomly-selected non-Blum primes that confirm conjecture (2.5), (2.6).

Conjecture 2.3. Consider EC

$$y^2 = (x^3 + x) \bmod p, \tag{2.7}$$

where p is a prime and $p \bmod 4 = 1$; $p = C^2 + F^2$; where C is *odd* (2.1).
If

$$C \bmod 4 = 2 \pm 1, \tag{2.8}$$

then respectively

$$\#E = p \pm 2C. \tag{2.9}$$

Therefore, (2.8)–(2.9) in an equivalent form

$$\#E = p + 2C \times (C \bmod 4 - 2). \tag{2.10}$$

Remark 2.4. EC (2.3) considered by C.F. Gauss has a remarkable property: if $p = 1777$, then $\#E = 1855$ {C.F. Gauss was born in 1777 and died in 1855} (see Table 2.1). The same property holds for EC (2.7).

Conjecture 2.5. Consider EC (2.1), where

$$a = \pm 1. \tag{2.11}$$

If p is a prime and $p \bmod 4 = 1$; $p = C^2 + F^2$, where C is *odd*, then

$$\#E = p + 2C[(C + F(1 - a)/2) \bmod 4 - 2]. \tag{2.12}$$

Corollary 2.6. Equation (2.12) implies that if $F \bmod 4 = 0$, then ECs (2.3) and (2.7) have equal number of points (see Table 2.1).
The identity (2.12) can also be presented as

$$\#E = p \pm 2C \quad \text{if} \quad \begin{cases} (C + F) \bmod 4 = 2 \pm 1 & \text{and} \quad a = -1, \\ C \bmod 4 = 2 \pm 1 & \text{and} \quad a = 1. \end{cases} \tag{2.13}$$

3. Examples of Points on ECs (2.1)

Case 1. Let

$$a := -2^{4k+1}, \quad \text{select} \quad x := 2^{2k+1}, \tag{3.1}$$

therefore,

$$y^2 = x(x^2 - a) = 2^{2k+1}(2^{4k+2} - 2^{4k+1}) = 2^{6k+2} \quad \text{and} \quad y = 2^{3k+1}. \tag{3.2}$$

Hence, for every integer $k \geq 0$ point $(2^{2k+1}, 2^{3k+1})$ is on the EC$y^2 = x(x^2 - a) \bmod p$, if a satisfies (3.1).

Case 2:

If $x = 2^w$ and $a = 2^{2w}$, then $x^2 + a = 2^{2w} + 2^{2w} = 2^{2w+1}$. \tag{3.3}

Thus, $y^2 = x(x^2 + a) = 2^{3w+1}$. Therefore, if w is *odd*, then

$$y = 2^{(3w+1)/2}. \tag{3.4}$$

Case 3: Let $x^2 - a = xb^2$; select

$$a := x(x - b^2). \tag{3.5}$$

Thus,

$$y^2 = x(x^2 - a) = x^2 b^2.$$

Therefore, $y = bx$, i.e., point (x, bx) is on EC

$$y^2 = x(x^2 - a) \bmod p. \tag{3.6}$$

Hence, if $a = 5$, or $a = 6$, or $a = -3$, then respectively $(5, 10)$, $(3, 3)$, $(3, 6)$ are the points on (3.6).

4. Points Counting on ECs with $a = 2^d$

Consider an EC

$$y^2 = (x^3 + 2^d x) \bmod p, \tag{4.1}$$

where the exponent $d \geq 0$ is an integer, $\#E(2^d)$ denotes the number of points on the EC (4.1), and p is a non-Blum prime {i.e., $p \bmod 4 = 1$}. Suppose that $p = C^2 + F^2$; where C and F are integers and C is *odd*. The ECs (4.1) have the following cyclic properties.

Conjecture 4.1. If

$$F \bmod 8 = 0, \tag{4.2}$$

then $\#E(2^d)$ is independent of the exponent d, i.e., is the same for every d; moreover, if

$$C \bmod 4 = 2 \pm 1, \quad \text{then} \ \#E(2^d) = p \pm 2C.$$

Conjecture 4.2. If

$$F \bmod 8 = 4, \tag{4.3}$$

then

$$\#E(2^{2k}) = \#E(1), \quad \text{and} \quad \#E(2^{2k+1}) = \#E(2). \tag{4.4}$$

If $C \bmod 4 = 1$, then for *even* d $\#E(2^d) = p - 2C$
and for *odd* d $\#E(2^d) = p + 2C.$ (4.5)
If $C \bmod 4 = 3$, then for *even* d $\#E(2^d) = p + 2C$
and for *odd* $d\#E(2^d) = p - 2C.$ (4.6)

Table 4.1 contains all cases listed in (4.3)–(4.6).

Conjecture 4.3. If $F \bmod 8 = 2$ or $F \bmod 4 = 6$, then the number of points on the EC is equal

$$p \pm 2C \ \text{if} \ d \ \text{is} \ \textit{even} \quad \text{and} \quad p \pm 2F \ \text{if} \ d \ \text{is} \ \textit{odd}. \tag{4.7}$$

In addition, for every integer k

$$\#E(2^{4k}) = \#E(1), \tag{4.8}$$

$$\#E(2^{4k+1}) = \#E(2), \tag{4.9}$$

$$\#E(2^{4k+2}) = \#E(4), \tag{4.10}$$

$$\#E(2^{4k+3}) = \#E(8). \tag{4.11}$$

If $C \bmod 4 = 1$, then for every $k\#E(2^{4k}) = p - 2C$
and $\#E(2^{4k+2}) = p + 2C.$ (4.12)
If $C \bmod 4 = 3$, then $\#E(2^{4k}) = p + 2C$
and $\#E(2^{4k+2}) = p - 2C.$ (4.13)

Table 4.1 $\#E(2^d)$ if $F \bmod 8 = 4$.

	$d = 2k$	$d = 2k + 1$
$C \bmod 4 = 2 \pm 1$	$\#E(2^{2k}) = p \pm 2C$	$\#E(2^{2k+1}) = 2p - \#E(2^{2k})$

Table 4.2 $\#E(2^d)$ if $F \bmod 8 = 2$ or 6.

$C \bmod 4 = 2 \pm 1$	$\#E(2^{4k}) = p \pm 2C$	$\#E(2^{4k+2}) = 2p - \#E(2^{4k})$
$F \bmod 8 = 4 \pm 2$	$\#E(2^{4k+1}) = p \pm 2F$	$\#E(2^{4k+3}) = 2p - \#E(2^{4k+1})$

Table 4.3 $\#E(2^d)$ on $y^2 = (x^3 + 2^d x) \bmod p$.

C	F	p	$d = 0$	$d = 1$	$d = 2$	$d = 3$
7	2	53	67; $p + 2C$	49; $p - 2F$	39; $p - 2C$	57; $p + 2F$
5	6	61	51; $p - 2C$	73; $p + 2F$	71; $p + 2C$	49; $p - 2F$
3	8	73	79; $p + 2C$	79	79	79
9	4	97	79; $p - 2C$	115; $p + 2C$	79	115
1	10	101	99; $p - 2C$	81; $p - 2F$	103; $p + 2C$	121; $p + 2F$
3	10	109	115; $p + 2C$	89; $p - 2F$	103; $p - 2C$	129; $p + 2F$
11	6	157	179; $p + 2C$	169; $p + 2F$	135; $p - 2C$	145; $p - 2F$
1	16	257	255; $p - 2C$	255	255	255
11	14	317	339; $p + 2C$	345; $p + 2F$	295; $p - 2C$	289; $p - 2F$
31	4	977	1,039; $p + 2C$	915; $p - 2C$	1,039	915
13	42	1,933	1,907; $p - 2C$	1,849; $p - 2F$	1,959; $p + 2C$	2,017; $p + 2F$
17	62	4,133	4,099; $p - 2C$	4,257; $p + 2F$	4,167; $p + 2C$	4,009; $p - 2F$

If $F \bmod 8 = 2$, then $\#E(2^{4k+1}) = p - 2F$ and $\#E(2^{4k+3}) = p + 2F$.

$$(4.14)$$

If $F \bmod 8 = 6$, then $\#E(2^{4k+1}) = p + 2F$ and $\#E(2^{4k+3}) = p - 2F$.

$$(4.15)$$

Table 4.2 contains all identities listed in (4.7)–(4.15). Table 4.3 provides numeric examples for 12 moduli p and four exponents d.

5. Points Counting on Dual EC with $a = -2^d$

Consider an EC

$$y^2 = (x^3 - 2^d x) \bmod p, \tag{5.1}$$

where the exponent $d \geq 0$ is an integer; and $p \bmod 4 = 1$.

Suppose that $p = C^2 + F^2$, where C and F are integers and C is *odd*.

Definition 5.1. The EC (5.1) is called *dual* to the EC (4.1) and vice versa. Let $\#G(2^d)$ be the number of points on (5.1). Then the mutually dual ECs have the following properties.

Conjecture 5.2. For every non-negative integer d holds

$$\#G(2^d) = \#E(2^{d+2}). \tag{5.2}$$

The identity (5.2) and identities for the EC (4.1) imply numerous equivalent identities for the EC (5.1). These identities are provided in the following section.

6. Further Generalization of Gauss Theorem

Conjecture 6.1. If $F \bmod 8 = 2$ or $F \bmod 8 = 6$, then the number of points $\#G(2^d)$ on EC (5.1) is equal

$p + 2C$ or $p - 2C$ if d is *even* and $p + 2F$ or $p - 2F$ if d is *odd*. (6.1)

In this case for every integer k

$$\#G(2^{4k}) = p \pm 2C, \quad \text{if } C \bmod 4 = 2 \pm 1, \tag{6.2}$$

$$\#G(2^{4k+1}) = p \pm 2F, \quad \text{if } F \bmod 8 = 4 \pm 2, \tag{6.3}$$

$$\#G(2^{4k+2}) = 2p - \#G(2^{4k}), \quad \text{if } C \bmod 4 = 2 \pm 1, \tag{6.4}$$

$$\#G(2^{4k+3}) = 2p - \#G(2^{4k+1}), \quad \text{if } F \bmod 8 = 4 \pm 2. \tag{6.5}$$

{see Tables 6.1 and 6.2}.

Conjecture 6.2. For every integer k the following identities hold:

if $F \bmod 8 = 4$ and $C \bmod 4 = 2 \pm 1$, then

$$\#G(2^{2k}) = p \pm 2C, \tag{6.6}$$

and

$$\#G(2^{2k+1}) = p - (\pm 2C). \tag{6.7}$$

Table 6.1   Values of $\#G(2^d)$ for *even* d.

	$d = 4k$	$d = 4k + 2$
$C \bmod 4 = 1$	$\#G(2^{4k}) = p + 2C$	$\#G(2^{4k+2}) = 2p - \#G(2^{4k})$
$C \bmod 4 = 3$	$\#G(2^{4k}) = p - 2C$	$\#G(2^{4k+2}) = 2p - \#G(2^{4k})$

Table 6.2   Values of $\#G(2^d)$ for *odd* d.

	$d = 4k + 1$	$d = 4k + 3$
$F \bmod 8 = 2$	$\#G(2^{4k+1}) = p + 2F$	$\#G(2^{4k+3}) = 2p - \#G(2^{4k+1})$
$F \bmod 8 = 6$	$\#G(2^{4k+1}) = p - 2F$	$\#G(2^{4k+3}) = 2p - \#G(2^{4k+1})$

Table 6.3   Values of $\#G(2^h)$.

	$F \bmod 8 = 0$	$F \bmod 8 = 4$
$C \bmod 4 = 2 \pm 1$	$\#G(2^d) = p \pm 2C$ for every d	$\#G(2^{2k}) = p \pm 2C,$ $\#G(2^{2k+1}) = 2p - \#G(2^{2k})$

Table 6.4   Number of points on EC $y^2 = (x^3 - 2^d x) \bmod p$.

p	C	F	$d = 0$	$d = 1$	$d = 2$	$d = 3$
53	7	2	39; $p - 2C$	57; $p + 2F$	67; $p + 2C$	49; $p - 2F$
61	5	6	71; $p + 2C$	49; $p - 2F$	51; $p - 2C$	73; $p + 2F$
97	9	4	79; $p - 2C$	115; $p + 2C$	79	115
101	1	10	103; $p + 2C$	121; $p + 2F$	99; $p - 2C$	81; $p - 2F$
109	3	10	103; $p - 2C$	129; $p + 2F$	115; $p + 2C$	89; $p - 2F$
113	7	8	127; $p + 2C$	127	127	127
257	1	16	*255*; $p - 2C$	255	255	255
977	31	4	1,039; $p + 2C$	915; $p - 2C$	1,039	915
1933	13	42	1,959; $p + 2C$	2,017; $p + 2F$	1,907; $p - 2C$	1,849; $p - 2F$
4133	17	62	4,167; $p + 2C$	$4,009; p - 2F$	4,099; $p - 2C$	4,257; $p + 2F$

Conjecture 6.3. For every non-negative integer d the following identities hold:

$$\text{if } F \bmod 8 = 0, \text{ then } \#G(2^d) = p \pm 2C \quad \text{if } C \bmod 4 = 2 \pm 1. \tag{6.8}$$

Table 6.3 contains all cases listed in (6.6)–(6.8).

Table 6.4 provides numeric examples for various cases of C and F of the EC (5.1).

7. Counting of Points $V(p, a)$ on EC

$$y^2 = (x^3 - ax) \bmod p \tag{7.1}$$

Let $V(a, p)$ denote the number of points on EC (7.1). The case, where a is a power of two, is analyzed in Secs. 4 and 5.

Let us consider discrete logarithm problem

$$2^w = a (\bmod p). \tag{7.2}$$

Conjecture 7.1. If *two* is a generator of a group based on prime modulus p, and integer w is discrete logarithm of a group modulo p (7.2), then

$$V(p, a) = \#G(2^{w \bmod 4}). \tag{7.3}$$

Proof follows from observation that

$$y^2 = x(x^3 - a) \equiv x(x^3 - 2^w) \bmod p. \tag{7.4}$$

Table 7.1   Number of points $V(p, a)$ on EC $y^2 = (x^3 - ax) \bmod p$; $\mathrm{ord}(2) = 12$.

a	1,3,9	2,5,6	4,10,12	7,8,11
$p = 13$	7	17	19	9

Table 7.2   Number of points $V(p, a)$ on EC $y^2 = (x^3 - ax) \bmod p$; $\mathrm{ord}(2) = 28$.

a	1,7,16,20, 23,24,39	2,3,11,14, 17,19,21	4,5,6,9, 13,22,28	8,10,12,15, 18,26,27
$p = 29$	39	33	19	25

Table 7.3

w	1	2	3	4	5	6	7	8	9
$2^w \bmod 53$	2	4	8	16	32	11	22	44	35
w	10	11	12	13	14	15	16	17	18
$2^w \bmod 53$	17	34	15	30	7	14	28	3	6

For instance, 2 is a generator for $p = 13, 29, 37, 53, 61$, therefore there exists w for every $1 \le a \le p - 1$.

Conjecture 7.2. For every p and every $|a| \ge 1$ there are at most four different values of $\#V(p, a)$, which are equal either $p + 2C$ or $p - 2C$ or $p + 2F$ or $p - 2F$.

Conjecture 7.3. If n is a Blum prime or a product of two Blum primes, and m is an odd integer, then hyper-EC

$$y^2 = x^m + ax (\bmod n), \tag{7.5}$$

has n points for every integer a.

Several thousands of CEs confirmed all conjectures. *Two* is a primitive element for $p = 53$; therefore, every $1 < a < 53$ can be presented as $2^w \bmod 53 = a$.

8. Effect of Doubling in EC

$$y^2 = (x^3 + a \times 2^d x) \bmod p$$

For every integer $a > 2$ the doubling of a and increment $d := d + 1$ demonstrate certain cyclic properties, although they are not the same as in the cases analyzed in Sec. 7; for details see the two following tables each

Table 8.1 Numeric examples for EC given by Eq. (8.1).

C	F	p\d	d = 0; a = 3	d = 1; a = 6	d = 2; a = 12	d = 3; a = 24
7	2	53	49; p − 2F	39; p − 2C	57; p + 2F	67; p + 2C
5	6	61	71; p + 2C	49; p − 2F	51; p − 2C	73; p + 2F
9	4	97	115; p + 2C	79; p − 2C	115	79
1	10	101	81; p − 2F	103; p + 2C	121; p + 2F	99; p − 2C
3	10	109	115; p + 2C	89; p − 2F	103; p − 2C	129; p + 2F
11	6	157	135; p − 2C	145; p − 2F	179; p + 2C	169; p + 2F
11	14	317	345; p + 2F	295; p − 2C	289; p − 2F	339; p + 2C
31	4	977	969; p − 2F	985; p + 2F	969	985
13	42	1,933	1,959; p + 2C	2,017; p + 2F	1,907; p − 2C	1,849;p-2F
17	62	4,133	4,009; p − 2F	4,099; p − 2C	4,257; p + 2F	4,167; p + 2C

Table 8.2 Numeric examples for EC given by Eq. (8.2).

C	F	p\d	d =0; a = 5	d = 1; a = 10	d = 2; a = 20	d = 3; a = 40
7	2	53	57; p + 2F	67; p + 2C	49; p − 2F	39; p − 2C
5	6	61	71; p + 2C	49; p − 2F	51; p − 2C	73; p + 2F
9	4	97	89; p − 2F	105; p + 2F	89	105
1	10	101	99; p − 2C	81; p − 2F	103; p + 2C	121; p + 2F
3	10	109	115; p + 2C	89; p − 2F	103; p − 2C	129; p + 2F
11	6	157	169; p + 2F	135; p − 2C	145; p − 2F	179; p + 2C
11	14	317	289; p − 2F	339; p + 2C	345; p + 2F	295; p − 2C
31	4	977	969; p − 2F	985; p + 2F	969	985
13	42	1,933	2,017; p + 2F	1,907; p − 2C	1,849; p − 2F	1,959; p + 2C
17	62	4,133	4,009; p − 2F	4,099; p − 2C	4,257; p + 2F	4,167; p + 2C

with 40 numeric examples. See also Remark 8.1 and Proposition A.2 in the Appendix.

$$\#E(a) \text{ in } y^2 = (x^3 + a \times 2^d x) \bmod p, a = 3. \tag{8.1}$$

$$\#E(a) \text{ in } y^2 = (x^3 + a \times 2^d x) \bmod p, \ a = 5. \tag{8.2}$$

Remark 8.1. Although

$$\{d = 1; a = 10\} \text{ is equivalent to } \{d = 2; a = 5\};$$

$$\{d = 2; a = 20\} \text{ is equivalent to } \{d = 4; a = 5\},$$

$$\{d = 3; a = 40\} \text{ is equivalent to } \{d = 6; a = 5\},$$

yet,

$$\{d = 4; a = 5\} \text{ is not equivalent to } \{d = 0; a = 5\},$$

and

$$\{d = 6; a = 5\} \text{ is not equivalent to } \{d = 2; a = 5\}.$$

Analogous observations follow from analysis of examples in Table 8.1, where $a = 3$.

9. Generation of Complex Primes via Points Counting on ECs

Since a Gaussian (C, F) is a prime if and only if its norm

$$N := C^2 + F^2, \tag{9.1}$$

is prime, in a naïve approach we can first select a non-Blum prime p, and then solve the Diophantine equation with integer unknowns C and F representing p as a sum of two integer squares. The complexity of such algorithm is of order $O(\sqrt{p})$. Instead we can apply the generalization of Gauss Theorem described above in Conjections 4.1–4.3 (for further details see Tables 10.1 and 10.2 in the next section).

Algorithm 9.1.

Step 1: Select a prime $p \bmod 4 = 1$.

Step 2: Find number of points $\#E$ on EC

$$y^2 = x^3 + ax \pmod p, \quad \text{where } a = \pm 1. \tag{9.2}$$

Step 3: Compute

$$R := |p - \#E|/2, \quad S := \sqrt{p - R^2}, \tag{9.3}$$

Step 4: If R is *odd*, then

$$(C, F) := (R, S), \quad \text{else } (C, F) := (S, R). \tag{9.4}$$

Example 9.2. Let $p = 2,097,593$ and $a = 1$, then $\#E = 2,099,359$; and $(C, F) = (883, 1148)$.

Example 9.3. Let $p = 433,494,437$, $a = -1$, then $\#E = 433,459,015$, therefore $(C, F) = (17711, 10946)$.

10. CEs

Table 10.1   Generation of complex primes (C, F) via EC $y^2 = x^3 + ax(\bmod p)$.

EC	P	#EC	C	F	$(C+F)\bmod 4$	$F\bmod 4$
$a = -1$	1,000,133	999,559	287	958	1 {GT}	2
$a = +1$	1,000,133	1,000,707	287	958	1 {**GGT**}	2
$a = \pm1$	1,000,249	1,001,359	555	832	3 {**GGT**}	0
$a = -1$	1,000,253	999,559	347	938	1 {GT}	2
$a = +1$	1,000,253	1,000,947	347	938	1 {**GGT**}	2
$a = \pm1$	1,000,289	1,000,255	17	1,000	1 {**GGT**}	0
$a = \pm1$	2,097,593	2,099,359	883	1,148	3 {**GGT**}	0
$a = -1$	3,010,349	3,013,159	1,405	1,018	3 {**GGT**}	2
$a = +1$	3,010,349	3,007,539	1,405	1,018	3 {**GGT**}	2
$a = -1$	3,276,509	3,278,599	1,045	1,478	3 {**GGT**}	2
$a = +1$	3,276,509	3,274,419	1,045	1,478	3 {**GGT**}	2
$a = \pm1$	10,006,001	9,999,999	3,001	1,000	1 {**GGT**}	0
$a = -1$	433,494,437	433,459,015	17,711	10,946	1 {GT}	2

Legend: GT = Gauss Theorem; GGT = Generalized Gauss Theorem.

Table 10.2   Generation of complex primes (C, F) via EC $y^2 = x^3 - 2x(\bmod p)$.

p	#E	C	F	#E
780,291,637	780,320,985	23,769	14,674	$p + 2F$
77,777,677,777	77,778,071,955	197,089	197,316	$p + 2C$
5,600,748,293,801	5,600,745,487,503	14,003,149	1,905,760	$p - 2C$
59,604,644,783,353,249	59,604,645,200,773,363	208,710,057	126,667,900	$p + 2C$
99,194,853,094,755,497	99,194,852,763,595,215	165,580,141	267,914,296	$p - 2C$

11. Complexity Analysis

Currently the Schoof–Elkies–Atkin (SEA) algorithm is the best known algorithm that counts points on an EC with expected running time $O(\log^4 p)$ (Schoof, 1995; Rubin and Silverberg, 2002). Therefore, if, for instance, p is of order $O(2^{1024}) = O(10^{307})$, then

$$O(\log^4 p) = O(2^{40}) = O(10^{12}). \tag{11.1}$$

Since the SEA algorithm does not work if $a = 1$ and $b = 0$ (Dewaghe, 1998), consider an EC $y^2 = x^3 + ax \bmod p$ with $|a| \neq 1$ and an algorithm with complexity $O(\log^m p)$ that counts points on this curve. Since there are algorithms with complexity $O(\log^8 p)$ that counts points for every EC, therefore $m \leq 8$. Thus

$$O(\log^m p) = O(2^{10m}) = O(10^{3m}). \tag{11.2}$$

(11.2) implies that in the worst case the problem can be solved with complexity $O(10^{24})$.

12. Concluding Remarks

The counting of points on the ECs $y^2 = x^3 + ax(\bmod p)$ is implemented on applets that were developed by my collaborator from Bangladesh Dr. Shiblee Sadik (currently at Amazon.com) and by my former graduate student Bharat Saraswat. Both of them independently developed software for the implementation of my algorithms that are used in these applets. Since these algorithms require storage that is a monotone increasing function of modulus p, their time complexity is a limitation on the order of p that is currently close to $O(10^{20})$. However, using a trade-off between time and space complexity, the calculators can be enhanced by their implementation on available Petaflop computers. Such implementation on the currently available computers with 10 or more petaflops can enhance the applets to $O(10^{30})$ or even larger orders.

Aleksey Koval of IBM (private communication, 2014) proposed a non-deterministic procedure that generates the complex primes. Here is the example of such Gaussian prime (873397278450747484694, 61623984910577 9061699), and its corresponding norm $N = 11425743576310858836260419\,1$ 7617888613040237.

As it follows from the CEs provided in the Tables A.1–A4 of the Appendix, it is not clear how to predict the cycles in the EC $y^2 = x^3 + b^d x(\bmod p)$ if the base b is not a power of 2. Further analysis is required, but this is beyond the scope of this book.

Appendix

A.1. Analysis of Periodicity in EC $y^2 = x^3 + b^d x(\bmod p)$ with Base $b = 3, 7, 11, 13$

In Tables A.1–A.3, $p = 53, 61, 73, 89, 97, 101, 109, 257, 317, 1913$ and 4133.
In general, for every k

$$\#E(1) = \#E(3^{4k}), \#E(3) = \#E(3^{4k+1}), \#E(3^2)$$
$$= \#E(3^{4k+2}), \#E(3^3) = \#E(3^{4k+3}).$$

There are four possible cycles:

(A) $p + 2C, p + 2F, p - 2C, p - 2F$, {see $p = 317, 1913$},
(B) $p + 2C, p - 2F, p - 2C, p + 2F$, {see $p = 53$},

Table A.1 Number of points $\#E(3^d)$ in $y^2 = (x^3 + 3^d x) \bmod p$.

p (C,F)	$p=53$ $(7,2)$	$p=61$ $(5,6)$	$p=73$ $(3,8)$	$p=89$ $(5,8)$	$p=97$ $(9,4)$	$p=101$ $(1,10)$	$p=109$ $(3,10)$	$p=257$ $(1,16)$	$p=317$ $(11,14)$	$p=1913$ $(43,8)$	$p=4133$ $(17,62)$
$d=0$	67; $p+2C$	51; $p-2C$	79; $p+2C$	79; $p-2C$	79; $p-2C$	99; $p-2C$	115; $p+2C$	255; $p-2C$	339; $p+2C$	1999; $p+2C$	4099; $p-2C$
$d=1$	49; $p-2F$	71; $p+2C$	67; $p-2C$	105; $p+2F$	115; $p+2C$	81; $p-2F$	115	289; $p+2F$	345; $p+2F$	1929; $p+2F$	4009; $p-2F$
$d=2$	39; $p-2C$	51	79	99; $p+2C$	79	103; $p+2C$	115	259; $p+2C$	295; $p-2C$	1827; $p-2C$	4167; $p+2C$
$d=3$	57; $p+2F$	71	67	73; $p-2F$	115	121; $p+2F$	115	225; $p-2F$	289; $p-2F$	1897; $p-2F$	4257; $p+2F$

Table A.2 $\#E(7^d)$ in $y^2 = (x^3 + 7^d x)\bmod p$.

C	F	p	d = 0	d = 1	d = 2	d = 3
3	8	73	79; $p + 2C$	89; $p + 2F$	67; $p - 2C$	57; $p - 2F$
1	16	257	255; $p - 2C$	289; $p + 2C$	259; $p + 2F$	225; $p - 2F$
11	14	317	339; $p + 2C$	295; $p - 2C$	339	295
31	4	977	1,039; $p + 2C$	915; $p - 2C$	1,039	915
13	42	1,933	1,907; $p - 2C$	1,959; $p + 2C$	1,907	1,959
17	62	4,133	4,099; $p - 2C$	4,009; $p - 2F$	4,167; $p + 2C$	4,257; $p + 2F$

Table A.3 $\#E(11^d)$ in $y^2 = (x^3 + 11^d x)\bmod p$.

C	F	p	d = 0	d = 1	d = 2	d = 3
3	8	73	79; $p + 2C$	57; $p - 2F$	67; $p - 2C$	89; $p + 2F$
1	16	257	255; $p - 2C$	255; $p - 2C$	255	255
11	14	317	339; $p + 2C$	339$p + 2C$;	339	339
31	4	977	1,039; $p + 2C$	915; $p - 2C$	1,039	915
13	42	1,933	1,907; $p - 2C$	1,849; $p - 2F$	1,959; $p + 2C$	2,017; $p + 2F$
17	62	4,133	4,099; $p - 2C$	4,009; $p - 2F$	4,167; $p + 2C$	4,257; $p + 2F$

Table A.4 $\#E(13^d)$ in $y^2 = (x^3 + 13^d x)\bmod p$.

C	F	p	d = 0	d = 1	d = 2	d = 3
3	8	73	79; $p + 2C$	57; $p - 2F$	67; $p - 2C$	89; $p + 2F$
1	16	257	255; $p - 2C$	259; $p + 2C$	255	259
11	14	317	339; $p + 2C$	345; $p + 2F$	295; $p - 2F$	289; $p - 2C$
31	4	977	1,039; $p + 2C$	985; $p + 2F$	915; $p - 2C$	969; $p - 2F$
13	42	1,933	1,907; $p - 2C$	1,959; $p + 2C$	1,907	1,959
17	62	4,133	4,099; $p - 2C$	4,099; $p - 2C$	4,099	4,099

(C) $p - 2C$, $p + 2F$, $p + 2C$, $p - 2F$, {see $p = 89, 257$},

(D) $p - 2C$, $p - 2F$, $p + 2C$, $p + 2F$, {see $p = 101, 4133$}.

Suppose we need to find $\#E(p, b = 3)$ $y^2 = x^3 + 3x(\bmod p)$, for $p = 29, 61, 4093$.

Since $a = 2$ is a generator for these primes, then every DLP $2^w = 3 \bmod p$ has a solution:

If $p = 29$, then $w = 5$; therefore $\#E(29, 3) = \#E(29, 2^5) = \#E(29, 2^1) = 25$.

If $p = 61$, then $w = 6$; therefore, $\#E(61, 3) = \#E(61, 2^6) = \#E(61, 2^2) = \#E(61, 4) = 71$.

If $p = 4093$, then $w = 12$;

therefore,

$$\#E(4093, 3) = \#E(4093, 2^{12}) = \#E(61, 2^0) = \#E(4093, 1) = 4147.$$

Conjecture A.1. For every b and every *even* d the number $\#E$ of points equals either $p + 2C$ or $p - 2C$; however, for every b and for every *odd* d the number of points $\#E$ equals either $p + 2F$ or $p - 2F$, or $p + 2C$, or $p - 2C$.

Proposition A.2. For every integer b, d and p the ECs

$$y^2 = (x^3 \pm b^d x) \bmod p \quad \text{and} \quad y^2 = (x^3 \pm b^{d \bmod 4} x) \bmod p \qquad \text{(A.1)}$$

have equal number of points.

Proof is provided in the Appendix of Chapter 4 of this book. The proof demonstrates how to establish one-to-one correspondence between these two ECs for every p.

Conjecture A.3. For every integer a and p the number of points $\#E$ on EC

$$y^2 = (x^3 \pm ax) \bmod p \qquad \text{(A.2)}$$

is equal either $p + 2C$ or $p - 2C$ or $p + 2F$ or $p - 2F$.

Chapter 24

Space Complexity of Algorithm for Modular Multiplicative Inverse

1. Introduction

In certain computational systems the amount of space required to execute an algorithm is even more restrictive than the corresponding time necessary for solution of a problem. In Chapter 1 we considered the algorithm for modular multiplicative inverse (MMI). In this chapter computational *space* complexity of that algorithm is considered and analyzed. A tight upper bound for bit storage required for execution of the algorithm is provided. It is demonstrated that for range of numbers used in public-key encryption systems, the size of bit storage does not exceed a 2K-bit threshold in the worst-case. This feature of the Enhanced-Euclid algorithm (EEA) allows designing special-purpose hardware for its implementation as a subroutine in communication secure wireless devices.

2. Algorithm for MMI

Operation of MMI is essential for public-key encryption, modular arithmetic (Menezes *et al.*, 1997) and for applications based on the Chinese Remainder Theorem (Knuth, 1997).

2.1. *Definition*

Operation of multiplicative inverse modulo n is a basic operation in modular arithmetic. An integer x is called a MMI of p_1 modulo p_0 (Knuth, 1997), if it satisfies equation

$$p_1 x \bmod p_0 = 1. \tag{2.1}$$

2.2. *EEA*

Consider integer variables L, M, S, t and Boolean variable c;

Assign $L := p_0$; $M := p_1$; $c := 0$;

repeat $t := \lfloor L/M \rfloor$, $S := L - Mt$, $c := 1 - c$, $L := M$, $M := S$,

$$(2.2)$$

push t {onto the top of the stack},	(2.3)

until either $S = 1$ or $S = 0$,

if $S = 0$, **then** $\gcd(p_0, p_1) = M$, **output** *"MMI does not exist"*, $M = \gcd(p_0, p_1)$},

else assign $S := 0$, $M := 1$,

repeat	**pop** t {from the top of the stack},

$$L := Mt + S, \ S := M, \ M := L, \tag{2.4}$$

until the stack is *empty*;

output

if $c = 0$ **then** $MMI := L$ **else** $MMI := p_0 - L$.

For more details see (Verkhovsky, 1998; Verkhovsky, 2010).

The algorithm is valid for both cases: for $p_0 > p_1$ or $p_0 < p_1$.

In the latter case, assign $p_1 := p_1 \bmod p_0$.

Validity of the EEA is discussed in (Verkhovsky, 1998) and its time complexity is analyzed in (Verkhovsky, 2010). Although both analysis and computer experiments demonstrate that the EEA is faster than the Extended-Euclid algorithm (Knuth, 1997), the EEA requires the *storage of stack* (see (1.3)–(1.4)). The worst-case *space* complexity of the EEA is analyzed if

$$p_0 > p_1. \tag{2.4}$$

3. Bit-Storage Requirement for Stack

3.1. *Direct problem*

Let $N(p_0, p_1)$ be the number of bits required to store the stack. Find a maximal p_0 such that for *all* values of p_1 satisfying (1.5) the EEA does not require more than s bits for storage of the stack. Consider optimization problems:

$$Q(s, p_0) := \max_{2 \le p_1 < p_0} N(p_0, p_1) \le s, \tag{3.1}$$

and let

$$q(s) := \max_{p_0} Q(s, p_0). \tag{3.2}$$

3.2. *Dual problem*

In order to analyze space complexity of the EEA let us consider a sequence $\{n_0, n_1, \ldots, n_k, \ldots\}$ generated in accordance with the following rules: let $a > b \geq 1$, $n_{k+1} := q_k n_k + n_{k-1}$, where all $q_k \geq 1$ and $n_1 := a, n_0 := b$, and for all $k \geq 1$ n_k are integers. Then for every $k \geq 1$

$$(n_{k+1}, n_k) = (n_k, n_{k-1}) \begin{pmatrix} q_k & 1 \\ 1 & 0 \end{pmatrix}. \tag{3.3}$$

Therefore, for every integer

$$r \geq 1 (n_{r+1}, n_r) = (a, b) \prod_{k=1}^{r} \begin{pmatrix} q_k & 1 \\ 1 & 0 \end{pmatrix}, \tag{3.4}$$

and

$$n_{r+1} = (a, b) \prod_{k=1}^{r} \begin{pmatrix} q_k & 1 \\ 1 & 0 \end{pmatrix} (1, 0)^T.$$

Suppose that a memory that stores an array of quotients $\{q_1, q_2, \ldots, q_{r-1}, q_r\}$ has restricted capacity, i.e., it cannot store more than s bits. Consider the following optimization problem:

Find

$$n(r, s) := \min_{\{q_k : k=1,\ldots,r\}} (a, b) \prod_{k=1}^{r} \begin{pmatrix} q_k & 1 \\ 1 & 0 \end{pmatrix} (1, 0)^T, \tag{3.5}$$

under constraint

$$\sum_{k=1}^{r} \lfloor \log_2 2q_k \rfloor = s, \tag{3.6}$$

where integers a, b, r and s in (3.5) and (3.6) are specified parameters.

Here $\lfloor \log_2 2q_k \rfloor$ is the number of bits required for storing the quotient q_k, and (3.6) describes the constraint that the total allowed bit-storage for r quotients is equal s.

Let

$$n(s) := \min_r n(r, s). \tag{3.7}$$

Therefore, for every integer s

$$q(s) = n(s)(2.2). \tag{3.8}$$

4. Properties of Optimal Quotients

Consider $\{q_1, q_2, \ldots, q_{r-1}, q_r\}$ (3.3), then the following properties hold:

Proposition 4.1. Every optimal q_k must be exact powers of *two*.

Proof. Let us assume that the statement is incorrect. This implies that for the same s, the value of $n(s)$ would be larger. □

Indeed, consider for all $k \geq 1$

$$q_k = 2^{i_k} \leq q_k' < 2^{i_k+1}.$$

Then for all $k \geq 1$ the inequality $n_k \leq n_k'$ holds. Here $n_0' := b, n_1' := a$ and all n_k' are generated iteratively as $n_k' := q_{k-1}' n_{k-1}' + n_{k-2}'$. At the same time both arrays of quotients require the same size of bit storage.

Let $E_0 := I$ {identity matrix} and for all $i \geq 1$

$$E_i := \begin{pmatrix} 2^{i-1} & 1 \\ 1 & 0 \end{pmatrix}. \tag{4.1}$$

Then (3.5) can be rewritten as

$$n(r, s) := \min_{\text{all } q_k} (a, b) \prod_{k=1}^{r} E_{i_k} (1, 0)^T. \tag{4.2}$$

Proposition 4.2. Since a spectral radius of matrix E_1^2 is larger than the spectral radius of matrix E_2, the sequence $\{n_0, n_1, \ldots, n_k, \ldots\}$, generated by an array of length $2m$ with all $q_k = 1$, grows faster than the sequence generated by an array of length m with all $q_k = 2$. Yet both arrays require the same storage. Hence all $q_k = 2$ generate smaller n_{r+1} than the *unary* array of the quotients. This observation provides a simple way to find an *upper bound* $h(s)$ for $n(s)$. Indeed, $h(0) = 2, h(2) = 5$, and for all $s \geq 2$

$$h(2s) = 2h(2s - 2) + h(2s - 4). \tag{4.3}$$

Let

$$H(s) := h(2s), \text{ then } H(0) = 2, H(1) = 5, H(s) := 2H(s - 1) + H(s - 2). \tag{4.4}$$

Representing the upper bound $H(s)$ as $H(s) = \alpha \rho^s + \beta \sigma^s$ (Harkin, 1957; Lueker, 1980), and using (4.4), we derive that

$$h(s) = \left(1 + 3\sqrt{2}\right) \left(\sqrt{1 + \sqrt{2}}\right)^s / 4 + o(s). \tag{4.5}$$

For $s = 40$ $h(40) = 93,222,358$, while the exact upper bound $n(40) = 80,198,051$ (see (8.17)), i.e., the relative difference between $h(40)$ and $n(40)$ is more than 16%. However, for larger values of s this difference is significantly increasing, namely

$$\lim_{s \to \infty} h(s)/n(s) = \infty.$$

Let us now consider properties of control variables that help to determine their optimal values.

5. Diagonally-Decreasing Matrices

5.1. *Definition*

$R = \{r_{ij}\}_{m \times n}$ is a diagonally decreasing matrix {or D-matrix, for short}, if $r_{ij} > r_{kl}$ for every $i \le k$ and $j \le l$.

Hence for every $k \ge 1$, E_k are D-matrices.

5.2. *Properties of D-matrices*

(1) A product of D-matrices is a D-matrix.
(2) Transposed D-matrix is also a D-matrix.

Let us consider function

$$F(X, u, w) := (1, u)X(1, w)^T, \tag{5.1}$$

where $X \ge 0$ is a two-dimensional square matrix {all further inequalities involving matrices are considered entry-wise} , scalars $u > 0$ and $w \ge 0$.

Remark 5.1. For the sake of simplicity in forthcoming inequalities wherever it is necessary, we use a normalization

$$(a, b)X(c, d)^T = ac(1, b/a)X(1, d/c)^T = ac\Phi(X, u, w), \tag{5.2}$$

where $u := b/a, w := d/c$.

Let

$$F(X) := \Phi(X, ., .). \tag{5.3}$$

It is easy to verify that

$$\text{if } X \ge Y > 0, \quad \text{then } F(X) \ge F(Y). \tag{5.4}$$

For example, since

$$E_1^2 \ge E_2, \quad \text{then } F(E_1^2) \ge F(E_2). \tag{5.5}$$

6. Decomposition

Proposition 6.1. Let

$$0 < u < 1, \quad 0 \le w < 1, \tag{6.1}$$

then the inequality

$$F(E_{k+m}) - F(E_k E_m) > 0, \tag{6.2}$$

holds if

$$k \ge 1, \quad m \ge 1, \quad k + m \ge 3, \quad \text{and} \quad w = 0. \tag{6.3}$$

Proof. Consider

$$F(E_{k+m}) - F(E_k E_m) = (1, u)(E_{k+m} - E_k E_m)(1, w)^T > 0, \tag{6.4}$$

and find under what conditions it holds. Let $x := 2^{k-1}$, $y := 2^{m-1}$, then

$$E_{k+m} - E_k E_m = \begin{pmatrix} 2xy & 1 \\ 1 & 0 \end{pmatrix} - \begin{pmatrix} x & 1 \\ 1 & 0 \end{pmatrix}\begin{pmatrix} y & 1 \\ 1 & 0 \end{pmatrix} = \begin{pmatrix} xy & 1 \\ 1 & 0 \end{pmatrix} - \begin{pmatrix} 1 & x \\ y & 1 \end{pmatrix}. \tag{6.5}$$

Therefore, definitions (5.1) and (5.3), and Eqs. (6.4), (6.5) imply the inequality

$$(2^{k-1} - u)(2^{m-1} - w) > (1 - u)(1 - w) + uw. \tag{6.6}$$

On the other hand, if (6.6) holds, then (5.4) also holds. In addition, it is sufficient to observe that (6.6) indeed holds if $k \ge 1, m \ge 1, k + m \ge 3$, and $w = 0$.

However, (6.6) does *not* hold if $k = m = 1$.   Q.E.D.

7. Transposition

Proposition 7.1. The inequality

$$(1, u)(E_k E_m - E_m E_k)(1, w)^T > 0 \tag{7.1}$$

holds if

$$(k - m)(w - u) > 0. \tag{7.2}$$

Proof. Let

$$x := 2^{k-1}, \quad y := 2^{m-1}, \quad X := \begin{pmatrix} x & 1 \\ 1 & 0 \end{pmatrix} \quad \text{and} \quad Y := \begin{pmatrix} y & 1 \\ 1 & 0 \end{pmatrix}.$$

Thus,

$$XY - YX = \begin{pmatrix} 0 & x - y \\ y - x & 0 \end{pmatrix} = (x - y) \begin{pmatrix} 0 & 1 \\ -1 & 0 \end{pmatrix}. \tag{7.3}$$

Therefore, inequality

$$(1, u)(XY - YX)(1, w)^T > 0, \tag{7.4}$$

holds if

$$(x - y)(w - u) > 0. \tag{7.5}$$

Hence, inequality (7.1) can be rewritten as

$$(2^{m-1} - 2^{k-1})(u - w) > 0, \tag{7.6}$$

and (7.6) holds if

$$\text{sign}(m - k) = \text{sign}(u - w). \qquad \text{Q.E.D.}$$

In addition, inequality (7.6) implies that if $w = 0$, then inequality (7.1) holds if $k < m$.

Let

$$E := E_2 E_1, \quad E(1, v)^T = \lambda(1, v)^T, \tag{7.7}$$

where λ is the largest eigenvalue of E.

Since $E = \begin{pmatrix} 3 & 2 \\ 1 & 1 \end{pmatrix} > 0$, i.e., with all positive elements, then by Perron–Frobenius Theorem (Perron, 1907) its largest eigenvalue $\lambda > 0$ with positive corresponding eigenvector $(1, v)$, where $v > 0$ (7.7). Indeed, $\lambda = 2 + \sqrt{3}$, and $v = (\sqrt{3} - 1)/2$.

8. Optimal Control Variables

8.1. *Cases* $s = 0, 1, 2$

It is easy to verify that $n(0) = 2, n(1) = 3$. To find $n(2)$ we must compare two cases only. From the Decomposition Theorem it follows that $(a, b)E_1^2 \geq (a, b)E_2$ for all $a > 0$ and $b > 0$.

Hence, $q_1^0 = 2$, and if $(a, b) = (2, 1)$, then $n(2) = 5$.

8.2. *Case* $s = 3$

Let $X := E_3$ and $E := E_2 E_1$, then

$$(2,1)E_3(1,0)^T > (2,1)E_1E_2(1,0)^T > (2,1)E_2E_1(1,0)^T, \qquad (8.1)$$

or after normalization

$$(1,1/2)E_3(1,0)^T > (1,1/2)E_1E_2(1,0)^T > (1,1/2)E_2E_1(1,0)^T$$

$$\equiv (1,1/2)E(1,0)^T. \qquad (8.2)$$

Here $u = 1/2$ and $w = 0$. Since in (8.2) $w = 0$, then the left-most inequality follows from the Decomposition (Proposition 6.1) and the right-most inequality follows from the Transposition (Proposition 7.1).

Thus, the optimal control variables are $q_1^0 = 2$, $q_2^0 = 1$ and $n(3) = 7$.

8.3. *Case* $s = 4$

The following scheme shows that there are two local minima. Indeed, consider $X := E_4$. Using the Decomposition and Transposition Theorems, we can decrease the value of function $F(X)$. This procedure leads to two local minima. Let $A \Rightarrow B$ mean that $F(A) \geq F(B)$, i.e.,

$$E_2 E_1^2 \Leftarrow E_3 E_1 \Leftarrow E_4 \Leftarrow E_1 E_3 \Leftarrow E_1^2 E_2$$
$$\Downarrow \qquad\quad \Downarrow \qquad\quad \Downarrow \qquad\quad \Downarrow \qquad\quad \Downarrow$$
$$E_2^2 \qquad E_1 E_2 E_1 \quad E_2^2 \quad E_1 E_2 E_1 \quad E_2^2$$

Direct comparison implies that

$$F(E_2^2) > F(E_1 E_2 E_1) \equiv F(E_1 E). \qquad (8.3)$$

Hence the optimal control variables are equal $q_1^0 = q_3^0 = 1$ and $q_2^0 = 2$. Thus, $n(4) = 11$.

8.4. *Case* $s = 5$

Consider $X := E_5$. Systematically applying decomposition and transposition, it is possible to demonstrate, that there are two local minima: $E_2 E_1 E_2$ and $E_2 E$ only (7.7) {see the diagrams below} . The direct comparison shows that $E_2 E$ delivers the global minimum.

Proposition 8.1 Let p_0 and p_1 be a pair that requires s bits of storage:

$$L := (2,1), \quad R := (1,0)^T, \quad s = 3m+j, \quad 0 \leq j \leq 2 \quad \text{and} \quad \sum_{\{all\ k\}} i_k = s,$$

$$(8.4)$$

then

$$\min_{\{all\ q\}} L \prod_i E_{q_i} R = LE_j E^m R. \tag{8.5}$$

Proof. {by induction over m}

1. $m = 0$: for $j = 1$ and $j = 2$ we proved in Subsection 7.1 that $LE_j R$ is the minimum.

   For $j = 3$ we proved in (6.1)–(6.2) that

   $$L(E_3 - E_1 E_2)R > 0,$$

   and that

   $$L(E_1 E_2 - E_2 E_1)E^m R > 0,$$

   i.e., LER is the minimum.

2. Let for $m = 0, 1, \ldots, k$ $LE_j E^m R$ be the minimum if $j = 0, 1, 2$; $\{E_0 := I,$ (4.1)$\}$ and correspondingly $E_j E^m$ be the optimal control strategy.

3. Let us insert matrix E_3 into $LE_j E^k R$ and prove that the following two inequalities hold:

   $$LE_j E^k (E_3 - E_1 E_2)R > 0, \tag{8.6}$$

   and

   $$LE_j E^k (E_1 E_2 - E_2 E_1)R > 0. \tag{8.7}$$

   Let

   $$LE_j := (a_{0j}, b_{0j}), \quad \text{and for all } m(a_{mj}, b_{mj}) := (a_{0j}, b_{0j})E^m. \tag{8.8}$$

Here L, E_j, E and R are D-matrices, {see the Definition 4.1} . Hence LE_j and $LE_j E^k$ are also D-matrices, {as products of D-matrices} , i.e., $a_{ij} > b_{ij} > 0$ for all $i = 0, 1, 2, \ldots$

Dividing the inequalities (8.6) and (8.7) by a_{kj}, we can respectively rewrite them as

$$(1, u_{kj})(E_3 - E_1 E_2)(1, 0)^T > 0, \tag{8.9}$$

and as

$$(1, u_{kj})(E_1 E_2 - E_2 E_1)(1, 0)^T > 0. \tag{8.10}$$

Then inequality (8.9) holds by the Decomposition Theorem because $w = 0$, $0 < u_{kj} < 1$, and $u_{kj} := b_{kj}/a_{kj}$. On the other hand, inequality

(7.10) holds by the Transposition Theorem because $u_{kj} > w = 0$. Therefore, $LE_jE^k(E_2E_1)R = LE_jE^kER = LE_jE^{k+1}R$ is the minimum and E_jE^{k+1} is the optimal control strategy. Q.E.D.

Remark 8.1. Another (more tedious) way to prove the Theorem is to consider an induction over m and j. Firstly, we make an assumption that for all $m = 0, 1, \ldots, k$ and for all $j = 0, 1, 2$ LE_jE^mR is the minimum and E_jE^m is the optimal strategy. Then we prove that for every $1 \leq i \leq m$

$$F(E_jE^iE_1E^{m-i}) > F(E_jE^{i-1}E_1E^{m-i+1}) > \cdots > F(AE^m). \quad (8.11)$$

Here

$$E_0 := I, \quad A := E_{j+1}, \text{ if } j = 0 \text{ or } j = 1, \quad \text{and} \quad A := E \text{ if } j = 2.$$

The application of all transpositions is based on the following propositions, provided here without proofs.

Proposition 8.2. For every $j = 0, 1, 2$ and for every $i = 1, 2, \ldots$

$$u_{0j} > u_{1j} > \cdots > u_{ij} > \cdots > v > \cdots > w_l > \cdots > w_1 > w_0 = 0, \quad (8.12)$$

if

$$u_{0j} > v = (\sqrt{3} - 1)/2. \quad (8.13)$$

Here all u_{ij} are defined in (5.2) and (8.8), and v satisfies condition $(1, v)E^T = \lambda(1, v)$, i.e., v is the second component of a normalized eigenvector of matrix E, corresponding to the largest eigenvalue λ of E (Perron, 1907). Direct computation shows that indeed the inequalities $u_{0j} > v$ are satisfied for every $j = 0, 1, 2$.

Therefore,

$$F(E_jE^iE_1E^{m-i}) > F(E_jE^{i-1}E_1E^{m-i+1}), \quad (8.14)$$

holds for every $i = 1, \ldots, m$.

Let $n(s)$ be the minimal p_0 that requires no more than s bits of storage for the stack. The minimal values $n(s)$ are generated by the following optimal quotients q_k^0:

1. If $s = 3m$, then for every $k \geq 1$

$$q_k^0 = 1 + k \bmod 2. \quad (8.15)$$

2. If $s = 3m + r$, and $r = 1, 2$, then $q_1^0 = r$, and for every $k \geq 2$

$$q_k^0 = 2 - k \bmod 2. \quad (8.16)$$

Examples:

$$n(0) = 2, \ n(1) = 3, \ n(2) = 5, \ n(3) = 7, \ n(4) = 11, \ n(5) = 17,$$
$$n(6) = 26, \ n(7) = 41, \ n(8) = 63, \ n(9) = 97, \ n(10) = 153,$$
$$n(11) = 235, \ n(12) = 362, \ n(13) = 571, \ n(14) = 877, \tag{8.17}$$
$$n(15) = 1412, \ldots n(20) = 12,863, \ldots n(40) = 80,198,051.$$

9. Iterative Relations for Tight Upper Bound $n(s)$

Since for $i = 0, 1, 2$

$$n(3m + i) = (2,1)E_i E^m(1,0)^T, \tag{9.1}$$

let us find telescopic relations for $n(s)$ in the following form (Perron, 1907):

$$n(3m + i + 2) = x_i n(3m + i + 1) + y_i n(3m + i), \tag{9.2}$$

where x_i and y_i must satisfy equations

$$(2,1)(A_{i+2} - x_i A_{i+1} - y_i A_i)E_2 E^m(1,0)^T = 0, \tag{9.3}$$

where

$$A_i = \begin{cases} E_i, & i = 0, 1, 2 \\ E, & i = 3 \\ E_1 E, & i = 4 \end{cases} . \tag{9.4}$$

From these equations we find all x_i and y_i and establish the following telescopic relations for $n(s)$:

$$4n(3m) = -n(3m - 1) + 11n(3m - 2), \tag{9.5}$$

$$11n(3m + 1) = 18n(3m) - n(3m - 1), \tag{9.6}$$

$$n(3m + 2) = -n(3m + 1) + 4n(3m), \quad \text{(Lueker, 1980)}. \tag{9.7}$$

Therefore,

$$n(3m - 2) = [n(3m) + n(3m - 3)]/3, \tag{9.8}$$

$$n(3m - 1) = [-n(3m) + 11n(3m - 3)]/3, \tag{9.9}$$

and finally,

$$n(3m) = [n(3m + 3) + n(3m - 3)]/4,$$

or

$$n(3m + 3) = 4n(3m) - n(3m - 3). \tag{9.10}$$

10. Closed-Form Expressions for $n(s)$

Direct substitution shows that

$$n(3m) = \left[\left(2 + \sqrt{3}\right)^{m+1} + \left(2 - \sqrt{3}\right)^{m+1}\right]/2, \qquad (10.1)$$

satisfies (9.10) for every integer $m \geq 0$.

Using (9.8), (9.9) and (10.1), we can find closed-form expressions for

$$n(3m - 2) = \left[\left(2 + \sqrt{3}\right)^m \left(1 + 1/\sqrt{3}\right) + \left(2 - \sqrt{3}\right)^m \left(1 - 1/\sqrt{3}\right)\right]/2, \quad (10.2)$$

and for

$$n(3m - 1) = \left[\left(2 + \sqrt{3}\right)^m \left(3 - 1/\sqrt{3}\right) + \left(2 - \sqrt{3}\right)^m \left(3 + 1/\sqrt{3}\right)\right]/2. \quad (10.3)$$

The tight-upper bound on the required bit-storage is deducible from the following:

Proposition 10.1. The bit-storage required by EEA for storage of the stack in the worst case satisfies the equation:

$$\max_{2 \leq p_1 < p_0} N(p_0, p_1) = 3\left(\log_{2+\sqrt{3}} p_0\right)[1 + o(p_0)], \qquad (10.4)$$

Proof. Since $\left|2 - \sqrt{3}\right| < 1$, then definitions (3.1)–(3.2) and formulas (10.1)–(10.3) imply (10.4).   □

11. Asymptotic Rate of Growth per Bit

Let $s = 3m + i$; represent $n(s)$ in a form

$$n(3m + i) = a_i u^{3m+i} + o(m). \qquad (11.1)$$

The asymptotic rate of growth u equals to $r(E)$, where $r(E)$ is a spectral radius of matrix E, (Hartmanis and Stearns, 1965; Fortnow and Homer, 2003; Goldreich, 2008), i.e., the largest root of equation

$$\begin{vmatrix} 3 - \lambda & 2 \\ 1 & 1 - \lambda \end{vmatrix} = 0.$$

Since $\lambda_{1,2} = 2 \pm \sqrt{3}$, then

$$u = \sqrt[3]{2 + \sqrt{3}} = 1.5511335. \qquad (11.2)$$

This observation independently verifies the stronger results of (10.1)–(10.3). Indeed, we can find the asymptotic rate of growth/bit by taking into account that $(2 - \sqrt{3})^m \to 0$ in (10.1)–(10.3) for large m. Finally, since $\sqrt{1 + \sqrt{2}} > \sqrt[3]{2 + \sqrt{3}}$, then the tight upper bound $n(s)$ grows slower than $h(s)$ (4.5).

Main Theorem: Let $N(p_0)$ denote the maximal number of bits required to store all quotients in the stack if the modulus equals p_0, and let $u := \sqrt[3]{2 + \sqrt{3}}$.

If

$$p_0 \in [a_0 u^{3m}, a_1 u^{3m+1} - 1], \quad \text{then } N(p_0) \le 3m.$$

If

$$p_0 \in [a_1 u^{3m+1}, a_2 u^{3m+2} - 1], \quad \text{then } N(p_0) \le 3m + 1.$$

If

$$p_0 \in [a_2 u^{3m+2}, a_0 u^{3(m+1)} - 1], \quad \text{then } N(p_0) \le 3m + 2, \tag{11.3}$$

where $a_0 = 1/2, a_1 = (3 - 1/\sqrt{3})/2$, and $a_2 = (1 + 1/\sqrt{3})/2$.
Proof follows from (10.1)–(10.4) and (11.1).

12. Concluding Remarks

As it follows from the observed results, EEA requires very small bit-storage for its execution. This storage does not exceed a 2K-bit level for public-key encryption algorithms, dealing with numbers p_0 and p_1 of range $(10^{100}, 10^{400})$. As it is demonstrated in numerous computer experiments, the average bit-storage is actually 40% *smaller* than 2K. Therefore, the EEA is executable if necessary by a custom-built chip with small memory (Ivey *et al.*, 1992). This property of EEA is especially important for a potential implementation of encryption if integrated-circuit memory is limited {smart cards, PC cards, smart phones, wearable computers, tablets, etc.}.

In the analysis provided above, it is not considered storage space, required for delimiters separating the quotients in the stack. The way to resolve the retrieval problem is to use a dynamic *prefix* coding for the quotients (Vitter, 1987; 1989). Since in the prefix coding there are no two codes such that one code is a prefix of another code, the quotients can be retrieved from the stack without delimiters.

Appendix

A.1. *Analysis and examples*

$$E_5 \Rightarrow E_1 E_4 \Rightarrow E_1 E_3 E_1 \Rightarrow E_1^2 E_2 E_1 \Rightarrow E_2^2 E_1, \qquad (A.1)$$

$$E_5 \Rightarrow E_3 E_2 \Rightarrow E_1 E_2^2 \Rightarrow E_2 E_1 E_2 \Rightarrow E_2^2 E_1, \qquad (A.2)$$

$$E_5 \Rightarrow E_2 E_3 \Rightarrow E_2^2 E_1. \qquad (A.3)$$

Equations (A.1)–(A.3) show that $E_2^2 E_1$ delivers the global minimum.

For comparison let us consider sub-sequences 2-1-2 in Table A.2 and 2-2-1 in Table A.3.

In bold are indicated the values of $n_k(20), n_k(15), n_k(10), n_k(5)$, where $k = 1, 2, 3$. They are the same in cases 2-2-1 and 2-1-2, and 11.6% smaller in case 1-2-2. Indeed: $14,357/12,863 = 15,76/1,412 = 1.11615$,

$$E_1^3 E_2 \Rightarrow E_2 E_1 E_2 \Leftarrow E_2 E_1^3 \qquad E_2^2 E_1$$

$$\Uparrow \qquad\qquad \Uparrow \qquad\qquad \Uparrow \qquad \Uparrow$$

$$E_1^2 E_2 E_1 \Leftarrow E_1^2 E_3 \qquad E_3 E_2 \Leftarrow \qquad E_3 E_1^2 \Rightarrow E_2 E_1^3$$

$$\Uparrow \qquad \Uparrow \qquad \Uparrow$$

$$E_1 E_2^2 \Leftarrow E_1 E_4 \ \Leftarrow\ E_5 \Rightarrow E_4 E_1 \ \Rightarrow\ \ E_2^2 E_1$$

$$\Uparrow \qquad \Downarrow \qquad \Downarrow \qquad\qquad \Uparrow$$

$$E_1 E_2 E_1^2 \Leftarrow E_1 E_3 E_1 \qquad E_1 E_3 E_1 \ \Rightarrow\ E_1^2 E_2 E_1$$

Fig. A.1   Direct comparison of local minima.

Table A.1   Optimal quotients {sub-sequence 1-2-2}.

12,863	9,046	3,817	**1,412**	993	419	**155**	109	46	**17**	12	5	2	1
Stack	1	2	2	1	2	2	1	2	2	1	2	2	***

Table A.2   Sub-sequence 2-2-1 of quotients.

14,357	5,311	3,735	**1,576**	583	410	**173**	64	45	**19**	7	5	2	1
Stack	2	1	2	2	1	2	2	1	2	2	1	2	***

Table A.3   Sub-sequence 2-1-2 of quotients.

14,357	6,058	2,241	**1,576**	665	246	**173**	73	27	**19**	8	3	2	1
Stack	2	2	1	2	2	1	2	2	1	2	2	1	***

$173/155 = 1.116123$, $19/17 = 1.11765$. Although the ratio is small, yet for $s = 200$ $n_2(200)/n_1(200) = 3.00064 \approx 3$. and for $s = 2000$

$$n_2(2000)/n_1(2000) = 3.00064^{10} = 59175.66.$$

A.2. Separability: Proof of Proposition 8.1

Let

$$(d_0, e_0) = (1,0), (d_k, e_k)^T = E^k(1,0)^T,$$

$$w_k := e_k/d_k. \tag{A2.1}$$

(a) If $w_0 < v$, then for every $k \geq 1$

$$w_k < v. \tag{A2.2}$$

(b) If $u_0 > v$, then for every $k \geq 1$

$$u_k > v. \tag{A2.3}$$

Proof. {by induction} : Consider $w_0 = 0 < v$, then $w_1 = 1/3 < v$.
Let

$$w_i < v \quad \text{for all } 1 \leq i \leq k \quad \text{and} \quad w_{k+1} \geq v, \tag{A2.4}$$

then from definition (8.1)

$$w_{k+1} = (1 + w_k)/(3 + 2w_k) > v. \tag{A2.5}$$

Therefore,

$$w_k \geq (3v - 1)/(1 \quad 2v) - \left(\sqrt{3} - 1\right)/2.$$

The contradiction proves Part (a) of Proposition 8.1. Part (b) of this Proposition can be analogously proved. Q.E.D.

A.3. Exact Presentation for Tight Upper Bound

A.3.1. Auxiliary arrays $t_i(k)$

Let $s = 3m + i$, $i = s \bmod 3$.
Let

$$w(s) = w(3m + i) = g_i u^s + h_i v^s. \tag{A3.1}$$

Consider auxiliary sequences

$$t_i(m) = \begin{cases} \alpha_i x_i^m + \beta_i y_i^m & \text{if } m \text{ is } even \\ \gamma_i x_i^m + \delta_i y_i^m & \text{if } m \text{ is } odd \end{cases}, \tag{A3.2}$$

where $\alpha_i, \beta_i, \gamma_i, \delta_i, x_i$ and y_i are unknowns, and

$$|y_i| < 1. \tag{A3.3}$$

Yet, let

$$t_i(2m) = 2t_i(2m - 1) + t_i(2m - 2), \quad \text{and}$$
$$t_i(2m + 1) = t_i(2m) + t_i(2m - 1) \tag{A3.4}$$

that satisfy the following initial conditions:

$$t_i(0) = \begin{cases} 1 & \text{if } i = 0 \\ 2 & \text{if } i = 1, 2 \end{cases}, \quad t_i(1) = \begin{cases} 2 & \text{if } i = 0 \\ 3 & \text{if } i = 1. \\ 5 & \text{if } i = 2 \end{cases} \tag{A3.5}$$

Then all unknowns must satisfy the following two systems of equations

$$\begin{cases} \alpha_i x_i^2 - 2\gamma_i x_i - \alpha_i = 0 \\ \gamma_i x_i^2 - \alpha_i x_i - \gamma_i = 0 \end{cases}, \tag{A3.6}$$

and

$$\begin{cases} \beta_i y_i^2 - 2\delta_i y_i - \beta_i = 0 \\ \delta_i y_i^2 - \beta_i y_i - \delta_i = 0 \end{cases}. \tag{A3.7}$$

System of equations (A3.6) is consistent for every $i = 0, 1, 2$ if and only if $\gamma_i = \pm\alpha_i/\sqrt{2}$. Indeed, multiply the first equation in (A3.6) by γ_i and the second equation by α_i and subtract one from another. Since $x_i \neq 0$, then $\alpha_i^2 = 2\gamma_i^2$.

Analogously, system of equation (A3.7) is consistent for every $i = 0, 1, 2$ if and only if $\delta_i = \pm\beta_i/\sqrt{2}$. These observations imply that for every $i = 0, 1, 2$ $x_i = \pm\sqrt{2 + \sqrt{3}}$, $y_i = \pm\sqrt{2 - \sqrt{3}} = 1/x_i$, and $|y_i| < 1$.

Values of α_i and β_i for every $i = 0, 1, 2$ can be determined from the initial conditions (A3.5). For example, $\alpha_0 = (1 + \sqrt{3})/2$ and $\beta_0 = (1 - \sqrt{3})/2$.

Finally, select $\alpha_i = \pm\sqrt{2}\gamma_i$ and $\beta_i = \pm\sqrt{2}\delta_i$.

Then

$$t_i(m) = \begin{cases} \alpha_i(\pm x_i)^m + \beta_i(\pm 1/x_i)^m, & \text{if } m \text{ is } even \\ [\pm\alpha_i(\pm x_i)^m + \beta_i(\pm 1/x_i)^m]/\sqrt{2}, & \text{if } m \text{ is } odd \end{cases}, \tag{A3.8}$$

where in all expressions either *plus* sign or *minus* sign must be taken simultaneously. This observation renders a simplification for (A3.8):

$$t_i(m) = \begin{cases} \alpha_i x_i^m + \beta_i/x_i^m, & \text{if } m \text{ is } even \\ (\alpha_i x_i^m + \beta_i/x_i^m)/\sqrt{2}, & \text{if } m \text{ is } odd \end{cases}. \tag{A3.9}$$

Chapter 25

New Algorithm Can Be Computed

1. Introduction

In this chapter using a simple example we demonstrate that algorithms not only compute, but *can* also *be computed*. For the sake of brevity, we discuss how to compute an algorithm that multiplies two complex numbers faster, than the direct multiplication. We indicate that the same approach of a parametric representation of algorithms can be applied to *compute* algorithms for multiplication of polynomials.

2. Multiplication of Complex Numbers

Let us consider multiplication of two complex numbers G and H:

$$GH := (a + bi)(c + di) = A + Bi, \quad \text{where } A := ac - bd, \quad B := ad + bc.$$
$$\tag{2.1}$$

Let us demonstrate that in order to find GH we need to perform *three* {rather than *four*} multiplications of their components a, b, c, and d. The goal is to find how to compute A and B, {rather than to compute ac, ad, bc, and bd, and only then A and B}.

Consider for $k = 1, 2, 3$

$$p_k := (ax_k + by_k)(cu_k + dv_k), \tag{2.2}$$

$$\sum_{k=1}^{3} p_k s_k = ac - bd, \tag{2.3}$$

$$\sum_{k=1}^{3} p_k t_k = ad + bc, \tag{2.4}$$

where for $k = 1, 2, 3$, s_k, t_k, u_k, v_k, x_k, and y_k are *unknown parameters* that can assume three values only: -1, 1, or 0.

Substituting all p_k from (2.2) into (2.3) and (2.4), and then collecting all terms with the components ac, ad, bc, and bd, and finally equalizing the left and right parts in Eqs. (2.3) and (2.4), we find that all parameters must satisfy the following nonlinear system of equations:

$$\begin{cases} s_1 u_1 x_1 + s_2 u_2 x_2 + s_3 u_3 x_3 = 1 \\ s_1 u_1 y_1 + s_2 u_2 y_2 + s_3 u_3 y_3 = 0 \\ s_1 v_1 x_1 + s_2 v_2 x_2 + s_3 v_3 x_3 = 0 \\ s_1 v_1 y_1 + s_2 v_2 y_2 + s_3 v_3 y_3 = -1 \end{cases} , \qquad (2.5)$$

$$\begin{cases} t_1 u_1 x_1 + t_2 u_2 x_2 + t_3 u_3 x_3 = 0 \\ t_1 u_1 y_1 + t_2 u_2 y_2 + t_3 u_3 y_3 = 1 \\ t_1 v_1 x_1 + t_2 v_2 x_2 + t_3 v_3 x_3 = 0 \\ t_1 v_1 y_1 + t_2 v_2 y_2 + t_3 v_3 y_3 = 1 \end{cases} . \qquad (2.6)$$

There are 18 variables and 8 equations {independent of the inputs a, b, c and d}. Therefore, there are 10 independent variables, i.e., there are at most $3^{10} = 59,049$ possible combinations. This number can be further reduced by taking into account symmetrical properties of Eqs. (2.2)–(2.6).

A set of all variables s_k, t_k, u_k, v_k, x_k, and y_k that satisfies all equations in (2.5) and (2.6), *parametrically* describes an algorithm for multiplication of complex numbers. Thus, the system of equations (2.5) and (2.6), solved once, leads to discovery of an algorithm, i.e., *algorithms can be computed.*

The system of equations (2.5) and (2.6) implies that

$$\sum_{k=1}^{3} (s_k + t_k)(u_k + v_k)(x_k + y_k) = 2, \qquad (2.7)$$

and that the number of required additions D satisfies the inequality

$$D \leq \sum_{k=1}^{3} (|s_k| + |t_k| + |u_k| + |v_k| + |x_k| + |y_k|) - 8. \qquad (2.8)$$

Table 2.1 provides an example of a solution to the system of equations (2.5) and (2.6).

Table 2.1 Feasible variables.

k	s_k	t_k	u_k	v_k	x_k	y_k
1	0	1	1	1	1	-1
2	1	1	1	0	0	1
3	1	-1	0	1	1	0

Thus, $p_1 = (a - b)(c + d)$, $p_2 = bc$, $p_3 = ad$, hence

$$A = p_2 + p_3, \quad B = p_1 + p_2 - p_3. \tag{2.9}$$

Therefore, the computed algorithm requires *three* multiplications and $D = 5$, while the direct multiplication of two complex numbers requires *four* multiplications of real numbers and *two* additions. It is also easy to check that the identity (2.7) holds.

Addition of two n-digit-long real integers requires $T_a(n) = \Theta(n)$ digital operations {table look-ups}. Multiplication of two n-digits-long real integers requires $T_m(n) = \Theta(n^2)$ digital operations {table look-ups}. Since $T_m(n) \gg T_a(n)$, then the speed-up of time complexity is equal

$$S = \frac{4T_m(n) + 2T_a(n)}{3T_m(n) + 5T_a(n)} = 4(1 + o(n))/3 \approx 1.333\ldots, \tag{2.10}$$

i.e., 33.3% faster.

Although faster algorithms for multiplication of polynomials and for matrix multiplication are described in Winograd (1973), Pan (1984), and Strassen (1969) respectively, neither an explanation nor a systematic methodology is provided *how* these algorithms were discovered. In some sense, *the parametric representation is a meta-algorithm*, which provides a systematic methodology helping *to discover new algorithms*.

An analogous parametric approach can be applied to compute faster algorithms for multiplication of polynomials, for matrix multiplication and for arithmetic operations with multi-digit large integers. The latter is especially important for encryption algorithms.

3. Multiplication of Polynomials of mth Degree

A "traditional" algorithm has time complexity $T_0(m) = \Theta(m^2)$.

Let $T_1(m)$ be time-complexity required to multiply two polynomials of degree m. Firstly, we can compute an algorithm for multiplication of two *quadratic* polynomials, which requires *six* (rather than *nine*) multiplications of their coefficients. Then, using divide-and-conquer approach, we can apply this algorithm recursively, taking into account that

$$T_1(m) = 6T_1(m/3) + o(m), \quad T_1(1) = 1. \tag{3.1}$$

The recursive relation (3.1) (Dobrushkin, 2010) implies that

$$T_1(m) = \Theta(m^{1+\log_3 2}) = \Theta(m^{1.631\ldots}), \tag{3.2}$$

which is substantially faster, than the direct multiplication with complexity $T_0(m) = \Theta(m^2)$.

By considering *first-degree* polynomials as basic blocks for polynomial multiplication, we can compute an algorithm, that requires *three* (not *four*) multiplications.

Using the recursion

$$T_2(m) = 3T_2(m/2) + o(m), \quad T_2(1) = 1,$$

we reduce the complexity to

$$T_2(m) = \Theta(m^{1.585}). \tag{3.3}$$

4. Reduction of Complexity

Let us consider

$$\sum_{k=1}^{3} (s_k + t_k)(u_k + v_k)(x_k + y_k) = 2. \tag{4.1}$$

I. Let

$$A(k) := (s_k + t_k)(u_k + v_k)(x_k + y_k).$$

Using symmetricity of constraints on control parameters, we can reduce the number of possible combinations.

Let us consider only cases where $A(1) \leq A(2) \leq A(3)$. Since every parenthesis can only assume values -2, -1, 0, 1, or 2, then every $A(k)$ can only be -8, -4, -2, -1, 0, 1, 2, 4 or 8.

Thus only eight combinations are possible:

$$-8 < 2 < 8, \quad -4 < -2 < 8, \quad -4 < 2 < 4, \quad -2 < 0 < 2,$$
$$-2 < 2 = 2, \quad -1 = -1 < 4, \quad 0 = 0 < 2, \quad \text{or} \quad 0 < 1 = 1.$$

The first combination is not feasible, because it requires that all

$$s(k) = -1, \quad \text{and} \quad t(k) = -1,$$

and all other variables are equal *one*. However, these variables do not satisfy any of the equations in (2.5) and (2.6).

II. More complicated case is multiplication of quadratic and linear polynomials i.e., case 3×2. It is easy to find an algorithm that performs polynomial multiplication (PM, for short) for *five* multiplications of components:

$$t := (a + b)(c + d + e), \quad q := ac, \quad r := bd,$$
$$s := bf, \quad p := (a + b)(c + d).$$

Then

$$A = ac = q, \quad D = s, \quad B = p - q - r, \quad C = t - (A + B + D).$$

III. Let us now consider 3×3 case, i.e., multiplication of two quadratic polynomials.

Consider

$$t := (b + c)(e + f), \quad q := ad, \quad r := cf, \quad s := (a + b)(d + e), \quad u := be$$

and

$$p := (a + b + c)(d + e + f).$$

Then

$$A = q, \quad m := s - u, \quad B = m - q, \quad C = p - (m + n),$$
$$D = t - (u + r), \quad E = r.$$

Hence, 6 multiplications and 14 additions are used.

To reduce complexity in (3.2), it is necessary to find $\log_3 x < 1.585$. That requires *five* or less multiplications. It is easy to find A, B, C, D and E using *six* multiplications:

Five multiplications would reduce the exponent in complexity to 1.465.

Let us consider a formal parametric approach in order to find an algorithm for fast PM of *two quadratic polynomials*.

Let

$$P_2(x) = \sum_{i=1}^{3} a_i x^i \quad \text{and} \quad Q_2(x) = \sum_{r=1}^{3} b_r x^r. \tag{4.2}$$

Consider

$$p_k := \left(\sum_{i=1}^{3} a_i u_{ik} \right) \left(\sum_{r=1}^{3} b_r w_{rk} \right), \tag{4.3}$$

$$q_t := \sum_{k=1}^{n} p_k s_{kt} = \sum_{k} \sum_{i} \sum_{r} a_i b_r u_{ik} w_{rk} s_{kt}, \tag{4.4}$$

$$q_t := \sum_{k=1}^{n} p_k s_{kt} = \sum_{i,r} a_i b_r \left(\sum_{i} u_{ik} w_{rk} s_{kt} \right), \tag{4.5}$$

$$q_1 := \left(\sum_{k} u_{ik} w_{rk} s_{k1} \right) = \begin{cases} 1, & i = r = 3 \\ 0 & \text{otherwise} \end{cases}, \tag{4.6}$$

$$q_2 := \left(\sum_{k} u_{ik} w_{rk} s_{k2} \right) = \begin{cases} 1, & i + r = 5 \\ 0 & \text{otherwise} \end{cases}, \tag{4.7}$$

$$q_3 := \left(\sum_k u_{ik} w_{rk} s_{k3} \right) = \begin{cases} 1, & i + r = 4, \\ 0 & \text{otherwise} \end{cases}, \tag{4.8}$$

$$q_4 := \left(\sum_k u_{ik} w_{rk} s_{k4} \right) = \begin{cases} 1, & i + r = 3, \\ 0 & \text{otherwise} \end{cases}, \tag{4.9}$$

$$q_5 := \left(\sum_k u_{ik} w_{rk} s_{k5} \right) = \begin{cases} 1, & i =, r = 1 \\ 0 & \text{otherwise} \end{cases}. \tag{4.10}$$

In general, for every $t = 1, 2, \ldots, 5$

$$q_t = \sum_{k=1}^{n} u_{ik} w_{rk} s_{tk} = \begin{cases} 1, & \text{if } i + k = 7 - t \\ 0 & \text{otherwise} \end{cases}. \tag{4.11}$$

The following identity holds:

$$\sum_{k=1}^{n} \left(\sum_{i=1}^{3} u_{ik} \sum_{r=1}^{3} w_{rk} \sum_{t=1}^{5} s_{kt} \right) = 9. \tag{4.12}$$

The system of equations has 55 unknowns $\{15 \ u_{ik}\text{'s}, 15 \ w_{rk}\text{'s}, 25 \ s_{kt}\text{'s}\}$ and 45 independent equations. Thus, there are 10 degrees of freedom.

Since each unknown can assume only ± 1 or 0, then $3^{10} = 59,049$ independent combinations must be checked in order to find a solution to the system of equations.

III. Case 4×4, i.e., multiplication of two cubic polynomials. We can do it for nine multiplications using recursive approach.

Compute *nine* products:

$$\begin{aligned}
p_1 &= ae, \quad p_2 = bf, \quad p_3 = cg, \quad p_4 = dh, \\
p_5 &= (a+b)(e+f), \quad p_6 = (c+d)(g+h), \\
p_7 &= (a+c)(e+g), \quad p_8 = (b+d)(f+h), \\
p_9 &= (a+b+c+d)(e+f+g+h).
\end{aligned}$$

Then the diagonals are

$$\begin{aligned}
A &= ae, \quad B = (a+b)(e+f) - A - bf, \\
C &= (a+c)(e+g) - A - cg + bf, \\
D &= (a+b+c+d)(e+f+g+h) - (A+B+C+E+F+G), \\
E &= (b+d)(f+h) - bf - dh + cg, \\
F &= (c+d)(g+h) - G - cg, \quad G = dh.
\end{aligned}$$

Remark 4.1. Every expression in products is with positive components, only the combinations of products have negative coefficients -1. That can reduce substantially the number of different candidates for solutions. This may not be correct if we try to compute $A, B, \ldots, G$ for *eight* multiplications or fewer. To reduce complexity in (3.2) it is necessary to make multiplication for *eight* operations. *Eight* operations reduce the exponent to 1.5.

5. Meta-Algorithm

To discover an algorithm, consider the system of equations:

for $i = 0, 1$

      for $r = 0, 1$

            for $t = 0, 1, 2$ **do**

{input}: **if** $i + r = t$ **then** $q(i, r, t) = 1$

                else $q(i, r, t) = 0$,

{solve the system of equations}:

$$
u(i,0)w(r,0)x(t,0) + u(i,1)w(r,1)x(t,1)
$$
$$
+ u(i,2)w(r,2)x(t,2) = q(i,r,t), \tag{5.1}
$$

All variables $= \{-1, 0, 1\}$.

The system of equations (25) can be written in a more explicit form:

if $(i = r = t = 0)$ **or** $(i = 0, r = 1, t = 1)$ **or** $(i = 1, r = 0, t = 1)$

            or $(i = 1, r = 1, t = 2)$

    then $u(i,0)w(r,0)x(t,0) + u(i,1)w(r,1)x(t,1)$

    $+ u(i,2)w(r,2)x(t,2) = 1$,

{totally 4 equations},

    else $u(i,0)w(r,0)x(t,0) + u(i,1)w(r,1)x(t,1)$

    $+ u(i,2)w(r,2)x(t,2) = 0$,

{totally eight equations}.

Hence, all together there are 12 equations and 21 variables.

Definition 5.1. A combination of variables is called **feasible**, if it satisfies the system of equations (5.1).

Remark 5.2. Not all these combinations of variables are *feasible*! Actually only relatively small number of combinations is feasible.

Quick check: A feasible combination of variables must satisfy the following equation:

$$\sum_{k=0}^{2} [u(0,k) + u(1,k)][w(0,k) + w(1,k)][x(0,k) + x(1,k) + x(2,k)] = 4.$$

$$(5.2)$$

6. Example of Feasible Solution

An example of a feasible combination of variables is presented in Tables 6.1–6.3.

Table 6.1 $u(i,k)$.

$k \backslash i$	$i = 0$	$i = 1$
$k = 0$	-1	0
$k = 1$	-1	1
$k = 2$	0	1

Table 6.2 $w(r,k)$.

$k \backslash r$	$r = 0$	$r = 1$
$k = 0$	1	0
$k = 1$	1	-1
$k = 2$	0	1

Table 6.3 $x(t,k)$.

$k \backslash t$	$t = 0$	$t = 1$	$t = 2$
$k = 0$	-1	-1	0
$k = 1$	0	1	0
$k = 2$	0	1	1

7. Enumeration of Combinations of Variables

Consider

$$z = \sum_{k=0}^{2} 3^k u(0,k) + 3^3 \sum_{k=0}^{2} 3^k u(1,k) + 3^6 \sum_{k=0}^{2} 3^k w(0,k) + 3^9 \sum_{k=0}^{2} 3^k w(1,k)$$

$$+ 3^{12} \sum_{k=0}^{2} 3^k t(0,k) + 3^{15} \sum_{k=0}^{2} 3^k t(1,k) + 3^{18} \sum_{k=0}^{2} 3^k t(2,k) + 1.$$

Remark 7.1. The above formula demonstrates the relationship between z and all variables $u(i,k), w(r,k), x(t,k)$.

Variable z is changing on interval $[1, 3^{21}]$, i.e., z is counting all possible combinations. Given a combination, one can find a corresponding *counter z*.

It is easy to find the counter z for simple cases. Say, if all variables are equal *zero*, then $z = 1$.

If all variables are equal *one*, then $z = (3^{21} - 1)/2 + 1$.

If all variables are equal 2, then $z = 3^{21}$.

Remark 7.2. if a variable $x = 2$ then $x = -1$.

vars:

for $k = 0, 1, 2$ $\quad u(0, k) = \{0, 1\}, w(0, k) = \{0, 1\},$

$\quad\quad\quad\quad\quad\quad\quad u(1, k) = \{-1, 0, 1\}, w(1, k) = \{-1, 0, 1\},$

for $k = 0, 1, 2,$ $\quad$ **for** $t = 0, 1, 2$ $\quad x(t, k) = \{-1, 0, 1\}.$

Since **for** $k = 0, 1, 2$ $u(0, k) = \{0, 1\}$, $w(0, k) = \{0, 1\}$, i.e., these variables can assume two values only, hence there are $2^6 = 64$ combinations for these variables. Remaining 15 variables can assume three values each, thus there are 3^{15} combinations for these variables.

The total number N of combinations of variables to check is equal $N = 64 \times 3^{15}$. This is 11.4 times smaller, than the previously considered.

In general, if the counter z is given, one can find the corresponding combination of values of all variables:

procedure $\{CombinationOfValuesOfVariables\}$

for $z = 1, 3^{21}$ **do**

$\quad u(0, 0) = z \bmod 3,$ **if** $u(0, 0) = 2$ **then** $z := z + 1,$ $\{$**goto** to the next combination$\}$,

$$z := [z - u(0, 0)]/3,$$

$\quad u(0, 1) = z \bmod 3,$ **if** $u(0, 1) = 2$ **then** $z := z + 1,$ $\{$**goto** to the next combination$\}$,

$$z := [z - u(0, 1)]/3,$$

$\quad u(0, 2) = z \bmod 3,$ **if** $u(0, 2) = 2$ **then** $z := z + 1,$ $\{$**goto** to the next combination$\}$,

$$z := [z - u(0, 2)]/3,$$

$\quad u(1, 0) = z \bmod 3,$ **if** $u(1, 0) = 2$ **then** $u(1, 0) = -1,$

$$z := [z - u(1, 0)]/3,$$

$$\cdots\cdots\cdots\cdots\cdots\cdots\cdots$$

$\quad u(1, 2) = z \bmod 3,$ **if** $u(1, 0) = 2$ **then** $u(1, 2) = -1,$

$$z := [z - u(1, 2)]/3,$$

$w(0,0) = z \bmod 3$, **if** $w(0,0) = 2$ **then** $z := z + 1$, {**goto** to the next combination},

$$z := [z - w(0,0)]/3,$$

$w(0,2) = z \bmod 3$, **if** $w(0,2) = 2$ **then** $z := z + 1$, {**goto** to the next combination},

$$z := [z - w(0,2)]/3,$$

$$w(1,0) = z \bmod 3, \text{ \textbf{if} } w(1,0) = 2 \text{ \textbf{then} } w(1,0) = -1,$$

$$z := [z - w(1,0)]/3, \text{ etc.}$$

8. Reduction of CPU Time

(1) **If** *quick check* (5.2) does not hold, **then** $z := z + 1$ {**goto** the next combination},

   else check the system of equations (5.1).

(2) **If** at least one equation does not hold, **then** $z := z + 1$:   {**goto** the next combination}.

(3) There are *no* feasible solutions on the interval $[1, 3^3 + 3^6 + 3^9 + \cdots + 3^{18}]$.

Although the problem is time consuming, it must be solved only once to discover an algorithm. The existing Petaflop computers, and Exaflops, forthcoming in couple years, and not so distant quantum computers can become efficient tools for this type of automated research.

Chapter 26

Search for Period of Odd Function

1. Introduction and Problem Statement

In algorithms searching for a minimum or maximum of a periodic function of one variable it is assumed that the period is known (Verkhovsky, 1986; 1989).

However, if the period is unknown, many efficient algorithms are not applicable.

A survey of methods detecting a period of a function is provided in Cohen (1993). Another detailed survey of ideas is provided in Sedgewick et al. (1982). They include "baby-step giant-step" algorithm (Shanks, 1972), Pollard rho-method (Pollard, 1975), Floyd's cycle-searching algorithm and Brent's modifications (Brent, 1980). Rho-method is based on an idea of random mapping described in Knuth (1981). The ideas on random mapping are summarized in Flajolet and Odlyzko (1990).

In this chapter, we have considered a search algorithm for a period of odd functions. The ideas discussed below were published in Verkhovsky (2002).

Let us consider two modes of computation:

- Recursively-computable function
- Random-access computable function

Definition 1.1. A function $f(x)$ is a periodic if for every x and every integer m holds $f(x) = f(x + mp)$, where an integer p is its period;

Definition 1.2. A function $f(x)$ is *odd* symmetric if for every x

$$f(x) = -f(-x); \tag{1.1}$$

Examples of *odd* functions with known periods:

$$\cos x = -\cos(\pi/2 - x); \quad \sinh x = -\sinh(-x); \quad \sin x = -\sin(\pi/2 - x).$$
$$(1.2)$$

In the following considerations we assume that

1. $f(x)$ is computable for every *integer* x; in more general case $f(x)$ is computable for every $x := ks$ where k are integers and s is a fixed positive number.
2. For every integer $u f(x)$ is one-to-one function on an interval $[u, p + u]$: for every integer v there is one and only one w such that $f(v) = w$; and for every w there is at most one v such that $v = f^{-1}(w)$.
3. Let $1 \leq p \leq h$, where h is known.

The goal is to describe an algorithm that finds the minimal integer p using the smallest number of probes of the function $f(x)$.

Properties of $f(x)$:

1. $f(0) = 0$.
2. $f(x) = -f(p - x)$. Indeed, since $f(x) = -f(-x)$; then the definition of periodic function implies that for every x

$$f(x) = -f(-x) = -f(p - x). \tag{1.3}$$

3. If $f(x) = f(z) \neq 0$, then $z - x = kp$. $\hspace{2cm}$ (1.4)
4. If $f(x) = -f(z)$, then $x + z = kp$, where k is an integer. $\hspace{1cm}$ (1.5)

2. Search for Period p

Theorem 2.1. Let us consider n points $x_1 < x_2 < \cdots < x_n$: where $x_1 = 1$; $x_2 = 2; \ldots, x_m = m$; and for every $k = 1, \ldots, s$

$$x_{m+k} := 3m + 1 + (k - 1)(2m + 1), \tag{2.1}$$

then for every integer u on the interval $[1, 2m + s(2m + 1)]$ there exists at least one pair of points (x_i, x_j) such that

$$\text{either } x_i + x_j = u, \text{ or } x_i - x_j = u; \text{ or } 2x_i = u. \tag{2.2}$$

3. Selection of Optimal Search Parameters

Since $p \leq h$, then it is sufficient to select such m and n that

$$2m + n(2m + 1) = h. \tag{3.1}$$

To minimize the total number of probes $s = m + n$, express $n = (h - 2m)/(2m + 1)$ and find the first derivative of

$$s(m) = m + (h - 2m)/(2m + 1).$$

Then from $s'(m) = 0$ we derive

$$m^o = \sqrt{(h + 1)/2} - 1/2. \tag{3.2}$$

Therefore,

$$n^o = (\sqrt{h/2} - 1)[1 + o(h)]. \tag{3.3}$$

Example 3.1. Let $p < h = 20,000$; then $m = 10$, i.e., for $i = 1, \ldots, 100$ $x_i = i$ and $x_{101} = 300$; $x_{102} = 501$; $x_{103} = 702$; $\ldots$; $x_{199} = 20,000$.

Suppose that $p = 11,067$; then the period p is detectable since $f(x_{155}) = f(x_{87})$, i.e.,

$$p = x_{155} - x_{87} = 11154 - 87 = 11067. \tag{3.4}$$

4. The Problem

Proposition 4.1. Let S be a set of all search strategies σ and F be a set of all odd symmetric functions f; let $N(f, \sigma, h)$ be the number of probes of function f required to find its period p if we use the search strategy σ and $1 \le p \le h$; and let $W(\sigma, h)$ be the largest number of probes required in the worst case of function f if the search strategy σ is applied; then

$$W(h, \sigma) = \max_{f \in F} N(f, \sigma, h). \tag{4.1}$$

Proposition 4.2. Let $B(h)$ be the smallest number of probes in the worst case of function f required to find its period p if we use the *best* search strategy σ^o and $1 \le p \le h$, then

$$B(h) = W(h, \sigma^o) = \min_{\sigma \in S} W(h, \sigma) = \min_{\sigma \in S} \max_{f \in F} N(f, \sigma, h). \tag{4.2}$$

5. Search for Optimal Search Strategy σ^o

Let

$$1 \le p \le h - 1. \tag{5.1}$$

The problem: Let $M = \{u_1, u_2, \ldots, u_m\}$ be a set of m integer and let $1 \le u_1 < u_2 < \cdots < u_m$.

Let for all $1 \leq i < k \leq m$

$$u_i + u_k = a_{ik}; \quad A = \{a_{ik}\}, \tag{5.2}$$

$$u_k - u_i = d_{ik}; \quad D = \{d_{ik}\}, \tag{5.3}$$

$$b_i = 2u_i, \quad \text{and} \quad B = \{b_i\}. \tag{5.4}$$

Then each set A and B has $m(m-1)/2$ distinct elements. The goal is to select all variables $\{u_1, u_2, \ldots, u_m\}$ in such a way that the union of all four sets $C = A \cup B \cup D \cup M$ will have the largest contiguous interval $[1, c(m)]$ of integers.

Let $|N|$ denote the number of elements in the set N, then

$$|A| + |B| + |D| + |M| = m^2 + m \geq |C|, \tag{5.5}$$

since not all elements in the sets A, B, D, and M are distinct.

Hence, the upper bound for $c(m)$ is determined by inequality:

$$c(m) \leq m(m+1). \tag{5.6}$$

Example 5.1. If $m = 2$, then $c(2) = 5$. Indeed, select $u_1 = 1$, $u_2 = 4$, then $C = \{1, 2, 3, 4, 5\}$.

In Table 5.1 $u_0 = m$, $u_1 = 3m + 2$, $u_2 = 5m + 4$, $u_3 = 7m + 5$, $u_4 = 9m + 7$, $u_5 = 11m + 8$, and for $k \geq 5$

$$u_{k+1} = u_k + 2m + \begin{cases} 2, & k \bmod 3 \neq 1 \\ 1, & k \bmod 3 = 1 \end{cases}. \tag{5.7}$$

Table 5.1   Computation of all gaps.

	$u_k(m)$	Gaps as function of m
$k = 0$	m	$2m + 1 = u_3 - u_2$
$k = 1$	$3m + 2$	$4m + 3 = u_3 - u_1$
$k = 2$	$5m + 4$	*There is no gap*
$k = 3$	$7m + 5$	$8m + 6 = u_1 + u_2$
$k = 4$	$9m + 7$	*There is no gap*
$k = 5$	$11m + 8$	$12m + 9 = u_1 + u_4$
$k = 6$	$13m + 10$	$14m + 11 = u_2 + u_4$
$k = 7$	$15m + 12$	*There is no gap*
$k = 8$	$17m + 14$	$18m + 15 = u_1 + u_7$
$k = 9$	$19m + 16$	$20m + 17 = u_2 + u_7$

Chapter 27

Optimized Search for Maximum of Function on Large Intervals[*]

In this chapter, we have considered a parallel algorithm that detects a maximizer of a unimodal function $f(x)$ defined and computable at every integer point on an unbounded semi-interval $(0, \infty)$. The algorithm consists of two modes: scanning and detecting. Search diagrams are introduced as a way to describe parallel searching algorithms on unbounded intervals. Dynamic programming equations, combined with a series of liner programming problems, describe relations between results for every pair of successive evaluations of the function in parallel. Properties of optimal search strategies are derived from these equations. Complexity analysis shows that, if the maximizer is located on a priori unknown interval $(n - 1, n]$, then in the worst case it can be detected within this interval for the number $c_p(n)$ of parallel evaluations of $f(x)$ equal $\lceil 2 \log_{p/2+1}(n + 1) \rceil - 1$, if the number of processors p is *even*. However, if p is *odd*, then $c_p(n) = \lceil 2 \log_{u(p)}(n + 1) \rceil - 1 + o(n)$, where for a large number of processors $u(p) \to (p + 3)/2$. The optimal parallel search algorithm for a maximizer of a unimodal unbounded function is provided in constructive terms.

1. Introduction and Problem Statement

The unbounded search problem, as described in Bentley and Yao (1976), is a search for a key in a sorted unbounded sequence. The goal of the optimal

[*]I express my appreciation to Willard Miranker, Shmuel Winograd and Henryk Wozniakowski for their comments and discussions.

unbounded search is to find this key for a smallest number of comparisons in the worst case. The authors describe an *infinite* series of sequential algorithms (i.e., using a single processor), where each algorithm is more accurate, than the previous algorithm. In Beigel (1990), the unbounded search problem is equivalent to the following two-player game. Player A chooses an arbitrary positive integer n. Player B may ask whether the integer x is less than n. The "cost" of the searching algorithm is the number of guesses that B must use in order to determine n. The goal of the player B is to use a smallest number of these guesses in the worst case. This number is a function $c(n)$. The author of that paper provides lower and upper bounds on the value of $c(n)$. More results on nearly-optimal algorithms are provided in Reingold and Shen (1991a), and then these results are generalized for a transfinite case in Reingold and Shen (1991b).

As pointed out in Goldstein and Reingold (1993), the problem formulated in Beigel (1990) is equivalent to the search for a maximizer of an unimodal function $f(x)$, where $x \in (0, \infty)$. The goal of the search is to minimize the number of required evaluations of a function $f(x)$ (*probes*, for short) in the worst case, if the maximizer is located on *a priori* unspecified interval $(n - 1, n]$, and where n is a positive integer number. In Goldstein and Reingold (1993), the authors consider the unbounded discrete unimodal *sequential* search for a maximizer. Employing an elaborate apparatus of Kraft's inequality (Goldstein and Reingold, 1993), inverse Fibonacci Ackermann's function and, finally, a repeated diagonalization, they construct a series of algorithms that eventually approach lower bounds on the function $c(n)$.

The general theory of optimal algorithms is provided in Traub and Wozniakowski (1980) and Nemirovsky and Yudin (1983). The problem where f is a unimodal function, defined on a *finite* interval, is analyzed by many authors, and the optimal algorithm is provided and analyzed in Beamer and Wilder (1970), Chasan and Gal (1976), Kiefer (1953), Oliver and Wilde (1964), and Witzgall (1972). Optimal parallel algorithms, searching for a maximum of a unimodal function on a *finite* interval, are discussed in Avriel and Wilde (1966), Gal and Miranker (1977), and Karp and Miranker (1968). The case where f is a *bimodal* function is discussed and analyzed in Verkhovsky (1989), Veroy and Verkhovsky (1986; 1988). The case where additional information is available is studied in Gal (1971) and Neymark and Strongin (1966). The optimal search algorithm for the maximum of a unimodal function on a finite interval is generalized for a case of multi-extremal function in Horst and Pardalos (1994), Shubert

(1972), and Timonov (1977). In all these papers, the optimal algorithms are based on the mere fact that a maximizer (minimizer) is located on *a priori known finite* interval K (called the interval of uncertainty). The algorithms employ a procedure that shortens the interval of uncertainty K after every probe. Complexities of related problems are functions of the size of interval K. Search algorithms for two-dimensional and multidimensional unimodal functions are considered respectively in Hoffman and Wolfe (1985) and Kuzovkin (1968).

In this chapter, we consider a parallel algorithm finding a maximizer (or a minimizer) of a function f defined on an *unbounded* interval I of R and computable at every point $x \in I$. Without loss of generality, we assume that $I = (0, \infty)$. It is easy to see that an algorithm, that detects a maximizer, cannot employ the same or analogous strategies as in the finite case, since the interval of uncertainty is infinite.

Definition 1.1. A unimodal function has the following properties: (1) there exists a positive number s, such that $f(x_1) < f(x_2) < f(s)$ for all $0 \le x_1 < x_2 < s$ and $f(s) > f(x_1) > f(x_2)$ for all $s < x_1 < x_2 < \infty$; (2) $f(x)$ is not constant on any subinterval of I. The point s is called a *maximizer* of the function $f(x)$. It is not required that f be a smooth or even a continuous function.

The goal of this chapter is to describe and analyze an algorithm that

(1) detects an interval of length t (t-interval, for short) within which a maximizer of f is located;
(2) uses a minimal number of parallel probes (*p-probes*, for short) in the worst case for the t-detection.

Definition 1.2. An algorithm is called *balanced* if it requires an equal number of probes for both stages (scanning and detection).

Definition 1.3. The described algorithm is minimax (optimal) in the following sense: let F be a set of all unimodal functions $f \in F$ defined on I; S_t be a set of all possible strategies s_t that detect a t-interval that contains a maximizer s of function f; and let $N(f, s_t)$ be the number of p-probes that are required for detection of the maximizer on t-interval using strategy s_t. Then a minimax strategy s_t^o detects the maximizer for a smallest number of p-probes in the worst case of the unbounded function f (Veroy and Verkhovsky, 1986).

Definition 1.3 implies that

$$N(s_t^o) = \min_{s_t \in S_t} \max_{f \in F} N(f, s_t). \tag{1.1}$$

Remark 1.4. Although s is *a priori* unknown to the algorithm designer, it is assumed that its value is *fixed*. Otherwise, the algorithm designer will not be able to provide any algorithm for t-detection of s. Indeed, the adversary can generate a function f that is increasing on any finite subinterval $(0, v) \subset I$.

2. Choice of Next Evaluation Point

2.1. *Sequential search: (single processor case)*

Proposition 2.1. *Let us consider two arbitrary points, L and R that satisfy inequalities $0 < L < R < \infty$. If $f(L) < f(R)$, then a maximizer is greater than L; if $f(L) > f(R)$ then a maximizer is smaller than R; if $f(L) = f(R)$, then a maximizer is greater than L and smaller than R, i.e., $s \in (L, R)$ (Kiefer, 1953; 1957).*

Proof follows immediately from unimodality of the function f.

If $f(L) \geq f(R)$, then a maximizer s is detected on a finite interval, i.e., $s \in (0, R)$. Therefore for t-detection of the maximizer s we can employ Kiefer's algorithm for sequential search (Karp and Miranker, 1968; Kiefer, 1953; 1957) for parallel search.

Let now f be evaluated at two points $q_i := L$ and $q_j := R$, where $0 < L < R < \infty$ and let $f(L) < f(R)$. Two strategies are possible in this case: to evaluate f either at a point $M \in (L, R)$ or at a point $M > R$; {there is no reason to evaluate f at $q < L$, since the Proposition 2.1 guarantees that if $f(L) < f(R)$, then a maximizer is greater than L.

Let us consider a function f with the following properties:

(1) It is increasing on the interval $(L, R - \varepsilon)$.
(2) $f(R - \varepsilon) = f(R) - \delta$, where ε and δ are positive and arbitrary small numbers.
(3) $\lim_{x \to \infty} f(x) = [f(R - \varepsilon) + f(R)]/2$.

Remark 2.1. It is important to keep in mind that we consider worst cases. A further analysis explains a rationale for the choice of function f and the choice of arbitrarily small ε and δ.

2.2. *Comparisons of possible scenarios and the outputs*

Let us consider four scenarios:

A: $q = M \in (L, R)$; **B:** $q = M \notin (L, R)$; $\{M > R\}$; **C:** $s \in [R - \varepsilon, R]$; **D:** $s \notin [R - \varepsilon, R]$.

Two possible outputs: **E:** $f(small) \geq f(large)$; **F:** $f(small) < f(large)$.

(1) **ACE** vs. **BCE:** For many $x = M \in (L, R)$ we can always select such small ε that $M < R - \varepsilon$. Hence for the ACE case detection is impossible, yet for the BCE case the detection is guaranteed by unimodality of $f(x)$.

(2) **ADE** vs. **BDE:** For the ADE case detection is impossible by the same arguments as for the ACE case. Yet for the BCE case detection is guaranteed by unimodality of $f(x)$. In this case $s \in (L, M)$.

(3) **ACF** vs. **BCF:** The interval $(L, M]$, eliminated in the ACF case, is a *proper part* of the interval $(L, R]$, eliminated in the BCF case.

(4) **ADF** vs. **BDF:** the same as in the previous case, i.e., the interval $(L, M]$, eliminated in the ACF case, is also a proper part of the interval $(L, R]$, eliminated in the BCF case.

All four comparisons show that evaluation at a point $M > R$ in all cases provides more information than evaluation at a point $M \in (L, R)$: in the worst case, evaluation at $M \in (L, R)$ provides no information since predictably $f_L < f_R$. It is obvious from the above, that in all cases there is no reason to consider the next evaluation inside interval (L, R).

2.3. *Multiprocessor case*

Let us consider the same function $f(x)$ as in the single processor case. Let evaluation be done at points $M_1, \ldots, M_p$, where p is the number of available processors.

Consider four scenarios:

A: All or a part of the points $M_1, \ldots, M_p$ are *inside* the interval (L, R).

B: All the points $M_1, \ldots, M_p$ are *outside* the interval (L, R), i.e., every point $M_1, \ldots, M_p$ is larger than R; **C:** $s \in [R - \varepsilon, R]$; **D:** $s \notin [R - \varepsilon, R]$.

2.4. *Possible outputs in the worst case*

For both AC and AD scenarios $f(x)$, ε and δ can be selected in such a way, that for all $1 \leq i \leq p$, for which $M_i \in (L, M)$, the inequality $f(M_i) < f(R)$ holds. Hence, taking into account that we are dealing with the worst case, all evaluations inside the interval (L, M) are predictable and, as a result, do not provide any information. That is why all evaluations must be done outside the interval (L, R) if $f(L) < f(R)$.

3. Search as Two-Player Game with Referee

3.1. *Sequential search:* $(p = 1)$

Let us consider two players A and B and a referee. Their game consists of two phases. At *the beginning*, the player A selects a value $s > 0$ and informs the referee about value of s. The player B selects a value t and lets it become known to the player A and to the referee. At *the first phase*, B sequentially selects positive and distinct points $q_1, q_2, \ldots, q_i$. The referee *terminates the first phase* if there are two points q_j and q_k such that $s < q_j$ and $s < q_k$. *The second phase begins* from a state (u_1, v_1, w_1) where $u_1 := q_{j_1}$; $v_1 := q_{j_2}$; $w_1 := q_{j_3}$, where $q_{j_1}, q_{j_2}, q_{j_3}$ are the three largest points.

At the second phase, B selects points and A selects intervals. Let the game be in the state (u_j, v_j, w_j) of the second phase. *The second phase terminates* if $|w_j - u_j| < t$. Otherwise B selects a point x_j such that $u_j < x_j < w_j$ and $x_j \neq v_j$. Then A eliminates either the left-most or the rightmost subinterval (Verkhovsky, 1989). The goal of the player B is to minimize the number of points required to terminate the game. The goal of the player A is to maximize the number of these points.

The adversarial approach for interpretation of the optimal search algorithms is also considered in Beigel (1990) and Gal (1974).

Remark 3.1. It is easy to see that B is an algorithm designer and A is a user that selects the function of f and t is a required accuracy.

3.2. *Multiple-processor search:* $(p \geq 2)$

An optimal parallel search algorithm with p processors has an analogous interpretation. In this case, at the first phase of the game, the player B on his move selects p different points on the interval. The referee *terminates the first phase* if there are at least two points to the right from s. At the beginning of the second phase, the player A selects any two adjacent subintervals and eliminates all other subintervals. In general, at the second phase, B selects points and A selects intervals. More specifically, the player B on his move selects p different points on the interval and the player A on her move selects any two adjacent subintervals and eliminates all other subintervals. The goal of the game is the same as in the case of a single processor case. It is obvious that on the first case of the game the player B must select all points in an increasing order from one p-probe to another.

Remark 3.2. At first, we will describe the optimal unbounded searching algorithm with one processing element (PE, for short). Only after that we will describe and discuss the parallel minimax unbounded search with p PEs. As it will be demonstrated, the case where p is an *even* integer is simpler than the case where p is *odd*.

4. Structure of Unbounded Sequential Search

In the case, if it is known a priori that $s \in K$ and $|K| < \infty$, we can t-detect a maximizer s for at most $(\log_\alpha |K|/t)[1 + o(|K|/t)]$ probes, where

$$\alpha = (1 + \sqrt{5})/2; \tag{4.1}$$

(Verkhovsky, 1989; Veroy and Verkhovsky, 1986).

However, the situation is more complicated, if f is defined on the unbounded interval $I = (0, \infty)$. In this case we divide the entire interval I onto an infinite set of finite subintervals of uncertainty $I_1 := (0, q_1]; I_2 := (q_1, q_2]; \ldots; I_k := (q_{k-1}, q_k]; \ldots$ where

$$I = \bigcup_{k=1}^{\infty} I_k. \tag{4.2}$$

In this chapter we will demonstrate that a minimax search algorithm consists of two major modes: a *scanning* (or expanding) mode and a *detecting* (or contracting) mode. Let us assume for the sake of simplicity of notations that $f_k := f(q_k)$ for all integer k, i.e., f_k is a result of the kth probe.

Definition 4.1. A search algorithm is in the *scanning mode* while for all $q_1 < q_2 < \cdots < q_k$ the function f satisfies the inequalities $f_1 < f_2 < \cdots < f_k$.

In the scanning mode we probe the intervals $I_1, I_2, \ldots, I_k, \ldots$ until the mode terminates. While in the scanning mode we consider a set of probing states $p_1, p_2, \ldots, p_k$ where f has been evaluated at the points $q_1 < q_2 < \cdots < q_k$.

Definition 4.2. A search algorithm is in lth *probing state* $p_l = \{r_{l-1}, r_l\}$ of the scanning mode if the lth interval of uncertainty $I_l = (q_{l-1}, q_l]$ be eliminated and q_{l+1} is the next evaluation point. Here,

$$r_{l-1} := q_l - q_{l-1} = |I_l|; \quad r_l = q_{l+1} - q_l = |I_{l+1}|.$$

Remark 4.3. If $f_l \geq f_{l+1}$, then the search changes into the detecting mode with an initial state $\{r_{l-1}, r_l\}$ (Verkhovsky, 1989). However, if $f_l < f_{l+1}$, then the search moves to the p_{l+1} probing state. As a result, the interval of uncertainty I_{l+1} is eliminated (since $s \notin I_{l+1}$) and the interval I_{l+2} is next to be examined. Since at any probing state the search can change into the detecting mode, the dilemma is whether to select the I_{l+2} interval as small as possible (in preparation for this change) or, if the search continues to stay in the scanning mode, to select I_{l+2} as large as possible. The dilemma indicates that there must be an optimal choice of I_{l+2}.

In the detecting mode, we can use an optimal strategy (Kiefer, 1953; 1957; Verkhovsky, 1989), which locates s on a t-interval. To design a minimax search algorithm, we must select all $q_1 < q_2 < \cdots < q_{k+1}$ in such a way, that the total number of required probes on both modes is minimal in the worst case.

Definition 4.4. We say that a set of points (q_i, q_j, q_k) is a *detecting triplet* if

$$q_i < q_j < q_k \quad \text{and} \quad f_i < f_j \geq f_k. \tag{4.3}$$

If (q_i, q_j, q_k) is a detecting triplet and f is a unimodal function, then a maximizer s satisfies the inequality $q_i \leq s \leq q_k$ (Veroy and Verkhovsky, 1986).

Definition 4.5. In further consideration $U(b, c)$ means the minimal total number of required probes for both modes in order to t-detect a maximizer s in the worst case if $s \in (b, c]$.

Theorem 4.6. *If f is an unimodal function and $s \in (F_{m-1} - 1, F_m - 1]$, but this is a priori unknown, then for all $m \geq 3$ s is t-detectable for $2(m-2)$ probes in the worst case, i.e.,*

$$U(F_{m-1} - 1, F_m - 1) = 2(m - 2), \tag{4.4}$$

Where $m - 1$ probes are used on the scanning mode and $m - 3$ probes on the detecting mode. Here, F_m is the mth Fibonacci number.

Proof. {by induction}: We will demonstrate that *in the scanning mode* the optimal evaluation points $q_1^o, q_2^o, \ldots, q_{k-1}^o, q_k^o$ must satisfy these properties: $q_1^o := 1, q_k^o - q_{k-1}^o := F_k$, for every $k \geq 2$, i.e.,

$$q_k^o := \sum_{i=1}^{k} F_i = F_{k+2} - 2. \tag{4.5}$$

$\square$

Remark 4.7. First, we demonstrate how to find an approximation a of s that satisfies inequality $|s - a| \le t$, i.e., $a - t \le s \le a + t$. Then we will show how to adjust the algorithm, if $s \in (n - 1, n]$.

I. Let $s \in (F_2 - 2, F_3 - 2] = (0, 1]$. Consider $1 \le q_1 < q_2 \le 2$; then $f_1 > f_2$. Hence, from the Lemma, it follows that $s \in (0, q_2)$. Then $a = q_2/2$ implies that $a \in (0, 1]$; therefore $|s - a| \le 1 = t$. It is easy to verify that, if $s \in (0, 1 + \delta)$ and $\delta > 0$, then, in the worst case, two probes are not sufficient for detection of s on t-interval. Indeed, the adversary can select such s and f that satisfy the following inequalities: $1 < q_1 < s < q_2$ and $f_1 < f_2$. Hence, in that case, s is t-detectable on $(0, 1]$ interval after two probes.

II. Let assume that if $s \in (F_m - 2, F_{m+1} - 2)$ and $m \le k$, then s can be t-detected for $\bigcup_s (F_m - 2, F_{m+1} - 2) = 2m - 1$ probes. If $m = k$, then k probes were used on the scanning mode and $k - 3$ probes on the detecting mode.

III. Let $s \in (F_{k+1} - 1, F_{k+2} - 1]$, but it is *a priori* unknown. Let for all $i = 1, 2, \ldots, k+1, k+2$ the probes are taken in the points $q_i := F_{i+2} - 1$.

In this case the following inequalities hold $f_1 < f_2 < \cdots < f_k < f_{k+1} \ge f_{k+2}$.

Since $f_k < f_{k+1} \ge f_{k+2}$, then (q_k, q_{k+1}, q_{k+2}) is a detecting triplet, and, as a result, the search is in the detecting state $\{F_{k+1}, F_{k+2}\}$. Therefore, using the optimal search algorithm, we can detect s with accuracy $t = 1$ for additional k evaluations of f. Hence, the smallest total number of required probes for both modes equals $U_t(F_{k+1} - 2, F_{k+2} - 2) = 2k - 1$. Thus, by induction we proved the Theorem 4.1.

5. Optimal Balanced Sequential Search

5.1. *The algorithm*

Assign a required accuracy t; {the scanning mode of the algorithm begins};

$$L := t; \quad R := 2t;$$

$$\textbf{while } f(L) < f(R) \textbf{ do begin}$$

$$temp := L; \quad L := R; \quad R := R + temp + t; \tag{5.1}$$

{(5.1) generates a sequence of probing states $\{F_1, F_2\}, \ldots, \{F_{k-1}, F_k\}\}$; end;
{the maximizer s is detected: $s \in (temp, R)$; the algorithm is in the detecting state $\{L - temp, R - L\};\}$;

{the following steps describe the optimal detecting algorithm-see [Verkhovsky, 1989]}; assign

$$A := temp; \quad B := R; \quad R := A + B - L; \tag{5.2}$$

repeat

if $f(L) > f(R)$ **then** $temp := L; \ L := 2R - B; \ B := R;$

$$R := temp; \ \{s \in (A, R)\}; \tag{5.3}$$

else $temp := R; \ R := 2L - A; \ A := L;$

$$L := temp; \ \{s \in (L, B)\}; \tag{5.4}$$

{(5.3) and/or (5.4) generate a sequence of detecting states $\{F_{k-1}, F_k\}, \ldots, \{F_1, F_2\}\}$;

until $(B - A)/2 \leq t;$

assign $a := (A + B)/2;$ {a is the approximation of the maximizer: $|s - a| \leq t\};$

stop.

The algorithm described above we call V-algorithm.

5.2. *Optimality of sequential search*

Theorem 5.1. *The number of required probes for t-detection of a maximizer described in Theorem 3.1 is minimal in the worst case.*

Proof. The algorithm consists of the scanning and detecting modes. On the scanning mode (SM) the search is sequentially in the probing states $p_1, p_2, \ldots, p_m$ where

$$p_1 := \{F_1, F_2\}, \ldots, p_m := \{F_m, F_{m+1}\}. \tag{5.5}$$

On the other hand, on the detecting node (DM) the algorithm is in the detecting states $\{F_m, F_{m+1}\}, \ldots, \{F_1, F_2\}$. It is known that all detecting states $\{F_m, F_{m+1}\}, \ldots, \{F_1, F_2\}$ are optimal (there is no other strategy that can t-detect s for a smaller number of probes). At the same time the entire SM is a mirror image of the DM. Indeed, from the beginning to the end of the SM the search goes from the probing state $\{F_1, F_2\}$ to the probing state $\{F_m, F_{m+1}\}$, while on the DM the search goes from the detecting state $\{F_1, F_2\}$ to the detecting state $\{F_1, F_2\}$. Thus, both modes (scanning and detecting) are optimal and, hence, the entire algorithm is optimal. $\qquad \square$

6. Complexity of Sequential Minimax Search

Let us compare the optimal search algorithms for two cases:

(1) The maximizer $s \in (b, F_m - 1]$, but this is *a priori* unknown; here b is a positive integer;

(2) It is known *a priori* that $s \in (0, F_m)$. Let $B(b, c)$ be the minimal total number of required probes for t-detection of s in the worst case if $s \in (b, c)$.

From the Theorem 6.1, if $b = F_{m-1} - 1$ and $m \geq 2$, then

$$U(F_{m-1} - 1, F_m - 1) = 2(m - 2). \tag{6.1}$$

However, if $b = 0$, then the following inequality holds:

$$U(0, F_m - 1) \leq 2(m - 2). \tag{6.2}$$

Therefore, if $m \geq 4$, then $B(0, F_m) = m - 2$, otherwise

$$B(0, F_m) = 0. \tag{6.3}$$

Then (6.1) and (6.3) imply that for every

$$m \geq 4 \quad U(0, F_m - 1) \leq 2B(0, F_m) = 2(m - 2). \tag{6.4}$$

In general, if $s \in (u, b] \cup (F_{m-1} - 1, F_m - 1]$, but this is *a priori* unknown, then

$$U(a, b) = 2\lceil \log_\alpha(b\sqrt{5}) \rceil [1 + o(b)] = \Theta(\log b), \tag{6.5}$$

where α is defined in (4.1).

The equality (6.5) follows from the fact that

$$F_m = (\alpha^m - \sigma^m)/\sqrt{5}, [13, 14]. \tag{6.6}$$

Here, $\sigma = |(1 - \sqrt{5})/2| < 1$ then $\lim \sigma^m = 0$ if $m \to \infty$.
Thus,

$$F_m = \alpha^m/\sqrt{5}[1 + o(\alpha)]. \tag{6.7}$$

If $F_{m-1} \leq P \leq F_m - 1$, then

$$U(F_{m-1} - 1, P) = 2(m - 2). \tag{6.8}$$

The complexities (6.1) and (6.5) can be further reduced if any prior information is available (Gal, 1971; Neymark and Strongin, 1966), or if a searching algorithm is based on a randomized approach (Rabin, 1976; Wardi, 1989).

Theorem 6.1. *Let in the worst case $c(n)$ be the minimal number of probes required to detect s on a priori unknown interval $s \in (n - 1, n]$. If*

$$F_{m-1} \leq 2n \leq F_m - 1, \tag{6.9}$$

then

$$c(n) = 2(m - 2). \tag{6.10}$$

Proof. First of all, the relations (6.1), (6.2), (6.5) and (6.8) are based on the previously made *Assumption* that $t := 1$. From this assumption follows that maximizer is detectable on an interval of length two, $\{a - 1 \leq s \leq a + 1\}$. In order to find the complexity of the algorithm if $s \in (n - 1, n]$, the scale of the search must be decreased twice, i.e., we must select $t := 1/2$. Two cases must be considered: $\qquad\qquad\qquad\qquad\qquad\qquad\qquad\square$

Case 1. If

$$(F_{m-1} - 1)t < n - 1; \quad n \leq (F_m - 1)t \quad \text{and} \quad t := \frac{1}{2}, \tag{6.11}$$

then (6.5) implies (6.10).

Case 2.

$$(F_{m-1})t \leq n \leq (F_m - 1)t \quad \text{and} \quad (F_{m-1} - 1)t > n - 1, \tag{6.12}$$

i.e., the case where $(F_{m-1} - 1)t$ is in the middle of the interval $(n - 1, n]$. It occurs if $m \bmod 3 = 0$. In this case the left half of the interval $(n - 1, n]$ is out of the interval $[(F_{m-1} - 1)t, (F_m - 1)t]$, i.e., $(n - 1, n - 1/2] \not\subset ((F_{m-1} - 1)t, (F_m - 1)t]$ and, as a result, fewer probes are required for t-detection of s. However, in the worst case, the maximizer may be on the right half of the interval $(n - 1, n]$, hence $c(n) = 2(m - 2)$ for both cases.

Table 6.1

$4 \leq n \leq 6$	$494 \leq n \leq 798$	$60,697 \leq n \leq 98,208$
$c(n) = 10;$	$c(n) = 30;$	$c(n) = 50.$

From (6.8) it follows that

$$c(n) = 2\lceil \log_\alpha(2n\sqrt{5}) \rceil [1 + o(n)] - 4. \tag{6.13}$$

7. Estimated Interval of Uncertainty

In many applications, an upper bound value Q on maximizer s can be estimated from a feasibility study. Let $T = \alpha\sqrt{Q/\sqrt{5}} = d\sqrt{Q}$.

Theorem 7.1. *If $s \leq T/\alpha$, then V-algorithm requires fewer probes, than Kiefer's algorithm (Kiefer 1957); if $T/\alpha < s \leq T$, then Kiefer's algorithm and V-algorithm require the same number of probes; if $T < s \leq Q$, then Kiefer's algorithm requires fewer probes than V-algorithm. Here, $d = \alpha/\sqrt[4]{5} = 1.082\ldots$.*

Proof. Let $T := F_m - 1$ and $Q := F_{2m-2}$; then in the worst case

$$U(0, F_{m-1} - 1) < U(F_{m-1} - 1, F_m - 1) = B(0, F_{2m-2}) = 2(m - 2). \tag{7.1}$$

. It is easy to check that the proof follows from (6.7) and from the fact that

$$F_{2m-2} = (F_m/\alpha)^2 \sqrt{5}[1 + o(m)]. \tag{7.2}$$

$\square$

8. Parallel Search: Basic Properties

If several processors are available, then as it is indicated in Verkhovsky (1995) the algorithm can be executed in a parallel mode (Avriel and Wilder, 1966; Karp and Miranker, 1968). Although the optimal search policies in both papers are in essence identical, the formulation of the problem is different. The proof of optimality of the search is more detailed in Karp and Miranker (1968). An idea of a parallel algorithm searching for a maximum of a unimodal function on an unbounded interval, based on an application of the Kraft's inequality formalism, is provided in Beigel (1990). The authors indicate that the approach they used to construct an infinite series of near-optimal algorithms for the unbounded search with a single processor can be expanded for a multiprocessor case. However, no details are provided.

The search algorithm described in this chapter is based on the following properties.

Lemma 8.1. Let us consider p arbitrary points $q_1, \ldots, q_p$ that satisfy inequalities

$$0 < q_1 < \cdots < q_p < \infty. \tag{8.1}$$

Let

$$f_i := f(q_i). \tag{8.2}$$

If

$$f_1 < f_2 < \cdots < f_{p-1} < f_p, \tag{8.3}$$

then maximizer s is greater than q_{p-1}.

If

$$f_1 > f_2 > \cdots > f_{p-1} > f_p, \tag{8.4}$$

then s is smaller than q_2.

If

$$f_1 < \cdots < f_{j-1} < f_j \geq f_{j+1} > \cdots > f_p, \tag{8.5}$$

then s is greater than q_{j-1} and does not exceed q_{j+1}, i.e.,

$$s \in (q_{j-1}, q_{j+1}]. \tag{8.6}$$

In the latter case we say that (q_{j-1}, q_j, q_{j+1}) is a detecting triplet of the search (see Definition 3.3).

Proof follows immediately from unimodality of function f.

9. Search on Finite Interval: Principle of Optimality

Definition 9.1. $I_m^p(u, v)$ is a minimal in the worst case interval of uncertainty containing maximizer s that can be detected after m p-probes if the search starts from the detecting state $\{u, v\}$.

9.1. *Properties of $I_m^p(u, v)$*

(a) $I_m^p(u, v) > I_l^p(u, v)$ if $m < l$,   (Effectiveness of p-probes);

(b) $I_m^p(u_1, v_1) > I_l^p(u_2, v_2)$ if $u_1 \geq u_2$; $v_1 \geq v_2$,   (Monotonicity of uncertainty);

(c) $I_m^p(u, v) = I_m^p(v, u)$,   (Symmetricity);

(d) $I_m^p(u, v) > I_m^q(u, v)$ if $p < q$,   (Efficiency of parallelization);

(e) $I_m^p(cu, cv) = c I_m^p(u, v)$ for every $c > 0$,   (Homogeneity).

9.2. *Case: $p = 2$*

Lemma 9.2. Let $u \geq v$; then

$$
I_m^2(u, v) = \min \left\{
\begin{aligned}
&\min_{y_1 < v, y_3 < v} \max \left\{ I_{m-1}^2[u - y_1, \max(y_1, y_3)], \right. \\
&\left. \qquad I_{m-1}^2[y_3, \max(u - y_1, v - y_3)] \right\}; \\
&\min_{y_1 + y_2 < u} \max \left\{ I_{m-1}^2[y_2, \max(y_1, u - y_1 - y_2)], \right. \\
&\left. \qquad I_{m-1}^2[u - y_1 - y_2, \max(y_2, v)] \right\}.
\end{aligned}
\right. \tag{9.1}
$$

Proof. There are only three ways to decompose the intervals u and v using two evaluations (semicolons indicate the previous points that separate u and v):

(1) $\{u, v\} \to [y_1; y_2, y_3, y_4] \to [u; y_2, y_3, v - y_2 - y_3]$; where

$$
y_1 = u; \quad y_2 + y_3 + y_4 = v; \tag{9.2}
$$

(2) $\{u, v\} \to [y_1, y_2; y_3, y_4] \to [y_1 u - y_1; y_3, v - y_3]$; where

$$
y_1 + y_2 = u; \quad y_3 + y_4 = v; \tag{9.3}
$$

(3) $\{u, v\} \to [y_1, y_2, y_3; y_4] \to [y_1, y_2, u - y_1 - y_2; v]$, where

$$
y_1 + y_2 + y_3 = u; \quad y_4 = v. \tag{9.4}
$$

The following recursive equation is derived from the decomposition (9.2)–(9.4):

$$I_m^2(u,v) = \min \begin{cases} \min_{y_2,y_3} \max[I_{m-1}^2(u,y_2), I_{m-1}^2(y_2,y_3), \\ \qquad\qquad I_{m-1}^2(y_3, v - y_2 - y_3)]; \\ \min_{y_1,y_3} \max[I_{m-1}^2(y_1, u - y_1), I_{m-1}^2(u - y_1, y_3), \\ \qquad\qquad I_{m-1}^2(y_3, v - y_3)]; \\ \min_{y_1,y_2} \max[I_{m-1}^2(y_1, y_2), I_{m-1}^2(y_2, u - y_1 - y_2), \\ \qquad\qquad I_{m-1}^2(u - y_1 - y_2, v)]. \end{cases} \quad (9.5)$$

Taking into account that $u + y_2 > v + y_2 > y_2 + y_3$ and that $u + y_2 > v > v - y_2$ we can eliminate the second and the third terms in the upper branch of the functional Eq. (9.5).

On the other hand the first term of the upper branch in (9.5) can itself be eliminated since

$$\min_{y_2 < v} I_{m-1}^2(u, y_2) \geq \min_{y_1 < u} I_{m-1}^2(u - y_1, y_1). \quad (9.6)$$

In addition, $\min_{0 < y_1 < u} I_{m-1}^2(y_1, u - y_1) \geq \min_{0 < y_3 < v}(y_3, v - y_3)$. Hence, Eq. (9.5) is reduced to Eq. (9.1). All that proves Lemma 9.1. $\square$

Theorem 9.3. *Let $u \geq v$, then*

$$I_m^2(u,v) = \begin{cases} I_{m-1}^2\left(v, \dfrac{u - v}{2}\right) & \text{if } u > v; \\ I_{m-1}^2(u - z, z); & 0 < z < u \quad \text{if } u = v. \end{cases} \quad (9.7)$$

Proof. Since, in the worst case, the adversary can select two adjacent intervals with the largest sum, from optimality point of view, one must select the intervals in such a way that every two adjacent intervals have equal sums. It implies that the alternating intervals must have equal lengths:

$$y_1 = y_3 = w; \quad y_2 = y_4 = z.$$

Hence, (9.7) implies that $y_1 = u - y_1 - y_2 = w; y_2 = v$.
Thus

$$y_1 = (u - v)/2 \quad \text{if } u > v.$$

However, if $u = v$, then $y_1 = y_3 = z; u - y_1 = v - y_3 = u - z$.

Let us consider for every $k = 1, \ldots, p+1$ a pair of equations:

$$\sum_{i=1}^{k} y_i = u, \qquad \sum_{i=k+1}^{p+2} y_i = v, \qquad (9.8)$$

where for all $i = 2, \ldots, p+2$ $y_i > 0$. $\qquad\square$

Lemma 9.4.

$$I_m^p(u, v) = \min_{1 \le k \le p+1} \max_{1 \le i \le p+1} \min_{y_i, y_{i+1}} I_{m-1}^p(y_i, y_{i+1}). \qquad (9.9)$$

Proof. There are $p + 1$ ways to represent the intervals u and v as sums in (9.8). The following dynamic programming equation describes recursive relations between the detecting states

$$I_m^p(u, v) = \min_{1 \le k \le p+1} \min_{y_1, \ldots, y_{p+2}}$$

$$\times \max[I_{m-1}^p(y_1, y_2), I_{m-1}^p(y_2, y_3), \ldots, I_{m-1}^p(y_{k-1}, y_k),$$

$$I_{m-1}^p(y_k, y_{k+1}), \ldots, I_{m-1}^p(y_{p+1}, y_{p+2})],$$

where all control variables $y_1, \ldots, y_{p+2}$ must satisfy constraints (9.8). Considering the worst case, a user *can* select such a function f, that the algorithm *must* select a pair of adjacent intervals with the largest sum. $\square$

9.3. *Odd number of processors*

Theorem 9.5. *If $p = 2r - 1$; and $u \ge v$, then*

$$I_m^{2r-1}(u, v) = \begin{cases} I_{m-1}^{2r-1}[(r - k + 1)v - ku, ku - (r - k)v]/k, \\ \qquad k/(r - k + 1) < v/u \le k/(r - k); \\ I_{m-1}^{2r-1}[(r - k)v - ku, (k + 1)u - (r - k)v]/(r - k), \\ \qquad k < (r - k)v/u \le (k + 1); \end{cases}$$

$$(9.10)$$

where for all $1 \le k \le \lfloor r/2 \rfloor$ $(r - k + 1)v - ku \ge ku - (r - k)v$ in the upper branch of (9.10) and for all $0 \le k \le \lfloor r/2 \rfloor$ $(r-k)v-ku \ge (k+1)u-(r-k)v$ in the lower branch of (9.10).

Proof. Since an algorithm designer's goal is for a given number of p-probes to maximize an interval on which s can be located within a unit interval, it is obvious to select all the intervals in such a way that any two adjacent intervals would have the same sum. This search strategy means that the intervals $y_1, y_2, y_3, \ldots, y_p, y_{p+1}, y_{p+2}$ must have alternate values: $y_1 = w$; $y_2 = z$; $y_3 = w$; $\ldots$, i.e., in general, for all $1 \leq i \leq p/2$ $y_{2i-1} = w$; $y_{2i} = z$. $\qquad\square$

9.4. *Even number of processors*

Theorem 9.6. *If $p = 2r$ and $u \geq v$, then for all $1 \leq k \leq \lfloor r/2 \rfloor$ the following dynamic programming equations holds:*

$$
I_m^{2r}(u,v) = \begin{cases} I_{m-1}^{2r}[(r-k+1)v - ku, (k+1)u - (r-k)v]/(r+1), \\ \qquad\qquad k/(r-k+1) < v/u \leq (k+1)/(r-k); \\ I_{m-1}^{2r}[(u+v)/(r+1) - z, z], ku = (r-k+1)v, \\ \qquad\qquad 0 < z < (u+v)/(k+1). \end{cases}
$$
$$(9.11)$$

where in the upper branch of the equation $(r-k+1)v - ku \geq (k+1)u - (r-k)v$.

Proof. Analogous to the proof of the Theorem 9.4. $\qquad\square$

9.5. *Optimal detecting states*

Definition 9.7. If there exists a pair of positive numbers c and d such that $c > d$ and for all non-negative numbers u and v $u + v \leq c + d$ and $I_m^p(u,v) = I_m^p(c,d)$, then $\{c,d\}$ is an *optimal* detecting state.

The following two propositions can be proved by induction:

(a) $\qquad\qquad I_m^{2r-1}(c_m, d_m) = I_{m-1}^{2r-1}(d_m, c_m/r - d_m),$

which means that

$$c_{m-1} := d_m; \quad d_{m-1} := c_m/r - d_m;$$

(b) $\qquad I_m^{2r}(c_m, d_m) = I_{m-1}^{2r}[(c_m + d_m)/(r+1) - d_m, d_m], \qquad (9.12)$

which means that

$$d_{m-1} := d_m = z; = \quad c_{m-1} := (c_m + d_m)/(r+1) - d_{m-1}. \qquad (9.13)$$

Remark 9.8. d_m is constant in (9.13).

(a) and (b) imply the *defining rules* (9.12) and (9.13) for optimal detecting states $\{c_k, d_k\}$; here $0 < z < 1$; $t := 1$; $d_0 := z$; $c_0 := t - z$; $r := \lceil p/2 \rceil$.

9.6. *Optimal detecting states: defining rules*

Definition 9.9. Let $\{c_k, d_k\}$ be the optimal detecting state starting from which s can be located for k additional p-probes.

Proposition (a) and (b) imply the *defining rules* for optimal detecting states $\{c_k, d_k\}$:

$$0 < z < 1; \quad t := 1; \quad c_0 := t - z; d_0 := z; \quad r := \lceil p/2 \rceil; \tag{9.14}$$

if p is odd, then for all

$$k \geq 1 \quad c_k := r(c_{k-1} + d_{k-1}); \quad d_k := c_{k-1}; \tag{9.15}$$

if p is even, then for all $k \geq 0$

$$d_k := z;$$

$$c_k := (r+1)(c_{k-1} + d_{k-1}) - d_{k-1} = (r+1)c_{k-1} + rd_{k-1} = t(r+1)^k - z. \tag{9.16}$$

Both these rules for odd and even p can be generalized in the following form:

$$\phi = (p+1) \bmod 2; \quad c_k := \lceil (p+1)/2 \rceil c_{k-1} - \phi d_{k-1};$$

$$d_k := (p \bmod 2)c_{k-1} + \phi d_{k-1}. \tag{9.17}$$

Example 9.10. Let $p = 3$; $t = 1$ and $z = 1/2$;
then

$$c_0 = 1/2; \quad d_0 = 1/2; \quad r := 2;$$

$$c_1 := 2(1/2 + 1/2) = 2; \quad d_1 := 1/2;$$

$$c_2 := r(c_1 + d_1) = 2(2 + 1/2) = 5; \quad d_2 := c_1 = 2;$$

$$c_3 := r(c_2 + d_2) = 2(5 + 2) = 14; \quad d_3 := c_2 = 5;$$

$$c_4 := r(c_3 + d_3) = 2(14 + 5) = 38; \quad d_3 := c_2 = 14; \dots$$

Example 9.11. Let $p = 4$; $t = 1$ and $z = 1/2$;
then

$$c_0 = 1/2; \quad d_0 = 1/2; \quad r := 2;$$

$$d_1 := 1/2; \quad c_1 := 3(c_0 + d_0) - d_0 = 3(1/2 + 1/2) - 1/2 = 5/2 \equiv 3 - 1/2;$$

$$d_2 := 1/2; \quad c_2 := 3(c_1 + d_1) - d_1 = 3(5/2 + 1/2) - 1/2 = 17/2 \equiv 3^2 - 1/2;$$

$$d_3 := 1/2; \quad c_3 := 3(c_3 + d_3) - d_3 = 3(17/2 + 1/2) - 1/2 = 53/2 \equiv 3^3 - 1/2.$$

10. Search Diagrams

A diagram introduced below is a convenient way to describe the unbounded search algorithms. The following list explains lists of meanings of every element of the diagram:

(1) SS_k is a scanning state of the search before the $(k+1)$th p-probe is taken;
(2) DS_k is a detecting state of the search when the kth p-probe is taken;
(3) $\exists$ is a *conditional operator* "**if** a detecting triplet exists, **then** change the search into the detecting mode **else** continue the scanning mode";
(4) *Arrows* $\xrightarrow{F}$ or $\rightarrow$ indicate continuation of the scanning mode;
(5) *Arrow* $\downarrow$ indicates that the search is changed into the detecting mode;
(6) *Arrow* $\leftarrow$ indicates continuation of the detecting mode;
(7) W is an *operator* that selects a next detecting triplet;
(8) *Parentheses* indicate intervals of uncertainty as a result of a p-probe on the scanning or detecting mode;
(9) *Indices outside the parenthesis* indicate how many p-probes are currently taken on the scanning mode;
(10) *Square brackets* show new intervals and the interval of uncertainty from the previous p-probe;
(11) *Semicolon* indicates the position of the point of function evaluation, taken at the previous state of the search;
(12) *Commas* indicate positions of current evaluation points. Then the algorithm can be described as the following *search diagram*:

$$\textbf{start} \rightarrow SS_0 \rightarrow \underset{\downarrow}{\exists} \xrightarrow{F} SS_1 \rightarrow \underset{\downarrow}{\exists} \xrightarrow{F} SS_2 \rightarrow \underset{\downarrow}{\exists} \xrightarrow{F}$$

$$\dots \xrightarrow{F} SS_k \rightarrow \underset{\downarrow}{\exists} \xrightarrow{F} SS_{k+1} \rightarrow \dots$$

$$\textbf{end} \leftarrow W \leftarrow DS_0 \leftarrow W \leftarrow DS_1 \leftarrow \dots \leftarrow W \leftarrow DS_{k-1} \leftarrow \dots$$

$$(10.1)$$

11. Optimal Intervals between Evaluation Points

11.1. *Linear programming problems*

Let $y_{1j}, y_{2j}, \dots, y_{p-1,j}, y_{pj}$ be intervals between the points of evaluations $q_{1j}, q_{2j}, \dots, q_{p-1,j}, q_{pj}$ on the jth p-probe of the scanning mode, i.e., for all $i = 1, \dots, p$ $y_{ij} := q_{ij} - q_{i-1,j}$; $q_{0j} := q_{p,j-1}$; and $q_{01} := 0$. The following linear programming problem determines optimal values of all intervals that maximize the size of an interval B_1, on which s is detectable within a unit interval for one p-probe only:

$$B_1 = \max(y_{11} + \cdots + y_{p-1,1}), \qquad (11.1)$$

subject to the following constraints:

$$y_{11} + y_{21} \leq 1, y_{21} + y_{31} \leq 1, \ldots, y_{p-1,1} + y_{p1} \leq 1, \qquad (11.2)$$

and all variables are positive. It is easy to check that optimal variables must satisfy the following rules: for all odd i $y_{i1} = y_{11}$; and for even i $y_{i1} = 1 - y_{11}$.

Then

$$B_1 = \begin{cases} r - 1 & \text{if } p \text{ is } odd \\ r - z & \text{if } p \text{ is } even. \end{cases} \qquad (11.3)$$

In all further discussions, unless it is stated otherwise, we consider $y_{11} = 1 - z$; and $y_{21} = z$.

Hence, if p is even, then

$$\lim_{z \to 0} B_1(z) = r. \qquad (11.4)$$

Before we consider a general case, let us find a maximal interval B_2 on which s is detectable within a unit interval for two p-probes. The following linear programming problem determines optimal intervals that maximize the size of interval B_2. There are possible two strategies: (1) to locate $s$within a unit interval for two p-probes or (2) to detect s on a finite interval for one p-probe and then to locate it within a unit interval for one more p-probe.

11.2. *Search diagrams*

The first strategy can be described as the following linear programming problem: to find

$$B_2 = \max(y_{11} + \cdots + y_{p,1} + y_{12} + \cdots + y_{p-1,2}) \qquad (11.5)$$

subject to the following constraints:

$$y_{11} + y_{21} \leq c_0 + d_0, \quad y_{21} + y_{31} \leq c_0 + d_0, \ldots, y_{p-1,1} + y_{p1} \leq c_0 + d_0$$

$$y_{12} + y_{22} \leq c_0 + d_0, y_{22} + y_{32} \leq c_0 + d_0, \ldots, y_{p-1,2} + y_{p2} \leq c_0 + d_0; \qquad (11.6)$$

and all variables are positive.

For the second strategy select $y_{11}^* := r; y_{21}^* := 1 - z$.

Then from search diagram

$$(0, \infty) \to [r, 1 - z, \ldots, r, 1 - z, r, \infty] \to \exists \xrightarrow{F}$$

$$end \leftarrow \{z, 1 - z\} \leftarrow [1 - z; z, 1 - z, \ldots, 1 - z, z, \infty] \leftarrow \{1 - z, r\}.$$

The total interval b_1^*, within which s is detectable for two p-probes, in this case is equal $(r + 1 - z)r - (1 - z)$. Although $b_1^* > b_1$, the latter strategy is not optimal. Indeed, if $s \in (0, r - 1)$, it can be detected by both strategies. However, the first strategy requires only one p-probe. Yet the second strategy requires two p-probes. Hence the case with two p-probes is trivial: the strategy determined for one p-probe earlier must be repeated twice.

Let us introduce the following notations:

q_{ij}^k = the ith point of the function evaluation on jth p-probe if s is to be detected within a finite interval for k p-probes and then to be located within a unit interval for additional $k - 1$ p-probes;

y_{ij}^k = is the ith interval between the $(i - 1)$th and ith points of the function evaluation on the jth p-probe if s is to be detected for k p-probes and then to be located within a unit interval for additional $k - 1$ p-probes.

Then for all

$$1 \le i, j \le p \quad y_{ij}^k := q_{ij}^k - q_{i-1,j}^k; \quad \text{where for all } k \ q_{01}^k = 0. \tag{11.7}$$

b_k = the maximal interval, on which s is detectable within a finite interval for k p-probes and after that is t-detectable (within a unit interval) for additional $k - 1$ p-probes.

Let us consider an infinite sequence of linear programming problems:

$$LP(1)\text{: to find} \quad B_1 := \max \sum_{i=1}^{p-1} y_{i1}^1, \tag{11.8}$$

where all positive variables y_{i1}^1 satisfy the following constraints:
for all $1 \le i \le p - 1$

$$y_{i1}^1 + y_{i+1,1}^1 \le e_0, \tag{11.9}$$

$$LP(2)\text{: to find} \quad B_2 := \max \left(\sum_{j=1}^{2} \sum_{i=1}^{p} y_{ij}^2 - y_{p2}^2 \right), \tag{11.10}$$

where all positive variables y_{i1}^2 and y_{i2}^2 satisfy the following constraints:

for all $1 \leq i \leq p-1$

$$y_{i1}^2 + y_{i+1,1}^2 \leq e_0; \quad y_{i2}^2 + y_{i+1,2}^2 \leq e_1; \quad y_{i1}^2 < y_{i1}^1; \quad y_{02}^2 := y_{p1}^1; \quad (11.11)$$

$$LP(k): \text{ to find } \quad B_k := \max \left(\sum_{j=1}^{k} \sum_{i=1}^{p} y_{ij}^k - y_{pk}^k \right), \quad (11.12)$$

where all positive variables y_{ij}^k satisfy the following constraints:
for all $1 \leq i \leq p-1$ and all

$$1 \leq j \leq k; \quad y_{ij}^k + y_{i+1,j}^k \leq e_{j-1}; \quad y_{ij}^k \leq y_{ij}^{k-1}; \quad y_{0j}^k = y_{p,j-1}^k. \quad (11.13)$$

Let, in addition, $b_0 := 0$, then the following dynamic programming equations show recursive relations between B_j and B_{j-1} for all

$$j \geq 1: \quad B_j = \max \left[B_{j-1} + \sum_{i=1}^{p-1} y_{ij}^j \right]. \quad (11.14)$$

Since it is *not* known *a priori* how many p-probes are required for detection of maximizer s on a finite interval, hence the optimal search policy must be independent of k.

Let y_{ij} be the variables that describe this optimal search policy. Such a policy must satisfy constraints for *all* i, j, and k.

It is obvious that for all natural j and k, and all $1 \leq i \leq p$ these constraints are:

$$y_{ij} + y_{i+1,j} \leq y_{ij}^k + y_{i+1,j}^k \leq e_{j-1}; \quad y_{ij} \leq y_{ij}^k; \quad \text{and} \quad y_{0j} = y_{p,j-1}.$$
$$(11.15)$$

It is possible to show by induction that the optimal y_{ij}^o satisfy the following conditions: $y_{ij}^o := h_k$ for all odd i and $y_{ik}^o := g_k$ for all even i. The values of g_k and h_k are provided in the upcoming sections this chapter.

12. Search Diagrams for Optimal Algorithms

12.1. *Odd p*

12.1.1. *Defining rules*

$$0 < z < 1; \quad t := 1; \quad g_0 := z; \quad h_0 := t - z; \quad r := \lceil p/2 \rceil; \quad \text{for all } k \geq 1$$

$$g_{k+1} := h_k; \quad h_{k+1} := r(g_k + h_k); \quad (12.1)$$

$$(0, \infty)_0 \rightarrow [h_0, g_0, \ldots, h_0, g_0, h_0, \infty] \rightarrow \exists \xrightarrow{F}$$
$$\downarrow$$

$$\text{end} \leftarrow \{g_0, h_0\}_0 \leftarrow$$

$$\rightarrow (g_0, \infty)_1 \rightarrow [g_1; h_1, g_1, \ldots, h_1, g_1, h_1, \infty] \rightarrow \exists \xrightarrow{F} (g_2, \infty)_2 \rightarrow \ldots$$

$$\leftarrow [h_0; g_0, \ldots, h_0, g_0, h_0] \leftarrow \{g_1, h_1\}_1$$

$$\ldots \rightarrow (g_k, \infty)_k \rightarrow [g_k; h_k, g_k, h_k, \ldots, g_k, h_k, \infty]$$

$$\rightarrow \exists \xrightarrow{F} (g_{k+1}, \infty)_{k+1} \rightarrow \ldots$$

$$\leftarrow \{g_{k-1}, h_{k-1}\}_{k-1} \leftarrow [h_{k-1}; g_{k-1}, h_{k-1}, g_{k-1}, \ldots, h_{k-1}, g_{k-1}, h_{k-1}]$$

$$\leftarrow \{g_k, h_k\}_k \leftarrow \ldots \tag{12.2}$$

Remark 12.1. $\underbrace{[g_k; h_k, g_k, h_k, \ldots, g_k}_{w_k}, h_k, \infty]$ indicates interval w_k that is
excluded from the further search after kth p-probe.

12.1.2. $p = 3$

$$0 < z < 1; \quad t := 1; \quad g_0 := z; \quad h_0 := t - z;$$

$$(0, \infty)_0 \rightarrow [1 - z, z, 1 - z, \infty] \rightarrow \exists \xrightarrow{F} (1 - z, \infty)_1$$

$$\rightarrow [1 - z; 2, 1 - z, 2, \infty] \rightarrow \exists \xrightarrow{F} (2, \infty)_2 \rightarrow$$

$$\textbf{end} \leftarrow \{z, 1 - z\}_0 \leftarrow [1 - z; z, 1 - z, z, 1 - z] \leftarrow \{1 - z, 2\}_1 \tag{12.3}$$

$$[2; 6 - 2z, 2, 6 - 2z, \infty] \rightarrow \exists \xrightarrow{F} (6 - 2z, \infty)_2$$

$$\rightarrow [6 - 2z; 16 - 4z, 6 - 2z, 16 - 4z, \infty] \rightarrow \exists \xrightarrow{F} \ldots$$

$$\leftarrow [2; 1 - z, 2, 1 - z, 2] \leftarrow \{2, 6 - 2z\}_2$$

$$\leftarrow [6 - 2z; 2, 6 - 2z, 2, 6 - 2z] \leftarrow \{6 - 2z, 16 - 4z\}_3 \leftarrow \ldots$$

12.2. *Even number of processors: $\{p = 2r\}$*

12.2.1. *Detecting mode*

Let the search be in the $(k + 1)$th detecting state. It means that at most
$k + 1$ p-probes are required for t-detection of the maximizer s. p-probes
will divide the larger interval c_{k+1} into $p + 1$ alternating subintervals

$d_k, c_k, d_k, c_k, \ldots, c_k, d_k$. In the kth detecting state, the search will be either in $\{d_k, c_k\}$ state or in the $\{c_k, d_k\}$ state. Both these states are equivalent, i.e., they require the same number of p-probes for t-detection and symmetrical choice of probes. Schematically it can be described by the following way:

$$\{d_{k+1}, c_{k+1}\} \rightarrow [c_k; d_k, c_k, d_k, c_k, \ldots, d_k, c_k, d_k] \rightarrow \{d_k, c_k\}. \qquad (12.4)$$

For more details see *the search diagrams*. Here, a semicolon separates the "leftover" interval d_{k+1} of the previous state, from the new subintervals $d_k, c_k, d_k, c_k, \ldots, c_k, d_k$, where the pair (d_k, c_k) is repeated r times.

It is important to notice for further application that the detecting states described above are not unique. Indeed, let us consider the search with $p = 6$ and let the search be in a detecting state $\{x, 8 - x\}$, where x is an integer variable, $1 \le x \le 7$. Then for any x, the maximizer s is t-detectable after one p-probe only: divide the left interval into x equal subintervals using $x - 1$ probes and divide the right interval into $8 - x$ equal intervals using $8 - x - 1$ probes. Let $x = 5$. Applying the schematic description of search we have that $\{5, 3\} \rightarrow [1, 1, 1, 1, 1; 1, 1, 1] \rightarrow \{1, 1\}$. If $x = 1$, then $\{1, 7\} \rightarrow [1; 1, 1, 1, 1, 1, 1, 1] \rightarrow \{1, 1\}$. In general, consider for any even p a detecting state $\{1, 2(r + 1)^k - 1\}$. Let us divide the right interval onto p subintervals with alternating length equal $2(r + 1)^{k-1} - 1$ and one. Then from the schematic description one can see that

$$\{1, (r + 1)^k - 1\}$$
$$\rightarrow [1, 2(r + 1)^k{}^{-1} - 1, 1, 2(r + 1)^{k-1} - 1, 1, 1, \ldots, 1, 2(r + 1)^{k-1} - 1]$$
$$\rightarrow \{1, 2(r + 1)^{k-1} - 1\} \rightarrow \{1, 2(r + 1) - 1\} = \{1, p + 1\}$$
$$\rightarrow [1; 1, 1, \ldots, 1, 1] \rightarrow \{1, 1\}.$$

Thus the detecting state $\{1, 2(r + 1)^k - 1\}$ is the optimal detecting state starting from which s can be t-detected for k p-probes.

12.2.2. *Scanning mode*

Let us select first p probes $q_1, q_2, \ldots, q_p$. Let for all natural k and for all $1 \le i \le p$ $y_{ik} := q_{ik} - q_{i-1,k}$. If maximizer $s \in (0, q_{p-1,1}]$, then s will be detected on a finite interval after the very first p-probe if for all $2 \le i \le p$ $q_{i1} - q_{i-2,1} \le 1$. Schematically the scanning mode can be described by the following way.

12.2.3. *Detecting rules*

$0 < z < 1$; $t := 1$; $g_0 := z$; $h_0 := t - z$; $r := p/2$; for all $k \geq 0$ $g_k := z$;
$h_k := t(r + 1)^k - z$;

$$(0, \infty)_0 \to [h_0, g_0, \ldots, h_0, g_0, \infty]$$

$$\to \underset{\downarrow}{\exists} \xrightarrow{F} (g_1, \infty)_1 \to [g_1; h_1, g_1, \ldots, h_1, g_1, \infty] \to \exists_{\downarrow} \xrightarrow{F} (g_2, \infty)_2 \to \ldots$$

$$\mathbf{end} \leftarrow \{g_0, h_0\} \quad \leftarrow [g_0; h_0, g_0, \ldots, h_0, g_0] \leftarrow \{g_1, h_1\} \leftarrow \ldots$$

$$\ldots \to (g_k, \infty)_k \to [g_k; h_k, g_k, h_k, \ldots, h_k, g_k, \infty]$$

$$\to \underset{\downarrow}{\exists} \xrightarrow{F} (g_{k+1}, \infty)_{k+1} \to \ldots$$

$$\ldots \leftarrow \{g_{k-1}, h_{k-1}\}_{k-1} \leftarrow [g_{k-1}; h_{k-1}, g_{k-1}, \ldots, h_{k-1}, g_{k-1}, h_{k-1}]$$

$$\leftarrow \{g_k, h_k\}_k \leftarrow \ldots \tag{12.5}$$

Remark 12.2. $\underbrace{[g_k; h_k, g_k, \ldots, h_k, g_k, \infty]}_{w_k}$ indicates interval w_k that is
excluded from the further search after the kth p-probe.

12.2.4. $p = 4$

$0 < z < 1$; $t := 1$; $g_0 := z$; $h_0 := t - z$; $r := p/2$; for all $k \geq 0$ $g_k := z$;
$h_k := t(r + 1)^k - z$;

$$(0, \infty)_0 \to [1 - z, z, 1 - z, z, \infty] \to \underset{\downarrow}{\exists} \xrightarrow{F} (z, \infty)_1$$

$$\to [z; 3 - z, z, 3 - z, z, \infty] \to \underset{\downarrow}{\exists} \xrightarrow{F} (z, \infty)_2 \to \ldots$$

$$\mathbf{end} \leftarrow \{z, 1 - z\}_0 \leftarrow [z; 1 - z, z, 1 - z, z, 1 - z] \leftarrow \{z, 3 - z\}_1 \leftarrow \ldots$$

$$\to (z, \infty)_k \to [z; 3^k - z, z, 3^k - z, z, \infty] \to \underset{\downarrow}{\exists} \xrightarrow{F} (z, \infty)_{k+1}$$

$$\to [z; 3^{k+1} - z, z, 3^{k+1} - z, z, \infty] \to \underset{\downarrow}{\exists} \xrightarrow{F}$$

$$[z; 3^{k-1} - z, z, 3^{k-1} - z, z, 3^{k-1} - z] \leftarrow \{z, 3^k - z\}_k$$

$$\leftarrow [z; 3^k - z, z, 3^k - z, z, 3^k - z] \leftarrow \{z, 3^{k+1} - z\}_{k+1} \leftarrow \ldots$$

13. Optimal Parallel Search

13.1. *Inter-processor communication network*

(1) All PEs are connected with a linear bus;
(2) Two adjacent PEs share a memory unit (MEM, for short), i.e., PE(i) and PE($i + 1$) are connected with MEM(i) and can read from it concurrently.

13.2. *The algorithm*

13.2.1. *Inter-processor communication*

(1) All PEs are connected with a linear bus;
(2) two adjacent PEs share a memory unit (MEM), i.e., PE(i) and PE($i+1$) are connected with MEM(i) and can concurrently read from it.

13.2.2. *Pseudo-code*

Assign $t := 1; p; \{t$ is the scale of search; p is the number of PEs$\}; r := \lceil p/2 \rceil;$
$g := z; h := t - z; base := 0; e := g + h; A := 0; f(A) := -\infty;$

{beginning of the scanning mode};

    par for $i = 1$ **to** p **begin** $q_i := base + \lceil i/2 \rceil h + \lfloor i/2 \rfloor g; f_i := f(q_i);$

    For every i $PE(i)$ transmits f_i to adjacent processors $PE(i - 1)$ and $PE(i + 1);$

end;

    while $f_{p-1} < f_p$ **do**

        begin {update the base and steps}; $base := base + q_p; \sigma := g[(p + 1) \bmod 2];$

            $g := h(p \bmod 2) + \sigma; h := e[r + (P + 1) \bmod 2] - \sigma;$

            par begin for $i = 1$ **to** p $q_i := base + \lceil i/2 \rceil h + \lfloor i/2 \rfloor g; f_i := f(q_i);$

            $PE(i)$ transmits f_i to adjacent processors $PE(i-1)$ and $PE(i+1);$
            end;

        end;

{end of the scanning mode};

    where $f_{j-1} < f_j \geq f_{j+1}$ **do**

        $A := q_{i-1}; B := q_i; C := q_{i+1}; flag := 1;$ broadcast $A; B; C; f(B);$

flag **elsewhere** *null*; {data-conditional masking scheme}; {(q_{j-1}, q_j, q_{j+1}) is an initial detecting triplet; A and C are points adjacent to B; $f(q_{p+1})$ is an evaluation by a dummy $PE(p+1)$}; {$f(q_{p+1}) := \infty$}; **end** {computation of new steps};

     $e := g + h$; **if** p is odd **then** $g := h$; $h := re$ **else** $h := (r+1)e - g$;

     for $i = 1$ **to** p **begin** $q_i := base + \lceil i/2 \rceil h + \lfloor i/2 \rfloor g$; $f_i := f(q_i)$;

     end {of the scanning mode};

     $PE(i)$ broadcasts (A, B, C) and *flag*; $PE(j \neq i)$ receives (A, B, C); {beginning of the detecting mode};

     repeat

     if p is odd   **then begin** $e := h/r$; $h := g$; $g := e - h$; **end**

                           else begin $e := g + h$; $e := e/(r+1)$; $h := e - g$; **end**;
                            $q_0 := B$;

     if {$B - A < C - B$} **then** {case {d, c}}

     begin par for $i = 1$ **to** p

     $q_i := q_0 + \lceil i/2 \rceil h + \lfloor i/2 \rfloor g$; $q_{p+1} := C$; $A := q_{i-1}$; $B := q_i$; $C := q_{i+1}$;
        end

     else {case {d, c}}

     begin par for $i = 1$ **to** p

     $q_i := q_0 - \lceil i/2 \rceil h - \lfloor i/2 \rfloor g$; $q_{p+1} := A$; $A := q_{i+1}$; $B := q_i$; $C := q_{i-1}$;
        end

     where $f(B) \geq \max(f(A), f(C))$ **do**

     broadcasts (A, B, C) **elsewhere** receives (A, B, C);

     until $|A - C| \leq t$; **end** {of the search: $s \in (A, C)$}

13.3. *Optimality of parallel search*

Theorem 13.1. *The algorithm is optimal.*

Proof. The proof follows from an observation that the scanning states $\{g_k, h_k\}$ are mirror images of the detecting states $\{c_k, d_k\}$. Since it is known that the detecting states $\{c_k, d_k\}$ are optimal (Avriel and Wilder, 1966; Karp and Miranker, 1968), hence the scanning states $\{g_k, h_k\}$ are also optimal. As a result, the entire search algorithm is optimal.   □

14. Basic Parameters and Relations

14.1. *Basic parameters*

a_k = interval added before kth p-probe is computed;
g_k = smaller interval on the kth scanning state of the search;
h_k = larger interval on the kth scanning state of the search;
w_k = interval of uncertainty excluded from the search after the kth p-probe;
t_k = total interval added before the kth p-probe is computed;
b_k = total interval excluded from the search as a result of k p-probes.

14.2. *Basic relations: {odd p}*

$$a_k = \lceil p/2 \rceil h_k + \lfloor p/2 \rfloor g_k = rh_k + (r-1)g_k = r(g_k + h_k) - g_k;$$

$$a_k := h_k - h_{k-2}; \tag{14.1}$$

w_k satisfies the following recursive relations for all $k \geq 3$:

$$w_k = a_k - h_k + g_k; \; w_k := h_k - h_{k-1}; \tag{14.2}$$

$$t_k := (h_{k+1} - h_1)/r; \tag{14.3}$$

b_k satisfies the following recursive relations for all $k \geq 3$:

$$b_k = b_{k-1} + w_k; \quad b_k := t_k - h_{k-1}. \tag{14.4}$$

14.3. *Basic relations: {even p}*

$$g_k := z; \quad h_k := (r+1)^k - z; \quad w_1 := r - 2; \quad w_k := r(r+1)^{k-1} - z;$$

$$b_k := \sum_{i=1}^{k} w_i = \sum_{i=1}^{k-1} r(r+1)^i - z = (r+1)^k - z. \tag{14.5}$$

15. Complexity Analysis

15.1. *Fundamental relations*

Let us consider for all $k \geq 1$ sequences h_k, v_k, δ_k with the following defining rules:

$$h_k := v_k - \delta_k z; \quad h_k = r(h_{k-1} + h_{k-2}); \tag{15.1}$$

where

$$v_{-1} := 0; \quad v_0 := 1; \quad \delta_{-1} := -1; \quad \delta_0 := 1 \quad \text{and} \quad 0 < z < 1. \tag{15.2}$$

From (15.1) follows that

$$v_k := r(v_{k-1} + v_{k-2}); \quad \delta_k := r(\delta_{k-1} + \delta_{k-2}). \tag{15.3}$$

It is easy to demonstrate by induction that for all

$$k \geq 1 \quad \delta_k = rv_{k-2}. \tag{15.4}$$

Therefore

$$h_k = v_k - rv_{k-2}z. \tag{15.5}$$

If $p = 1$, then $v_k = F_k$, where all F_k are the Fibonacci numbers, and every v_k can be computed using the following formula:

$$v_k = \beta u^k + \omega w^k; \tag{15.6}$$

where u and w are roots of the equation

$$x^2 - r(x - 1) = 0 \tag{15.7}$$

and β and ω satisfy the equations:

$$\beta + \omega = v_0 = 1; \quad \beta u + \omega w = v_1 = r. \tag{15.8}$$

From (15.7)

$$u = (r + \sqrt{r(r+4)})/2 = r + 1 - \delta(p);$$
$$w = (r - \sqrt{r(r+4)})/2; \quad r = (p+1)/2. \tag{15.9}$$

For all $p|x_1| > 1 > |x_2|$; $u = x_1; w = x_2$. Indeed, from the Viete's theorem

$$w = -r/u. \tag{15.10}$$

Since $u > r$, then $-1 < w < 0$. From (15.9) and (15.10)

$$v_k = \beta u^k + o(u). \tag{15.11}$$

From (15.8)

$$\beta = [r(r+4) + (r-2)\sqrt{r(r+4)}]/2r(r+4). \tag{15.12}$$

Here,

$$\lim_{p \to \infty} \beta(p) = 1/2; \quad \lim_{p \to \infty} \delta(p) = 0; \quad \text{i.e.,} \quad \lim_{p \to \infty} u(p)/(r+1) = 1. \tag{15.13}$$

The latter, (15.13), limit means that for a large number of processors $u(p) = (p+3)/2$.

Table 15.1

p	$p = 1$	$p = 5$	$p = 9$
$u(p)$	$(1 + \sqrt{5})/2 = 1.618$	$(3 + \sqrt{21})/2 = 3.791$	$(5 + \sqrt{45})/2 = 5.854$

15.2. *Maximal interval analyzed after m parallel probes*

Theorem 15.1. *If $s \in (v_{m-1} - 1, v_m - 1)$, then m p-probes are required in the worst case to detect the maximizer on a final interval.*

Proof follows from (15.8) and (15.11).

Theorem 15.2. *If p is odd, then*

$$c_p(n) = \lceil 2\log_{u(p)}[(v_m - 1)/\beta(p)] \rceil - 1 = \lceil 2\log_{u(p)}[(n + 1)/\beta(p)] \rceil - 1,$$
(15.14)

and, if p is even, then

$$c_p(n) = \lceil 2\log_{r+1}(v_m - 1) \rceil - 1 = \lceil 2\log_{r+1}(n + 1) \rceil - 1.$$
(15.15)

Proof. If $s \in (n - 1, n) \subset (v_{m-1} - 1, v_m - 1]$, then $c(n) = 2m - 1$. Then the proof follows from (15.8) and (15.11) respectively. □

16. Speed-up and Efficiency of Parallelization

Let

$$b_{m(p)-1} < n \le b_{m(p)} \quad \text{and} \quad b_{m(1)-1} < n \le b_{m(1)},$$
(16.1)

then for large $m(p)$ and $m(1)$ holds that

$$m(p)\log u(p) = m(1)\log u(1).$$
(16.2)

On the other hand,

$$c_p(n) = 2m(p) - 1 \quad \text{and} \quad c_1(n) = 2m(1) - 1.$$
(16.3)

Let's define the speed-up of parallelization as

$$s_p(n) = c_1(n)/c_p(n),$$
(16.4)

then (16.2) and (16.3) imply that

$$s_p(n) = \frac{\log u(p)}{\log u(1)}.$$
(16.5)

If efficiency of parallelization is defined as

$$e_p(n) := s_p(n)/p, \qquad (16.6)$$

then

$$e_p(n) = c_1(n)/[pc_p(n)] = \frac{\log u(p)}{p \log u(1)}. \qquad (16.7)$$

Since for the large number of processors

$$u(p) \rightarrow \lceil p/2 \rceil + 1, \qquad (16.8)$$

then for a large n

$$s_p(n) = \frac{\log(p/2 + 1)}{\log[(1 + \sqrt{5})/2]} = \Theta(\log p). \qquad (16.9)$$

Finally,

$$e_p(n) = \frac{\log \sqrt[p]{p/2 + 1}}{\log[(1 + \sqrt{5})/2]} = \Theta(\log \sqrt[p]{p}). \qquad (16.10)$$

Chapter 28

Topological Design of Satellite Communication Networks

1. Introduction and Problem Definition

Modern satellite communication networks consist of terrestrial users interconnected via terrestrial links (cable or wireless) with earth antennae or more sophisticated equipment. The latter communicate via broadcasting with one or several satellites. Widely spread "dishes" provide only one-way quality communications and only in exceptional cases. That is why in many specific cases more complex and more expensive hardware like earth stations (ESs) are required. Medium or small "size" users cannot financially afford an individualized ES. And alternative for them is to share an ES with several other users, (Gilbert, 1967; McGregor and Shen, 1977). Only large corporations, major governmental offices, and, in general, large business organizations can afford individual ESs.

Multiple military units must be interconnected during combat operations and other activities with appropriate centers of command via C^3I/BM (command, communication, control, intelligence/battle management) system. Satellite communication networks can be substantial parts of such system. More than one ES (stationary or mobile) is required in this case since the area of operation can be vast, and/or survivability of the system might otherwise be jeopardized.

Communications nowadays is a very competitive business. To reduce its expense, and to make it more economically attractive to potential customers, a communication company must decide how many ESs of each type is needed, where to allocate them, and how the customers must be interconnected with these earth stations. A correct decision can save tens or even hundreds of millions of dollars annually, and hence can attract more users, (Gilbert, 1967; McGregor and Shen, 1977; Verkhovsky, 1988; 1989).

This problem, if formulated in different terms, has numerous applications and was investigated from diverse points of view by many researchers (Baumol and Wolfe, 1958; Christofides and Viola, 1971; Cooper, 1963; Dearing *et al.*, 1976; Eisenmann, 1962; Eyster *et al.*, 1973; Fang Kai-tai and Ma Feng-shi, 1982; Francis and White, 1974).

From a computational point of view, the problem is NP-complete, since brute force algorithms or other known techniques that decide how the cluster all users require an exponential time-complexity (Johnson *et al.*, 1978; Verkhovsky, 1989).

This chapter describes an algorithm that solves the problem with very high approximation for a polynomial time complexity. First results were provided in Verkhovsky (1983) and in the UK Journal of Telecommunication Management.

2. Problem Statement

(1) Let us consider locations of n users which are specified by coordinates $P_i = (a_i, b_i)$ $i = 1, \ldots, n$. Each user is characterized by a "volume" of incoming and outgoing communication flow w_i ("weight" of ith user's flow).

(2) Let S_k be a set of all users P_i connected with kth switch-ES C_k, and (U_k, V_k) be coordinates of C_k.

(3) $f(w_i, P_i, C_i)$ is a cost function of a transmission link connecting ith user P_i and kth swtich-ES C_k.

(4) The minimal total cost of all terrestrial links and all switches-ESs is

$$\min_{S_1, \ldots, S_m} \left[\min_{u_1, \ldots, u_k} \right] \sum_{i \in sk} \sum \sum_{i \in S_k} f(w_i, P_i, C_i) + q_k \left(\sum w_i \right) \right], \quad (2.1)$$

where $q_k \sum_{i \in S_k} w_i$ is a cost of kth switch-ES as a function of all outgoing and incoming flows. Thus problem (2.1) requires a clustering analysis in order to find an optimal clusters (subsets) $S_1, \ldots, S_m$. Survey on models and algorithms related to clustering is provided in Kusiak *et al.* (1986).

A clustering in general has been studied and described in Diday and Celenx (1981), Diehr (1985), Stantel (1986), and Tamura (1982). Nonparametric clustering and related problems and applications are considered in Alvo and Goldberg (1986) and Huang and Chen (1986).

3. Special Cases

1. Let the number m of switches-ESs be fixed, a cost of every switch-ES be either small or flow-independent, and let their locations be specified. Then it is easy to find S_k. Indeed,

$$S_k = \left\{ i : \min_{1 \le j \le m} f(w_i, P_i, C_i) = f(w_i, P_i, C_i) \right\}. \tag{3.1}$$

2. If all S_k are known, it is easy to find the optimal allocation of the kth switch/ES;

$$\min_{(u_k, v_k)} \sum_{i \in S_k} f(w_i, P_i, C_i) \quad \text{for } k = 1, \dots, m. \tag{3.2}$$

3. If $f(w_i, P_i, C_k) = dist(P_i, C_k)$,

then (3.2) is known as a *Weber problem*. This problem has been investigated by many authors (Baumol and Wolfe, 1958; Bellman, 1965; Christofides and Viola, 1971; Cooper, 1963; 1967; Francis and White, 1974; Kuhn, 1973; McGregor and Shen, 1977).

The difficulties appear when the clusters S_i are not known, the cost of a switch/ES is neither small nor flow-independent, and the number m of switches/ESs and their best location (u_k, v_k) for every k are not known either.

4. Linear Switching Cost Function

If $q_k \sum_{i \in S_k} w_i = q_k \sum_{i \in S_{2k}} w_i + q_k \sum_{i \in S_{2k+1}} w_i$ for all S_{2k} and S_{2k+1} such that $S_{2k} \cap S_{2k+1} = \emptyset$ and $S_{2k} \cup S_{2k+1} = S_k$ for all $k = 1, \dots, m$, that $q_k(.)$ is a linear function of network flow. In this case it is clear that an optimal partitioning on sub-networks is not effected by switching costs. These properties immediately imply that more clusters the better from transmission-cost-wise point of view since $g_k > g_{2k} + g_{2k+1}$.

Case $m = 2$: It is important to stress that there is substantial difference between the two cases $m = 1$ and $m = 2$. In the case where $m = 2$ the problem can be solved by repetitive application of the algorithm for the Weber problem. This must be done for all possible pairs of clusters S_1 and S_2. There are $2^{n-1} - 1$ different ways to partite n points into two subsets S_1 and S_2 and, for each clustering, two allocation problems must be solved. Thus, the total time complexity of a brute force approach is $O(2^n)$.

5. Binary Parametric Partitioning

In this section, we provide an example of a procedure which divides a centralized network N_1 with one switch S_1 into two sub-networks N_2 and N_3 with two switches-earth stations.

Step C1: Consider $m = 1$ and solve the problem

$$\min_{(u,v)} \sum f(w_i, P_i, C) \tag{5.1}$$

to find the common "center of gravity" C_0 for all n points.

Step C2: Consider a straight line L and rotate it around C_0. For every angle x of rotation, the line L divides all points P_i into two clusters $S_1(x)$ and $S_2(x)$.

Remark 5.1. To simplify the programming effort, consider polar coordinates (ρ_i, d_i) for each of the n points with respect to point C_0 as the origin of the coordinate system. Here, ρ_i is an angular coordinate of P_i.

Consider $x_i := \rho_i - 180°$; then sort all x_i in ascending order. If $x_i = \rho_i$ then $ch_i = 1$ else $ch_i = 0$. Then $S_1(x) = \{i : (x_i \leq x \text{ and } ch_i = 1) \text{ or } (x_i > x \text{ and } ch_i = 0)\}$. Also other points belong to $S_2(x)$.

Step C3: Compute

$$g_k(S_k(x)) = \min_{C_k} \sum f(w_i, P_i, C_k) \quad \text{for } k = 1, 2 \text{ and } i \in S_k(x). \tag{5.2}$$

Step C4: Compute

$$H(x) := g_1(S_1(x)) + g_2(S_2(x)) + q_1 \left(\sum w_i\right) + q_2 \left(\sum w_i\right), \tag{5.3}$$

for $i \in S_1(x)$ and $i \in S_2(x)$.

Remark 5.2. It is easy to check that rotation of the line L around point C_0 divides all n points onto two clusters, $S_1(x)$ and $S_2(x)$, by exactly n different way as the angle x changes from $0°$ to $180°$.

Step C5: Compute

$$h(x_r) := \min_{0 \leq x \leq 180°} h(x). \tag{5.4}$$

Step C6: If $f(w_i, P_i, C_1) > f(w_i, P_i, C_2)$ for $i \in S_1(x_r)$, then reassign $i \in S_2(x_r)$.

If $f(w_i, P_i, C_2) > f(w_i, P_i, C_1)$ for $i \in S_2(x_r)$, then reassign $i \in S_1(x_r)$.

Step C7: Using (5.4) find optimal locations of C_1 and C_2 for new values of $S_1(r_2)$ and $S_2(r_2)$.

Remark 5.3. $S_1(r_2)$ and $S_2(r_2)$ are defined as the best partitioning.

Numerical examples illustrating applications of the algorithm are provided below in several tables. Hundreds of computer experiments for $n = 25, 50, 100, 150, 200, 300$ and 600 indicate that the steps $C6$ and $C7$ do not create instability in the parametric partitioning algorithm (Verkhovsky, 1986).

6. Complexity of Algorithm

If the cost function of a terrestrial link is proportional to its length and to the size of flow that it can handle, i.e., if $(w_i, P_i, C_k) = w_i \times dist(P_i, C_k)$; then the problems (5.1) and (5.2) can be rewritten as an iterative process

$$(u, v) = T(u, v). \tag{6.1}$$

This idea was introduced by several authors including the author of this book. Its convergence was demonstrated in Bellman (1965), Cooper (1967), Kuhn (1973), McGregor and Shen (1977), Ostresh (1978), Verkhovsky (1986) and other publications.

It is known that each iteration of (6.1) requires $O(|S|)$ time complexity, where $|S|$ is the cardinality of set S. Hence for every fixed x the time-complexity to solve (5.1) is of order

$$O(|S_1(x)|) + O(|S_2(x)|) - O(n). \tag{6.2}$$

Therefore, the time-complexity to find $\min h(x)$ is equal

$$T(n) = n \times O(n) = O(n^2). \tag{6.3}$$

Numerous computer experiments demonstrated close to quadratic growth of the time-complexity for the algorithm C1–C7. For example, the average times to run the algorithm C1–C7 for $n = 25, 50, 100, 150, 200, 300$ and 400 are $T(25) = 1.23\,\text{s}$, $T(50) = 4\,\text{s}$, $T(100) = 13\,\text{s}$, $T(150) = 29\,\text{s}$, $T(200) = 52\,\text{s}$, $T(300) = 115\,\text{s}$, $T(400) = 192\,\text{s}$ (Verkhovsky, 1986).

7. Binary Partitioning and Associated Binary Tree

Let t_1 be a minimal total transmission cost for a network N_1 with one switch and the cost of this switch to be q_1. Let us consider an algorithm which subdivides the network N_1 on two sub-networks N_2 and N_3 with corresponding transmission costs t_2 and t_3 and q_2 and q_3 are corresponding costs of associated switches-ESs. We assume that the algorithm subdivides N_1 on two subnets in such a way that $t_2 + t_3 + q_2 + q_3$ is minimal.

For further consideration we represent the binary partitioning as a binary tree where a root represents a cluster (set) of all users S_1 and associated with it the network N_1. In general a kth node of the binary tree represents a cluster S_k and associated with it a network N_k. Two children of the kth node represent two sub-networks N_{2k} and N_{2k+1} of the network N_k (result of the binary partitioning).

Let $h_k = q_k + t_k$, where h_k be a hardware cost of the network N_k. It is clear from the essence of the problem that for every

$$kq_k \geq q_{2k}, \quad q_k \geq q_{2k+1} \quad \text{and} \quad t_k \geq t_{2k} + t_{2k+1} \tag{7.1}$$

since each sub-network N_{2k} and N_{2k+1} has a smaller number of users than N_k.

8. Non-Monotone Cost of Hardware

It is obvious that, if $h_k > h_{2k} + h_{2k+1}$, then the partitioning on two clusters (sub-networks) is cost-wise advantageous.

On the other hand, $h_k < h_{2k} + h_{2k+1}$ does *not* imply that any further partitioning is not cost-wise beneficial. To illustrate this let us consider a network N_k and six its sub-networks N_{2k}, N_{2k+1}, N_{4k}, N_{4k+1}, N_{4k+2}, N_{4k+3} (see Table 8.1).

The case where $h_k = 460$ is obvious: since $h_k > h_{2k} + h_{2k+1}$, then the binary partitioning of N_k on two sub-networks is gainful. However, a local analysis of hardware costs does not provide a correct insight if $h_k = 43$. Indeed, $h_k > h_{2k} + h_{2k+1}$ implies only that there is no reason to subdivide the network N_k into two sub-networks N_{2k} and N_{2k+1}. Further analysis demonstrates

$$h_k > h_{4k} + h_{4k+1} + h_{4k+2} + h_{4k+3} = 100,$$

Table 8.1

Sub-network N_1	N_k	N_{2k}	N_{2k+1}	N_{4k}	N_{4k+1}	N_{4k+2}	N_{4k+3}
Transmission cost t_1	310; 340	130	150	60	30; 50	50	40
Switch-ES cost q_1	120	90	80	50	70	60	40
Hardware cost h_1	430; 460	220	230	110	100; 120	110	80

and

$$h_k > h_{2k} + h_{4k+2} + h_{4k+3} = 120.$$

Therefore, this example illustrates that for a proper partitioning one needs to apply a global rather than a local analysis.

Definition 8.1. A network N_k is *indivisible* if there is no cost-wise advantage to divide it onto *any* number of sub-networks.

Definition 8.2. An optimal topology of a satellite communication network is determined if we know all indivisible sub-networks of the initial network N_1.

9. Dynamic Programming Algorithm

9.1. *Bottom-up mode*

(1) Assign for k-node a label $L_k = h_k$, and a final label F_k, $k = 1, 2, \ldots, m$.
(2) For all leaves $F_k = L_k$.
(3) If both children of a kth node have final labels, then compute

$$F_k = \min(L_k, F_{2k} + F_{2k+1}).$$

(3) Stop if F_k is computed.

9.2. *Top-down-depth-first mode*

Starting from $k = 1$ we find all nodes for which $F_l = L_l$.

It is easy to observe that a network N_l for which $F_l = L_l$ is indivisible, and, as a result, there is no reason to further continue an investigation of its sub-tree.

9.3. *Numerical example*

To simplify the example we assume as initial conditions specified by a network designer that sub-networks N_6, N_{10}, N_{11}, N_{17}, N_{18}, N_{28}, N_{30}, N_{32}, N_{33}, N_{39}, N_{58}, N_{59}, N_{62}, N_{63}, N_{76}, N_{77} are not further divisible. In the following considerations, we treat them as the network leaves and indicate that in bold. Here all values of t_k and q_k are computed on the basis of considerations described in (2.1); (3.1), (3.2), (7.1)–(5.4), and in (6.1). In accordance with the algorithm, $F_k = L_k$ for all leaves.

After all final labels F_k are known we find that an optimal cost-effective partitioning consists of the sub-networks N_5, N_6, N_{14}, N_{16}, N_{17}, N_{18}, N_{30},

Table 9.1

Sub-network N_k	N_1	N_2	N_3	N_4	N_5	N_6	N_7	N_8	N_9	N_{10}	N_{11}
t_k	2,350	1,010	1,200	490	410	400	650	220	280	200	200
q_k	350	290	230	250	140	200	210	130	120	100	130
$L_k = h_k$	2,700	1,300	1,430	740	550	600	860	350	400	300	330
F_k	2,480	1,190	1,290	640	550	600	690	320	320	300	330

Table 9.2

N_k	N_{14}	N_{15}	N_{16}	N_{17}	N_{18}	N_{19}	N_{28}	N_{29}	N_{30}	N_{31}	N_{32}
t_k	240	260	90	100	110	90	100	120	100	120	40
q_k	120	120	60	70	80	50	80	90	60	70	30
$L_k = h_k$	360	380	150	170	190	140	180	210	160	190	70
F_k	360	330	150	170	190	130	180	190	160	170	70

Table 9.3

N_k	N_{33}	N_{38}	N_{39}	N_{58}	N_{59}	N_{62}	N_{63}	N_{76}	N_{77}
t_k	40	40	40	30	50	40	50	10	20
q_k	50	20	40	50	60	30	50	10	10
$L_k = h_k$	90	60	80	80	110	70	100	20	30
F_k	90	50	80	80	110	70	100	20	30

N_{39}, N_{62}, N_{63}, N_{76}, N_{77}. It is easy to see from the Tables 9.1–9.3 that the minimal total cost of all hardware (transmission links plus switches-ESs) is equal

$$550 + 600 + 360 + 150 + 170 + 190 + 160 + 80 + 70 + 100 + 20 + 30 = 2480.$$

10. Statistical Properties of Cost-Function $h(x)$

About 1,800 of computer experiments for $n = 10, 20, 25, 50, 75, 100,$ 150, 200, 250, 300, 400 illustrated that $h(x)$ has rather stable statistical properties:

(1) $h(x)$ is a bimodal function of $x \in (0, 180°)$ if $n \gg 10$ and if $h(x)$ has a spread (the interval between its minimum and maximum) larger than 5%;

(2) It has more than one local minimum if $h(x)$ has a spread smaller than 5% or the number of users is small ($n < 25$).

These properties can be used to construct a more elaborate algorithm that requires significantly less computation than the thorough parametric search over $x \in (0, 180°)$.

11. Optimal Algorithm for Large n

It is easy to observe that the parametric partitioning requires in general case exactly n rotations of the separable line. As a result, time-complexity $f(n)$ to divide n users onto two clusters is equal $f(n) = an^2 + o_1(n)$ for large n. However, if the properties of $h(x)$ can be employed, this complexity can be substantially reduced. In [69, 70], we described an optimal algorithm for search of the global minimum on a discrete periodic bimodal function. This algorithm requires $O(\ln n)$ rotations of the separable line L.

As a result, $f(n) = bn \ln \ln n + o_2(n)$ for large n, provided, that $h(x)$ is a bimodal function. Since it is not known *a priori* whether this property holds, it can happen (with small probability) that after $O(\ln n)$ rotations we will find a local rather than a global minimum. However, this is possible with great probability if the spread of $h(x)$ is small, and, as a result, the relative difference between local and global minima is also small.

12. Average Complexity of Parametric Partitioning

Let $a(n)$ be a computational complexity to divide a set of n users on several clusters (sub-networks). Thus from [71] it is clear that the following recursive equations holds:

$$a(1) = 0; \quad a(2) = f(2); \quad a(n) = \sum_{k=1}^{n-1} p(k, n)[a(k) + a(n - k)] + f(n);$$

where

$$a(n) = O[n(\ln n)^2]; \quad \text{if } f(n) = O(n \ln n);$$

and

$$a(n) = O(n^2); \quad \text{if } f(n) = O(n^2).$$

References

Ablayev, F. and Karpinski, M. (2003). A lower bound for integer multiplication on randomized ordered read-once branching programs. *Journal of Information and Computation*, 186, 78–89.

Adleman, L.M. and DeMarrais, J. (1993). A sub-exponential algorithm for discrete logarithms over all finite fields. *Journal of Mathematics of Computation*, 61(203), 1–15.

Adleman, L., Manders, K. and Miller, G. (1977). On taking roots in finite fields. In *Proceedings of the 18th IEEE Symposium on Foundations of Computer Science*. New York, NY: IEEE Press.

Adleman, L.M., Pomerance, C. and Rumley, R.S. (1983). On distinguishing prime numbers from composite numbers. *Journal of Annals of Mathematics*, 117, 173–206.

Agrawal, M., Kayal, N. and Saxena, N. (2002). *PRIMES is in P*. Manuscript.

Aldini, A., Roccetti, M. and Gorrieri, R. (2003). On securing real-time speech transmission over the internet: an experimental study. *Journal of Applied Signal Processing*, 1(1), 1027–1042.

Alford, W.R., Granville, A. and Pomerance, C. (1994). There are infinitely many Carmichael numbers. *Annals of Mathematics*, 139(3), 703–722.

Alvo, M. and Goldberg, M. (1986). A nonparametric approach for clustering. In *Proceedings of the Eighth International Conference on Pattern Recognition*, Paris, France.

Avriel, M. and Wilde, D.J. (1966). Optimal search for a maximum with sequences of simultaneous function evaluations. *Journal of Management Science*, 12(9), 722–731.

Bach, E. (1984). Discrete logarithms and factoring. Technical Report: CSD-84-186, University of California, Berkeley, CA.

Bach, E. and Shallit, J. (1996). *Algorithmic Number Theory, Efficient Algorithm*. Vol.1. Cambridge, MA: MIT Press.

Barrett, P. (2001). *Making, Breaking Codes*. Upper Saddle River, New Jersey, NJ: Prentice Hall.

Barreto, P. and Voloch J. (2006). Efficient computation of roots in finite fields. *Journal of Designs, Codes and Cryptography*, 39, 275–280.

Baumol, W.J. and Wolfe, P. (1958). A warehouse-location problem. *Operational Research*, 6(2), 252–263.

Beamer, J.H. and Wilde, D.J. (1970). Minimax optimization of unimodal function by variable block search. *Journal of Management Science*, 16, 629–641.

Beigel, R. (1990). Unbounded searching algorithm. *Society for Industrial and Applied Mathematics Journal of Computing*, 19(3), 522–537.

Bellman, R. (1956). An application of dynamic programming to location-allocation problems. *Society for Industrial and Applied Mathematics Review*, 7(1), 126–128.

Bentley, J.L. and Yao, A.C.C. (1976). An almost optimal algorithm for unbounded searching. *Journal of Information Processing Letters*, 5, 82–87.

Bernstein, D. (2008). Fast multiplication and its applications. In J.P. Buhler and P. Stevenhagen (Eds.), *Algorithmic Number Theory: Lattices, Number Fields, Curves and Cryptography* (pp. 325–384). New York, NY: Cambridge University Press.

Blake, I. (1999). *Elliptic Curves in Cryptography*. London Mathematical Society Lecture Notes, Series 265. Cambridge University Press.

Boncompagni, B. (Ed.) (1857). *Scritti di Leonardo Pisano*, Vol.1, (pp. 283–285). Rome.

Brent, R.P. (1980). An improved Monte-Carlo factorization algorithm. *Journal of BIT Numerical Mathematics*, 20, 176–184.

Brent, R.P. (1985). Some integer factorization algorithms using elliptic curves. In *Proceedings of Ninth Australian Computer Science Conference*.

Bressoud, D.M. (1989). *Factorization and Primality Testing*. New York, NY: Springer-Verlag.

Brown, D.C., Trinidad, K. and Borja, R.R. (2008). NASA successfully tests first deep space Internet. http://www.nasa.gov/home/hqnews/2008/nov/HQ-08-298_Deep_space_internet.html.

Buhler, J., Lenstra, H.W. and Pomerance, C. (1993). Factoring integers with the number field sieve. In A.K. Lenstra and H.W. Lenstra (Eds.), *The Development of the Number Field Sieve*, Lecture Notes in Mathematics, Vol. 1554, Berlin-Heidelberg, New York: Springer-Verlag.

Carmichael, R.D. (1910). Note on a new number theory function. *Bulletin of American Mathematical Society*, 16, 232–238.

Chasan, D. and Gal, S. (1976). On the optimality of the exponential function for some minimax problems. *SIAM Journal of Applied Mathematics*, 30(2), 324–348.

Chateauneuf, M., Ling, A. and Stinson, D.R. (2003). Slope packings and coverings, and generic algorithms for the discrete logarithm problem. *Journal of Combinatorial Designs*, 11(1), 36–50.

Christofides, N. and Viola, P. (1971). The optimum location of multi-centers on a graph. *The Quarterly Journal of Operational. Research*, 22(1), 145–154.

Churchill, R.V., Brown, J.W. and Verhey, R.F. (1976). *Complex Variables and Applications*, 3rd Edn. New York, NY: McGraw Hill.

Cipolla, M. (1903). Unmetodo per la risolutionedellacongruenza di secondo grado, *Rendicontodell Accademia Scienze Fisiche e Matematiche*, Napoli, Ser.3, Vol. IX, 154–163.

Cohen, H. (1993). Pollard's rho-method for detecting periodicity. In *A Course in Computational Algebraic Number Theory*, Chapter 8 (pp. 419–422). Springer-Verlag.

Cook, S.A. (1966). On the minimum computation time of functions. PhD Thesis, Harvard University, Cambridge, MA.

Cooper, L. (1963). Location-allocation problems. *Operational Research*, 11(3), 331–343.

Cooper, L. (1967). Solution of generalized locational equilibrium models. *Journal of Regional Science*, 7(1), 1–18.

Coppersmith, D. and Shamir, A. (1997). Lattice attacks on NTRU. *Advances in Cryptology* — EUROCRYPT 1997, Lecture Notes in Computer Science, Vol. 233 (pp. 52–61). Springer-Verlag.

Coron, J., Lefranc, D. and Poupard, G. (2005). A new baby-step giant-step algorithm and some applications to crypt analysis. In *Lecture Notes in Computer Science*, Vol. 3659 (pp. 47–60). Berlin-Heidelberg: Springer.

Crandall, R. (1994). Method and apparatus for public key exchange in a cryptographic systems. *U.S. Patents* 5159632 (1992); 5271061 (1993); 5463690.

Crandall, R. and Pomerance, C. (2001). Prime numbers: A computational perspective. *The Quadratic Sieve Factorization Method* (pp. 227–244). Berlin: Springer.

Cross, J.T. (1983). The Euler's φ-function in the Gaussian integers. *Journal of American Mathematics*, 55, 518–528.

Curts, R. (2003). *Building a Global Information Assurance Program*. Boca Raton, FL: Auerbach Publications.

Davis, P.S. and Ray, T.L. (1969). A branch-bound algorithm for the capacitated facilities location problem. *Naval Research Logistics Quarterly*, 16(3), 331–344,

Dearing, P.W., Francis, R.L. and Lowe, T.J. (1976). Convex location problem on tree networks. *Journal of Operational Research*, 24(4), 628–641.

Dewaghe, L. (1998). Remarks on the Schoof — Elkies — Atkin algorithm. *Mathematics of Computation*, 67(223), 1247–1252.

Diday, E. and Celenx, G. (1981). Optimization in cluster analysis. *Mathematical Methods of Operational Research*, 43, 327.

Diehr, G. (1985). Evaluation of a branch and bound algorithm for clustering. *Journal of Society for Industrial and Applied Mathematics on Scientific and Statistical Computing*, 6(2), 268–284.

Diffie, W. and Hellman, M. (1976). New directions in cryptography. *Institute of Electrical and Electronic Engineers Transactions on Information Theory*, 22(6), 644–654.

Dobrushkin, V. (2010). *Methods in Algorithmic Analysis*. Boca Raton, FL: CRC Press.

Dubner, H. (1989). A new method for producing large Carmichael numbers. *Mathematics of Computation*, 53, 411–414.

Eisenmann, K. (1962). The optimum location of a center. *Society for Industrial and Applied Mathematics Review*, 4(4), 394–395.

ElGamal, T. (1985). A public-key cryptosystem and a signature scheme based on discrete logarithms. *Institute of Electrical and Electronic Engineers Transactions on Information Theory*, 31(4), 469–472.

Elkamchouchi, H., Elshenawy, K. and Shaban, H. (2002). Extended RSA cryptosystem and digital signature schemes in the domain of Gaussian integers. *The Eighth International Conference on Communication Systems*, Washington, DC.

El-Kassar, A.N., Rizk, M., Mirza, N. and Wada, Y. (2001). El-Gamal public key cryptosystem in the domain of Gaussian integers. *International Journal of Applied Mathematics*, 7(4), 405–412.

Enge, A. and Gaudry, P. (2000). A general framework for sub-exponential discrete logarithm algorithms. Research Report LIX/RR/00/04, Luxembourg Internet eXchange (LIX), Kirchberg, Luxembourg.

Euler, L. (1911–1944). *Opera Omnia*, Series prima, Vols. I–V.

Eyster, J.W., White, J.A. and Wierwille, W.W. (1973). On solving multi-facility location problems using a hyperboloid approximation procedure. *Transactions of the American Institute of Electrical Engineers*, 5(1), 1–16.

Falby, N., Fulp, J., Clark, P., Cote, R., Irvine, C., Dinolt, G., Levin, T., Rose, M. and Shifflett, D. (2004). Information assurance capacity building: A case study. In *Proceedings IEEE Workshop on Information Assurance*, U.S. Military Academy.

Fang, K.-T. and Ma, F.-S. (1982). Splitting in cluster analysis and its application. *Acta Mathematicae Applicatae Sinica*, 5(4), 339–345.

Francis, R.L. and White, J.A. (1974). *Facility Layout and Location*. Englewood Cliffs, NJ: Prentice Hall, Inc.

Flajolet, P. and Odlyzko, A. (1990). Random mapping statistics. *Advances in Cryptology* — EUROCRYPT 1989 Lecture Notes on Computer Science, Vol. 434 (pp. 329–354).

Follett, R.H. (1991). Letter to NIST regarding DSS, 25 November.

Fortnow, L. and Homer, S. (2003). A short history of computational complexity. *Bulletin of the European Association for Theoretical Computer Science*, 80, 95–133.

Furukawa, E., Kawazoe, M. and Takahashi, T. (2004). Counting points for hyper-elliptic curves of type $y^2 = x^5 + ax$ over finite prime fields. In *Annual International Workshop on Selected Areas in Cryptography*, Ottawa, Ontario, Canada.

Gal, S. (1971). Sequential minimax search for maximum when prior information is available. *SIAM Journal of Applied Mathematics*, 21(4), 590–595.

Gal, S. (1974). A discrete search game. *SIAM Journal of Applied Mathematics*, 27, 641–648.

Gal, S. and Miranker, W.L. (1977). Optimal sequential and parallel search for finding a root. *Journal of Combinatorial Theory, Series A*, 23(1), 1–14.

Garrett, P. (2004). *The Mathematics of Coding Theory*. Pearson Prentice Hall.

Gaudry, P. (2003). A comparison and a combination of SST and AGM algorithms for counting points of elliptic curves in characteristic 2. *Advances in Cryptology — EUROCRYPT 2003*, Lecture Notes in Computer Science, Vol. 2656 (pp. 311–327). Springer-Verlag.

Gauss, C.F. (1863). *Disquisitiones Arithmeticae (arithmetical investigations)*. New Haven, CT: Yale University Press.

Gauss, C.F. (1965). Theoria residuorum biquadraticorum. 1832, Göttingen, Germany. *Untersuchungen über höhere Arithmetik (Disquisitiones Arithmeticae and other papers on number theory)*, 2nd Edn. (pp. 534–586). Chelsea New York.

Gentry, C., Johnson, J., Szydlo, M. and Stern, J. (2001). Cryptanalysis of the NTRU signature scheme (NSS) from Eurocrypt 2001. *Advances in Cryptology — ASIACRYPT 2001*, Lecture Notes in Computer Science, Vol. 2248 (pp. 1–20). Springer-Verlag.

Gentry, C. and Szydlo, M. (2002). Analysis of the revised NTRU signature scheme R-NSS. *Advances in Cryptology — EUROCRYPT 2002*, Lecture Notes in Computer Science, Vol. 2332 (pp. 299–320). Springer-Verlag.

Gethner, E., Wagon, S. and Wick, B. (1998). A stroll through the Gaussian primes. *American Mathematics Monthly*, 105(4), 327–337.

Gilbert, E.N. (1967). Minimum cost communication networks. *Bell System Technical Journal*, 2209–2229.

Goldreich, O. (2008). *Computational Complexity: A Conceptual Perspective*. Cambridge, MA: Cambridge University Press.

Goldstein, A.S. and Reingold, E.M. (1993). A Fibonacci-Kraft inequality and discrete unimodal search. *Society for Industrial and Applied Mathematics Journal on Computing*, 22(4), 751–777.

Gordon, D.M. and McCurley, K.S. (1993). Massively parallel computation of discrete logarithm. *Advances in Cryptology — CRYPTO 1992*, Lecture Notes in Computer Science, Vol. 740 (pp. 312–323).

Gorodetsky, V., Skormin, V. and Polyack, L. (Eds.) (2001). *Information Assurance in Computer Networks: Methods, Models, and Architecture for Network Security*. Saint Petersburg, Russia: Springer.

Hadden, R.W. (1994). *On the Shoulders of Merchants: Exchange and the Mathematical Conception of Nature in Early Modern Europe*. New York, NY: State University of New York Press.

Hamill, J., Deckro, R. and Kloeber, J. (2005). Evaluating information assurance strategies. *Decision Support Systems*, 39(3), 463–484.

Hankerson, D., Menezes, A. and Vanstone, S. (2003). *Guide to Elliptic Curve Cryptography*. New York, NY: Springer-Verlag.

Hardy, D.W. and Walker, A.C.L. (2003). *Applied Algebra: Codes, Ciphers and Discrete Algorithms*. Prentice Hall.

Harkin, D. (1957). On the mathematical works of Francois–Edouard–Anatole–Lucas. *Enseignement Mathematique*, 3(2), 276–288.

Hartmanis, J. and Stearns, R.E. (1965) On the computational complexity of algorithms. *Transactions of the American Mathematical Society*, 117, 285–306.

Hoffman, A.J. and Wolfe, P. (1985). Minimizing a unimodal function of two integer variables. *Mathematical programming, II. Math. Programming Studies*, 25, 76–87.

Hoffstein, J., Pipher, J. and Silverman, J. (1998). NTRU: A ring-based public key cryptosystem. *Algorithmic Number Theory*: Third International Symposium, Lecture Notes in Computer Science, Vol. 1423 (pp. 267–288). Berlin-Heidelberg: Springer-Verlag.

Hoffstein, J., Pipher, J. and Silverman, J. (2001). NSS: an NTRU lattice-based signature scheme. *Advances in Cryptology — EUROCRYPT 2001*, Lecture Notes in Computer Science, Vol. 2045 (pp. 211–228). Berlin-Heidelberg: Springer-Verlag.

Hoffstein, J., Pipher, J. and Silverman, J.H. (2008). *An Introduction to Mathematical Cryptography*. New York, NY: Springer-Verlag.

Horner, W.G. (1819). A new method of solving numerical equations of all orders by continuous approximation. *Philosophical Transactions of Royal Society of London*, 109, 308–335.

Horst, R. and Pardalos, P.M. (1994). *Handbook of Global Optimization*. Norwell, MA: Kluwer Academic Publishers.

Howgrave-Graham, N., Nguyen, P., Pointcheval, D., Proos, J., Silverman, J., Singer, A. and Whyte, W. (2003). The impact of decryption failures on the security of NTRU encryption. *Advances in Cryptology — CRYPTO 2003*, Lecture Notes in Computer Science, Vol. 2729 (pp. 226–246). Berlin-Heidelberg: Springer-Verlag. http://en.wikipedia.org/wiki/Safe prime.

Huang, Z. and Chen, Z. (1986). A new clustering method by bipartite graph theory. In *Proceedings of the Eighth International Conference on Pattern Recognition*, Paris, France.

Ivey, P., Walker, S.N., Sternm, J.M. and Davidson, S. (1992). An ultra-high speed public key encryption processor. In *Proceedings of IEEE Custom Integrated Circuits Conference*, Boston, MA.

Jacobson, M., Koblitz, N., Silverman, J., Stein, A. and Teske, E. (2000). Analysis of the xedni calculus attack. *Designs, Codes and Cryptography*, 20, 41–64.

Jacobson, M., Menezes, A. and Stein, A. (2001). Solving elliptic curve discrete logarithm problems using Weil descent. *Journal of the Ramanujan Mathematical Society*, 16, 231–260.

Jaulmes, E. and Joux, A. (2000). A chosen cipher text attack against NTRU. *Advances in Cryptology — CRYPTO 2000*, Lecture Notes in Computer Science, Vol. 1880 (pp. 20–35). Berlin-Heidelberg: Springer-Verlag.

Johnson, D.S., Lenstra, J.K. and Rinooy Kan, A.H.G. (1978). The complexity of the network design problem. *Networks*, 8(4), 279–285.

Joux, A. (2000). A one round protocol for tripartite Diffie — Hellman. *Algorithmic Number Theory:* Fourth International Symposium, Lecture Notes in Computer Science, Vol. 1838 (pp. 385–393). Berlin-Heidelberg: Springer-Verlag.

Kak, S. (2007). The cubic public-key transformation. *Circuits Systems Signal Processing*, 26(3), 41–47.

Kaliski, B.S. (1991). Letter to NIST regarding DSS, 4 November.

Karatsuba, A. and Ofman, Y. (1962). Multiplication of multi-digital numbers by automatic computers. *Doklady Akad. Nauk SSSR*, 14(145), 293–294.

Karp, R. and Miranker, W.L. (1968). Parallel minimax search for a maximum. *Journal of Combinatorial Theory*, 4, 59–90.

Kiefer, J.C. (1953). Sequential minimax search for a maximum. In *Proceedings of American Mathematical Society*.

Kiefer, J.C. (1957). Optimal sequential search and approximation methods under minimum regularity assumptions. *SIAM Journal of Applied Mathematics*, 5, 105–136.

Kirsch, M. (2008). *Tutorial on Gaussian arithmetic based on complex modulus.* http://wlym.com/~animations/ceres/InterimII/Arithmetic/ComplexModulus.html.

Knuth, D.E. (1981). *The Art of Computer Programming: Semi-numerical Algorithms*, 2nd Edn, Vol. 2. New York, NY: Addison-Wesley.

Knuth, D.E. (1997). *The Art of Computer Programming, Fundamental Algorithms*, 3rd Edn, Vol. 1. Reading, MA: Addison-Wesley.

Koblitz, N. (1987). Elliptic curve cryptosystems. *Mathematics of Computation*, 48(177), 203–209.

Koblitz, N. (1989). Hyper-elliptic cryptosystems. *Journal of Cryptology*, 1(3), 139–150.

Koblitz, N. (1994). *A Course in Number Theory and Cryptography*, 2nd Edn. New York, NY: Springer.

Koblitz, N. and Menezes, A. (2004). A survey of public-key cryptosystems. Research Report, University of Waterloo, Department of Combinatorics and Optimization.

Koblitz, N., Menezes, A. and Vanstone, S. (2000). The state of elliptic curve cryptography. *Designs, Codes and Cryptography*, 19(2–3), 173–193.

Kocher, P., Jaffe, J. and Jun, B. (1999). Differential power analysis. *Advances in Cryptology — CRYPTO 1999*, Lecture Notes in Computer Science, Vol. 1666 (pp. 388–397). Springer Verlag.

Krantz, S.G. (1999). Modulus of a complex number. *Handbook of Complex Variables* (pp. 2–3). Boston, MA: Birkhäuser Publishing Ltd.

Kuhn, H.W. (1973). A note on Fermat's problem. *Journal of Mathematical. Programming*, 5(4), 98–107.

Kusiak, A., Vannelli, A. and Kumar, K.R. (1986). Clustering analysis: models and algorithms. *Control and Cybernetics*, 115(2), 139–154.

Kuzovkin, A.I. (1968). A generalization of Fibonacci search to the multidimensional case. *Èkonomkai Matematicheskie Metody*, 4, 931–940.

LaMacchia, B.A. and Odlyzko, A.M. (1991). Computation of discrete logarithms in prime fields. *Designs, Codes and Cryptography*, 19(1), 47–62.

Lauder, A.G.B. (2004). Counting solutions to equations in many variables over finite fields. *Foundations of Computational Mathematics*, 4(3), 221–267.

Lauder, A.G.B. and Wan, D. (2008). Counting points on varieties over finite fields of small characteristics. In J.P. Buhler and P. Stevenhagen (Eds.), *Algorithmic Number Theory* (pp. 579–612). Cambridge, MA: Cambridge University Press.

Lehman, S. (1974). Factoring large integers. *Mathematics of Computation*, 28, 637–646.

Lehmer, D.H. (1969). Computer technology applied to the theory of numbers. In *Studies in Number Theory* (pp. 117–151). Englewood Cliffs, NJ: Prentice Hall.

Lencier, R., Lubicz, D. and Vercauteren, F. (2006). Point counting on elliptic and hyper-elliptic curves. In H. Cohen, and G. Frey (Eds.), *Handbook of Elliptic and Hyper-elliptic Curve Cryptography* (pp. 407–453). Boca Raton, FL: Chapman & Hall/CRC.

Lenstra, A.K., Lenstra, Jr. H.W. and Lovasz, L. (1982). Factoring polynomials with integer coefficients. *Mathematische Annalen*, 261, 513–534.

Lenstra, A.K. and Lenstra, Jr. J.H.W. (1993). *The Development of the Number Field Sieve*. Lecture Notes in Mathematics, Vol. 1554 (pp. 95–102). Berlin: Springer-Verlag.

Lenstra, A.K. and Shamir, A. (2000). Analysis and optimization of the TWINKLE factoring device. *Advances in Cryptology — EUROCRYPT 2000*, Lecture Notes in Computer Science, Vol. 1807 (pp. 35–52). Berlin-Heidelberg: Springer-Verlag.

Lenstra, Jr. H.W. (1987). Factoring integers with elliptic curves. *Annals of Mathematics*, 126(3), 649–673.

Leon-Garcia, A. and Widjaja, I. (2000). *Communication Networks*. McGraw Hill.

Van der Linden, F.J. (1982). Class number computations of real Abelian number fields. *Mathematics of Computation*, 39(160), 693–707.

Lueker, G.S. (1980). Some techniques for solving recurrences. *Computing Surveys*, 12, 410–436.

Maurer, U. and Wolf, S. (1999). The relationship between breaking the Diffie — Hellman protocol and computing discrete logarithms. *SIAM Journal on Computing*, 28(5), 1689–1731.

McClenon, R.B. (1919). Leonardo of Pisa and his Liber Quadratorum. *American Mathematical Monthly*, 26(1), 1–8.

McCurley, K. (1990). Discrete logarithm problem. In *Cryptology and Computational Number Theory* (pp. 49–74). Providence, RI: American Mathematical Society.

McGregor, P. and Shen, D. (1977). Network design: an algorithm for the access facility location problem. *IEEE Transactions on Communications*, 25, 61–73.

Menezes, A., Okamoto, T. and Vanstone, S. (1993). Reducing elliptic curve logarithms to logarithms in a finite field. *IEEE Transactions on Information Theory*, 39, 1639–1646.

Menezes, A., Van Oorschot P.C. and Vanstone, S.A. (1997). *Handbook of Applied Cryptography*. Boca Raton, New York, London Tokyo: CRC Press.

Miller, V.S. (1985). Use of elliptic curves in cryptography. *Advances in Cryptology — CRYPTO 1985*, Lecture Notes in Computer Science, Vol. 218 (pp. 417–426). Berlin-Heidelberg: Springer.

Mollin, R.A. (1998). *Fundamental Number Theory with Applications*. Boca Raton, FL: CRC Press.

Mollin, R.A. (2001). *An Introduction to Cryptography.* Boca Raton, FL: Chapman & Hall/CRC.

Montgomery, P.L. (1992). A FFT extension of the elliptic curve method of factorization. PhD Thesis, University of California, Los Angeles.

Müller, V., Stein, A. and Thiel, C. (1999). Computing discrete logarithms in real quadratic congruence function fields of large genus. *Mathematics of Computation,* 68(226), 807–822.

National Institute of Standards and Technology (1994). NIST FIPS PUB 186, Digital Signature Standard. U.S. Department of Commerce.

Nemirovsky, A.S. and Yudin, D.B. (1983). *Problems Complexity and Method Efficiency in Optimization.* New York, NY: Wiley-Interscience.

Neymark, Y.I. and Strongin, R.T. (1966). Informative approach to a problem of search for an extremum of a function. *Technicheskaya Kibernetika,* 1, 7–26.

Nishihara, N., Harasawa, R., Sueyoshi, Y. and Kudo, A. (2009). A remark on the computation of cube roots in fi rem fields. eprint.iacr.org/2009/457.

Nishihara, N., Harasawa, R., Sueyoshi, Y. and Kudo, A. (2013). Root computation in finite fields. In *IEICE Transactions on Fundamentals,* E96-A(6), 1081–1087.

NIST SP 800-37 (2004). *Guide for the Security Certification and Accreditation of Federal Information Systems.*

Odlyzko, A.M. (2000). Discrete logarithms: the past and the future. *Designs, Codes and Cryptography,* 19(2–3), 129–145.

Oliver, L.T. and Wilde, D.J. (1964). Symmetric sequential minimax search for a maximum. *Fibonacci Quarterly,* 2, 169–175.

Ong, E. and Kubiatowicz, J. (2005). Optimizing robustness while generating shared secret safe primes. Lecture Notes in Computer Science, Vol. 3386 (pp. 120–137). Berlin-Heidelberg: Springer.

Ostresh, L.M. (1978). On the convergence of a class of iterative methods for solving the Weber location problem. *Operations Research,* 26(4), 597–609.

Perron, O. (1907). ZurTheorie der Matrizen. *Mathematische Annalen,* 64, 276–288.

Pinch, R.G.E. (1993). The Carmichael numbers up to 10^{15}. *Mathematics of Computation,* 61, 381–391.

Pocklington, H.C. (1914/1916). The determination of the prime or composite nature of large numbers by Fermat's Theorem. In *Proceedings of the Cambridge Philosophical Society.*

Pollard, J. (1974). Theorems on factorization and primality testing. *Mathematical In Proceedings of the Cambridge Philosophical Society,* 76, 521–528.

Pollard, J. (1975). A Monte Carlo method for factorization. *BIT Numerical Mathematics,* 15(3), 331–334.

Pollard, J. (1993). Factoring with cubic integers. *The Development of the Number Field Sieve,* Lecture Notes in Mathematics, Vol. 1554 (pp. 4–10). Berlin-Heidelberg: Springer.

Pollard, J. (2000). Kangaroos, monopoly and discrete logarithms. *Journal of Cryptology,* 13(4), 437–447.

Pomerance, C. (1985). The quadratic sieve factoring algorithm. *Advances in Cryptology*, In *Proceedings of Eurocrypt 1984*, Lecture Notes in Computer Science, Vol. 209 (pp. 169–182). Berlin: Springer-Verlag.

Pomerance, C. (1982). Analysis and comparison of some integer factoring algorithms. In H. W. Lenstra, and R. Tijdeman (Eds.), *Computational Methods in Number Theory*, Vol. 154, (pp. 89–139). Math Centre Tracts — Part1. Amsterdam: Math Centrum.

Pomerance, C. (1996). A tale of two sieves. *Notices of the American Mathematical Society*, 43(12), 1473–1485.

Pomerance, C. (1998). Paul Erdös, number theorist extraordinaire. *The Notices of the American Mathematical Society*, 45(1), 19–23.

Pomerance, C. and Crandall, R. (2001). Section 7.4: elliptic curve method. *Prime Numbers: A Computational Perspective* 1st Edn, 301–313 Springer.

Pomerance, C., Smith, J. W. and Tuler, R. (1988). A pipeline architecture for factoring large integers with the quadratic sieve algorithm. *SIAM Journal on Computing*, 17(2), 387–403.

Proos, J. and Zalka, C. (2003). Schor's discrete logarithm quantum algorithm for elliptic curves. *Quantum Information and Computation*, 3, 317–344.

Proposed Federal Information Processing Standard for Digital Signature Standard (1991). Federal Register, 56 (169), 42980–42982.

Rabin, M.O. (1976). Probabilistic algorithms. In *Algorithms and Complexity* (pp. 21–39). San Diego, CA: Acad. Press.

Rabin, M. (1979). Digitized signatures and public-key functions as intractable as factorization. MIT/LCS Technical Report, TR-212.

Reingold, E.M. and Shen, X. (1991a). More nearly-optimal algorithms for unbounded searching, part I. The finite case. *SIAM Journal of Computing*, 20(1), 156–183.

Reingold, E.M. and X. Shen (1991b). More nearly-optimal algorithms for unbounded searching, part II. The transfinite case. *SIAM Journal of Computing*, 20(1), 184–208.

Rivest, R., Shamir, A. and Adleman, L. (1978). A method of obtaining digital signature and public-key cryptosystems. *Communication of ACM*, 21(2), 120–126.

RSA Factoring Challenge. http://en.wikipedia.org/wiki/RSA_Factoring Challenge.

Rubin, K. and Silverberg, A. (2002). Ranks of elliptic curves. *Bulletin of the American Mathematical Society* (N.S.), 39(4), 455–474.

Satoh, T. (2000). The canonical lift of an ordinary elliptic curve over a prime field and its point counting. *Journal of the Ramanujan Mathematical Society*, 15, 247–270.

Satoh, T., Skjernaa, B. and Taguchi, Y. (2003). Fast computation of canonical lifts of elliptic curves and its application to point counting. *Finite Fields and Their Applications*, 9, 89–101.

Schirokauer, O. (2000). Using number fields to compute logarithms in finite fields. *Mathematics of Computation*, 69(231), 1267–1283.

Schoof, R. (1985). Elliptic curves over finite fields and the computation of square roots mod p. *Mathematics of Computation*, 44, 483–494.

Schoof, R. (1995). Counting points of elliptic curves over finite fields. *Journal Theory des Nombres Bordeaux*, 7(1), 219–254.

Schor, P.W. (1997). Polynomial-time algorithms for prime factorization and discrete logarithms on a quantum computer. *SIAM Journal on Computing*, 26, 1484–1509.

Sedgewick, R., Szymanski, T.G. and Yao, A.C. (1982). The complexity of finding cycles in periodic functions. *SIAM Journal of Computing*, 11, 376–390.

Semaev, I. (1998). Evaluation of discrete logarithms in a group of p-torsion points of an elliptic curve in characteristic p. *Mathematics of Computation*, 67, 353–356.

Shamir, A. and Tromer, E. (2003). Factoring large numbers with the TWIRL device. *Advances in Cryptology — CRYPTO 2003, Lecture Notes in Computer Science*, Vol. 2729 (pp. 1–26). Berlin-Heidelberg: Springer-Verlag.

Shanks, D. (1969). Class number, a theory of factorization and genera. *Proc. Symposium of Pure Mathematics*, 20, 415–440. Providence, RI: American Math. Society.

Shanks, D. (1972). Five number theoretical algorithms. *Congressus Numerantium*, Vol. VII (pp. 51–70). Winnipeg: University of Manitoba.

Shanks, D. (1993). Euler's phi function. In *Solved and Unsolved Problems in Number Theory*, 4th Edn. (pp. 68–71).

Shoup, V. (1992). Searching for primitive roots in finite fields. *Mathematics of Computation*, 58, 369–380.

Shroyer, L. (1992). Letter to NIST regarding DSS, 17 Feb 1992.

Shubert, B.O. (1972). A sequential method seeking the global maximum of a function. *SIAM Journal of Numerical Analysis*, 3, 43–51.

Silverman, J. (2000). The xedni calculus and the elliptic curve discrete logarithm problem. *Designs, Codes and Cryptography*, 20, 5–40.

Silverman, J. and Suzuki, J. (1998). Elliptic curve discrete logarithms and the index calculus. *Advances in Cryptology — ASIACRYPT 1998, Lecture Notes in Computer Science*, Vol. 1514 (pp. 110–125). Berlin-Heidelberg: Springer-Verlag.

Silvermanand, J.H. and Tate, J. (1992). *Rational Points on Elliptic Curves* (pp. 128–129). New York, NY: Springer-Verlag.

Silverman, R.D. (1987). The multiple polynomial quadratic sieve. *Mathematics of Computation*, 48, 329–339.

Smart, N. (1999). The discrete logarithm problem on elliptic curves of trace one. *Journal of Cryptology*, 12, 193–196.

Soland, R.M. (1974). Optimal facility location with concave costs. *Operational Research*, 22(2), 373–382.

Stantel, L.E. (1986). A recursive Lagrangian method for clustering problems. *European Journal of Operational Research*, 27(3), 332–342.

Stinson, D.R. (2005). *Cryptography: Theory and Practice*, 3rd Edn. Boca Raton, FL: CRC Press.

Stinson, D.R. (2002). Some baby-step giant-step algorithms for the low Hamming weight discrete logarithm problem. *Mathematics of Computation*, 71(237), 379–391.

Tamura, S. (1982). Clustering based on multiple paths. *Pattern Recognition*, 15(6), 477–483.

Terr, D.C. (2000). A modification of Shanks'baby-step giant-step algorithm. *Mathematics of Computation*, 69(230), 767–773.

Teske, E. (1998). Speeding up Pollard's rho method for computing discrete logarithms. *Algorithmic Number Theory*: Third International Symposium, Notes in Computer Science, Vol. 1423 (pp. 541–545). London: Springer-Verlag.

Timonov, L.N. (1977). Search algorithm for a global extremum. *Technicheskaya Kibernetika*, 3, 53–60.

Tonelli, A. (1891). Bemerkungüber die Auflösungquadratischer Congruenzen. Nachrichten von der KöniglichenGesellschaft der Wissenschaften und der Georg-Augusts-UniversitätzuGöttingen, 344–346.

Toom, A. (1963). The complexity of a scheme of functional elements realizing the multiplication of integers. *Soviet Mathematics Doklady*, 7(3), 714–716.

Traub, J.F. and Wozniakowski, H. (1980). *A General Theory of Optimal Algorithms*. San Diego, CA: Acad. Press.

Verkhovsky, B. (1983a). Large scale network architecture synthesis: Interactive strategy. *International Journal of General Systems*, 9(2): 73–87.

Verkhovsky, B. (1983b). Distributed packet switching queuing network design. *Computers and Electrical Engineering*, 10(3), 137–147.

Verkhovsky, B. (1986). An optimal algorithm for search of extrema of a bimodal function. *Journal of Complexity*, 2, 323–332.

Verkhovsky, B. (1989). Optimal search algorithm for extrema of a discrete periodic bimodal function. *Journal of Complexity*, 5, 238–250.

Verkhovsky, B. (1995). Parallel minimax unbounded searching for a maximum of a unimodal function. Research Report, CIS-95-03, NJIT, 1–24.

Verkhovsky, B. (1997). Optimal algorithm for search of a maximum of n-modal function on infinite interval. In D. Du and P.M. Pardalos (Eds.), *Minimax and Applications* (pp. 245–261). Kluwer Academic Publisher.

Verkhovsky, B. (1998). Hardness of cryptanalysis of public keys cryptosystems with known timing of modular exponentiation. *Advances in Computer Cybernetics*, Vol. VI, 80–84.

Verkhovsky, B. (1999) Enhanced Euclid algorithm for modular multiplicative inverse and its complexity. *Advances in Computer Cybernetics*, 6, 51–57.

Verkhovsky, B. (2001). Overpass-crossing scheme for digital signature. In *International Conference on System Research, Informatics and Cybernetics*. Baden-Baden, Germany.

Verkhovsky, B. (2002). Search for a period of odd symmetric function. *Research Report*, CIS 02-02, NJIT.

Verkhovsky, B. (2004). Multiplicative inverse algorithm and its space complexity. *Annals of European Academy of Sciences*. Liege, Belgium, 2, 110–124.

Verkhovsky, B. (2008a). Information assurance and secure streaming algorithms based on cubic roots of integers. In *The Fifth International Conference on Information Technology: New Generations* (ITNG-08), IEEE Computer Society, Las Vegas, USA.

Verkhovsky, B. (2008b). Entanglements of plaintext streams and cubic roots of integers for network security. *Advances in Decision Technology and Intelligent Information Systems (IIAS)*, IX, 90–93.

Verkhovsky, B. (2008c). Information assurance protocols: efficiency analysis and implementation for secure communication. *Journal of Information Assurance and Security*, 3(4), 263–269.

Verkhovsky, B. (2009a). Integer factorization: Solution via algorithm for constrained discrete logarithm problem. *Journal of Computer Science*, 5(9), 674–679.

Verkhovsky, B. (2009b). Accelerated cyber-secure communication based on reduced encryption/decryption and information assurance protocols. *Journal of Telecommunication Managements*, 2(3), 284–293.

Verkhovsky, B. (2009c). Selection of entanglements in information assurance protocols and optimal retrieval of original blocks. *Journal of Telecommunications Management*, 2(2), 186–194.

Verkhovsky, B. (2009d). Fast digital signature hybrid algorithm based on discrete logarithm, entanglements of plaintext arrays and factorization. In Y. Polyanskov (Ed.), *7th International Conference on Mathematical Modeling in Physics, Technology, Socio-Economic Systems and Processes*, Ulyanovsk, Russia.

Verkhovsky, B. (2009e). Control protocols providing information assurance in telecommunication networks. *Journal of Telecommunications Management*, 2(1), 59–68.

Verkhovsky, B. (2010a). Hybrid authentication cyber-system based on discrete logarithm, entanglements and factorization. *International Journal of Communications, Network and System Sciences*, 3(7), 579–584.

Verkhovsky, B. (2010b). Potential vulnerability of encrypted messages: decomposability of discrete logarithm problems. *International Journal of Communications, Network and System Sciences*, 3(8), 639–644.

Verkhovsky, B. (2011a). Double-moduli Gaussian encryption/decryption with primary residues and secret controls. *International Journal of Communications, Network and System Sciences*, 4(7), 475–481.

Verkhovsky, B. (2011b). Space complexity of algorithm for modular multiplicative inverse. *International Journal of Communications, Network and System Sciences*, 4(6), 357–363.

Verkhovsky, B. (2011c). Integer factorization of semi-primes based on analysis of a sequence of modular elliptic equations. *International Journal of Communication, Network and System Sciences*, 4(10), 609–615.

Verkhovsky, B. (2011d). Information protection based on extraction of square roots of Gaussian integers. *International Journal of Communication, Networks and System Sciences*, 4(3), 133–138.

Verkhovsky, B. (2011e). Protection of sensitive messages based on quadratic roots of Gaussians: Groups with complex modulus. *International Journal Communications Network and System Sciences*, 4(5), 287–296.

Verkhovsky, B. (2011f). Cubic root extractors of Gaussian integers and their application in fast encryption for time-constrained secure communication. *International Journal of Communications, Network and System Sciences*, 4(4), 197–204.

Verkhovsky, B. (2011g). Satellite communication networks: Configuration design of terrestrial sub-networks. *Journal of Telecommunications Management*, 3(4), 360–373.

Verkhovsky, B. (2012). Deterministic algorithm computing all generators: application in cryptographic systems design. *International Journal of Communications, Network and System Sciences*, 5(11), 715–719.

Verkhovsky, B. and Koval, A. (2008). Cryptosystem based on extraction of square roots of complex integers. In S. Latifi (Ed.), (pp. 1190–1191). In *Proceedings of 5th International Conference on Information Technology: New Generations*, Las Vegas, Nevada.

Verkhovsky, B. and Mutovic, A. (2005). Primality testing algorithm using Pythagorean integers. In *Proceedings of International Computer Science and Information Systems Conference*, Athens, Greece.

Verkhovsky, B. and Rubino, R. (2012). Corporate intranet security: packet-level protocols for preventing leakage of sensitive information and assuring authorized network traffic. *International Journal of Communications, Network and System Sciences*, 5(5), 517–524.

Verkhovsky B. and Sadik, S. (2010). Accelerated search for Gaussian generator based on triple prime integers. *Journal of Computer Science*, 5(9), 614–618.

Veroy B. (1986). Optimal algorithm for search of extrema of a bimodal function. *Journal of Complexity*, 2(4), 323–332.

Veroy, B. (1988a). Average complexity of a divide-and-conquer algorithms. *Information Processing Letter*, 29(6), 319–326.

Veroy, B. (1988b). Optimal search algorithm for a minimum of a discrete periodic bimodal function. *Information Processing Letters*, 29(5), 233–239.

Voas, J. and Wilbanks, L. (2008). Information and quality assurance: an unsolved, perpetual problem for past and future generations. *IT Professional*, 10(3), 10–13.

Wardi, Y. (1989). Random search algorithms with sufficient descent for minimization of functions. *Mathematics of Operations Research*, 14(2), 343–354.

Weil, A. (1949). Number of solutions of equations in finite fields. *Bulletin of American Mathematical Society*, 55, 497–508.

Williams, H.C. (1972). Some algorithms for solving $x^q = N(\bmod p)$. In *Proceedings of the Third Southeastern Conference on Combinatorics, Graph Theory and Computing*, Florida Atlantic University, Boca Raton, FL.

Williams, K.S. and Hardy, K. (1993). A refinement of H.C. Williams' q-th root algorithm. *Mathematics of Computation*, 61(203), 475–483.

Witzgall, C. (1972). Fibonacci search with arbitrary first evaluation. *Fibonacci Quarterly*, 10, 113–134.

Xu, Z. and Sun, J. (2010). *Video Encryption Technology and Application* (pp. 1–99). New York, NY: Nova Science Publishers Inc.

Zadeh, N. (1973). On building minimum cost communication networks. *Networks*, 3(3), 315–331.

Zanoni, A. (2010). Iterative Toom — Cook methods for very unbalanced long integer multiplication. In *Proceedings of the 2010th International Symposium on Symbolic and Algebraic Computation*, ISSAC.

Zuccherato, R. (1998). The equivalence between elliptic curve and quadratic function field discrete logarithms in characteristic 2. *Algorithmic Number Theory Seminar ANTS-III*, Lecture Notes in Computer Science, Vol. 1423 (pp. 621–638). Berlin: Springer.

Zhengjun Cao, Qian Sha and Xiao Fan. (2011). *Adleman–Manders–Miller Root extraction method revisited*. arXiv:1111.4877v1 [cs.SC] 21 November.